# LABOR IN THE TOURISM AND HOSPITALITY INDUSTRY

## Skills, Ethics, Issues, and Rights

*Advances in Hospitality and Tourism*

# LABOR IN THE TOURISM AND HOSPITALITY INDUSTRY

## Skills, Ethics, Issues, and Rights

**Abdallah M. Elshaer**
**Asmaa M. Marzouk**

AAP | APPLE ACADEMIC PRESS

Apple Academic Press Inc.
3333 Mistwell Crescent
Oakville, ON L6L 0A2 Canada

Apple Academic Press Inc.
1265 Goldenrod Circle NE
Palm Bay, Florida 32905 USA



*Exclusive worldwide distribution by CRC Press, a member of Taylor & Francis Group*



International Standard Book Number-13: 978-1-77188-731-1 (Hardcover)
International Standard Book Number-13: 978-0-42946-509-3 (eBook)



**Library and Archives Canada Cataloguing in Publication**

Title: Labor in the tourism and hospitality industry : skills, ethics, issues, and rights / Abdallah M. Elshaer, Asmaa M. Marzouk.

Names: Elshaer, Abdallah M., author. | Marzouk, Asmaa M., author.

Series: Advances in hospitality and tourism book series.

Description: Series statement: Advances in hospitality and tourism book series | Includes bibliographical references and index.

Identifiers: Canadiana (print) 20190076119 | Canadiana (ebook) 20190076186 | ISBN 9781771887311 (hardcover) | ISBN 9780429465093 (eBook)

Subjects: LCSH: Tourism. | LCSH: Labor supply.

Classification: LCC G155.A1 E47 2019 | DDC 331.11/9191—dc23

**Library of Congress Cataloging-in-Publication Data**

Names: Elshaer, Abdallah M., author. | Marzouk, Asmaa M., author.

Title: Labor in the tourism and hospitality industry : skills, ethics, issues, and rights / Abdallah M. Elshaer, Asmaa M. Marzouk.

Description: Oakville, ON ; Palm Bay, Florida : Apple Academic Press, 2019. | Includes bibliographical references and index.

Identifiers: LCCN 2019010131 (print) | LCCN 2019010324 (ebook) | ISBN 9780429465093 (ebook) | ISBN 9781771887311 (hardcover : alk. paper)

Subjects: LCSH: Tourism--Employees--Supply and demand. | Hospitality industry--Employees--Supply and demand. | Labor turnover. | Employee rights.

Classification: LCC HD5716.T64 (ebook) | LCC HD5716.T64 E57 2019 (print) | DDC 331.7/6191--dc23

LC record available at https://lccn.loc.gov/2019010131

Apple Academic Press also publishes its books in a variety of electronic formats. Some content that appears in print may not be available in electronic format. For information about Apple Academic Press products, visit our website at **www.appleacademicpress.com** and the CRC Press website at **www.crcpress.com**

# *Dedication*

*"To the memory of my uncle Abdallah, the smart man whom I still miss every day."*

Abdallah M. Elshaer

*"To my lovely mom, the special person in my life, she always gives me the power to be better. My mother, I promised you one day I will make you proud of me, now I'm in the beginning of achieving the promise, I love you very much, God bless you."*

Asmaa M. Marzouk

# ABOUT THE AUTHORS

**Abdallah M. Elshaer, PhD**

Abdallah M. Elshaer is a lecturer in the Hotel Studies Department, Faculty of Tourism and Hotels at the University of Sadat City, Egypt, where he has been a faculty member since 2011. Currently, he is a PhD researcher at the Pamplin College of Business, Virginia Tech University, USA.

He received his bachelor degree in tourism and hotels management from Menoufia University, Egypt, in 2009, and an MS degree in hotel studies from the University of Sadat City, Egypt, in 2013. His Master's thesis was titled, "Introducing Lean Six Sigma to Achieve Continuous Service Improvement in Fast Food Restaurants." While, his PhD thesis' title is "Introducing Continuous Emergency Management (CEM) Based on Statistical Process Control (SPC) In Tourist Governmental Organizations and Hospitality Industry."

His research interests lie in challenges of the tourism and hospitality industries, service operations management, and foodservice operations. He is the author of a number of papers. He is teaching many courses, which include fundamentals of tourism and hospitality industry, hotel service management, business statistics, marketing management for services, and human resources management.

**Asmaa M. Marzouk, PhD**

Asmaa M. Marzouk is a lecturer in the Tourism Studies Department, Faculty of Tourism and Hotels, University of Sadat City, Egypt, since 2011. She graduated from the Faculty of Tourism and Hotels, Menoufia University in 2010.

She received her MSc degree in tourism studies from the University of Sadat City, Egypt, in 2014, under the title, "The Impact of WiMAX on Developing Location-based Services in Tourism." Her PhD thesis' title is "The Influence of Augmented Reality and Virtual Reality Combinations on Tourist Experience".

For the last 6 years, she has taught a wide range of courses, which include tourism management, information and communication technologies in tourism, travel agencies management, basics of tourism and hotels, and tourism marketing. Her research interests concentrate on labor issues, information and communication technologies in tourism, tourism management, and marketing. She published a number of research papers on information and communication technologies and labor issues.

# ADVANCES IN HOSPITALITY AND TOURISM BOOK SERIES



This series reports on research developments and advances in the rapidly growing area of hospitality and tourism. Each volume in this series presents state-of-the-art information on a specialized topic of current interest. These one-of-a-kind publications are valuable resources for academia as well as for professionals in the industrial sector.

**BOOKS IN THE SERIES:**

**Food Safety: Researching the Hazard in Hazardous Foods**
Editors: Barbara Almanza, PhD, RD, and Richard Ghiselli, PhD

**Strategic Winery Tourism and Management: Building Competitive Winery Tourism and Winery Management Strategy**
Editor: Kyuho Lee, PhD

**Sustainability, Social Responsibility and Innovations in the Hospitality Industry**
Editor: H. G. Parsa, PhD
Consulting Editor: Vivaja "Vi" Narapareddy, PhD
Associate Editors: SooCheong (Shawn) Jang, PhD,
Marival Segarra-Oña, PhD, and Rachel J. C. Chen, PhD, CHE

**Managing Sustainability in the Hospitality and Tourism Industry: Paradigms and Directions for the Future**
Editor: Vinnie Jauhari, PhD

**Management Science in Hospitality and Tourism: Theory, Practice, and Applications**
Editors: Muzaffer Uysal, PhD, Zvi Schwartz, PhD, and
Ercan Sirakaya-Turk, PhD

**Tourism in Central Asia: Issues and Challenges**
Editors: Kemal Kantarci, PhD, Muzaffer Uysal, PhD, and Vincent Magnini, PhD

**Poverty Alleviation through Tourism Development: A Comprehensive and Integrated Approach**
Robertico Croes, PhD, and Manuel Rivera, PhD

**Chinese Outbound Tourism 2.0**
Editor: Xiang (Robert) Li, PhD

**Hospitality Marketing and Consumer Behavior: Creating Memorable Experiences**
Editor: Vinnie Jauhari, PhD

**Women and Travel: Historical and Contemporary Perspectives**
Editors: Catheryn Khoo-Lattimore, PhD, and Erica Wilson, PhD

**Wilderness of Wildlife Tourism**
Editor: Johra Kayeser Fatima, PhD

**Medical Tourism and Wellness: Hospitality Bridging Healthcare (H2H)©**
Editor: Frederick J. DeMicco, PhD, RD

**Sustainable Viticulture: The Vines and Wines of Burgundy**
Claude Chapuis

**The Indian Hospitality Industry: Dynamics and Future Trends**
Editors: Sandeep Munjal and Sudhanshu Bhushan

**Tourism Development and Destination Branding through Content Marketing Strategies and Social Media**
Editor: Anukrati Sharma, PhD

**Evolving Paradigms in Tourism and Hospitality in Developing Countries: A Case Study of India**
Editor: Bindi Varghese, PhD

**The Hospitality and Tourism Industry in China: New Growth, Trends, and Developments**
Editor: Jinlin Zhao, PhD

**Labor in Tourism and Hospitality Industry: Skills, Ethics, Issues, and Rights**
Abdallah M. Elshaer, PhD, and Asmaa M. Marzouk, PhD

**Sustainable Tourism Development: Futuristic Approaches**
Editor: Anukrati Sharma, PhD

# ABOUT THE SERIES EDITOR

Mahmood A. Khan, PhD, is a Professor in the Department of Hospitality and Tourism Management, Pamplin College of Business at Virginia Tech's National Capital Region campus. He has served in teaching, research, and administrative positions for the past 35 years, working at major US universities. Dr. Khan is the author of several books and has traveled extensively for teaching and consulting on management issues and franchising. He has been invited by national and international corporations to serve as a speaker, keynote speaker, and seminar presenter on different topics related to franchising and services management.

Dr. Khan has received the Steven Fletcher Award for his outstanding contribution to hospitality education and research. He is also a recipient of the John Wiley & Sons Award for lifetime contribution to outstanding research and scholarship; the Donald K. Tressler Award for scholarship; and the Cesar Ritz Award for scholarly contribution. He also received the Outstanding Doctoral Faculty Award from Pamplin College of Business.

He has served on the Board of Governors of the Educational Foundation of the International Franchise Association, on the Board of Directors of the Virginia Hospitality and Tourism Association, as a Trustee of the International College of Hospitality Management, and as a Trustee on the Foundation of the Hospitality Sales and Marketing Association's International Association. He is also a member of several professional associations.

# CONTENTS

# ABBREVIATIONS

| | |
|---|---|
| B2B | business to business |
| B2C | business to customer |
| CSE | commercial sexual exploitation |
| CSR | corporate social responsibility |
| DEAs | disability employment advisers |
| EWD | employees with disabilities |
| F/B | food and beverage |
| GDP | gross domestic product |
| GDS | global destination systems |
| HR | human resource |
| HRM | human resource management system |
| ICT | information and communication technology |
| ILO | International Labor Organization |
| ISO | International Organization for Standardization |
| IT | information technology |
| OECD | Organization for Economic Cooperation and Development |
| PWD | people with disabilities |
| SA | social accountability |
| SICTA | Standard International Classification of Tourism Activities |
| SMEs | small and medium enterprises |
| SWOT | strengths, weaknesses, opportunities, and threats |
| THB | trafficking of human beings |
| Three R's Rule | recognize, reward, and repeat |
| TVPA | Trafficking Victims Protection Act |
| UDHR | Universal Declaration of Human Rights |
| VET | vocational education and training |
| WOM | word of mouth |
| WTO | World Tourism Organization |

# PREFACE

Nowadays, the tourism industry is considered as one of the fastest growing global industries. It has already outpaced other industries, such as agricultural science, mining, and even retail. According to the International Labor Organization, more than 255 million people around the world are currently involved in this industry as workers and employees, such progress will reach a total of 296 million to global employment by 2019, and by 2022, travel and tourism will employ 328 million people—creating 73 million new jobs. Therefore, understanding how to create and maintain a solid workforce is increasingly vital as economics of nations are dependent on human resources.

An organization's workforce is arguably its greatest asset. A workforce is an asset capable of being cultivated to achieve and maximize its organizational objectives. At the same time, it is one of the few elements that competitors cannot copy. However, the organizations are suffering as a result of poor investment in the human resource, as they are usually regarded by many organizations as temporary business assets. Therefore, leaders and managers must handle their workforce as their organization's most valuable asset and not just only as a cliché, to say, "Our workforce is our most valuable asset." The employers must treat them as sovereign human beings and stakeholders and not consider them as "assets" owned by the company. Consequently, this book is developed to be as a plea for the more serious study of labor in tourism industry. If, as is often said, tourism is where the jobs of the future lie, then we need to know a lot more about it.

Subsequently, there is a two-fold reason for this book. In the first place, it attempts to open up our thinking on the status of labor in tourism industry in order to understand the very important and constrained parameters of managing workforce-related issues in organizations, manpower planning, and forecasting estimates that include investigative techniques in a way that may offer insight to workforce managing in both tourism and tourism education. These purposes are pursued simultaneously, as the rendering of economic development imposes simultaneity without boundary adopting and developing workforce development strategies, as there is a clear linkage between workforce development and engagement and firm performance, including profit. However, too often leaders' decisions, policies, and actions tell a very different story. Instead of valuable assets, leaders' behaviors often tell a story of employees as an expense to be minimized and leveraged to extract all the productivity possible to maximize profit. Such thinking and behaviors of managers toward their employees firstly kill their creativity; as companies that need to make a step forward should take care of the internal customer (workforce) first; so, the inside "strength" needs to be considered at all levels. Secondly, such action may eventually cause organizations to lose some of their skilled employees' "costs." For example, labor turnover in the hospitality industry often averages as much as 200–300% per year. As when an organization loses a good employee it causes the other employees to have a reason for thinking, "why would that person leave this place, and is there something wrong with this environment that I should be worried about?" Consequently, other employees start looking for another opportunity. The disastrous consequences may entail the customers too. In case the customers trust an employee and if that employee leaves, the customers begin to ask themselves the very same questions that other employees had, "is there something wrong that I am unaware of?" And in turn, the customers start to outlook for another place. Such unaccountable behavior of employers in managing their workforce asset is depicted in the follows quote "killing the goose that laid the golden egg." Since, the ripple effect of losing a good employee is tremendous and it goes well beyond what is regularly quantified. Therefore, investing in the organization's employees is the starting point. If an organization wants loyalty, it has to start giving some. Investing in human resources is the key to business success.

This textbook provides both profound understandings of the workforce in tourism and hospitality industry; issues that face labor in the tourism and hospitality industry; and the relevant treatment of essential topics, in addition to investigating the importance of ethics dimension and labor rights. The philosophy and techniques of this approach run as a theme through the text. This is an academic text which is analytical in tone and which looks at behavior from the perspective of the industry, the employee, and the job, in addition, search in the reasons of that behavior. It uses economic, sociological, and psychological analysis and takes a pragmatic stance on the challenges of the workforce. It offers readers, whether they are students, managers, planners, or educationalists, an in-depth understanding of labor in tourism as a whole and in its specifics.

Initially, this book will analyze the specifics of the labor market of the tourism and hospitality industry and in the same line, it presents discussion about the current status of the industry's organizations and how they are suffering labor shortage (qualitative or quantitative) and their actual needs from their labor markets. The gap that exists and the imbalance occurring between tourism labor market and the requirements of the organizations of the industry pushed us to examine the ethics topic on both sides, in addition to focusing on issues responsible for recording high rates of labor turnover. By heeding the reasons of the labor shortage in the industry, two reasons were found: one is linked to the characteristics of the industry and another is associated with HRM policies and practices. The increasing labor issues within the tourism and hospitality industry coincided with a similar general increase in ignoring the labor rights. From understanding the holistic view of labor skills, ethics, issues, and rights, further insights and conclusions were drawn regarding the sufficient practices that must be adhered by human resource management. Thus, this book will be of value to students and adult educators, as it provides them of what skills they must cultivate that are highly appreciated in the industry, and make them aware of their rights to advocate, in case it is depreciated. Additionally, senior human resources practitioners who engage in professional positions in the tourism industries will get significant benefits as it gives a holistic view which starts from the labor market that supplies their organizations to the costs that stem from leaving the employees their companies. Then, it will help them in handling labor-related issues such as labor shrinking in their organizations and enhancing their organizations' image through their human capital asset.

**—Abdallah M. Elshaer**

# INTRODUCTION

Tourism has become critical in driving economic development in many countries. Unplanned tourism development can lead to negative impacts both on society as a whole and the labor market in particular. The World Tourism Organization has observed that tourism activities are highly dependent on the availability and quality of labor, which is a key factor in providing services and enhancing quality. So, labor force is the most important assets for any kind of institutions. The tourism and hospitality industry is considered one of the sectors that rely on the human element in the provision of services; the critical importance of employees' involvement in the quality process of an organization is based on the belief that the best process innovation ideas come from people actually doing the job.

Financial performance in business is intricately dependent on the productivity of the people in the organization. One of the main factors in the progress of any tourism industry component is the development of human capital. So, the organization must work for ensuring its employee satisfaction on a regular basis with the same conviction applied to measuring guest satisfaction, as the first will determine the latter.

We believe that human capital is the sum of knowledge, experience, skills, and practical experiences that provide different types of profit and competitive advantage in the face of competition; this is the result of accumulated investments in the particular asset of human health, knowledge, skills, and talent. The tourism business practice is focused on their own business interests. They need specialists, who possess specific skills, able to quick profession adaptation, maintain an ethical conduct, and have the service mentality. Tourism involves a wide range of different activities, types of establishments, employment contracts, and working arrangements. There are also often significant differences between regions in a country and between the seasons of the year. Informal employment, ethical concerns, and high labor turnover all pose challenges and bring troubles into the work environment. According to World Economic Forum, shortage of skilled labor could cost the tourism, hospitality, and leisure industry (THL) a loss of $610 billion and 14 million jobs by 2024. The THL industry typically has high employee turnover and below-average attraction for potential employees. The unique nature of human capital requires vigilant and proficient consideration and management. Organizations should seek wisdom in their management of human capital. Developing and maintaining a fair, equitable, and effective human resource management system (HRM) can motivate staff and increase their level of job satisfaction and efficiency, which can result in developed customer engagement and simultaneously a good business image that lead to maximizing the financial returns (Fig. 1). Organizations that have an effective HRM are able to attract employees with high skills and good ethical behaviors, as such organizations definitely put a great deal of focus on respecting labor rights and developing ideal organizational culture. In a well-designed organizational climate, the workforce is the "bridge" between objectives development and objectives implementation.

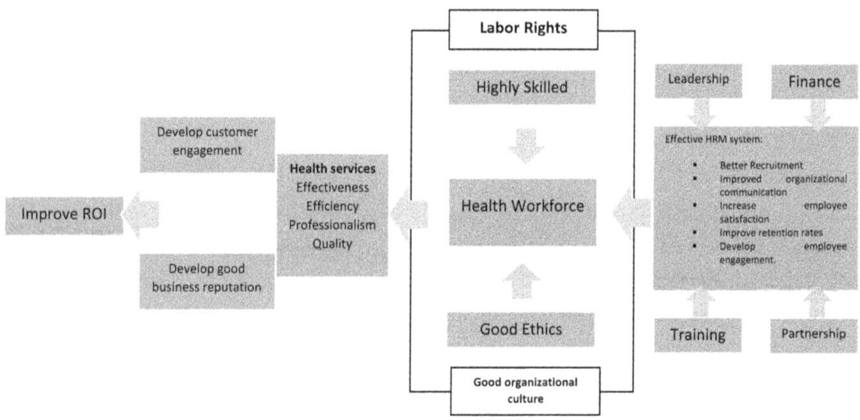


**FIGURE 1** The health framework of workforce.

**Source:** The Authors.

Skilled labor has become a strategic theme and is needed in the tourism industries. The tourism industries lack in structured employee competency development programs. Similarly, the developmental role of tourism cannot, or should not, be extolled without knowledge and understanding of tourism employment as a whole and its specifics, issues, and rights. In other words, the achievement of development in the tourism industries depends primarily on the status of its labor markets, in addition to the conditions of employment and the current status of the workforce within the industry's organizations.

The kind of questions that are always asked about the status of workforce include what are the specific characteristics of tourism labor markets? What are the main reasons behind the high rates of labor turnover? What does an organization's workforce represent? Why their status is relatively low or marginalized position in the industry? We address these issues by arguing the importance of understanding tourism labor markets and by showing how they can be understood in a more qualitative way. Tourism is a labor-intensive, seven-days-a-week industry, which depends on an adequately supplied and skilled workforce to service its global customer base.

It is also true in the labor-intensive industry that effective utilization of human resource can give an organization its competitive edge; however, the tourism industry generally, and hospitality businesses specifically, suffer from relatively high staff attrition rates based on a perception of relatively low pay rates, difficult working hours, uncertainty of employment, and lack of career path. So, leaders of some tourism and hospitality organizations need strategic HRM practices to enhance employee productivity and avert a future loss of labor while improving corporate financial performance. So, our book gives a profound understanding of the status of human resource involved in tourism industries, their skills, ethics, issues, and rights.

This book is divided into four parts. The first part looks at labor in the industry as a whole and concentrates on its primary features, such as diversity, skill, and productivity, in addition to studying the reasons of the gap between the labor supply and demand. This section begins with Chapter 1 highlighting the significance of tourism and hospitality industry in employment creation and in turn on its contribution to the world's economy. Chapter 2 turns around the critical analysis of labor supply and demand with the purpose of identifying the characteristics of the labor markets in order to investigate the problem of labor imbalance between the labor market and the requirements of the industry's organizations. In a sense, this chapter forms the qualitative heart of many of the structural arguments used elsewhere in the book.

Chapters 3 and 4 are on the employment skills which determine the future demand for skills and competencies.

Chapter 3 looks at labor skills and the different categories of skills required in the industry. It identifies skills and qualifications urgently needed for tourism in general. It goes on to raise the important issue of the relationship between achieving a high standard of service quality and having a specific type of skills, in addition to discussing the educational and training responses in order to meet the needs of the industry. Chapter 4 begins with showing the types of labor shortage within the tourism industries. The qualitative and quantitative labor shortage in tourism labor markets led to the term "multiskilling" in popular employers and HR discourse to mean a range of things and is associated with learning processes and beyond, but not excluding, education and training. The term multiskilling offers labor the prospect of learning new skills and provides for job variety. In addition, the chapter will highlight the reasons of occupational disequilibrium in labor markets and the organizations' reactions to tackle labor/skills shortages.

Regarding the occupational disequilibrium, business ethics may have a potential contribution in labor-related development perspective. Especially the workforce actions and behaviors represent a panacea to the challenges generated by service characteristics such as intangibility and heterogeneity. So, the ethical conducts must be addressed in tourism literature. Also, it is certainly unrealistic to expect a development "tool," such as tourism, to be a solution to all the problems and challenges that may face the industry, while the scale of tourism-related ethics also remains an ignored matter.

Part 2 is about ethics in tourism and hospitality industry. Chapter 5 explores in detail the work ethics and its components. Work ethic is one of the five most important employability skills that must be given a great attention by the employers; on the other hand, educational settings should seek to cultivate it into its graduates. Also, the chapter discusses the ethical issues in the organizations involved in the industry and presents some examples of ethical issues within the organization while highlighting the degree of morality that the employees have and their contribution in generating such troubles. Chapter 6 describes the importance of involving the workforce in ethical initiatives and how such ethical rules, standards, and actions to a large extent influence the workforce and their performance, in addition to the position of the organization within the society that will be influenced accordingly, as complex and serious ethical issues affect this broad industry whether they are internal or external issues.

Part 3 tries to explore the conundrums surrounding the high rate of labor turnover in tourism industries and the current loss of longer serving skilled workers that coincide with a shortage of job seekers who are not interested in pursuing their career in tourism industries. Chapter 7 investigates the reasons behind employees leaving their jobs in the industry's organizations in notable numbers. The hospitality and tourism industry is plagued with high turnover, which has both direct costs (e.g., recruitment and training) and indirect costs (e.g., overtime and reduced customer satisfaction). The chapter tries to give an answer to the essential question "what are the challenges that face labor force in the tourism and hospitality industry?" In a response to this question, Chapters 8–13 present a series of challenges that significantly influence the workforce commitment and performance, challenges that tourism labor suffer from primarily associated with the characteristics and image of the industry, for example, the seasonal characteristics of the industry is considered one of the main challenge that prevents skilled employees and employees with family burden to join the industry. Also, the image of the industry as a symbolic value and high profile has reflected on its resilience to threats and emergencies (natural or human made) and made the industry a target for destructive actions which in turn prevent the new laborers to join the industry or the current workforce to continue in the industry. In support of this perspective, we argue that the issues which confront managers and employers on a daily basis are contingent upon a wider picture beyond the scope of their specific responsibilities. This argument does not demean the impacts of negative organizational behavior nor devalue the role of human resource management in contributing to generating and maximizing the labor issues. There are challenges associated with management policies such as low pay, discrimination practices, managing cultural diversity in work environment that result in more clashes among the workforce members, and the new technology adoption that represents a significant challenge for the employees in the middle and low levels.

These series of challenges were followed by ideas and solutions. It is our hope that leaders in organizations will consider these insights when they deal with the ever-present challenges of growing and surviving in today's volatile business environment.

Finally, Part 4 investigates the rights of labor. The term "rights" is used throughout this part and particularly in Chapter 15, so it is appropriate to begin by the question: what are the workforce rights and what does it mean for HRM practitioners in the industry? In our book, we explored this question by delving into the forms of labor trafficking in the tourism industries which is presented in Chapter 14. According to International Labor Organization, three out of every 1000 people worldwide are in forced labor. The chapter also highlights the reasons that make the tourism and hospitality organization an ideal place for trafficking actions. In response to the workplace challenges created by influences such as globalization, workforce mobility, the individualization of work, the term "right" has been created. Chapter 15 discusses legislation that is created in order to create legal protections for labor force and ensure a social justice. The term has come about in response to the workplace challenges created by influence such as globalization, workforce mobility, and the individualization of work.

Finally, drawing together the various concepts, themes, and issues introduced and discussed throughout the book, the conclusion considers the human assets as the unique power that is impossible to be copied if managed and treated efficiently. As such, it raises a number of important points that may encourage further debate amongst students, academic and practitioners of tourism while, more generally, it is hoped that this book as a whole will contribute to further understanding and knowledge of the inherent processes that shape the tourism labor market and identifying the reasons of gaps between the labor market and the practice field, in addition to the status and challenges that face the involved workforce and in turn affect both the life of millions of families in particular and the advancement of industry in many countries.

The conclusions of this book may contribute to social change by keeping more workforce gainfully engaged, increasing the dignity and prosperity of tourism employees and their families, and reducing the undesirable effects of unemployment on the society, accordingly, keeping the tourism industry as the economy of all eras.

# PART I

# Labor Skills

CHAPTER 1

# THE SIGNIFICANCE OF THE TOURISM AND HOSPITALITY INDUSTRY IN EMPLOYMENT CREATION

*"Tourism grants the poorest of the poor the simplest means to live in dignity. It puts money in the hand of petty shop-keepers, drivers, beach vendors, photo makers, and other miserable works."*

## 1.1 INTRODUCTION

The history of tourism and hospitality industry extends for thousands of years. Tourism and hospitality industry represents one of the most dynamic and growing industries in countries all over the world. Specifically, the hospitality industry has existed for almost 4000 years. According to the International Labor Organization (ILO, 2010), international tourism includes business and professional travel, visiting friends and relatives, religious travel, and health treatments of travelers crossing a border and spending one or more nights in the host country. Thus, the movement of guests and customers affected the revenue of global hotel industry, in particular, to touch US $553.8 billion in 2018 (Statista, 2017). Teng (2013) described the hospitality industry as an enterprise with a purpose to provide service and products in order to satisfy a full range of needs such as food, beverages, and accommodations. In details, the hospitality industry consists of various service activities that include accommodation, restaurants, event planning, theme parks, transportation, cruise lines, and others.

The various components of the hospitality industry in addition to specific segments of transport, travel agencies, and tour operators are all considered by most organizations to belong to the "tourism-characteristic industries" and are therefore subsumed under tourism. Such various activities involve numerous guest–host interactions that involve the needs of a diverse group of people (Teng, 2013). Therefore, many groups of employees and workers run these establishments with various responsibilities, such as directors of operations, management or leadership roles, hosting and service, facility maintenance, and marketing positions (Ruizalba et al., 2014).

Generally, tourism is considered an extremely labor intensive and a significant source of employment. Although some academics consider tourism and hospitality jobs are characterized by low-status jobs with low payments and poor working conditions, the industry having a higher amount of human capital invested than it is in other industries (Baum, 1996). It is among the world's top creators of jobs requiring varying degrees of skills and allows for quick entry into the workforce for youth, women, and migrant workers.

It accounts for 30% of the world's export service (ILO, 2010). Consequently, the tourism industry and its informal components offer a significant number of employment opportunities to job seekers with little skills or with or no formal training and who do not want to be involved in long-term employment commitments (e.g., students). In addition, the tourism industry provides opportunities for migrants to find jobs as well as for workers who have family responsibilities. Tourism can provide an opportunity for those facing significant social and capability disadvantages in a way that is not always offered by other environments.

Hence, the tourism industry employs a significant number of workforce worldwide (Grobelna, 2015). As a result, concerning the contribution to international gross domestic product (GDP) and the number of jobs creation, the tourism industry has already outpaced other industries, such as agricultural science, mining, and even retail (Vasquez, 2014). For example, in the Pacific, tourism contributes greatly to GDP. In Fiji, the sector offered to employ over 40,000 people and contributed significantly to foreign exchange savings. In 2005, US $1 million created about 63 jobs in Fiji (Narayan et al., 2010). In Egypt, every million dollars invested in hotels created 18 direct and 12 indirect jobs (Egyptian National Competitiveness Council, 2008).

According to Vasquez (2014), the travel, tourism and hospitality economy contribute in pumping trillions of dollars to the international GDP. At a global level, experts and industry professionals anticipate profits and revenues from the tourism and hospitality industry will continue to grow. The hospitality and tourism industry creates many job opportunities around the globe and extensively contributes to many countries' GDP.

## 1.2 THE INDUSTRY'S CONTRIBUTION TO THE WORLD'S ECONOMY

Tourism is now world's largest industry with its wide range of constituent sub-sectors and various activities. The tourism and hospitality industry as a whole (of which the hospitality industry is a part) remains one of the world's most important drivers of economic growth and development, accounting for nearly 9% of worldwide GDP (ILO, 2010).

Travel and Tourism is an export sector, attracting foreign currency to a country in the form of international guests and customers. In 2016, global visitor exports accounted for 6.6% of total world exports (a total of US $1.4 trillion) and almost 30% of total world services exports (World Travel and Tourism Council, 2017). So, the economy flourish and tourism are intrinsically correlated to each other as tourism and hospitality organizations have long-term socioeconomic impacts on the host economy and community regarding the employment and community development branch (Keyser, 2002). Being a socioeconomic phenomenon, tourism acts both as an engine of economic development and a social force, impacting a wide range of other industries; from the demand-side, tourism refers to the activities of guests and their role in the acquisition of goods and services. At the same time, tourism can also be viewed from the supply side. According to World Travel and Tourism Council (2017), travel and Tourism's impact includes the movement of people for both leisure and business, domestically and internationally. So, it will then be understood as the set of service and productive activities that cater mainly to guests and customers (WTO and ILO, 2014). In 2016, 76.8% of all travelers spend was as a result of leisure purpose, compared to 23.2% from business travel. The sector contributed US $7.6 trillion to the global economy. This was equal to 10.2% of the world's GDP.

In 2017, the total contribution of Travel and Tourism to the world's economy is expected to grow by 3.5% (World Travel and Tourism Council, 2017). Moreover, it is much of the labor-intensive type of industry as it offers many work opportunities for a large number of people. Consequently, today the world tourism industry is becoming a major attraction for job seekers. The tourism impacts on employment go beyond employment in sectors, in which tourists directly spending their money, such as lodging establishments, restaurants, recreation and entertainment premises, and airlines. The establishments which receive tourists also buy goods and services from other sectors that generate indirect employment in those sectors through multiplier effect (Keyser, 2002). Generally, the significance of the tourism industry for economic development, employment creation, and poverty alleviation is being increasingly recognized. The tourism sector has experienced the fastest growth rate in comparison to other sectors of the global economy in recent years and is reported to account "for more than one-third of the total global services trade" (ILO, 2011). Figure 1.1 shows the tourism significance in countries' development.

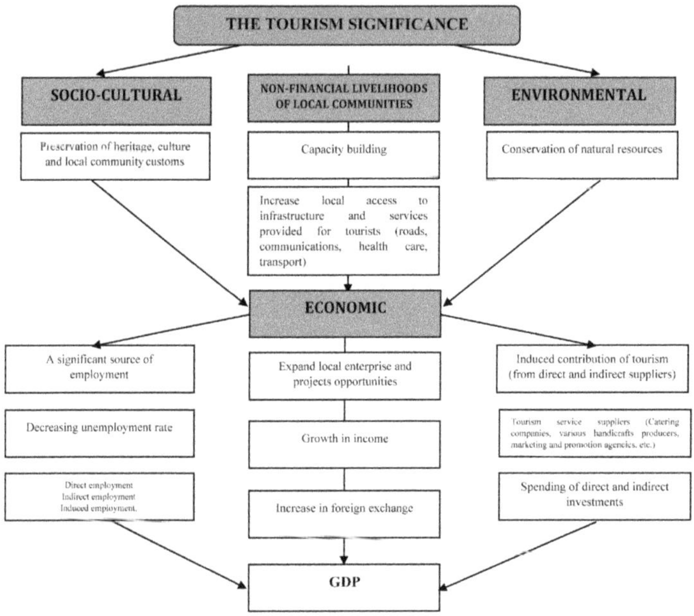


**FIGURE 1.1** The tourism significance in economic development.
**Source:** The Authors.

## 1.3 POTENTIAL OF TOURISM IN CATERING EMPLOYMENT

Tourism and hospitality industry is highly labor-intensive and, numerically, a significant source of employment (Fig. 1.1). People are clearly central to the effective operation and further development of the tourism industries as a whole. As a service industry, many tourism products include people as an integral part of the expertise offered, whether as performers or as members of the cultural environment (WTO and ILO, 2014). Thus, tourism has a significant effect on those areas that has surplus labor. It has a great influence on local population employment. Thus, there is a positive relationship between the growth of tourism and creating employment opportunities, and this helps in minimizing the extremities of poverty. The industry's projected growth and development will help stimulate economic gains that are critically needed around the world. Economic development means jobs, and jobs bring much more than a paycheck: they bring dignity to individuals, tax revenue to governments, new consumers to businesses, and invested citizens to communities. Thus, the industry outlook brings hope not only to hospitality sector businesses but also to each destination in which industry businesses thrive.

In the accommodation industry, for instance, globally there is an average of one employee for each hotel room. A new job created in the hospitality industry generates 1.5 jobs along the supply chain in the tourism-related economy, with a proportionate economic help to local communities (ILO, 2010; WTO, 1997). Further, it also stimulates the growth of employment in other industries. There are three workers indirectly dependent on each person working in hotels, such as textile workers, laundry workers, gardeners, shop staff for souvenirs and others, as well as airport employees.

Taking its wider indirect and induced impacts into account, in 2016, travel and tourism directly contributed US $2.3 trillion and 109 million jobs worldwide (approximately 1 in 10 of all jobs). The sector contributed US $7.6 trillion to the global economy and supported 292 million jobs in 2016 (World Travel and Tourism Council, 2017). More than 255 million people around the world currently work in the sector, and the industry will contribute a total of 296 million to global employment by 2019 (ILO, 2011), and by 2022, travel and tourism will employ 328 million people—creating 73 million new jobs (ILO, 2010). Such statistics indicate that tourism industry is the world's largest employer, the industry is entering an exciting phase. In addition, while other industries struggle to recover from the global economic downturn, tourism industry has proved resilient. The hotel sector bounced back quickly from its 2009 decline, despite the crisis, global employment in the tourism industry increased by about 1% between 2008 and 2009 and is predicted to show continuous increase (Datamonitor, 2011). This growth and success of the industry primarily depend on the quality of organizations' workforce. Stemming from the earlier statements, by its nature, tourism is about people (tourism products and services are about people).

Because the tourism industries are comprised of production and service dimensions, the creation and delivery of services from the organization to the customer are dependent on the employees and workers (Holston-Okae, 2017), in addition to other factors such as natural resources, infrastructure, and capital to ensure delivery and quality of its products and services. Taylor (2002) argued that customers and guests yearn for that personal touch and humane encounters with the employees during service. Guests and customers also are people, subject to changes in their behavior, demands, and decision-making. Such changes are difficult to predict and anticipate. Therefore, labor should be treated as human capital not as variable costs. A high-quality skilled workforce will ensure greater competitiveness and innovation, improve job prospects, and ease the process of adjustment in changing markets (WTO and ILO, 2014). Consequently, tourism is recognized as a many-sided and rapidly expanding economic activity relying predominantly on the labor force.

The service sector is seen as increasingly important for most of the economics in many countries. In the United States, for example, the accommodation and food service industry employ around 12.5 million people (7.61% of the total workforce). Table 1.1 offers a recent profile of employment in the industry in the United States and includes estimates for growth from 2008 to 2018. The United States Bureau of Labor Statistics expects the industry to account for 7.42% of employment in 2018 and to grow by 7.3% between 2008 and 2018 (ILO, 2010).

**TABLE 1.1** Employment in the Accommodation and Food Services Industry, by Occupation, and Percent Distribution, 2008 and Projected Change, 2008–2018.

| **Industry** | **Employment 2008** | | **Employment 2018** | |
|---|---|---|---|---|
| | **Number (thousands)** | **% Occupations** | **Number (thousands)** | **% Occupations** |
| Accommodation including hotels and motels | 1,857.3 | 1.23 | 1,956.7 | 1.18 |
| Food services and drinking places | 9,631.9 | 6.38 | 10,370.7 | 6.24 |

**Source:** The Author, based on ILO, 2010.

The often-cited benefit of tourism industries is the creation of job opportunities, so, employment in the tourism sector has received much attention (Robson, 2002). In the tourism industries, in terms of employment relations, the industry is characterized by diversity, complexity, interlinkage, and fragmentation; thus, employment refers to all the jobs (or persons engaged) in both tourism-characteristic activities and non-tourism-characteristic activities (WTO and ILO, 2014).

As compared to other economic activity, the tourism industry is an important source of job creation and countries are interested in its development for this reason, as it provides direct and indirect employment opportunities.

Tourism creates large number of direct jobs in tourist establishment like hotels, restaurants, tourist shops, travel agencies and also in transport, handloom, and handicraft industries in the destinations. It also generates certain category of workers like interpreters, guides, tour operators etc. Those directly employed in the tourism industry create indirect employment in certain other sectors through their demand for goods and services. Direct occupations are not the only jobs linked to the industry's activities, there are also many jobs that have indirect relationships with the sector (e.g., taxi drivers, other means of transport, tourist guides, or gift shops). These relationships created many types of employment contracts that include full-time, part-time, temporary, casual, and seasonal employment within the sector. The sector often crosses the fluid boundaries between the informal economy and the formal economy, with a number of formal establishments offering black market jobs (ILO, 2010).

As tourism and hospitality industry is not an industry in the traditional sense of the word, measuring tourism employment is particularly complex. The World Tourism Organization (WTO) has developed a classification methodology entitled the Standard International Classification of Tourism Activities (SICTA) in order to reduce confusion and avoid misunderstanding the core issue of tourism. Within SICTA classification, businesses in tourism are classified according the principal activity of the organization. Occupations in tourism and hospitality industry in turn can be easily identified in such as hotels and motels, camping sites, hostels, health-oriented accommodation facilities, restaurants, bars, fast food, nightclubs, taxi services, airline and car rental companies, travel agencies, amusement parks, etc. (WTO, 1997). As a result, tourism employment can be categorized at three separate levels depending on involvement into tourism supply-side (Keyser, 2002) as follows:

### 1. *Direct Employment*

Occupations that arise from direct contact with customers and tourists and cater for tourist demand like front offices in accommodation establishments, restaurants, travel agencies, tourism information offices, aircrafts, cruise lines, resorts, or shopping outlets.

### 2. *Indirect Employment*

Tourism and hospitality industry support indirect employment. It is more or less dependent on other companies in other industries or sectors, such as:

- catering companies that provide supplies and materials,
- construction companies that build and maintain tourist facilities,
- infrastructure companies,
- aircraft manufacturers,
- various handicrafts producers,
- marketing and promotion agencies,
- accounting service offices, etc.

*3. Induced or Ancillary Employment*

It means that industry growth and the general development of tourism at specific destination will stimulate the growth of employment in other areas, such as educational institutions, training academies, municipal authorities, medical establishments, police and security services, taxi and bus drivers, etc.

Being tourism and hospitality a labor-intensive industry, tourist organizations offer opportunities for employment for certain types of individuals, as follows:

- ➢ Low competent labor: Workers with little qualification in general. Applied sociological research claimed that tourism skill sets tend to have many people enter tourism field from other industries (WTO and ILO, 2014).
- ➢ Minority groups: Workers with some disabilities, ethnic minority groups and migrants, unemployed youth, long-term unemployed, as well as women with family responsibilities who can take only part-time jobs.
- ➢ Old aged workers: These types of job opportunities are considered more suitable for old aged people who are seeking for flexible job opportunity; in turn, such employment seems an important source of income for them.
- ➢ Low experienced labor: The industry is considered a good opportunity for those who entering the labor market for the first time, who are experiencing work transitions, or having difficulties in finding employment elsewhere. For example, opportunities for street vending in high-traffic areas for tourists generate livelihoods predominantly for women and children in developing countries, in such activities as food stalls, sales of trinkets, and artisan crafts (ILO, 2010).
- ➢ Small investors: In addition to the easy access to the tourism and hospitality industry jobs, tourism businesses are often individually,

or family owned (Economic and Social Commission for Asia and the Pacific, 1990). Small- and medium-scale enterprises typically require less capital to provide good service, providing people who typically cannot afford to start their own business with an opportunity to do so (Aviation, 2011).

Hence, tourism employment is a measure of the number of jobs directly attributable to tourism demand in tourism and non-tourism industries, held by employees, self-employed, and contributing family workers. Besides direct contributions to global employment, as shown in Figure 1.1, the industry also has a positive impact on livelihoods of local people in tourism destinations. In recent years, studies have shown a growing trend in the expansion of the benefits of tourism beyond the confines of traditional tourist attraction sites to local communities (Snyman, 2012). To sum up, tourism and hospitality industry give an impulse to the country's overall economic and social development by earning large sums of foreign exchange besides the vast potentiality for generating employment. The following section gives a brief discussion on the two main categories of workforce that are supported in the tourism industry.

### *1.3.1 CREATING JOB OPPORTUNITIES FOR YOUTH*

Tourism is an income multiplier (Kumar, 2005). If both domestic and international tourists visit a destination, its youths would be employed in accommodation establishments, restaurants, bars, discotheques (leisure), sea resorts, beaches, transport organizations, airlines, and tourist agencies. This list is not comprehensive. Further, local residents can also be employed in those industries that support the tourism industry of the state (Shukla and Ansari, 2013). The industry is particularly dependent on its ability to hire young men and women between ages 15 and 24, who make up the largest share of employees in the industry (Chapter 2, Young Workers).

Tourism and hospitality industry's potential to realize growth and make significant contributions to the economic development of destination areas around the world hangs on one condition: its ability to rapidly fill hundreds of thousands of new positions with qualified people. Thus, attracting young people who possess the technical skills, non-technical skills, and passion to provide exceptional guest service will prove more important than ever. In contrast to other industries, employment tends to be oriented toward people under 35 years of age, half of which are 25 or under, and a large number of this percentage are women. Every year, 120 million young people enter the workforce with enormous potential to lead productive and engaged lives and help drive real economic growth around the globe (ILO, 2012). In Spain, for example, 43.4% of workers in the sector are aged 25–34 (ILO, 2010). The United States Bureau of Labor Statistics reported a higher number of workers aged between 16 and 20 than those aged 20 and above working in food preparation and service-related occupations (ILO, 2010).

It is widely recognized that tourism and hospitality rely heavily on youth employment; however, for a variety of reasons, most youth still suffer to enter the labor market of the tourism industry.

Today's shockingly high levels of youth unemployment are driven by many factors, including lack of information about employment opportunities as well as networks needed to become connected in the workplace (Billett, 2011). They also lack strategic understanding of how to traverse the labor market in identifying and using job and training opportunities.

The ILO characterized the current state of youth unemployment as a "social and economic catastrophe" for nations across the globe (ILO, 2012) as more than 75 million of young people face significant barriers to finding decent work, locking them into a cycle of displacement and frustration. In Europe, about 5.5 million young people under 25 years of age are unemployed. The youth unemployment rate at 22.4% is twice as high as for the whole working population and nearly three times as high as the rate for the adult active population. In Spain and Greece, youth unemployment has reached almost 50% (BusinessEurope, 2012).

The barriers to employing young people at the rate required for industry growth can be found in three simple statements (Sweet et al., 2010):

- Youth do not know about the nature and extent of meaningful careers the hospitality industry offers. The lack of preparedness for the workplace makes employers averse to employing young people due to the potential of underperformance that can affect an organization's business performance. In addition, there are also questions about the work ethic of youths (Oxenbridge and Evesson, 2012).
- Youth are not suitably qualified for tourism job opportunities. Many young job seekers lack the necessary skills and adequate or sufficient training opportunities (ILO, 2011). This has been blamed on the disconnect between educational curricula and requirements of the workplace.
- Youths are not knowledgeable about how the workplace operates and fail to utilize the time spent in school to prepare their career

path. Furthermore, they fail to use their time in school to prepare appropriately for realistic career paths. Often, youths that have gone through formal training programs come out with the theoretical knowledge that fails to prepare them adequately for practical skills and knowledge required for the work environment. Added to the foregoing is the lack of both generic and soft skills "such as cooperation, communication, critical thinking, creativity, and a focus on the needs of the enterprise" required in the workplace (Mirza et al., 2014).

- The industry attracts qualified youth but does not retain an optimal number of them; effectively, most youths lack the communication and social capital that is significant to enable them to be successful in business (ILO, 2011).

In turn, the result is long-term workforce challenges that can only lead to societal unrest, economic instability, and lost generations. One such factor is "a lack of information, networks, and connections among youth, especially youth from families lacking a significant social capital" (ILO, 2011).

The following points identifies ways to meet the industry's key youth employment goals and gain other advantages through supporting the pre-employment initiatives: (1) teaching young people about the job market, (2) establishing job-shadowing programs and internships, and (3) educating youth about the lasting value of acquiring experience in the hospitality industry, and investing in on-the-job activities: (1) offering convenient and flexible opportunities for training, mentoring, and apprenticeships, (2) ensuring that training opportunities account for a diversity of team member backgrounds, (3) engaging youth in their communities, and (4) engaging them on the job, and finally activating partnerships programs between businesses, government, and education and training providers (Taylor, 2002).

### 1.3.2 CREATING JOB OPPORTUNITIES FOR WOMEN

Tourism industry is among the world's top job creators and allows for quick entry into the workforce especially for youth, women, and migrant workers. Jobs in tourism and hospitality industry were always attractive and highly appreciated. Job opportunities arising out of the growing tourism and hospitality industry cover a range of sectors and activities. Consequently, tourism industries provide entry points for women, youth, migrants, and old-aged groups' employment. It plays important role in job creation, especially in seasonal women employment. It provides women with employment and opportunities for creating self-employment in small- and medium-size income generating activities. Alternative tourism businesses are often individually, or family owned and tends to allow for more contact between locals and guests. Often, women use their existing skills to open small-scale businesses such as guesthouses and restaurants (Aviation, 2011; Gentry, 2007), thus creating paths toward minimizing poverty of women and local communities in developing countries.

The tourism industry is also considered to be oriented toward recruiting young, female workers in order to maintain its glamorous image. Likewise, the perceived glamour of tourism work is thought to be a key factor in attracting women into the workforce. Generally, tourism is seen as being a "female-friendly" work environment which is more attractive to women than to men because of the nature of the work involved. (Chapter 2, Female Workforce).

This industry has created opportunities for women who otherwise had little or no employment opportunity by allowing women to use stereotypes regarding their work to their advantage. It is believed that they are well suited for household responsibilities; many have used these ideas to open their own guest houses and restaurants (Gentry, 2007).

This view of tourism employment, as positively attractive and more suitable for their nature, provides employers with a useful explanation for the number of women working in poorly paid jobs within the industry. Their justification is that women are happy to accept the poor conditions because the work is glamorous. In many countries, females represent a majority of workers in the sector but, at the same time, find themselves significantly under-represented in higher paid and managerial positions. Such segregation is enhanced by the low status women within their societies that subsequently is reinforced and reflected in the mass industry (Jordan, 1997), for example, in Caribbean, most of the top managerial members were brought in from North America or Europe because they felt that Caribbean's did not have the experience and skills needed to serve in upper-level management. Generally, mass tourism is frequently predestined for maintaining traditional notions about female gender roles by segregating employment such that women's domestic skills and what are believed to be "feminine characteristics" become commodities. (Chapter 13, Occupational Gender Segregation).

The International Labor Office (ILO, 2010) highlighted the challenges faced by women in the tourism and hospitality workplace when it noted that the divergence between qualifications and workplace reality is observable for women, who make up between 60 and 70% of the labor force. Unskilled or semi-skilled females are more likely to experience poor working conditions, inequality of opportunity and treatment, violence, exploitation, stress, and sexual harassment." This assessment is supported by a number of complementary sources, notably the United Nations World Tourism Organization (UNWTO, 2011) in a report which highlights both the opportunities and challenges, which face women with respect to employment in tourism. Therefore, it can be concluded that women's employment in tourism is segregated both horizontally (women and men are placed in different occupations) and vertically (women are concentrated in the lower levels in occupations with few opportunities for upward mobility), with the majority of female workers located in subordinated posts, receiving lower levels of payment (Parrett, 2004).

Accordingly, one of the sector's key challenges is to ensure decent work conditions, reduce uncertainty, and support moves toward greater gender equality in the opportunities, remuneration, and working conditions available to women in tourism and hospitality industry. The success of the sector depends on staff commitment, loyalty, and efficiency, all of which are shown through interactions with customers. Thus, employers must give a good attention to the women employment issues and the surrounding conditions.

## REFERENCES

Aviation: The Real World Wide Web. Oxford Economics, 2011. [Online] www.oxfordeconomics.com (accessed Nov 7, 2017).

Baum, T. Unskilled Work and the Hospitality Industry: Myth or reality? *Int. J. Hosp. Manag.* **1996,** *15* (3), 207–209.

Billett, P. Youth Social Capital: Getting on and Getting Ahead in Life. Doctoral Thesis, School of Social Sciences, Media and Communication, University of Wollongong, 2011. [Online] http://ro.uow.edu.au/cgi/viewcontent.cgi?article=4535andcontext=theses (accessed NOV 15, 2017).

Business Europe. "Creating Opportunities for youth: How to Improve the Quality and Image of Apprenticeship.", 2012. [Online] https://www.businesseurope.eu/sites/buseur/files/media/imported/2012 00330-E.pdf (accessed Oct 26, 2017).

Datamonitor. *Global Hotels and Motels Industry Profile;* New York, 2011. http://datamonitor.com/ (accessed Jan 13, 2019).

Economic and Social Commission for Asia and the Pacific. Guidelines on Input–Output Analysis of Tourism, New York, 1990.

Egyptian National Competitiveness Council. Towards a competitive Egypt: Where Everybody Wins, in The Egyptian Competitiveness Report, Cairo, May 2008, p. 85.

Gentry, K. Belizean Women and Tourism Work–Opportunity or Impediment? *Ann. Tour. Res.* **2007,** *32* (2), 477–496.
Global Employment Outlook. "Global Spill-Overs from Advanced to Emerging Economics Worsen the Situation for Young Job Seekers," Geneva: ILO, 2012.
Grobelna, A. Intercultural Challenges Facing the Hospitality Industry: Implications for Education and Hospitality Management. *J. Intercult. Manag.* **2015,** *7* (3), 101–117.
Hinds-Smith, S. Competency Requirements of Managers in Hotels in Jamaica: The Implications of Soft Skills, MSc Thesis; Rochester Institute of Technology, 2009.
Holston-Okae, B. L. "Employee Turnover Intentions in the Hospitality Industry," 2017. [Online] http://scholarworks.waldenu.edu/cgi/viewcontent.cgi?article=4883andcontext=dissertations (accessed Oct 20, 2017).
ILO. Developments and Challenges in the Hospitality and Tourism Sector, Global Dialogue Forum for the Hotels, Catering, Tourism Sector (23–24 November)," Geneva, Switzerland, 2010.
ILO. Women and Men in the Informal Economy: A Statistical Picture, ILO, Geneva, 2002.
ILO. Employment in the Tourism Industry to Grow Significantly, 2011. [Online] http://www.ilo.org/global/publications/magazines-and-journals/world-of-workmagazine/articles/WCMS_157893/lang--en/index.htm (accessed Nov 23, 2017).
Jordan, F. An Occupational Hazard? Sex Segregation in Tourism Employment. *Tour. Manag.* **1997,** *18* (8), 525–534.
Keyser, H. *Tourism Development*; Oxford University Press: Oxford, 2002.
Mirza, F. M.; Jaffri, A. A.; Hashmi, M. S. An Assessment of Industrial Employment Skill Gaps among University Graduates in the Gujrat-Sialkot Gujranwala Industrial Cluster, Pakistan, 2014. [Online] http://pdf.usaid.gov/pdf_docs/pnaed263.pdf (accessed Aug 23, 2017).
Narayan, P. K.; Narayan, S.; Prasad, A.; Prasad, B. C. Tourism and Economic Growth: A Panel Data Analysis for Pacific Island countries. *Tour. Econ.* **2010,** *16* (1), 169–183.
Oxenbridge, S.; Evesson, J. Young People Entering Work: A Review of the Research. *ACAS Res. Papers* 2012. [Online] http://www.acas.org.uk/media/pdf/5/2/Young-people-entering-work-a-review-of-the research-accessible-version.pdf (accessed Oct 26, 2017).
Robson, E. A Nation of Lace Workers and Glassblowers? Gendering of the Maltese Souvenir Handicraft Industry. In *Gender/Tourism/Fun*; Swain, M.; Momsen, J., Eds.; Elmsford: Cognizant, 2002, pp109–117.
Ruizalba, J. L.; Bermúdez- González, G.; Rodríguez-Molina, M. A.; Blanca, M. J. Internal Market Orientation: An Empirical Research in Hotel Sector. *Int. J. Hosp. Manag.* **2014,** *38*, 11–19.
Shukla, P. K.; Ansari, A. A. "Role of Tourism Industry in Employment Generation in Gujarat: A Geographic Assessment." *Int. J. Res. Human. Arts Literature* **2013,** *1* (2), 1–8.
Snyman, S. L. The Role of Tourism Employment in Poverty Reduction and Community Perceptions of Conservation and Tourism in Southern Africa. *J. Sustain. Tour.* **2012,** *20* (3), 395–416.
StatistaGlobalHotelIndustryRetailValuefrom2010to2018(inbillionUSdollars),2017.[Online] https://www.statista.com/statistics/247264/total-revenue-of-the-global-hotel-industry/. (accessed Dec 19, 2017).
Sweet, S.; Pitt-Catsouphes, M.; Besen, E.; Hovhannisyan, S.; Pasha, F. Talent Pressures and the Aging Workforce: Responsive Action Steps for the Accommodation and Food Services Sector. [Online] http://www.bc.edu/research/agingandwork/metaelements/pdf/publications/TMISR04_Accommodation.pf (accessed Oct 21, 2017).

Taylor, S. *People and Organization Employee Resourcing*; Prentice-Hall: Sidney, Australia; 2002.

Teng, C. C. Developing and Evaluating a Hospitality Skill Module for Enhancing Performance of Undergraduate Hospitality Students. *J. Hosp. Leisure, Sport, Tour. Edu.* **2013,** *13* (1), 78–86.

UNWTO. Global Report on Women in Tourism 2010, Madrid, 2011.

Vasquez, D. Employee retention for Economic Stabilization: A Qualitative Phenomenological Study in the Hospitality Sector. *Int. J. Manag. Econ. Soc. Sci.* **2014,** *3* (1), 117.

Wilks, D.; Hemsworth, K. Soft Skills as Key Competencies in Hospitality and Higher Education: Matching Demand and Supply. *Tour. Manag. Stud.* **2011,** *7*, 131–139.

World Tourism Organization and International Labor Organization. Measuring Employment in the Tourism Industries – Guide with Best Practices; UNWTO, Madrid: 2014.

World Tourism Organization. International Tourism: A Global Perspective, Madrid, 1997.

World Travel and Tourism Council. "Travel and Tourism Global Economic Impact and Issues 2017."[Online]https://www.wttc.org/-/media/files/reports/economic-impact-research/2017 documents/global-economic-impact-and-issues-2017.pdf (accessed Oct 20, 2017).

# CHAPTER 2

# A CRITICAL ANALYSIS OF LABOR SUPPLY AND DEMAND IN THE TOURISM AND HOSPITALITY INDUSTRIES

*"The managerial notion: 'protect the job, not the workers' may be the main reason behind the imbalance phenomenon of labor demand and supply."*

## 2.1 INTRODUCTION

The nature of tourism and hospitality jobs requires special type of employees; it imposes appropriate employee structure to be engaged in all types of job positions and levels. Frontline employees who have a direct contact with guests and customers, most important attention has to be paid to them, no matter on job position: whether the property manager, receptionist, waiter, housekeeper, sales manager, banquet manager, animator, etc. Service is "care for the guest" and it is a task and duty of every person who contacts with guests, so the "philosophy of caring" must be reflected on the employees' attitudes and behaviors. In line with the philosophy of caring that tourism and hospitality labor must have and must apply during their work, hospitality jobs demand long working hours, provide seasonal employment, and have poor job security.

What is strange is that the tourism and hospitality industry ask the employee to act according to the caring philosophy when dealing with guests and customers, while, at the same platform, the organizations treat the employee according to the negligence philosophy; managers ask the employee to strive in serving guests and customers to the degree that keep the customer highly satisfied and retain them as a loyal customer, on the other hand, the organizations neglect his issues (low payment, provide a low level of job satisfaction, and limited opportunities for advancement).

Hence, the logical outcome of this discrepancy as stated by the International Labor Office (ILO) (2010) is the rapid turnover of staff. Then, there is an imbalance between the labor supply and demand of tourism and hospitality industries, these industries became relying on a flexible workforce based on part-time, fixed term, temporary contracts, and agency work far more than any other industry.

## 2.2 LABOR IN THE TOURISM AND HOSPITALITY INDUSTRY

Tourism is a rapidly growing phenomenon and tourism activities, taken as a whole, are accounting for a significant share of economic activity in most countries. This upward trend looks likely to continue into the future. In addition to other factors such as natural resources, monuments, outstanding attractive places, infrastructure, and capital, the tourism industries are heavily dependent on the human factor to ensure delivery and quality of its products and services. In other words, tourism industry is about people; visitors are people, subject to changes in their behavior, demands, and decision-making. Such changes are difficult to predict and anticipate. Also, tourism products and services are also about people. Furthermore, many tourism products include people as an integral part of the expertise offered, whether as performers or as members of the cultural environment.

Subsequently, human factor is clearly central to the effective operation and further development of the tourism industries as a whole (World Tourism Organization and International Labor Organization, 2014). So, tourism and hospitality industry is known to be labor intensive. Labor intensity, however, varies according to some factors such as (Kusluvan 2003):

- Level and type of the organization or the establishment,
- The type and stage of tourism and hospitality development, and
- Infrastructural development.

Commonly, employment is of major importance in the economic analysis of productive activities and this is true also of tourism. The focus on employment in the tourism industries is further justified by the fact that tourism industries have matured into a major consumer market experiencing increasing global and national competition, market turbulence and ever changes in consumer behavior and then in his preferences that will be reflected in his demand accordingly.

Typically, the industry consists of a number of diverse sectors including travel agencies, tour operators, transportation, accommodation establishments, food and beverage organizations, and attractions which require a variety of occupational skills and competencies. Subsequently, tourism is considered as the collection of activities, services, and industries that deliver a travel experience including attractions, lodging establishments, transportations, food and beverages properties, retail shops, entertainment, business and other hospitality services provided for individuals or groups of traveling away from home (Dayananda, 2014).

In 2013, the contribution of Travel and Tourism in the global economy reached 9.5% of global GDP; while, approximately 266 million jobs (8.9% of total employment) were supported by Travel and Tourism in 2013 (1 in 11 of all jobs in the world) (The World Travel and Tourism Council, 2014). It has become recognized that the good use of human power and attempting to raise labor skills have the greatest impact on maximizing the production and achieving the organizations' progress, so, there is no doubt that the human element is a determining factor for the degree of progress in any community. Therefore, labor should not be treated simply as variable costs, but as human capital. A loyal skilled labor will ensure greater competitiveness and innovation, improve job prospects and ease the process of adjustment in highly competitive and changing markets.

Employment in tourism and hospitality industries refers to all the jobs or individuals engaged in both tourism-characteristic activities and non-tourism-characteristic activities in all organizations and properties in tourism industries (Martin 2013). The concept of tourism employment, in accordance with the Martin, refers to employment strictly related to services and goods acquired by customers and travelers and produced by either tourism organizations or other industries (2013).

Respectively, and according to Keyser employment in tourism industries can be categorized into three separate levels depending on their involvement in or contribution to tourism supply-side into direct, indirect and induced employment (2002) as follows:

- ✓ Direct labor: Employees who are in contact with tourists and guests, and cater for tourist demand (Front offices in hotels, restaurants, travel agencies, tourism information offices, aircrafts, cruise lines, resorts, or shopping outlet),
- ✓ Indirect labor is in the tourist supply sector, but does not result directly from tourist expenditure;

✓ Induced labor is the additional employment resulting from the effects of the tourism multiplier (Infrastructure, aircraft manufacturers, various handicrafts producers, marketing agencies, and accounting services) which are more or less dependent on the tourist organization providing direct employment for their revenue (see Chapter 1, Potential of Tourism in Catering Employment).

Thus, the number of employed in tourism and hospitality industry will be underestimated when, for example:

- Catering companies providing raw materials for the production of tourism-related goods and services are left out of the picture and therefore indirect tourism-characteristic jobs are excluded.

On contrary, the number of employed will be overestimated when:

- Labor engaged in an establishment belonging to a tourism industry also participate in the establishment's non-tourism-characteristics activities.

Thus, tourism-generated expenditure creates employment in a range of sectors requiring an equally varied mix of skilled and unskilled staff. The issue of recruitment for the tourism industry can be illustrated by explaining the specifics of the tourism labor markets.

## 2.3 SPECIFICS OF THE TOURISM AND HOSPITALITY INDUSTRY'S LABOR MARKET

Tourism is not a recognized industry in the Standard Industrial Classification and most countries' national accounts would not list tourism as a separate entity. This, of course, is largely due to the fact that tourism is a "multiproduct industry" with strong linkages to other economic sectors (Riley, 2002).

The true dimensions of the tourism industry clearly stretch beyond the hospitality sector as the industry would not function without a number of other sectors and operators who together from this complex industry. The tourism industry also includes a number of other sectors and activities, namely:

- Transport
- Travel agencies, tour operators

- Tourist attractions
- Conference business
- Tour guides
- Tourist information services
- Souvenir shops
- Relevant government offices
- NGOs
- Educational establishments

Therefore, tourism and hospitality industry has the ability to attract surplus labor and to generate employment opportunities especially in developing countries; so, tourism and hospitality industry is labor intensive especially it relies heavily on its human resources to deliver service and product. The hospitality industry, in particular, is one sector that can hire hundreds of employees in a small establishment. However, a closer look at the characteristics of the workforce raises some interesting specifies, as following:

### *1. Shortage of labor*

Many tourism and hospitality businesses around the world have expressed considerable concern about the impacts of labor shortages on their businesses. Labor shortages and their impact on the industry in almost every geographic location are consistently among the most difficult challenges noted by industry professional. In many cases, tourism and hospitality activities expansion is limited not by financial factors, but rather by human resources.

The most commonly used indicators for labor shortages are the qualitative and the quantitative indicators (Estruch-Puertas and Zuppi, 2009):

- ✓ Quantitative indicator, unfilled vacancies (and a range of related indicators); and
- ✓ Qualitative indicator, skills gaps.

A number of challenges resulting from the labor shortage whether it's a qualitative or quantitative shortage that tourism and hospitality organizations are experienced are identified by the study conducted by Sentis Market Research Inc. (2014) as follows:

- ➢ Some river rafting and kayaking operators could not offer all the trips that visitors were seeking due to a shortage of qualified guides (Quantitative shortage),

- Some restaurant managers indicated that they had to close down for one shift (breakfast, lunch or dinner) or had to shut down for one extra day per week due to a shortage of servers and/or cooks (Qualitative shortage),
- Some hoteliers reported that they had to shut down the wing of a hotel due to a shortage of housekeeping staff, and other hotel workers (Quantitative shortage),
- Some businesses could not respond to all visitor requests, possibly missing reservations as a result (Qualitative and Quantitative shortage),
- Some operators had to forgo opportunities to expand their business and/or open a new business due to uncertainties about their ability to hire enough staff (Quantitative shortage),
- Some restaurant managers indicated that they had to turn down business, such as requests for catering services (Quantitative shortage),
- Some management indicated that, due to a shortage of servers, they were forced to assist on "the floor", taking management away from key activities, such as participating in important business development activities (Quantitative shortage).

Thus, shortage occurring in the workforce of tourism and hospitality industry brought a dramatic sequences in tourism and hospitality industry as recorded by Sentis Market Research Inc' study. The study estimated $918 to $1030 million in lost tourism spending (or gross revenue) across the province because of the inability of these businesses to operate at full capacity due to labor shortages. This, in turn, resulted in much larger losses, when indirect and induced economic impacts are considered. Impacts are also felt with regard to lost taxation revenue for all three levels of government (Thornton and Econometric Research Limited, 2016). Accordingly, tourism and hospitality organizations' managers have no choice except to recruit employees from both the primary and secondary labor markets in order to mitigate the unpleasant sequences of labor shortage (see Chapter 4, Reasons of Occupational Disequilibrium in Labor Markets).

## *2. Secondary labor markets*

Bauder (2006) argued that the labor market can be split into primary and secondary markets. The primary labor market consists of job seekers who are specialized in the industry through education, training, and experience; in the hotel industry, these include managers, chefs, receptionists, and bar staff.

While, the secondary labor market consists of people who are interested in the industry, but do not feel committed to a career in a particular industry.

Secondary markets are more unstable than the primary markets filled with secure jobs built on developed and educated human capital. However, hospitality organizations' managers have no choice except to rely on the secondary labor market to fill the vacancies gaps in their business.

The secondary labor market consists mainly of women, young people and ethnic minorities. The very nature of the secondary market acts to encourage mobility—where there is diversity of opportunity and accessibility, irrespective of the level of pay, there is increased mobility (Greve, 1994). Thus, staff are recruited from the secondary labor market often look for jobs merely to earn an income and not to pursue a career. Moreover, shift or part-time work deviate traditional work and life patterns. Such people are described as low skilled labor. Yunis (2009) confirmed that in Austria, qualifications of employees in tourism are significantly below the average. In 2007, 31.9% had only finished the compulsory education (in the national economy: 13.4%), 33.9% have at most a degree of a vocational training (national economy: 44.7%). The share of university graduates stood in 2007 at only 3.1% (national economy: 13.1%).

## 3. *Female workforce*

Tourism employment is considered positively attractive to women. This claim may be true because of the nature of the work involved. Thus, tourism industry is considered a "female friendly" industry which is more attractive to women according to Obadić and Marić (2009). The justification of tourism and hospitality organizations' employers was that women are happy to accept the poor conditions because the work is glamorous. According to ILO's estimation, women account for 46% of wage employment in tourism globally and up to 90% if including catering and accommodation (Saarinen et al., 2013). However, at the same time, another negative side of tourism labor market exists. Namely, women are still under-represented in the managerial structures (Witz and Savage, 1992) and the pay they get of these sectors.

According to Purcell (1996), the occupational segregation in hospitality industry in specific is justified by three main elements explaining employers to recruit women for particular types of work: labor price, sex and gender.

- Concerning the labor price; one example of this type of justification is the generalization by some employers that the disproportionately high concentration of women in low-paid, part-time jobs is primarily attributable to women's preference for these patterns of employment. Women, it is argued, seek these jobs in order to accommodate their domestic/family commitments.
- While, the worker's gender from the point of views of many employers contribute significantly in the amount of money they will get and the type of work he/she will adhere especially in developing countries where there are significant limits between female and male workers.
- The problem of gender differences in wages is especially grave in hospitality sector. As compared to male colleagues, women earn less not just when entering the world of work, but also, when reaching a career-peak position. In other words, they earn less even doing the same kind of tasks with the same level of responsibility.
- In addition, Mckenzie Gentry (2007) claimed that the gender-segregated employment is a common practice in the tourism industry. Numerous respondents in different studies mentioned that sex was important factors governing work in tourism. For instance, it is familiar that hotel domestic workers, waitress, room attendants, cleaners, travel agency salespersons, and cooks were generally female.

In addition to the three previous reasons, there is another justification for the predominance of women in tourism occupations which is ethical factors. Several studies (Peterson et al., 2001) have tested the proposition that females are more ethical than males. This assumption is supported by Landry et al. (2004) because they believe that this is based on the reality of females identifying and understanding the "nuances" of ethical dilemmas. Adebayo (2005) stressed that the ethical reference point chosen by each gender is based on the differences in the socialization techniques instilled throughout their developmental stages in life. Consequently, females tend to be more friendly, unselfish and submissive, and thus their perception is focused on caring or maintaining relations, while disapproving of those who threaten this position. In contrast, males are generally taught to be independent, assertive, fierce and aggressive in their perceived automatic obligations of financially providing –usually for their mothers –and subsequently their new family (child and/or child mother). (see Chapter 13, Tackling Workplace Discrimination).

### 4. *Young workers*

The hospitality and tourism industry has to relied upon young job seekers for its entry-level hourly jobs, and this is related to the demand for unqualified workers. It obviously varies according to the tourism sub-sectors, as shown in the following examples (Yunis, 2009):

> Australia: The Accommodation, Cafes and Restaurants industry has relatively young workforce, with more than one third (35.9%) of workers aged 15 to 24 years, compared with the average of 17.7% for all industries. Youth aged between 15 and 24 years experienced the strongest employment growth in this industry in the five years to 2007 (up by 31,600 people).
>
> Canada: Youth aged 15–24 years, occupied 39% of employee tourism jobs. Youth are disproportionately represented in the Food and Beverage services as well as in the Recreation and Entertainment industry.
>
> France: In the Hotel-café-restaurant sub-sector, which employs around 800,000 people, the proportion of young workers aged 15–29 years is quite high: 43.8% against 19.8% for the whole economy.

### 5. *Less committed workforce (high rate of labor turnover)*

As mentioned above, most of the workforce affiliated to tourism and hospitality industry belongs to the secondary labor market, accordingly, Bauder (2006) argued that labor markets of the tourism industry are far from perfect. The nature of labor market whether it is a primary or secondary market contributes critically to shaping the turnover rate of employees in the various industries.

- In the primary market, the whole of the workforce is motivated to serve their employer diligently through wages, health benefit, job security, and pension. This kind of job market consists majorly of blue-collar and white-collar jobs. This sector is characterized by high-status jobs which are better paid. Employers in this sector offer the best terms and condition and the jobs are considered mainly occupational. The employees in this sector attempt to prove themselves to their employees by portraying their abilities, skills and academic prowess. Turnover in this sector is minimal. On the other hand,

- Turnover is significantly high in the secondary sector as employees either leave or are replaced quickly. Jobs in this sector are mostly low-skilled, require relatively little training and can be learned relatively quickly and on the job. In this sector, there are few barriers to job mobility because jobs are unattractive and there are fewer incentives to stay on. Wages are low, and the terms and conditions are quite poor. Because specific professional skills are not required, employees in this sector switch jobs and employers with considerable ease. Many employees in the hospitality industry belong in this sector.

Subsequently, industry professionals and employers are beginning to feel the impact of a shrinking labor force in the service industry. Most of the studies reviewed indicate that labor market plays a significant role in determining employee turnover. However, most of the researchers do not exploit the phenomena of supply and demand of labor in determining labor turnover as an independent variable. They have viewed labor market as a sub-factor of other greater factors.

In general, CIPD (2005) introduced several reasons explaining why the high turnover rate in the tourism and hospitality industry, in addition to the characteristics of the secondary labor market that reflected on its members to the degree that made the employees hired from the secondary market have no stability in any industry:

The labor pool for the hospitality industry often consists of untrained, unskilled workers. Higher skilled employees are harder to find and even those employees are highly vulnerable as they seek better opportunities.

- Many employees are young, students or female workers or immigrant people simply using hospitality jobs as either a fallback or a stepping stone to other careers.
- It is the attraction of a new job or the prospect of a period outside the workforce which "pulls" them, employees are just waiting for the right opportunity to leave
- They are "pushed" due to dissatisfaction in their current jobs to seek alternative employment opportunities.
- Young employees are more likely to switch jobs as compared to their older counterparts who prefer job security.

Turnover also can be influenced by the nature of service industry, specifically hospitality jobs that are considered easy access jobs, in this industry, employees' competencies depend on skills acquired during training and working (Sarah et al., 2012), as long they got experienced and have the soft and hard skilled that qualify them to work in a better place, they leave.

After identifying the main themes of labor market of tourism and hospitality industry organizations and why these organizations rely on the secondary labor market and low skilled young labor. The next step is exploring the analysis of labor supply and demand.

## 2.4 A CRITICAL ANALYSIS OF LABOR SUPPLY AND DEMAND

The significant imbalance between skilled labor supply and demand in tourism and hospitality industry around the world is well recognized, but disturbingly, there is little evidence to prove reverse in this imbalance in the future (Beesley et al., 2013). The imbalance between skilled labor supply and demand in tourism and hospitality industry imposing deep investigation to catch the causes that led to increasing and expanding this issue. To get involved in the issue, first we should shed the light on three very important themes related closely to the investigated issue of labor supply and demand as follows:

### *2.4.1 THE GLAMOR/AUREOLE OF TOURISM AND HOSPITALITY INDUSTRY*

Tourism is basically a service industry and human resources are of essential significance to the success of a tourism destination. For every country, tourism is a very important economic activity because it generates employment. Tourism is generally and globally acknowledged as being one of the (very) few economic sectors that has more than significant growth prospects and therefore is characterized as a catalyst for welfare and prosperity of employees involved in working in different tourist and hospitality organizations. The attractiveness of the industry is identified as flexible hours, opportunities for minorities and females and the opportunity to learn new skills. In addition, the opportunity to travel, meet people from different cultures and backgrounds, foreign language use, and task variety are also identified.

Multi-skilling and flexible working makes tourism employment attractive to people of all skill levels, and to those seeking easy access job and looking for a wide range of non-standard working patterns. Tourism also provides workers with an opportunity to travel abroad and to learn foreign languages.

Moreover, the tourism industries are characterized by diversity both on the basis of intra-national and international criteria and have a major impact on the sector labor. The organization's type, their ownership, and the markets they serve illustrate the factors which contribute to attract employees to get involved in tourism sector. The glamorous image of tourism and hospitality industry pushed the youth to imagine working in the industry will enable them to:

- ✓ Meeting new people.
  This is a perfect chance to practice your soft skills and learn to effectively communicate across various different cultures.
- ✓ Income will be high in tourist destinations which attract large numbers of visitors; where customers spend more time and money, especially, the customers usually leave tips for employees.
- ✓ An opportunity to start a career without any experience or education. That doesn't mean you should have some basic understanding of the industry or possess the necessary features like an open mind and being an easy-going kind of person. And mind that you won't jump into a management position right away. It requires some training courses and takes a lot of experience and knowledge, and if you aim that high and don't want to climb up the career ladder for ages, you'd better enroll on a degree program.
- ✓ The enormous satisfaction you get from making other people feel welcome and happy.

Subsequently, today's generation of graduates hold distinctive perceptions of and ideals toward work and then there appears to be a gap between hospitality graduates' perceptions and the reality of the workplace (Richardson, 2009), this gap is an expected outcome which is attributed to societal change and generational shifts in thinking and expectations (Solnet and Hood, 2008). While there are some negative conceptualizations associated with industry on the other side, some of the experts interested in the industry developed a number of common perceptions of the sector (Expert Group on Future Skills Needs, 2015), for example:

- The idea that jobs in the sector are only a "stop-gap" while studying
- Working in hospitality is not considered by some as a viable career choice
- There is also a societal and family focus on completing education. This is influenced by parental judgement and by the advice of some school guidance counsellors.

Dodds and Joppe (2005) claimed that this sector is known for low pay (for example, in the European Union, it is less than 20% of the average salary), difficult working conditions (irregular schedules, Sunday/holiday work, unpaid overtime), and many clandestine jobs. Women make up 70 percent of the labor force in tourism and there are numerous cases of youth or child workers (half the workers in the sector are up to 25 years old). Hence, there are some cons of working in the industry are as following (Lindsay and McQuaid, 2004; Szivas et al., 2003; Choi et al., 2000):

- It is a 24/7 business creating a work-life imbalance for employees especially for those having family responsibilities (long unsociable hours),
- Working weekends and holidays. This may include some of the big and special events like Christmas, your friends' birthdays, weddings, and if you're unlucky, your own birthday too.
- Poor wages, shifts, sexual discrimination, and narrow job function.
- Stressful working environment. That makes part of any job based only contacting and serving people. That is because we are not machines, and anything can go wrong when the human factor is involved.
- Low skilled work and lack of training opportunities.
- The lack of clear career paths (and/or slow progression) within the tourism and hospitality industry further impacted on both recruitment and retention.

Thus, form the point of view of experienced workers, hospitality employment is often seen as a transitory job whilst completing studies or as a stepping stone to another career (Duncan et al., 2013; Solnet and Hood, 2008), that trend destroyed the aureole of working in tourism industry.

### 2.4.2 NATURE OF THE OPERATION "SERVICE"

Tourism and international travel become popular all over the world and people themselves considered that travel is human rights, on the other side, destinations are worried much to meet the needs and wants of tourists to offer high standard of services in the destinations; tourists have a wide choice of holidays; international standards and quality assurance system are being set by national and international tourism and hospitality associations to provide standardized and quality customer services thereby ensuring sustainable development in the sectors.

All the aforementioned cases require a certain type of labor who have the willingness to serve others and offer them the highest level of satisfaction. However, any service definition and conception is still problematic. Finding an ideal definition and a corresponding list of characteristics is very difficult, if not impossible. The definition that is selected here to discuss is defined by Lehtinen (1984 in Lehtinen, and Järvinen, 2015): "Service, actually a service-like marketed entity, is a benefit providing object of transaction that is a more or less abstract activity or process of activities essentially produced, marketed and consumed in a simultaneous interaction." In addition to the service characteristics, there are the traveler's characteristics, the cultural diversity that distinguish the travelers' experience itself which demands well-developed communication and high interpersonal skills in employees.

Subsequently, the service process requires personal interaction that has increased the pressure on the employees and workers; also most services consist of various processes, which the employee has to follow. Hence, it can be said that working in the service sector and especially in hospitality organizations requires employees with special abilities, requires those who have both the vocational and soft skills, the above service definition by Lehtinen (1984) contains three basic characteristics usually connected to services, namely:

1. abstract nature, that is, intangibility,
2. the simultaneousness of production, consumption, marketing (inseparability), and
3. the interactive nature.

In addition to the mentioned characteristics that make service process more challenging, the hotel and restaurant and transport and communications sectors stand out as generally having less favorable work conditions than other service industries within the service sector. Working environment conditions in such service sector also tend to be as bad as or less favorable than in the other sectors.

For example, a higher proportion of workers in these sectors report working long hours and having no additional financial benefits than do workers in manufacturing. The spread of jobs involving unpleasant work tasks, monotonous work, limited work autonomy or limited working-time flexibility is also roughly similar.

In addition, the proportion of workers not feeling secure in their jobs is higher in the hotel and restaurant sector than in manufacturing, although the proportion is lower than in agriculture and construction. This claim is also confirmed because tourism and hospitality have all the characteristics of services. In general, for the sake of analyzing the term of service associated in hospitality industry operations, three characteristics of services are of great significance: First, all tourism services are intangible. Oxford Dictionary defines it as (1) something that cannot be touched or seen, (2) something that cannot be precisely defined and formulated, and (3) something that is unable to be grasped mentally. While, the Cambridge International Dictionary of English says: "immaterial, impossible to be seen or touched, but real, and therefore difficult to be explained or shown."

This causes an increase in the uncertainty level. Customers draw the conclusion of the service mainly from the service employee and workers actions and attitudes. So, it is very important for the service labor to tangibilize the service. Customers evaluate the service during the time the service is delivered to them "encountering time," and this also put extra pressure on labor staff involved in the hospitality and tourism.

The inseparability of tourism services is a second important characteristic. Production and consumption take place on the properties or in the equipment of the producer, and not in the residence of the customer. As a consequence, the employee of the tourism suppliers has some consumer contact and is seen by the tourists to be an inseparable aspect of the service product. Whereas goods can be tested and guaranteed, and product performance can be enforced by consumer protection laws, this is much more difficult with tourism services.

The inseparability has direct consequences not only on the customers but hard impacts on the staff providing the service. So, the performance in a hotel is determined by the attitude of the staff, and normal guarantees or legal enforcement cannot be expected. Indeed, the attitude of the staff (e.g., friendliness, helpfulness) is often a vital element in delivering tourism products. Human beings are not machines, and one group of hotel tourists may be very satisfied with the staff's behavior whereas another group arriving a week later may have a lot of complaints; perhaps owing to the staff's pressure of work. Together with climate, attitude is to a large extent responsible for the heterogeneity of performance. Heterogeneity is directly related to the characteristic of inseparability.

For our purpose, perishability is the most important character of services with respect to tourism. For this reason, the following paragraph is dedicated to this characteristic. The perishability of tourism products can best be illustrated by a practical example. An accommodation establishment with 100 rooms has a production capacity of 100 rooms for rent every day, and the manager is required to sell this full capacity every day. Logically, on most days of the year, he will not be successful. Unlike goods, the manager cannot save the unsold rooms in stock for the next day, and nor can he reduce the capacity. Supply in tourism is relatively inflexible, and rooms that are not rented are totally lost - or "perishable". All hotels staff and transport operators face the same situations of matching perishable supply to the available demand. The production capacity that is not sold on a particular day is lost and can never be recovered. As a direct consequence of perishability, it is not possible to create a stock of hotel rooms, restaurant tables or plane seats.

In order to cope with the perishable character of tourism products, many owners and managers created restrictive specification for the jobs of the organizations they own or manage, and this obviously reflects on the performance of the staff, and increase the pressure of the work environment because they all the time required not to meet the specification but also to exceed to get their customers not only highly satisfied but to guarantee that he will come again.

Subsequently, service sector labor need to have special characteristics, the most important is creativity and flexibility to be able to manage effectively every single encounter with the customers and to convince him to get the service—because service unlike the goods, it needs a speaker to speak in behalf, and to keep their organization brand name into the customers mind, in addition to be able to compete up with the various special characteristics of service environment (Table 2.1).

**TABLE 2.1** Characteristics that Distinguish Services from Goods.

| | Goods | Services | |
|---|---|---|---|
| | Machine | Human | |
| | Manufacturing | Performance | |
| **Homogeneity** | Material | Experience | **Heterogeneity** |
| | Can be delivered home | Require movement to get it | |
| | Tangible | Intangible | |
| | Expected | Unexpected | |

**Source:** The Authors.

From the above, the term service holds many challenging meanings that need to be addressed effectively, also, it should be taken into account that customer and guest expectations and their perceptions of service quality vary, so employees should be able to and can evaluate and adapt as best they can to the needs of guests. Besides individual capabilities and commitment of employees to achieve a high quality of service, teamwork is a very important aspect of this issue and can help a lot to cope up with the service process challenges. Teamwork in many companies in the tourism and hospitality industry is an important prerequisite for successes and leadership.

### *2.4.3 THE CHARACTERISTICS OF WORK*

The nature of working in the organization of the hospitality industry is complicated, the organizations involved in the tourism and hospitality industries are subject to on-going restructuring and evolutionary change. According to Hjalager and Baum (1998), there are major labor market and skills implications of such change as businesses reshape the range of services they offer or respond to fashion and trend imperatives in the consumer marketplace (Warhurst et al., 2000). Vertical diversity in hospitality work is represented by a more traditional classification that ranges from unskilled to semi-skilled, and from skilled to supervisory and management. This "traditional" perspective of work and, therefore, skills in hospitality is partly described by Riley (1996) in terms that suggest that the proportionate breakdown of the workforce in hospitality is as follows:

- Managerial level—6%,
- Supervisory level—8%,
- Craft (skilled) level—22%, and
- Operative level (semi-skilled and unskilled)—64%.

All the workforce involved in tourism and hospitality industries whatever their positions in their organizations must understand the nature of their work and act accordingly, tourism and hospitality employee is a person that takes care of the guests during their visit, who is responsible to enable them to spend their time as much as more pleasant, and fulfilled, after which they will leave with feeling of satisfaction. Therefore, an employee can appear in different roles and tasks that come out of his/her main job task to take care of guests' needs.

However, Riley claimed that the internal labor market of the tourism and hospitality industries is very weak (1996), he justified that his workforce structure has to a number of weak externalities including educational requirements, points of entry into the workforce, workplace pay differentials and level of trade union membership. This analysis has important ramifications for the status of hospitality work, and the perceived attractiveness of the sector both for employment and educational/training opportunity.

Keep and Mayhew (1999) summarized a list of the characteristics of hospitality work that tend to confirm Riley's weak internal labor market attribution:

- informal recruitment practices;
- the tendency to low wages, except where skills shortages act to counter this;
- rare incidence of equal opportunities policies and male domination of higher-level positions, and better paid work;
- prevalence of unsocial hours and family unfriendly shift patterns;
- poor or non-existent career growth structures;
- failure to adopt formalized "good practice" models of human resource management and development;
- lack of any significant trade union presence;
- high levels of labor turnover;
- difficulties in recruitment high skilled employees; and
- difficulties in retention.

### 2.4.4 INAPPROPRIATE MANAGEMENT STYLE

Another perspective that can be considered one of the most important approaches in understanding the imbalance phenomenon of labor supply and demand is the management style. The management practices and procedures refer to all the activities concerning a company's human resources: selection, recruitment, job description, personnel assessment, reward and benefit systems, training and career progression. So, inadequate management practices and procedures are considered as the main risk source from the employees' point of view.

The management controls everything relating to the employees and this makes them a vital partner in shaping work condition; they control payment, time commitments, job satisfaction, organizational structure, jobs skills, education, and training level and even the management style. Inappropriate management style uses inappropriate corporate philosophy and leadership style, considering staffs as a cost rather than an asset, unplanned recruitment, little due attention for staff turnover, imported workforce, rigid leadership which is against the concept of democracy, and inadequate trainings are some managerial procedures that are considered irresponsible (Dayananda, 2014).

Further, managerial level in tourism industries involves a disproportionately high degree of owner or proprietors, as well as own-account workers (self-employed), that is, those who work on a contractual basis for a specified period of time.

Thus, the labor profile of large hospitality organizations generally shows a flat occupational pyramid in that the majority of the jobs are low-skill positions (Cooper and Kleinschmidt, 1994) (Fig. 2.1). This structure results in two main outcomes:

1. Reinforcing the power of the managerial level to use whatever they want against their employees, and
2. Lack of career development and lack of staff motivation as the opportunities for promotion are very limited.

The flat occupational pyramid profile of hospitality organization contributed significantly in reinforcing the unfavorable managerial notion that seeks to protect only the job, not the employee, and this may be one of the main reasons of creating working environment full of confusion, fear, and espionage, in turn creating an employee who does not feel job security and thus, recording high rates of labor turnover in tourism and hospitality sector.

Also, the full power that employees involved in the managerial level are enjoying may push them to commit unacceptable incidents, according to The Kroll Global Fraud Report, about 30% of senior or middle management employees are accused of fraud and theft actions.

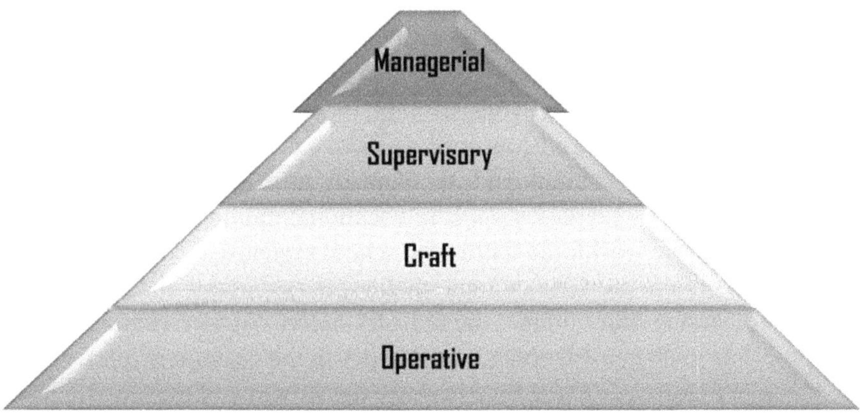


**FIGURE 2.1** Labor profile of large hospitality organizations.

**Source:** The Authors.

Furthermore, managers according to Peceri often face accusations of discrimination on the basis of age, gender, race, and belief often leading their organizations to lose employees and also to lose their customers as a result of the bad reputation concerning human rights, and also this may lead to complaints that may result in lawsuits (2010).

The cost of legal actions is enormous and time consuming, no hospitality organization wishes to face a lawsuit. So, management must give their employees an equal treatment because the managerial style and job design not only influences the degree of employee commitment to the organization but add to the organization revenues.

A significant need for industry managers is to learn better management techniques that would aid in retaining the most valuable, well-trained workforce, effectively helping the industry compete in the competitive hospitality market with ease (Brown et al., 2015). In particular, high turnover could be detrimental and disruptive to the hospitality organizations (Faldetta et al., 2013).

Almost without exception, any commentary on labor supply and demand in the tourism industry will first note the nature of the industry and the wrong managerial style have contributed critically to the labor imbalance, these factors also supported by the unreal picture of the industry that has been rooted in the minds of young job seekers (Fig. 2.2).

As already mentioned, this spans across all facets of the tourism industry, but within the hospitality sector, this is perhaps most pronounced in organizational terms. This point is made, not to reignite the debate, but to acknowledge some of the unique characteristics of tourism as an economic sector and how these defining characteristics have contributed to the current human resource crisis confronted by the hospitality industry (Beesley et al., 2013).

To sum up, a labor market consists of all industry sectors, their personnel requirements and skill needs, as well as those currently outside the actual labor force, whether unemployed, temporarily unable to work because of illness or injury, or undergoing specific vocational training, or more general preparation for the workforce within the school systems. Within the tourism labor market, there are fundamental challenges (structural and perceptual) relating to, among other things, the industry nature, service characteristics, inappropriate management style, and changes in the customers' preferences as shown in Figure 2.2. These factors shape the structure of the tourism labor force, making it difficult to maintain high permanent staffing levels.

Thus, according to International Labor Office (2001), there is a generic tendency to operate on the basis of a core staff and to employ the labor

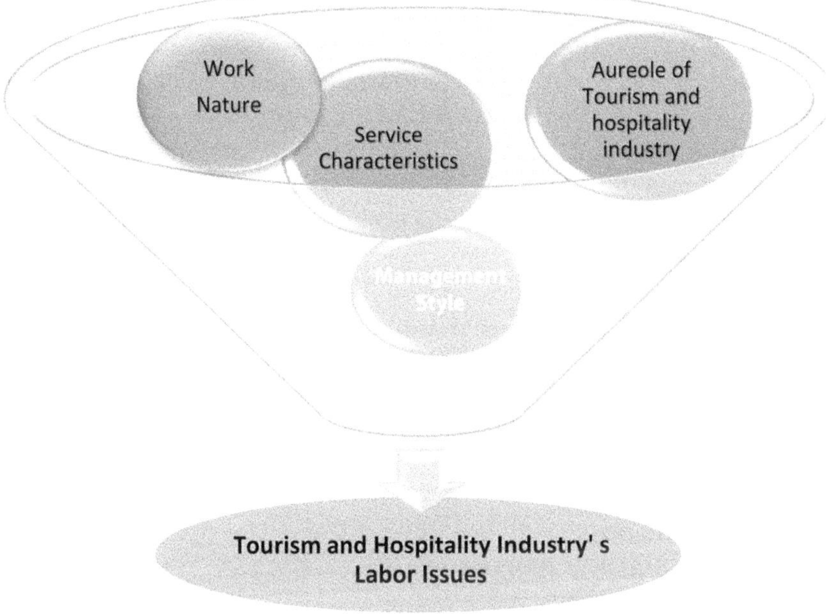


**FIGURE 2.2** Factors of the imbalance of labor supply and demand.
**Source:** The Authors

needed for day-to-day operations under atypical contractual arrangements, and this created the imbalance between the labor supply and demand in the industry.

The tourism and hospitality industries are characterized by the predominance of on-call, casual, temporary, seasonal, and part-time employment related to insecurity, comparatively low pay (frequently below the national average), job instability, limited career opportunity, a high level of subcontracting and outsourcing, and a high turnover rate. Keep and Mayhew (1999) noted that "the aim of many who enter the sector is to eventually start up their own business." Others may choose to do so after careers in different areas of employment or enterprise, perhaps for "lifestyle" reasons (Andrew et al., 2001).

This type of employment has clear implications for human resource practices where:

- training courses budgets,
- career growth/progression opportunities,

- strategic human resource plans, and
- required skill levels

vary dramatically as a function of organizational size. Without doubt the organization size and also the area where the organization is located affect significantly on the labor skills supply and demand; small-to-medium sized enterprises located in regional areas differ sharply from those located internationally. Small-to-medium sized enterprises are also affected noticeably by the labor crisis.

In one word, each of aforementioned factors presents a particular challenge in the effective management of workforce within the hospitality sector; in turn, they have created a critical imbalance in labor supply and demand, not just in the recruitment process, but also in retention system. To address this imbalance in labor supply and demand it is necessary to understand the factors controlling the process of labor supply and demand.

## 2.5 LABOR DEMAND AND SUPPLY WITHIN THE TOURISM AND HOSPITALITY INDUSTRY

Tourism contributes to economic growth and job creation. However, many of these jobs are seasonal or part-time, require low levels of skill and offer wages no better than minimum wage rates. Most jobs are in the accommodation industry, restaurants, and bar jobs, especially in food and beverage outlets. Many job seekers get their first job in tourism because of the widespread availability of jobs but there is little job security or opportunity for career progression.

Globally, in the accommodation industry, there is an average of one employee for each room in hotels. One job in the core tourism industry creates about one and a half additional (indirect) jobs in the tourism-related economy.

Being a human-resource intensive sector, tourism offers opportunity to get a job for persons entering the labor market for the first time or having difficulties in finding a job elsewhere, such as low-skilled workers, people with disabilities and workers with little qualification in general, ethnic minority groups and migrants, unemployed youth, long-term unemployed, as well as women with family responsibilities who can take only part-time jobs. So, the tourism and hospitality industries are characterized by diversity, complexity, interlinkage, and fragmentation in terms of employment relations. Direct employment is not the only way linked to the sector's activities (e.g., hotels and restaurants employees); there are also many jobs that have indirect relationships with the sector (e.g., taxi drivers, other means of transport, tourist guides, gift shops). Also, diversity of the labor market covers many different characteristics, including age, disability, race, religion, sex, values, educational level, ethnic culture, social class, and economic status (Morrison et al., 2006).

These relationships influence the many types of workplace contracts that include full-time, part-time, temporary, casual and seasonal employment and have significant implications for "Human Resource Procedures" within the industries. The sector often crosses the boundaries between the informal economy and the formal economy, with a number of formal establishments offering black market jobs. Tourist movements generate livelihoods predominantly for women and children in developing countries.

Like any other market, the labor market consists of a supply side and a demand side. Consistent with the law of supply and demand (as price rises, quantity demanded falls and quantity supplied rises), the demand curve has a negative slope and the supply curve has a positive slope (LaFaive, 2001):

- **The labor supply** of the population, referred to as the economically active population or labor force, has two components: employed individuals and unemployed persons. It merely indicates how much labor workers are willing to offer at various prices. The supply curve for each worker will be different as each worker has different opportunity costs and preferences.

The labor market consists of people doing productive work for wages. labor in the tourism sector involved people who are working and getting a certain wage from either or both direct and indirect tourism-related businesses such as accommodation establishments, restaurant workers, handicraft production, construction jobs created by the demand for new hotels, guesthouses or the expansion of the airports or other forms of transportation, superior quality shops and so on are engaged in the tourism labor market.

It is also important to highlight that the sector and its informal components provide a significant number of jobs to workers with little or no formal training and who do not want to enter long-term employment commitments (e.g., students). In addition, the sector provides opportunities for migrants to find jobs as well as for workers who have family responsibilities. Tourism can provide an opportunity for those facing significant social and capability disadvantages in a way that is not always offered by other environments (ILO, 2010).

Generally, tourism activities are highly dependent upon the availability and quality of labor resources. An understanding of labor tourism markets is thus of primary importance to the tourism industry in both developed and developing countries. Subsequently, it is very important to assure a balance of the labor supply and demand for sustainable tourism development.

- **The labor demand** of enterprises and other production units, too, can be broken down into two components: jobs (filled posts) and job vacancies (unfilled posts). The demand curve for each organization will differ as each firm faces different labor substitutes (differing rates of potential capital substitution, for instance), preferences, demand curves for the business profit, and alternative employment for their resources.

Generally, the following section explains the different factors that shape labor demand of organizations involved in tourism and hospitality industries.

### *2.5.1 LABOR DEMAND*

Tourism as a demand-side phenomenon refers to the activities of visitors and their role in the acquisition of goods and services. Tourism creates opportunities for many small and micro-entrepreneurs, be they in the formal or the informal sector. They generate a substantial share of total jobs. Large tourism enterprises are concentrated in accommodation and transport activities. In most of the cases, large international hotel and leisure chains which pick up the major part of the profits import their tourism employees and managers. By contrast, local populations benefit only from low or semi-skilled, poorly paid jobs (cooks, maintenance workers, room attendants, barmen, gardeners, bus drivers, etc.) (Dodds and Joppe, 2005).

Here are the factors that control demand of labor:

#### *A. Enterprises' Size*

Small and Medium Enterprises (SME) are necessary to the tourism economy and workforce employment. The industry is characterized by a high share of micro, small, and medium enterprises (MSMEs) (Table 2.2). However, according to Ackah and Vuvor (2011), there is no universal definition for SMEs because the definition depends on who is defining it and where it is being defined.

For example, in Canada SME is defined as an enterprise that has fewer than 500 employees and small enterprise as one that has less than 100 employees. On the other hand, the World Bank defines SMEs as having no more than 500 employees. So, in order to perfectly define SMEs, two main ways must be followed:

1. the number of employees in an enterprise and/or
2. the enterprises fixed assets.

According to ILO (2010), more than 2.5 million SMEs are estimated to be involved in tourism industry in Europe. The sector in Spain, for example, is composed of 43.4% of hotel chains with more than 50 employees compared to 56.6% with one to 50 employees (ILO, 2010). Unlike the more general European picture of tourism enterprises, businesses in North America, emerging Asian destinations, Australia, the United Kingdom, and some Nordic countries are more strongly influenced by large hotel chains that employ more than 250 people (ILO, 2010).

**TABLE 2.2** Tourism Enterprises' Size and Employment Contribution.

| Enterprises' size | No. of employees | Annual work unit | Annual turnover |
|---|---|---|---|
| Micro | Up to 5 | ≤ 10 | ≤ €2 Million |
| Small | 5–19 | ≤ 50 | ≤ €10 Million |
| Medium | 20–250 | ≤ 250 | ≤ €50 Million |

**Source:** The Authors, based on European Commission, 2005.

The importance of the SME sector is well recognized worldwide due to its significant contribution to gratifying various socioeconomic objectives, such as higher growth of employment, output, promotion of exports and fostering entrepreneurship. According to Keskin et al. (2010), SMEs contribute to over 55% of GDP and over 65% of total employment in developed countries.

SME's and informal enterprises account for over 60% of GDP and over 70% of total employment in developing countries, while they contribute over 95% of total employment and about 70% of GDP in middle-income countries. Also, it is apparent that SMEs play an important role in all countries' economies of The Organization for Economic Cooperation and Development (OECD), they makeup over 95 percent of enterprises and account for 60 to 70 percent of jobs in most OECD countries (https://www.oecd.org/cfe/smes/2090740.

pdf). Specifically, in European Union countries, there are some 25 million small businesses, constituting 99% of all businesses; they employ almost 95 million people, providing 55% of total jobs in the private sector (Keskin et al., 2010).

Thus, according to ILO, there is solid empirical evidence confirming that SMEs are a major job creation engine (2015). Moreover, an important contribution is on exports and on productivity growth (OECD, 2004). The actual importance of SMEs is emerged to adapt the changing conditions of competition and innovation with the globalization process. SMEs, in many studies, are seen as key actors in innovation systems and are important in increasing the competitive and innovative capacity of the countries/regions.

### *B. Rate of Labor Turnover*

Bolch (2001) defined labor turnover, as the movement of people in and out of a business, measures the extent of change in the workforce due to accession (total number of employees added to employment) and separation (severance of employment at the instance of workers or employers) during a particular period of time. While Beam's (2009) definition is the ratio comparison of the number of employees a company must replace in a given time period to the average number of total employees.

There are many reasons that employees may leave an organization is due to unsatisfactory performance appraisals. Low pay is a good reason as to why an employee may be lacking in performance. Unequal or substandard wage structures fall under this category as well. "When two or more employees perform similar work and have similar responsibilities, differences in pay rate can drive lower paid employees to quit. In a like vein, if you pay less than other employers for similar work, employees are likely to jump ship for higher pay, if other factors are relatively equal (Handelsman, 2009).

Another reason that employees leave is the lack of benefits available to them through the company in which they work. High employee turnover could also be due to no potential opportunity for advancements or promotions. Employees prefer other organizations which may provide them with higher posts and increased compensation packages (Rampur 2009). If the job is basically a dead-end proposition, this should be explained before hiring so as not to mislead the employee. The job should be described precisely, without raising false hopes for growth and advancement in the position.

Employees still seek to work in a suitable and appropriate work environment (Handelsman, 2009).

A bad match between the employee's skills and the job can also be a reason for an employee to leave an organization. ""Employees who are placed in jobs that are too difficult for them or whose skills are underutilized may become discouraged and quit. Inadequate information about skill requirements that are needed to fill a job may result in the hiring of either under skilled or overqualified workers." (Handelsman, 2009). Moreover, employees may leave an organization due to the lack of projects or assignments that do not require their full potential. "Employees would certainly leave if they do not get a real experience and knowledge and are just placed on the 'bench'. Other causes which contribute to employee turnover are lack of employee motivation, work pressure, job stress, partiality and favoritism, employee egos and attitudes, poor employee management." (Rampur, 2009) (see Chapter 7, Causes of Turnover).

Although high rate of labor turnover affects negatively on the business' performance and profits, some turnover is good. As cited in Rampur (2009), George Zografos, Chief Executive Officer of the Z Donut Company claimed that relating to employee turnover, there are a host of good and bad issues. New employees do bring in new ideas, attitudes and keep the organization fresh and current. Also, money is not the only motivator.

Employers would be able to retain and attract well-qualified and talented personnel if they could to identify the cause that makes their employees leave the organization and make it would make them competitive points. Here are some tips on how to control employee turnover in your organization:

- Identify the cause that makes the employees leave the organization (Zografos, 2006).
- Provide an employee-friendly work environment (Pires, 2009); work environment, respect, responsibility, and camaraderie play a huge role in keeping an employee.
- Attract well-qualified and talented employees at good salaries (Rampur, 2009),
- Hire persons seeking stability, older people better than kids labor (Pires, 2009).
- Notify the employees of the all benefits like compensation package, long-term care and life insurance (Nugent, 2009).

- Devise motivational tools, challenge your employees, and award them (Pires, 2009), staff need to get motivated because employees generally want to do a good job, it follows that they also want to be appreciated and recognized for their works. Even the most seasoned employee needs to be told what he or she is doing right once in a while (Shamsuzzoha, 2007).
- Provide excellent supervision, incompetent supervisors are often one of the first issues linked to employee turnover and try to recognize employee success, it is important to let your employees know that their work does not go unnoticed (Pires, 2009).

## *C. Seasonality Phenomenon*

Employment levels in tourist destinations follow the seasonality of tourism demand in most tourist destinations and resorts. Most tourism destination and resorts have a "high" season when employment levels and tourist visitation and spending are at a peak, and a "low" season when employment and tourist visitation and spending is the lowest. Biedermann defined seasonality as "a prevalent characteristic in travel and tourism marked by sharp variations in demand depending on the time of the year" (2008, 41).

As cited in (Morse and Smith, 2015), Baron (1975) specified the causes of variation (seasonality) in tourism demand into four categories:

1. natural Climate Seasonality,
2. institutional Seasonality,
3. calendar Effects, and
4. sociological and Economic Causes (cited in Morse and Smith, 2015).

The seasonal fluctuation of capacity use of tourism destinations and resources brings a local shift of the working area (e.g., from ski destinations in winter to the lakes or coasts in summer). This requires a high degree of flexibility of the labor tourism markets, but also the need to consider, in highly seasonal destinations, developing plural-activity skills for local populations (Yunis, 2009). Unfortunately, seasonality or temporal demand fluctuations generated many terms of unfavorable consequences of, whether they should be expressed in terms of:

- ➢ accommodation terms (bed nights),
- ➢ destination statistical reports (total numbers of visits),

- tourist organization financial returns (monthly income generated), or
- the economic indicators (unemployment rate).

However, the most acceptable measure in this section is the unemployment rate. Seasonality phenomenon is considered a main factor in labor crisis; it generates a high level of unemployment in the tourism labor market. This fact is confirmed by the data used to analyze the employment and unemployment levels in many destinations around the world, where, part-time jobs as a new pattern of employment aroused as a result of low tourist demand (Table 2.3), part-time jobs are the logic results of low weekday demand versus high demand on weekends for many tourism businesses (e.g., restaurants, hotels, etc.). This fluctuation along the week makes it difficult for businesses to employ all their workers on a full-time basis.

**TABLE 2.3** Part-time Jobs as a Pattern of Employment.

| Country | Part-time job% | Year | Sub-sectors |
|---|---|---|---|
| Canada | 36% | 2006 | Hotels, restaurants, and Cafés |
| Australia | 48.1% | – | The accommodation, cafés, and restaurants |
| France | 55% | – | Hotel and restaurants |
| Spain | 17% | 2008 | Hotel and restaurants |

**Source:** The Authors, based on ILO, 2009.

However, the nature of part-time/casual employment entails poorer conditions of work, high staff turnover, and in some instances less professional performance. Consequently, the seasonality of the hospitality industry is highly related to labor turnover (Arnoux-Nicolas et al., 2016). So, most studies have identified seasonality and systematic fluctuations in tourist demand as problems to be modified or reduced in tourism destinations and communities. Problems associated with the economic impacts of seasonality are focused on problems during the off-peak season such as the loss of profits and cutting off jobs that would create unemployment due to the idle use of resources and facilities.

Several countries reported efforts to extend the high season by creating new tourism products that attract tourists all the year around. This would solve the seasonality of employment, as well as help to secure a better return on investment (see Chapter 8, Managing Seasonality).

## D. Vulnerability of Tourism Industries to Emergencies

There is no universally accepted definition of what constitutes an emergency. However, it appears that three elements must be present according to Henderson (2006):

- a triggering event causing significant change or having the potential to cause significant change; the perceived inability to cope with this change; and
- a threat to the existence of organizations, as well as of tourists and members of the tourism industry.

Every emergency/crisis is unique, displaying a remarkable range and variety (Henderson, 2006), yet characteristics generally cited include unexpectedness, urgency, and danger. Thus, employment opportunities in tourism and hospitality are affected by different difficult situations that the tourism and hospitality industry faced.

Causes of many tourism emergencies can be traced to developments in the economic, political, sociocultural and environmental domains which affect demand and supply in generating and destination countries. For instance, terrorist attacks are happening in different tourist destinations, for example, ISIS, Bokhara, Alishavave, etc.; prevalence of new contagious diseases such as the so-called Ebola and Zika virus; world economy crises and technological advancement in tourism and hospitality sectors such as the application of e-business, e-marketing, and virtual tourism. Emergencies that strike tourism industry usually share these attributes although certain crisis situations can be predicted and lack immediacy.

Thus, crises generated within the industry can also be analyzed under the headings of economic, sociocultural and environmental when tourism has negative impacts in these fields (Henderson, 2006). Due to these reasons, many tourism and hospitality industries are incurring loss in their business. This is the main reason that employers are firing the workforces, which gives rise to unemployment rate (Aynalem et al., 2016) (see Chapter 9, Tourism and Emergency).

Emergencies occur at all levels of tourism operations with varying degrees of severity, from much publicized environmental, economic and political disasters through to internally generated risks such as work accidents and sudden illness (Beeton, 2001). Unfortunately, the sector of travel and tourism is very susceptible to a wide range of internal and external forces and is impacted heavily by crisis events resulting in negative tourist perceptions (Pforr and Hosie, 2009).

**TABLE 2.4** Financial Crisis Impacts on Tourism Regions.

| Regions | Impacts % | Comments |
|---|---|---|
| Europe | Down 6% | Tourism regions in Central, Eastern, and Northern Europe were particularly badly hit compared to Western, Southern and Mediterranean Europe |
| Asia and the Pacific | Down 2% | The second half of 2009 saw a 3% growth |
| The Americas | Down 5% | The last quarter of 2009 saw a notable growth |
| The Middle East | Down 6% | The middle east had a positive second half in 2009 |
| Africa | Up 5% | Africa was the only stronger performer, particularly sub-Saharan destinations |

**Source:** The Authors, based on UNWTO, 2009.

Economic downturn and recession, fluctuating exchange rates, loss of market confidence and withdrawal of investment funds can all create a tourism crisis.

Such crises had resulted that the businesses have reported a downturn in sales of lodging, foodservice, events, and other hospitality products and some have closed their doors forever.

The decline resulted not only from the decreased number of customers in hotels, restaurants, conference, convention centers etc., but also from a significant decline in the average expenditure per guest (Pizam, 2009). Because of the global economic crisis, the hospitality and tourism industry experienced a serious downturn in sales and profitability. For example, the worldwide financial crisis in 2009 influenced sharply the performance of various global regions in the world (Kapiki 2012). For more specific information see Table 2.4.

However, according to UNWTO (2017), tourism has shown extraordinary recovery in recent years, despite many challenges, particularly those related to safety and security. Yet, international travel continues to grow strongly and contribute to job creation and the wellbeing of communities around the world (Table 2.5).

**TABLE 2.5** 2016 Regional Results of Tourist Arrivals.

| Regions | International arrivals | Increase% |
|---|---|---|
| Europe | 620 million | 5% |
| Asia and the Pacific | 303 million | 8% |
| Americas | 201 million | 4% |
| Africa | 58 million | 8% |
| Middle East | 54 million | 4% |

**Source:** The Authors, based on UNWTO, 2017.

Despite the good indication that shown in the previous table, if the tourism organizations are well prepared and equipped to such bad triggering events, the number of arrivals would be the double and the tourism will be stamped as the economy of all eras.

The following fishbone diagram (Fig. 2.3) summarizes the causes that affect labor demand of tourism and hospitality industry that mentioned above in details.

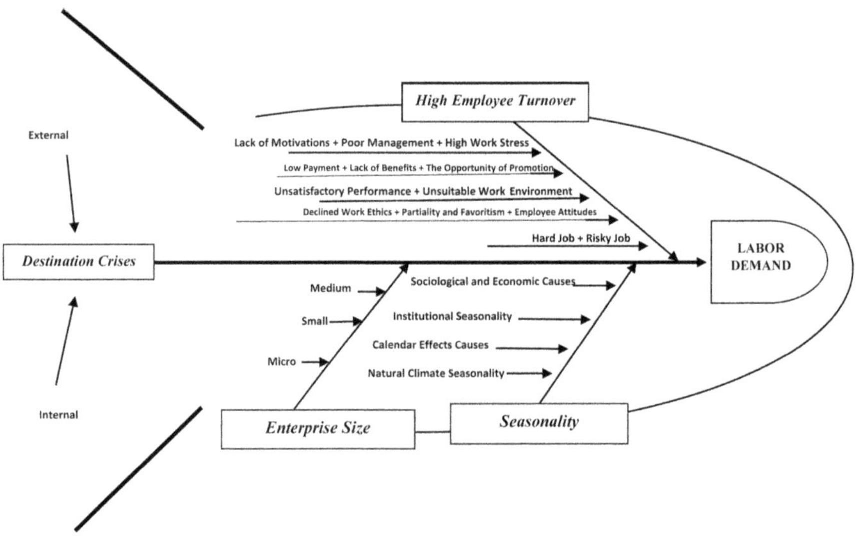


**FIGURE 2.3** Labor demand of tourism and hospitality industry.
**Source:** The Authors.

### 2.5.2 LABOR SUPPLY

The tourism industry is playing an increasingly significant important role in the economy of many countries, contributing, to their economic growth and job creation. This requires more and more attention, not only to quality in products and services but also to quality of labor, which is one of the major assets of this industry.

Labor force employment rate in any country depends on two basic elements which are (El-ashry and Delal 2010):

1. Population size, age structure, and annual growth rate.
2. Labor force characteristics and their structure.

Based on the involvement or contribution tourism supply side, employment opportunities in tourism and hospitality sectors can be created either directly or indirectly (Dayananda, 2014). Direct Employment opportunities are the total number of job opportunities supported by directly in travel and tourism.

For example, employment by accommodation establishments, food and beverage outlets, travel agencies, tourism information offices, museums, protected areas such as national parks, palaces, religious sites, monuments, aircrafts, cruise lines, resorts or shopping outlets, souvenirs, photography, sightseeing tours, farmhouses, rural inns, and guesthouses local transportation (state-owned airlines and railways, private transport facilities), Guides, cooks and scouts. Tourism and hospitality also supports indirect employment in activities catering companies, construction companies that build and maintain tourist facilities, as well as necessary infrastructure, aircraft manufacturers, various handicrafts producers, marketing agencies, accounting services, which are more or less dependent on the companies providing direct employment for their revenues (UNWTO, 2011).

#### 2.5.2.1 COMPOSITION OF TOURISM LABOR MARKETS

The next section clarifies the shape of the labor market supplying the tourism and hospitality industries with labor:

#### 1. Child Labor

Tourism sector by its nature and necessity attracts children to work as laborers. Most of them have been seen working in hotels and restaurants as bellboy, housekeeper, maintenance worker, garden workers, cleaner, laundry cleaners, kitchen helpers, and porters. Away from the hotel properties, many children also are found selling newspapers, flowers, and other goodies at most historic monuments frequently visited by visitors in many countries. According to the International Labor Organization's (ILO) Global Report 2006, Tourism affects the lives of 218 million children (Sharma et al., 2012).

Plüss (1999) gathered information from more than 300 experts and came to the conclusion that child labor in tourism is a "very widespread phenomenon" (Plüss, 1999). The number of children and youths working for tourism (including the informal sector) is actually much higher than 10% according to EED Tourism Watch (2002). A high proportion of them are working in the informal sector and employment conditions vary greatly. Working conditions in tourism are generally not good, working hours are generally long, jobs are not secure, employment is seasonal, wages are low, very little unionization and collective bargaining is possible, labor laws are often broken and there is a lack of opportunities for training for tourism workers (ILO, 2011). However, employment possibilities in tourism industry are plentiful and children are hired in different tourism sectors such as hotels, catering/food and beverage, excursions/activities/entertainment, transport, souvenir production and souvenir sales (Pluss, 1999).

Working in tourism put the children into a vulnerable position where (Pluss, 1999):

- The majority of children and young people working in tourism experience mentally and physically stressful working conditions.
- Children's health is affected due to bad working conditions (unsocial, long working hours and crazy shifts).
- The lack of schooling and training in tourism puts their future at risk.
- The children are highly exposed to be sexually abused and exploited.

In alignment with Pluss, EED Tourism Watch (2002) pointed out that even though not all "young employees in tourism are exploited" their jobs in tourism prevent millions of children from completing their education. The work is often difficult and dangerous, pays little or nothing and prevents chances for education. Worse still, in many cases, the work is considered hazardous and exploitative.

## 2. *Immigrant Labor*

Globalization has created a link between the growing demand for labor in the tourism sector and labor migration. As a consequence of globalization, and particularly in developed countries in some regions like Australasia, Europe, and North America, ethnic and cultural minority groups tend to be numerically overrepresented in tourism and hospitality workforce (ILO, 2010). However, the number of migrant workers can diverge from that of the total population for which they account, depending on many factors such as:

- governmental policies in the country of destination,
- better job opportunities,
- time of arrival of the successive migration waves,
- the size of the family component in migration flows, and
- selection criteria linked to age or qualifications.

Over the past decade, the proportions have essentially followed the same trend. It is greater in the United States, Canada, Australia, Austria, Germany, and Luxembourg, whereas it is smaller in Denmark, France, the Netherlands and Norway (Jeanv and Jimenez 2007). Hospitality employers have traditionally seen value in a transient workforce (Capita Consulting, 2011). For example, in the United Kingdom, migrant workers participate significantly in shaping the sector's traditional employment model (21% of the current workforce was born overseas), in the United States, in 2016, there were 27.0 million foreign-born persons in the US labor force, comprising 16.9% of the total immigrant workforce.

Such minority groups are able to gain employment in occupations that require low skills level or can obtain jobs within the informal sector; something that may not be possible in other sectors of the economy. In tourism context, migrant workers tend to be concentrated in "back of house" functions, or in elementary occupations where there is little or no interaction with customers, such as cooks, kitchen assistants, room attendants, and cleaners (Anderson et al. 2007). However, certain groups of migrant workers can occupy good positions, according to Anderson (2007), certain groups of migrant workers were occupying 'front of house' positions when they aesthetically matched their employers' requirements.

In a survey conducted by Capita Consulting (2011), about 47% of hospitality employers stated that they believed the sector was too reliant on transient workers. There is limited evidence to suggest that some employers have used Eastern European migrants as a "safety valve" (Smedley, 2007) to manage the consequences of labor market shortages.

The temporary employment of foreign workers introduces flexibility into the labor market and contributes thereby to relieving sectoral labor shortages in the host countries. This is particularly the case in-service sectors, where many countries face shortages especially in hospitality industry. Increased temporary labor immigration can also have the effect of dissuading employers, particularly in seasonal activities, from resorting to the use of expensive workers. Labor migration, when properly governed, can help to fill labor shortages in high- skills and low skills parts of the market, rejuvenate populations, and promote entrepreneurship, dynamism, and diversity in destination and originating countries.

On a negative note, there are instances of institutionalized discrimination within the tourism sector that tend to work against ethnic minority groups in terms of payment and career progress within the industry. This is clearly illustrated in the case of the hotel sector in Hawaii (Adler and Adler, 2004), but is also evident in countries which depend heavily on unskilled, temporarily expatriate workers in the sector. (see Chapter 13, Race Discrimination).

Although migrants' employment can help organizations to achieve its financial goals, it has hazardous impacts on the economy of countries and also on the performance of the organizations:

1. The differences in skills between migrants and natives influence:
    - Unemployment rate, and relative wages among workers in the host economy. The magnitude of the impact on relative wages depends on the changes in the relative supply of different categories of workers, and on the degree of substitutability among them. If relative wages do not adjust, immigration may also influence the distribution of unemployment rates by skill category.
    - Low skilled employees, without doubt, affect the performance of the organizations in terms of:
        - offering a low standard quality of service and
        - creating some kind of chaos and confusion in work environment that influence the final outcome of the work team; this is because of the limited skills or the different backgrounds and cultures of migrant workers.
2. The mobility nature of migrant workers
   If there is an economic downturn or better opportunities develop elsewhere, migrant workers may well decide to move elsewhere, and

their supply of labor will reduce (Caterer, 2007), in Eastern Europe for example, migrants intend to stay in the United Kingdom for only a limited period of time before returning to their home countries (Anderson et al., 2007), accordingly, placing the hospitality and other sectors in potentially very vulnerable positions where organizations will be understaffed, the case that will influence on the performance of the business greatly.

3. The profile of migrant workers
   The population of migrant workers does not constitute a homogeneous group. Changes in foreign labor and its main characteristics (race, skill level, cultures, educations, and beliefs) may cause some conflicts in work environments.

Hence, in order to compete and adapt to new market environments, it is important to invest in the workforce. This is important as it should support the case for a greater focus on developing retention policies of employees which will benefit all hospitality workers; it particularly helps arguments for older worker recruitment and retention (Capita Consulting, 2011).

Although, human resources are the most valuable asset of the tourism industry, paradoxically, the will to invest in education and training in some of the major sectors is relatively low compared with most other industries. The suggestion made by Skills Minister David Lammy that British employers should invest in training rather than developing a reliance on migrant workers (Caterer, 2007). However, unfortunately for obvious reasons, such as seasonality, limited career opportunities and often poor labor conditions, little attention is given by employers to develop reliable retaining policies for native skilled employees. Too often human resource planning in the tourism industry is based on short-term thinking, so migrant employment is expected to be in progress especially in the hospitality industry in developed countries.

### 3. *Female Workers*

For similar reasons to other groups (young and migrant workers), female workers are targeted by employers because they are prepared to work flexibly and for lower wages either because it fits in with family or care obligations (Lucas 2004), or because it is the only work that is available to them.

In addition, female workers are highly valued in the service sector, especially in jobs that require direct contact with guests and customers, so many of the skills that employers value in the service encounter are perceived as more feminine. This would explain a preference for 'attractive,' younger women in a 'front of house role,' while 'back of house' jobs, such as housekeeping, are also perceived as gender-specific roles, with women being preferred to men.

Although female workers make up between 60 and 70% of the labor force according to International Labor Office (2010), the female share of the total workforce has declined in the last 15 years, such that the proportion of male workers has increased. This may because of the divergence between qualifications and workplace reality for women. Female workers tend to work in the most vulnerable jobs, where they are more likely to experience poor working conditions, inequality of growth opportunity and treatment, violence, exploitation, stress, and sexual harassment. Female workers are on average paid 25% less in the sector than male workers for comparable skills. In Spain, female workers earn 76.52% of the average monthly salary of male workers (ILO, 2010) (see Chapter 13, Gender Stereotyping in the World of Tourism Industry). They also suffer segregation in terms of access to education and training.

In one word, it is not in practice and feasible to achieve the ideal scenario of having sufficient high-quality labor available for 24 hours a day. While demand is very often defined as being 'feast or famine,' wage costs would be prohibitive, so having the ability to vary and adjust working patterns to respond to changes in demand remains paramount. This explains employers' reliance on all three groups, and why they value young workers' and migrants' flexibility (Lucas and Keegan 2007) and female workers' role in jobs that depend on the encounter with the customers.

#### *2.5.2.2 FACTORS CONTROLLING LABOR SUPPLY*

There are in fact a variety of factors that contribute significantly in determining and influencing the supply labor market of the tourism industry, of which poor career prospects, low pay, unsocial working hours and physical stress appear to play a part. In addition to working hours that are irregular for half of all employees in the tourism industries, most of whom perform work on Sundays and in the evenings and almost half of whom also work at night.

Here are the factors that control the shape of tourism industries' labor market:

## *1. Policies of Filling Job Vacancies*

Increasing competition entails more emphasis on cost-reduction and efficiency in business operations. As most of the owners and managers are considered cost-minded, they identified two directions to reduce costs relating human resources. The cost-minded tourism and hospitality managers measure and scale the pros and cons of each direction and its impact on the budget than on the quality of service and products delivered. The two main directions that are adopted by most of the organizations' managers are as follows:

1. Robotic labor
2. Low-cost labor

These two directions shaped the labor market of tourism and hospitality industries in low skilled groups (young workers and women) and the minorities groups (migrants and workers with disabilities) (Fig. 2.4).

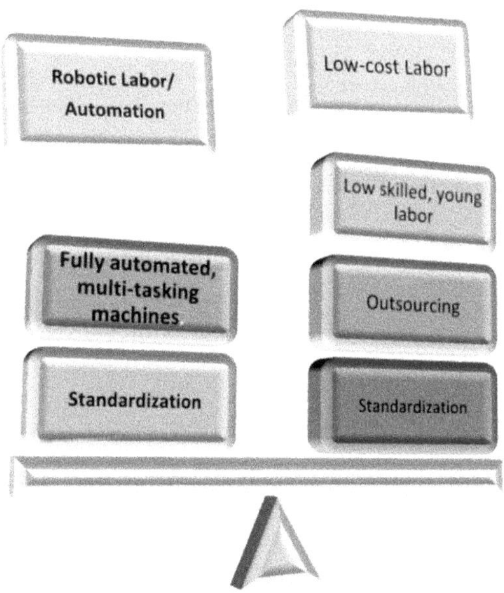


**FIGURE 2.4** Managers measure for labor cost reduction.
**Source:** The Authors.

### A. *Robotic labor or automation system*

As technology has advanced in recent years, employers can sometimes alter the production process to replace workers with equipment, where the types of tasks performed by machines have also changed; formerly, machines typically replaced humans in tasks that require physical abilities, not soft skills such as lifting and moving.

Recently, a restaurant in India "Chennai Restaurant" becomes the first to hire robots as waiters, the orders are placed on iPhones/Tablets conveniently located on every table, and are sent to the kitchen directly. Once the order is ready, it is delivered to the customers by designated robot waiters. Robots man 20 tables without any issues. They are battery-operated and are controlled through sensors.

More recently, computer-based technology permits machines to perform more sophisticated tasks. So, most of owners and managers of large corporations have the intention to generalize the automation systems in their organizations. Frohm et al. (2005) defined Robotic Labor or Automation as the allocation of tasks between the human and the technology, as shown in Figure 2.5. Dependence on the automation system imposes that human share does not exceed 25% of operation duties, while, it relies heavily on multi-function machines, computerized procedures, and the standardized operations, therefore minimizing or cutting the jobs off.

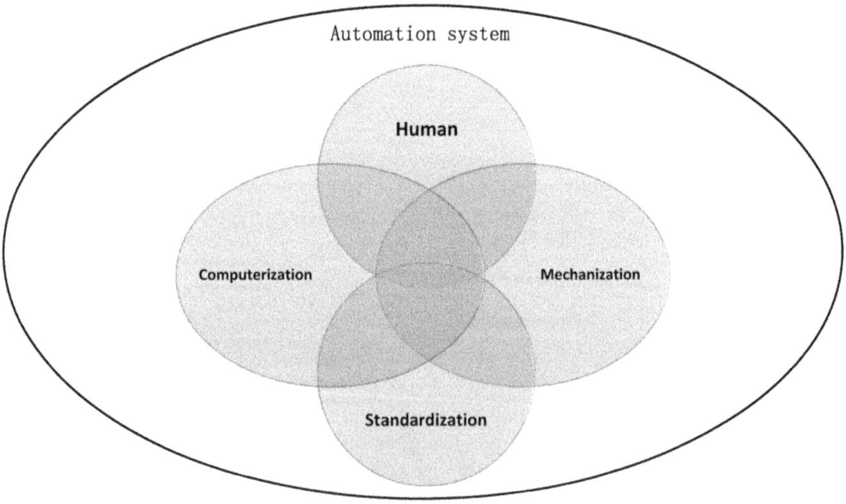


**FIGURE 2.5** Automation system pillars.
**Source:** The Authors.

Smith and Anderson (2014) in their study claimed that a Pew Research Center study asked 1896 experts about the impact of emerging technologies. The results revealed that about half of experts (48%) expected that the multitasking machines and computers will take place significant numbers of both blue-collar workers (food service workers and cookers) and white-collar workers (supervisors and line managers). Where labor presence is limited, or machine is the replacement of a human worker. There are several reasons for one system to be automated and thus they are (Mishev, 2006):

- reducing labor cost,
- increasing the productivity,
- mitigation of the effect of labor shortages,
- reduction routines of manual and clerical tasks,
- improving worker's safety,
- improving production quality,
- reducing manufacturing lead time,
- accomplishing a process that cannot be done manually.

On the other hand, depending intensively on multitasking machines and computers will lead to vast increases in income inequality, masses of people who are effectively unemployable, and breakdowns in the social order" (Smith and Anderson, 2014), in addition to the increase in automation doesn't necessarily result in more efficient productivity (Frohm et al., 2005).

### B. *Low-cost labor*

Labor costs are defined as the ratio of a worker's total compensations to labor productivity (Felipe and Kumar, 2011). Worker' total returns are classified mainly to financial returns (Wage or salary, Compensations, Profit Percentage, Piece Rate, Commissions, severance and termination pay, employers' contributions to pension schemes, etc.) and non-financial returns (employers' contributions to casualty, insurance plans, security Plans, etc.) and in some cases, payroll taxes as well as fringe benefits taxes, etc. (see Chapter 7, Pay and Compensations).

$$\text{Labor cost \%} = \frac{\text{Worker's total returns}}{\text{Worker's productivity}} \times 100$$

Higher labor costs (higher wage rates and employee benefits) make workers better off, but they can reduce organizations' profits, the number of jobs, and the hours each person works.

Labor cost may be broadly classified as direct labor cost and indirect labor cost:

- Direct Labor Cost: Labor cost that is expended in the production of a product and easily identified and allocated to a cost unit i.e. a specific job, contract, work order, or any other unit of cost.
- Indirect Labor Cost: Labor cost that is expended on the wages of workmen who are not directly engaged in the production process and can be easily identified with a cost unit.

Generally, labor cost is one of the major direct costs in every organization. The labor costs are costs which are bearing by the organization in every process of human resource management such as costs of selection, hiring people, wrongful termination lawsuits, rehiring costs. In the service sector, labor costs are more than material costs but in some sector, the material costs are more than labor cost.

Labor is classified as the largest variable cost for hotels. Employers do not react instantly when labor costs increase. It takes a while before they believe that the increase is not just a temporary aberration.

So, managers struggle to keep labor costs down and profits up. Although it is tempting to cut staff to reduce costs (Singh, 2014), service quality may suffer when the property is understaffed, so organizations and managers have two ways to follow for the sake of reducing labor costs (cutting workers or hiring low-cost labor), generally the choice between cutting workers or hiring low skilled workers at low pay depends on the cost of each, the most important consideration is the total product of workers. After all, it is the total number of worker-hours across the economy that determines how much is produced—the GDP.

➢ Cutting workers or hours:

Hiring new workers at the rate that is stated by the organization takes time, in addition to the governmental restrictions on layoffs that make cutting jobs an uneasy task. Despite these restrictions, the evidence is very clear that things move fairly quickly. In the United States, at least, half of the cuts in employment when labor costs increase occur in the first six months, while in Europe the adjustment is slower, but not greatly so (Hamermesh, 1993).

➢ Hiring low-cost labor:

From the perspective of the economy: An increase in wage rates reduces employment and hours, and an increase in the fixed costs of a worker reduces the total number of hours worked. Any increase in labor costs, regardless of its source, will lead employers to cut the total number of employees.

In order to avoid cutting the total number of employees that may bring some lawsuits issues with the government or even human rights organizations, most of the employers prefer to hire low or semi-skilled labor at moderate wages instead of cutting them, this notion is proved by Riley who claimed that a large proportion of jobs in tourism and hospitality are semi-skilled or unskilled with about two thirds or 64% of jobs in the hotel, restaurant and catering sector (1996). Employers need to achieve flexibility in order to minimize costs and to address the vastly fluctuating demands that are placed upon the organizations at differing times of the day, week, month or year. These needs are met and well-served by young workers, female workers and migrants (Lai and Baum 2005). Accordingly, the employer's nominal definition predominates, contributes to a low labor market status (Korczynski, 2002). Consequently, the shape of service sector work is constituted by a high proportion of women, young workers and migrants in the sector's labor force. Unfortunately, these groups have less power in employment relations and are likely to be disadvantaged in the process of the social construction of skill and other job-related opportunities.

## 2. *Seasonality Phenomenon*

Seasonality is generally viewed as a problem that limits the economic returns that can be obtained from tourism and prevents the optimum economic benefits that might be gained if a destination and the organization were able to attract tourists year-round. Highman and Hinch (2002) described seasonality as one of the most predominant challenges, yet least understood features of tourism. While Butler (2014) defined seasonality as a "temporal imbalance in the phenomenon of tourism, which may be expressed in terms of dimensions of such elements as numbers of tourists, expenditure of visitors, traffic on highways and other forms of transportation, employment rates, and admissions to attractions". Seasonality dramatically influences industry employment, leading to widespread seasonal employment, underemployment, and unemployment.

The seasonal tourism employment is defined as "a non-permanent paid job that will end at a specified time or in the near future, once the seasonal peak has passed" (Marshall, 1999). These seasonal positions often recur on an annual basis, influenced by the labor demands of seasonal industries (Perusse, 1997).

In Atlantic Canada, for example, seasonality is a pervasive feature of the tourism industry. According to Jolliffe and Farnsworth (2003), the provinces areas located on the eastern seaboard, is hardly affected by seasonality, they economically activate only in summer. In much of the region (Newfoundland and Labrador, Prince Edward Island (PEI), Nova Scotia (NS) and New Brunswick (NB), the season runs from late June until the first weekend in September. This short season determines to a large extent the type of the labor force entering the industry.

So, seasonality impacts relating to employment come significantly in hiring employees from the second labor market where unskilled or semi-skilled labor force, also, those who have no experience in the tourism field or even not interested in such service sector, just taking jobs as an entry point in their working life. This type of employment will influence the success of the business negatively. For human resource (HR) managers, this creates a cyclical employment environment requiring extraordinary resources devoted to recruitment, selection, training, and retention of staff.

However, there are many characteristics of seasonality that enable its causes to be identified and thus may help in modifying its occurrence (Butler, 2014).

The most significant case it is generally regular and consistent, occurring at the same time for roughly the same duration each year. This means that unlike some other negative influences on tourism, both at the local level such as natural disasters, security issues or epidemics, or at the global level such as economic recession and war, seasonality is predictable and in a sense "reliable" in terms of it being able to be anticipated and ideally, mitigated.

This should mean that steps to counter its presence and or its effects should be easier to conceive and to implement. The fact that success to date has been very limited suggests that perhaps the wrong steps have been taken which may stem from tackling the wrong "problems". This phenomenon made the employees think before making the decision of involving into the industry.

### 3. *Unequal Treatment*

There is no equal treatment for all type of employees. For example, gender inequality is manifested in the sectors according to ILO-UNDP (cited in Thomas, 2013). Although, female workers perform 66 percent of the world's work, produce 50 percent of the food, but earn 10% of the income and own 1% of the property. Women are under-represented in managerial and senior positions, the lower levels and occupations with few career development opportunities being dominated by women while key managerial positions are dominated by men. Such circumstances are avail due to the fact that employers make employment decision on stereotypical assumption about specific jobs that suit only men or women and thus occupation gender segregation occurs (Burrell et al., 1997). Gender segregation leads to unequal career rewards for men and women (Reskin and Bielby, 2005).

In addition, there are a number of factors besides gender discrimination, that impede women's career advancement, including lower access to land, capital, and education than men, lower training and educational opportunities, and exclusion of women from informal networks. Moreover, promotion systems in most tourism companies operate on the basis of informal and non-written criteria and the decisions that senior management makes about promotion usually depend on middle managers' recommendation.

Such promotion procedures further contribute to gender segregation (Jordan, 1997). All these discriminative actions decreased the women involvement in work environment of tourism industries in the last 15 years (ILO, 2010), so, a significant portion of females tend to work at home or family enterprises unprotected by law, women face discrimination and overload of work at business enterprises and family life. In developing countries, women situation gets worse, additional factors such as widespread poverty, poor maternal health, and lack of sociocultural factors have prevented women from being empowered as economic actors. Businesses can be located at some distance from residential areas, particularly in poorer countries and communities, imposing both travel and time costs on women who frequently have limited access to both financial and time-flexibility resources (UNWTO, 2011).

So, it is recommended to take steps to identify talent not on the gender basis but rather on transparent access to higher organizational positions for both sexes (Baum, 2013) and achieving gender equality.

According to ILO (2010), gender equality means the demand to assure equal conditions for both men and women—their full rights to benefit from economic, political, cultural and social development. However, when talking about equal opportunities it is not just about impartiality that pertains individuals but rather about the successful development of the contemporary society. Also, social dialog to encourage the reduction of wage gaps is required (Baum, 2013).

### 4. *Inappropriate Management Style*

As claimed by Griffin and DeLacey (2002), the other challenges are inappropriate management style/corporate philosophy and leadership style such as unplanned recruitment, little due attention for human resources' issues such as staff turnover, recruitment procedures, and policies, inadequate training. In addition, a leadership style that considers staffs as a cost rather than an asset, and rigid leadership that is against the concept of democracy.

### 5. *Poor Wages and Hardworking Condition*

Work conditions refer to the working environment in which employees have to perform their tasks and duties. Consumer expectations and their demand patterns in hotels and restaurants require working conditions that are frequently characterized as stressful and unsocial working hours.

These conditions include low hourly rates of pay, long and crazy working hours (50 hours per week) in the form of split shifts, weekend shifts, nightshifts, or work during holiday periods, little or no adequate breaks during peak season periods and overtime work without extra money (Griffin 2002).

These working conditions heighten stress on employees and workers with family responsibilities, particularly women who carry most of the care responsibility and burden for children and the elderly as well as for household chores. Therefore, it has been shown that 50% of employees are having the intention to change jobs and that only 45% of the workforce was engaged in their jobs (Zingheim and Schuster, 2008). They felt that an organization must have total compensation policies, not just focus on pay and benefits. Sturman (2006, p. 9) researched hotel pay and performance and stated that "both 'how' one is paid, and 'how much' one is paid can influence performance"). Equitable total compensation can lead to increased profits because motivated managers and employees help to increase hotel sales, customer satisfaction, and overall condition and cleanliness of the hotel. Hence, a system must be in place to make the organization attractive to the high performers. Organizations that have a competitive compensation package can have a sustainable competitive advantage because of lower turnover, more engaged employees, and higher revenues through engaged employees.

## 6. Demeaning Jobs

Also, the tourism and hospitality industry nature generate service jobs which are "demeaning" in their nature, such jobs require the employee to clean and wipe bathrooms, mobbing the corridors and lifting heavy stuff. In addition, low wages impose workers to depend extensively on tipping, this push workers to behave in a certain way that put them in a beg position. Such jobs are low skilled, low paid, provide a low level of job satisfaction and limited opportunities for advancement. Employees in the hotel sector have been described as "uneducated, unmotivated, untrained, unskilled and unproductive" (Williams and Shaw, 1988). Such criticism is mainly in reference to back-line jobs such as room attendants and kitchen porters. The hotel industry remains one where experience carries more weight than paper qualifications.

## 7. Industry Image

Although it is encouraging to see many of the worldwide chains organizations adopting a clear strategic human resource approach, providing enhanced work-life balance for employees (Choi and Dickson, 2010) and this may seduce young people because of the glamor/aureole of the industry, the reality is the poor image of the hospitality industry is one of the largest factors that is frequently cited in the literature. The hospitality industry is dominated by small business and that little has changed since 1997 when Wood described the industry as "largely exploitative, degrading, poorly paid, unpleasant, insecure and taken as a last resort." (Baum, 2006, p 198) A compounding factor here is the increasing demand for low-cost tourism, which encourages the use of low-cost labor, and reinforces poor perceptions held towards working conditions within the tourism and hospitality industry

## 8. Labor Expectations

Several societal changes over the past few decades have impacted greatly on employees' definitions of what constitutes their perceptions, this new generation does not have the patience to wait for promotion. In addition, even if training and education provide them with the right skills, the requisite behaviors do not necessarily follow, and they often seem to lack a work ethics, motivation, willingness, passion, and, as said before, realistic expectations.

Today's generation of hospitality employees holds vastly different expectations toward work than those of previous generations. Consequently, as noted in Whitelaw et al. (2009), there seems to be a gap between candidates and the reality of the market.

For example, today's graduates are ambitious, with over 80% expecting a promotion within two years of commencing work (McCrindle and Hooper, 2006).

According to McCrindle and Hooper (2006), the three most important aspects of employment for today's graduates are:

- interesting work (work in leisure activities with foreign customers),
- positive relationships with colleagues, and
- continuous opportunities for learning.

Subsequently, employers must develop good procedures in order to retain this generation of employees. Solnet and Hood (2008) suggested providing job variety, feedback and establishing suitable reward systems, flexible work actions, autonomy, career growth opportunities, and empowerment.

Generally, tourism employment is often challenged by one or more of the above factors; seasonality, during some months of the year the number of tourists and customers is very low so that tourism and hospitality business sectors cut staffs and their number significantly reduced, part-time and/or excessive hours of work; low-paid (or unpaid) family labor; and informal or sometimes illegal labor of some group of minorities (migrant workers or child labor) where measurement is notably more difficult.

Furthermore, employment opportunities in tourism and hospitality are affected by different difficult risks and hazards that the industry faced. For instance, terrorist attacks are happening in different tourist destinations, the prevalence of new contagious disease, world economic crises and technological advancement in tourism and hospitality sectors such as the application of e-business, e-marketing, and virtual tourism.

Due to these reasons, many tourism and hospitality sectors are struggling in the field of human resources. The employers are firing out the workforces, which give rise to unemployment rate and also in peak season make the industry easy accessible to low-cost labor being utilized to mitigate the shortage, an outcome that enables many tourism and hospitality businesses to ignore issues of skills development and general workplace enhancement (Baum, 2007), and so a vicious circle is formed. This is the main reason of why the tourism labor market is characterized as low skilled, young, and diversified market. The above does not cover all possible situations but illustrates the multiple pitfalls to avoid and difficulties to tackle in measuring employment in the tourism industries.

## 2.6 CHARACTERISTICS OF TOURISM LABOR MARKET

Determining the special characteristics of tourism labor market on a global basis cannot, or should not, be an easy task. This is especially true when considering that the views that claim that the tourism labor market is various and sometimes opposing. The developed analysis of the labor supply and demand gave us some lights to figure out the characteristics of the tourism labor market.

Generally, the image of tourism as a generator primarily of low-wage and low-skill employment is true except for the technical, managerial, and professional levels that require education and training which command compensation commensurate with these qualifications (UNWTO, 1997).

According to Wall and Mathieson (2006), tourism employment characteristics can be summarized as follows:

- Employment and income impact are significantly related,
- The characteristics of tourism labor market vary by tourist activity; some activities are more labor-intensive than others,
- Many jobs are self-employed, particularly if the enterprises are small,
- Tourism employment is characterized by being low-wage jobs,
- Tourism and hospitality employment commonly requires low skill levels in addition to low entry requirements,
- Part-time and casual jobs are very popular in the industry,
- Tourism employment is highly seasonal,
- Tourism may hire people from other sectors (secondary labor market) and,
- Tourism employment is structured by gender; many jobs in most tourism tasks are held by women, young worker particular the low-paid, part-time and seasonal positions.

The effects of tourism employment are frequently not visible and hence not recognized, while the characteristics of a broad number of tourism occupations may concur with commonly held beliefs (Choy, 1995), they may also differ significantly from each other.

There is a consensus about the qualities of tourism employment and the characteristics of its labor market. The characteristics and qualities of tourism labor are not to be defined exclusively by the alleged "nature" of tourism, but also by enterprises size, political and sociocultural conditions in the destination community. In addition, the specific conditions of the destination area play a vital role in defining the characteristics of employment of any type of tourism.

Based on the existing analysis, general observations about what seems to be the "inherent" characteristics of tourism and hospitality labor market. The main characteristics of labor market that supply tourism and hospitality industry are as follows:

### A. *Younger Workers*

One of the main features of tourism employment not commonly cited in the literature is that of under-age labor or young workers. In a few countries, the issue of child work is regulated. However, child labor still exists in many countries illegally. Young workers find tourism jobs are best suitable for their physical abilities and skills and experience because of:

- low skill/experience levels,
- physical nature of the job,
- unsocial working hours, and
- low pay.

Many hospitality jobs are considered "entry level" (particularly in the restaurant and bar sectors) and suited to young people, where nearly 40% of hospitality businesses are restaurants; while pubs, bars, and nightclubs make up nearly a third of the remaining businesses (Capita Consulting, 2011).

The age profile of the industry in these businesses, in particular, reflects this and it has a significant impact on the age profile of the tourism sector as a whole.

One alternative available source of labor is older workers. Many employers in the hospitality industry do not see increasing workforce age diversity through the employment of older workers as a priority, but some do recognize this is an issue which now deserves attention. As a result of predomination of young workers on the industry' jobs, old workers are underrepresented in the workforce as a whole, with only 14 percent of employees being 50 years old and older (People 1st, 2006).

Traditionally, hospitality employers have had a negative impression of older workers with the aesthetic appearance and attitude of younger people being preferred (Lucas and Keegan 2008 forthcoming) which means that most of older workers in the hotels, public sector catering, and travel sectors operate "behind the scenes".

### *B. Female Workers*

Although in some cultures tourism work is considered a man's activity (Tucker, 2007), it is skewed because of culture, beliefs, and values of the few countries with extremely low participation by women. However, according to informants, the domination of males is justified on the basis that many activities require special physical effort, which represents a difficulty for women. However, women and men share the same percentage 50% of jobs in some countries like the USA. However, others advocated that tourism employment is highly gendered.

There are a large number of women working in the tourism industry, it has been estimated that over 70% of tourism employees are women (ILO, 2010; Marshall, 2001). Although gender-based classification of labor exists in several employment sectors (McKenzie, 2007), tourism employment has been reported as being highly gendered.

It seems that tourism employment help a variety of female workers. Young, single mothers, divorced or older one, were able to find employment and some are even able to start their own business. However, many of the women perceived tourism to be an industry which is still male-dominated at senior management levels, despite the number of women employed. They do not agree that a climate of equal opportunities already exists (Jordan, 1997). Female workers tend to work in the most vulnerable jobs, where they are more likely to experience poor working conditions, inequality of opportunity and treatment, violence, exploitation, stress, and sexual harassment (Baum, 2013). Generally, it follows that the tourism sector is often criticized for providing only low-wage, seasonal employment, but it should be made clear that if there were to be no tourism many workers, especially women in the economy would be unemployed.

### *C. Limited Skills Labor*

In spite of the growing complexity of the customer/employee interaction, driven by technology and the information age that impose having skilled human resources in the future, employees are not required to hold specific qualifications for working at most occupations in tourism and hospitality industry. Entry requirements are not difficult to be met in terms of academic education, because no proof of even basic education is needed to work. In a time, the customer, armed with more information, will expect frontline and other hospitality staff to be at least as knowledgeable about the attractions areas and the organization's offerings as they are themselves.

In fact, most of the staff have limited skills, they only received basic education at public schools. So, this m may be difficult in an industry characterized by low-skilled, low-paid personnel and a high degree of cultural and behavioral diversity among its employees (Wang and Wang, 2009).

It should be concluded that it may be easy to analyze the labor markets of the tourism industries but also it is more difficult to measure labor supply in the tourism industries than is the case for many other industries. The reason being that tourism labor is often characterized by depending on more than one labor market with various demographic factors as mentioned above so a small hospitality organization may involve direct and indirect labor; high skilled and unskilled, men and women, and employees from different cultures and backgrounds.

## 2.7 FACTORS OF IMPROVING THE TOURISM LABOR MARKET

The following section will highlight the collaboration factor, which if effectively addressed would in large part improve the current (and future) tourism labor market. This factor is discussed in light of interventions that industry, government, and education providers might facilitate in order to reverse labor shortage trends.

Effective collaboration needs to take place between industry and education providers, between industry and government policymakers and administrators, and between industry and potential employees. While there are number of organizations and agencies that do engage in collaborative undertakings to increase understanding of current and future issues within the sector and in turn, develop appropriate solutions, the stakeholders frequently have loyalties and different agendas that lie outside of the sector (Baum and Szivas, 2008).

Tri-lateral stakeholders (involving industry, the government, and education providers) need to understand how and why their roles might differ from those within their originating organization. The high failure rate of collaborative tourism research projects is frequently attributed to the complexities associated with a fragmented sector and issues relating to power and politics that emerge as individuals struggle to accept differing roles, and individual agendas take precedence over collective outcomes.

## *The role of industry and government*

There is a clear need for industry to improve its image if it is to attract quality employees. Industry needs to promote itself to the community (e.g., to schools) and emphasize its contribution to the community and to the economy, and create opportunities for continuous development, thereby acknowledging the need for lifelong learning, and the relationship it holds to a knowledge-based economy. To achieve this industry will need to (Robinson and Beesley, 2010; Nuemann and Banghart, 2001):

- Create a "career culture" and initiate incentive systems that recognize not just performance, but also tenure.
- Provide internship programs to develop employees' skills.
- Introduce apprenticeships across various dimensions of tourism work and specifically hospitality work.
- Demonstrate a career path to employees to reduce the ambiguity and then mitigating turnover.
- Place emphasis on critical thinking and problem-solving skills as core graduate competencies, then it would be prudent to
- Cooperate with governmental authorities and institutions, there is a clear need for government policy to incentivize and support industry initiatives.

However, this is clearly not a panacea to cure workforce ills, it also requires the support of education providers.

## *The role of education providers*

Education providers need to be aware and more responsive to changing markets and industry needs, and produce graduates that recognize the fickle work environment in which they are embedded, and give them the skills (both vocational and technical) that equip them to be not just reactive, but also proactive to a constantly changing environment.

Generally, the desired outcomes are dependent on one primary factor—the capacity for industry, education and government sectors to communicate effectively and seek solutions pursuant to a common goal. Communication between participating stakeholders and broader business needs to be developed in ways so that the policies and procedures presented have relevance and might be translated into immediate application.

If solutions developed are to be optimized maximally, not only do findings need to be disseminated in a way that proves the uptake of knowledge among stakeholders and the broader business community, but also dissemination efforts must demonstrate the value of strategic planning and how to engage it. This implies the need for an "educative" component to build into the communication of new knowledge that might provide solutions to tourism labor issues.

Stakeholders come from separate public and private sector organizations whereby participants may be participating at either an enterprise or destination level (Faulkner 2002). This challenge may not seem to hold much incentive to establish a tri-lateral collaboration to address the labor crisis. So, in order to achieve success when addressing the tourism and hospitality labor issues, the struggle between values and interests within these alliances must lead to the formulation of outcomes serve the industry as a whole, not a particular stakeholder.

## REFERENCES


Ackah, J.; Vuvor, S. "The Challenges Faced by Small and Medium Enterprises (SMEs) in Obtaining Credit in Ghana." MSc Thesis, School of Management, 2011.

Adebayo, D. O. Gender and Attitudes Toward Professional Ethics. A Nigerian Police Perspective. *Afr. Secur. Rev.* **2005,** *14* (2), 21–36.

Adler, P. A.; Adler, P. E. Paradise Laborers. Hotel Work in the Global Economy, Ithaca, Cornell University Press, 2004.

Andrew, R.; Baum, T.; Morrison, A. The Lifestyle Economics of Small Tourism Businesses. *J. Travel Tour. Res.* **2001,** *1,* 16–25.

Arnoux-Nicolas, C.; Sovet, L.; Lhotellier, L.; Di Fabio, A.; Bernaud, J. Perceived Work Conditions and Turnover Intentions: The Mediating Role of Meaning of Work. *Front. Psychol.* **2016,** *7,* 704–720.

Aynalem, S.; Birhanu, K.; Tesefay, S. Employment Opportunities and Challenges in Tourism and Hospitality Sectors. *J. Tour. Hosp.* **2016,** *5* (257), 1–11.

Baron, R. V. *Seasonality of Tourism–A Guide to the Analysis of Seasonality and Trends for Policy Making*, 2nd ed., The Economist Intelligence Unit Ltd. London, 1975.

Bauder, H. *Labor Movement: How Migration Regulates Labor Markets*. New York: Oxford University Press, 2006.

Baum, T. "Reflections on the Nature of Skills in the Experience Economy: Challenging Traditional Skills Models in Hospitality." *J. Hosp. Tour. Manag.* **2007,** *13* (2), 124–135.

Baum, T. International Perspective on Women and Work in Hotels, Catering and Tourism. International Labor Office: Geneva, 2013.

Baum, T.; Szivas, E. HRD in Tourism: A Role for Government? *Tour. Manag. J.* **2008,** *29,* 783–794.

Beam, J. What is Employee Turnover? 2009. [Online] http://www.wisegeek.com/what-is-employee turnover.htm (accessed 15 Nov, 2017).

Beesley, L.; Davidson, M. A Critical Analysis of Skilled Labor Supply and Demand in the Australian Hospitality Industry. *J. Quality Assur. Hosp. Tour.* **2013,** *14* (3), 264–280

Beeton, S. Horseback Tourism in Victoria: Cooperative, Proactive Crisis Management. *Curr. Issues Tour.* **2001,** *4* (5), 403–421.

Biederman, P. S. *Travel and Tourism: An Industry Primer*. Pearson Education: Upper Saddle River, 2008.

Bolch, M. *The Coming Crunch*. Human Resource Training Magazine, 2001, *196* (2628), pp 42–46.

Bridget, A.; Clark, N.; Parutis, V. "*New EU Members? Migrant Workers Challenges and Opportunities to UK Trade Unions: A Polish and Lithuanian Case Study.*" Trades Union Congress: London, 2007.

Brown, E. A.; Thomas, N. J.; Bosselman, R. H. Are they Leaving or Staying: A Qualitative Analysis of Turnover Issues for Generation Y Hospitality Employees with a Hospitality Education? *Int. J. Hosp. Manag.* **2015,** *46,* 130–137.

Butler, R. Addressing Seasonality in Tourism: The Development of a Prototype, the Punta del Este Conference, May 2014.

Capita Consulting. The Case for Recruiting and Retaining Older Workers: A Business Imperative for the Hospitality Sector, 2011. [Online] https://www.instituteofhospitality.org/Knowledge_Pack_HOSPITALITY_Dec2011_v2 (accessed Oct 20, 2017).

Caterer. Do Not Depend on Migrants, Lammy Warns Employers, 2007. [Online] www.caterersearch.com. (accessed 15 Nov, 2017).

Choe, Y.; Dickson, D. R. A. Case Study into the Benefits of Management Training Programs: Impacts on Hotel Employee Turnover and Satisfaction Level. *J. Hum. Resour. Hosp. Tour.* 2010, *9* (1), 103–116.

Choi, J.; Woods, R. H.; Murrmann, S. K. International Labor Markets and the Migration of Labor Forces as an Alternative Solution for Labor Shortages in the Hospitality Industry. *Int. J. Contemp. Hosp. Manag.* **2000,** *12* (1), 61–66.

Choy, D. The Quality of Tourism Employment, *Tour. Manag. J.* **1995,** *16* (2), 129–137.

CIPD. Employee Turnover and Retention, 2005. [Online] http://www.cipd.co.uk/subjects/hrpract/turnover/empturnretent.htm?IsSrchRes=1 (accessed 06 Aug, 2017).

Cooper, R. G.; Kleinschmidt, E. J. Determinants of Timeliness in Product Development. *J. Prod. Innovat. Manag.* **1994,** *11* (5), 381–396.

Dayananda, K. Tourism and Employment: Opportunities and Challenges in Karnataka—Special Reference to Kodagu District. *IOSR J. Human. Soc. Sci.* **2014,** *19* (11), 1–11.

Deloitte. It is 2008: Do You Know Where Your Talent Is? Why Acquisition and Retention Strategies Don't Work, 2004. [Online] www.deloitte.com/dtt/cda/doc/content/US_Talent MgmtPOV_2.11.05.pdf (accessed 06 Aug, 2017).

Desouza, K. C.; Awazu, Y. Knowledge Management at SMEs: Five Peculiarities. *J. Knowl. Manag.* **2006,** *10* (1), 32–43.

Dodds, R.; Joppe, M. CSR in the Tourism Industry? The Status of and Potential for Certification, Codes of Conduct and Guidelines, Study Prepared for the CSR Practice Foreign Investment, Advisory Service Investment Climate Department, 2005. [Online] http://www.ifc.org/ifcext/economics.nsf/AttachmentsByTitle/CSR+in+the+Tourism+Industry/$FILCSR+in+the+Tourism+Industry.pdf (accessed Aug 9, 2017).

Duncan, T.; Scott, D.; Baum. 'The Mobilities of Hospitality Work: An Exploration of Issues and Debates.' *Ann. Tour. Res.* **2013,** 41, 1–19.

EED Tourism Watch. RIO +10: Red Card for Tourism? 2002. [Online] http://www.eed.de (accessed Nov 27, 2017).

El-ashry, F.; Delal, M. Population Research and Studies, CAPMAS, 2, 2010.
Estruch-Puertas, E.; Zupi, M. Assessment of Data Sources and Methodology Development for Measuring Foreign Labor Requirements in the Russian Federation. Working Paper: Geneva, ILO, 2009.
European Commission. The New SME Definition: User Guide and Model Declaration Section. Brussels: Office for Official Publications of the European Communities, 2005.
Expert Group on Future Skills Needs. Assessment of Future Skills Requirements in the Hospitality Sector in Ireland, 2015–2020, Executive Summary Report, 2015. [Online] http://www.skillsireland.ie/Publications/2015/Assessment%20of%20Future%20Skills%20Requiremnts%20in%20the%20Hospitality%20Sector%20in%20Ireland,%202015-2020.html (accessed Sep 8, 2017).
Faldetta, G.; Fasone, V.; Provenzano, C. Turnover in the Hospitality Industry: Can Reciprocity Solve the Problem? Revista de Turismo y Patrimonio Cultural: Pasos, 2013, 11, pp 583–595.
Faulkner, L. L. Developing the Optimal Path Test Method: A Quantifiable Approach to Usability. Proceedings of the International Conference on Practical Software Quality Techniques/Practical Software Testing Techniques, 2002.
Felipe, J.; Kumar, U. Unit Labor Costs in the Eurozone: The Competitiveness Debate Again, Levy Economics Institute, 2011. [Online] http://www.levyinstitute.org/pubs/wp_651.pdf (accessed Aug 10, 2017).
Frohm J.; Lindström, V.; Bellgran, M. A. Model for Parallel Levels of Automation within Manufacturing, 18th International Conference on Production Research, Italy, 2005.
García-Pozo, A.; Campos-Soria, A.; Sánchez-Ollero, J.; Marchante-Lara, M. The Regional Wage Gap in the Spanish Hospitality Sector Based on a Gender Perspective. *Int. J. Hosp. Manag.* **2012,** *31* (1), 266–275.
Greve, H. R. Industry Diversity Effects on Job Mobility, *Acta Sociol.* **1994,** *37* (2), 119–139
Griffin, T.; DeLacey, T. Green globe: sustainability accreditation for tourism. In Sustainable Tourism: A Global Perspective; Harris, R.; Griffin, T.; Williams, P., Eds., 2nd ed.; Elsevier: Oxford, 2002.
Hamermesh, D. *Labor Demand. Princeton*; Princeton University Press: NJ, 1993.
Hamermesh, D. S. Do labor costs affect companies' demand for labor? 2014. [Online] https://ideas.repec.org/a/iza/izawol/journly2014n3.html (accessed 15 Aug, 2017).
Handelsman, J. Understanding and Remedying Employee Turnover, 2009. [Online] Business Owner's Toolkit:http://www.toolkit.com/news/newsDetail.aspx?nid=138turnover (accessed Nov 15, 2017).
Henderson, C. J. *Managing Tourism Crises*. Butterworth-Heinemann, Elsevier: UK, 2006.
Hjalager, A.-M.; Baum, T. Upgrading Human Resources: An Analysis of the Number, Quality and Qualifications of Employees Required in the Tourism Sector, Paper for the High-Level Working Group on Tourism and Employment. Brussels: Commission of the European Union, 1998.
ILO. Developments and Challenges in the Hospitality and Tourism Sector, Global Dialogue Forum for the Hotels, Catering, Tourism Sector (23–24 November 2010), Geneva, Switzerland, 2010.
ILO. Small and Medium-Sized Enterprises and Decent and Productive Employment Creation, International Labor Conference 104th Session, Geneva, 2015.
ILO. Sectoral Activities Department: Issues Brief: Gender (Geneva). [Online] www.ilo.org/public/english/dialogue/sector/papers/tourism/gender.pdf (accessed July 24, 2017).
ILO. ABC of Women Worker's Rights and Gender Equality, Geneva, 2010.

International Labor Organization. Development and Challenges in Tourism and Hospitality Sector; International Labor Organization: Geneva, Switzerland, 2010.
Jean, B.; Manfredi, S.; Rollin, H.; Price, L.; Stead, L. Equal Opportunities for Women Employees in the Hospitality Industry: A Comparison between France, Italy, Spain and the UK. *Int. J. Hosp. Manag.* **1997,** *16* (2), 161–179
Jolliffe, L.; Farnsworth, R. Seasonality in Tourism Employment: Human Resource Challenges. *Int. J. Contemp. Hosp. Manag.* **2003,** *15* (6), 312–316.
Jordan, Fiona. An occupational hazard? Sex Segregation in Tourism Employment. *Tour. Manag. J.* **1997,** *18* (8), 525–534.
Kamau, S.; Waudo, J. Hospitality Industry Employer's Expectation of Employees' Competences in Nairobi Hotels. *J. Hosp. Manag. Tour.* **2012,** *3* (4), 55–63.
Kapiki, S. The Impact of Economic Crisis on Tourism and Hospitality: Results from a Study in Greece. *Central Eur. Rev. Econ. Finance*, **2012,** *2* (1), 19–30.
Keep, E.; Mayhew, K. Skills Task Force Research Group; The Leisure Sector: London: DfEE, 1999.
Keskin, H.; Sentürk, C.; Sungur, O.; Kiris, H. M. The Importance of SMEs in Developing Economies, 2nd International Symposium on Sustainable Development, June 8-9 2010, Sarajevo.
Keyser, H. *Tourism Development*, Oxford University Press: Oxford, 2002.
Kim J. H. Career expectations and Requirements of Undergraduate Hospitality Students and the Hospitality Industry, MSc Thesis; AUT University: Auckland, New Zealand, 2008.
Korczynski, M. *Human Resource Management in Service Work;* Palgrave Macmillan: London, 2002; 1–237
Kroll Global Fraud Report. 2016/2017 Annual Edition. [Online] www.kroll.com/.../fraud/Fraud (accessed 5 Nov, 2017).
Kusluvan, S. Multinational Enterprises in Tourism: A Case Study of Turkey. PhD Dissertation; Strathclyde University, the Scottish Hotel School: Glasgow, 2003.
LaFaive, M. D. Supply and Demand and the Labor Market, 2001. [Online] https://www.mackinac.org/3818 (accessed Nov 9, 2017).
Lai, P.; Baum, T. Just-In Time Labor Supply in the Hotel Sector: The Role of Agencies. *Employee Relat.* **2005,** *27* (1), 86–103.
Lehtinen, U. On Defining Service. In Services Marketing: Nordic School Perspectives: Proceedings of the XIIth Annual Conference of the European Marketing Academy; Grönroos, C., Gambeson, E., Eds.,1984.
Lehtinen, U.; Järvinen, J. The Role of Service Characteristics in Service Innovations, *NJB J.* **2015,** *64* (3), 168–181.
Leydesdorff, L.; Meyer, M. The Decline of University Patenting and the End of the Bayh-Dole Effect. *Scientometrics* **2010,** *83* (2), 355–362.
Lindsay, C.; McQuaid, R. W. Avoiding the 'McJobs': Unemployed Job Seekers and Attitudes to Service Work. *Work Employment Soc.* **2004,** 18, 297–319.
Lucas, R. *Employment Relations in the Hospitality and Tourism Industries,* Routledge: London, 2004.
Lucas, R.; Keegan, S. Young Workers and the National Minimum Wage. *Equal Opportun. Int. J.* **2007,** *26* (6), 573–589.
Lucas, R.; Keegan, S. Forthcoming. Probing the Basis for Differential Pay Practices of Younger Workers in Low Paying Hospitality Firms. *Hum. Resour. Manag. J.* **2008,** *18* (4), 386–404.

Marshall, J. Women and Strangers: Issues of Marginalization in Seasonal Tourism. *Tour. Geogr.* **2001,** *3* (2), 165–186.
Martin, T. Human Resource Module of the Tourism Satellite Account, 2012. [Online] www.statcan.gc.ca/pub/13-604-m/13-604-m2013072-eng.pdf (accessed Nov 3, 2017).
McCrindle, M.; Hooper, D.; Gen, Y. Attracting, Engaging and Leading a New Generation at Work; University of Tasmania: Hobart, 2006.
McKenzie, K. Belizean Women and Tourism Work. Opportunity or Impediment? *Ann. Tour. Res.* **2007,** *34* (2), 477–496.
Mishev, G. Analysis of the Automation and the Human Worker, Connection between the Levels of Automation and Different Automation Concepts, 2006. [Online] (accessed 15 Nov, 2017).
Morrison, M.; Lumby, J.; Sood, K. Diversity and Diversity Management: Messages from Recent Research. *Edu. Manag. Adm. Leader.* **2006,** *34*, 277–295.
Morse, S. C.; Smith, E. M. Employment Impacts of Off-Peak Seasonal Tourism Development. *Bus. Econ. J.* **2015,** *6* (150).
Neumann, B. R.; Banghart, S. Industry-University 'consultantships': An Implementation Guide. *Int. J. Edu. Manag.* **2001,** *15* (1), 7–11.
Nugent, A. Using Voluntary Benefits Strategically Can Help Employers Address Goals of Retaining Employees and Controlling Costs. *Benefit. Quart.* 2009, *25* (2), 7–10.
Obadić, A.; Marić, I. The Significance of Tourism as an Employment Generator of Female Labor Force. *Significance Tour.* **2009,** *1*, 93–114.
OECD [Organisation for Economic Co-operation and Development], Small and Medium-Sized Enterprises in Turkey Issues and Policies, OECD Publications, 2004. [Online] http://www.oecd.org/dataoecd/5/11/31932173.pdf (accessed Nov 10, 2017).
OECD. Is Migration Good for the Economy?, Migration Policy Debates, 2014. [Online] https://www.oecd.org/migration/OECD%20Migration%20Policy%20Debates%20Numero%202.pdf (accessed Oct 20, 2017).
Peceri, R. Promoting Organizational Effectiveness: Managerial Conduct Perspective. *Cornell Hotel Restaur. Adm. Quart.* **2010,** *10* (5), 157–351.
People 1st. Skill Needs Assessment for the Hospitality, Leisure, Travel and Tourism Sector, UK Report. London: People 1st, 2006.
Peterson, D.; Rhoads, A.; Vaught, B. C. Ethical Beliefs of Business Professionals: A Study of Gender, Age and External Factors. *J. Bus. Ethics* 2001, 31, 225–232.
Pforr, C. and Hosie, P. *Crisis Management in the Tourism Industry*; Ashgate, UK, 2009.
Pires, M. 9 Steps to Reducing Employee Turnover, 2009. [Online] http://www.articlesbase.com/human-resources-articles/9-steps-to-reducing-employee-turnover 747936.html (accessed Nov 20, 2017)
Pizam, A. The Global Financial Crisis and Its Impact on the Hospitality Industry. *Int. J. Hosp. Manag.* **2009,** *28* (3), 301.
Plüss, C. Quick Money: Easy Money? A Report on Child Labor in Tourism, 1999. [Online] http://akte.ch/ (Accessed: AUG 19, 2017).
Purcell, K. The Relationship between Career and Job Opportunities: Women's Employment in the Hospitality Industry as a Microcosm of Women's Employment. *Women Manag. Rev.* **1996,** *11* (5), 17–24.
Rampur, S. Causes of Employee Turnover, 2009. [Online] http://www.buzzle.com/articles/causes-of employee-turnover.html (accessed Nov 19, 2017).

Reskin, B.; Bielby, D. A Sociological Perspective on Gender and Career Outcomes. *J. Econ. Perspect.* **2005,** *19* (1), 71–86.

Richardson, S. A. Used and Unappreciated: Exploring the Role Work Experience Plays in Shaping Undergraduate Tourism and Hospitality Students' Attitude Towards a Career in the Industry, PhD Thesis; Griffith University: Nathan, Queensland, 2009.

Riley, M. *Human Resource Management in the Hospitality and Tourism Industry*, 2nd ed., Oxford: Butterworth-Heinemann, 1996.

Riley, M., Ladkin, A., and Szivas, E. *Tourism Employment: Analysis and Planning*. Channel View Publication, 2002; pp 10–11.

Robinson, R. N.; Beesley, L. G. Linkages between Creativity and Intention to Quit: An Occupational Study of Chefs. *Tour. Manag. J.* **2010,** *31* (6), 765–776.

Saarinen, J.; Rogerson, C.; Manwa, H. *Tourism and the Millennium Development Goals: Tourism, Local Communities, and Development*; Routledge: London and New York, 2013, p 68.

Sentis Market Research, Temporary Foreign Worker Program Survey of Employers, Commissioned by go2HR, September, 2014.

Shamsuzzoha, A. Employee Turnover-a Study of its Causes and Effects; University of Vaasa: Finland, 2007.

Sharma, A1.; Kukreja, S.; Sharma, A2. Impact of Labor Laws on Child Labor: A Case of Tourism Industry. *Int. J. Adv. Manag. Econ.* **2012,** *1* (3), 47–55.

Singh, V. Impact of Labor Cost in Overall Performance of Hotels and Restaurants. *Int. J. Enhanced Res. Manag. Comput. Appl.* **2014,** *3* (9), 25–29.

Smedley, T. Say Hello, Wave Goodbye. People Management, 2007, 25.

Smith, A.; Anderson, J. AI, Robotics, and the Future of Jobs, *Pew Research Center*, August 6, 2014.

Solnet, D.; Hood, A. Generation Y as Hospitality Employees: Framing a Research Agenda., J. Hosp. Tour. Manag. **2008,** *15*, 59–68

Sturman, M. C. Using Your Pay System to Improve Employees' Performance: How You Pay Makes a Difference. Cornell Hospitality Report, 2006, 6(13), pp 1–16.

Szivas, E.; Riley, M.; Airey, D. Labor Mobility into Tourism. Attraction and Satisfaction. *Ann. Tour. Res.* **2003,** *30*, 64–76.

The World Travel and Tourism Council (WTTC). Travel and Tourism Economic Impact. Geneva 22, Switzerland, 2014.

Thomas, B. International Perspectives on Women and Work in Hotels, Catering and Tourism, Bureau for Gender Equality. International Labor Office, 2013.

Thornton and Econometric Research Limited Tourism Labor Shortage Economic Impact Study, 2016. [Online] https://www.go2hr.ca/sites/default/files/legacy/reports/go2HR-2016-Tourism-Labor Shortage-Economic-Impact-Study.pdf (accessed Nov 3, 2017).

Tucker, H. Undoing shame: Tourism and Women's Work in Turkey. *J. Tour. Cult. Change* **2007,** *5* (2), 87–105.

UNWTO. Employment in the Tourism Industries: Measurement Issues and Case Studies. Fifth UNWTO International Conference on Tourism Statistics, Bali, Indonesia, 2009.

UNWTO. Global Report on Women in Tourism 2010. [Online] http://www2.unwto.org/sites/all/files/pdf/folleto_globarl_report.pdf (accessed Oct 26, 2017).

UNWTO. *Global Report on Women in Tourism;* 2011. [Online] http://cf.cdn.unwto.org/ (accessed Jan 14, 2019)

UNWTO. Sustained Growth in International Tourism Despite Challenges. [Online] http://www2.unwto.org/press-release/2017-01-17/sustained-growth-international-tourism-despite challenges (accessed Nov 16, 2017).

UNWTO. United Nations World Tourism Organization Annual Report, Madrid: World Tourism Organization, 2013. [Online] www.unwto.org (accessed Oct 27, 2017).

Wall, G.; Mathieson, A. Tourism: Change, Impacts and Opportunities, Harlow: Pearson Education, 2006.

Wang, J. Z.; Wang, J. Issues, Challenges, and Trends, that Facing Hospitality Industry. *Manag. Sci. Eng.* **2009,** *3* (4), 53–58.

Warhurst, C.; Nickson, D.; Witz, A.; Cullen, A. M. Aesthetic Labor in Interactive Service Work: Some Case Study Evidence from the New Glasgow. *Serv. Ind. J.* **2000,** *20* (3), 1–18.

Whitelaw, P.; Paul, B.; Jeremy, B.; Grant, C.; Michael, D. Training Needs of the Hospitality Industry, 2009. [Online] http://citeseerx.ist.psu.edu/viewdoc/download?doi=10.1.1.546.3207&rep=rep1&type=pdf. (accessed Aug 23, 2017).

Williams. A.; Shaw, G. Tourism: Candy Floss Industry or Job Generator? *Town Plan. Rev.* **1988,** *59*, 81–103.

Witz, A.; Savage, M. *The Gender of Organizations; in Gender and Bureaucracy*, Blackwell Publishers/The Sociological Review: Oxford, 1992.

World Tourism Organization and International Labor Organization. Measuring Employment in the Tourism Industries—Guide with Best Practices, UNWTO, Madrid, 2014.

Yunis, E. Tourism an Engine for Employment Creation: The Fifth UNWTO International Conference on Tourism Statistics: Tourism and Employment: An Overview by UNWTO. Bali, Indonesia, 2009.

Zingheim, P. K.; Schuster, J. R. Developing Total Pay Offers for High Performers. *Compensat. Benefits Rev.* **2008,** *40*, 55–59.

Zografos, G. Employee Turnover Statistics Remain a Great Tool. *Franchising World*, 2006, 38(1), p 36.

# CHAPTER 3

# LABOR SKILLS AND TRAINING IN THE TOURISM AND HOSPITALITY INDUSTRY

*"The tourism and hospitality world is nonexistent without groups, this means that the characteristics of the brain's right hemisphere are the most important now: interpersonal skills (communication, emotional, empathy, big-picture thinking, and the ability in finding a common ground)."*

## 3.1 INTRODUCTION

In the economy of the world, the hospitality sector is one of the fastest growing industries. In modern hospitality business, it is all about competence in people, and especially the employees' skills. The level of service quality depends on the skills of employees. The skills are about knowledge, qualities, and thoughts, which lead to a property's survival and development. However, the hospitality industry faces real challenges in matching its skill requirements to the changing labor market in every country and elsewhere. According to Baum (2002), the hospitality sector cannot readily be ignored regarding the skill mismatch problem because it accommodates a significant number of workforce, up to 10% of the global workforce are employed in tourism and hospitality-related work.

Burns (1997) has categorized the hospitality employment into "skilled" and "unskilled" categories arguing that this separation is something of a social construct, especially in postmodernist case. Some voices advocate that service sector occupations especially hospitality industry's jobs tend to be undervalued and accordingly they justify that skills are not important compared to other sectors and industries. The low social recognition of these jobs contributed significantly to shaping their low status. Although such occupations as delivering pizzas, waiters, and security guards certainly do not appear to require many special skills, their skills, when objectively defined, were not as limited as is normally assumed. Employees in the service sectors should possess different types of skills enough to produce a high-quality product and convince the customers to afford it, their success based on their technical and soft skills in satisfying the customers. They should have a range of skills, knowledge, and attitudes that affect a major part of their jobs which impacts on service quality excellence. Interactive service jobs depend upon skills located within each employee, especially emotional skills that can be appeared in the quality of the verbal communication (Hochschild, 1989), and are often exploited as an "invisible" skills. Such skills tend to be tacit, derived from experience, and not objectified in qualifications and they tend to be very different from the benchmark skills traditionally identified in manufacturing sector. Ritzer (1993) argued that working in the hospitality environment requires more than an ability to operate a cash register; emotional demands are made of employees to constantly be in a positive, joyful, and even playful mood (p. 240). In parallel with Ritzer, Poon (1993) noted that new employees in hospitality must be trained to be loyal, flexible, tolerant, amiable, and responsible. At every successful tourism establishment, it is the employees that stand out. Technology cannot substitute for welcoming employees. Subsequently, there is great emphasis on the interpersonal skills in lower status service sector. Consequently, the skilled employee is someone who is qualified to practice an explicit body of knowledge and has the intention to learn the new (Thompson et al., 2000).

Hospitality occupations (and subsequently the skills that it requires for its delivery) involve diversity in both horizontal and vertical terms (Baum, 2002):

- Horizontal diversity proves how the industry is expanded from fast food outlets and bed and breakfast institutions to elite resorts and "style" hotels and clubs.
- Vertical diversity is reflected in the range of vocational, technical, service, supervision, and managerial tasks.

Organizational structure is used to help divide tasks, specify the job for each department, and delegate authority within and among departments. Even within the same organization "under the one roof," hospitality occupations involve diversity in both horizontal and vertical terms. Every hotel, for example, whether it is big or small, needs considering the diversity of employees' skills in the hotel organizational structure to carry out its daily operations. Keep and Mayhew (1999) presented the occupational typology developed by Reich (1991) that identified three discrete vertical categories of occupations in hotels as follows:

1. High-level manipulators or analysts.
2. A dwindling group of those engaged in routine production.
3. A group providing interpersonal services—waiters and hotel receptionists among others.

Effective job specifications increase work efficiency, productivity, and profit. Each hotel organizes workforce in different ways. A medium-size hotel organizational structure basically segmented into six divisions: finance, front office, human resources, food and beverage (F/B), sales, and logistics.

### *Financial*

The finance department's role is to prepare and interpret financial statements, record financial transactions, and deal with cost accounting and cost control.

### *Front Office*

The front office department handles customer service including front desk service, reservation, concierge, telephone, laundry, and housekeeping service. A hotel's front office is where guests are greeted when they arrive, where they get registered and assigned to a room, and where they check out. It is almost the most important department as it often offers direct contact with customers.

### *Human Resources*

The human resource department is given the responsibility to handle employees' issues, manage recruitment process, arrange staff training, make promotion and disciplinary decisions, and check staff absenteeism.

### *Food and Beverage*

The F/B department is responsible for all of the dining rooms, restaurants, bars, kitchen, clean-up services, etc. Here, F/B department is divided into two parts: kitchen and restaurant. Kitchen department is responsible for food preparation including main food, dessert, side food, and beverage.

Restaurant department's role is to provide dining room operation, waiter service, food runner, busboys, and clean-up service.

### Sales

The responsibility for sales department is to sell the hotel facilities and services to individuals and groups. They sell rooms, food, beverage, or special service such as massage and laundry to potential customers through advertising channels or direct contacts.

### Logistics

The logistics department is responsible for tracking for daily supplies, purchasing appliances, and keeping security; the responsibilities of this department may be included in other department duties, such as F/B, front office departments, or even financial department according to the burden of each departments and the vision of the management.

Skills that fall within the first category are most highly valued in society. Hospitality work, on the face of it, falls, in part, into the second category (chefs) and predominantly into the growing third category. However, first category skills were also found to be lacking as were decision-making, problem-solving, and control of information. Food and beverage skills and other functional skills such as housekeeping and customer care were also in need of a revamp.

## 3.2 EMPLOYABILITY SKILLS

Hospitality work environment is critically characterized in both the popular press and in research-based academic sources as dominated by a low skilled labor (Wood, 1997). On the other hand, Shaw and Williams (1994) argued that referring to employees involved in the industry as the uneducated, unmotivated, untrained, unskilled, and unproductive labor force is brutal criticism and unfair classification. However, Bradley et al. (2000) applied this epithet to the wider service or new economy in questioning assumptions about a skills revolution in Britain, noting that "jobs commonly retain a low-skill character, especially in the fastest-growing sectors" (p. 129). All employees, irrespective of rank, lack even the most basic understanding of the levels of service expected by all guests but especially international guests (Agut et al., 2003). In addition, based on personal experience, there appears to be a chronic shortage of skills in many hospitality occupations and this possibly suggests that these are not cultivated in the workforce during their training.

In other words, the technical (hard) and nontechnical (soft) skills are required to be grown up during their educational life in order to meeting the requirements of employability skills. It was reported by DIISRTE (2013) that business and industry required a broader range of skills and recommended communication, problem-solving skills, teamwork, initiative and enterprise, planning and organizing skills, self-management, learning, and technology as employability skills.

Employability skills are technical and nontechnical competences that are fundamental requirements for employment in the current competitive job market. Overtoom (2000, p. 2) defined employability skills as the "transferable core skill groups that represent essential functional and enabling knowledge, skills, and attitudes required by the 21st century workplace." Employability skills as defined by Gowen (1992) refer to those skills and qualities needed by workers to effectively respond to the literacy demands of the workplace and to successfully implement job duties, learn, train, and apply learning on the job. According to Keller et al. (2011), the employability skills are a classification of attributes and skills, in which attributes speak to nonskill-related behaviors and attitudes, whereas skills refer to the ability to carry out a technical task. Employability skills encompass a wide array of skills that include technical and nontechnical competencies (Ju et al., 2012). Jackson (2013) suggested that employability skills, also known as "professional, core, generic, key, and nontechnical skills," enhance the work readiness of new graduates (p. 272).

The primary objective of any hospitality organization is to highly satisfy its customers by providing a prompt and high-quality service (Boella and Goss-Turner, 2005); so, a number of academics have claimed that in diverse countries, the employers may expect employees to possess a different set of skills in the workplace. This implies that all employees and workers must initially be carefully selected, sufficiently trained, and motivated to be committed to submit a high-quality performance. The nature of service process enhances the promotion of the notion of hiring multiskilled workforce. Multiskilled employee is not only able to provide more effective and efficient service but also has a major part in shaping the perceptions and experiences of customers and guests. Davids and Fredericks (2004) mentioned that multiskilling is the acquirement of skills, qualities, knowledge, competency, and experiences, which empower the individual to perform tasks beyond the scope of their immediate and traditional job requirements.

So, filling job vacancies of the hospitality industry by multiskilled employees in case of labor shortage is very vital for the business success. The ease of movement from one task to another is the main feature of the multiskilled employees; their skills facilitate both the sideways and upward mobility of employees from one post to a different one (Reche and Fuentes, 2006), in order to perform a variety of tasks and participate in decision-making and thus add value to the organization as a whole (Kalleberg, 2001).

These extra successful tasks accomplished by a multiskilled employee made Haas et al. (2001) claim that productivity in organizations can be increased by 5% or more and total hiring of employees can be reduced by 35% where multiskilling exists. Multiskilling thus awards the organization with highly flexible and adaptable employee in addition to the clear financial benefits.

The validity of multiskilling depends significantly on the nature and the characteristics of each market and organizations; so, Ladkin (2005) ascertained that organizations managers must identify and specify skills and competencies they expcct from the employees and workers and only when their expectations match their perception, does service quality result, which ultimately raise the customers satisfaction and benefits the business. In case the workforce needed are correctly identified and if they are truly committed to, and passionate about their workplace, multiskilling will be an effective important tool to help hospitality industry operations to cope with problematic changes. In addition to a set of desired skills being taught, there is also a need, for example, to develop reachable career paths for employees so as to increase employee engagement. This will also aid in the drive to retain employees who are well qualified longer. However, the multiskilled employees can only benefit the organization if the work environment, work organization, job design, and strength management to use the skills obtained are in place.

Despite the fact that multiskilling can improve the business productivity and financial savings, Ingram and Fraenkel (2006), on the other hand, argued that it may also to an extent lower the quality of service by reducing the number of "point of service" staff.

To lay a foundation in which this discuss can take place, it is necessary to define the term "multiskilling" which is viewed from a number of diverse perspectives.

Clark (1989) stated that "Programs of multiskilling generally involve workers on a particular occupational, craft or skill category progressively picking up the capability to perform additional tasks, usually performed by workers in another functional or occupational area within the organization" (p. 13). Subsequently, a multiskilled worker is an individual who possesses relevant qualities and acquires a range of skills, competencies, and knowledge in other working areas. Accordingly, it is not necessary that the worker should possess mastery level skills in multiple working areas. However, the worker should be productive and effective in the other disciplines other than his or her primary task (Burleson et al., 1998).

Hence, multiskilled employees are able to serve the organization in a wider range of operational areas, which cut across traditional occupational boundaries by having an increasing pool of skills (Matias-Reche and Fuentes-Fuentes, 2006), and a loyal multiskilled employee is a valuable asset for any organization.

## 3.3 MULTISKILLING IN THE HOSPITALITY INDUSTRY

For many hospitality organizations, the high diversity of workforce and the lenient practices of employment process are causing considerable challenges in terms of experiencing labor shortage or having low skilled employees. Powell and Wood (1999) claimed that one of the most critical problems in the hospitality industry worldwide is the "brain drain" since the skilled and competent employees in hospitality industry are effortlessly transferable to others.

The labor market skills logically influence the skills profile of hospitality. The weak internal labor market characteristics impose downward pressures on the skills expectations that organizations and its customers expect, in turn, influences the quality and level of service that the labor delivers. Therefore, it is becoming a vital issue for human resource managers to handle the employment practices strategically in the hospitality industry operations. Hrebiniak (2005) confirmed that the efficient and effective implementation of daily operations relies heavily on the optimal human resource management (HRM) in the hospitality operations in general. Considering multiskilling in the process of hiring to meet the demand of providing service quality, excellence is a strategic option for human resource professionals in the industry. The attainment of supplementary task-related skills and experience, which empower an employee to perform a broader range of tasks and functions within an organization, may refer to multiskilling.

The optimal allocating and utilizing the existing multiskilled workforce lead to a greater efficiency and greater profits for the business. According to Sommerville (2007), multiskilling enhances the capabilities of employees and serves to benefit both the organization and the customers; it strengthens the organization competitive advantage and meets the customers' expectations.

So, competence in a variety of skills is needed to prevent the functional lacking in terms of guest expectations and service quality provision to the customers; in order to do so, employees must be trained and compensated; employees should be given incentives in order to be motivated to acquire extra skills and do various tasks. In addition, they should acquire the necessary skills which will eventually allow them to perform all the required tasks of a number of working areas whether it is related or not to their job specifications of the current functional areas of operation when the need arises, also it is important that the competency and skill levels of all multiskilled trained employees should be uniform.

Multiskilling would certainly include the acquisition of valued skills and appropriate professional attitudes. The foundation of the appropriate professional behavior is to be punctual, careful, reliable, and trustworthy.

The absence of these aspects will impact negatively on the performance of the multiskilled employee who is thus wasted. In general, multiskilling offers labor the prospect of learning new skills and provides for job variety. Of course, all required skills are fine-tuned by learning and constant practices and interaction with other coworkers. Moreover, all the employees need to be given regular feedback relating to their newly acquired skills.

Generally, there are three distinct approaches of multiskilling (Wood, 1993) (see Fig. 3.1): first, vertical multiskilling, which relates to the acquiring of extra skills at a higher level of difficulty; second, cross-skilling, which relates to the acquiring of skills of a similar level of complexity but beyond the traditional boundaries of the daily operations; and third, horizontal multiskilling, which relates to acquiring other skills related to another working area which are similar in levels of complexity.

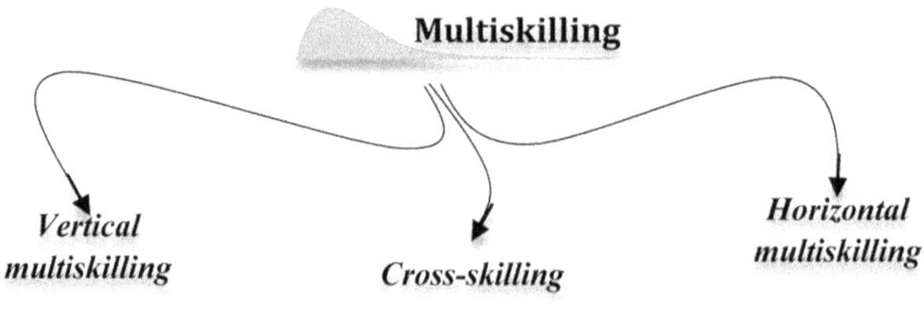


**FIGURE 3.1** Multiskilling approaches.

**Source:** The Authors.

In the hospitality industry, multiskilling is a very useful program allowing the business to manage in service environments that are unstable due to a plethora of impacts from both the micro- and macroenvironments. The hospitality organizations provide the convenient conditions that suit promoting multiskilling across organization departments, for example, when a large number of guests are expected, the supervisor supports the flexibility of allocating the employees to engage in pressing tasks.

Nankervis and Compton (2006) promoted the notion of deploying function flexibility strategy adoption in managing the workforce that fills the gaps and enhances the productivity of employees; such strategy suggests that employees who are functionally flexible through the effective practice of multiskilling are highly likely to perform their duties efficiently and thus less likely to be part of a high turnover rate of staff (Nicolaides, 2013). Therefore, in order to mitigate and control any unexpected situation, multiskilling should initially encompass employees and workers from middle management down to the most vocational levels in each of the departments of a hotel, including the front desk, housekeeping, laundry services, engineering, stewarding, culinary or F/B service, and even security and health and safety aspects. There is no doubt that hotels, in particular, need to vigorously promote multiskilling notion in the workplace.

Research conducted by Burgess and Aitken (2004) in their survey of employers confirmed that conflict resolution skills, functional skills, computer skills, and basic good work habits were the expected skills employees should possess. Additionally, they also noted what were considered to be chronic skill shortfalls including chef skills, kitchen control, general housekeeping, management techniques, sales techniques, and most importantly customer service quality provision.

Cotton (2002) has stated a number of skills that hospitality employees are expected to have, including communication, self-management, relationship-building, persuasion, planning and organizing, analyzing information, commercial acumen and flexibility, and decision-making skills. Gilmore and Gregor (2001) also identified a number of characteristics that are desirable to exist in the work environment such as adherence to an ethical code of conduct, suitably attired employees, integrity, honesty, fairness, respect, and harmonious working relationships that are important skills to impart. Only when employees and workers have attained thorough skills, will quality service improve. Baum (2006) show leadership and develop competencies associated with interpersonal, problem-solving, and self-management skills.

These skills are rated as having the greatest impacts on the success of the organization as a result of multiskilling; consequently, this skill as well as others should be imparted by industry. Other skills have been identified that after reviewing of a total of 18 hotels ranging from 4 to 5 stars ratings (Burgess and Aitken, 2004), there should also be a focus on the improvement of skills in areas such as languages, nonverbal communication and business etiquette, adaptation skills, cultural skills, host culture values, and stress management. On the face of it, there is little about hospitality work and the skills it requires that is unique to the sector. There is, however, a studied argument, for example, Lashley and Morrison (2000), as well as Seymour (2000) confirmed how important the emotional labor in the hospitality work context is. Service staff is responsible for managing their emotions, feelings, and attitudes in the workplace (Diefendorff and Richard, 2003).

The employees are expected to be an actor in order to convey the positive emotions, such as friendliness and kindliness to enhance customer loyalty and experiences (Ashkanasy et al., 2002), especially those who are involved in front-line working areas (Hochschild, 1983); they are required to handle the feelings of their customers and themselves. Groth et al. (2009) mentioned some of the emotional feelings and attitudes that are required such as smiling and creating eye contacts and performing real caring to customers' demands. An ability to cope with such demands must be recognized as a "skill" par excellence.

Bates and Phelan (2002) mentioned that an American organization "Jobs for American Graduates", started in 1980, examined the topic of workplace competencies. A primary objective is to secure a quality job that will lead to a good career. The core competencies are as follows:

1. **Resources:** identifies, organizes, plans, and allocates resources.
    - Time: selects goal-relevant activities, ranks them, allocates time, and prepares and follows schedules.
    - Money: uses or prepares budgets, makes forecasts, keeps records, and makes adjustments to meet objectives.
    - Materials and facilities: acquires, stores, allocates, and uses materials or space efficiently.
    - Human resources: assesses skills and distributes work accordingly, evaluates performance, and provides feedback.
2. **Interpersonal:** works with others.
    - Participates as a member of a team: contributes to group effort.
    - Teaches others new skills.
    - Serves clients/customers: works to satisfy customers' expectations.
    - Exercises leadership: communicates ideas to justify position and persuade and convince others; responsibly challenges existing procedures and policies.

- Negotiates: works toward agreements involving exchange or resources, resolves divergent interests.
- Works with diversity: works well with others from diverse backgrounds.

3. **Information:** acquires and uses information.
   - Acquires and evaluates information: identifies need for data, obtains it from existing sources or creates it, and evaluates its relevance and accuracy.
   - Organizes and maintains information: organizes, processes, and maintains written or computerized records and other forms of information in a systematic fashion.
   - Interprets and communicates information: selects and analyzes information and communicates the results to others using oral, written, graphic, pictorial, or multimedia methods.
   - Uses computers to process information: employs computers to acquire, organize, analyze, and communicate information.
4. **Systems:** understands complex relationships.

- Understands systems: knows how social, organizational, and technological systems work and operate effectively with them.
- Monitors and corrects performance: distinguishes trends, predicts impacts on system operations, diagnoses systems' performance, and corrects malfunctions.
- Improves or designs systems: suggests modifications to existing systems and develops new or alternative systems to improve performance.

5. **Technology:** works with a variety of technology.
   - Selects technology: judges which set of procedures, tools, or machines, including computers and their programs, will produce the desired results.
   - Applies technology to tasks: understands overall intent and proper procedures for setup including computers and their programming systems.

Riley et al. (2002) noted that skill is always surrounded by disagreements because perceptions of skill are highly subjective and relative. Who is or who is not skilled is inevitably an issue.

The skill definition, in general, is the ability of an employee to use his/her knowledge efficiently in execution or performance of the daily tasks. So, skills can be in many forms; generic, vocational, technical, and soft skills.

Each form is closely related to another and the effect of every type of those skills goes each way, but, from my point of view, the generic skill is foundation that every employee should have, while the soft skills are the difference maker; it is the qualitative ones that differentiate among the manager, the employee, and worker, and who make a decision and who implement it.

So, it may be concluded that a paradigm shift has occurred in terms of the skills required for hospitality occupations. Figure 3.2 shows the skills needed to exist in the work environment of tourism and hospitality industry.

Figure 3.2 outlined a presentation of most necessary skills required to exist in the work environment of the industry; the two categories of employability skills—technical and nontechnical skills—represent the two corners stone that the service employees must establish in their personality; they represent the foundations of the skills paradigm in the tourism and hospitality context.

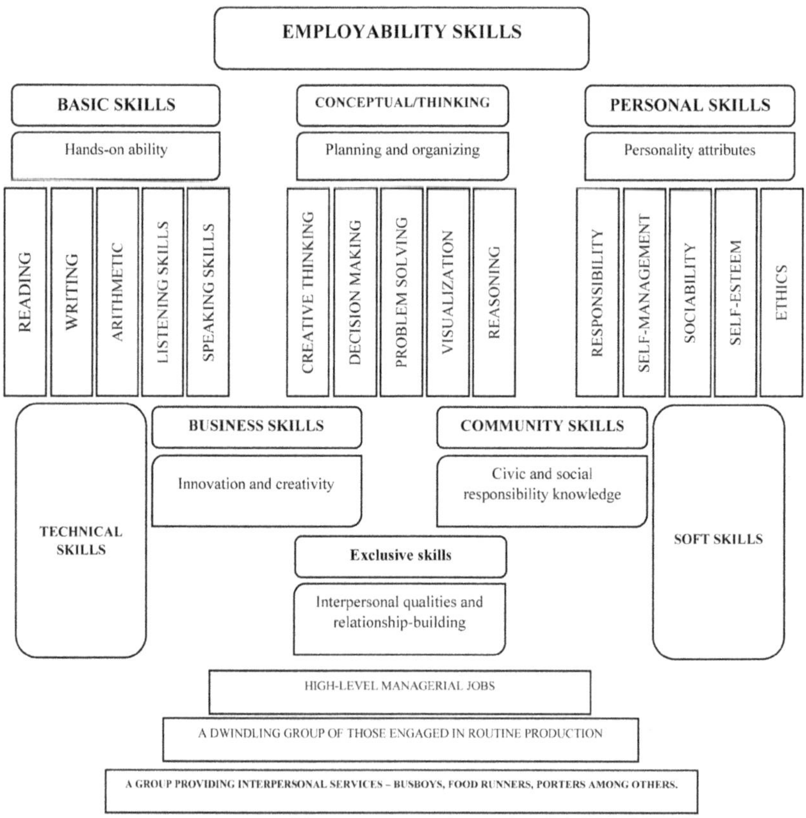


**FIGURE 3.2** Skills paradigm within tourism and hospitality context.

**Source:** The Authors.

As depicted in the figure, there are three job levels, and they were figured as three stair steps; if you are at the ground step, this means that you are still away from the skills cave and, in turn, you still lose the treasure. Employability skills are stated in terms of technical and nontechnical skills. The technical skills are occupational or vocational, technology, literacy, and numeracy skills; however, nontechnical skills are soft skills.

In reality, all these aspects play a part in shaping our understanding of skills and they are further overlaid with the social construction that tradition, gender, and ethnicity impose on our interpretation of who is skilled employee and who is not.

### *3.3.1 HARD SKILLS WITHIN HOSPITALITY INDUSTRY*

Weber et al. (2009) claimed that hard skills are corresponding to the skills in the technical and administrative categories. Basically, when employees use the term hard skills, they typically are referring to the definition of skill as defined by Random House Dictionary: the ability, coming from individual's knowledge, practice, aptitude, to do specific occupations well.

This definition is confirmed by the technical skills' definition that was developed by Omar et al. (2012) who claimed that skills needed to perform specific tasks refer to technical skills. Dixon et al. (2010) claimed a similar definition of hard skills but added that hard skills can be measured and quantified. So, competent excellence in performing a trade or craft job requires manual dexterity or special training or knowledge express generic or technical or hard skills (http://dictionary.reference.com/browse/skills). Thus, hard skills can be considered are those achievements that are included on a résumé, such as education, knowledge, work experience, and level of expertise (Investopedia, 2012). Table 3.1 explains in detail the different definitions of skills that may be enrolled as hard skills.

Although skills shortages in hospitality industry are increasingly seen in terms of generic rather than specific technical skills, historically, skills in hospitality industry were seen almost exclusively in terms of their technical requirements, and this formed the basis of the training agenda pursued by educational institutions all over the world and especially in the developing countries through funded aid programs, for much of the 20th century. Jobs in hospitality were constructed on the basis of an accumulation of skills required for specific technical tasks (Baum, 2002). Thus, it was highlighted that there is a great emphasis on what can be classified as generic

**TABLE 3.1** Hard Skills Group.

| **Hard skills** | | |
|---|---|---|
| Hard skills are also referred to as technical, generic, and vocational skills (Dixon et al., 2010). To add to a better understanding of hard skills, Laker and Powell (2011) associated working with equipment and software as using hard skills | | |
| **Generic skills** | **Vocational skills** | **Technical skills** |
| The skills are necessary to function in routine work environment:<br>- written communication skills<br>- critical thinking, and<br>- interactions skills (Tribble, 2009; Badcock et al., 2010) | The skills refer to the technical, hands-on, job-specific skills (Davis, 2009). Skills taught in vocational education focus on "know-how or practical expertise" rather than theoretical knowledge; vocational skills are related to a trade, for example, catering, carpentry, and electrical engineering (Mucunguzi, 2013) | The skills are also known as occupationally specific skills that workers must possess in order to function in specific tasks (Guy et al., 2008). Hargis (2011) stated that technical skills are also known as hard skills, which are defined as "job specific tasks directly necessary for successful completion of the job," for example, electricity, robotics, and computer technology (p. 1) |

**Source:** The Authors.

skills—communications, problem-solving, and customer service in addition to job-specific skills (HtF, 2000). Qualifications and Curriculum Authority (2000) identified key skills as

- communications,
- information technology,
- working with others, and
- improving own learning and performance.

These key skills represent capabilities that have, traditionally, been identified as "normal" expectations within hospitality field at operational and management levels, and a specific focus on the development of these skills.

Odgers and Baum (2001) conducted a study in 4–5-star hotels in seven European countries investigating the skill requirements in the frontline jobs; the results showed that they recruit on the basis of hard skills rather than soft skills. They added that even 5-star hotels accept the reality of the marketplace and are willing to recruit staff without front office experience provided as long as they have good generic skills such as education and a willingness to learn. Warhurst et al. (2000) noted that esthetic criteria also feature in the recruitment of front-line staff for hospitality work. In brief, the recruitment criteria within the hospitality industry increasingly focus on the triangular nature of skills—technical, generic, and esthetic.

However, Hospitality Training Foundation (HtF, 2000) continues to report employer demands for improved hard skills as a priority. Recommendations to tackle the generic skills gap include

- recruitment practices need to encompass generic skill requirements,
- building generic skills development into full-time education programs,
- funding for training providers to deliver key skills and develop appropriate aptitudes and attitudes within young people, and
- ensuring providers are developed to be able to deliver key skills.

Generally, the nature of the job (the degree of direct contact with the customer) and the type of business that is involved (accommodation establishment, F/B outlets, etc.) determine the priority of each dimension of the hard skills that are on the top of job requirements such as:

- Dexterity dimensions.
- Knowledge dimensions.

- Communication dimensions.
- Esthetic dimensions.

### 3.3.2 SOFT SKILLS WITHIN HOSPITALITY INDUSTRY

Although the term soft skills have been around a long time in both business and educational institutions, in corporate meetings, and in curriculum development (Evenson, 1999), soft skills are difficult to define and measure, because it is relative based on thc domain in which the skills are demonstrated (Yaacoub et al., 2011). So, soft skills usually are reflected in practices and tasks that employees have perfected, such as keyboarding with speed and accuracy or wiring the electronics in an automotive system.

Thus, the real soft skills definition is not about skills in the traditional common sense but it's about personal traits, attitudes, and behaviors rather than technical aptitude or knowledge. Brungardt (2009) defined soft skills as nontechnical skills that are based on personal competencies and interpersonal skills. The Collins English Dictionary defines the term soft skills as "desirable qualities for certain forms of employment depend on the individual's common sense, the ability to deal with others, and the positive flexible attitude, instead of depending on the acquired knowledge" (http://dictionary.reference.com/browse/soft/skills). Another definition was developed by Klaus (2007) who defined soft skills as personal, social, communication, and self-control behaviors.

Therefore, soft skills contribute significantly in guiding individuals to use technical skills and factual knowledge effectively as it is based on self-awareness, trustworthiness, self-control, integrity, and problem-solving competencies. Higher education institutions around the world are acknowledging that soft skills are the distinctions between obtaining and retaining jobs. Another significant main feature that distinguishes soft skills from hard skills is that soft skills are not limited to one's profession. Unlike hard skills, which are about a person's skill set and ability to perform a certain type of task or a specific job, soft skills are interpersonal (Parsons, 2008) that also able to promote improvement in job performances (Hargis, 2011). Soft skills are continually developed through practical application during one's approach toward everyday life and the workplace (Arkansas Department of Education, 2007).

Be it nontechnical skills and based on the personality trait in the first place (see Table 3.2), it enhances the individuals' career navigation by improving their personal interactions and in turn improves their job performance

(Klaus, 2007; Parsons, 2008). In a study conducted in the United Kingdom and United States, it is having been found that generic interpersonal and human relations competencies are very important, while technical competencies were seen as less important (Raybould and Wilkins, 2006).

On the same lines, hospitality managers in Australia confirmed generic domains of interpersonal relations, self-management, and problem-solving as the most important while the 10 most important descriptors included dealing effectively with customer problems and maintaining professional ethical standards (Raybould and Wilkins, 2006). Changing market and globalization prompt the need for higher levels of competence in the workforce. The competitive nature of the job market makes this need a priority (Davis, 2009).

**TABLE 3.2** Soft Skills and Nontechnical Skills.

| Soft skills | Nontechnical skills |
|---|---|
| Soft skills are the nontechnical, intangible, personality-specific skills that determine one's strengths as a leader, facilitator, mediator, and negotiator. It includes | Those skills/competencies including ability to work with others (Brungardt, 2009) by which good working relations between coworkers are created in order to satisfy customers (Tribble, 2009). It includes |
| - communication, work ethics, critical thinking, and problem-solving (Hargis, 2011)<br>- teaming skills (Fogle, 2011; Tribble, 2009) | - communication, problem-solving, leading and inspiring others, and decision-making or management (Brungardt, 2009)<br>- creativity and teamwork (Boahin and Hofman, 2013)<br>- initiative, critical thinking, ethical behavior, emotional intelligence, and work ethic (Jackson and Hancock, 2010) |

**Source:** The Authors.

Soft skills are interrelated with employability and are relevant in the field of tourism and hospitality; there is a wide array of soft skills' employers expect from the potential labor force. It is of some significance to mention the crucial importance of soft skills in the hospitality industry since hospitality is almost by definition an international industry; cross-cultural competencies have been identified as fundamental. This pushed the researchers to shed the light on some competencies and skills that are very essential to the success of the hospitality business. Johanson and Woods (2008) emphasized the ability to cope with emotional demands to empathize with customers and possess emotional intelligence (Raybould and Wilkins, 2006). Emotional intelligence is considered an essential skill for successful entry into level managers by hospitality recruiters and university educators (Staton-Reynolds, 2009). Seymour (2000) had adopted the "emotional demands" notion in her study as an additional dimension of hospitality skills. Her work builds upon the earlier work of Hochschild (1983) who introduced the concept of emotional work within the services economy arguing that service providers are required to manage their emotions for the benefit of customers. The competencies identified as essential by Kay and Russette (2000) include recognizing customer problems, showing enthusiasm, maintaining professional and ethical standards, cultivating a climate of trust, and adapting creatively to change.

Stumpf (2007) reported the many subsets of soft skills as follows:

- honesty,
- self-improvement,
- interpersonal relations,
- team building,
- communications,
- career preparation,
- leadership,
- problem-solving skills,
- critical thinking,
- communication skills,
- self-discipline,
- self-confidence,
- good work ethic, and
- showing courtesy.

Chung-Herrera et al. (2003) developed competency model based on two dimensions:

- self-management (comprising ethics, time management, flexibility, adaptability, and the like) and
- strategic positioning (comprising awareness of customer needs, commitment to quality, concern for the community).

Thus, hospitality students and employees should be educated and trained in good manners, civility, and proper speech, in addition to conceptual and technical skills and hospitality competence (Pizam, 2011). Generally, a wider cross-section of relevant soft skills that identified as important for employability was derived. The following paragraphs provide a detailed exploration of the top commonly noted soft skills related to jobs in the fields of tourism and hospitality.

### 3.3.2.1 SOFT SKILLS: PEOPLE SKILLS

The core component of soft skill is people skills (Klaus, 2010). People skills according to Lei (2011) are how to interact and work with others in a way that enables you to a meaningful work relationship, influence others perception of you and your work, and motivate their actions.

The individual's relationship with others is highly determined by the interpersonal characteristics that are considered one facet of soft skills; however, many authors equate interpersonal skills with soft skills (James and James, 2004). According to Sheikh (2009), interpersonal skills are the most important skills at all levels of the job. Another facet of the soft skills is personal qualities and career attributes (Perreault, 2004). Personal attributes might include individual's personality, likeability, time management prowess, and organizational skills (Parsons, 2008). On the other hand, career/job attributes can include communication, teamwork, leadership, and customer service (James and James, 2004). Therefore, soft skills are made up of the combination of interpersonal (people) skills and personal (career) attributes.

Therefore, employee skills are the foundation of good customer relations, and customer service skills are critical to professional success of any business. Employee skills promote a positive attitude, efficient behaviors, effective communication, respectful interaction, and the ability to remain composed in difficult situations (Evenson, 1999). The entry into the tourism and hospitality industry requires some essential competencies; the core competencies deemed essential go back to the beginning of 1990s. Tas in Roy (2009) identified 36 competencies which were narrowed to 5 core competencies, namely, self-management, communication, interpersonal relations, leadership, and critical thinking.

The following section presents the common soft skills focusing on how to deal with guests and customers:

#### 3.3.2.1.1 Communication Skills

Despite the high importance of other nontechnical skills such as creativity, problem-solving, and teamwork (Boahin and Hofman, 2013), communication is the top-rated nontechnical skill (Gokuladas, 2010). Rudolph (1999) investigated the most desirable competencies in the hospitality industry context and concluded that the highest rated competencies were in the areas of communication.

According to John (2009), communication is considered the most important interpersonal skill in today's global business environment. With a good communication skill, the service employee is able to actively listen to customers and convey ideas in writing and verbally to any audience (Klein, 2009) in a way that achieve the goals intended. This also includes language skills if the spoken language at work is not your native language. Beer (2009) demonstrated the importance of positive communication with the diverse backgrounds and concluded that effective communication in another language, cross-cultural sensitivity, and adaptability are some of the most important skill.

Although communication is often assumed as a fundamental skill, which everyone knows and is able to do it in an effective way, but that assumption is usually a way of reality.

Griffin (2012) as supported by Fogle (2011) advocated that employers reported that business graduates from an educational institution lacked having the soft skill, especially communication skills.

The lack of communication skill has been the reason for stimulating many tragedies and crises that have taken place within many service industries, especially in financial and health-care sectors, and the wider environment in recent years (Jelphs, 2006).

Business professionals and employers continue to criticize and blaming against the educational institutions for inability to support the key soft skills—verbal and nonverbal communication skills, work ethic, problem-solving, critical thinking, attendance, positive attitude, and teamwork, which were judged the most deficient skills (Arkansas Department of Education, 2007; Westray, 2008). As one employer said, "We want somebody who shows up on time, somebody who works hard and someone who's trainable" (Arkansas Department of Education, 2007, p. 13). Ju et al. (2012) emphasized the role of schools and colleges in providing adequate training for students in basic literacy skills, mathematics, and communication skills. The business at all levels is in a big need of resourceful employees with soft skills (John, 2009) with interpersonal qualities (Rodas, 2007) who can motivate, collaborate, and empathize with their peers and their customers (Klaus, 2010).

In a survey conducted by Mitchell et al. (2010) with the purpose of capturing the business educators' perceptions of the importance of specific soft skills for success in today's workplace, the results were that ethics and general communication skills rated extremely important, with 57% stressing written communication and 56% indicating time management and organization skills as extremely important. Communication skills are coupled with the emotional intelligence and considered the most important skills to be required by hospitality labor. However, Fournier and Ineson (2009) found that IT competency was the least regarded. Stovall and Stovall (2009) agreed with Yaacoub et al. (2011) that communication skill is a necessary skill for successful performance in modern work environments. Other researchers concurred that in such global competitive environment with its technological advancements, management skills, and diverse cultures, employees must be fully prepared and equipped with excellent communication, problem-solving, and critical thinking skills (Shafie and Nayan, 2010).

#### *3.3.2.1.2 Teamwork Skills*

Teamwork is another crucial skill in hospitality and should be part of multiskilling in order to achieve a sustainable quality of service. Teamwork is the ability to work with anyone from diverse culture and backgrounds (Raftopoulos et al., 2009).

As the employee is able to work effectively with coworkers with different skill sets, personalities, work styles, or motivation level to achieve better team outcomes, this means that the employee has a significant teamwork skill. Raftopoulos et al. (2009) claimed that graduates and employers reported that the ability to work with others effectively is an important work-readiness skill.

Robles (2012) supported Raftopoulos et al. (2009) and Falconer and Pettigrew (2003) who claimed that effective teamwork is among the top 10 work-readiness skills. Robles added that business executives and employers want to recruit employees who will add value to the workplace with a composite of soft skills and who will embrace teamwork. Organizations are seeking to recruit employees who pay a significant attention to relations with their colleagues and superiors.

Teamwork encompasses flexibility, adaptability, cooperativeness, and respectfulness. Showing respect for others is an important factor in building a good team work skill. According to Ju et al. (2012), showing respect for others, among other skills, is identified as relevant for employment. The level of respect for self and others is stated to a large extent by the body language and the tone of the conversations. The business world is nonexistent without groups; this means the work stability requires from the employees to have teamwork skills. Teamwork is the synonymous to working collaboratively in groups; therefore, the use of groups in educational organizations should not only build collaborative skills but also enhance other positive interpersonal relationships and skills.

#### *3.3.2.1.3 Work Ethic*

Work ethic is one of the most five important employability skills that educational settings should seek to cultivate into its graduates (Ju et al., 2012). This notion also supported by other many researchers such as Heimler (2010) and Robles (2012) who argued that work ethic is one of the key soft skills required in the workplace and the students are required to possess. Ethical standards are also showed as a significant part of the required bundling of hospitality skills. As cited in Wilks and Hemsworth (2011), individuals should demonstrate ethical standards and strong values.

Work ethics is defined as an employee's attitudes toward work, which includes their responsibility, attendance, accountability, punctuality, and dress code (Heimler, 2010). Additionally, the characteristics of work ethic include professionalism (maturity and business etiquette), realistic expectations of job requirements, and career advancement. In addition, interpersonal skills and dependability are seen by Adams (2007) as work ethics. Ju et al. (2012) confirmed that the "ability to be on time" is a highly recommended work ethic skill.

Work ethics is related significantly to employability skills (Adams, 2007). Adams also supported the implementation of employability skill-bundled curriculum, which fills the gaps of workplace expectations in many aspects such as interpersonal skills, initiatives, and independence skills.

Another perspective is reported by human resource managers, that is, labor ethics influence significantly on the job performance and then on the career advancement (Heimler, 2010) (see Chapter 5, Ethics in Tourism and Hospitality Industry).

#### *3.3.2.1.4 Interpersonal Relationship Skills*

Klein (2009) claimed that organization representatives must demonstrate a satisfactory level of interpersonal skills to meet customers' expectations; therefore, interpersonal skills are strongly correlated with high level of job success. Interpersonal skill is referred as social skills; these skills are closely related to communication skills. Interpersonal skill is primarily focused on how you made the other feel. So, it can be defined as the necessary skills that aloe an employee to work with others and include dealing with diversity of cultures and backgrounds, negotiation, and customer service (Heimler, 2010). Subsequently, interpersonal skills' matters are the individual ability to build trust with coworkers and customers by developing emotional empathy conduct, in addition to the ability in finding a common ground (Lei, 2011).

#### 3.3.2.1.5 Decision-Making Skills

Decision-making skill is closely dependent on the individuals' confidence and knowledge. According to Shafie and Nayan (2010), decision-making skill is considered as an important criterion of employability skills. So, many researchers like Rivera and Schaefer (2009) and Kazilan et al. (2009) called for paying a good attention to improve decision-making skills among students in the educational institutions.

#### 3.3.2.1.6 Self-management

Self-management is considered the third most important employability skill required in the work environment (Shafie and Nayan, 2010). Self-management is the ability of the employee to plan, control emotions, and execute job-related activities in order to achieve tasks or goals in an established time frame (Williams, 2015). It is also defined as an individual's ability to "assess self accurately, set personal goals, monitor progress, and exhibit self-control" (Bates and Phelan, 2002, p. 125).

#### 3.3.2.1.7 Critical Thinking Skills

Critical thinking must be paid critical attention by the employers during the recruitment process. Critical thinking is necessary in managing the business relations and controlling unpleasant situations. Heimler (2010) referred to critical thinking skill as the ability to think creatively to identify key concepts, generate solutions to problems, and to make decisions. It was reported that education professionals and human resource managers agreed that graduates and employees need additional training in the area of critical thinking, although the college graduates were not certain about training in critical thinking skills.

##### *3.3.2.1.8 Problem-Solving Skills*

Mason et al. (2009) advocated that problem-solving skills represented one of the generic skills that enhance individuals' employability. Problem-solving skill helps employees to identifying the problems, creating, and implementing solutions and the evaluation of the results (Arensdorf, 2009). So, graduates must consider the problem-solving skills as an important soft skill that is required urgently in the work environment. Harris and Rogers (2008) purported that problem-solving skills should begin at an early age and encouraged at most advanced educational levels.

#### *3.3.2.2 SOFT SKILLS: MANAGEMENT SKILLS (LEI, 2011)*

*Growth Mindset*

Difficult situations are representing an opportunity to learn for employees with growth mind; thus, such types of employees perceive unpleasant situations as an opportunity for improvement instead of blaming or changing others.

*Self-Awareness*

Behaviors and actions of an employee are significantly and positively shaped by the high awareness and perception of himself, others, and the work environment conditions. Self-awareness is about understanding what drives anger, motivates, embarrasses, frustrates, and inspires others (both internal and external clients). Self-awareness includes a holistic understanding of all the dimensions and factors of the work environment.

*Emotion Regulation*

Managing and regulation of emotions, especially negatives ones at work, enables the employees to think clearly and objectively and act reasonably.

*Self-Confidence*

Self-confidence is considered one of the most important skills that characterize the successful employee and contribute significantly to mobility up into the managerial positions. Self-confidence includes the belief of one's abilities to accomplish hard tasks. Self-confidence not only affects the employee but also his peers and coworkers; they believe in him as a hero who has access to unlimited power.

*Stress Management*

Stress management helps in making accurate decisions in any challenging situations, staying healthy, calm, and balanced; reduce your stress level; and increase your productivity and supports your physical and emotional health, all of which you need for a fulfilling, successful career.

*Resilience*

The employee who is able to bounce back after a disappointment or failing in accomplishing something and the ability to continue to move onward and upward is urgently required especially in jobs related to sales and marketing activities.

*Persistence and Perseverance*

Maintain the same energy and dedication in your performance to learn, do, and achieve in your work despite challenges, failures, and opposition.

*Perceptiveness*

Employees in the field of tourism and hospitality industry especially those who are working in the front-line positions and have a direct contact with the guests and customers are in a great need to such skills, the skills of developing cognitive or emotional empathy of other people's situation and perspective. Giving attention to the unspoken cues, thinking about others and what they are feeling, and watching and understanding others' action and intentions can fulfill the organizations' long-term goals. If you misinterpret other's intention or do not try to put yourself in their shoes, you can easily encounter difficulties dealing with people and not even know why.

*Patience*

The ability to step back for a while in a rushed or crisis situation in order to think clearly that has a positive influence on your performance and reactions and lead to taking action that fulfills your long-term goals.

## 3.4 SKILLS SHORTAGE REASONS

The hospitality industry has a significant part in creation of extra employment. In order to ensure the industry contribution in jobs creation, it is important to identify current skills shortages to be mitigated and to anticipate future skill requirements. There are stated gaps in basic skills and experience at entry and junior level, and at management level.

Some of the reasons stated by stakeholders for the skill gaps in the hospitality sector are as follows (Expert Group on Future Skills Needs, 2015):

- insufficient numbers of labor market supply,
- imbalance between academic and hands-on training individuals,
- shortage of basic and specialized practical skills,
- the right level of experience, and
- the relatively poor reputation and perception of the sector.

It is important to mention that the hospitality industry provides many employment opportunities for a range of skills. These opportunities include skilled professionals and entrepreneurs, people with high levels of customer service and customer-facing skills, and technical skills in areas such as marketing, accountancy, and specialist services, as well as junior entry-level kitchen and front-of-house staff.

Other specific skill gaps identified by hospitality businesses included:

- management skills:
  - revenue managers with considerable knowledge,
  - food and beverage supervisors with management skills,
  - HR skills,
  - marketing and sale skills,
  - general management skills for business owners.
- specialized reception and front-of -house skills,
- bar staff with waiting skills for food service and modern drink skills,
- executive housekeepers,
- sales and marketing executives,
- customer service-mindedness and up-selling skills, and
- specialist knowledge:
  - employment and human rights law,
  - licensing law,
  - consumer law,

- social responsibility concerns,
- minimum pricing,
- raw materials and food allergens.

There is some variance highlighted in relation to skills gaps by geographic location, although not always higher in remote locations. According to businesses, without action, the same key skills gaps are anticipated to increase over time.

Nevertheless, the reputation and perceptions of the industry should be improved based on systematic investment by both business establishments and educational institutions in further skills development and enhanced HRM processes to further professionalize the sector and continue to build employee development and respect, loyalty, and retention.

## 3.5 MEETING THE NEEDS OF INDUSTRY: EDUCATIONAL AND TRAINING RESPONSE

Skill shortage is a major barrier for many job seekers desiring enter the job market of hospitality industry, including literacy, numeracy, and basic information and communication technology skills. Many developed economies see 100% enrollment in upper secondary schools; however, yet nearly one in five students do not acquire a minimum level of basic skills that enables them to function well in society (OECD, 2012). Accordingly, a significant mismatch in skills youth possess and the skills workplace need is highly reported; such shortage in skills is felt acutely by employers in all industries, and they are especially pronounced in the hospitality sector. As a result of the low level of education and training they got from their educational institutions, many employees leave work since they feel they do not have the required skills and they thus become unstable at work and seek other forms of employment which appears more suitable for their skills and knowledge (Mobley, 1982). In the United States, for example, 38% of employers in the hospitality sector reported that the low skill levels of new employees posed a moderate or great business risk, compared with 25% of organizations in other sectors (Sweet et al., 2010). Frequently, "skills mismatch" refers not to a lack of technical skills but to a lack of the life skills (i.e., "soft" skills) required to carry out their jobs and successfully interact with coworkers, supervisors, and customers (Wilks and Hemsworth, 2011).

Hospitality industry workers must be able to rapidly adapt to accommodate a degree of diversity unheard of in other lines of work. Not surprisingly, communication skills, cross-cultural competencies, adaptability, ability to manage guest and customers problems with understanding and sensitivity, and maintaining a professional demeanor are crucial to staff at all levels of the industry (Hinds-Smith, 2009). Thus, the industry professionals' challenge is to find young candidates with such potential, assess their qualifications, and give them the training to bridge any gaps in basic, technical, and life skills. Recognition of the need to investment in skills development in hospitality and tourism industry is significantly increased among the industry professionals to fill skill gap of graduates; this investment cannot bring new without considering the educational institutions.

Historically, education and training for hospitality has developed over the last few decades, developing from early European apprenticeship programs and beginning to take root in universities in the early 1900s in the United States and rather later in Europe (Barrows and Johan, 2008). Nevertheless, it may be said that hospitality management's higher education is still immature when compared with more traditional fields and has yet to establish its identity as an academic subject. Hospitality educational institutions have often been reluctant to grant courses the same status as other subjects; this may because the hospitality education is still vocational (Rudolph, 1999) which produced a graduate who lacked the requisite soft skills. Employers often express concern about recruiting such employees, for example, there are many cases where the human resource manager refused to hire those who displayed impolite telephone manners (Bhanot, 2009). Busby (2001) analyzed the content of tourism degrees in the United Kingdom and concluded what he described as vocationalism. Such hand on skills plays an important role in ensuring employability of the graduates as it includes the development of specific skills in hospitality and travel-related areas. In addition, it influences the mobility of the employees to the higher managerial positions in hospitality organizations; the results of a study investigated the careers of hotel managers conducted by Ladkin (2000) which showed that F/B experience (Chef) remains the single dominant career characteristic of successful general managers, although the revenue contribution of F/B department is relatively less important than that of accommodation (Horwath and Horwath, 1999). Hospitality management not only has many of the features common to other forms of management but also still has unique attributes that require technical-vocational instruction (Raybould and Wilkins, 2006). Managers in the hospitality industry value practical and operational skills as well as on-job training, which may be acquired easily within the workplace (ILO, 2001). Ladkin noted that few successful general managers have experience in room, accounting, and marketing departments prior to their entry into managerial level. So, both soft skills and high formal qualifications from new entrants are not highly regarded within the hospitality industry; researchers suggested that employers greatly value soft skills as relevant employability skills.

Meeting the soft skills needs of the workforce must be of concern to educators and employers. Although education institutions' role is to produce skilled graduates ready for employment, the successful reduction of skills mismatching in the context of the tourism and hospitality industry requires creation and adopting a comprehensive long-term strategy that involves public–private partnerships among governments, employers, and unions to continuously develop and improve the use of skills, the involved stakeholders need to shoulder some of the responsibility (Maxwell et al., 2010).

The development of skills to meet the needs of various stakeholders in tourism and hospitality industry must be based on a partnership between the industry and the educational/training institutions, with each playing a critical complementary role. Such partnerships contribute in minimizing unemployment rate as it works on matching graduates' skills to organizations requirements. ILO predicts that youth unemployment rates will fall in developed economies from 17.5% in 2012 to 15.6% in 2017 (ILO, 2012); so, to keep this progress, the burden of investment in educational and training programs must be shared between both the public sector and the private enterprises to create a skilled graduate. In case of bringing education and working environment closer together, a successful skilled graduate will be the expected outcomes of that strategy. A coordinated strategy is required that builds hard and soft skills through high-quality education while involving all relevant stakeholders in the skill-matching process throughout an individual's life.

Generally, addressing projected skills demand is likely to necessitate a combination of approaches (Expert Group on Future Skills Needs, 2015).

In relation to training, some of the reasons suggested for skills gaps included the

- provision of additional education and training programs,
- provision of greater numbers of accessible and flexible continuing professional development, apprenticeship, and career traineeship schemes,
- retraining of unemployed former hospitality sector workers,
- increasing staff retention and reducing the high extent of exit from certain occupations, and
- increasing the attractiveness of employment opportunities and take-up of vacant positions.

### 3.5.1 TRAINING FOR FILLING THE SKILL GAP

The hospitality industry operates in a very competitive environment catering to continual and swiftly changing consumer trends. The development of the technologies and the whole business environment impose both managers and employees to be more skilled and qualified; even if they are good employees today, you could be out of the line some other day if you do not keep studying.

Many managers are viewed lack the knowledge, experience, and skills that make them unable to meet their responsibility for training and skilling of staff. Managers lack competence in skills and knowledge and this is a critical gap in their technical skills. Agut et al. (2003) in a study of Spanish hotels claimed that financial skills and computer skills were found to be lacking in the managerial level. Also, other skills requiring attention through multiskilling included communication and motivational skills, understanding and considering the organization mission and vision, and the expectations and behavior of different types of guests and customers.

So, both the managers and employees are requiring multiskilling in both technical and nontechnical aspects of work. Generally, managers specifically should possess generic managerial competences that empower them to self-regulate and self-control themselves in their job development and also possess the knowledge and skills that enable them to function effectively. For this reason, hospitality programs must be especially keen in adapting to these shifts, responding to them by a reliable collaboration among the industry' stakeholders that aim to produce programs that make practical sense to the graduates and provide them the desired skill sets for the job market they enter. Therefore, organizations need organized staff training if they want to be competitive among others (Wang, 2010). When the organization trains their own staff, by providing and forming a harmonious atmosphere, accurate work specification, and the passion of work, team spirit will be built between employees and management team within the process.

Therefore, staff training is essential in many ways as follows (Wang, 2010):

- employees will be armed with professional knowledge, experienced skills, and valid thoughts;
- motivates and inspires workers by providing them all needed information in work as well as help them to recognize how important their jobs are, and subsequently, the productivity is going to be increased.

Hospitality businesses stated that they have responded to skills gaps with initiatives such as (Expert Group on Future Skills Needs, 2015):

- increased emphasis on in-house/on-the-job training tailored to immediate needs,
- overseas recruitment (often through personal contacts of existing staff),
- induction programs for entry-level jobs,
- basic skills training and up-skilling of existing staff within organizations,
- reskilling existing staff for new roles within the organization,
- personal training plans for all staff,
- development of career progression and retention initiatives,
- there is a broad consensus about the importance of balance between a strong vocational education and training system (including apprenticeships and traineeships with significant practical work content) to complement more general hospitality management and academically focused courses.

Achieving such previous initiatives and more require collaborative efforts among the hospitality industry stakeholders is the solution to this fall of skills (Economist Intelligence Unit, 2009).

#### *3.5.1.1 ROLE OF THE EDUCATIONAL INSTITUTIONS*

Although hospitality is one of the oldest industries and hospitality education itself was born out of a need to supply the hospitality industry with skilled managers and is often driven by industry standards (Nelson and Dopson, 2001), it has a comparatively short life in higher education. However, hospitality higher education programs in general is a specialized area of study that aims at preparing students for careers in the hospitality industry; thus, most undergraduate hospitality programs are specialized rather than general, and their courses lack the optional business perspective (Pavesic, 1991). As a result of the growth of the hospitality industry, it is crucial that hospitality degree programs have a clear understanding of the industry employers' expectations and job requirements of the skills and the competencies that the graduates should possess. The hospitality programs must proliferate rapidly and allocate adequate resources to prepare students, as employers desire of hiring graduates who got highly training and personal development; this, in turn, leads to an increase in employee commitment and to job satisfaction in general. It is imperative that graduates become cognizant and encourage other students to acquire at least the basics of soft skills. In some instances, the graduates do not possess the soft skills relevant to the workplace, especially in the changing demands of employers; the traditional focus was on the development of generic skills in core hospitality areas, and this remains the rationale and priority within programs in many countries.

Therefore, the trend of hospitality programs must move away from vocational subjects such as cooking and hotel operations to managerial subjects such as quality management and technological applications (Breakey and Craig-Smith, 2007). Baum (1997) claimed that educational providers must respond to labor market needs and tailor their skills programs provision to prepare the graduates with the solid skills to successfully enter the labor market, rather than attempting to be "all things to all hospitality activities." Hospitality education programs must seek to bring together vocational training and academic education as students need more than a certain level of schooling; they need an adequate quality of training and specific type of skills to be competitive in the hospitality workforce.

Hence, college and university graduates need to have relevant soft skills because there is no guarantee that employers will assume the responsibility of providing such training. Educational institutions should equip its graduates with a combination of hard and soft skills; education should include excellent reading skills, computer literacy and proficiency with software, sensitivity to and appreciation for other cultures and backgrounds, good teamwork skills, stress management, team management, and coping with changes (Rudolph's, 1999). In order to maintain a clear commitment to the development of skills, level of education and training must be given a good attention. The US Department of Labor has set aside $2 billion to excess community college students' career preparation but questioned whether the teaching of soft skills will be incorporated (Dutton, 2012).

To ensure exploitation of the full potential of the skills, the education and training providers must guide their students in choosing their fields of study. Accordingly, higher education hospitality programs have developed in similar ways, from a limited choice of subjects to multiple options. Moreover, as the universal trend is to incorporate hospitality management within business colleges, courses may include management and hotel and food service operations. Tourism subjects tend to be taught in different departments. Some programs offer a selection of more specialized subjects. Indeed, a growing trend is to offer a greater number of optional specializations (Breakey and Craig-Smith, 2007). Moreover. Educational institutions must develop continuing training programs for its students trying to create a real work environment inside their classrooms. In the United Kingdom, the training approach "real work environment" was developed within the educational institutions with only limited formal and assessed exposure to the industry during the program. This ensures the students obtain knowledge and skills and increases their ability to adjust to be able to work in such changing and competitive environment (Walker, 2007).

#### *3.5.1.2 ROLE OF THE ORGANIZATIONS*

Employers must assume the responsibilities and work for reinforcing the transition of graduates from school to work and maintaining and improving skills throughout their working lives. Although organizations that incorporate youth development into their business models can reap gains beyond filling staffing needs, there are some employers still reluctant to incur additional expenses to train unprepared graduates to fill vacancies, and seeking for capturing high ethically and experienced employees (Rao et al., 2011). Hinkin and Tracey (2000) confirmed that poor training and support, badly planned working environments, cause the high rates of turnover in the industry workforce. Thus, the hospitality organizations feed the educational requirements and support college and school training activities. Organization must adopt the implementation of educational and training programs "apprenticeship system," where students spend the majority of their training time in the workplace with a short, normally 8-week release period to college within any one year.

This system was developed in Germany. Such systems serve in supporting multiskilling notion that is adopted by the majority of hospitality organizations as a result of skills shortage in hospitality industry. Multiskilling, cross-deployment, and the use of the latest technology are generally at the top of the initiatives that most hospitality organizations are looking at to increase the levels of productivity of their employees. Employees will become more creative and innovative and also serve the role of grooming them for supervisory positions. Multiskilling is generally perceived to be a very cost-cutting way to enable hospitality organizations to deal with the cyclical discrepancies in the demand for seasonal employees (Baum, 2006), also it leads to improved profitability and reduces the risks and crisis at work environment and violations of safety issues. Wastage is minimized, especially in F/B operations.

Knox and Walsh (2005) have shown that especially five-star hospitality institutions are always seeking to improve their internal labor market through making improvements in skills training provisions and employee career development programs. Hospitality organizations use this system with the purpose of providing a high-quality service; multiskilling empowers employees and helps them to better understand their tasks in the broadest sense and it encourages self-confidence and self-development. Multiskilled employee is able to maintain desirable standards that give him the ability to learn a wide range of problem-solving skills and generally makes them more productive and this consequently upgrades the employees' salaries. Also, multiskilling training helps reducing the employees' turnover rates since the employees in this case will be able to cope with the challenges on a day-to-day basis (Kelliher and Riley, 2003). Managing employees' experience in their place of work will lead to solve the customers' experience of service quality provisions (Bowen, 1993). Hence, employees are more likely to be positive and more receptive to customers and their needs and wants, where multiskilling is in place. The multiskilling training of employees together from diverse departments enhances the team's work spirit. The extent of their respective involvement depends upon the objectives of the organization and level of training as well as upon the system in which such training is located.

## REFERENCES

Adams, D. Filling the Gap between a Magnet High School Workplace Readiness Curriculum and the Workplace. *Ph.D. Dissertation*; Minnesota, United States: Cappella University, 2007.

Agut, S.; Grau, R.; Peiro, J. M. Competency Needs among Managers from Spanish Hotels and Restaurants and Their Training Demands. *Int. J. Hospitality Manage.* **2003,** *22* (3), 281–295.

Arensdorf, J. The Perceptions of Employability Skills Transferred from Academic Leadership Classes to the Workplace: A Study of the FHSU Leadership Studies Certificate Program. *Ph.D. Dissertation*, Kansas State University, 2009.

Arkansas Department of Education. *Combined Research Report of Business Leaders and College Professors on Preparedness of High School Graduates*, 2007.

Ashkanasy, N. M.; Hartel, C. E.; Daus, C. S. Diversity and Emotion: The New Frontiers in Organizational Behavior Research. *J. Manage.* **2002,** *28* (3), 307–338.

Badcock, P. T.; Pattison, P. E.; Harris, K. Developing Generic Skills through University Study: A Study of Arts, Science and Engineering in Australia. *High. Educ.* **2010,** *60* (4), 441–458.

Barrows, C. W.; Johan, N. Hospitality Management Education. In *The Sage Handbook of Hospitality Management*; Wood, R. C., Brotherton, B., Ed.; London: Sage Publications Ltd., 2008; pp 146–162.

Bates, R. A.; Phelan, K. C. Characteristics of a Globally Competitive Workforce. *Advances in Developing Human Resources* **2002,** *4* (2), 121–132.

Baum, T. No Frills but Sound Business Sense: A Look at Economy-Sector Trends in Travel and Tourism. In *Insights;* English Tourist Board: London, 1997; Vol. 9, pp 49–56

Baum, T. Reflections on the Nature of Skills in the Experience Economy: Challenging Traditional Skills Models in Hospitality. *J. Hospitality Tour. Manage.* **2006,** *13* (2), 124–135.

Baum, T. Skills and Training for the Hospitality Sector: A Review of Issues. *J. Vocat. Educ. Train.* **2002,** *3* (54), 343–364.

Beer, D. J. Global Competency in Hospitality Management Programs: A Perfect Recipe for Community Colleges. *Ph.D. Dissertation*; Chicago, IL: Louis University, 2009.

Bhanot, S. Importance of Soft Skills for an Employee and for the Organization. *SIES J. Manage.* **2009,** *6* (1), 18–22.

Boahin, P.; Hofman, A. A Disciplinary Perspective of Competency-Based Training on the Acquisition of Employability Skills. *J. Vocat. Educ. Train.* **2013,** *65* (3), 385–401.

Boella, M. J.; Goss-Turner, S. *Human Resource Management in the Hospitality Industry: An Introductory Guide*; Amsterdam: Elsevier, 2005.

Bowen, R. C. The Use of Occupational Therapists in Independent Living Programs. *Am. J. Occup. Ther.* **1993,** *48,* 105–112.

Bradley, H.; Erickson, M.; Stephenson, C.; Williams, S. *Myths at Work*; Cambridge: Polity Press, 2002.

Breakey, M. N.; Craig-Smith, S. J. Hospitality Degree Programs in Australia: A Continuing Evolution. *J. Hospitality Tour. Manage.* **2007,** *14* (2), 102–118.

Brungardt, C. J. College Graduates' Perceptions of Their Use of Teamwork Skills: Soft Skill Development in Fort Hays State University Leadership Education. Ph.D. Dissertation,Kansas State University, 2009.

Burgess, C.; Aitken, L. *Report on Core Research on Unitizing Curricula*, 2004. http://www.isda/curriculam/core/interim (accessed Oct 23, 2017).

Burleson, R. C.; Hass, C. T.; Tucker, R. L. Multiskilled Labor Utilization Strategies in Construction. *J. Constr. Eng. Manage.* **1998,** *124* (6), 480–489.

Burns, P. M. Hard-Skills, Soft-Skills: Undervaluing Hospitality's 'Service with a Smile'. *Progress Tour. Hospitality Res.* **1997,** *3*, 239–248.

Busby, G. Vocationalism in Higher Level Tourism Courses: The British Perspective. *J. Furth. Higher Educ.* **2001,** *25*, 29–43.

Chung-Herrera, B. G.; Enz, C. A.; Lankau, M. Grooming Future Hospitality Leaders: A Competency Model. *Cornell Hotel Restaur. Adm. Q.* **2003,** *44* (3), 17–25.

Clark, N. *Study of Multiskilling Training Initiatives in Australian Industry*; New South Wales Department of Industrial Relations and Employment, Australia, 1989.

Cotton, B. *Industry and Education in Partnership in Graduate Employability* (online), 2002. Conferencereportlondonfile;//C:\WINDOWS/Desktop/Graduate%20Employability%20 inHospitalityonference (accessed Oct 25, 2017).

Davids, Z.; Fredericks, G. H. *Aspects of Multiskilling Contributing to Service Quality Provision within Academic Libraries*; Cape Town: University of Western Cape, 2004.

Davis, T. The Challenge of Change: A Case Study of the Institutionalization of Employability Skills at Guilford Technical Community College. Ph.D. Dissertation, Western Carolina University, United States, North Carolina, 2009.

Diefendorff, J. M.; Richard, E. M. Antecedents and Consequences of Emotional Display Rule Perceptions. *J. Appl. Psychol.* **2003,** *88* (2), 284–294.

DIISRTE. Department of Industry, Innovation, Science, Research and Tertiary Education (2013) Core Skills for Work Developmental Framework: the Framework. Canberra, ACT: Commonwealth of Australia, 2013.

Dixon, J.; Belnap, C.; Albrecht, C.; Lee, K. The Importance of Soft Skills. *Corp. Finan. Rev.* **2010,** *14* (6), 35–38.

Dutton, G. Taking Soft Skills for Granted? *Training* **2012,** *49* (5), 48–50.

Economist Intelligence Unit. Skills to Compete: Post-Secondary Education and Business Sustainability in Latin America (online), 2009. http://graphics.eiu.com/upload/eb/DellFedEx_Skills_WEB.pdf (accessed Oct 20, 2017).

Evenson, R. Soft Skills, Hard Sell Techniques: Making Education and Career Connections. *SAGE J.* **1999,** *74* (3), 29–31.

Expert Group on Future Skills Needs. Assessment of Future Skills Requirements in the Hospitality Sector in Ireland, 2015–2020. *Executive Summary Report* (online), 2015. www.skillsireland.ie (accessed Sept 8, 2017).

Falconer, S.; Pettigrew, M. Developing Added Value Skills within an Academic Programme through Work Based Learning. *Int. J. Manpower* **2003,** *24* (1), 48–59.

Fogle, C. D. Employers' Perceptions of Business Graduates from Historically Black Colleges and Universities. *DBA Dissertation*, Walden University, 2011.

Fournier, H.; Ineson, E. Closing the Gap between Education and Industry: Skills and Competencies for Food Service Internships in Switzerland Hospitality and Industry Management (online), 2009. http://scholarworks.umass.edu/sessions/wednesday/11 (accessed Aug 25, 2017).

Gilmore, J.; Gregor, M. B. Developing Professionalism in a Hospitality Undergraduate Programme. *Hospitality Tour. Educ.* **2001,** *13* (3), 14–19.

Gokuladas, V. K. Technical and Nontechnical Education and the Employability of Engineering Graduates: An Indian Case Study. *Int. J. Train. Dev.* **2010,** *14* (2), 130–143.

Gowen, S. *The Politics of Workplace Literacy: A Case Study*; New York: Teachers College Press, 1992.

Griffin, M. Y. Manufacturing Mississippi's Workforce: An Assessment of Employability Skills as Perceived by Faculty and Senior Students of Four-Year Manufacturing Related Degree Programs. Ph.D. Dissertation. The University of Southern Mississippi, 2012.

Groth, M.; Hennig-Thurau, T.; Walsh, G. Customer Reactions to Emotional Labor: The Roles of Employee Acting Strategies and Customer Detection Accuracy. *Acad. Manage. J.* **2009,** *52* (5), 958–974.

Guy, B. A.; Sitlington, P. L.; Larsen, M. D.; Frank, A. R. What Are High Schools Offering as Preparation for Employment? Career Development for Exceptional Individuals. *SAGE J.* **2008,** *32* (1), 30–41.

Haas, C. T.; Rodriguez, A. M.; Glover, R.; Goodrum, P. M. Implementing a Multiskilled Workforce. *Constr. Manage. Econ.* **2001,** *19*, 633–641.

Hargis, K. B. Career and Technical Education Program Alignment with Local Workforce Needs. Ph.D. Dissertation, Eastern Kentucky University, 2011.

Harris, K.; Rogers, G. Soft Skills in the Technology Education Classroom: What Do Students Need? *Technol. Teacher* 19-24, 2008 (online) file:///C:/Users/ABDALLAH/Downloads/SoftSkillsintheTechnologyeducation%20(1).pdf (accessed Mar 5, 2019).

Heimler, R. Attitudes of College Graduates, Faculty, and Employers Regarding the Importance of Skills Acquired in College and Needed for Job Performance and Career Advancement Potential in the Retail Sector. Ed.D. Dissertation, Dowling College, New York, 2010.

Hinds-Smith, S. Competency Requirements of Managers in Hotels in Jamaica: The Implications of Soft Skills. M.Sc. Thesis, Rochester Institute of Technology, 2009.
Hinkin, T. R.; Tracey, J. B. The Cost of Turnover: Putting a Price on the Learning Curve. *Cornell Hotel Restaur. Adm. Q.* **2000,** *41* (3), 14–21.
Hochschild, A. R. *The Managed Heart: Commercialization of Human Feeling*; Berkeley, CA: University of California Press, 1983.
Hochschild, A. Reply to Cas Wouters' Review Essay on The Managed Heart, Theory. *J. Cult. Soc.* 1989, 6, 439–445.
Horwath and Horwath. *Worldwide Industry Study*; London: Horwath and Horwath, 1999.
Hospitality Training Foundation (HtF). *Delphi Study of the Hospitality Industry—Final Summary*; London: HtF, 2000.
Hrebiniak, L. G. *Making Strategic Work: Leading Effective Execution and Change*; Hoboken, NJ: Wharton School Publishing, Pearson Education, Inc., 2005.
ILO-Global Employment Outlook. *Global Spill-Overs from Advanced to Emerging Economics Worsen the Situation for Young Job Seekers*; Geneva: ILO, 2012.
Ingram, A.; Fraenkel, S. Perceptions of Productivity among Swiss Hotel Managers: A Few Steps Forward?. *Int. J. Contemp. Hospitality Manage.* **2006,** *18* (5), 439–445.
International Labor Organization (ILO). *Human Resource Development, Employment and Globalization in the Hotel, Catering and Tourism Sector: Report for Discussion at the Tripartite Meeting on the Human Resource Development, Employment and Globalization in the Hotel, Catering and Tourism Sector*; Geneva: International Labor Organization (online), 2001. http://www.ilo.org (accessed Sept 5, 2017).
Investopedia. *Hard Skills*, 2012 (online). http://www.investopedia.com/terms/h/hard.skills.asp#axzz1lMzgjWjK (accessed Oct 10, 2017).
Jackson, D. Student Perceptions of the Importance of Employability Skill Provision in Business Undergraduate Programs. *J. Educ. Bus.* **2013,** *88* (5), 271–279.
Jackson, D.; Hancock, P. Nontechnical Skills in Undergraduate Degrees in Business: Development and Transfer. *Educ. Res. Perspect.* **2010,** *37* (1), 52–125.
James, R. F.; James, M. L. Teaching Career and Technical Skills in a "Mini" Business World. *Bus. Educ. Forum* **2004,** *59* (2), 39–41.
Jelphs, K. Communication: Soft Skill, Hard Impact? *Clin. Manage.* **2006,** *14*, 33–37.
Johanson, M. M.; Woods, R. H. Recognizing the Emotional Element in Service Excellence. *Cornell Hospitality Q.* **2008,** *49* (3), 310–316.
John, J. Study on the Nature of Impact of Soft Skills Training Program on the Soft Skills Development of Management Students. *Pac. Bus. Rev.* **2009,** 19–27.
Ju, S.; Zhang, D.; Pacha, J. Employability Skills Valued by Employers as Important for Entry-Level Employees with and without Disabilities. *SAGE J.* **2012,** *35* (1), 29–38.
Kalleberg, A. L. Organizing Flexibility: The Flexible Firm in a New Century. *Br. J. Ind. Relat.* **2001,** *39* (4), 479–504.
Kay, C.; Russette, J. Hospitality-Management Competencies-Identifying Managers' Essential Skills. *Cornell Hospitality Q.* **2002,** *41* (2), 52–63.
Kazilan, F.; Hamzah, R.; Bakar, A. R. Employability Skills among the Students of Technical Vocational Training Centers in Malaysia. *Eur. J. Soc. Sci.* **2009,** *9* (1), 147–160.
Keep, E.; Mayhew, K. The Assessment: Knowledge, Skills and Competitiveness. *Oxford Rev. Econ. Policy* **1999,** *15*, 1–15.
Keller, S.; Parker, C. M.; Chan, C. Employability Skills: Student Perceptions of an IS Final Year Capstone Subject. *ITALICS* **2011,** *10* (2), 4–15.

Kelliher, C.; Riley, M. Beyond Efficiency: Some By-Products of Functional Flexibility. *Serv. Ind. J.* **2003,** *23* (4), 98–113.

Klaus, P. Communication Breakdown. *Calif. Job J.* **2010,** *28*, 1–9.

Klaus, P. *The Hard Truth about Soft Skills: Workplace Lessons Smart People Wish They'd Learned Sooner*. New York, NY: Klaus and Associates, 2007.

Klein, C. R. What Do We Know about Interpersonal Skills? A Meta-Analytic Examination of Antecedents, Outcomes, and the Efficacy of Training. *Ph.D. Dissertation*; Orlando, FL: University of Central Florida, 2009.

Knox, A.; Walsh, J. Organisational Flexibility and HRM in the Hotel Industry: Evidence from Australia. *J. Human Res. Manage.* **2005,** 15 (1), 57–75.

Ladkin, A. Careers and Employment. In *An International Handbook of Tourism Education, University of Surrey, UK*; Airey, D., Tribe, J., Eds.; Amsterdam: Elsevier, 2005.

Ladkin, A. Vocational Education and Food and Beverage Experience: Issues for Career Development, *Int. J. Contemporary Hospitality Manage.* **2000,** *12* (4), 207–218.

Laker, D. R.; Powell, J. L. The Differences between Hard and Soft Skills and Their Relative Impact on Training Transfer. *Hum. Resour. Dev. Q.* **2011,** *22* (1), 111–122.

Lashley, C.; Morrison, A. *Franchising Hospitality Services.* Oxford: Butterworth-Heinemann, 2002.

Lei, H. *Soft Skills List—28 Skills to Working Smart* (online), 2011. http://bemycareercoach.com/soft-skills/list-soft-skills.html (accessed Sept 14, 2017).

Mason, G.; Williams, G.; Cranmer, S. Employability Skills Initiatives in Higher Education: What Effects Do They Have on Graduate Labor Market Outcomes? *Educ. Econ.* **2009,** *17* (1), 1–30.

Matias-Reche, F.; Fuentes-Fuentes, M. M. The Internal Labor Market and the Employment of Temporary Help Workers in Spain. *Pers. Rev.* **2006,** *35* (4), 378–396.

Maxwell, G.; Scott, B.; Macfarlane, D.; Williamson, E. Employers as Stakeholders in Postgraduate Employability Skills Development. *Int. J. Manage. Educ.* **2010,** *8* (2), 1–11.

Mitchell, G. W.; Skinner, L. B.; White, B. J. Essential Soft Skills for Success in the Twenty-First Century Workforce as Perceived by Business Educators. *Delta Pi Epsil. J.* **2010,** *52*, 43–53.

Mobley, W. H. *Employee Turnover: Causes, Consequences and Control;* Addison-Wesley Publishing: Philippines, 1982.

Mucunguzi, J. *Vocational Skills Key to Job Creation for Young People: Deputy Secretary-General. Commonwealth* (online), 2013. http://thecommonwealth.org/media/news/vocational-skills-key-job-creation-young-people-deputy-secretary-general (accessed Oct 12, 2017).

Nankervis, A. R.; Compton, R. L. Performance Management: Theory in Practice? *Asia Pac. J. Hum. Resour.* **2006,** *44* (1), 83–101.

Nelson, A. A.; Dopson, L. R. Future of Hotel Education: Required Skills and Knowledge for Graduates of U.S. Hospitality Programs beyond the Year 2000. *J. Hospitality Tour. Educ.* **2001,** *13* (5), 58–67.

Nicolaides, A. The Use of Multiskilling in the Southern African Hospitality Environment. *Asian J. Bus. Manage. Sci.* **2013,** *3* (4), 64–83.

Odgers, P.; Baum, T. *Benchmarking of Best Practice in Hotel Front Office*; Dublin: CERT, 2001.

OECD. *Better Skills, Better Jobs, Better Lives: A Strategic Approach to Skills Policies;* OECD Publishing: Paris; 2012.

Omar, M. K.; Bakar, A. R.; Rashid, A. M. Employability Skill Acquisition among Malaysian Community College Students. *J. Soc. Sci.* **2012,** *8* (3), 472–478.

Overtoom, C. *ERIC Clearinghouse on Adult, C. H. Employability Skills: An Update* (online), 2000. http://files.eric.ed.gov/fulltext/ED445236.pdf (accessed Aug 23, 2017).
Parsons, T. L. *Definition: Soft Skills* (online), 2008. http://searchcio.techtarget.com/definition/soft skills (accessed Nov 3, 2017).
Pavesic, D. V. Another View of the Future of Hospitality Education. *Cornell Hotel Restaur. Adm. Q.* **1991,** *32* (4), 8–9.
Perreault, H. Business Educators Can Take a Leadership Role in Character Education. *Bus. Educ. Forum* **2004,** *59*, 23–24.
Pizam, A. The Domains of Tourism and Hospitality Management. In *Paper Presented in the Plenary Section at the First International Conference on Tourism and Management Studies*, Faro, 2011.
Poon, A. *Tourism, Technology and Competitive Strategies*; Wallingford: CAB, 1993.
Powell, S.; Wood, D. Is Recruitment the Millennium Time Bomb for the Industry Worldwide? *Int. J. Contemporary Hospitality Manage.* **1999,** *11* (4), 138–139.
Pukelis, K.; Pileicikiene, N. Study Programme Quality Peculiarities at Some Lithuanian Universities and Colleges: Study Outcomes Paradigm. In *Quality of Higher Education;* Lithuanian University: Slovenia, 2010; p 7.
Qualifications and Curriculum Authority. *Key Skills* (online), 2000. http://www.qca.org.uk/nq/ks/keyskills (accessed Aug 13, 2017).
Raftopoulos, M.; Coetzee, S.; Visser, D. Work-Readiness Skills in the Fastest Sector. *S. Afr. J. Hum. Resour. Manage.* **2009,** *7* (1), 119–126.
Rao, A.; Shah, S.; Aziz, J.; Jaffari, A.; Ejaz, W.; Ul-Haq, I.; Raza, S. Employability in MNCs: Challenge for Graduates: Interdisciplinary. *J. Contemporary Res. Bus.* **2011,** *3* (4), 189–200.
Raybould, M.; Wilkins, H. Generic Skills for Hospitality Management: A Comparative Study of Management Expectations and Student Perceptions. *J. Hospitality Tour. Manage.* **2006,** *13* (2), 177–188.
Reche, F.; Fuentes, M. The Internal Labor Market and the Employment of Temporary Help Workers in Spain. *J. Personal Rev.* **2006,** *35* (4), 378–396.
Reich, R. *The Work of Nations: Preparing Ourselves for 21st Century Capitalism*; New York, NY: Vintage Books, 1991.
Riegel, C. D. The Causes and Consequences of Turnover in the Hospitality Industry. In *Hotel management and operations*; Rutherford, D. G., Ed.; New York: John Wiley and Sons, 2002; pp 469–476.
Riley, M.; Ladkin, A.; Szivas, E. *Tourism Employment: Analysis and Planning*. Clevedon: Channel View Publications, 2002.
Ritzer, G. *The McDonaldization of Society*; Thousand Oaks, CA: Pine Forge Press, 1993.
Rivera, L. M.; Schaefer, M. B. The Career Institute: A Collaborative Career Development Program for Traditionally Underserved Secondary (6–12) School Students. *J. Career Dev.* **2009,** *35* (4), 406–426.
Robles, M. M. Executive Perceptions of the Top 10 Soft Skills Needed in Today's Workplace. *Bus. Commun. Q.* **2012,** *75* (4), 453–465.
Rodas, D. J. What Business Students Should Know. *Chron. Higher Educ.* **2007,** *54* (4), 39.
Roy, J. S. An Analysis of Business Competencies Important for Entry-Level Managers in Destination Marketing Organization. *Ph.D. Dissertation*; Minneapolis, MN: School of Business and Technology, Capella University, 2009.

Rudolph, R. D. Desirable Competencies of Hospitality Graduates in Year 2007. *Ph.D. Dissertation*; Princeton, NJ: Cornell University, 1999.

Sweet, S.; Pitt-Catsouphes, M.; Besen, E.; Hovhannisyan, S.; Pasha, F. *Talent Pressures and the Aging Workforce: Responsive Action Steps for the Accommodation and Food Services Sector* (online), 2010. http://www.bc.edu/research/agingandwork/metaelements/pdf/publications/TMISR04_Accommodati n.pdf (accessed Dec 3, 2017).

Seymour, D. Emotional Labor: A Comparison between Fast Food and Traditional Service Work. *Int. J. Hospitality Manage.* **2002,** *19*, 159–171.

Shafie, L.; Nayan, S. Employability Awareness among Malaysian Undergraduates. *Int. J. Bus. Manage.* **2010,** *5* (8), 119–123.

Shaw, G.; Williams, A. Critical Issues in Tourism: A Geographical Perspective. Oxford: Blackwell, 1994.

Sheikh, S. *Alumni Perspectives Survey: Comprehensive Data Report*; Reston, VA: Graduate Management Admission Council (online), 2009. http://www.gmac.com/~/media/Files/gmac/Research/Measuring%20Program%20ROI/APR09Alumn _CDR_Web.pdf (accessed Aug 25, 2017).

Sommerville, K. L. *Hospitality Employee Management and Supervision, Concepts and Applications*; Hoboken, NJ: John Wiley and Sons, 2007.

Staton-Reynolds, J. A Comparison of Skills Considered Important for Success as an Entry Level Manager in the Hospitality Industry According to Industry Recruiters and University Educators. Ph.D. Dissertation, Oklahoma State University, 2009.

Stoner, G.; Milner, M. Embedding Generic Employability Skills in an Accounting Degree: Development and Impediments. *Account. Educ.* **2010,** *19* (1/2), 123–138.

Stovall, D. C.; Stovall, P. S. Professional Accountants: Void of "Soft Skills"? *Bus. Rev. Cambr.* **2009,** *14* (1), 99–104.

Stumpf, J. M. Meeting the Needs: Does Technical College Education Meet the Needs of Employers? E.D. Dissertation; Minnesota, United States: University of Minnesota, 2007.

Thompson, P.; Warhurst, C.; Callaghan, G. Human Capital or Capitalizing on Humanity? Knowledge, Skills and Competencies in Interactive Service Work. In *Managing Knowledge*; Prichard, C., Chumer, H., Willmott, R., Hull, R., Eds.; London: Palgrave, 2000; pp 122–140.

Tribble, L. S. S. The Importance of Soft Skills in the Workplace as Perceived by Community College Instructors and Industries. Ph.D. Dissertation. Mississippi State University, 2009.

Walker, J. R. *Introduction to Hospitality Management*, 2nd ed.; Hoboken, NJ: Pearson Education, Inc., 2007.

Wang, T. Educational Benefits of Multimedia Skills Training. *J. TechTrends* **2010,** *54* (1), 47–57.

Warhurst, C.; Nickson, D.; Witz, A.; Cullen, A. M. Aesthetic Labor in Interactive Service Work: Some Case Study Evidence from the 'New Glasgow. *Serv. Ind. J.* **2000,** *20* (3), 1–18.

Weber, M. R.; Finley, D. A.; Crawford, A.; Rivera, D. An Exploratory Study Identifying Soft Skill Competencies in Entry-Level Managers. *Tour. Hospitality Res.* **2009,** *9* (4), 353–361.

Westray, V. Job Readiness Training: A Qualitative Study of Program Graduates in Rural South Carolina. Ph.D. Dissertation, Cappella University, Minnesota, 2008.

Wilks, D.; Hemsworth, K. Soft Skills as Key Competences in Hospitality Higher Education: Matching Demand and Supply. *Tour. Manage. Stud.* **2011,** *7*, 131–139.

Williams, A. M. Soft Skills Perceived by Students and Employers as Relevant Employability Skills. Ph.D. Dissertation, Walden University, 2015.

Wood, R. C. *Working in Hotels and Catering*, 2nd ed.; London: Routledge, 1997.

Wood, S. The Japanese Model: Post-Fordism or Japanimation of Fordism? Towards a New Productive Model. Paris: Syros, 1993.

Yaacoub, H. K.; Husseini, F.; Choueiki, Z. Engineering Soft Skills: A Comparative Study between the GCC Area Demands and the ABET Requirements. *Competit. Forum* **2011,** *9* (1), 88–99.

## CHAPTER 4

# LABOR SHORTAGE IN THE TOURISM AND HOSPITALITY INDUSTRY

*"You can't be in the service community... without realizing there's a big shortage of talent."*

### 4.1 INTRODUCTION

Without doubt, a strong tourism and hospitality industry is fundamental to global economic prosperity. For example, the hospitality industry is entering an era of growth and development, with global business travel spending hitting record-breaking levels. The hospitality industry accounts for 1 out of every 10 jobs worldwide. Even stronger growth is projected for 2017, pushing the combined travel and hospitality market closer to $381 billion by the end of 2017 according to Deloitte Center for Industry Insights' report 2017 Travel and Hospitality Industry Outlook (Spragg, 2017).

Despite this favorable position, the industry is facing some familiar, yet significant, challenges, as tourism and hospitality industry suffer labor and skills shortage, which is impacting business operations and impeding investment and growth (Spragg, 2017). Labor force has been found to be an important determinant of economic development and explanatory of international differences in aggregate economic growth or productivity (Kneller and Stevens, 2005; Madsen, 2010).

Labor shortages and their impact on the industry in almost every geographic location are consistently among the most difficult challenges noted by industry stakeholders. In many cases, tourism and hospitality activities expansion is limited not by financial factors, but rather by human resources crisis in terms of qualitative shortage or quantitative shrinking. According to the International Society of Hospitality Consultants, which recently convened to brainstorm tourism and hospitality industry issues and ranked them according to influences, it was found that a shrinking labor force is the number one challenge facing the global hospitality industry. Subsequently, the problem of attracting and retaining skilled workers is increasingly becoming a global challenge, once an issue only, in an isolated number of markets. In addition, other factors such as wage levels, failure to adequately address worker satisfaction and a reputation for long hours and demography are all cited as contributing factors in creating this crisis. Creative hospitality professionals have begun to develop innovative strategies for capturing and keeping high-quality staff (Wang and Wang, 2009).

## 4.2 SKILLED LABOR SHORTAGE IN TOURISM INDUSTRY

Changes in the supply of and demand for occupational labor or even skills are normal features of market economies. Some component of the variation is always random while other components may be determined by a number of factors and may include trend and/or cyclic components.

- The trend components of demand may be apparent over the long term only. They may be a result of changes in technology, work organization, shifts in consumer tastes, commodity price changes, or demographic shifts.
- Changes in supply may be due to factors such as changes in labor demographic characteristics, education and training provision and changes in preferences for various forms of work and to demographic changes including aging and emigration and immigration.

A hierarchical structure for occupational classifications or skills is often used with each skill's setting determined by the level of knowledge needed and the autonomy of decision-making involved in completing the job tasks. The definition of an occupation has two dimensions—the set of tasks done by a person occupied in it and the bundle of skills and knowledge an employee in the occupation should possess. Therefore, there is no common agreement on definition or measurement method at the international level of labor or skills shortage (Shah and Burke, 2005). Nonetheless, a number of terms are used, sometimes interchangeably, to indicate human resource crisis: imbalances in skills availability on the labor market is an example, also mentions are made of labor shortage, labor shrinking, skills shortage, skills mismatch, or skills gap. However, operative definitions are generally agreed and established in line with organizational policy objectives. Thus, it has become clear that it is important to distinguish between shortages of skills in existing staff and shortages of workers in the labor market with appropriate skills (Mason and Wilson, 2003). These have been called "qualitative shortage or internal skill gaps" and "quantitative shortage or external skill gaps," respectively (Forth and Mason, 2004). Figure 4.1 shows the different terms that describe the two types of skills shortages in work environment. Generally, the most commonly used indicators for labor or skill shortages are (Estruch-Puertas and Zuppi, 2009):

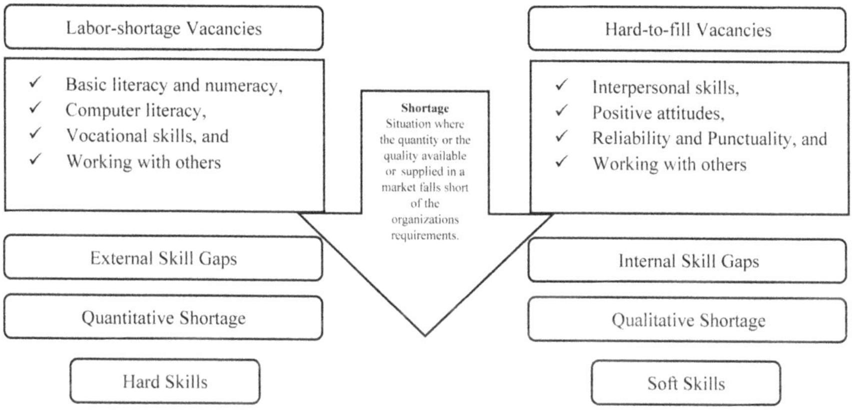


**FIGURE 4.1** Skills shortages terms.
**Source:** The Author

## *Unfilled vacancies*

A shortage occurs when the demand for labor for a particular occupation is greater than the supply of available skilled workers who are willing to work under existing work environment conditions, and if the supply is greater than demand then there is a surplus. In practical industries, shortages have always been interpreted directly, in terms of difficulties in filling vacancies. In general, a shortage in an occupation is the aggregation of hard-to-fill vacancies across firms. These vacancies are those that remain unfilled after a certain time in spite of all reasonable efforts by employers. A shortage may be evident only in particular tasks in an occupation, it does not have to be across the whole occupation. Furthermore, it may be restricted to particular geographical locations.

### *Skills gaps*

The difficulty in filling vacancies with appropriately skilled applicants means that there is a skill shortage in the labor market. Skills gaps, on the other hand, arise where members of the existing workforce are seen to lack the skills and knowledge necessary to meet business needs. Skills gaps are far greater in number than skills shortages; it is also important to measure skills gaps by sector and occupation.

Skills imbalances and mismatches can take various forms: skill shortages or gaps occur when there is “excess” demand for skills; unemployment, inactivity, “over-qualification,” or “under-employment,” where there is insufficient demand (Shah and Burke, 2005). The same source points out that it is important to measure skills or labor shortages by sector and occupation to identify those activities in which they do have a significant impact. Here, this means that shortage has two facets: the hard (quantitative labor shortages) and the soft (qualitative labor shortages) meaning (Zimmer, 2012).

Hard facet means that there is insufficient workforce in the organization to the degree that causes delaying and sometimes hindering the flow of production (a shortfall in the total number of individuals in the labor force), while, the soft shortage, denotes that there a full team able to cover all the departmental and sectoral vacancies, but some of them lose the skills and knowledge needed to perform tasks efficiently (mismatch between workers and jobs in the industry). In terms of a range of skills, employers have traditionally been viewed as demanding “softer” skills more than “harder” from their employees and wanting them to have the “right” positive attitude (Burns, 1997). Dealing with customers is seen as an inherent attribute or skill rather than an ability that can be learned, in contrast to the “harder” or more technical skills of food preparation or operating technical equipment.

In nutshell, when demand for a skill grows faster than supply, the concept of dynamic shortage arises. Arrow and Capron (1959) explored some factors that cause dynamic shortage such as:

- low elasticity of supply,
- rapid and persistent rise in demand, and
- the slow reaction of labor market.

## *4.2.1 QUALITATIVE LABOR SHORTAGE*

In the 21st century, skills have become the global precious currency. In such world, people languish on the margins of society, technological progress does not translate into economic growth and development, and countries can no longer compete in an increasingly knowledge-based global society without proper investment in skills and competencies. Skills are the qualifications that individuals have, and then skills enhance the ability of the worker to perform specified tasks or the ability to perform a productive task at a certain level of competence, and its acquisition and maintaining through formal education and practicing. But this "currency" depreciates as the requirements of labor markets grow and individuals lose the skills they do not use. Skills do not automatically convert into jobs and growth (OECD, 2012). Such excessive demand and the low skills of labor market members in addition to the limited capabilities of employer to switch their organizations labor demand composition or generate substitute labor market (e.g., sourcing labor from different locations or sectors) definitely lead to skills shortages in their work environment. Labor demand and labor supply are in equilibrium, but there is simultaneously a large share of unfilled vacancies, caused by qualitative discrepancies between supply and demand in which qualitative characteristics of the supply do not match with the qualitative characteristics that are set by the employers. However, an employee can acquire skills in other ways, including various forms of informal learning and on-the-job experience.

The term skill may be open to a number of interpretations by employers (Bosworth et al., 1992). For some, it may refer to the ability to learn tasks rather than an acquired skill. Other employers may place a higher value on personality skills exhibited at an interview rather than on past experience or certified skills. This can be happening in service sector jobs especially the front line that imposes a direct touch with customers. It may also happen that the employer is looking for a particular type of person, perhaps in his or her own image, rather than for the skills necessary to undertake a particular job.

As a skill is associated with a particular task, a person who does not possess such a skill is unlikely to be able to carry out the tasks of his job or will be less productive than somebody who does possess this skill. Skills shortages can be due to a significant geographical imbalance and shortfall in the number of skilled people.

These qualitative characteristics first and foremost refer to personality skills, and may also be related to work experience, age, gender, and work preferences. Subsequently, skills shortages arise in a situation in which organizations face difficulties in recruiting staff with the skills needed. Green et al. (1998) showed some employers valued motivational and attitudinal skills very highly and indicated a deficiency of these skills among their employees according to the analysis of Employer Manpower and Skills Survey in Britain.

Nowadays, skill shortages are often portrayed as a major problem for the economies of many countries. Gore (2005) asserted that the employability of potential applicants became a multifaceted concept, as the current work environment requires and emphasizes quality and innovation, for which human, rather than physical capital, is particularly important. Employers not only want individuals with the appropriate skills and attributes, but also, they have perceptions about which particular groups of employees and workers may have these features, and those that may not, such as the unemployed and workers on Government training schemes (Lucas and Keegan, 2008).

Recent industry professional claims and employment theories argue that the role of employees has dramatically changed over the past century. Human relations theories (Maslow, 1943; Hertzberg, 1959; McGregor, 1960) view employees as key organizational assets, rather than expendable commodities, who can create fundamental value by inventing new products, developing production stream, or building strong customers relationships. Changes in skill profiles happen at all levels of qualifications and across all departments within any organization operating in the service sector.

Thus, kills can be classified into two main categories; general and specific, although, the boundary between the two is often blurred.

- Generic skills are this type of skills that every applicant must have to be able to enter the labor market. General skills include those that are now known as generic including basic literacy and numeracy, but increasingly computer literacy. General skills are transferable or portable across a range of different occupations.

It was reported also a shortage in generic and vocational skills in hospitality organizations by People 1st National Skills Survey (2006), about 40% of chefs working in hospitality did not have the minimum level qualification required, which raises issues about their lack of training in food preparation and hygiene practices. Although it is difficult to define what skills are required because there are many different kinds of chefs, not to mention types and styles of cooking, work as chefs and cooks is the other occupation employers report as being difficult to fill.

Pratten and O'Leary (2007) claimed that the reasons for the shortage in numbers of chefs are generic and related to the issues of labor in hospitality industry as a whole, in particular, low pay, poor conditions and unsociable hours. The issue of low skilled cooks and chef (Deskilling and standardization) has resulted in many organizations now outsourcing the production of food, such that reduced the chef's role to one of reheating "cook-chill" or "cook-freeze" foods (Robinson and Barron, 2007). This highlighted that educational institutions need to reflect in their curriculum more about the realities of the current-day roles of chefs to reflect the strict rules and rigid way of working in a commercial kitchen.

– Other skills which differ from an organization to another in different sector or even in the same sector is "employability skills," these include interpersonal skills, positive attitudes, reliability and punctuality and working with others and in teams, in another word, such skills also known as hard-to-fill vacancies that arise due to poor attitude or personality, lack of motivation.

In the context of hospitality industry, Kent (2006) claimed that 17% of employers believed their "front of house" staff did not possess the soft skills necessary to deliver high standard of service (customer service) that enable them to build strong relationship with customers (lacking personal skills) to meet their business needs and that young people, in general, did not have adequate communication skills. Thus, it can be argued that this highlights the shortfall of recruiting by personality, skills, abilities and aesthetic qualities, among other skills.

Service organizations highly value "softer" skills that have been termed "emotional intelligence," whereby employees have an array of non-cognitive skills which make them creative, self-motivated and understanding of their own emotions and those of others (customers and coworkers) (Dulewicz and Higgs, 2000).

Emotional intelligence encompasses attitudes, skills, and personality which are crucial in successful service encounters (Varca, 2004). In relation to experience, some employers seeking to build a successful relationship with customers claimed that personality is the most important factor that makes them neglect any other factor like experience in hiring job seeker (Dench et al., 2006). This dimension of labor market demand has advanced further with more recent indications showing that employees now also have to demonstrate the "right" personality and aesthetic qualities, that is, having "certain capacities and attributes that favorably appeal to customers' visual or aural senses" (Nickson et al., 2005), which gives them a competitive advantage over others.

Although soft skills are often difficult to develop without a good grounding in generic skills, in particular, the basic generic skills, employers value soft skills over hard skills; they prefer to have employees with creativity and critical thinking skills, enthusiasm, commitment, stamina and responsibility over technical skills (Rowley and Purcell, 2001), and value the "right" personality over qualifications (Nickson et al., 2005).

### *4.2.2 QUANTITATIVE LABOR SHORTAGE*

A shortage occurs when the demand for labor exceeds labor supply either permanently or for a specific period of time, resulting in a large amount of vacancies. Labor shortages are a concern because they may result in economic incompetence due to a loss of potential output and a suboptimal use of the available workforce (Barnow et al., 2013). However, there is no universal agreement about the definition of labor market shortages in the literature (OECD, 2003).

There are various definitions suggested in the academic literature. Shah and Burke (2003) defined labor shortage as "A shortage occurs when the demand for workers for a particular occupation is greater than the supply of workers who are qualified, available and willing to work under existing market conditions." In 2013, two more definitions were developed, Behan et al. defined skills shortage as a situation in which there is a shortage or an insufficient number of trained/skilled individuals in the domestic market to meet the demand for an occupation, while, Barnow et al. view labor shortages as "a sustained market disequilibrium between supply and demand in which the quantity of individuals demanded exceeds the supply available and willing to work at a particular wage and working conditions at a particular place and point in time." Recently, specifically in 2015, Gusciute et al. (2015) expressed shortages as a proportion of total employment stock:

- low refers to a shortage of less than 1per cent of total employment stock,
- medium, a shortage of 1–3%,
- high, a shortage of greater than 3%.

Broadly speaking, labor shortages refer to a situation in which labor demand exceeds labor supply.

Generally, organizations may suffer shortages of particular workers, or difficulties in filling vacancies, either because there are not enough of them or else those who are available do not possess skills now deemed necessary by employers. Shortages of the first type are quantitative while those of the second type are qualitative. Thus, in a slack labor market, if overqualified people fill positions then the market may not show an imbalance. In contrast, in a tight labor market whose skills do not match the ideal for their organizations, if the employers accepted hiring applicants a shortage exists and if refused also a shortage exists, and subsequently the organization experiences profit fall accompanying the substandard performance.

## 4.3 SHORTAGE AND PERFORMANCE

Four skills were considered among the array of possibilities for skills improvement in the organizations: job-specific tasks, oral communication, knowledge of a foreign language, and manual dexterity. However, there are essentially two elements to the link between skills and the performance. First, skills represent the foundation of the success of the firm's production. Employees with higher skills have more human capital and so produce greater output.

A number of researchers found highlighted the positive relationship between skill and education in particular and social returns and the overall performance of the organization (Psacharopoulos and Patrinos, 2004; McMahon, 2004). The direct impact of high skill levels not only increase organization productivity but also enhance synergies across the different departments and productive inputs, such as other workers, physical and knowledge capital, and new technologies.

Skills are an important determinant of firms, industries, and overall economic performance. Shortages of skilled labor directly constrain production and prevent firms from meeting demand and using available inputs efficiently (Stevens, 2007). Indirectly, skill shortages inhibit innovation and the use of new technologies. This may have longer-term impacts on the way firms do business, in terms of their location, size, structure, production methods and product strategy (Mason and Wilson, 2003; Durbin, 2004; Mason, 2005).

Knowledge spillovers is another way of skills, through which, skilled labor increases the productivity of other workers (Audretsch and Feldman, 2004). Spillovers occur when other employees and workers pick up skills through observation, interaction or tuition. These spillovers can occur within the organization and across the boundaries of the firms through direct relationships with all involved stakeholders (Audretsch and Feldman, 2004). For a long time, it has been suggested that skilled labor is more complementary with capital than unskilled labor (Papageorgiou and Perez-Sebastian, 2004).

Over time, old skills may disappear, and because of the changing mode and perception of customers, technological and organizational changes, new ones may be developed. In times of very rapid technological changes, the shelf life of some skills diminishes quickly, and skill obsolescence becomes a problem. To avoid future skill shortages, countries need to devise strategies based on well-informed policy decisions, educational vocational strategies, social dialogue and coordination among ministries and between employers and training providers.

This discussion of the nature of skills has been included because as will be seen below some notions of skills shortage are to do with the absence of particular skills among current employees in work environment rather than a shortage of numbers of employees available for work.

Labor shortages can result from a number of different causes. In this section, we discuss the reasons why the labor market for a particular occupation in a disequilibrium situation.

## 4.4 REASONS OF OCCUPATIONAL DISEQUILIBRIUM IN LABOR MARKETS

### *4.4.1 REASONS OF QUANTITATIVE SHORTAGES*

In case of quantitative labor shortage, the total number of individuals available in the labor market (total supply of labor) in an economy falls short of the total demand for labor in that economy, this shortage can be measured at a regional, at a national level. Although the quantitative shortages do not seem a big issue nowadays, the consequence of demographic developments in future may shrink the labor force in some countries while simultaneously labor demand increases as the economy expands.

Identifying particular types of quantitative labor shortages is useful for establishing which mechanisms explain these shortages and what policy responses may be considered. Generally, we can distinguish two types of quantitative shortages:

#### *4.4.1.1 DECLINE IN THE NUMBER OF AVAILABLE WORKERS*

The decline in available individuals in labor market can be caused by the general decline in the active population of working age; this decline can be caused naturally due to aging and the low fertility rate and also by emigration.

#### *4.4.1.1.1 Emigration*

Without doubt emigration of people in working age from a region or country negatively influence on the labor market in the country of origin especially if the emigrants of young and educated workers, on the other side, it also reduces potential labor market shortage in the destination country. This process improves the average skill level of labor market in destinations countries, in turn, employers are able to offset labor shortages, accumulate skills. While the sending countries experience a "brain drain" and shortage in labor supply (Exenberger, 2007).

The motives for people to leave their countries of origin vary as follows:

- economic factors: Poverty or unemployment,
- personal factors: Ambitious personality, high career prospects, or freedom constraints,
- social factors: Social instability or bad living conditions,
- political factors: Insecurity, instability, or persecution.

#### *4.4.1.1.2 Demographic Characteristics*

In addition to emigration of young workers, demographic characteristics is also another factor contributing in labor market shortage. Due to a low and/or declining fertility rate in the past decades, the inflow of young people into the labor market may be smaller than the outflow of older workers who retire, resulting in a natural decline of the population of working-age.

In some countries, if there will be no compensation by increasing number of migrants, labor shortage may be an endemic crisis as a result of population decline (Shah and Burke, 2003). Following a recent study of Horbach (2014), without migration effects, German population (between the age of 15 and 66) would shrink from now 55 million to 30 million in 2060. Including migrations, the most optimistic scenario shows that population in 2060 will be 45 million.

#### *4.4.1.1.3 Decrease in the Participation Rate*

Labor shortage may be the outcome of the limited participation of society members in labor markets, two groups are identified to have a lower contribution in the labor markets, as follows:

*Skill obsolescence of older workers*

Due to a loss of physical ability and the skills, older workers lose their job and become unemployed, this may result in a permanent departure from the labor market and subsequently, occupations vacancies arise.

*Marginal groups*

Other sociodemographic groups such as women, low-skilled immigrants, and people with disabilities are considered marginal and at a risky group. These groups constitute a notable part in the labor market, however, employers may ignore them and claim that labor demand and labor supply are in disequilibrium position. This may because the negative stereotypes about this groups that the employers have, in case of women they may think that their family commitments influence negatively on their performance in the job. Also, employers may look at people with disabilities as an overload on the business in terms of special treatment and disability aid plan required for them.

#### *4.4.1.2 INCREASE IN THE DEMAND FOR LABOR*

An increase in demand for labor in a particular industry does not necessarily result in declining in labor market. If the supply of labor to an industry can respond to the increased demand, the result will be a new equilibrium with more workers employed and a higher wage rate than at the previous equilibrium.

The increase in the demand for labor occurs for several reasons:

- An increase in the demand for particular goods and services;
  Perhaps the most likely reason for an increase in the demand for labor is an increase in the demand for the goods or services. An increase in the demand for the product can result from (Barnow et al., 2013):
  - an increase due to aging societies,
  - an increase in the income or wealth of consumers,
  - a change in the composition of the population of buyers, or
  - changes in the tastes and preferences of consumers.
- An increase in the prices of substitute factors of production;
  The demand for a given type of labor will also increase if the price of a non-labor factor (automation systems) increases and labor can be used as a substitute in the production process.

#### 4.4.1.3 A GEOGRAPHICAL MISMATCH BETWEEN REGIONS

Geographical mismatch arises when the locations where job openings are available are poorly matched with potential employees. It occurs when different regions in one country have different critical labor market characteristics; when labor market is tight (low-skilled workers) in a region, while there is a surplus in another, when there are very little young educated individuals in a country, while there is an overabundance in another.

It worthy to mention that, sometimes, maybe some constraints over the mobility of individuals whether within the same country or across national borders, which keep the issue still exists. Labor mobility may be constrained by:

- people's unwillingness to move and relocate,
- social life stability of people,
- restricted policies that regulate labor movements in the country of destination,
- language barriers,
- the ambiguity of foreign opportunities, and
- the difficulties in recognizing foreign qualifications.

### 4.4.2 REASONS OF QUALITATIVE SHORTAGES

Even without a quantitative labor shortage, there may still be qualitative shortages in particular occupations or industries whilst disappear in other occupations or industries. Qualitative labor shortages occur if the labor demand in a specific occupation is higher than the labor supply in the same sector/occupation in terms of qualities, skills, competencies, and attitudes. Thus, there is a mismatch between the particular characteristics of the labor supply and the particular characteristics of the labor demand, resulting in a shortage in a specific segment of the labor market. The clear reason for qualitative labor market shortages is skill mismatch. However, skill mismatch is a broader category than skills shortages (OECD, 2003), as we will explain in the next section. Table 4.1 shows the different types of skill mismatches.

**TABLE 4.1** Definition of Various Types of Skill Mismatches.

| Types | Definitions |
|---|---|
| *Skill mismatch* | The level of qualification or education is less or more than required |
| Vertical mismatch | The type/field of education or skills is inappropriate for some occupations |
| Horizontal mismatch | |
| *Skill gap* | Type or level of skills is different from that is required to adequately perform specific types of tasks |
| *Skill shortage* | Demand for a particular type of skill exceeds the supply of labor market with that skill |
| *Skills obsolescence* | Skills or knowledge previously used in a job are no longer required and/or skills have deteriorated over time, this occurs because of not keeping up with the new in the workplace and in the industry. Old and female workers may be characterized by skills obsolescence because of their lack of connection to professional and old boy networks |

**Source:** The Author, based on (ILO, 2014).

#### *4.4.2.1 SKILL MISMATCH*

In case of a skill mismatch, employers may also decide to hire undereducation, under-qualified, or under-skilled workers. In such cases, the occurrence of undereducation or underqualification may be an indication of skill mismatch. Skill mismatch can be defined as an imbalance between the supply and demand of particular skills within a specific sector, a specific occupation, or at particular skill levels. The ILO (2014) distinguishes between horizontal skill mismatch, meaning that the type or field of education or skills is inappropriate for the job, and vertical mismatch, meaning that the level of education or qualification is less or more than required by employers.

On the other hand, under particular conditions, the employees may have more education or better qualifications than is needed for their job. In this case, skill mismatch translates into overeducation or overqualification of employees, and vice versa.

#### *4.4.2.2 SKILL GAP*

The literature on the definition of skills gaps is ambiguous. Skills gaps are used to describe the qualitative mismatch between the supply or availability of labor force and the requirements of the organizations (Strietska-Ilina, 2008). Shah and Burke defined skill gap as "a situation where employers are hiring workers whom they consider under-skilled or that their existing workforce is under-skilled relative to some desired levels" (2003, p 19), while Strietska-Ilina (2008) emphasizes "the existence" rather than "a situation."

When employers or managers feel that their employed workforce have inadequate skills types/levels to meet their business requirements and objectives, skills gaps exist, or where new recruits appear to be qualified but actually they are not able to perform their tasks and duties as expected from them or to accomplish their jobs as planned. Recruitment difficulties cover all forms of recruitment problems faced by employers (Strietska-Ilina, 2008), including the situation in which employers cannot hire qualified staff to perform given duties even though there is a sufficient supply of labor in the market (Shah and Burke, 2003).

### *4.4.2.3 SKILL SHORTAGE*

In tourism context, skill shortage varies by location, organization, and season. A skill shortage is considered one of the consequences of a skill mismatch. Healy et al. (2011) claimed that skills shortages refer to "a situation where employers in specific sectors cannot find suitably qualified workers," and therefore "the job is often left vacant and there is no match or mismatch between a worker and a job."

Skills shortages can be both cyclical and structural:

- Cyclical shortage: At times of economic growth, as more recruitment occurs, more difficulties in finding the "right" candidates are experienced.
- Structural shortage: At times of economic downturns, as more voluntary staff turnover happens, significant shrinking in labor force.

Generally, in the following, we discuss the various factors of skill shortages from two main perspectives, skills shortage that is due to changes in skills required for jobs, and skills shortages that are due to changes in the skill composition of the labor supply.

#### 4.4.2.4 CHANGES IN SKILLS REQUIRED FOR JOBS

### 1. *Skills shortages due to technological change*

Ongoing technological development increases the demand for a particular type of skilled labor. Skills shortages may be due to a scarcity of the skills required for certain technologies lines and systems. Quintini (2011) observed that emerging technological changes, such as the adoption of new technology, can create needs for new skills that are not immediately available in the labor market, giving rise to skills shortages until the educational institutions are able to meet the new skill requirements.

Also, skill shortage is expected to continue occur if poor organizational restructuring process kept hiring applicants who previously worked in declining sectors, such as agriculture and infrastructure, they may not be easily employable in jobs in growing sectors such as hospitality, health, and education, which require interpersonal skills, communication skills or problem-solving skills (CEDEFOP, 2014).

### 2. *Stakeholders' practices*

#### *A. Stakeholders' restrictions*

The labor supply curve for an occupation might decline because of restrictions on entry into the relevant labor market. Such restrictions may be commanded by the government (through licensing requirements and restricting the number of licenses granted), by professional organizations that set tight standards and rules for practice, by labor unions, or by educational and training institutions (e.g., universities, community colleges).

In the tourism and hospitality context, the main restriction may be the nature of the work environment of the tourism and hospitality jobs (e.g., the crazy shift that affect negatively on the employee's social life balance, the stress resulting from seeking satisfying customers every encounter they experience, low wages associated with working in the hospitality firms, etc.).

#### *B. Skills shortages caused by recruitment rigidity*

Skills shortages may result from poor investments in hiring, especially for small-medium enterprises -SMEs, which lead employers to overestimate candidates at the recruitment stage and hire under-skilled workers.

- **Recruitment method**. Discrepancies between the recruitment channels used by employers to attract skilled labor and the search strategies pursued by skilled job-seekers.

Although the informal hiring channels (friendship, kinship, and collegial ties) have been found to reduce vacancy duration compared to more formal recruitment methods, it always brings the wrong employee into the workplace.

- **Slowness in the adjustment of wages.** Adjusting wages as a response to changes in the supply or demand for certain skills may not ensue, and even if it does, it may be slow, thus resulting in skills shortage in work environment. Institutional and regulatory arrangements are among the factors that hinder the process of wage adjustment. According to OECD (1994), the following factors increase the wage-related adjustments stickiness:
  - The existence of a wages agreement within the company, industry or the whole economy (Accords in Australia in the 1980s and early 1990s)
  - Contracts of employment between employers and employees,
  - The ability of their organization to afford extra expenses related to its personnel especially employers fear that higher salaries for new recruits will have a flow-on effect on salaries of existing staff.
  - Lack of transparency of the market.

  Another cause of skills shortages is when the equilibrium wage for a particular skill is below some minimum level. Here the minimum wage must match the wage equivalent of public social welfare benefits payments (Roy et al., 1996).

- **Adjustment of training.** There are several reasons why the adjustment of the numbers and mix of training in educational institutions may be slow, as follows:
  - the recognition process of the shortages,
  - preparing the internal budgetary processes in public vocational education and training (VET) and higher education institutions, and
  - the patterns of the current educators.

### *3. Skills shortages caused by increasing replacement demand*

Increasing in replacement demand may result in skills shortage in work environment, jobs vacant due to the departure specific groups of workers must be filled by new more skilled workers. Employers must put some working specific groups into consideration, and be prepared for their moving, such groups as following:

- old workers entering retirement,
- young casual workers backing to school,
- women withdrawing due to childbirth and childrearing,
- individuals with chronic disease who may face some health troubles, and
- occupational and job mobility.

However, replacement demand tends to be low in relatively new occupations that have recently established. Increasing replacement demand may also be due to a lack of skill upgrading during the career and skill obsolescence.

### *4.4.2.5 CHANGES IN THE SKILL COMPOSITION OF THE LABOR SUPPLY*

#### ***1. Skills shortages caused by the "wrong" educational choices of students.***

An important source of skill mismatches is a discrepancy between the fields of study that students choose or are able to choose and the type of qualifications that employers demand. This phenomenon is known as horizontal mismatch. In choosing a course direction, many students do not take into account the expected future demand for different fields of study. As far as they do base their field of study on labor market prospects, they tend to focus on current labor market shortages or surpluses instead of on the projected future shortages. According to Heijke (1996), this may result in so-called cobweb or pork cycles, in which periods with shortages and periods with surpluses of workers with particular qualifications replace each other.

Skill mismatches can also occur when insufficient educational institutions exit, or if they offer programs of insufficient quality to meet the standards of the labor market, limiting the options of VET, for example.

Changes in the skill composition of the labor supply may also result in a vertical mismatch. In some countries, such as France, the increasing share of the labor force with tertiary qualification does not match a production structure that still requires a relatively large share of low-qualified workers, giving rise to labor shortages in low-skilled jobs or to a skill mismatch resulting in overeducated workers. On the contrary, countries with a small share of tertiary degree jobseekers, such as Italy, may register skill imbalances in higher labor market segments (World Economic Forum, 2014).

#### *4.4.2.6 INFORMATION MISMATCH BETWEEN LABOR MARKET AND EMPLOYERS*

Information asymmetries can result in labor shortages; imperfect information flows lead not only to the shortage of skilled labor in the local labor market but also resulting in a lack of transparency on the labor market.

Information mismatch may result from both sides' activities:

- recruitment activities by employers who fail to reach their target, or
- job search ways by job seekers that fail to locate available jobs.

Information mismatch may also entail workers who are currently employed in jobs that do not match their level of qualifications or skills and who may be qualified for and willing to move to a better suitable position.

#### *4.4.2.7 MISMATCH BETWEEN PREFERENCE OF LABOR MARKET AND THE JOBS OFFERED*

Sometimes, labor market members are unwilling to take up certain jobs despite the fact that these jobs match their qualifications and skills profile and are located in the relevant geographical region, this contributes creating a shortage in work environment.

This means that the full potential of the workforce is not fully utilized because labor market's preferences differ from the available occupations. Various factors may divert people from certain available jobs.

Preference mismatch can be related to the objective and to the subjective characteristics of particular jobs, in short, the attractiveness of a job control the number of applicants to get positions in some sectors compared to another especially in developing countries, where the community value and appreciate those who are working inside four walls (office) and dealing with some papers, regardless the amount of money he/she gets at the end of each month, while, those who belong to field working environment do not enjoy the same appreciation.

#### 4.4.2.8 PREFERENCE MISMATCH DUE TO WORKING CONDITIONS

According to Haskel and Martin (2001), the sectoral or occupational labor shortages may occur because specific occupations or do not offer attractive working conditions (e.g., risky tasks, demanding tasks, long hours, and low wages). They also advocated that firms and organizations that offer a higher wage relative to the average wage within the same sector in a given geographical area rarely experience labor shortage incidents.

Lack of flexibility in working hours also influence the preference for jobs, inflexibility may hinder combining work with caring responsibilities. Thus, in some industries that combine between low wages and poor working conditions, employers may be forced to hire underqualified personnel for lack of interest from more suitable candidates.

## 4.5 REACTION TO LABOR/SKILLS SHORTAGES

Both demand-side and supply-side factors are associated with the appearance of skills shortages. Quintini (2011) observed that, in order to eliminate the shortage of skills levels, organizations must make some adjustments such as wage rigidities, cooperating with educational establishments for adjusting the education systems, encouraging of geographical mobility and information flow for applicants.

In line with Quintini, Healy et al. (2011) claimed that recruiting standards change in response to fluctuations in the business cycle and, when demand is buoyant, and the labor market is tight, employers may be forced to modify their hiring standards downward, increasing the incidence of undereducation and underfilling to cope with the real world of labor market. The firms or organizations reaction to labor shortage take a time to respond precisely to that issue that threatens not only the organization performance but also the whole economy of countries, Arrow and Capron used the rise ratio of wage as an indicator to speed of reaction of any organization to tackle labor shrinking, they defined reaction speed as the ratio of the rate of wage rise to the excess of demand over supply (1959). And they also stated a number of factors that contribute originating slow reaction time:

- **Firstly,** it takes time for employers to recognize the existence of a shortage at the current wage rate. In this case, if the initial recruitment efforts fail, they often try the strategy of increasing advertising expenditure in the hope of attracting suitable applicants. This strategy is likely to fail if the equilibrium wage has indeed increased.

- **Secondly,** it takes time for employers to decide on the level for a new wage rate and the number of employees to hire at the new rate, and also to make decisions about the current employed staff wages.
- **Thirdly,** the time taken for information flow to labor market (supply-side) regarding new opportunities (slow recognition of opportunities) and the time taken by them to take advantage of those opportunities (enter to the occupation and training system) adds to the time lag.

With respect to the previous factors, there may be confusion in employers' minds over their ability to attract labor and the concept of existing skill gaps or deficiencies in current employment, which have more to do with training inadequacies than experiencing shortages. When a labor shortage has been established, governments have tried to address it in various ways (Ducanes and Abella, 2008). Over time, countries could respond to such crisis in a number of ways, including:

A. induce existing workers to work longer hours,
B. postpone old workers retirement,
C. invest in physical capital or to automate,
D. outsourcing and relocating,
E. admitting foreign migrant workers,
F. admitting price and/or quantity adjustment, and
G encourage those who are unemployed or not part of the labor force to join the workforce.

The previous solutions that adopted by some governments help significantly in controlling and limiting labor shortage in work environment and reduce the negative consequences to a critical extent, at the same time, entities and organizations must move forward in proposing and implementing some strategies relating workers in order to kill this phenomenon.

Because employers will note the problems first, as they are unable to fill vacancies at current policies and strategies, employers must take actions to deal with the unfilled positions. Some actions are more costly or less reversible than others, so employers are likely to undertake these actions first. In particular cases, of course, some of the potential actions may be inapplicable or employers may undertake the actions in a different order.

Organizations and establishments must turn their Human Resources initiatives into a competitive advantage by building a dynamic workplace environment and culture that is aligned with the values of the modern workforce. This includes reevaluating existing hiring procedures, the promotion process, career development, and workplace culture. In addition, the organization must have a deep look into their recruiting practices, consider their wages and compensation package, check working conditions, and revise the training system. Generally, each entity's needs and corresponding solutions will vary as well. However, it is likely a two-pronged approach is needed to succeed.

This following section describes some of the actions that firms are likely to take to deal with the labor shortage.

### *4.5.1 IMPROVING RECRUITING EFFORTS*

A logical first step to fill vacancies is not only to increase but also to improve recruiting efforts and practices. Although employers will incur short-term costs in expanding recruiting, there are no long-term or permanent costs involved (Barnow et al., 2010).

Recruiting practices can be enhanced through several ways, including:

1. Establish an attractive organizational climate (ethical climate in particular) and promoting social programs (e.g., social corporate responsibility) that gain the respect of the community and then serve as a competitive advantage for the organization especially to attract skilled employees.
2. Use Word-of-Mouth (WOM) Marketing tool.
   By building a strong WOM foundation (e.g., sufficient levels of satisfaction, trust and commitment) in the organization work environment enables the organizations to use their employees as brand ambassadors who are willing to share the influential image of the organization to others.
3. Increase advertising efforts in the usual channels.
   For example, employers who advertise in newspapers can increase the frequency of the advertisements or the size of the advertisements to attract more attention to vacancies.
4. Expand the geographical area.
   Employers who believe that the problem is local rather than regional or national can increase the geographical scope of their recruiting efforts.

5. Use public and private employment agencies.
   Firms that do not already do so can make use of public and private employment agencies. Public agencies, referred to as the employment service or job service, are free to both workers and employers.

### 4.5.2 *REDUCE ENTRY REQUIREMENTS FOR THE JOB*

Sometimes, the plentiful skilled individuals in labor market make the organizations to set the minimum hiring qualifications higher than necessary. In the tight labor market, such high entry requirements make it difficult for the organization to respond quickly to the occurring shortage in the work environment. Therefore, reducing the minimum hiring standards is another method of filling occupations vacancies.

This may appear harming for the quality of the production that in turn will reflect on the quality of the image of the organization. But, the reduced entry requirements for any job means that the organizations are able to reduce the wages offered or at least avoid increasing wages, subsequently, the savings from reduced wages of low skilled workers may go to establishing a dynamic and effective training system in case the productivity of fewer workers is lower.

Therefore, in some cases, the firm may have to hire applicants from the most prestigious schools or have had a minimum grade point average or test score cutoff, and these requirements may not be necessary (Barnow et al., 2010).

### 4.5.3 *RESTRUCTURE TASKS TO INVOLVE CURRENT WORKERS IN OTHER OCCUPATIONS*

If employers have difficulty filling vacancies with current workers in one occupation, it is sometimes possible to restructure the work to make use of workers in other working areas. In some cases, complex jobs can be decomposed into simpler tasks that can be handled by a few workers or less skilled workers. However, delegating tasks to the current workers must not last for a long time because of two main reasons:

i. Employers may report skills gaps during the adjustment process, shortages are more likely to occur for high-skill occupations than low-skill occupations (Barnow et al., 2010), thus, customers may report complaints concerning the quality of the product (service).
ii. It may incur extra if the current workers asked the management for any compensations.

### 4.5.4 EXTEND USE OF OVERTIME

A relatively very simple solution to the problem of filling vacancies is to have current employees work more hours. This solution is conditional on the period of adjustment; if the employers predict that the problem will not last for a substantial period of time, this approach is likely to be propitious (Barnow et al., 2010).

### 4.5.5 ROBOTIC LABOR OR AUTOMATION SYSTEM

In case of experiencing a labor shortage, companies may need to take advantage of lower cost technology and automate routine job tasks. Substituting technology for labor is sometimes a viable solution of dealing labor shortage. As technology has advanced in recent years, the types of tasks performed by machines have also changed (see Chapter 2, Robotic Labor or Automation System).

Employers can sometimes alter the production system to replace workers with machines. Formerly, machines typically replaced employees in unskilled tasks such as lifting and moving. According to Barnow et al. (2010), more recently, computer-based technology permits machines to perform more sophisticated tasks. Artificial intelligence "expert system" models even permit computers to substitute for professional judgment under certain circumstances. In the travel and hospitality context, the airline industry has fully adopted this concept and is already deploying automation technology across its operations.

To implement this strategy at the operational level within the hospitality industry, an organization will need to ask this basic question before it posts each new job: Do we need another hire, or can this job be automated through technology? (Spragg, 2017) Although, there are obviously limits to how much technology can substitute for workers, in many situations technology will be used to substitute for workers for reasons other than difficulty in filling job openings.

### 4.5.6 TRAIN WORKERS FOR THE JOBS

According to Richardson (2007), training can be used for two main purposes:

i. Alleviating shortages whether it is of qualitative or quantitative type.
ii. Improving working conditions that will result in enhancing the quality of the product (service).

Offering training for an occupation is often a major commitment for employers, and it is typically not provided unless most other strategies fail. This is highlighted by Kent (2006) who identified a "sector paradox" in that a third of organizations are not engaging in any labor training. Yet nearly two-thirds of them recognize the business benefits of training and a quarter states they will not train staff.

For some occupations, training is traditionally performed by organizations (employers), either:

- formally through apprenticeship or other training programs,
- informally through on-the-job training,
- universities and schools;
  - in universities, training for entry-level jobs is performed for professional occupations, and
  - vocational schools and trade schools for skilled craft and service occupations.

Employers who traditionally do not train their own workers may resort to offering or sponsoring training if they are experiencing difficulty filling vacancies. There are several related reasons why employers are reluctant to offer occupational training:

- First, the training is generally time-consuming. In some certain occupations, training may not resolve the problem immediately, as training takes some time. Training new employees for a skilled occupation can sometimes take months, and by the time the staff is trained, the problem of filling vacancies may have disappeared.
- Failure the training program to produce graduates that meet the requirements of the organizations particularly where the skills imparted by the training are of a general nature or when focusing some skills over others (generic skills over technical or the opposite), Mitchell and Quirk (2005) observed, the efficiency of the training may not be as expected or not perfect.
- Establishing and operating a training course to bring new employees into an occupation is costly. So, employers must feel confident that they can regain their investment before they are willing to underwrite these costs.
- Training new recruits for occupations with vacancies associated with several risks for employers. The individuals selected may not be able to successfully complete the training course, or if the skills

are transferable to other employers, they may quit shortly after they are trained (Barnow et al., 2010).

### 4.5.7 IMPROVE WORKING CONDITIONS

Improving working conditions is not only an effective way to reduce turnover of current employees but also to attract new workers. Working conditions include some factors such as (Barnow et al., 2010);

- recognition and appreciating the workers' role in the organization,
- ensuring standards of safety factors in work environment,
- social working hours,
- reliable and safe equipment and facilities,
- adequate level and type of supervision,
- involvement degree in operation of the organization, and
- training to deal with stress related to the job.

The adjacent benefit of improving working conditions is that productivity may increase as well. Although, ensuring adequate working conditions is very crucial in order to achieve high performance and reaching the organization's goals, but, still, some employers adopt this strategy only when crisis exists; high turnover is often associated with occupations with bad working conditions, high stress, low wages, or low prestige.

In hospitality industry context, unsocial working hours is the main undesirable feature of working condition. Some occupations may require split shifts (e.g., Hotel front desk employees), night and weekend work (e.g., restaurants and bars), or downtime between productive periods (e.g., housekeepers).

Employers sometimes deal with these crazy working conditions by offering incentives for work at undesirable times, but they often believe they cannot afford a sufficiently high shift differential to eliminate the problem (Barnow et al., 2010).

### 4.5.8 OFFER BONUSES

Although this approach is not commonly used, employers sometimes offer new employees bonuses for joining their organizations, but these bonuses must go only to highly skilled employees. In hard to fill jobs, signing bonuses are similar to paying current employees bonuses for recruiting new employees, except that bonuses go to the new employees rather than the current employees.

Signing bonuses are most frequently used when employers feel that they are under extreme pressure to fill vacancies in the short run. This way is more beneficial for employers than raising wages because it is a one-time cost and only affects the employees added to the occupation of interest. The disadvantage for employers is that the employees enticed by such incentives may not be as interested in long-term careers with the organization, and they may be moving to other organization offering similar bonuses (Barnow et al., 2010).

### 4.5.9 IMPROVE WAGES

The shortage in labor may be unreal if it can be eliminated through raising wages and employers are not willing to increase the pay to eliminate labor shrinking. Improving labor wages is costly and often takes time. The price/wage mechanism is the most determinant factor of the equilibrium of demand and supply of labor market. Therefore, at the current wage level, there will be an imbalance between the supply of and demand for particular skills at any given time and geographical area.

In standard economic theory, a labor shortage is assumed to stimulate an increase in the wage offered by employers, resulting in an increase of supply and a reduction of demand, until equilibrium is restored, and the market clears again (Barnow et al., 2013). However, it is problematic for an organization to pay higher wages to new employees because this would also force the employer to raise the wages of the personnel already employed by the firm. So, employers are generally reluctant to increase wages for several reasons, as follows:

- **First**, an increase in wages will affect the entire workforce in the organization, not just the new workers the organization wishes to attract. Thus, the employer affords costs for more than just the added new workers.
- **Second**, based on the equity factor, increasing wages for the specific type may impose doing the same action for workers in other departments that may do not suffer shortage as well.

  Thus, if the organization increases wages for one occupation because of difficulties in filling vacancies, wages may have to be increased for other occupations as well to maintain what are viewed as proper differentials.

- **Another problem** with raising wages is that wages tend to be "sticky" in terms of moving down. That is, once market conditions change, employers will generally have less flexibility to reduce wages later.
- **Finally**, raising wages might not be an effective way of recruiting in the short run if supply is not responsive to changes in wages (i.e., the supply is inelastic). In the extreme case, if the supply is totally fixed in the short run, higher wages cannot induce any change in the num ber of workers qualified to fill vacancies.

In a highly competitive market with small margins to play with, organizations may initially try to offset shortages through non-wage adjustments because at first increased product demand may be considered temporary. Initially, and in the short term, the organization may rely on the internal labor market for a solution. They include the adjustment to working hours per employee and capital utilization intensity. However, if wages do not adjust, or adjust rather slowly, labor market imbalances are likely to exist. The adjustment of wages as a reason for labor shortage has been confirmed by Junankar (2009) who claimed that the labor market would respond with large increases in wage rates in the standard neoclassical economics.

### *4.5.10 CONTRACT OUT THE REGION*

If the organizations unable to attract all the workers it needs in particular occupations, the employers may be able to contract out the work to another employer who is not experiencing a shortage in workforce. In some instances, the labor problem may be regional in nature, and the firm can contract out the work to a firm in another region of the country (Barnow et al., 2010).

## REFERENCES

Arrow, K. J.; Capron, W. M. Dynamic Shortages and Price Rises: The Engineer-Scientist Case. *Quart. J. Econ.* **1959,** *73* (2), 292–308.

Audretsch, D. B.; Feldman, M. P. Knowledge Spillovers and the Geography of Innovation. In *Handbook of Regional and Urban Economics*; Duranton, J., Henderson, J. V., Strange, W. C., Eds.; Science Direct, Elsevier, Edward Elgar: Cheltenham, UK, 2004; Vol. 4, pp 2713–2739.

Barnow, B. S.; Schede, J.; Trutko, J. W. Occupational Labor Shortages: Concepts, Causes, Consequences, and Cures, Alfred P.; Sloan Foundation, 2010. [Online] http://capitalresearchcorporation.com/assets/pdf/publications/1EJT/1.01EJT/Occupational%20Labo%20Shortages-%20Concepts,%20Causes,%20Consequences,%20and%20Cures-2010-09.pdf (accessed Aug 5, 2017).
Barnow, B. S.; Trutko J.; Piatak, J. S. Conceptual Basis for Identifying and Measuring Occupational Labor Shortages. In *Occupational Labor Shortages: concepts Causes, Consequences, and Cures;* W.E. Upjohn Institute for Employment Research: Kalamazoo, MI, 2013. http://doi.org/10.17848/9780880994132.
Burns, P. Hard-Skills, Soft-Skills: Undervaluing Hospitality Service with a Smile. *Progr. Tour. Hosp. Res.* **1997,** *3* (3), 239–248.
CEDEFOP. Skill Mismatch: More Than Meets the Eye. Briefing Note, 2014.
Dench, S.; Hurstfield, J.; Hill, D.; Akroyd, K. *Employers' Use of Migrant Labor.* Home Office Report: London, 2006.
Ducanes, G.; Abella, M. Labor Shortage Responses in Japan, Korea, Singapore, Hong Kong, and Malaysia: a Review and Evaluation. ILO-EU Asian Programme on the Governance of Labor Migration Working Paper No. 2; ILO: Bangkok; 2008.
Duffy, J.; Papageorgiou, C.; Perez-Sebastian, F. 'Capital-Skill Complementarity? Evidence from Panel of Countries'. *Rev. Econ. Stat.* **2004,** *86* (1), 327–344.
Dulewicz, V.; M. Higgs. Emotional Intelligence: A Review and Evaluation Study. *J. Manag. Psychol.* **2000,** *15* (4), 341–372.
Durbin, S. Workplace Skills, Technology Adoption and Firm Productivity: A Review, New Zealand Treasury Working Paper, 2004.
Estruch-Puertas, E.; Zupi, M. Assessment of Data Sources and Methodology Development for Measuring Foreign Labor Requirements in the Russian Federation. Working Paper; ILO: Geneva; 2009.
Exenberger, A. 'Migration from Africa to Europe in the Age of Globalization'. In *Africa and Fortress Europe. Threats and Opportunities*; Gebrewold, B., Ed.; Ashgate: Hampshire; 2007, pp 107–126.
Forth, J.; Mason, G. Information and Communication Technology (ICT) Skill Gaps and Company-Level Performance: Evidence from the ICT Professionals Survey 2000-2001; National Institute of Economic and Social Research: London. NIESR Discussion, 2004, p 236. [Online] http://www.niesr.ac.uk/pubs/dps/dp236.PDF (accessed Aug 5, 2017).
Gore, T. Extending Hospitality or Solving Employers' Recruitment Problems? Demand-Led Approaches as an Instrument of Labor Market Policy. *Urb. Stud.* **2005,** *42* (2), 341–353.
Gusciute, E.; Quinn, E.; Barrett, A. Determining Labor and Skills Shortages and the Need for Labor Migration in Ireland; The Economic and Social Research Institute: Dublin; 2015. [Online] www.emn.ie (accessed Nov 23, 2017).
Haskel, J.; Martin, C. Technology, Wages, and Skill Shortages: Evidence from UK Micro Data. *Oxford Econ. Papers* **2001,** *53* (4), 642–658.
Healy J.; Mavromaras, K.; Sloane, P. J. Skill Shortages: Prevalence, Causes, Remedies and Consequences for Australian Businesses. Final Report, 2011.
Heijke, H. *Labor Market Information for Educational Investments*; ROA: Maastricht; 1996.
Horbach, J. Determinants of Labor Shortage—with Particular Focus on the German Environmental Sector; IAB-Discussion Paper, Institute for Employment Research, 2014.
ILO. Skills Mismatch in Europe: Statistics Brief. International Labor Office; Department of Statistics: Geneva; 2014.

Junankar, P. N. Was There a Skills Shortage in Australia? Discussion Paper, IZA: Bonn, Germany, 2009.

Kalamazoo; Barnow, B. S.; Trutko, J.; Piatak, J. S., Eds.; Upjohn Institute for Employment Research: MI: W.E.; 2013, pp 1–34.

Kent, M. C. *Knitting with Fog, Assessing Whether the Education System is Meeting the Needs of the Sector*. People 1st: London; 2006.

Kneller, R.; Stevens, P. Frontier Technology and Absorptive Capacity: Evidence from OECD Manufacturing Industries. *Oxford Bull. Econ. Stat.* **2006,** *68* (1), 1–21.

Lucas, R. (2008). Is Low Unionization in the British Hospitality Industry Due to Industry Characteristics? *Int. J. Hosp. Manag.* 2006, *28* (1), 42–52.

Madsen, J. B. The Anatomy of Growth in the OECD Since 1870. *J. Monetary Econ.* **2010,** *57* (6), 753–767.

Mason, G. In Search of High Value-Added Production: How Important are Skills? Investigations in the Plastics Processing, Printing, Logistics and Insurance Industries in the UK; Department for Education and Skills: London; 2005.

Mason, G.; Wilson, R. Employers Skill Survey: New Analyses and Lessons Learned, Report NALL1; Department for Employment and Skills, London, 2003. [Online] http://www.dfes.gov.uk/research/data/uploadfiles/RR663.pdf (accessed Nov 12, 2017).

Mason, G.; Wilson, R. Employers Skill Survey: New Analyses and Lessons Learned, Report NALL1, Department for Employment and Skills: London; 2013.

McMahon, W. M. The Social and External Benefits of Education. In *International Handbook on the Economics of Education*; Johnes, G., Johnes, J., Eds.; Edward Elgar: Cheltenham, 2004.

Mitchell, W.; Quirk, V. Skill Shortages in Australia: Concepts and Reality, Centre of Full Employment and Equity Working, University of Newcastle; 2005, pp 5–16.

Nickson, D. *Human Resource Management for the Hospitality and Tourism Industries*; Oxford: Butterworth-Heinemann, 2007.

Nickson, D.; Warhurst, C.; Dutton, E. The Importance of Attitude and Appearance in the Service Encounter in Retail and Hospitality. *Manag. Serv. Quality* **2005,** *15* (2), 195–208.

OECD. OECD Jobs' Study: Evidence and Explanations; OECD: Paris, 1994.

OECD. Better Skills, Better Jobs, Better Lives: A Strategic Approach to Skills Policies. OECD Publishing: Paris; 2012.

OECD. Demographic Change in the Netherlands: Strategies for Labor Markets in Transition. OECD Local Economic and Employment Development (LEED) Working Paper Series. OECD Publishing: Paris, 2013.

OECD. Employment outlook; OECD: Paris, 2003.

OECD. Labor Shortages and the Need for Immigrants: A Review of Recent Studies. OECD Publishing: Paris, 2003.

OECD. Sickness, Disability and Work, Breaking the Barriers: A Synthesis of Findings across OECD Countries. OECD Publishing: Paris 2010.

People 1st. The Hospitality, Leisure, Travel and Tourism Sector: Key Facts and Figures, 2006a. [Online] http://www.people1st.co.uk/key-facts.html (accessed Oct 20, 2017).

Pratten, J.; O'Leary, B. Addressing the Causes of Chef Shortages in the UK. *J. Eur. Ind. Train.* **2007,** *31* (1), 68–78.

Psacharopoulos, G.; Patrinos, H. Human Capital and Rates of Return. In *International Handbook on the Economics of Education*; Johnes, G., Johnes, J., Eds.; Edward Elgar: Cheltenham, 2004.

Quintini, G. Over-qualified or Under-skilled: A Review of Existing Literature, OECD Social, Employment and Migration Working Papers; OECD Publishing: Paris, 2011; p 121.

Richardson, S. What is a Skill Shortage? National Centre for Vocational Education Research: Adelaide, 2007.

Robinson, R. N.; Barron, P. E. Developing a Framework for Understanding the Impact of Deskilling and Standardization on the Turnover and Attrition of Chefs. *Int. J. Hosp. Manag.* **2007,** *26* (4), 913–926.

Rowley, G.; Purcell, K. As Cooks Go, She Went: Is Labor Churn Inevitable? *Int. J. Hosp. Manag.* **2001,** *20* (2), 163–185.

Roy, R.; Henson, H.; Lavoie, C. *A Primer on Skill Shortages in Canada, R-96-8E, Human Resources Development Canada*; Hull, Canada, 1996.

Shah, C.; Burke, G. Skill Shortages: Concept Measurement and Implications. *Aust. Bull. Labor*, **2005,** *31* (1), 44–71.

Shah, C.; Burke, G. Skill Shortages: Concepts, Measurement and Implications. Monash University, Centre for the Economics of Education and Training, Working Paper: Clayton, 2003; p 52.

Spragg, T. Hospitality Industry Labor Shortage: A Mixed Methods Investigation, College of Business-Business and Hospitality, Oregon State University. [Online] http://osucascades.edu/sites/osucascades.edu/files/research/labor_shortage_tmm.pdf (accessed Oct 5, 2017).

Stevens, P. A. Skill Shortages and Firms' Employment Behavior. *Labor Econ.* **2007,** *14* (2), 231–249.

Strietska-Ilina, O. Skill Shortage, Fourth Report on Vocational Education and Training Research in Europe: Background Report; 2008, 1, p 8.

Varca, P. E. Service Skills for Service Workers: Emotional Intelligence and Beyond. *Manag. Serv. Quality* **2004,** *14* (6), 457–467.

Wang, J. Z.; Wang, J. Issues, Challenges, and Trends, that Facing Hospitality Industry. *Manag. Sci. Eng.* **2009,** *3* (4), 53–58.

World Economic Forum. Matching Skills and Labor Market Needs. Building Social Partnerships for Better Skills and Better Jobs. World Economic Forum Global Agenda Council on Employment, 2014.

Zimmer, H. Labor Market Mismatches. *Economic Review*; National Bank of Belgium: Brussels, 2012; pp 55–68.

# PART II
# Labor Ethics

# CHAPTER 5

# ETHICS IN THE TOURISM AND HOSPITALITY INDUSTRY

*"Failure of Service Process = Unethical Service Provider."*

## 5.1 INTRODUCTION

In such ongoing changing competitive market, tourism and hospitality organizations must come up with ways to stay ahead of their competitors other than the traditional ways. Nowadays, most guests and customers believe that most of services and products are reasonably alike in terms of quality, and service providers are alike in terms of performance. In addition to the flexible strategy of prices that organization may use in stimulating demand, tourism and hospitality experts and managers must develop other strategies to retain a loyal customer or guest. Hospitality and tourism organizations must strive to create collaborative relationships and better partnerships with their guests and consumers. In regard to these relationships, there has been a lot of discussion in the last few years regarding ethical practices and standards prevailing the climate of hospitality and tourism businesses. Finally, it has been supposed that those businesses that do what is ethical and moral to their employees and customers generate benefits (Wallace, 2005), not immediately, it may be long-term benefits.

Today, ethics is among the vital topics (Buff and Yonkers, 2005). The terms "ethics" and "morality" are used interchangeably; both morality and ethics loosely have to do with distinguishing the difference between "good and bad" or "right and wrong." There is a slight difference between ethics and morality; while ethics deals in general with principles of right or wrong conduct, morals refer to what is right and good conduct and character.

Ethics indicate how individuals should behave, as it is based on moral obligation and duties. It distinguishes what is right from what is wrong and promotes individuals to do what is right, it is more concerned with standards of conduct acceptable to a group, a profession, or members of an organization (Sinclair, 1993); so, ethics refers to behavioral rules and standards. They also defined ethics as the philosophical study of morality, and morality consists of beliefs involving right and wrong, good and bad. Also, Noe et al. (2004) adopted the same perspective in defining ethics considering it as the fundamental principles of right and wrong; it is the behavior that is consistent with those principles. Some of the values that define ethical principles include honesty, integrity, trustworthiness, keeping promises, fairness, fidelity, caring for others, accountability, the pursuit of excellence, leadership, responsibility, and respect for others. These values guide us to the origin of the word "ethics;" it stems from the Greek word "ēthos" which means "custom, habit, significance, disposition" (Holjevac, 2008). So, ethics values according to the great philosophers are permanent and should be respected, cultivated, and applied by everyone and everywhere (Holjevac, 2008). In consistent with the obligatory notion of ethics values, Valentine and Barnett (2003) claimed that doing ethics is inevitable, it is not limited to some people and demonstrated in some certain situations (Chapter 6, Ethical Employees); ethics values must be considered not only in ones' lives but also in their work according to the great philosophers.

Holjevac (2008) added that uprightness, wisdom, kindness, and faithfulness belong to the category of permanent values which consist of the real values of today according to Confucius.

According to Oxford Advanced Learner, ethics' definition is "the science which deals with morals." Ethics is the systematic approach of the fundamental principle of the moral law, or as normative science of human morals (Akatan et al., 2008). Based on Akatan et al.'s definition, ethics is a normative science basically, as distinct from the descriptive or empirical sciences. Moral principles that form the subject matter of ethics are about the way people ought to behave in terms of integrity, being self-disciplined and the commitment to their organization and their team. It follows that ethics, primarily is the critical investigation of the norms of conduct to which human attitudes and actions ought to conform.

Many theories have been developed to explain how people behave when faced with ethical situations, whereas ethical theorists created normative perspectives and approaches that prescribed standards of behavior and codes of conduct. More specifically, there are two major approaches to business ethics the descriptive and the normative (Carroll and Buchholtz, 2006; Donaldson et al., 2002):

- Descriptive ethics refers to "what is" the ethical behavior of individuals, organizations, and society.
- Normative ethics defines principles and values that guide behavior and decisions. It is sometimes known as the study of "what should to be."

Generally, all employees involved in working in service sector especially tourism and hospitality industry should possess these values as they are critical in the success of any organization (Stevens and Fleckenstein, 1999), also as these values are part of their work that depends on the first place on the philosophy of care. In line with customers' caring notion, a related term was created—business ethics; Barsh and Lisewski (2008) referred to business ethics as "the systematic process that commercial organizations use in order to evaluate actions as right or wrong." They also suggested that business ethics encompasses a wide range of themes that managers and employees must face.

## 5.2 ETHICS DIMENSIONS

In preparing to write this section of the book, I was convinced that, in order to better understand ethics as an essential component of the human condition, I was compelled to look deeper than the limitations of relations in tourism industry, and deeper still than the conventional material on ethics. My reading led to developing the following conceptualization about what constitute the human ethical conducts and its impacts on the individual's relations, providing a holistic base from which to improve human morality nature.

As a consequence of the maturity of the tourism products and services, the level of competition has increased. According to the latest UNWTO (2017) World Tourism Barometer, international tourism demand remained robust in 2016 despite challenges. International tourist arrivals grew by 3.9% to reach a total of 1235 million; this contributed largely in creating more jobs for the residents.

Every society consists of people who are connected to some common goals and whose activities are regulated so that these objectives are successfully implemented through the institutions of society. The most influential institutions in modern societies are economic institutions. They determine how and who would produce various goods and services, how the jobs would be organized, which resources would be used, and how the products and revenue would be distributed among members of society. The nature of tourism industry is based on the sociality and the interaction of the elements of the experience (stakeholder groups), the intersection of many competing interests shapes the basis for the impacts that we experience in tourism and hospitality industry.

The main groups involved in these interactions include customers, residents of the destination, and the organization employees (see Table 5.1). As a service employee, you may think of customer contacts, for example, as those in which you have to deal with courteous, shy, coward, stingy, negative, rude, angry, complaining, or aggressive people. These contacts range along a series of negative (hostile) to positive (symbiotic) and are specified by time, space, situational factors, resource allocation, and a whole host of other elements. Still, the ethical component is the main common factor that contributes strongly to shape the type of interactions and control its efficiency.

The main issues of business ethics can be classified into three areas: the relationship between business subjects and customers, the relationship between employers and employees, and the nature and value of business organizations and the market (Njegovan, 2009).

The combinations of these interactions are extensive and are affected significantly by ethical behavior, the various cultural backgrounds, and changing values of the stakeholders (staff, customers, and the locals) which mean that perceptions of right and wrong might differ and the right answer is not always obvious.

These are just a few of the types of potential interactions among the industry stakeholders. However, in the field of hospitality, the most important interaction occurs between the customer and employee; hospitality revolves around relationships between two persons, one who requests and expects a high-quality and honest service and the other person is expected to meet that request in a professional manner. From the point of view of customers and guests, the display of attitudes and emotions by service employees is the main part of the service process (Grove et al., 1992). Customers expect certain types of emotions by employees (Tsai and Huang, 2002); when the customers' expectations are met by the behavioral attitudes and performance of the employees, the result is a successful service process and a highly satisfied customer.

From time to time, the employee will also be called upon to help customers who can be described in one or more of the following ways:

- Boorish customers.
- Lack knowledge about your product, service, or policies.
- Dissatisfied with your item.

**TABLE 5.1** The Industry Interactions Combination.

| | |
|---|---|
| **1 The customers' own personal or existential experiences** | |
| **1.1** | Interactions with other customers |
| **1.2** | Interactions with residents of the destination |
| **1.3** | Interactions with tourism employees |
| **2 Destination residents' interactions** | |
| **2.1** | Interactions with tourists |
| **2.2** | Interactions with his community |
| **2.3** | Interactions with tourism employee |
| **3 Employees' interactions** | |
| **3.1** | Interactions with tourists |
| **3.2** | Interactions with coworkers |
| **3.3** | Interactions with residents |

**Source:** The Author.

- Demanding.
- Talkative.
- Internal customers with special requests.
- Speak English as a second language.
- Elderly and need extra assistance.
- Have a disability.

Each of the above categories can be difficult to handle, depending on your knowledge, experience, and abilities, but mainly depending on ethics and morality.

Grandey (2005) claimed that if customers perceive the patience, sincerity, courage, and just behavior of employees, their satisfaction will be significantly higher. Therefore, compared with unethical conducts displays by employees, ethical emotional conducts will easily induce a positive effect on the customers.

So, a key to successfully serving all type of customers is to behave ethically, as follows:

- Treat each person as an individual.
- Avoid stereotyping people according to their behavior.
- Do not mentally classify customers according to the way they speak or act or look—and then treat everyone in a "group" the same way through an ethical frame.

The notion that we cannot always be angelic in our actions, there is a side to human behavior that allows us to be more self-interested, especially in the realm of service sector or perhaps after having spent thousands of dollars on a business. Every organization seeks to have employees work as the first and impressive marketing tool in boosting the image of the organization to others. So, the goal of any organization is to have employees behave in a manner consistent with the organization's mission and goals (aligning absolutely with the core values, adhering to a code of ethics, and matching actions with beliefs across a variety of situations) (Pattison and Edgar, 2011).

Here are the four main components of ethics that should be the characteristics of every person involved in the service sector, especially those employees who are having a direct contact with guests and customers.

### 5.2.1 PATIENCE

Patience means being patient and forgiving about the other person's follies, mistakes, and shortcomings. Patience is required to deal with all differences and incompatibilities in the life. Patience is a skill an employee in the service sector needs if a successful contact with customers and guests is required. Patience is a key element of success in the workplace. In order to deal with any situation that does not work out in your favor and therefore elicits strong feelings, patience is strongly required.

In the field of hospitality industry, employees may face unpleasant working conditions that require patience; they may have needed to work some extra hours due to urgency of some matters or may get stuck in a situation which causes the impulse to react quickly such as allotting to accomplish some tasks at the eleventh hour for certain urgent reasons. In such cases and especially when getting in contact with the customers, patience is highly treasured; when patience between parties no longer exists, things are said or actions are taken that are often regretted later. Due to emotions, these actions frequently destroy the relationships. The results are dissatisfied customers, upset work teams, and the expected profits going down the drain. In this situation, the business loses customers, lose referral opportunities, and lose money. So, a significant part of maintaining a successful relationship during customers' encounter is patience.

In general, work includes many problems whether it is related to working conditions or coworkers and supervisors or even the customers. However, if you embrace such situations and treat them patiently, you can create a good image for your organization in your customers' mind and also create a good image for yourself in your superiors and coworkers' mind. It causes you to gain their trust. If you gain the trust of your customers and managers alike, the chances of organizational growth are very positive.

### *5.2.2 SINCERITY*

Sincerity in dealing with customers is about providing product and/or services that reflect care, consideration, genuineness, and respect for customers. All these attributes would then reflect the culture and values of employees and then the organization, enabling it to gain more business from existing customers and guests and keeping their loyalty, stimulating new customers, and enhancing its market reputation in an unprecedented manner. Sincerity in customer service, therefore, would be the catalyst and stimulator for business excellence and prosperity.

### *5.2.3 COURAGE*

Courage is the will to take action in the face of fear. In order to make improvement in the organizations, courage must be enhanced; employees must be supported to share their true thoughts and feelings about their work and the organization to modify torsion and correcting mistakes subsequently improving the organizations' performance. This means that you have a genuine concern for the development of business potential with an appreciation for the interconnection of all living things.

On the other hand, if they do not share honestly, it is difficult to make improvements. A lack of courage can afflict anyone at work. Lack of courage can be the consequences of the following issues:

- Fear of loss outweighs the potential gains (employees may feel they have nothing to gain by providing thoughtful, honest answers).
- Embarrassing of speaking up in front of others.
- Punitive actions of managers to opinions that criticize his decisions.

Courage is usually classified based on the type of threat(s) faced:

- physical (risks and hazards related work conditions),
- moral (disapproval, opposition, or condemnation to stand up for what is right or ethical), and

– psychological (inner fears and struggles for personal gains or battling personal doubts).

However, some studies suggested that researchers classify courage based on the contexts and meaningful roles in one's life rather than solely on the type of threat or risks. Specifically, courage is categorized as (Wan, 2017)

1. work/employment courage,
2. patriotic, religion, or belief-based physical courage,
3. social–moral courage, and
4. family-based courage.

In general, courage is critical to everyone life's success. Employees must have courage so that they can look back on their career without the "what if's." Real courage is the difference maker.

### *5.2.4 JUSTICE*

Organizational justice can be defined as the role of fairness in organizations and is closely related to employees' perceptions of fair treatment in the organization (Costello and Hogan, 2002) and customers' perception of fair purchasing experience. High positive outcomes the organization will gain in case organizational justice is adopted; when employees are treated fairly, their productivity is expected to increase. At the same time, when customers perceive service justice, or that their service providers are being fair to them, positive outcomes are likely to occur. Organizational justice may be generally categorized into three subdimensions:

a. distributive justice,
b. procedural justice, and
c. interactional justice.

Although little research has examined how employees and customers of hospitality organizations form opinions about whether or not their company is just, justice requires the quite straightforwardness.

– In case of an employee is denied a promotion, the justice requires the manager to clearly explain the plentiful reasons for why it could not happen. The employee therefore has the basic background information needed to determine if the manager and organization were being fair or not.

– At the same time, if a hotel's guest claimed that he was denied extra amenities or special offers, the service providers must clearly explain the plentiful reasons for why it could not happen. The guest therefore has the basic background information needed to determine if the employee and the hotel were being fair.

There is a meaningful relationship between the theory of organizational justice and the organization development (Kong et al., 2010, 2011).

Establishing high ethical standards and keeping good principles within the tourist organizations can attract and retain both the best customers and employees. Employees attitudes that is based on the previous-mentioned ethics pillars will result in displaying high ethical conducts such as cooperation, honesty, respecting others, and value diversity that will in turn lead to generating a high-quality performance, high-quality work environment, and will reflect on the customers' satisfaction. Figure 5.1 combines the pillars of ethical conducts and the impacts.

Organizations having employees with good ethics will have a solid work ethics that are characterized by the following characteristics.

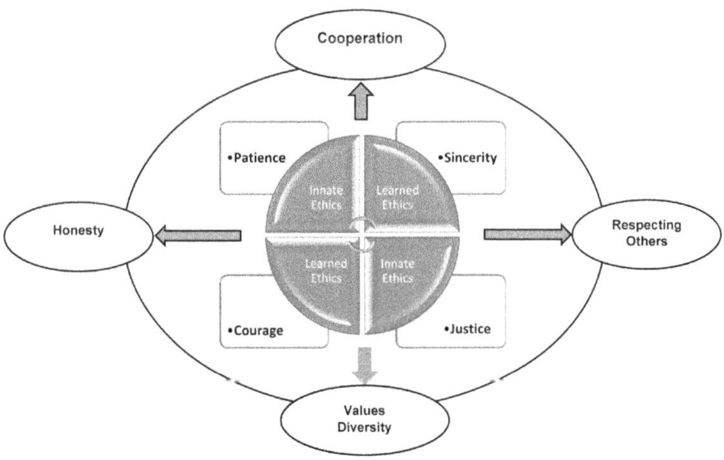


**FIGURE 5.1** Ethics conducts pillars.

**Source:** The Author.

### 5.2.5 HONESTY

Employees with strong ethics help greatly the organization to avoid work troubles that hinder the streaming of business, honesty of employees can prevent the following issues to creep into the workplace environment:

- stealing guests' property,
- stealing employees' property,
- sabotaging a coworker's section, and
- taking someone's idea to gain applause or compensation.

Highly ethical employees can keep and guard others' properties; employees with strong ethics refrain from lying or cheating to make others look bad in the hopes of making themselves appear smarter. In addition, they take responsibility for mistakes, admit failures, and keep the lines of communication open with everyone involved. Moreover, they enhance the success and reputation of their work.

### 5.2.6 VALUES DIVERSITY

Employees with strong ethics not only understand the importance of a diverse workplace but also work for improving the work team's performance. They value everybody's contributions—regardless of race, ability, age, gender, and this allows for more creativity and better problem-solving. Diversity in the workplace contributes to successful customers interactions.

### 5.2.7 RESPECTING OTHERS

An employee with a strong work ethic is conscientious of people's feelings and considerate of workers in a shared workspace. They rarely ineffective, they respect everyone's time, from coworkers to customers.

High ethics grant the employees success in their work and out of work environment; in the sector of service, someone with a strong work ethic can manage customer encounters wisely, uses time perfectly so that deadlines are met. Out of work environment, will keep personal relations successful and not harm others.

### *5.2.8 COOPERATION*

Having a good work ethic means the employees cooperate with each other. In case of stressful and unsatisfying or unenjoyable work, they will do what is necessary for the team and the organization instead of debating every issue and finding reasons why things cannot get done. They see the bigger picture and in turn, use strong conflict resolution skills to solve problems and manage the workload.

Professional attitudes and quality services offered by these highly moral practitioners and employees will subsequently build the customer' confidence in the organization and keep them coming in and returning back to the destination. Such an investment can ultimately contribute to better financial performance in the companies and benefit the tourism and hospitality industry as a whole and the economy in the long run (Carroll and Buchholtz, 2006).

## 5.3 BUSINESS ETHICS

Business organization consists of a group of people who are connected to some common goals, for the sake of achieving these goals, their activities must be regulated through the organizational rules and standards. According to Githui (2011), the most successful organizations are those which determine the following three major issues that control their business ethics:

1. how the jobs would be organized,
2. who would produce goods and services, and
3. which resources would be used.

In fact, the subject of business ethics is just the average, which is obtained by combining the labor moral and ethics and economic aspects of the business (Rosnana et al., 2013); so, work environment ethics represent a field of two different approaches:

1. personnel ethics and morality and
2. business/institution or economic ethics and rules perspective (Babin et al., 2000).

The ethical perspective, related to the labor personality, is based on moral values: patience, sincerity, courage, justice, honesty, dependability, rights, and duties, which can be characterized as good or morally right.

The institutions or business ethics is a form of applied ethics or professional ethics that examines ethical principles and moral or ethical problems that arise in a business environment. It related to the business rules, procedures, and quality. So, cost, price, profit, benefit, efficiency, and competition are the business perspective. Also, the restricted specifications of the product that determined in the business contract with guests or customers are considered a foundation of business ethics. Barsh and Lisewski (2008) referred to business ethics as "the systematic process that commercial organizations use to evaluate actions as right or wrong;" they also suggested that business ethics includes a wide range of themes and perspectives that managers and employees must face.

It is a well-known fact that business owners and managers should be aware of the corruption temptations faced by all levels of labor members and various stakeholders and must be vigilant to prevent any malpractices or corruption to take root. A single unethical situation or incident of corruption could ruin the hard-earned reputation and would be a heavy cost for the Industry to bear (Barsky and Nash, 2004). It would result in the loss of an organization's business and profits, loss of competitiveness in the industry, loss of jobs in the workforce, loss of trust by customers and loss of image for destinations (Beck et al., 2007).

Hall (1992) proposed that the proper application of ethics can change the workplace average to an excellent one (cited in Mathenge, 2013). However, it is noted that different tourism industry-related stakeholder groups may have vastly different perceptions of the importance of ethics in tourism and hospitality industry. Perhaps, the academics are perceived as being too idealistic and moralistic, while organization managers have the perception that an ethical approach will be bad for business in terms of cost. Some organizations view ethics as a constraint on their profitability, they consider that profits and ethics are inversely proportional. This may be true on the short term but on the long term, the hotel will be compensated for the money invested through the profits generated through increased employee morale and productivity (Pettijohn et al., 2008); high-organizational ethical standards and practices significantly minimize the cost of business transactions, establish customer loyalty, create trust with suppliers, maintain social capital, and successful team of employees. Hence, short-term expenses are justified by the positive long-term benefits of operating as an ethical organization.

Other than the increased productivity, code of conducts, and ethical practices are urgently needed to be adopted in tourism and hospitality organizations in order to keep fighting in such a competitive environment (Grynko, 2012), they need to develop ethical standards such as a protected environment, meeting customer demand, enhancing industry efforts and image, and assuring product quality. Such ethical standards and practices reputation in any business activity represent a competitive advantage.

Human is ethical animals; we sometimes fail to manage or behave properly, and we have a tendency to tell each other what they should do and to grade, evaluate, and compare (Bhatia, 2003). So, the public and private stakeholders of tourism and hospitality industry should cooperate in the implementation of ethical and moral principles and evaluate as well as monitor their impacts and effective application in their organizations. Tourism and hospitality-related stakeholders should consciously promote responsible business and ethical values common and/or acceptable to the customers and to the extent that is harmonious to their needs. The organizational codes state that "the members are obliged to practice good business principles and to promote ethical corporate principles" (Githui, 2012). According to ethical principles, the employees are requested "to avoid of any act or conduct felt to be offensive or injurious to the guests and customers, or likely to damage the local environment (Githui, 2012).

Although tourism studies researchers were largely inactive in the area of ethics in the late of 19th century (Fennell, 2006), there was a remarkable recognition of the importance of ethics in tourism (Holjevac, 2008).

Three events were seen to be instrumental in the development of an interest in tourism studies and ethics during the 1990s.

- The AIEST Congress in Paris (1992), which proposed the creation of a commission to deal with the ethical issues in tourism industry (Fennell, 2006; Pizam and Thornburg, 2000).
- The Rio Earth Summit of 1992, whose attendees committed themselves to Agenda 21. Chapter 30 of this plan is as follows:
  Business and industry, including transnational corporations, should be encouraged to adopt and report on the implementation of codes of conduct promoting best environmental practice, such as the International Chamber of Commerce's Business Charter on Sustainable Development and the chemical industry's responsible care initiative (Grynko, 2012).
- The internet conference in 1998 on tourism which identified key ethical issues facing the industry, from the ethics of destination promotion to cultural, religious, and environmental sustainability (Fennell, 2006).

- In October 1999, the General Assembly of the World Tourism Organization (WTO) in Santiago, Chile adopted the Global Code of Ethics for Tourism. The content of this international code which is binding to all WTO member states was systematized in the following 10 points (Jovičić et al., 2011):
  - Tourism's contribution to mutual understanding and respect among people and societies.
  - Tourism as means for individual and collective fulfillment.
  - Tourism, a factor of sustainable development.
  - Tourism—user of the cultural heritage of mankind and a factor of its improvement.
  - Tourism—a beneficial activity for countries, communities, and hosts.
  - Obligations of independent travel professionals responsible for development.
  - Right to tourism.
  - Liberty of tourist movements.
  - The rights of employees and entrepreneurs in the tourism industry.
  - Implementation of the Global Code of Ethics for Tourism.

In general, the key issue identified at and since that time has been how the negative impacts of the tourism industry might be decreased or mitigated and addressed by those engaged (tourists, students, employees, and stakeholders) in the industry. as tourism is not just an economic business or a series of activities which can be isolated from everyday employees' life or from their impact on people, as the vital fact that we travel to another culture and get involved into direct contact with the people raises a number of ethical issues.

Business ethics has always been heavily influenced by community and the work environment in which it flourished, the society, with its organizations, institutions, culture, habits, and values, has created an appropriate legal and behavioral environment that influence ethics in business. Business ethics is also influenced by personnel's conduct, which is again a product of community and social relations within which the moral opinion of persons is shaped in relation to what is good and right and what is not (Barsh and Lisewski, 2008). Thus, all stakeholders in these sectors as such are beings capable of actions that affect the ethical environment; the industry' stakeholders just need unity of purpose and a plan of action so that they can pave way for further penetrations and win the hearts of tourists, employees, and the locals (Githui, 2012). Managers should make their best to lead by example and put ethics into practice, as they have a critical role in the mitigation hoped for above.

## 5.4 THE PURPOSE OF BUSINESS ETHICS

Although ethics is considered an uncomfortable and disturbing issue as it focuses on direct our behavior, handling our attitudes, and controls our habits, it invades our behavioral tendencies, because people generally are uneasy with being told what to do. Because of this, there are few who are sensitive to the moral or ethical environment, namely the climate of ideas about how to live a good life (Bhatia, 2003).

Hence, the main question that its answer serves the purpose of this section is: Can the tourism and hospitality industry professionals avoid ethics, turn a blind eye, and reject to listen to the so-called fun police? The answer is no, actually there are three main reasons:

1. Ethics is a fundamental aspect of living as a social being, it is an integral part of social life. All humans engage, wittingly or not, in debates about what they consider to be right or wrong, who is right, and who has been wronged and all human societies have moral principles and codes which guide social life. In an increasingly competitive world, it becomes even more imperative that service providers are equipped to deal all groups of customers or guests.
2. The cost of running businesses in a corrupted environment is much higher than in environment with high integrity (Phau and Kea, 2007). As cited in Lim (2003), PricewaterhouseCoopers estimated the cost of corruption in 35 emerging and developing countries amount to as much as $500 billion between 1997 and 1998. Therefore, a work ethic, especially a positive work ethic, is important from a business perspective for the success of business because of the confidence it plants in guests and customers. The positive attitude and dedication to a customer's needs or creation of a product can boost the business' reputation as an organization that deals honestly and fairly. Ethics also work to build a moral compass within a business and helps discourage attitudes and business models that seek to cut corners in the name of making a profit.
3. The new civilizations consequences, such as conflicts of interest and the growing conflict in economics and business, cultural clashes and

contacts, and changes in communications and information technologies, ideologies conflicting and expressed political conflicts about world domination may lead to general decline in moral values and standards.

These reasons may arouse inevitable necessity about morality and ethics in business, the direct practice of business-ethical conduct (Carroll and Buchholtz, 2006). Hospitality managers' ethical perceptions often change and are complicated by certain factors such as demographic structure, religion, values, customs, manners, family, and culture (Peceri, 2010). So, ethical principles and rules were written in form of codes to guide behavior. Codes of ethics, codes of conduct, or codes of behavior are designed to anticipate and prevent certain specific types of behavior, for example, inappropriate actions, conflict of interest, self-dealing, and bribery. Any final analysis of the impact of a code must include how well it affects behavior. Contemporary social psychological research also strongly suggests that codes can guide or induce behaviors especially in developing countries that are critical to a functioning public service (White, 1999).

## 5.5 ETHICS IN TOURISM AND HOSPITALITY INDUSTRY

The subject of ethics is based on the moral rules of conduct in all business activities directed toward a successful and profitable business operation. According to Buff and Yonkers (2005), these standards are based on fundamental ethical principles and their content is expressed by the judgments of the wrong and right, good and bad, successful and unsuccessful business behavior. Heimler (2010, p 37) defined work ethic as an individual's disposition toward work and includes attendance, punctuality, motivation, the ability to meet deadlines, patience, attitude, and dependability. Therefore, the goal is to oblige all participants in the overall business processes on ethical behavior.

### *5.5.1 ETHICS IN TOURISM INDUSTRY*

Being tourism is the world's largest industry, tourism involves a wide range of activities that implies various practices in which the key values and drivers of globalization are demonstrated.

The globalization consequences and the modernity provoked the issues of ethical practices in the industry. By its nature, the tourism industry places customers and employees in tempting situations that contain abuse transactions and practices (Forster and Hegarty, 2009). Subsequently, there is a growing concern for business ethics in tourism and hospitality industry as professionals and managers are faced daily with ethical issues. Complex and interesting ethical issues influence this broad industry whose business ranges from restaurant operations to tourism-based businesses.

The origin of ethics in tourism industry appears to have developed because the nature of the tourism product that depends on environmental and cultural resources largely. Tourism industry involves activities that are continuously interacting with the natural systems (Costello and Hogan, 2002). Subsequently, this dependence and interaction cause unpleasant results for both the locals and their environment. Residents of the destinations may experience some of the negative consequence of tourism development occurring in their area, however, they also suffer of other consequences, as follows:

- *Erasing the cultural identity*: Tourism activities involve both direct and indirect contacts between local residents and tourists; such contacts affect the culture of the host communities because of the arising conflicts of values stemming from the invading of new culture and lifestyle to their community.
- *Displacing of community residents*: The expansions of tourism projects especially in scenic and secluded areas lead to displacing people as a result of the economic purposes.
- *Overuse of community resources*: Although the economic earnings of tourism such as jobs creation and invigorating the treasure of the involved stakeholders, it brings many negative consequences to the community, as follows:
    - increasing the demand on the raw materials necessary for operations of food outlets and accommodation establishments influence negatively on the prices,
    - the pressure on the public services (transportations, hospitals, etc.) affect the normality of locals' lives, and
    - organic and solid wastes produced by the hospitality organizations may contribute to environmental pollution and in turn on the quality of local's life.

- *Environmental impacts*: The aggressive use of natural resources stemming from clearance of various natural areas for the purpose of developing hotels and resorts. Tourist transportation and kitchens and laundries of hospitality establishments that use fossil fuels release a considerable amount of air pollutants and other greenhouse gasses. In addition to producing large quantities of solid wastes that contribute to environmental pollution.

As a result of these numerous ethical issues, the importance of applied ethics in the service industry in the last two decades has grown. There has been a global acknowledgment of the need to think about the concept of sustainable or responsible tourism as an effort to control the unfavorable impacts of the industry. Sustainable tourism has dual concerns; it is that form of tourism that creates better conditions for the local community to live and unique places for tourists to visit.

This form of tourism broadens the concept of sustainable or ecotourism to include environmental, ethical, and social considerations. The responsible tourism is defined according to World Tourism Organization (2002) as the form of tourism that relates all types of tourism with respect to the cultural and natural dimensions of the host destinations and the interests of all the involved parties.

This form of tourism creates more economic benefits for the host communities and improving the overall interests of the destination, and before of all, it reduces harmful environmental, social as well as economic impacts. Many countries such as India, Gambia, Sri Lanka, America, and United Kingdom as well as tourism organizations are by now practicing this form of tourism.

The ethics of any business whether it is a manufacturing or service is based on respect for the others' rights and interests and achieving successful interactions and quality working environment where business success, competitiveness, and profits do not depend on anything else other than the rights and duties that are applied in decision-making (Buff and Yonkers, 2005; Beck et al., 2007).

### *5.5.2 ETHICS IN HOSPITALITY INDUSTRY*

The intensity of hospitality industry business provoked a debate over the ethical issues in the hospitality businesses that range from restaurant operations to tourism-based businesses. There is a growing concern for business ethics in the hospitality industry as hospitality managers are faced with ethical dilemmas in their daily operations. By virtue of its nature, the hospitality industry places both customers and employees in tempting situations that may stimulate abuse. Ethical issues in hospitality industry reflect the challenges that happen in a cash-based, people-intensive industry. Managers today are suffering from the following ethical issues (Stevens, 2011):

- cash-transaction errors (theft, embezzlement, etc.),
- food-and-beverage pilfering,
- food mishandling,
- disappearing inventory, and
- unreported sales.

In addition, diversity issues, honesty, fairness, integrity, and good service all concern the hospitality professionals, who often seek to make a balancing act with competing values.

One of unethical problem that is very common in hospitality operations is theft. Theft and fraud actions are confirmed by Stevens (2011) as a key concern. Hospitality managers considered theft as both an issue at their own hotel and an industry problem; they had experienced both small and large thefts. In Stevens' (2001) study of hospitality ethical issues, theft was mentioned by hospitality human-resources managers as an ongoing problem. Opportunities to steal arise in several occasions mainly because of the widespread cash transactions and the industry's vulnerability to dishonesty practices. It was reported that 44% of restaurant employees and workers had stolen cash or merchandise from their organizations (Withiam in Stevens, 2011). In 2008, another study indicated that 1 out of 30 employees in the restaurants and food industry was caught stealing from his or her employer (Retail, Restaurants and Food Service, 2009). According to Crowell (2008), thefts from loading docks areas whether it is of a hotel or a catering company are especially common these days, as items are taken before they reach their destinations. Inside thefts in hospitality industry were also recorded as quite common incidents. For example, the financial controller of the Stafford Hotel, in London, was imprisoned after embezzling more than $500,000 to pay for his gambling debts (Stafford Hotels, 2009). In the United States, the average loss due to embezzlement is $385,000, and it takes 4.5 years to uncover (Stevens, 2011). Also, measly theft was recorded in hospitality organizations as frequented incidents, according to The Kroll Global Fraud Report (2017), toilet amenities, lamps, and TV are reported disappeared frequently, also, a manager lost several thousand dollars from a safe when two trusted employees did not follow protocols for placing money in the safe. One of them likely took the money, but the manager could not determine which one. Stevens (2011) also reported that managers mentioned problems with debit cards. Payment made with debit cards sometimes involve a "hold" or claim on several hundred dollars. The problem occurs when the debit-card company continues the hold on the cash for several days and the guests or customers leave the hotel. Generally, ethical violations are not new incidents; many have been taking place for a long time also. For instance, in 1898, Caesar Ritz and his Auguste Escoffier manager and chef, respectively, were discharged from London's Savoy Hotel for accepting less weighing raw materials deliveries and extorting commissions from suppliers thereby using the hotel for their own gain and profit (Fennell and Malloy, 2008; Forster and Hegarty, 2009).

The Kroll Global Fraud Report (2017) confirmed that junior employees in leisure and tourism segments of the industry are the most common perpetrators of fraud (45%) followed by ex-employees (33%) and senior and middle management (30%). Even managers themselves are not above reproach when it relates to ethical standards (Walsh and Swinfold, 2006); they indicated that reporters from the *London Times* captured fake online hotel reviews written by the owners and managers of the company in Scotland and Britain. Although they were caught guilty, they claimed that they have done nothing unethical. Additionally, another lawsuit filed against Hilton Hotels by Starwood Hotels and Resorts claimed corporate espionage and theft of business secrets. Hilton hired the former president of Starwood luxury brands, and the Starwood suit alleges that the executive took confidential information with him, allowing Hilton to develop its accommodation properties brand very quickly by using millions of dollars' worth of Starwood's research (Freed, 2009).

Figure 5.2 shows the most ethical challenges that face the hospitality industry (fraud and theft), and also list of perpetrators type involved in these dirty actions in descending way according to the frequency and the impact of the incident.

Therefore, it is notoriously noted in the field of the hospitality industry that dishonesty of all sorts (fraud, bribery, embezzlement, theft, etc.) is existing especially by part-time, underpaid employees.

Long working hours always associated with part-time employees put them in seductive opportunities where frequent cash transactions and events are unpredictable. To be fair, not only the craft and operational level of workers and employees who are involved in such humiliated, unethical actions but also managers and seniors got stuck in unethical actions.

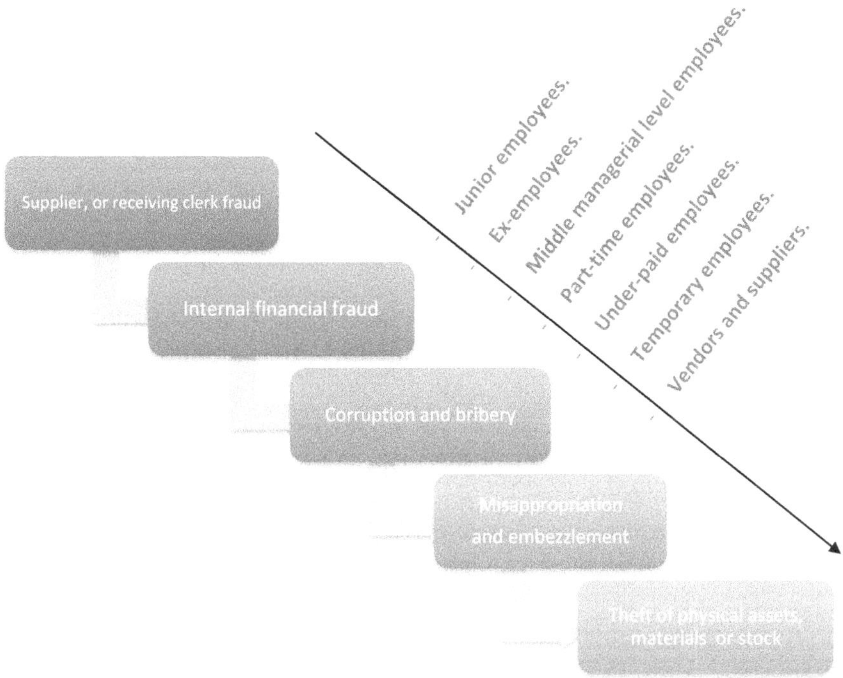


**FIGURE 5.2** Theft and fraud issues in hospitality industry.

**Source:** The Author.

Whitney (1990) showed that hospitality industry employees in a big need for a higher ethical consciousness compared to other industries, as well as a stronger ability to judge ethical issues according to the principles of the organization. Unlike other industries, hospitality is very diverse. It involves employees and managers from every racial, educational, cultural, social, age, sex, and religious background. Moreover, Hall (1992) mentioned that hospitality professionals need an international understanding of what is right and wrong and what is good and bad because hospitality embraces a large spectrum of beliefs and ethically acceptable behavior.

However, measuring the business ethics of hospitality industry is very challenging and complicated. In order to do so, many researchers measure the ethical climate of an organization, as it helps them to better understand the levels of business ethics which make them aware of their position and what they need to establish. Githui (2012) asserted the importance of engrained ethical values in motivating employees and workers in all sectors of business. Laufer and Robertson (1997) claimed that adopting ethical standards helps individuals recognize their organization fit. Other studies showed that adopting ethical values influences employee's affections for that organization. On the other hand, Fox (2000) through his study on hospitality employees confirmed that unethical climate lead to additional organizational costs.

#### 5.5.2.1 HOSPITALITY INDUSTRY ETHICAL CASES

Although most of the European hotels understand what is responsible and ethical and have publicized their code of ethics, these organizations are still below average in fulfilling their code of conduct and responsibilities to the public in the last few years. According to Patterson (2008), there have been an increasing number of ethical lawsuits against some of the hospitality organizations in Europe.

Miss Walton's story is a good example of hospitality industry ethical cases. Miss Walton worked as a housekeeper at The Nottingham Gateway Hotel. She worked for more than 13 h for 3 days as a housekeeper. Because of her pregnancy, she asked her supervisor for 3 days off, after the off, she was not allocated work. In front of the tribunal, the supervisor of Miss Walton claimed that there was no work, but another employee had been allocated the work. The tribunal found out that Miss Walton was treated unfairly because of her condition (Dozier, 2013).

Another example of unethical issues occurring in hospitality organizations is the discriminative practices. This case is classified as ageism case. Mr. Dell'Osa is the victim; a 69-year-old waiter, who was dismissed in 2009. The management of Money Island Hotel justified the decision that she is too old to be a waiter and was soon replaced by a younger waiter (Hall, 2000).

Such unethical practices not only ruin the name of the organizations but also have a huge cost involved. So, in the current competitive environment, initiating and implementing ethical practices are very important. Vitell and Hidalgo (2006) argued that there is a great relationship between ethical behavior and job satisfaction and career success. Koh and Boo's (2001) study of MBA students in Singapore showed that there is a strong association between organizational ethics and job satisfaction. In alignment with Koh and Boo (2001), Schwepker (2001) in his study on salespeople also demonstrated a significant relationship between ethical climate in an organization and job satisfaction. Out of tourism and hospitality context, a study of Joseph and Deshpande (1997) on nurses revealed that ethical environment is significantly associated with job satisfaction.

Hence, organizational ethics is one of the means through which managers can generate favorable job attitudes and behaviors and organizational outcomes. Therefore, the need for hotels to foster and promote an ethical working environment is more important than ever before. Studies have revealed that hospitality industry employees require a higher ethical perception than other industries and a stronger capacity to judge ethical issues as per the policies of the organization. So, Yang (2008) asserted the need for defining job-related ethical standard for hospitality employees.

## 5.6 EMPLOYEES AND ETHICS

Hospitality revolves around relationships between two persons one who requests and expects a high quality and honest service and the other person is expected to meet that request in a professional manner, that is, the professionalism in performing tasks and duties.

Undoubtedly, unethical practices not only undermine the image of the organization, they also destroy the business; when an unethical climate prevails the organization, disastrous consequences strike the business where the value and quality of goods and services produced by these organizations decline; makes a negative impression on customers; depicts an unattractive organization image for skilled employees, suppliers, and caterers; cause the enterprise to be blacklisted by the government; and makes the organization an easy prey for criticism in the media.

These consequences can occur as a result of one of the following actions (Yücel and Çiftci, 2012):

- Unfair treatment to employees.
- Ignoring customers' complaints.
- Insensitivity to the organizational business environment.
- Conducting misleading promotions and advertisements.

Thus, the views of hospitality organizations' professionals and managers on ethical issues occurring in the industry are very important, they are challenged each day to take such following decisions (Sims and Gegez, 2004):

- ensuring solving customers and guests' issues,
- ensuring the safety of its employees (arranging the business environment in accordance with health regulations),
- ensuring employee's problems (make hard decisions that may favor one group of employees over another),

- conducting a satisfactory remuneration and a merit-based selection and promotion policy,
- being tolerant of union activities,
- not monitoring the employees discreetly,
- refraining from emotional abuse directed toward employees' professional competence and reliability,
- disallowing racial and gender discrimination (not exploiting the labor of women and children, preventing acts of sexual harassment in the workplace), and
- providing social rights.

Such ethical decisions are among the main conditions of reliability and productivity of the organizations. Studies in the area of ethical behaviors (Harris, 1990; Yücel and Çiftci, 2012) suggested that attitudes toward business ethics are shaped by cultural differences as well as demographic characteristics. Other studies (Blanchard and Hodges, 2003; Arnould et al., 2004) confirmed that religion has a significant role in shaping human perception and attitudes toward ethical behavior. Basically, Relativism Theory suggested that ethical action and conducts are based on whether it is tolerated and sanctioned by the individual's family, culture, or tradition.

Here are some factors that shape the individuals' ethical actions and conducts.

### 5.6.1 EDUCATION LEVEL

In terms of business ethics, there has been a significant difference between less educated employees and higher educated employees (Giacalone, 2004), less educated employees were found to be less ethical.

In a study conducted by Kraft and Singhapakdi (1991), they compare the perception of ethics of undergraduate and postgraduate students. These students were given a situation in which they evaluate a supervisor who behaves unethically in order to maximize the outcomes; they found that the undergraduate students viewed the act as more ethical in case an increase in production happened, while postgraduate students, regarded the act as immoral even if the production was increased. It appears that the graduate students viewed the morality of the supervisor as fewer dependents on the outcome than did the undergraduates.

Crisis situation or cases that the business face a decline in profits also shows the significant differences between the behavior of more educated staff and others, it was found that employees having a high level of education tend to be less willing to engage in unethical situations. Unlike the majority of less educated employees, they may find an unethical attitude more than acceptable in certain situations (Kraft and Singhapakdi, 1991).

By looking at the literature, one can reach the conclusion that "education" makes a positive influence in business ethics attitudes and behavior. An increase in the level of education positively affects ethical business conduct.

### *5.6.2 GENDER*

Investigations of gender differences in ethics and morality have yielded conflicting debates; in a review completed by Ford and Richardson in Kum-Lung (2010) shows that out of 14 studies comparing males and females in terms of their ethical behavior, the results of 7 studies supported females being more ethical than males. The remaining seven studies found no significant difference between females and males in terms of their ethical behavior. However, as cited in Kum-Lung (2010), Borkowski and Ugras conducted meta-analysis on 47 studies. Their finding revealed that there are 49% of studies that yielded significant differences between females and males in terms of ethical behavior, 34% not significant, and 17% mixed results.

Hence, there are two strong sides debating about this relationship; it was claimed by Ergeneli and Arikan (2002) and McCuddy and Perry (1996) that there is no significant effect on ethical perceptions between males and females, while Gilligan (1982) asserted that there are contrasting differences between males and females with respect to their morality. In his study performed on business students from a public university, Harris (1990) claimed that females are less tolerant than males on unethical behavior. He relates this gender difference to the different ethical frameworks used by females and males.

Adebayo (2005) confirmed that the ethical reference point chosen by each gender is based on the differences in the socialization techniques instilled throughout their developmental stages in life.

So, the literature indicates that females are socialized to show not only compassion, but to be caring, while males are described as being more competitive and justice-oriented (Devonish et al., 2009; Sidani et al., 2009), which may have arisen due to the early socialization process (Gilligan, 1982). Consequently, females tend to be more friendly, gentle, and unselfish, and thus their perception is focused on caring or maintaining relations—usually for their mothers—and subsequently their new family (children); for example, Peterson et al. (2001) argued that women are assumed to view ethical dilemmas in terms of understanding relationships, responsibilities, and compassion for others. These features make them socialized and be ethically more sensitive (Bass et al., 1998). On the other hand, it is assumed that men learn to resolve ethical problems in terms of rules, rights, fairness, and justice. So, men are generally seen to be independent, assertive, and aggressive in their perceived automatic obligations of financially providing. Thus, males have been found to possess a stronger ethical view in issues relating to duty and justice but may ignore laws when placed in a situation where there is a choice between adhering to ethical conduct and the pursuit of wealth or self-interest goals, regardless of costs.

### *5.6.3 AGE*

Another key affecting on ethical behavior is age (Emerson et al., 2007). Certainly, with age, individuals get more experiences, and wisdom, so their perceptions of what is right and wrong are developed. Borkowski and Ugras (1998) found that ethical conducts seem to change with age. It was found that individuals' behavior and attitude tended to be more ethical with age (Emerson et al., 2007). Borkowski and Ugras (1998) concluded that 13 studies showed that older students responded more ethically than the younger students. Other empirical evidence shows that moral reasoning increases with age may be an important factor in moral judgment development (Dellaportas, 2006; Abdolmohammadi and Reeves, 2000). However, Rest and Narvaez (1994) found unusual gains in moral judgment with age, also it was claimed by Borkowski and Ugras (1998) that 2 studies of 15 showed that younger students were more ethical. The study found that fresher and juniors are more justice-oriented than MBAs; the MBAs tended to be more utilitarian in their approach to ethical dilemmas, but typically the review of the literature using university students generally find limited or no evidence in age differences (Rogers and Smith, 2001). So, age is a significant variable in the study of ethics.

### *5.6.4 RELIGIOSITY*

From a religious standpoint, the divinity's laws are absolutes and shape the whole of an individual's life. So, religion plays a significant ethical role in contemporary life; Hoffman and Moore (1988) asserted that religion is a strong determinant of values than any other predictor.

Religiosity is defined as "the extent to which an individual is committed to teachings of religion" (Johnson et al., 2001), this commitment must be reflected in individual's attitudes and behaviors (Weaver and Agle, 2002). Foxall and Goldsmith (1994) asserted that religious beliefs are intertwined with cognitive components to form the basis of knowledge that justifies and control attitude and behavior. So, religion is an innate value that defines how to do things right and provides a series of tools and techniques for social connections. It also represents a system of beliefs and practices on how people responds and interprets what they feel (Johnstone in Kum-Lung, 2010); so, it is considered the most basic building block for an individual's cognitive world (Delener, 1994). Thus, religion influences people's goals, decisions, motivations, purpose, and satisfaction. Functionalist theory in sociology commends religion as it promotes social solidarity and norms that reduce conflicts and impose sanctions against antisocial behavior (Light et al., 1989).

Hence, religiosity is expected to influence an individual's ethical beliefs in a positive way due to the fact that religiosity is a key personal characteristic. In other words, people with higher level of religiosity are expected to be more ethical in terms of their behaviors. Sidani (2005) concluded that unethical behavior is negatively correlated with the severity of penalties due to the fear of God's punishment in this life and hereafter. This results in adhering to virtue and morality. Furthermore, Kennedy and Lawton (1998) also uncovered a negative relationship between religiosity and willingness to engage in unethical behavior.

## 5.7 ETHICAL DECISION-MAKING IN THE HOSPITALITY SECTOR

During their daily operations, organizations' managers are confronted with a number of ethical issues that can leave a permanent impression either positive or negative in the minds of customers, employees, stakeholders, and the community. Generally, hospitality managers are confronted with ethical issues surrounding guest rights, labor rights, sexual harassment, departmental relations, yield management, empowerment, suppliers' relationships, equal opportunity, and public relations.

Therefore, ethical performance of an organization is critical managerial problems, management in any organization is responsible for setting the ethical tone for their organizations (Barsch and Lisewski, 2008), so ethics management is a critical aspect from a manager's perspective. Management should have a leading role in promoting ethical behaviors (Chonko et al., 2002); the organizational behavior literature shows that managers have a significant impact (positive or negative) on the ethical actions of employees. Management decisions greatly influence an organization's ethical performance by the establishment of right way that direct the ethical conduct of the entire organization (Foster and Hegarty, 2009).

Although management process and in particular setting organizational priority affects the realization of ethical conduct by identifying the values that the management deems as important, hospitality training basically focuses on foreign languages and processes; it fails to focus on ethics and morality. Hospitality managers must have certain personality traits which include honesty, integrity, loyalty, trustworthiness, fairness, respect for others, leadership, accountability, reputation, and commitment to excellence. Managers must reflect on their daily decision as well as their behavior to the business partners and customers (Walker, 2010).

Ethical decision-making is mainly influenced by two factors:

1. The severity of ethical issues that face the organization; ethical dilemmas are classified according to:
   - The participant of the crisis.
   - The consequences of the crisis.
2. The methodology of decision-making which include deontology and teleology.
   - Deontology is concerned with the notion of common principles and truths, which should be held on irrespective of the situation. Deontology is based on man's absolute duty toward mankind and how it is given priority over results, it argues that people faced with a challenge is in a position to respond constantly and in compliance with their moral principles and are happy with the decision made in full view of others.
   - On the other hand, teleology (consequentialism) is referred to as outcome-oriented ethics. It focuses on the purpose of each action and whether there is an intention for the action. It concentrates on examining past experiences in order to figure out the results of present actions.

A general distinction of these approaches is that deontology focuses more on means than the end while in teleology the end justifies the means. If hospitality managers adopt teleology approach to solve ethical dilemmas, severe penalties must also be applied in order to prevent forbidden behavior and then ensure the efficiency of decisions, therefore no need to understand how decisions are made.

Managers must understand how to manage the composition of the organization which includes human behavior, material resources, and profits. They must pay a great attention to the value component which includes morality ethics, managers are daily faced with the dilemma of either giving priority to the customer or profits. Although the main goal of the hospitality managers is to generate a profit; they, however, must do so in within the framework bearing in mind that they must offer customers value for their money.

Hospitality managers have the responsibility of maintaining the highest levels of services, guest satisfaction, and optimal financial return on investment. In order to meet these objectives, hospitality managers must seek to establish an ethical culture within their organizations; there is a positive relationship between profitability and ethics. The popularity of code of ethics used by the tourism and hospitality industry is a tool to offer guidance to industry stakeholders when making decisions.

## 5.8 IMPACTS OF ETHICS IN THE TOURISM AND HOSPITALITY INDUSTRY

### *5.8.1 FEWER LEGAL ISSUES*

Some organization select to cut costs by following unethical ways, such as:

- purchasing sub-standard materials,
- ignoring important work-safety practices,
- ignoring environmental laws,
- unsocialized wages, and
- tax evasions.

The effects of this type of neglect may include legal and financial consequences as well as damage to the organization's reputation. In contrast, when an organization focuses on maintaining high ethical standards, it will tend to face fewer legal problems related to its products or services. An organization that works to address such issues in a conscientious manner are less likely to face legal problems and in turn maximizing its financial status.

### 5.8.2 ENHANCES QUALITY

Ensuring the quality in the hospitality organizations require maintaining high standards and prevailing good rules. Quality is not a just a chance but a commitment; so, hospitality establishments and their management should always ensure the quality of their employees. Quality is made up of good employees who respect ethics and morality in both their work and in life. Therefore, ethics should be part of every activity in the hotel with definitions according to particular responsibility and work of every department. Ethics should cut across housekeeping, food and beverage, front office, purchasing, yield management, security, marketing, and public relations departments.

Excellent hospitality leaders must ensure that the vision, mission, values constitute an ethical climate, as well as the ethics of the hotel, which reflect a socially responsible culture (Smith and Colman, 2006).

Ethical leaders lead by example in restoring trust in business by stimulating ethical conduct of all the employees and taking necessary measures on the basis of facts and situations and having a clear understanding of ethical quality and progress of the hotel.

### 5.8.3 EMPLOYEE RETENTION

As opposed to other sectors, the hospitality sector is very diverse; it involves employees and managers from every racial, social, sex, cultural, age, educational, and religious background (Vallen and Casado, 2000). The industry also embraces a wider spectrum of ethically acceptable behavior and beliefs. Therefore, hospitality employees and managers need an international common understanding of what is acceptable and wrong. Adopting and implementing ethical values helps people realize their organization fit as well as influencing employee's affections for the organization. Unethical climate or practices often lead to extra organizational costs; thus, there is a need for hospitality businesses to promote an ethical environment in the working place to avoid this.

Hospitality organizations that are socially and ethically responsible can attract as well as retain skilled employees because the organization's practices and values are affect the values that such employees hold, which decreases the employees' turnover. Service employees' retention is directly related to the hospitality organization's ethical climate, high ethical practices reduce stress, increases trusts between employees thereby reducing conflicts, increasing job satisfaction, and enhancing employees' commitment.

The process of either recruiting or employees' turnover is very costly and time-consuming. When organizations continually have to replace their employees, the expense and disruption to work processes can have a damaging effect on the organization's overall productivity and profitability. The goal, therefore, is for an organization to retain its best employees on a long-term basis.

When the ethical climate prevails the organization (open, honest, and fair), talented workers will be more inclined to stay onboard with the organization (Chapter 7, Effects of Labor Turnover).

### *5.8.4 EMPLOYEE SATISFACTION*

Many researchers around the world have conducted job satisfaction in the hospitality industry. In addition, the literature has described job satisfaction in different ways through the years. Mathenge (2013) viewed job satisfaction as the combination of psychological and environmental circumstances that affect an employee to be satisfied with his or her work. It is also defined as a pleasurable emotional status resulting from the evaluation of one's job as achieving or facilitating one's job values (Locke in Mathenge, 2013). So, job satisfaction is the feelings of happiness employees have about their jobs. However, according to Cranny et al. (1992), there is a clear consensus in relation to defining job satisfaction.

That "consensus" definition described job satisfaction as "an emotional reaction to one's job, resulting from a comparison of actual outcomes with those that are expected, deserved, desired and so on."

Although there are a number of definitions and studies related to job satisfaction, very little research has been done on the methods measuring employee satisfaction levels (Mathenge, 2013). Perhaps that is because job satisfaction is a very complicated concept that includes a variety of different facets.

Generally, employees are one of the most important assets of any organization. Therefore, companies should try to take better care of their employees. Job satisfaction may be both

- internal, derived from internally rewards and compensations such as the job itself and opportunities for personal growth and accomplishment, and
- external, resulting from externally rewards such as satisfaction with organization policies, promotion opportunities, support, pay, supervision, fellow workers, and customers.

It is the role of the management to know what the employees think, how they perceive the organization culture, what they think of their working environment, whether they are satisfied with the existing procedures and policies, and of course if they consider their working environment as ethical or not.

The study by Barsky and Nash (2004) showed that job satisfaction was driven by emotions of the employees and their beliefs about their organization. In a study conducted by Aksu and Aktas (2005) to measure job satisfaction of the managerial level in first-class Turkish Hotels, they discovered that despite low salaries, long hours and little support from coworkers, the managers were highly satisfied with their jobs due to the nature of the work itself and the authority that came from managing the first-class facility.

In addition, the results showed that job satisfaction has been closely related to positive climate prevailing the work environment that in turn generated institutional outcomes such as the productivity, the degree of innovation, and reduced turnover. More specifically, Sledge et al. (2008) demonstrated that job satisfaction is linked to increased organizational performance and the ethical climate.

Ethical climate is conducted in several studies as a significant indicator for employees' job satisfaction; Donaldson et al. (2002) focused on a large nonprofit charitable organization and found that managers may be able to enhance their employees' job satisfaction by creating an ethical climate in the organization. Their results showed that apart from satisfaction with pay, an organization can influence all different facets of job satisfaction by manipulating its ethical environment.

Pettijohn et al. (2008) confirmed that if the organization's employees perceive that their employers are ethical, then that company's survey statistics will reveal that job satisfaction ratings are high, the turnover rate is low, and their intention to leave the organization is small. On the contrary, Jaramillo et al. (2006) argued that when employees consider their employers unethical, then job satisfaction levels may decrease, and turnover rates may rise. Therefore, hospitality managers should take a leading role in encouraging ethical behavior in their organizations (Smith and Colman, 2006). It is confirmed by Chiang et al. (2005) that job satisfaction greatly influences the employees' intention to stay with that organization. In turn, this will lead the employees to be more productive. In a study conducted on Korean Hotel employees by Choi's (2006), the findings were that there was a negative relationship between job satisfaction and turnover intention. This confirms that the absenteeism rates are strongly related to job satisfaction and job satisfaction strongly depends on an ethical organizational climate.

### *5.8.5 ORGANIZATIONAL COMMITMENT*

Employee commitment is an extent to which employee feels attached, loyal, and dedicated to the organization mission, goals, and objectives (Akintayo, 2010). It is considered a harmonious relationship with the work activity; it is a sign of how strong is the relationship between the employee and the organization. Biljan (2004) described organizational commitment as a "psychological bond" to the organization that influences people to act according to what is best for the organization and its interests. Most organizations have realized that the employees' commitment is fundamental in determining organization success (Zheng et al., 2010; Biljan, 2004); committed employee bring benefits to the organization in several ways which include but not limited to reduce absenteeism, promote employee active engagement, reduce intention to quite thereby resulting in sustained productivity and high profitability (Bhatti et al., 2011), struggle with the organization even in turbulent times, protects organization's assets as well as share its goals (Habib et al., 2010). Mathenge (2013) found that an important indicator of commitment is the level of satisfaction that the newcomers get during organizational assimilation. He also supported that employee's commitment to an organization depend heavily on his/her attitudes, and feelings, as well as involvement in that organization, whereas Pauline et al. (2008) claimed that organizational commitment is critically associated with the work-related ethics and behaviors of employees in organizations. Committed employees believe in and accept the ethical values and goals of the organization they work for. They are not only willing to keep working there but are also assiduous to provide high effort on their part in order to stay.

Therefore, there is a positive relationship between an organization's ethical climate that is based on specific rules and employees' commitment to that organization; such commitment empowers the employees to exert more efforts in their work (Janssen, 2004). Employee empowerment is closely associated with organizational commitment and that commitment exists at both the individual and organizational level.

## REFERENCES

Abdolmohammadi, M. J.; Reeves, M. F. Effects of Education and Intervention on Business Students' Ethical Cognition: A Cross Sectional and Longitudinal Study. *Teach. Bus. Ethics* **2000,** *4* (3), 269–284.

Adebayo, D. O. Gender and Attitudes Toward Professional Ethics. A Nigerian Police Perspective. *Afr. Secur. Rev.* **2005,** *14* (2), 21–36.

Akatan, M., G.; Burnaz, S.; Topku, Y. An Empirical Investigation of the Ethical Perceptions of Future Managers with a Special Emphasis on Gender—Turkish Case. *J. Bus. Ethics* **2008,** *82* (3), 573–586.

Akintayo, D. I. Work–Family Role Conflict and Organizational Commitment Among Industrial Workers in Nigeria. *J. Psychol. Couns.* **2010,** *2* (1), 1–8.

Aksu, A.; Aktas, A. Job Satisfaction of Managers in Tourism: Cases in the Antalya Region of Turkey. *Manage. Audit. J.* **2005,** *20* (5), 479–488.

Arnould, E.; Price, L.; Zikhan, G. *Consumers*, 2nd ed.; New York: McGraw-Hill, 2004.

Babin, B. J.; Boles, J. S.; Robin, D. P. Representing the Perceived Ethical Work Climate among Marketing Employees. *J. Acad. Mark. Sci.* **2000,** *28* (3),. 345–358.

Barsh, A.; Lisewski, A. Library Managers and Ethical Leadership: A Survey of Current Practices from the Perspective of Business Ethics. *J. Libr. Adm.* **2008,** *47* (3/4), 27–67.

Barsky, J.; Nash, L. Employed Satisfaction Tied to Emotions: Company Beliefs. *Hotel Motel Manage.* **2004,** *219* (20), 12.

Bass, K.; Barnett, T.; Brown, G. The Moral Philosophy of Sales Managers and Its Influence on Ethical Decision Making. *J. Pers. Sell. Sales Manage.* **1998,** *18*, 1–17.

Beck, J. A.; Lazer, W.; Schmidgall, R. Hotel Marketing Manager's Responses to Ethical Dilemmas. *Int. J. Hospitality Tour. Adm.* **2007,** *8* (3), 35–48.

Bhatia, S. K. *Business Ethics and Managerial Values*; Deep and Deep Publications Pvt. Ltd.: New Delhi, 2003.

Bhatti, K. K.; Nawab, S.; Akbar, A. Effect of Direct Participation on Organizational Commitment. *Int. J. Bus. Soc. Sci.* **2011,** *2* (9), 15–23.

Biljan, D. Employee Commitment in Times of Radical Organisational Changes. *Econ. Organ.* **2004,** *2* (2), 111–117.

Blanchard, K.; Hodges, P. *Servant Leader*; Thomas Nelson: Nashville, TN, United States, 2003.

Borkowski, S.; Ugras, Y. Business Students and Ethics: A Meta-Analysis. *J. Bus. Ethics* **1998,** *17*, 1117–1127.

Buff, C. L.; Yonkers, V. Using Student Generated Codes of Conduct in the Classroom to Reinforce Business Ethics Education. *J. Bus. Ethics* **2005,** *61* (2), 101–110.

Carroll, A. B.; Buchholtz, A. K. *Business and Society: Ethics and Stakeholder Management*, 6th ed.; Thomson/South-Western: Mason, OH, 2006.

Chiang, C. F.; Back, K. J.; Canter, D. D. The Impact of Employee Training on Job Satisfaction and Intention to Stay in the Hotel Industry. *J. Hum. Resour. Hospitality Tour.* **2005,** *4* (2), 99–118.

Choi, K. A. Structural Relationship Analysis of Hotel Employees' Turnover Intention. *Asia Pac. J. Tour. Res.* **2006,** *11* (4), 321–337.

Chonko, L. B.; Wortruba, T. R.; Loe, T. W. Direct Selling Ethics at the Top. *J. Pers. Sell. Sales Manage.* **2002,** *22* (2), 87–96.

Costello, H.; Hogan, I. Codes of Ethics in Hospitality and Tourism. *Int. J. Hospitality Manage.* **2002,** *2* (4), 243–268.

Cranny, C.; Smith, P.; Stone, E., Eds. *Job Satisfaction: How People Feel about Their Jobs and How It Affects Their Performance*; Lexington Books: New York, NY, 1992.
Crowell, C. The Art of Theft Prevention. *Hotel Motel Manage.* **2008,** *223* (14), 139.
Delener, N. Religious Contrasts in Consumer Decision Behavior Patterns: Their Dimensions and Marketing Implications. *Eur. J. Mark.* **1994,** *28* (5), 36–53.
Dellaportas, S. Making a Difference with a Discrete Course on Accounting Ethics. *J. Bus. Ethics* **2006,** *65* (4), 391–404.
Devonish, D.; Alleyne, P.; Cadogan-McClean, C.; Greenidge, D. An Empirical Study of Future Professionals' Intentions to Engage in Unethical Business Practices. *J. Acad. Ethics* **2009,** *7* (3), 159–173.
Donaldson, T.; Werhane, P. H.; Cording, M. *Ethical Issues in Business: A Philosophical Approach*, 7th ed.; Prentice Hall: Upper Saddle River, NJ, 2002.
Dozier, B. *Ethics in the Hospitality Industry* (online), 2013. https://barbradozier.wordpress.com/2013/06/17/ethics-in-the-hospitality-industry/ (accessed Aug 17, 2017).
Emerson, T.; Conroy, S.; Stanley, C. Ethical Attitudes of Accountants: Recent Evidence from a Practitioner' Survey. *J. Bus. Ethics* **2007,** *71*, 73–87.
Ergeneli, A.; Arikan, S. Gender Differences in Ethical Perceptions of Salespeople: An Empirical Examination in Turkey. *J. Bus. Ethics* **2002,** *40* (3), 247–260.
Fennell, D. A. *Tourism Ethics*; Channel View Publications: Clevedon, Buffalo, Toronto, 2006; p 9.
Fennell, K.; Malloy, J. Ecotourism and Ethics: Ethical Development Perspective. *J. Travel Res.* **2008,** *36* (4), 47–56.
Forster, K.; Hegarty, L. Ethical Decision Making. *J. Bus. Ethics* **2009,** *8* (6), 125–141.
Fox, J. Approaching Managerial Ethical Standards in Croatia's Hotel Industry. *Int. J. Contemp. Hospitality Manage.* **2000,** *12* (1), 70–74.
Foxall, G. R.; Goldsmith, R. E. *Consumer Psychology for Marketing*; Routledge: London, 1994.
Freed, J. Lawsuit Leaves Hilton's Brand Plans in Limbo. *Hotel Motel Manage.* **2009,** *224* (5), 1–53.
Giacalone, R. A. A Transcendent Business Education for the 21st Century. *Acad. Manage. Learn. Educ.* **2004,** *3* (4), 415–420.
Gilligan, C. *In a Different Voice: Psychological Theory and Women's Development*; Harvard University Press: Cambridge, MA, 1982.
Githui, D. Ethical Considerations in Human Resource Management in Kenya: Theory and Practice. *Public Policy Adm. Res.* **2011,** *1* (4), 8–20.
Githui, D. *Fundamentals of Business Ethics and Values: A Focus on Individual, Business Conduct and Environmental Concern in a Globalized Village*; International Institute of Science, Technology and Education (IISTE): New York, United States, 2012.
Grandey, A. A.; Fisk, G. M.; Mattila, A. S.; Jansen, K. J.; Sideman, L. A. Is Service with a Smile Enough? Authenticity of Positive Displays During Service Encounters. *Organ. Behav. Hum. Decis. Process.* **2005,** *96* (1), 38–55.
Grove, S. J.; Fisk, R. P.; M. J. Bitner, M. J. Dramatizing the Service Experience: A Managerial Approach. *Adv. Serv. Mark. Manage.* **1992,** *1*, 91–121.
Grynko, A. Ukrainian Journalists' Perceptions of Unethical Practices: Codes and Everyday Ethics. *Cent. Eur. J. Commun.* **2012,** *2* (9), 259–273.
Habib, A.; Khursheed, A.; Idrees, A. S. Relationship between Job Satisfaction, Job Performance Attitude towards Work and Organizational Commitment. *Eur. J. Soc. Sci.* **2010,** *18* (2), 257–267.

Hall, J. *Ethics in Hospitality Management*; Prentice Hall: Englewood Cliffs, NJ, 2000.

Hall, S. S. *Ethics in Hospitality Management: A Book of Readings*; Educational Institute of the American Hotel and Motel Association: East Lansing, MI, 1992.

Harris, D. Ethical Values of Individuals at Different Levels in the Organizational Hierarchy of a Single Form. *J. Bus. Ethics* **1990,** *9*, 741–750.

Heimler, R. Attitudes of College Graduates, Faculty, and Employers Regarding the Importance of Skills Acquired in College and Needed for Job Performance and Career Advancement Potential in the Retail Sector. *Ed.D. Dissertation*; Dowling College: New York, United States, 2010.

Hoffman, W. M.; Moore, J. M. *Business Ethics – Readings and Cases in Corporate Morality*; McGraw-Hill: New York, 1988.

Holjevac, I. A. Business Ethics in Tourism: As a Dimension of TQM. *Total Quality Manage.* **2008,** *19* (10), 1029–1041.

Janssen, O. The Barrier Effect of Conflict with Superiors in the Relationship between Employee Empowerment and Organizational Commitment. *Work Stress* **2004,** *18* (1), 56–65.

Jaramillo, F.; Mulki, J. P.; Solomon, P. The Role of Ethical Conflict on Salesperson's Role Stress, Job Attitudes, Turnover Intentions, and Job Performance. *J. Pers. Sell. Sales Manage.* **2006,** *26* (3), 271–282.

Johnson, B. R.; Jang, S. J.; Larson, D. B.; Li, S. D. Does Adolescent Religious Commitment Matter? A Reexamination of the Effects of Religiosity on Delinquency. *J. Res. Crime Delinq.* **2001,** *38* (1), 22–43.

Joseph, J.; Deshpande, S. P. The Impact of Ethical Climate on Job Satisfaction of Nurses. *Health Care Manage. Rev.* **1997,** *22* (1), 76–81.

Jovičić, A.; Pivac, T.; Dragin, A. Ethical Conduct of Employees in Tourist Organizations in Novi Sad (Serbia). *Turizam* **2011,** *15* (4), 135–147.

Kennedy, E. J.; Lawton, L. Religiousness and Business Ethics. *J. Bus. Ethics* **1998,** *17* (2),163–178.

Koh, H. C.; Boo, E. H. The Link between Organizational Ethics and Job Satisfaction: A Study of Managers in Singapore. *J. Bus. Ethics* **2001,** *29* (4), 309–324.

Kong, H.; Cheung, C.; Song, H. Hotel Career Management in China: Developing a Measurement Scale. *Int. J. Hospitality Manage.* **2011,** *30*, 112–118.

Kong, H.; Cheung, C.; Zhang, H. Q. Career Management Systems: What Are China's State-Owned Hotels Practicing? *Int. J. Contemp. Hospitality Manage.* **2010,** *22* (4), 467–482.

Kraft, K.; Singhapakdi, A. The Role of Ethics and Social Responsibility in Achieving Organizational Effectiveness: Students Versus Managers. *J. Bus. Ethics* **1991,** *10*, 679–686.

Kroll Global Fraud Report (online), 2017. www.kroll.com/.../fraud/Fraud (accessed Oct 21, 2017).

Kum-Lung, C. Attitude towards Business Ethics: Examining the Influence of Religiosity, Gender and Education Levels. *Int. J. Mark.* **2010,** *1*, 1.

Laufer, W. S.; Robertson, D. C. Corporate Ethics Initiatives as Social Control. *J. Bus. Ethics* **1997,** *16* (10), 1029–1047.

Light, D.; Keller, S.; Calhoun, C. *Sociology*; Alfred A. Knopf: New York, 1989.

Mathenge, G. D. Responsible Tourism and Hotel Management: An Empirical Analysis of the Ethical Dimensions in Tourism and Hospitality Industry in Kenya. *Am. Int. J. Contemp. Res.* **2013,** *3* (6), 18–19.

McCuddy, M. K.; Perry, B. L. Selected Individual Differences and Collegians Ethical Beliefs. *J. Bus. Ethics* **1996,** *15* (3), 261–272.
Njegovan, B. R. *Business Ethics*; Faculty of Technical Sciences: Novi Sad, 2009.
Noe, R. A.; Hollenbeck, J. R.; Gerhart, B.; Wright, P. A. *Fundamentals of Human Resource Management*; Me Grand-Hill International Edition Inc.: New York, NY, 2004.
Patterson, D. Research Ethics Boards as Spaces of Marginalization: A Canadian Story. *J. Qual. Inquiry* **2008,** *14* (1), 18–27.
Pattison, S.; Edgar, A. Integrity and the Moral Complexity of Professional Practice. *Nurs. Philos.* **2011,** *12* (2), 94–106.
Pauline, J.; Benzein, E.; Årestedt, K.; Berg, A.; Saveman, B. Families' Importance in Nursing Care Nurses' Attitudes—An Instrument Development. *J. Family Nurs.* **2008,** *14* (1), 97–117.
Peceri, R. Promoting Organizational Effectiveness: Managerial Conduct Perspective. *Cornell Hotel Restaurant Adm. Q.* **2010,** *10* (5), 157–351.
Peterson, D.; Rhoads, A.; Vaught, B. C. Ethical Beliefs of Business Professionals: A Study of Gender, Age and External Factors. *J. Bus. Ethics* **2001,** *31*, 225–232.
Pettijohn, C.; Pettijohn, L.; Taylor, A. J. Salesperson Perceptions of Ethical Behaviors: Their Influence on Job Satisfaction and Turnover Intentions. *J. Bus. Ethics* **2008,** *78* (4), 545–557.
Phau, I.; Kea, G. Attitudes of University Students Toward Business Ethics: A Cross-National Investigation of Australia, Singapore and Hong Kong. *J. Bus. Ethics* **2007,** *72*, 61–75.
Pizam, A.; Thornburg, S. W. Absenteeism and Voluntary Turnover in Central Lorida Hotels: A Pilot Study. *Int. J. Hospitality Manage.* **2000,** *19* (2), 211–217.
Rest, J. R.; Narvaez, D. *Moral Development in the Professions: Psychology and Applied Ethics*; Erlbaum: Hillsdale, NJ, 1994.
Retail, Restaurants and Food Service. Security. *Solut. Enterprise Secur. Lead.* **2009** *40* (11), 46.
Rogers, V.; Smith, A. Ethics, Moral Development and Accountants-in-Training. *Teach. Bus. Ethics* **2001,** *5*, 1–19.
Rosnana, H.; Saihanib, S; Nuryusmawati, M. Y. *Attitudes towards Corporate Social Responsibility among Budding Business Leaders*. *Proc. Soc. Behav. Sci.* **2013,** *107*, 2–58.
Schwepker, C. H. Ethical Climate's Relationship to Job Satisfaction, Organizational Commitment, and Turnover Intention in the Salesforce. *J. Bus. Res.* **2001,** *54* (1), 39–52.
Sidani, Y.; Abib, I.; Rawwas, M.; Moussawer, T. Gender, Age and Ethical Sensitivity: The Case of Lebanese Workers. *Gend. Manage.: Int. J.* **2009,** *24* (3), 211–227.
Sidani, Y. M. Women, Work, and Islam in Arab Societies. *Women Manage. Rev.* **2005,** *20* (7), 498–512.
Sims, R.; Gegez, E. Attitudes towards Business Ethics: A Five Nation Comparative Study. *J. Bus. Ethics* **2004,** *50* (3), 253–265.
Sinclair, A. Approaches to Organizational Culture and Ethics. *J. Bus. Ethics* **1993,** *12* (1), 63–73.
Sledge, S.; Miles, A. K.; Coppage, S. What Role Does Culture Play? A Look at Motivation and Job Satisfaction Among Hotels in Brazil. *Int. J. Human Res. Manage.* **2008,** *19* (9), 1667–1682.
Smith, P.; Colman, J. Ethics in the Tourism and Hospitality Industry. *J. Bus. Ethics* **2006,** *15* (11), 1175–1187.
Stafford Hotels. Stafford Hotels' Financial Chief Jailed for Two Years. *Cater. Hotelk.* **2009,** *199* (4595), 7.

Stevens, B. Hotel Managers Identify Ethical Problems: A Survey of their Concerns. *Hospitality Rev.* **2011,** *29* (2), 2.

Stevens, B. Hospitality Ethics: Responses from HR Directors and Students to Seven Ethical Scenarios. *J. Bus. Ethics* **2001,** *30* (2), 233–242.

Stevens, B.; Fleckenstein, A. Comparative Ethics: How Students and Human Resource Directors React to Real-Life Situation. *Cornell Hotel Restaur. Adm. Q.* **1999,** *40* (2), 69–75.

Tsai, W. C.; Huang, Y. M. Mechanisms Linking Employee Affective Delivery and Customer Behavioral Intentions. *J. Appl. Psychol.* **2002,** *87* (5), 1001–1008.

UNWTO. *Sustained Growth in International Tourism Despite Challenges* (online), 2017. http://www2.unwto.org/press-release/2017-01-17/sustained-growth-international-tourism-despite challenges (accessed Nov 16, 2017).

Valentine, S.; Barnett, T. Ethics Code Awareness, Perceived Ethical Values, and Organizational Commitment. *J. Pers. Sell. Sales Manage.* **2003,** *23* (4), 359–367.

Vallen, R.; Casado, F. Ethical Principles for the Hospitality Managers. *Cornell Hotel Restaur. Adm. Q.* **2000,** *1* (5), 44–45.

Vitell, S. J.; Hidalgo, E. R. The Impact of Corporate Ethical Values and Enforcement of Ethical Codes on the Perceived Importance of Ethics in Business: A Comparison of U.S. and Spanish Managers. *J. Bus. Ethics* **2006,** *64*, 31–43.

Walker, R. J. *Introduction to Hospitality Management*, 3rd ed.; Prentice Hall: Upper Saddle River, NJ, 2010.

Wallace, H. Current Issues: Business Ethics and Tourism: Responsible Management. *Int. J. Hospitality Manage.* **2005,** 263–268.

Wan, K. E. *Leadership and Courage*; Singapore: Civil Service College, 2017; 3–4.

Weaver, G. R.; Agle, B. R. Religiosity and Ethical Behavior in Organizations: A Symbolic Interactionist Perspective. *Acad. Manage. Rev.* **2002,** *27* (1), 77–98.

White, R. D. Public Ethics, Moral Development, and the Enduring Legacy of Lawrence Kohlberg: Implications for Public Officials. *Publ. Integr.* **1999,** *1* (2), 121–134.

Whitney, D. L. Ethics in the Hospitality Industry: With a Focus on Hotel Managers. *Int. J. Hospitality Manage.* **1990,** *9* (1), 56–68.

WTO. *Ethics and Social Dimensions of Tourism.* Eleventh Meeting of the World Committee on Tourism Ethics, Rome, 2002.

Yang, J. T. Effect of Newcomer Socialization on Organizational Commitment, Job Satisfaction, and Turnover Intention in the Hotel Industry. *Serv. Ind. J.* **2008,** *28* (4), 429–443.

Yücel, R.; Çiftci, G. Employees' Perceptions towards Ethical Business Attitudes and Conduct. *Turk. J. Bus. Ethics* **2012,** *5* (9), 151–161.

Zheng, W.; Sharan, K.; Wei, J. New Development of Organizational Commitment: A Critical Review (1960–2009). *Afr. J. Bus. Manage.* **2010,** *3* (2), 1–15.

# CHAPTER 6

# LABOR ETHICS AND SOCIAL RESPONSIBILITY IN THE TOURISM AND HOSPITALITY INDUSTRY

*"Great organizations have great employees."*

## 6.1 INTRODUCTION

Nowadays, most guests and customers believe that competing services and products are reasonably alike in terms of quality. Therefore, tourism professionals must realize that competing on the basis of quality and prices is not sufficient and may lead to an erratic market and uneven profits. In such continual changing competitive environment, tourism and hospitality organizations must develop new ways and policies to stay ahead of their competitors other than the traditional ways. Tourism and hospitality organizations clearly understand that the best way to capture and retain the loyalty of market is to create collaborative relationships and better partnerships with their consumers. In relation to these relationships, the best way is developing ethical practices by hospitality and tourism businesses. Commonly, it has been supposed that those organizations that do what is ethical and moral to their employees and clients generate benefits (Wallace, 2005), these benefits may be on the long term not immediately. Doing what is right is the basic of ethics and if applied properly, it can become the foundation for both the organization and the employees' pride and motivation (Hall in Mathenge, 2013); he also defined ethics in a very simple way, as "knowing what should to be done, and having the will and intention to do it."

Recognition and developing ethics codes in the tourism and hospitality business is necessary for the proper assessment of different standards that employees may adopt. However, the organization must pay attention and recognize "external" ethical considerations and the moral requirement to behave humanely and decently toward community and the environment in the course of business.

Many of these external ethical considerations arise from the fact that business exists in an environment and community and involves people, and that environment and the people have certain standards and rights must be followed and respected. People need such the moral right; they need to be treated with respect as human beings, that is, beings with the capacity to suffer, the ability to choose for themselves, and to have the chance to live a meaningful life. These moral imperatives may, in general, be equated with the human rights and the environmental standards that all organizations ought to respect. As such, they may be viewed as considerations out of business activities, which may limit or extend the business activity.

Thus, human rights and environment standards identify those things that businesses may not do in the otherwise legitimate pursuit of profit in the process of wealth creation. A great deal of business ethics can be conceptualized as working out the specific obligations of businesses with respect to the people and community of those involved in and affected by business activity, and working out how compliance with these obligations is best achieved. Stevens (2008) confirmed that all employees involved in tourism and hospitality should possess these morals as they are critical in the success of any organization.

This broad conception of business ethics, distinguishing its internal and external aspects and incorporating moral debate about the proper scope and mode of business regulation, may seem as a challenge to those who consider that the main issue in business is how to convert the talks and thoughts into real actions. It will certainly appear somewhat a significant issue to the business owners and managers who are grappling with the mix of conflicting pressures and humdrum routine that characterize their daily work.

## 6.2 ETHICS AND TOURISM INDUSTRIES

Tourism is a fast-growing industry; tourism is a key driver of socioeconomic progress through export revenues, the creation of jobs, and development of structures and infrastructure. Over the past six decades, tourism has experienced continued expansion and diversification, becoming one of the largest and fastest-growing economic sectors in the world. International tourist arrivals have shown virtually uninterrupted growth. According to UNWTO

(2014, 2017), tourist arrivals sharply increased in the last years especially between 1995 and 2013, as follows:

- in 1950, tourist arrivals were 25 million;
- in 1980, tourist arrivals were 278 million;
- in 1995, tourist arrivals were 528 million;
- in 2013, tourist arrivals were 1087 million; and
- in 2015, tourist arrivals were 1,235 million.

These millions of arrivals made tourism and hospitality industry a multi-billion dollars industry, so many experts have described the industry as a savior in many countries and regions. However, at the same time, the industry is associated with bringing some difficulties to the communities of destination; these difficulties and problems are the logical results of the conflict between the dollars (the commercial targets) and the ethical commitment (social and environmental ethics). Hence, it can be argued that the community hardship or prosperity (destiny) is controlled to a large extent by application degree of ethical rules and standards that the organization or the company adopt.

### 6.2.1 *INTERNAL ETHICAL ISSUES*

Internal ethical issues are about the companies' customers and employees, the policies of yield management, the departmental operations and performance, the quality of the product (service), and developing unusual working patterns.

Measuring the organizational ethics of a hotel organization, for example, may sound straightforward and easy in theory, but in reality, when it comes to practicing, it can be very challenging and complicated.

However, in order to do so, many researchers measure the ethical climate of an organization, as it helps them to better understand its levels of business ethics. Expression of unethical behavior depends on the individual and the organization in which the individual is employed.

In the field of hospitality industry context, Stevens (2001) asserted that the hospitality industry is open to unethical practices, as hospitality professionals are faced with ethical dilemmas in their daily operations. Both customers and employees (managerial, supervisory, craft, and operative) are placing in tempting situations because of the virtue nature of hospitality industry. They are frequently presented with morally ethically ambiguous situations such as overbooking, misappropriations, theft, mistreatment of others, racial prejudices, sabotage, benefit at the expense of guest supplementary service, and misleading information in the restaurant menus, hotel brochures, and websites. Some of these ethical challenges are not new and have been taking place for a long time.

### *6.2.2 EXTERNAL ETHICAL ISSUES*

The external issues revolve around the compelling governmental policies, adhering to the environmental laws and standards, and responding to the destination community development calls (Stevens, 2001).

Tourism nature depends largely on cultural and environmental resources; this in turn generates numerous ethical dilemmas that should be considered by tourism professionals. According to Costello and Hogan (2002), tourism nature generated many activities based on interacting with the social systems and the natural setting. Unfortunately, these activities brought negative consequences, for example:

- Tourists crave for scenic and secluded accommodation leads to increased clearance of various natural areas for the purpose of building hotels and resorts; thousands of people are forced to leave from their homes to make way for huge new tourism projects.
- Excessive use of resources, in many developing countries, for example, women must walk miles to get water because hotels siphon it off from the groundwater for their own overuse.
- The organic and solid wastes produced by these hospitality institutions may contribute to environmental pollution.
- The transportation of tourists from one attraction site to the other results in the use of fossil fuels which release a considerable amount of air pollutants and other greenhouse gasses.
- Organic and solid wastes produced by the hospitality industry may contribute to environmental pollution.
- In addition to the interactions with natural systems, tourism activities involve both direct and indirect contacts between local community and tourists. Such contacts between host communities and tourists cause various, ethically in nature, problems. Contacts between host communities and tourists cause importation of new culture and lifestyle, overcommercialization of cultural commodities, and conflict of values.

It is not just those suburban, marginalized destinations that are hit by the ugly side of tourism but places that are part of the mainstream (McGran, 2003).

These are just examples of the ethical issues that arise as a result of tourism projects expansions that ignore the social and environmental ethics, where economic priority in the name of tourism has given way to unthinkable human and environmental abuses. As a result of these consequences, the tourism and hospitality industry has a weak position in terms of social and environmental responsibility and ethical business conduct; there has been arisen public concern and elevated demand for more socially responsible and ethical practices (Enea, 2007).

These discrepancies and shortcomings have given rise to increased attention from industry professionals and policymakers; and thus during the last decade or so, the tourism industry has observed significant changes in business and regulatory environment that have stressed the importance of corporate social responsibility (CSR) and ethics, placed these issues on the business agenda of tourist organizations (Schwartz et al., 2008), and led them to act ethically and behave more responsible (Hall and Brown, 2008).

The dirty impacts that the tourism organizations leave behind have contributed significantly in promoting the concept of sustainable or responsible tourism that seek to reduce the harmful environmental, social as well as economic impacts, and at the same time creating more economic benefits for the host communities and improving the overall interests of the destination.

Social and environmental responsibility is largely associated with ethical business management and includes the obligation of management to create appropriate choices and take those actions which will contribute to the welfare of both the organization and the community. Thus, sustainable tourism has emerged as a key trend globally as consumer market trends shift toward ethical consumption. Responsible tourism is a form of tourism that relates all types of tourism with reverence to the destination, built, cultural, and natural environment and the interests of all the involved parties. This form of tourism broadens the concept of sustainable or ecotourism to include environmental, ethical, and social considerations (WTO, 2002). Various countries such as the United States, India, Gambia, Sri Lanka, and United Kingdom as well as tourism organizations are by now practicing this form of tourism. Hospitality organizations are starting to recognize that promoting their ethical position can be of great importance as it enhances their profits, public image, management effectiveness, as well as enhancing effective employee relations.

Another example of responding the industry to the ethical concerns is the emergence of ecotourism. Ecotourism has been created by professionals in the industry as an example of ethical tourism practice, in which the "no harm to the environment" is the main theme. Ecotourism depends primarily on the educational benefits for conservation and sustainability, and the conscious moral commitment to the importance of protecting the environment and the community characteristics (Pearson, 2010).

Ecotourism is slightly different from sustainable or responsible tourism and is more focused on ecological conservation and educating travelers on local environments and natural surroundings, whereas sustainable tourism focuses on travel that has minimal impact on the environment and host communities (Integra, 2012). So, ecotourism is considered more ethical form of practice (Pearson, 2010).

However, the allegation of sustainability and ecological conservation by some tourism organizations and professionals bring some questions about the sincerity of being them green and environmentally conscious or not! Along with this question, Lansing and DeVries (2007) have questioned the concept of sustainability in the industry. Does it fit the contours of accurate environmental practices or is it a gimmick used by marketers to get the popularity of ecotourism and the green movement? It has become fashionable to claim one's business as helping the environment, when, in reality, not all businesses measure up.

Concerning sustainable practices, Elan (2010) claimed that 63% of restaurant owners feel an ethical responsibility to conduct the sustainable practices in their restaurants, and 50% indicated that reducing the carbon footprint was of some or no importance to them. Another example that proves the tricks of sustainable practices in tourism organizations is "Greenwashing," when some organizations claimed that applying these environmental perspectives and asked their guests to reuse their towels to save the environment, whereas the organization did not engage in other sustainable practices (Pearson, 2010). Nevertheless, Dodds and Joppe (2005) found that demand for responsible tourism is price-sensitive; in other words, "the customer and the industry are driven by cost."

Also, ecotourism has received a lot of criticism that are as follows:

- Karwacki and Boyd (1995) claimed that ecotourism, in fact, is unethical – as those who accrue the greatest benefits are the socially advantaged and those who reap the least reward are the poor and disadvantaged.

- It undermines a developing nation's ability to feed itself or sustain growth through exports because tourism as an economic practice can supplant agriculture.
- Ecotourism also contributes to pollution.
- It facilitates the commodification of culture.
- It invariably ensures the concentration and monopoly of local resources lie in the hands of already established local elites.
- It often involves a top-down form of management that fails to address local community concerns and needs.

Ironically, as Wheeler (1994) has observed, ecotourism can in practice differ from other forms of tourism only in its claim to "higher moral ground."

Unethical practices not only negatively affect the host communities but also it will entail the organizations on the long term, when the destination lose its glamour; if the natural settings of hospitality and tourism activities are degraded, polluted, or lose its aesthetic qualities due to unethical planning and poor development, the quality of interactions between the destination community and tourist will lessen significantly. Therefore, the mitigation of these problems caused by the human unawareness or unethical human actions is very vital in order to prolong the quality of tourism and hospitality services and keep the organizations' image as it is "aesthetic center."

Thus, the tourism and hospitality industry need to operate in a socially, environmentally, and ethically responsible way that include all the stakeholders. The stakeholders should contribute to solving problems in society through stabilizing ethical and moral behavior. This will create an impact on the prevention and resolution of the surrounding environmental problems (Walker, 2010). But, poor employee training has also been identified as a main hinder to achieve the ethical goals, along with other factors, while management attempt to establish and conduct high ethical standards in their hospitality organizations, the information often does not always reach frontline employees (Stevens, 2001). So, improved ethical training reduces workplace problems and is recommended even in organizations with high turnover, as it reduces workplace problems (Poulston, 2008). In this sense, it is necessary to motivate employees and to implement properly and practically a code of ethics through ethical training, without the knowledge of employees about the contents of this code and its importance for the organization (Walker, 2010).

## 6.3 CORPORATE SOCIAL RESPONSIBILITY IN TOURISM SECTOR

Nowadays, the fact of each organization has to bear responsibility for its past, present, and future ethical behavior contributed in creating the concept of CSR as a corporate citizenship and corporate sustainability is extremely important in today's new era (Labbai, 2007). CSR is a particular set of procedures, practices, policies, and programs that are embedded into each aspect of the corporate activities, let it be daily transactions, supply, or decision-making (Labbai, 2007).

According Zenisek (1979), it is a "fit" between the two components of a "business ethics" and "societal expectations" of the private economic entities, which limits possible negative impacts of business activities on the society and its each individual member and maximizes their positive impacts (Smagulova et al., 2009).

Thus, the concept of CSR is a loosely defined term that seems to be a large umbrella, which includes a vast number of concepts as (Shahin and Zairi, 2007)

- philanthropy,
- human resources (HRs),
- environmental standards, and
- public and community relations.

However, the definitions of CSR differ from incorporating equity, human rights and welfare, protection of stakeholders' interests, and volunteerism, but common for most of them is that they include ethical business operations in some way. The concept of CSR may be hard to define because some of the practices included in the organization' CSR strategies today are not necessarily new CSR practices but old HR practices as ethics, compliance, diversity, and equity. It is therefore evident that some practices that used to be under HR are nowadays considered as CSR or that some HR practices at least overlap with CSR practices (Gond et al., 2011).

There exist some definitions that are more accepted and referred to than others. Based on an analysis of 37 definitions made by Dahlsrud (2008), the most frequent definition of CSR found on internet is from the Commission of the European Communities, which states that CSR is "a concept whereby organizations integrate social responsibility and environmental standards in their business operations and in their interaction with their stakeholders on a voluntary basis." This definition includes five aspects, where at least one or more of the aspects are common between most of the definitions that exist, namely, volunteerism, stakeholders, environmental, social, and economic concerns. Even though the concept covers more or less the same areas, it is hard to develop an unbiased definition due to the fact that CSR can be viewed as a social concept that adapts to the surrounding challenges of society.

CSR is biased toward the interests and challenges of those that engage in social responsibility practices; for this reason, hospitality organizations are engaged in different approaches of CSR such as (Smagulova et al., 2009):

- community involvement,
- HR management,
- fair business practices,
- energy saving,
- public relations,
- environmental products, and
- safety.

Therefore, managers recognize CSR as a concept that fits their business purposes, such as quality management, communication, and human rights, and they, therefore, adopt the term to align with their company's specific situation and challenges (Marrewijk, 2003).

UNWTO is also adopting the following CSR approaches in tourism and hospitality industry:

- *Sustainable tour*
  Tour operators' initiative for sustainable tourism development, which is promoting sustainable tourism by encouraging tour operator business to design and conduct environmentally, economically, and socially sustainable tours.

- *Child labor*
  Labor protection in tourism is another important CSR-related practices. So, UNWTO has established a task force that focuses on preventing sexual exploitation of minors, child labor, and the trafficking of children and young people in the industry.

CSR can make a significant contribution toward sustainable tourism development. This can allow the destination and organizations to minimize the negative impacts of tourism on the environment and on overall community while creating a favorable corporate image. Smagulova et al.

(2009) argued that important reasons for adopting and applying a CSR practices by hospitality industry are to maximize its economic and social benefits by

- justifying their existence within the society;
- fulfilling environmental laws and regulations;
- fair working conditions for employees;
- ensuring the loyalty of the customer, the employees and the community;
- creating good will in society; and
- improving community's life for improving long-run profitability (contributing to the welfare of local communities).

Subsequently, the concept of CSR has become a central part of corporate strategies for tourism business. For customers as well as for employees, the development of CSR strategies is becoming more and more important. To operate sustainably in future, it will be necessary for tourism businesses to continuously implement and successfully develop CSR strategies in the long term.

In accordance with tourism literature, the whole approach of CSR relates to a company's accountability to be responsible for all its business activities, operations, and impacts exposed on tourism stakeholders (Dodds and Joppe, 2005), which focuses on the accomplishment of sustainable development not only in economic sense but in social, environmental, and economic purports as well (TOI, 2002; Dodds and Joppe, 2005). According to many researchers, socially responsible tourism has initially been considered mainly from an environmental perspective only; and economic, social, and community aspects have relatively recently been incorporated in CSR concept (TOI, 2002; Dodds and Joppe, 2005; Enea, 2007) (see Fig. 6.1).

## 6.4 EMPLOYEES AND CORPORATE SOCIAL RESPONSIBILITY

Employee often wants more from a job than just performing their duties. CSR has the advantage that it makes work more meaningful for them. Several jobs can be meaningful in themselves, but for certain firms and industries, this meaningfulness can be hard to see. For these firms, CSR can be viewed as a solution that can help employees find their work meaningful, as it can give them a chance to positively affect some important issues (Bauman and Skitka, 2012). This can be connected to Maslow's theory of needs, where

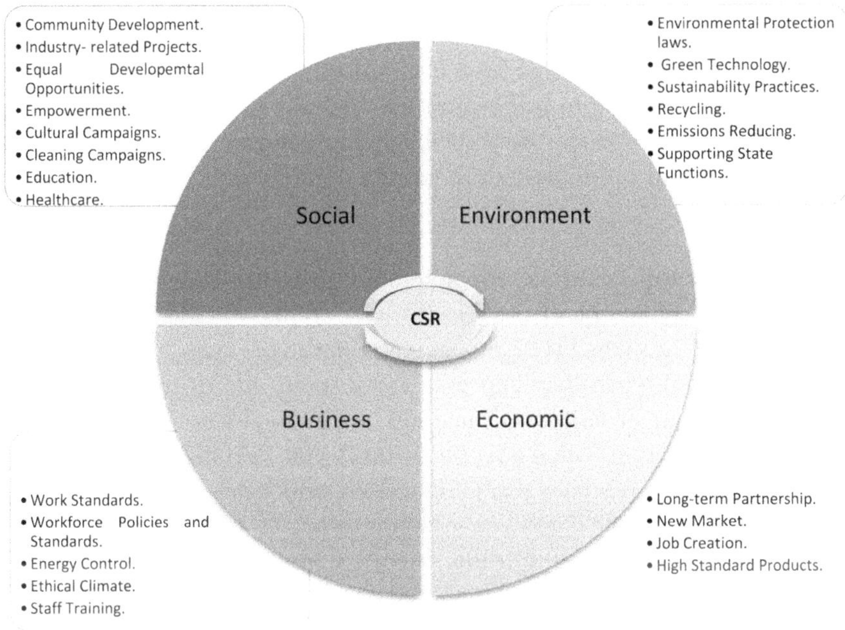


**FIGURE 6.1** The scope of corporate social responsibility.
**Source:** The Authors.

achievements and the desire to be useful and necessary in this world are included after the basic needs are covered (Rustad and Skar, 2015). Mirvis (2012) supported this view, as he argued that financial incentives will probably keep the employee on the job physically, but the money alone is not enough to keep a person on the job emotionally. So, in order to keep employees fully committed to their organization, it is becoming more and more usual that organization use CSR as a tool to recruit, retain, and engage employees (Mirvis, 2012).

Through a good CSR strategy, the organization can influence how both current and future employees look at the organization (Mirvis, 2012). On the other side, it was proved in a study conducted by PricewaterhouseCoopers that employee motivation is in fact highlighted as the second top factor that helps managers in making the business case for CSR, after reputation, which was rated as the top factor (Bhattacharya et al., 2008).

Bhattacharya et al. (2008) argued, in a similar manner as Mirvis (2012), that while a job gives returns in terms of payment, benefits, and advancement opportunities, incorporating CSR in the job environment can be a way for the organization to satisfy one or more high-order psychological needs of its employees. Human beings have basics needs, starting with survival and security and increasing to self-realization and self-esteem. Bhattacharya et al. (2008) uncovered at least four such higher order psychological needs that employees seek to fulfill through proximity to the firm's CSR initiatives, as follows:

1. **Gives opportunities for personal growth**: Personal growth is proved to be one of the reasons why employees desire to work for socially responsible organizations. Employees may feel emotionally rewarded when they express their responsibilities to other in their immediate or larger surroundings. Also, employees who work with CSR programs often adopt new skills that help them in their future career. The reason is that CSR-related work often involves tasks that are far from the employee's daily routine.
2. **Establishing a "reputation shield"**: Criticism against the organization and its operations can not only negatively affect the business but it can as well hurt employees' self-confidence. CSR initiatives help employees fight such negative rumors by teaching external stakeholders (or even themselves) about their organization's ethical values.
3. **Improving integration of work personal life**: Employees seek to improve the integration of their personal life and their work life so that they can move more smoothly between the two spheres. CSR can be a tool to fulfill this need, as the implementation of CSR can make employees feel that they to a greater extent can balance the needs of work and family.
4. **Building a bridge to the company**: Employees who work in distant locations have a tendency to feel isolated from the headquarter or regional offices. CSR is claimed to be a tool for the organization to demonstrate a commitment to employees and to provide a bridge between colleagues and all stakeholders at different locations.

On the other hand, its argued that Maslow's theory rarely applies directly to employees in everyday lives; almost everyone has different motivations concerning. Therefore, it might be hard for organizations to target CSR initiatives directly to employees' needs, as the employees often have motivations to do their job which precedes CSR practices.

## 6.5 THE INDUSTRY'S MORALITIES AND REALITIES

Tourism and hospitality industry is currently one of the top industries driving the global economy through its positive benefits such as employment opportunities, economic prosperity, and wealth, it has, with virtually all countries having an increase opportunity to play a part either as the source market or the tourist destination. As a result of the very complex environment which in the tourism industry operates, there is a huge potential of negative social and environmental impacts (Enea, 2007). Tough and aggressive competition, high turbulence, and volatility of the global tourism environment make tourism and hospitality organizations not always capable to manage their business operations in an ethical and socially responsible manner (Hall and Brown, 2008); a lot of employees deem unethical behavior indispensable to get ahead. Researchers have disclosed that some people consider themselves to be more ethical and moral than their colleagues in the workplace. The indispensable link between tourism and the social and physical environments implies that the industry survival largely depends on its capacity to not only maximize its benefits but also reduce its negative impacts on the destination community and environments (Butcher, 2008).

However, Boyd (1999) in his answer about the ability of tourism industry to put a side its dirty tricks and become ethical, he said "it has failed because of many aspects that are closely related to developing tourism projects and institutions;" such aspects are as follows:

- unfair labor practices,
- the displacement of local residents and indigenous people as a result of expansions operations of tourism projects,
- corruption of or disrespect for culture of destination communities,
- a myriad of other human rights:
    - child abuse (child labor),
    - migrant labor trafficking, and
    - female workers discrimination (wages and positions),
- environmental contamination.

Because of its environmental and socially destructive effects, lately the tourism industry has experienced elevated external pressures and has been challenged to respond to the rising problems promptly, ethically and responsibly (Tepelus, 2008); so during the past 5–6 years, interest in ethical issues for various branches and private companies has increased in order to improve the relationship to moral problems.

Organizations involved in tourism and hospitality industries must follow companies in other fields, such as Levi Strauss, Nike, and Reebok were some of the first to set up their own codes of conduct. Dozier (2013) argued that here is a growing concern for business ethics in tourism and hospitality industry as hotel professionals particularly are facing ethical dilemmas in their daily operations. According to Dodds and Joppe (2005), ethical practices and CSR standards have been originally established by the private sector organizations to act in response to escalated governmental and societal pressure. Luthar et al. (1997) defined ethics within the institutions and organizations as "codes, standards, rules or principles which provide guidelines for morally right behavior and attitudes in specific situations" (cited in Mathenge, 2013, p. 381).

Codes of ethics differ from the ethical rules. Codes of ethics aim at raising the employees' morality level. According to Beck et al. (2007), this means that ethics become institutionalized. The concept of a code derived from the Latin word "codex" which means the legal code. Code is a set of principles in the field of morals and professional ethics, as guidelines for professional work and public activities of all members of the organization. Codes of ethics have great importance for regulating the conduct of employees in organizations (Ratkovic, 2009). It is a set of rules, norms of moral character, which regulate the behavior.

Thus, codes of ethics should play an important role by directing, provide support, encourage, and assist in resolving of specific, morally controversial issues with which managers, employees, or members of a profession within the organization are faced.

Generally, since the 1990s, the primary change in the industry has been subjective rather than changes in practice or outcomes where ethical and moral debates have facilitated a shift from "fun tourism" to self-conscious "ethical" or "moral" tourism and where hedonistic pleasure is replaced by guilt and obligation (Butcher, 2008).

It might also be added that those who have expressed ethical concerns are also then cast as the "fun police" and questions are raised about the need for ethical codes or why industry operators should be concerned about ethics at all. More generally, the response to ethical concerns has been largely prescriptive, where various ethical codes and codes of conduct have been developed to address "impact" outcomes (Fennell, 2006). Code of ethics has been developed to provide moral guidance to organizational employees and customers of the services provided as a reaction to the increased concern and awareness of ethics in business contexts.

Codes of ethics are based on principles that explain and define a sense of responsibility, rather than prescribing precise conduct, and include actions formulated from a set of principles that incorporate values to serve as moral standard for everyday life. More specifically, Bligh (2006) suggested that codes are meant to translate more formal philosophical theories of ethics into standard guidelines and rules that can be applied to day-to-day actions and situations when making a decision in order to shape employee behavior and effect change through explicit statements of desired behavior.

However, little is known about the effectiveness of these codes, whether they lead to behavioral change, and/or whether they can address the specificities of a range of social encounters and interactions. As we will see, such efforts are important, but nonetheless limited, primarily because "tourism" is conceptualized as some "thing" that happens to people, rather than a social practice which people engage with and in. Here, following are some of key elements that have been identified with codes of conduct within any company or organization according to World Tourism Organization (WTO, 2017).

## *6.5.1 CODES OF CONDUCT IN GENERAL*

- A code of conduct should be part of the policy of the company; it relies on the support of the company management 100%.
- All the work staff and personnel must be informed of the contents of a code of conduct directly.
- The criteria of the code must be presented to all suppliers and all stakeholders clearly.
- Code of conduct must be implemented in the daily workplace.
- Code of conducts criteria must be applicable and controllable, so it may be necessary to set up an internal, functional reporting and control system.
- Control and follow-up by a third independent party is more or less necessary as a code of conduct that does not benefit from external monitoring, quite often loses its credibility.
- Balanced promotion is inevitable in order to make a deep impression on both the market and the community.
- Codes of conduct have been prioritize for acting more as public relations tool than as a means leading to an improvement of working conditions, problematic situations, etc.

It is worthy to say that codes are not designed for "bad" people, but for the persons who want to act ethically. The bad people will rarely follow a code, while most people—especially service sector—welcome ethical guidance in difficult or unclear situations (Levy and Park, 2011).

### *6.5.2 CODES OF CONDUCT IN THE TOURISM AND HOSPITALITY INDUSTRY*

World Travel and Tourism Council (2002) clearly identified that tourism and hospitality industries impact as involving water consumption, energy consumption, chemical use and atmospheric pollution, purchasing, and wastewater management. So, as a result of human and environmental violations, the commodification of daily life on a global scale, and the relationship between global and local environmental sustainability, there is a big need for the tourism industry to address the ethical and moral challenges provoked by travel and tourism practice. Employees and the organization they work for are the main determinants in determining what is ethical and what is not.

Ethics codes have a great importance in regulating the employee–organization relationship. In recent years, a large number of codes of ethics are regulating and organizing the human relationships and also the relationship between the companies and the host communities with the purpose of helping the operation' stakeholders to behave in ethical and morally responsible ways (Albaum and Peterson, 2006). Thus, the hospitality industry can initiate considerable changes in the physical environment.

Here are some examples of existing and planned ethical codes of conduct in the tourism industry:

#### *Global Code of Ethics for Tourism*

Tourism sector by its nature and necessity attracts children to work as laborers. According to Sharma et al. (2012), tourism affects the lives of 218 million children.

For instance, Plüss (1999) confirmed that working in tourism put the children into a vulnerable position where they are highly exposed to be sexually abused and exploited. Commercial sexual exploitation of children has been one of the major concerns prompting the international community to establish a "Global Code of Ethics for Tourism."

Global Code of Ethics for Tourism differs from WTO's "Tourism Bill of Rights and Tourist Code" (1985); it is considered as a follow-up, then it will seek to provide for a broader approach to social, economic, and environmental issues from the ethical perspective, while balancing responsibilities of all the social agents involved in tourism activities and development.

The code's criteria will provide for its voluntary application and monitoring, including by third parties (individuals, nongovernmental organizations, and certification bodies).

### *Social Accountability 8000*

Social Accountability 8000 was created by the Council on Economic Priorities Accreditation Agency in order to establish and promote ethical aspects in different activities including tourism activities. In preparing SA 8000, the Council on Economic Priorities Accreditation Agency has based on three major conventions:

1. International Labor Organization conventions,
2. convention on the Rights of the Child, and
3. the UN Declaration of Human Rights,

while, in its development, SA 8000 has had the following two standards as a model:

- ISO 9000 (quality assurance) and
- ISO 14000 (environmental revision).

### *Green Globe Certification*

Green Globe Certification was developed by the World Travel and Tourism Council for travel and tourism companies and tourism destinations with the aim of making it possible for the tourism industry to reach a higher degree of environmental awareness and apply that to their activities.

The program is based on Agenda 21's stated cultural, environmental, and social commitments (Agenda 21 is a globally prioritized collection of principles for sustainable development, Rio Earth Summit, 1992).

Although conduct codes can be brief, most often they are fairly lengthy and detailed. The rational for the detailed scope of the ethical code is that it is necessary to both protect the employee while at the same time protecting the reputation of the organization. Most codes of conduct focus on the "do nots" rather than on affirmative obligations.

Despite all these efforts, the right ethical action is not often clear, tourism and hospitality managers in a big need to gain a deeper understanding on various ethical issues and learnt different ways of dealing with them when they arise. The most important central moral perspectives in a number of organizational codes of ethics are respect for the public, respect for human dignity, honesty, and fairness. Every organization in its business activities should balance the four fundamental moral values (Jovičić et al., 2011):

1. Business activities must be characterized by the respect for public. This should mean that business activities look at potential consumers and the general public as an objective, not only as mean.
2. Business activities must be characterized by respect for human dignity and should show special concern for the less powerful and less able.
3. Business activities must be characterized by sincerity. Honesty should ensure openness, the will for the truth and fulfillment of promises.
4. Business activities must be characterized by correctness. Correctness should provide equal treatment and equal opportunity to all market participants.

These principles of business ethics should be an integral part and the foundation of any ethical code.

To conclude, the perceptions of tourism and hospitality industries toward adhering to ethics and code of conducts are still subjective, where in the tourism industry, the use of codes of conduct and other "attributes" of ethical and socially responsible practices have been limited to the theoretical form (Butcher, 2008). Some of the explanations for this low priority status can be attributed to the following reasons:

- the lack of generally accepted global principles and criteria (Dodds and Joppe, 2005),
- controversy on ethical and social responsible conceptual and operating framework (Enea, 2007; Tepelus, 2008),
- multifaceted character of tourism activities involving water consumption, energy consumption, chemical use and atmospheric pollution, purchasing, and wastewater management (Tepelus, 2008), and
- deficiency of assessment methods of the ethical and social responsible performance of tourist organizations (Hall and Brown, 2008).

However, concern for ethical behavior in the hospitality sector is quite more obvious than other tourism sector. So, the professionals of the tourist organization should think ethically and develop ethical patterns such as ethics management and developing social responsibility in order to protect the external environment and society from the tourism and hospitality organizations' hidden tricks. Since it has a direct implication to the industry, nowadays, an adopting and implementing code of ethics in tourism organizations is very important than before.

Harris' (2007) study has found out that 45% of travelers are more likely to book a holiday with a tour company that has a written code of ethics. As many as 55% of the sample noted that they would be willing to pay 5% more for holidays that guarantee applying the ethical codes. Another Tearfund study confirmed that 27% of UK tourists felt that a service employee's ethical policies were important to them in choosing who to travel with (Harris, 2007).

## 6.6 ESTABLISHING ETHICAL CLIMATE

As noted by Bhatia (2003), ethics is our code of conduct. These are set of rules and standards that guide our behavior and attitudes and control our actions. According to Sledge et al. (2008), management can create an ethical climate that positively influences ethical behavior in the organization by applying and enforcing codes of rules, approaches, perspectives, and policies on ethical behavior, as well as establishing a positive discipline where needed.

Organization with an ethical climate would typically have a more pleasant working environment, as it fosters ethical values such as trust and honesty (Schwepker, 2001); such positive ethical environment is preferred by employees. It has been confirmed that those employees who work in an ethical environment are more satisfied in their jobs, loyal to the organization, are less likely to look for work elsewhere, provide quality services to the customers who are already satisfied, and are less likely to look for any organization elsewhere. The stronger ethical climate brings less role stress, greater job satisfaction, and organizational commitment. This makes perfect sense since the organization with an ethical climate would typically have successful reactions whether from the employees, the market, or even the community.

Clarifying what types of behaviors, the organization wishes to develop and promote is considered the first step toward creating ethical business climate practices, also identifying what activities are considered unacceptable or prohibited in the workplace environment is very important. As part of this step, an organization should adopt a thorough, all-encompassing code of conduct.

A code of conduct outlines the specific actions that employees must take in order to comply with the values and philosophy of the organization; it also details the expectations the organization has for its employees' behavioral outcomes.

A proper code of conduct should provide guidelines on unacceptable personal behavior as it relates to bribes, harassment, frequent absences, and so on. As mentioned earlier in Chapter 5, it is important for an organization to carefully outline what behavioral standards it expects its labor force to uphold, lest misunderstandings or misinterpretations occur. Employees may claim that they have organizational or professional ethics, which guide their personal behavior; they guide their professional conduct, this may be true, but it is necessary to write ethical guidelines down.

In addition to clarifying and promoting the ethical values and philosophy of the organization, it is necessary to provide training for the employees in order to ensure establishing ethical climate and therefore promoting ethical culture in the organization. As such, many organizations require their employees to participate in rigorous ethics training programs.

The US government, for example, has specific guidelines for its employees regarding ethics training, including which federal agencies are required to afford annual or semiregular training and which agencies have flexibility in their training programs. Additionally, many states also require their employees to undergo ethics training programs on a regular basis. However, in order for these training programs to be successful, an organization must stand by its code of conduct, make its ethical guidelines clear to all employees, and enforce its stated policies equally without regard to position or status within the company. Employees want to do what is right and they want to be "normal." Even those who are hired with strong character and an ethical compass need guidance and support:

> "No matter how strong their values, employees cannot be expected to be naturally familiar with all of the laws and regulations that pertain to their work. Nor can they be expected to be automatically aware of the ethical ambiguities that they might face in a particular industry or position. However, if employees are aware of relevant ethical and legal issues, they will be more likely to ask the right questions and ultimately do the right thing when faced with a dilemma. Many people do the wrong thing simply because they are unaware—they do not know that they should be concerned or ask for help." (Treviño et al., 1999)

Sledge et al. (2008) demonstrated that the ethical climate of an institution drives its values and encourages expected behaviors which, in turn, lead to affecting the ethics of its employees. The role of ethical codes in the organization whatever it is belongs to the manufacturing or service sector is very important. Verbeke et al. (1996) demonstrated that the ethical standards of the organization drive its values and encourages expected behaviors which, in turn, lead to influencing the ethics of its employees. Schwepker (2001) suggested that by applying and enforcing codes of procedures, rules and policies on ethical behavior, as well as imposing positive and negative discipline where needed, "management can create an ethical climate that positively influences ethical behavior in the organization."

Table 6.1 presents two distinct but related concepts: ethical culture and ethical climate.

Ferrell and Gresham (1985) found that the climate for unethical conduct exists when the codes of ethics, policies, and directives of an organization that discourage unethical behavior are not supported and enforced. The role of ethical climate in the organization is very important. Therefore, an organization's code of ethics should also address the consequences of noncompliance with its stated policies. A company must uphold its side of the ethics agreement by enforcing the code of conduct equitably no matter who is responsible for the violation (cited in Mathenge, 2013).

The ethical dimension of a company's climate and culture, therefore, has a strong influence on the extent to which employees adhere to organizational standards and align their work with the core values and vision of the organization.

In addition, a strong, ethical climate, and culture is essential for complying with laws and regulations, increases productivity and employee retention, and serves as the foundation for an enduring, successful company.

## 6.7 ETHICAL LEADERSHIP AND THE SUCCESS OF THE BUSINESS

Every organization, large or small, private or public enterprise, struggles to acquire productivity so as to achieve success and maintain a valuable image in these present days of stiff organizational competitions. Ethical behavior and the prevailing system of employment relations are very crucial for general development, the production of goods and services in any work organizations.

Employees are one of the most important communication channels for organizations to promote and market the product and service to the customers and the community. Employees have a wide reach among external

**TABLE 6.1** Ethical Culture Versus Ethical Climate.

| | **Ethical culture** | **Ethical climate** |
|---|---|---|
| **Definition** | Strong ethical cultures make doing what is right a priority. Often, ethical culture is unwritten code of conduct by which employees learn what they should think and do (ERC, 2005). Ethical culture can also be defined as the extent to which an organization regards its values<br><br>Also, ethical culture teaches employees how to "do the right thing." Weber and Seger (2002) demonstrates that 86% of managers act at work based on moral standards that they perceive in their workplace | Stemming from the field of psychology and based on the dominant theory of ethical climate that been created in 1987 and its measures, ethical climate is concerned with the "collective personality" of the organization<br><br>Ethical climate can be defined as the prevailing perceptions of typical organizational rules, standards, practices, and procedures that have ethical content (Treviño et al., 2001) |
| **Perspective** | Just as ethical culture can be viewed as a subset of organizational culture literature | Ethical climate is an outgrowth of work done on organizational climate |
| **Prospects** | The ethical culture of the organization communicates acceptable limits, how employees ought to treat others, whether it is acceptable to question authority figures, if it is safe to report observed misconduct, and the importance of compliance with controls and safeguards. Treviño notes that ethical culture determines "how persons understand what is expected of them, and how things really get done" (Treviño et al., 1999) | Ethical climate literature investigates the ethics-related attitudes, perceptions, and decision-constituting processes in an organization<br><br>Ethical climate includes several dimensions: self-interest, company financial target, efficiency, friendship, team-interest, social responsibility, personal morality, rules and standard operating procedures, and laws and professional codes (Treviño et al., 2001) |
| **Impacts** | Ethical culture drives how employees conduct themselves. It also provides direction for day-to-day behavior | Ethical climate is considered as an informal organizational control system … or an instrument of domination. Hence, this approach is one of the easiest, most effective, and recommended ways to measure and evaluate how ethical an organization truly is |

**Source:** The Authors

stakeholder groups and are considered to be a highly credible source of information among external surroundings. Therefore, their image and word impact weights far more to customers and community than the words of a communication manager or of a glossy brochure (Lockwood, 2007). So, ethical employees are considered organizational valuable assets.

Workplaces in which employees at all levels strive toward self-transcending values and adhere to ethical obligations are, by performance, more success than those in which employees strive toward self-enhancing values or violate their ethical obligations. However, ethical behaviors seem to change with the place, at work or out of work (with family, with friends, in your neighborhood, etc.) (see Fig. 6.2). We probably all know people in our private lives who say one thing but do another. Although the individual's ethical behavior must be the same elsewhere and under any circumstances, workplace cultures are no different.

So, some individuals' behaviors and attitudes tend to be more ethical in certain situations and under specific circumstances. Some employees at their work show strict adhering and committing to ethical rules and develop ethical practices in some situations. For example, they demonstrate such behaviors and attitudes when they get involved in a contact with their supervisors and managers. Generally, relativists feel that moral actions depend upon the nature of the situation and the individuals involved, and when they judge others, they weigh the circumstances more than the ethical principle that was violated. Those types of people are perceived as skeptics and feel that ethics and moral principles do not influence their working performance. Such relativists are often less educated and less committed to religious rules; in addition, they are unwilling to earn or behave as a role model. Such type of employees significantly associated with any failure at their encountering with the customer in the field of service sector. It was argued by Levinson (2007) that employees who develop ethical attitudes in their work are more likely to create loyal customers.

Ethical employees are more successful to meet customer needs than others (Right Management, 2006) and, as a result, customer loyalty tends to be better in organizations having such type of employees (Pont, 2004). Ultimately, this may lead to what is sometimes termed "customer engagement," where sincere ethical conducts created a mental and emotional connection between the employees and the customer (Bates, 2004).

Generally, although human behavior consists of two main dimensions (discipline and indiscipline, good and bad, just and unjust, right and wrong), and the ethical behavior is influenced significantly of many factors such as demographics of factors of individuals, their educational, and religiosity levels, but working in service sector requires special type of people who have understand that caring of customers and guests is their main duty, this duty does not accept the negative dimension of human behavior at anyway. The proper application of ethics can change the workplace to an excellent one (Hall in Mathenge, 2013).

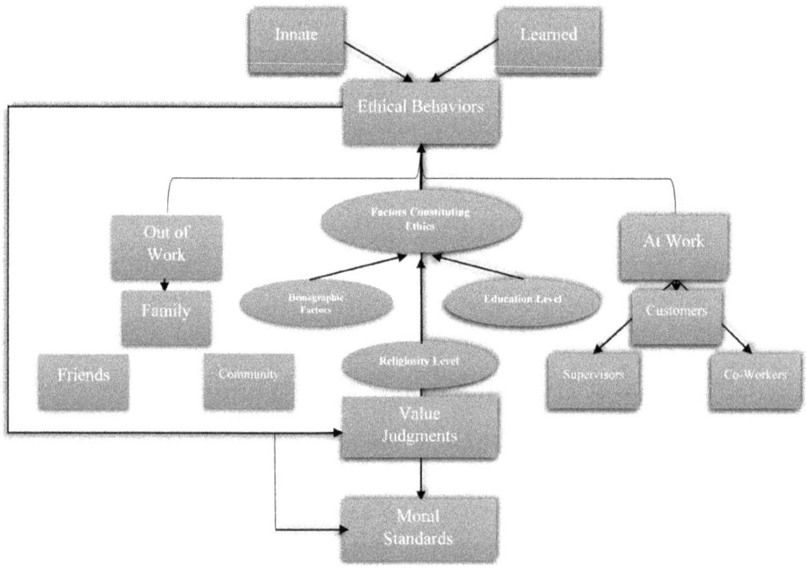


**FIGURE 6.2** Individual's ethics scope.

**Source:** The Authors

The relationship between ethics and productivity has been largely studied and various factors are responsible for this relationship. Some researchers argued that employees work attitude tends to be more favorable especially for organizations working in the service sector (Aluko, 2007; Kenrick et al., 2005; Salau et al., 2014), where friendliness, affection, recognition, harmony, and freedom are crucial for enhancing organizational productivity (Ogunbameru, 2004). However, where these are ignored, low morale and productivity becomes a common phenomenon.

In other words, how well organizations adhere to ethical standards, obviously, determines the well-being of all the stakeholders, the organization's productivity and subsequently the business profitability. Any behavior contrary to the expectations of these actors would rather hinder the trajectory of production processes and the development of the organizations. Therefore, the success of every organization is a dependent factor on employees' attitude toward increasing productivity of the organization.

### *6.7.1 ETHICAL LEADERSHIP*

In order to achieve a productive and successful workforce in the business sector in general, there are a number of issues that business professionals and managers must consider, such as

- recruitment procedures (discriminations issues, gendered hiring, etc.),
- employment contract (zero hours contract, temporary contract, etc.),
- employment types (casual, part-time),
- pay and compensations (low wages, financial and nonfinancial incentives, etc.),
- labor skills (apprenticeships problems, lack or inefficient training course, or programs),
- working hours (long working hours, unsocial shifts),
- working environment (modern slavery conditions),
- teamwork harmony (workforce diversity impacts, etc.), etc.

Negative examples of immoral behavior are like a "cancer" within organizations (Fisher and Lovell, 2003). Failing to be a good leader can bring disastrous consequences to the business environment; it can increase and maximize employee issues and in turn hinder the production and service process, increase turnover and decrease the likelihood of attracting new employees that cause labor shortage in the organization which end into two ways: hiring low skilled employees or experiencing closing down for some shifts. Generally, all these consequences associated increasing costs, employee turnover costs, costs of reduced employee productivity, or losing a part of work time that may extend to lose a segment of the market.

In the context of tourism and hospitality industries, there are a number of labor issues, which affect the business negatively. These include

- individual discrimination concerns prejudice (race, age, gender, etc.),
- fair wages (high dependence on tipping and service charges),
- female workers' rights,
- child labor,
- long working hours,
- inability to join trade unions, and
- importing of labor at low pay and displacement of traditional employment to benefit from tourism dollars.

According to Crane and Matten (2007), if leaders are perceived to be ruthless and inconsiderate in their business interactions with employees and customers, they are likely to get the message too. So, managers and supervisors must work on themselves to gain the skills of leadership. Customers and other stakeholders increasingly expect that organizations operating in the built environment behave ethically. Ethical behavior includes tackling corruption (e.g., compliance with the Bribery Act), acting transparently, having high standards of business ethics and human rights, and facilitating whistleblowing. A good leader has an idea of goodness and respective goals and is willing to hold on to these goals even in difficult times to develop an ethical business environment. In a study conducted by Treviño et al. (2003) on the understanding of executive ethical leadership, they found that ethical leaders are thought to be receptive and open, and possess traditional leadership traits such integrity, honesty, and trustworthiness. Leadership is defined as a process whereby an individual influences a group of individuals to achieve a common goal (Northouse, 2007). Theoretically, there are three basic ways to explain how people become leaders (Bass, 1990):

1. The trait leadership theory: trait theory is a situation where some personality qualities may lead people naturally into leadership roles.
2. Crisis theory: a crisis or important event may cause a person to rise to the occasion, which brings out extraordinary leadership qualities in an ordinary person.
3. The process leadership theory: the individual learns the leadership skills.

Organizations can achieve better employee attraction and retention when employees have the opportunity to work for truly responsible and ethical leader (Bower, 2003 cited in Upadhyay and Singh, 2010; Collins, 2011). Managers and supervisors who develop ethical conducts such as honest, credible, respectful, and fair positively influence on their subordinates (Kouzes and Posner, 2007 cited in Collins, 2010). De Hoogh and Den Hartog (2008) argued that ethical leaders not only stress moral values in their decision making, but they also define organizational norms and standards, encourage their employees to be adopt high ethical standards and behaviors, clarify to followers how their tasks and efforts will contribute to the achievement of important work unit goals, and live up the employees' expectations.

In addition, because ethical leaders ask, "What is the right thing to do?" When making decisions, employees learn to develop their critical sense and think strategically about the decisions they make, and this process enhances employee self-efficacy. By helping employees think through the decisions they make, ethical leaders help foster an important skill that employees can utilize when making decisions on their own—and this increased autonomy improves their self-efficacy beliefs. This is a situation whereby leaders engage in behavior that benefits others and refrains from behavior that can cause harm to their coworkers and the business (Toor and Ofori, 2009). So, ethical leadership can be defined as "the demonstration of normatively appropriate behavior through personal actions and interpersonal relationships, and the promotion of such conduct to employees through two-way communication, reinforcement and, decision-making" (Brown et al., 2005).

Incorporating the purpose, vision, and values of the organization within an understanding of ethical ideals is the main quality of the ethical leaders. They connect the goals of the organization with that of the internal employees and external stakeholders; also, they focus on moral values and social concerns in decision-making, consider the impact of organizational decisions on the outside world (Piccolo et al., 2010). Table 6.2 shows the many attributes that characterize ethical leadership according to some researchers.

It can be concluded that ethical leaders are those leaders that are sensitive to the interest of all employees without fear or favor. According to social exchange theory, employees tend to develop high-quality relationships based upon whom they interact with, how they interact with them, and their experiences with them (Cropanzano and Mitchell, 2005). In other words, when employees perceive that leaders act in their best interests and are caring, employees infer that leaders are committed to them. The result is enhanced high quality of performance and productivity because of high levels of loyalty, emotional connections, and mutual support (Bauer et al., 2006).

## 6.7.2 ETHICAL LEADERSHIP IMPACTS

### 6.7.2.1 SELF-EFFICACY

According to Bandura (1986), self-efficacy can be enhanced by four techniques (modeling, physiological motivation, verbal persuasion, and enactive mastery or personal attainments), each influenced by ethical leadership through social learning.

**TABLE 6.2** Ethical Leadership Characteristics.

| | Resick et al. (2006) | Freeman and Stewart (2006) | Tumlin and Connaughton (2009) | O'Connell and Bligh (2009) |
|---|---|---|---|---|
| 1 | Character and integrity | The articulation and adopting of organizational purposes and values | Leadership knowledge and ethical organizational standards | Use an ethical lens |
| 2 | Ethical awareness | Priority of organizational success rather than personal objectives or personal ego | Collective actions situations managing | On time ethical decisions |
| 3 | Community development | Developing high standard recruitment and retention policies | Observing and positively interacting with ethical leaders, who have demonstrated moral courage | Ability to make strategic decisions |
| 4 | Motivating | Building an ethical organizational climate | Evaluating the ethical standards of organization's team | Involve others when making decisions |
| 5 | Encouraging and empowering | Creating the concept of charitable ethics | Devise measures and develop incentives for the ethical behavior | Acts as role models' ethical behavior |
| 6 | Activating ethical accountability | Taking imaginative ethical decisions and supporting organization' stakeholders through the social responsibility approach | Enhancing the individuals' organizational values | Communicates the culture of ethics (orientation, holding employees accountable for acting ethically, providing training) |

**Source:** The Authors

Ethical leadership practices impose the manager to place employees in situations that facilitate growth and confidence in their job-related skills, subsequently enhancing their levels of self-efficacy through observational or indirect learning and persuasion (Zhu et al., 2004), so leaders who demonstrate moral conduct and act ethically play a significant role in developing and strengthening efficacy beliefs.

Anxiety and stress-associated working environment significantly is reduced because of developing ethical leadership climate within the organization that focuses on the process matters more than the outcomes, thereby enhancing employee's self-efficacy. Regarding personal attainments, ethical leaders are described as more caring about employees' best interests and thus want to see them perform well and achieving their potential (Brown et al., 2005). Such leader behavior is more likely to create a psychologically safe environment for employees to get direct feedback regarding their problems (Walumbwa et al., 2009). The result is feeling more confident in one's ability, leading to increased self-efficacy.

#### *6.7.2.2 ORGANIZATIONAL IDENTIFICATION*

The presence of trust and when the satisfaction of the individual's need for psychological security is ensured, employee will further identify themselves with their organization (Walumbwa et al., 2011).

Ethical leader behaviors promote the trust and make the employee feel job secure and then raise their identification with the workgroup or organization. The absence of competition within the organization raises the organizational identification with workforce (Mael and Ashforth, 1992).

#### *6.7.2.3 EMPLOYEE PERFORMANCE*

Employee performance is the vital element of any organization and the most important factor for the success of the organization and its performance. The performance is the combined efforts of all of the organization employees. The performance of the employee is highly affected by the leadership; ethical leadership can stimulate the workgroups for better performance as cited in Sabir et al. (2012). Leadership practices influence the employees' performance directly and sometimes indirect. So, leadership is broadly proved through research to be an important factor for the success of the organizations.

#### 6.7.2.4 TRUST

The employees' trust in their ethical leaders results in increasing the employee's compliance with organizational rules and laws, increasing the employees' flexibility to accept organizational changes, and improving employee contributions in terms of performance, intent to remain and civic virtue behavior (Ponnu and Tennakoon, 2009). Trust within an organization can contribute to creating greater efficiencies in relationships between leaders, employees, and top-level executives. On the other hand, workgroups are unlikely to follow leaders who show unethical behaviors and may likely take advantage of them (Sabir et al., 2012); so, low levels of trust can result in infighting and inefficient performance because of the status of organizational decay that prevails the work environment. Hence, there is no basis for the future in organizations that have little or no trust. So, trust is an important issue in organizations which has effect on performance and if broken is likely to has serious adverse effect.

#### 6.7.2.5 ATTRACTING AND RETAINING THE BEST EMPLOYEES

Lockwood (2007) argued that in the near future, there will be a shortage in the labor force. Thus, developing good policies concerning the human resources issues has become very important. The success of any company depends significantly on attracting, motivating, and retaining skilled employees. So, ethical leadership was found to play an important role in the success of the business today as well as in the long term.

Ethical leadership makes the organization a convenient work environment in which employees take pride in their organization and that they get highly satisfied with their job. In addition, employees that identify with their organization will aim for more success at work.

Satisfied employees that take pride in their company will in turn lead to a commitment to continue employment. Employees are extremely satisfied and committed with organizations that they believe in ethics and act in a socially responsible way (Bhattacharya et al., 2008).

#### 6.7.2.6 EMPLOYEE ENGAGEMENT

Barclays (2008) defined employee engagement as "the extent to which an employee feels a sense of attachment to the organization he or she works for, believes in its missions and supports its values." Engaged employees are more than just being satisfied or motivated so they want to give of their best to help it succeed because they have a sense of personal attachment. Also, they are considered as a good marketer for the organization they are affiliated because always speak positively about their organization and have an active desire to stay (Civil Service, 2008). The engaged employees differ from others; they have unique qualities that make them valuable assets for the organization, such qualities as (Macey and Schneider, 2006) follows:

- strive to meet the organization's needs,
- they are proactive, and takes initiative,
- try to reinforce and support the organization's culture and values,
- share the values of the organization, and
- stays focused and vigilant and always their efforts make a difference.

Macey and Schneider (2008) claimed that engagement is an "illusive force" that motivates an employee to achieve higher levels of performance. A study of 50,000 employees found that the performance of most engaged and committed employees is 20% better than their coworkers (Corporate Leadership Council, 2004). Likewise, Watson Wyatt's (2007) survey of 946 organizations across 22 countries found that employees who are highly engaged are more than twice as likely to be top performers than are other employees. As cited in (Sonnentag, 2003), Schaufeli et al. (2002) claimed that work engagement is a positive experience.

There are numerous outcomes of investing in improving employee engagement as follows:

*Employee retention*

Levinson (2007) also suggests that employees who are satisfied in their work are more likely to stay in the organization. It was claimed by Sonnentag (2003) that work engagement is indeed positively related to organizational commitment. Blessing White (2008) reported that 41% of engaged employees said that they would stay if the organization is struggling to survive.

*Employees' commitment*

Loyalty and attachment of an employee or group to an organization is defined as commitment. High levels of ethical leadership behavior are strongly linked to higher levels of employee's organizational commitment (Upadhyay and Singh, 2010). Organizational commitment is defined as a state in which an individual identifies with a particular organization and its goals and wishes to maintain membership in the organization.

### *Bottom-line profit*

Ethical leadership practices as mentioned before entail prevailing ethical culture within the organization, which affects significantly on employee engagement. The appeal of employee engagement to management links to bottom-line results (People Management, 2008). These results may manifest in various ways such as through increased high-quality products (service), customer loyalty, increased sales, or better retention levels (Cleland et al., 2008).

### *Successful organizational change*

Graen (2008) claimed that employee engagement plays a key role in aiding the successful implementation of organizational change and may be particularly important to enabling organizational flexibility in organization forced to adapt to the changing market.

## REFERENCES

Albaum, G.; Peterson, R. Ethical Attitudes of Future Business Leaders: Do They Vary by Gender and Religiosity? *Bus. Soc.* **2006,** *45* (2), 300–321.

Aluko, M. A. Factors That Motivate the Nigerian Workers. *JFE Soc. Rev.* **2007,** *5* (10), 55.

Bandura, A. *Social Foundations of Thought and Action: A Social Cognitive Theory*; Englewood Cliffs, NJ: Prentice Hall, 1989.

Barclays. *Definition* (online), 2008. www.business.barclays.co.uk/BRC1/jsp/brccontrol?task=articleFWvi6andvalue=7220andtarget=_bla kandsite=bbb#definition (accessed Nov 5, 2017).

Bass, B. From Transactional to Transformational Leadership: Learning to Share the Vision. *Organ. Dyn.* **1990,** *8* (3), 19–31.

Bates, S. Getting Engaged. *HR Mag.* **2004,** *49* (2), 44–51.

Bauer, T. N.; Erdogan, B.; Liden, R. C.; Wayne, S. J. A Longitudinal Study of the Moderating Role of Extraversion: Leader–Member Exchange, Performance, and Turnover during New Executive Development. *J. Appl. Psychol.* **2006,** *91*, 298–310.

Bauman, C. W.; Skitka, L. J. Corporate Social Responsibility as a Source of Employee Satisfaction. *Res. Organ. Behav.* **2012,** *32*, 63–86.

Beck, J. A.; Lazer, W. Schmidgall, R. Hotel Marketing Manager's Responses to Ethical Dilemmas. *Int. J. Hospitality Tour. Adm.* **2007,** *8* (3), 35–48.

Bhatia, S. K. *Business Ethics and Managerial Values*; Deep and Deep Publications Pvt. Ltd.: New Delhi, 2003.

Bhattacharya, C. B.; Sen, S.; Korschun, D. Using Corporate Social Responsibility to Win the War for Talent. *MIT Sloan Manag. Rev.* **2008,** *49* (2), 36–44

Blessing White. *The State of Employee Engagement*; Blessing White, 2008.

Bligh, M. C. Rebounding from Corruption: Perceptions of Ethics Program Effectiveness in a Public-Sector Organization. *J. Bus. Ethics* **2006,** *67* (4), 359–374.

Bower, M. Company Philosophy: The Way We Do Things around Here. *McKinsey Q.* **2003,** *2*, 111–117.

Boyd, S. Tourism: Searching for Ethics under the Sun. *Latin america Press* **1999,** *31* (33), 1–10.

Brown, M. E.; Treviño, L. K.; Harrison, D. A. Ethical Leadership: A Social Learning Perspective for Construct Development and Testing. *Organ. Behav. Hum. Dec. Process.* **2005,** *97*, 117–134.

Butcher, J. 'Ethical' Travel and Well-Being: Reposing the Issue. *Tour. Recreat. Res.* **2008,** *33* (2), 219–222.

Civil Service. *Introducing Engagement: Understanding the Concept and Practice of Employee Engagement* (online), 2008. www.civilservice.gov.uk/documents/pdf/engagements/Introducing_Engagement.pdf (accessed Aug 12, 2017).

Cleland, A.; Mitchinson, W.; Townend, A. *Engagement, Assertiveness and Business Performance – A New Perspective*; Ixia Consultancy Ltd.: Chipping Norton, UK, 2008.

Collins, D. Designing Ethical Organizations for Spiritual Growth and Superior Performance: An Organization Systems Approach. *J. Manage., Spirituality Relig.* **2010,** *7* (2), 95–117.

Corporate Leadership Council. *Driving Performance and Retention Through Employee Engagement*; Corporate Executive Board, Washington, DC, 2004. (Online) https://www.stcloudstate.edu/humanresources/_files/documents/supv-brown-bag/employee-engagement.pdf (accessed Mar 3, 2019).

Costello, H.; Hogan, I. Codes of Ethics in Hospitality and Tourism. *Int. J. Hosp. Manage.* **2002,** *2* (4), 243–268.

Crane, A.; Matten, D. *Business Ethics: Managing Corporate Citizenship and Sustainability in the Age of Globalization*, 2nd ed.; New York: Oxford University Press Inc., 2007.

Cropanzano, R.; Mitchell, M. S. Social Exchange Theory: An Interdisciplinary Review. *J. Manage.* **2005,** *31*, 874–900.

Dahlsrud, A. How Corporate Social Responsibility Is Defined: An Analysis of 37 Definitions. *Corp. Soc. Responsibility Environ. Manage.* **2008,** *15* (1), 1–13.

De Hoogh, A. H.; Den Hartog, D. N. Ethical and Despotic Leadership, Relationships with Leader's Social Responsibility, Top Management Team Effectiveness and Subordinates' Optimism: A Multimethod Study. *Leadership Q.* **2008,** *19*, 297–311.

Dodds, R.; Joppe, M. *CSR in the Tourism Industry? The Status of and Potential for Certification, Codes of Conduct and Guidelines*; CSR Practice Foreign Investment, Advisory Service Investment Climate Department, 2005. http://www.ifc.org/ifcext/economics.nsf/AttachmentsByTitle/CSR+in+the+Tourism+Industry/$FIL CSR+in+the+Tourism+Industry.pdf (accessed Aug 28, 2017).

Dozier, B. *Ethics in the Hospitality Industry* (online), 2013. https://barbradozier.wordpress.com/2013/06/17/ethics-in-the-hospitality-industry (accessed Dec 15, 2017).

Elan, E. *Cultivating a Green Image*; New York, NY Nation's Restaurant News, 2010; p 15.

Enea, C. The Tourism Industry of Ethics and Tourism. *Manage. Mark. Craiova* **2007,** *1*, 166–170.

ERC Ethics Resource Center. SURVEY FINDINGS 2005: Ethical Conduct Within Business, 2005. (Online) www.ethics.org/nbes/nbes2005/index.html (accessed Mar 1, 2019).

Fennell, D. A. *Tourism Ethics*; Channel View Publications: Clevedon, Buffalo, Toronto, 2006; p 9.

Ferrell, O. C.; Gresham, L. G. A Contingency Framework for Understanding Ethical Decision Making. *J. Mark.* **1985,** *49* (3), 87–96.

Fisher, C.; Lovell, A. *Business Ethics and Values*; Pearson Education Limited: Essex, 2003.

Freeman, R. E.; Stewart, L. *Developing Ethical Leadership, A Bridge Paper of Business Roundtable Institute for Corporate Ethics* (online), 2006. www.corporate-ethics.org (accessed Aug 20, 2017).

Gond, J. P.; Swaen, V.; El Akremi, A. The Human Resources Contribution to Responsible Leadership: An Exploration of the CSR–HR Interface. *J. Bus. Ethics* **2011,** *98* (1), 115–132.

Graen, G. B. Enriched Engagement through Assistance to Systems' Change: A Proposal. *Ind. Organ. Psychol.* **2008,** *1*, 74–75.

Grojean, M. W.; Resick, C. J.; Dickson, M. W.; Smith, D. B. Leaders, Values, and Organizational Climate: Examining Leadership Strategies for Establishing an Organizational Climate Regarding Ethics. *J. Bus. Ethics* **2004,** *55* (3), 223 -241.

Hall, D.; Brown, F. The Tourism Industry's Welfare Responsibilities: An Adequate Response?. *Tour. Recreat. Res.* **2008,** *33* (2), 213–218.

Harris, S. M. Green Tick TM: An Example of Sustainability Certification of Goods and Services. *Manage. Environ. Quality: Int. J.* **2007,** *18* (2), 167–178.

Integra. *Ecotourism vs. Sustainable Tourism* (online), 2012. http://www.integrallc.com/2012/08/13/ecotourism-vs-sustainable-tourism/ (accessed Oct 5, 2017).

Jovičić, A.; Pivac, T.; Dragin, A. Ethical Conduct of Employees in Tourist Organizations in Novi Sad (Serbia). *Turizam* **2011,** *15* (4), 35–147.

Karwacki, J.; Boyd, C. Ethics and Ecotourism. *Eur. Rev.* **1995,** *4*, 225–232.

Kenrick, D. T.; Neuberg, S. L.; Ciadini, R. B. *Social Psychology: Unraveling the Mystery*, 3rd ed.; Pearson Education Inc.: Upper Saddle River, NJ, 2005.

Kouzes, J. M.; Posner, B. Z. *The Leadership Challenge*; John Wiley and Sons: Hoboken, NJ, 2007.

Labbai, M. M. Social Responsibility and Ethics in Marketing. In *Proceedings of the International Marketing Conference on Marketing and Society*; IIMK, 2007.

Lansing, P.; Devries, P. Sustainable Tourism: Ethical Alternative or Marketing Ploy. *J. Bus. Ethics* **2007,** *72*, 77–85.

Levinson, E. *Developing High Employee Engagement Makes Good Business Sense* (online), 2007. www.interactionassociates.com/ideas/2007/05/developing_high_employee_engagement_makes_goodbusiness_sense.php (accessed Nov 15, 2017).

Levy, S. E.; Park, S-Y. An Analysis of CSR Activities in the Lodging Industry. *J. Hosp. Tour. Manage.* **2011,** *18* (1), 147–54.

Lockwood, N. R. Leveraging Employee Engagement for Competitive Advantage: HR's Strategic Role. *HR Mag.* **2007,** *53* (3), 1–11.

Lockwood, N. R. *Corporate Social Responsibility: HR's Leadership Role*; Society for Human Resource Management, 2004. (Online) http://www.mandrake.ca/bill/images/newsletter/documents/HR's%20Leadership%20Role.pdf (accessed Mar 2, 2019).

Luthar, H. K.; Bibattista, R. A.; Gautschi, T. Perceptions of What the Ethical Climate Is When What It Should Be: The Role of Gender, Academic Status, and Ethical Education. *J. Bus. Ethics* **1997,** *16* (2), 205–217.

Macey, W. H.; Schneider, B. The Meaning of Employee Engagement. *Ind. Organ. Psychol.* **2006,** *1*, 3–30.

Macey, W. H.; Schneider, B. The Meaning of Employee Engagement. *Ind. Organ. Psychol.* **2008,** *1*, 3–30.

Mael, F.; Ashforth, B. E. Alumni and Their Alma Mater: A Partial Test of the Reformulated Model of Organizational Identification. *J. Organ. Behav.* **1992,** *13*, 103–123.

Marrewijk, M. Concepts and Definitions of CSR and Corporate Sustainability: Between Agency and Communion. *J. Bus. Ethics* **2003,** *44* (2–3), 95–105.

Mathenge, G. D. Responsible Tourism and Hotel Management: An Empirical Analysis of the Ethical Dimensions in Tourism and Hospitality Industry in Kenya. *Am. Int. J. Contemp. Res.* **2013,** *3* (6), 18–19.

McGran, K. Taking Tourists for a Ride? *Toronto Star, Section B*, 2003.

Mirvis, P. Employee Engagement and CSR: Transactional, Relational and Developmental Approaches. *Calif. Manage. Rev.* **2012,** *54* (4), 93–117.

Northouse, G. *Leadership Theory and Practice*, 3rd ed.; Sage Publications, Inc.: Thousand Oak, London, New Delhi, 2007.

O'Connell, W.; Bligh, M. Emerging from Ethical Scandal: Can Corruption Really Have a Happy Ending? *Leadership* **2009,** *5* (2), 213–235.

Ogunbameru, O. A. *Organizational Dynamics*; Spectrum Books Ltd.: Ibadan, 2004.

Pearson, J. Are We Doing the Right Thing? *J. Corp. Citizenship* **2010,** *37*, 37–40.

Piccolo, R. F.; Greenbaum, R.; Den Hartog, D. N.; Folger, R. The Relationship between Ethical Leadership and Core Job Characteristics. *J. Organ. Behav.* **2010,** *31*, 259–278.

Plüss, C. *Quick Money-Easy Money? A Report on Child Labor in Tourism* (online), 1999. http://akte.ch/ (accessed Aug 19, 2017).

Ponnu, C. H.; Tennakoon, G. The Association between Ethical Leadership and Employee Outcomes the Malaysian Case. *Electr. J. Bus. Ethics Organ. Stud.* **2009,** *14* (1), 21–32.

Pont, J. Are They Really 'On the Job'? *Potentials* **2004,** *37*, 32.

Poulston, J. Hospitality Workplace Problems and Poor Training: A Close Relationship. *Int. J. Hospitality Manage.* **2008,** *20* (4), 412–427.

Ratkovic, N. B. *Business Ethics*; Robinson, D., Ed.; Novi Sad: University of Novi Sad Faculty of Technical Sciences, 2009.

Resick, C. J.; Hanges, P. J.; Dickson, M. W.; Mitchelson, J. K. A Cross-Cultural Examination of the Endorsement of Ethical Leadership. *J. Bus. Ethics* **2006,** *63* (4), 345–359.

Right Management. *Measuring True Employee Engagement*; Right Management, 2006.

Rio Earth Summit. Environment And Development. THE RIO DECLARATION, 1992. (Online) http://www.unesco.org/education/pdf/RIO_E.PDF (accessed Mar 1, 2019).

Rustad, M. J.; Skar, L. Involvement of Employees in Corporate Social Responsibility: An Explorative Case Study. Ph.D. Dissertation, Industrial Economics and Technology Management, Norwegian University of Science and Technology, Trondheim, Norway, 2015.

Sabir, M. S.; Iqbal, J. J.; Rehman, K. U.; Shah, K. A.; Yameen, M. Impact of Corporate Ethical Values on Ethical Leadership and Employee Performance. *Int. J. Bus. Soc. Sci.* **2012,** *3* (2), 163–171.

Salau, O. P.; Faiola, H. O.; Akin bode, J. O. Induction and Staff Attitude towards Retention and Organizational Effectiveness. *IOSR J. Bus. Manage.* **2014,** *16* (4), 47–52.

Schaufeli, W. B.; Salanova, M.; Gonzalez-Roma, V.; Bakker, A. B. The Measurement of Engagement and Burnout: A Two-Sample Confirmatory Factor Analytic Approach. *J. Happiness Stud.* **2002,** *3*, 71–92.

Schwartz, L.; Willison, D. J.; Emerson, C.; Szala-Meneok, K. V.; Gibson, E.; Weisbaum K. M.; Fournier, F.; Brazil, K.; Coughlin, M. Access to Medical Records for Research Purposes: Varying Perceptions Across Research Ethics Boards. *J. Med. Ethics* **2008,** *34* (4), 308–314.

Schwepker, C. H., Jr. Ethical Climate's Relationship to Job Satisfaction, Organizational Commitment, and Turnover Intention in the Salesforce. *J. Bus. Res.* **2001,** *54* (1), 39–52.

Shahin, A.; Zairi, M. Corporate Governance as a Critical Element for Driving Excellence in Corporate Social Responsibility. *Int. J. Quality Reliab. Manage.* **2007,** *24* (7), 753–770.

Sharma, A.; Kukreja, S.; Sharma, A. Impact of Labor Laws on Child Labor: A Case of Tourism Industry. *Int. J. Adv. Manage. Econ.* **2012,** *1* (3), 47–50.

Sledge, S.; Miles, A. K.; Coppage, S. What Role Does Culture Play? A Look at Motivation and Job Satisfaction among Hotels in Brazil. *Int. J. Hum. Resour. Manage.* **2008,** *19* (9), 1667–1682.

Smagulova, A.; Shegebayev, M.; Garkavenko, V.; Boolaky, M. Ethical Practices and Social Responsibility of Kazakhstani Tourism Business: A Pilot Study in the Tour Operator Sector. *Cent. Asia Bus. J.* **2009,** *2*, 12–23.

Sonnentag, S. Recovery, Work Engagement, and Proactive Behavior: A New Look at the Interface between Non-work and Work. *J. Appl. Psychol.* **2003,** *88* (3), 518–528.

Stevens, B. Hospitality Ethics: Responses from HR Directors and Students to Seven Ethical Scenarios. *J. Bus. Ethics* **2001,** *30* (2), 233–242.

Stevens, G. Ethical Issues in Hotel Human Resources. *J. Hospitality Tour. Educ.* **2008,** *12* (5), 56–78.

Tepelus, C. M. Social Responsibility and Innovation on Trafficking and Child Sex Tourism: Morphing of Practice into Sustainable Tourism Policies? *Tour. Hospitality Res.* **2008,** *8*, 98–115.

TOI. *Improving Tour Operator Performance: The Role of Corporate Social Responsibility and Reporting* (online), 2002. http://tilz.tearfund.org/webdocs/Website/Campaigning/Policy%20and%20research/Policy%20%20Tourism%20CSR%208%20Pager.pdf (accessed Aug 20, 2017).

Toor, S.; Ofori, G. Ethical Leadership: Examining the Relationships with Full Range Leadership Model, Employee Outcomes, and Organizational Culture. *J. Bus. Ethics* **2009,** *90*, 533–547.

Tumlin, G. R.; Connaughton, S. L. An Interdisciplinary Major in Ethical Leadership Studies: Rationale, Challenges and Template for Building an Adaptable Program. *J. Int. Leader.* **2009,** *2* (1), 91–128.

Treviño, L. K.; Brown, M.; Hartman, L. P. A Qualitative Investigation of Perceived Executive Ethical Leadership: Perceptions from Inside and Outside the Executive Suite. *Hum. Relat.* **2003,** *56* (1), 5–37.

Treviño, L.; Butterfield, K.; McCabe, D. The Ethical Context in Organizations: Influences on Employee Attitudes and Behaviors. *Next Phase Bus. Ethics* **2001,** *3*, 301–337.

Treviño, L.; Weaver, G.; Gibson, D.; Toffler, B. Managing Ethics and Compliance: What Works and What Hurts. *Calif. Manage. Rev.* **1999,** *41* (2), 131–151.

UNWTO, UNWTO Annual Report 2014, UNWTO, Madrid.

UNWTO. *Sustained Growth in International Tourism Despite Challenges* (online), 2017. http://www2.unwto.org/press-release/2017-01-17/sustained-growth-international-tourism-despite challenges (accessed Nov 16, 2017).

Upadhyay, Y.; Singh, S. K. In Favor of Ethics in Business: The Linkage between Ethical Behavior and Performance. *J. Hum. Value* **2010,** *16* (1), 9–19.

Verbeke, W.; Ouwerkerk, C.; Peelen, E. Exploring the Contextual and Individual Factors on Ethical Decision Making of Salespeople. *J. Bus. Ethics* **1996,** *15* (11), 1175–1187.

Walker, R. J. *Introduction to Hospitality Management*, 3rd ed.; Prentice Hall: Upper Saddle River, NJ, 2010.
Wallace, H. Current Issues: Business Ethics and Tourism: Responsible Management. *Int. J. Hospitality Manage.* **2005,** *4* (1), 263–268.
Walumbwa, F. O.; Cropanzano, R.; Hartnell, C. A. Organizational Justice, Voluntary Learning Behavior, and Job Performance: A Test of the Mediating Effects of Identification and Leader–Member Exchange. *J. Organ. Behav.* **2009,** *30*, 1103–1126.
Walumbwa, F. O.; Mayer, D. M.; Wang, P.; Wang, H.; Workman, K.; Christensen, A. L. *Linking Ethical Leadership to Employee Performance: The Roles of Leader–Member Exchange, Self-Efficacy, and Organizational Identification* (online), 2011. http://scholarship.sha.cornell.edu/articles/762 (accessed Oct 1, 2017).
Watson Wyatt. *Playing to Win in a Global Economy: Global Strategic Rewards Report and United States Findings*, Watson Wyatt Worldwide: Arlington, VA, 2007.
Weber, J.; Seger, J. E. Influences upon Organizational Ethical Subclimates: A Replication Study of a Single Firm at Two Points in Time. *J. Bus. Ethics* **2002,** *41* (1/2), 69–84.
Wheeler, M. Ethics and the Sports Business. *J. Bus. Ethics* **1994,** *3* (1), 8–15.
World Tourism Organization. *Code of Conduct for the Protection of Children from Sexual Exploitation in Travel and Tourism: Background and Implementation Examples* (online), 2017. https://www.unicef.org/lac/code_of_conduct.pdf (accessed Sept 21, 2017).
World Travel and Tourism Council. Global Code of Ethics for Tourism, 2002. (Online) http://ethics.unwto.org/content/global-code-ethics-tourism (accessed March 3, 2019).
WTO. Ethics and Social Dimensions of Tourism. Eleventh Meeting of the World Committee on Tourism Ethics, Rome, 2002.
Zenisek, T. J. Corporate Social Responsibility: A Conceptualization Based on Organizational Literature. *Acad. Manage. Rev.* **1979,** *4* (3), 359–368.
Zhu, W.; May, D. R.; Avolio, B. J. The Impact of Ethical Leadership Behavior on Employee Outcomes: The Roles of Psychological Empowerment and Authenticity. *J. Leadersh. Organ. Stud.* **2004,** *11*, 16–26.

# PART III

# Labor Issues

CHAPTER 7

# LABOR TURNOVER IN THE TOURISM AND HOSPITALITY INDUSTRY

*"Employees don't quit jobs, they quit work circumstances."*

## 7.1 INTRODUCTION

Nowadays, the hospitality industry is considered one of the fastest global industries experiencing an increase, contributing to more than one-third of the service business (ILO, 2010 cited in Bharwani and Butt, 2012). Hospitality industry is a broad category of fields in the service sector that includes accommodation, event planning, theme parks, transportation, cruise lines, and others in the tourism industry (Chon et al., 2013). Jagun (2015) proposed that almost all industrialized nations and even a good number of developing countries have experienced long economic expansions. Specifically, job growth will accompany the economic expansions translating directly into new jobs. Asela et al. (2017) stated that hospitality industry was known to be one of the major contributors to economy in many countries. Furthermore, the hotel sector emerged as a subsection of the industry that strengthened the business. According to Kusluvan (2003), one of the major benefits of the development of the hospitality industry in any economy is the provision of employment.

An increasing number of hospitality organizations were greatly influenced by the growing number of domestic and international tourists. Thus, the industry professionals must focus on the quality of human resource that will be in charge of providing the service for the customers. In order to provide high-quality service, the hospitality industry needs qualified human resources. This is because the industry is fully oriented to customer's satisfaction and the success of the hospitality organization can be seen from customer's satisfaction resulting from the services provided by its employees (Ameliya and Febriansyah, 2017). Primarily, the hospitality industry strongly depends on the human factor and direct contact with customers and guests. Human resources become the major role of the service process, playing a decisive part in enhancing the organizational image (Bharwani and Butt, 2012).

However, workers in hospitality industry face various challenges including those common to all service industry jobs and those specific to the hotel industry, which is characterized by small-scale organizations. Huge problems still exist in attracting and retaining a skilled labor force. According to Mwilu (2016), the two abiding things in this industry are a high staff turnover, which affects the ability to deliver a consistent brand experience and the fact that not enough jobseekers see the growing industry as somewhere to meet their expectations regarding their careers stability and personal growth.

The main problem that this chapter discusses is labor turnover. Turnover intention is one of the areas which is so popular that it has been researched in organizational analysis (Özbağ et al., 2014) and has unpleasant financial impacts on the organization in terms of selection and training, developing, maintaining, and retaining. Business organizations could lose some of their greatest assets when well-trained employees leave their work (Narayanan, 2016).

Labor turnover in the hospitality industry often averages as much as 200–300% per year. Woods (1997) expressed the issue of labor turnover in hospitality operations statistically by summarizing that the entire staff of a hospitality operation turnover two to three times per year.

Organizations with high levels of turnover rates for full-time employees experience poor customer-satisfaction ratings (Hurley, 2015) that reflect on the financial performance of the organization in terms of costs resulted by losing the customers and hiring new employees. So, in order to serve quality goods and services with a reasonable price, and compete with their competitors, managers and supervisors must control the labor expenses by satisfying their employees through considering their problems.

## 7.2 THE CONCEPT OF LABOR TURNOVER

Although the turnover of low skilled or complaining employees is an opportunity to hire new employees and stabilize the organization, organizations should know that employee turnover is a serious problem if the number continues to increase, as from the employer's perspective, the turnover of skilled employees is a big loss to the company. According to Musa et al.

(2014), labor turnover refers to the movement of people in and out of a business. However, the term is commonly used to refer only to "wastage" or the number of employees leaving. Frequently, managers refer to turnover as the entire process associated with filling a vacancy in case of the movement of workers out of the organization, whereas employees who transfer to other positions within the same organization are not considered in the calculation, as well as old workers who retired, had their job phased-out, or were terminated due to downsizing.

Generally, labor turnover can come in different forms:

- resignation,
- transfer out organizational units,
- retirement,
- termination, or
- death.

Also, there are some patterns that may be considered turnover cases or not according to the manager perceptions:

- internal transfers,
- promotions,
- pregnancy or illness vacations, and
- planned layoffs.

It is important to identify how to calculate the turnover rate and to define the parameters of a satisfactory ratio in the market. Turnover rates for employees can be measured and compared over time and across organizations using what is commonly referred to as the employee turnover index. The method used for calculating employee turnover differs among hospitality organizations, depending on their objectives.

Thus, there are different ways of measuring employee turnover:

- The term turnover is defined by Price (1977) as the ratio of the number of organizational workers who have left during the period being considered divided by the average number of workforce in that organization during that period. This definition emphasizes the number of employees who left the work and thus can be depicted as the workforce stability index and is expressed as follows:

$$\frac{\text{Number of employee exceeding 1 year}}{\text{Total number of employees a year ago}} \times 100 = y\%$$

Some organizations add in the number of new positions added during the year instead of who left the work in order to get a more accurate turnover figure.

- If it is organizational aim to detect and analyze turnover reasons, then they will consider both involuntary turnover (employee termination) and voluntary turnover (employees who leave of their own accord). If the employer wants to assess all costs associated with staff turnover, they should also consider internal transfers, promotions, retirement, planned layoffs, etc. (Steed and Shinnar, 2008).

  By considering the definitions of Price (1977) and Steed and Shinnar (2008), the separation or wastage rate, which expresses the number of leavers during a period (usually 1 year) as a percentage of the average number employed during that period, can be as follows:

$$\frac{\text{Number of leavers (involuntary + voluntary staff turnover) in a period of time}}{\text{Average number of workforce during the surveyed period}} \times 100 = y\%$$

- Another formula that excludes unavoidable employees' departure, calculating controllable turnover levels by separating avoidable from unavoidable employees' departures. Unavoidable separations are those occurring for reasons over which the organization has no control such as pregnancy, illness, and death. Thus, controllable turnover rate is then calculated as

$$\frac{\text{Number of job leavers in (a period of time)} - \text{Unavoidable employees' departure}}{\text{Average number of workforce}} \times 100 = y\%$$

According to Kuria et al. (2011), the result of the last formula is considered the most significant measure of the effectiveness of those who are managing human resources within the organizations; this is mainly because of the proportion of workers and employees' departure which management has a prominent opportunity to control the reasons causing their departure by adopting adequate managerial techniques in selection, training, supervision, improved working conditions, better wages, and opportunities for advancement.

Employee turnover has also been defined as the rotation of workers around the labor market; between organizations, jobs and occupations; and between the status of employment and unemployment (Abassi and Hollman, 2000). The more recent definition of labor turnover is set by Katsikea et al. (2015) who claimed that turnover is a reduction in the number of employees who plan to leave their work. So, labor turnover rate can be used as a parameter which indicates the overall health of an industry or an organization in terms of wages, ethical climate, working conditions, and other welfare facilities provided to the workers (Bolch, 2001); employees are more likely to stay when there is a stable work environment (Zuber, 2001).

Although labor turnover is one of the aspects that mostly studied in organizational research, very little is known regarding causes that generate turnover intention (Mitra et al., 1992). Zeffane (1994) defined turnover intention as a tendency or intention of personnel to quit their jobs. Also, Lambert et al. (2013) defined turnover intention as an employee's thoughts or plan to leave an organization, while Tett and Meyer (1993) defined turnover intention as an aware and considered willingness to leave the organization. The employee willingness to leave the organizations has many signs recorded by Karatepe (2013) described as follows:

- speak negatively about their work environment,
- limiting participation in the organization,
- avoiding involving in setting plans,

In addition to,

- changing in the attitude and behavior,
- increasing the rate of absenteeism, and
- pretending engaging in some social concerns.

Mobley (1977a) stated that the desire/intention to move can be early symptoms of turnover in a company. Labor turnover occurs in a gradual way; in any organization, any time, after joining the work, the employees start to evaluate and compare the existing gob environment, based on their evaluation, their decisions come to continue working in the organization or to quit (Mobley, 1977a). There are some independent factors upon which the employees evaluate their jobs; these include the pay package, organizations policies, personnel rules and regulations, the safety and hygiene factors, work monotony, and burnouts, including work environment, which plays a pivotal role on employees' satisfaction. Turnover intention reflects the probability that an employee will change his or her job within a certain time period (Hartog and Ophem, 1996).

Turnover intention may be classified into six categories (Asela et al., 2017) described as follows.

*a. Voluntary and involuntary turnover intention (Robbins et al., 2008)*

Voluntary turnover intention is a turnover that occurs when employee has own decision/choice to quit or when they leave organization at their own discretion in order to take other employment advantage that offers more attractive conditions. Voluntary turnover is caused by two main factors (Asela et al., 2017):

1. the current available job is uninteresting (job dissatisfaction, unfitting incentives, unmet job expectations, performance problems, situational constraints, socialization difficulties, greater degrees of job stress, and a lack of career advancement opportunities); or
2. the availability of other attractive employment alternatives.

Although involuntary turnover can be defined as the organizations' decision to cut off the working relationship, in this case, employees have no choice in their termination such as business downsizing, sickness, and family reasons and thus this type is uncontrollable for the employees who experience it. In the case of voluntary turnover intention, often, employees who leave on their own decision are the precious employees that the employers would like to retain. According to Phillips and Connell (2003), voluntary termination of employment is on the increase within the hospitality industry. So, such type of employees who have not been dismissed by the employer should be interviewed to determine the reasons of leaving. They must be interviewed at exiting time; this may reveal specific information regarding conditions of employment, competitors' conditions, and the quality or otherwise of supervision, training, and selection procedures.

*b. Functional and dysfunctional turnover*

Functional turnover intention is a turnover in which employees with poor and unskilled performance leave. Besides that, dysfunctional turnover is a turnover in which good performers leave.

*c. Avoidable turnover and unavoidable turnover intention*

Avoidable turnover occurs when employees are dissatisfied with wages, lack of training, workplace stress, relationship with management and other coworkers, working hours, and transport difficulties, whereas unavoidable turnover occurs from life decision that extends beyond an employer's control such as death, retirement, illness, pregnancy, and moving to a new area or a job transfer for a spouse.

All these abovementioned categories may be grouped under one of the following title: external turnover. In turn, another category will be added as follows.

### 7.2.1 INTERNAL TURNOVER AND EXTERNAL TURNOVER

Internal labor turnover involves employees leaving their current position and taking another one within the same organization (Kenya Bureau of Labor Statistics, 2009). Subsequently, internal turnover keeps the human resource asset in addition to increasing the motivation level of the employees as it can be controlled by many human resource mechanisms (e.g., internal recruitment policy or formal succession planning) through which the employees can try new tasks and work with other supervisors which in turn allow them to avoid any relational disruption of the work. Subsequently, internal turnover can be moderated and controlled by typical human resource mechanisms, such as an internal recruitment policy or formal succession planning.

Labor turnover gained a significant importance by many psychologists since such movements represented potential costs to organizations in terms of loss of valuable human resources and the disruption of ongoing activities (Cascio, 1991). So, it is necessary to take constructive action by measuring and monitoring turnover in order to maintain acceptable rate of labor retention. Fair (1992) suggested that employers must consider using leading indicator to detect turnover problems before they become hard to control issue if they really need to decrease the sequences of labor turnover issues in their organization. Intention to quit is an important leading indicator along with organizational engagement and job satisfaction data. According to Tracey and Hinkin (2008), employee turnover rates are usually affected by job dissatisfaction with the overall work environment, working conditions, and wages. Some special working groups are characterized by the symptoms of turnover most of times and wherever they work like women workers, old workers, child labor, and workers with chronic diseases.

Because of their responsibilities like housework, taking care of children and having a baby, female workers leave their jobs more than males (Doherty and Manfredi, 2001). Working hours whether the long working hours or the crazy ones are also among other reasons for women workers to leave their jobs in the hospitality organizations (Demir et al., 2007). Especially night shifts and inflexible working hours force women workers to quit their jobs.

So, women usually work at the entry-level jobs in hospitality establishments, accordingly get fewer salaries than their male coworkers.

According to a study conducted by Iverson (2000) in the United States, it was found that women managers in hotel establishments got very less pay than men managers whether in the beginning or top of their careers. Therefore, some female workers also do not want to return back to their jobs after having a baby (Demir et al., 2007).

The leading indicators can be necessary for early detection before turnover develops into a serious problem (Fair, 1992). Also, it is fundamental to understand the employment climate to develop labor retention and then reducing turnover causes. Such information empowers the management to consider solutions, changes, and improvements to their labor force; settling a high-quality working environment with a range of employee-valued benefits may also increase satisfaction levels and result in discouraging turnover behaviors (Mobley, 1977b). All the managerial levels of the organization should moreover accept the responsibility for eliminating the causes of turnover and managing retention.

## 7.3 EFFECTS OF LABOR TURNOVER

Human resources are recognized as one of the most important assets in service industry, as the hospitality industry is a unique one that exists to serve customers during their holiday time. This time is often spent in the form of hotels and restaurants, amusement parks, cruises, and more. In order to best serve customers' needs, hospitality organizations employ a vast variety of employees (e.g., entertainers, customer service representatives, and maintenance staff). Therefore, loss of human factor assets in terms of high level of turnover rate is considered a significant issue that confronts the organizations, management, and individuals as it jeopardizes the performance and profit of the organization (Guilding et al., 2014).

High turnover rate influences negatively on the level of service provided to the customers and on the hospitality organizations' performance (Hinkin and Tracey, 2000); employee turnover may influence organizational financial performance through five major cost categories: predeparture, recruitment, selection, orientation, and lost productivity (Narayanan, 2016); additionally, high employee turnover rates often result in business failure, an unsatisfied work environment, and lack of attractiveness to skilled workers (Surji, 2013). Moreover, high turnover harms the reputation in terms of losing the quality of product (service) resulting from losing the skilled labor and dominating the residual employee population composed of a high percentage of novice workforce (Amankwaa and Anku-Tsede, 2015). The lack of well-experienced and skilled human power affects negatively on the organizations' performance.

Worldwide researches have claimed that employee turnover is among the highest in the hospitality industry. Studies have shown that the average turnover level among nonmanagement hotel staff in the United States is about 50% and about 25% for management staff.

Estimates of average annual employee turnover range from around 60% to 300%, according to the research conducted by the American Hotel and Motel Association (Mwilu, 2016).

Also, the newly hired employees need adequate training programs that are considered costly for the employers. Thus, labor turnover represents a significant cost in terms of poor production practices and reduced performance standards, high replacement as well as recruiting and training programs costs (Hiemstra, 1990).

Cost of employee turnover depends basically on two factors.

### 1. *The size of the organization*

Larger organization experience more severe turnover problems than smaller. Small organizations are not part of a larger operation such as "chains." They are usually a single outlet, family-owned enterprises, operate as a sole establishment, more likely to hire individuals they know and more stable, whereas major chains or organizations use impersonal hiring procedure, and this will result in errors and attract employees that intend to move to other jobs in an attempt to gain experience or to advance their career. However, the negative consequences of labor turnover are similar for the establishment of all sizes (Lee-Ross, 1999).

### 2. *Job specialty (complexity of the job)*

CIPD (2005) noted that in cases where it is relatively easy to find and train new employees quickly and at relatively little cost, it is possible to sustain providing high-quality levels of service provision despite having a high turnover rate. On the other hand, however, when the job tasks are complicated, the skills are relatively scarce, and in turn, the recruitment process is costly issue and turnover is likely to be problematic from a management point of view. This is especially true of situations with strong customer interaction. This seems to be the issue bedeviling the hospitality organizations.

Hence, costs of labor turnover increase when employees are more specialized, more difficult to find, and require high standard of training courses. It is made up of some or all of the following components (Pranoto, 2011):

- Possible diversion of efforts of more highly skilled employees while waiting for the replacement.
- Payment or other employees' financial incentives while waiting for the replacement.
- Lost production while the employee is being replaced.
- Low-quality production during the training period.
- Cost of scrap and spoiled products during the training period.
- Cost of recruitment, selection.
- Uniform costs.
- Administrative cost.

Also, there are other factors that contribute significantly in determining the cost of turnover include experiences, qualifications, and type of hospitality property (Hinkin and Tracey, 2008).

Generally, many hospitality managers are convinced that excessive turnover is a costly phenomenon, but it is difficult to develop specific turnover cost numbers. That is not to say that researchers have not attempted to nail down the cost of turnover, but the fact remains that specific cost figures can be elusive (William and Davis, 1983). However, a group of statisticians at the Bureau of Labor Statistics in 2014 has tried to do so; they found that employee turnover costs work environment more than $25 billion a year (Holston-Okae, 2017). Organizations spend 30–50% of the yearly salary for entry-level employees, up to 150% of the salaries annually for middle-level employees, and as high as 400% of the annual salary to replace those in upper management positions (Bryant and Allen, 2013).

Therefore, in terms of personal, work-unit, and organizational readjustment, the organizational cost incurred by labor turnover can be tremendous due to members quitting their work and the subsequent hiring of replacement personnel (Darmon, 1990), new-hire training, and general costs for administration (Griffeth and Hom, 2004), in addition to the hidden costs of quality declining during the replacement period. Generally, the higher the turnover rate, the higher the expenditure will occur; staff turnover linked to two types of costs: direct costs and indirect costs (Fair, 1992).

The direct costs are associated with the loss of time and money to recruit, hire, and train employees. According to Lussier (2005), selecting, recruiting, and training new employees often spend a lot of money, whereas the indirect cost is the decline in the quality of performance, production, and services because the company has not found a replacement for the employee to perform work that had previously been left vacant behind by employees who quit or hire new employees who do not have experience and should be given training (Hinkin and Tracey, 2000).

Labor turnover costs are described in detail as follows:

1. *Direct costs (see Fig. 7.1):*
   - temporary staff costs,
   - management time and efforts,
   - separation costs (exit interviews and severance pay),
   - recruitment costs (advertising and search fees),
   - selection costs (interview and reference checking),
   - hiring costs (induction and initial training), relocation expenses, and
   - uniforms and lost productivity costs associated with both the unfilled vacancy and the learning curve associated with the new employee.

Beside the direct costs that are mentioned above, there are hidden costs that contribute to bulk of the cost and often these are overlooked as indirect costs. They include:

2. *Indirect costs:*
   - Low morale.
   - Lost skill sets.
   - Disgruntled customers and lost networks.
   - Stress and pressure on residual staff that in turn impact the employee's performance and make everyone less effective (less motivated, absenteeism, tardiness, less quality products and services) leading to customer dissatisfaction and ultimately customer defection, this is because the staff may be forced to do more unpaid hours or working back to back with no breaks in order to pick up the shortfall. In addition, managers should spend more time and efforts trying to keep the team on track.
   - Coverage costs.
   - When an employee leaves a job, employers cannot say no to bookings or offering an uncompleted product (service); employers definitely will have to pay overtime for someone to cover.
   - Employment brand.
     Employment brand is the image that the organization' prospective, current, and past employees have in their minds about the employment

experience at the organization. In any industry, any employee could finger point at least three businesses that have the reputation as poor employers; excessive turnover destroys the brand of the organization; it reduces organizations' ability to attract the skilled labor and having the brand continually advertising will do nothing to generate interest from candidate's long term.

Negative leaving people are also now able to air their grievances and opinions about the organization and its policies to the wider public through increased exposure on social networking sites on top of word of mouth (www.hospitalityrecruitmentsolution.com.au).

Although direct costs are relatively easy to measure, indirect costs are not so clear cut; this may lead many hotel professionals and executives fail to realize how serious a problem labor turnover can be due to the "hidden" nature of its costs and is difficult to quantify (Mwilu, 2016). So, Hinkin and Tracey (2000) have attempted to shed light on the structure and costs of turnover by classifying turnover costs into five categories: predeparture, recruitment, selection, orientation and training, and lost productivity.

High turnover organizations spend excessive amounts of resources on recruiting and replacing their workforce, whereas smart organizations invest in employee retention. Companies take a deep interest in their employee turnover rate because it is a costly part of running the business (Beam, 2009).

As mentioned before, organizations suffer direct and indirect expenses, which include the cost of advertising, headhunting costs, human resource wages, loss of productivity, new hire training, and customer retention, every time they have to replace an employee. These expenses can add up to anywhere from 30% to 200% of a single employee's annual wages or salary, depending on the industry and the job role being filled (Beam, 2009).

In their study about turnover culture, Iverson and Deery (1997) suggested that the costs of employee turnover are high and exponential according to job, ranging from A$4651 for a room attendant, A$4787 for food and beverage servers, A$9468 for cookers, to A$12,679 for managerial positions (cited in Mwilu, 2016).

Figure 7.1 shows how it cost to cover one vacancy when an employee leave; the figure assumes an internal management cost of $30/h (according to self-calculations depending Salary.com).

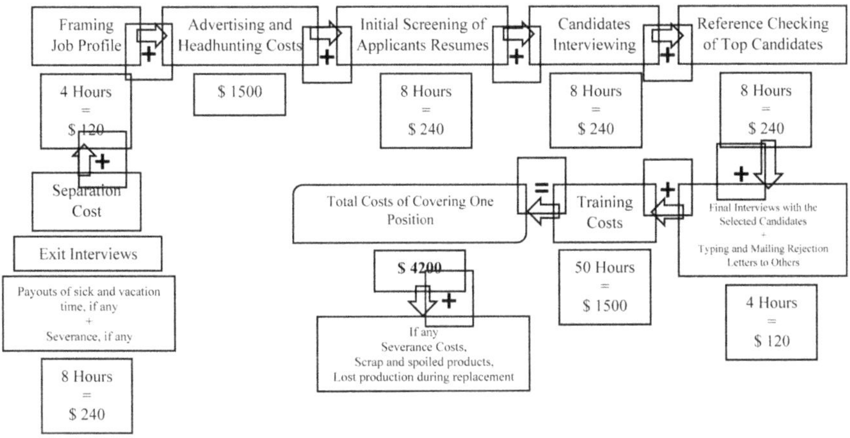


**FIGURE 7.1** Costs of an employee turnover in a middle-sized organization.
**Source:** The Authors.

The total costs could be applied as a minimum to most recruitment scenarios, although organizations vary in the size and brand and jobs also vary in the level and accordingly the costs could equate to at least double.

## 7.4 LABOR TURNOVER IN HOSPITALITY INDUSTRY

Without a doubt, labor force represents the main assets of hospitality organizations. Today, organizations generally admit the important contribution that their employees make in delivering the services. Being the hospitality industry is a labor-intensive one, labor costs on goods and services produced are very high; it means that labor expenses have an important share of total expenses (almost 40%).

The prominent labor-intensive feature of the hospitality industry made it experiences high levels of labor turnover; it has one of the highest employee turnover rates of any industry, making the issue a serious challenge for organizations in this sector. Labor turnover is seen as a significant factor when measuring the overall performance of the organizations, which management can mitigate (White, 1995). Low labor turnover is seen as an asset in the competitive market. High labor turnover is seen as a serious problem to be managed (Glebbeek and Bax, 2004). So, hospitality industry professionals should make every effort to control and decrease labor turnover as it seen as one area of cost which can be measured and benchmarked in order to drive down internal costs associated labor force as part of the price commitment.

In hospitality industry context, high employees' turnover rates are not country or region specific, it is a worldwide epidemic. In the United States, for example, Fortino and Ninemeier (1996) indicated that the national annual turnover rate ranges from 154% to 240%. In Ireland, a study by Ernst and Young (2013) showed that workforce in the hospitality industry in 2010 dropped by around 11%, employing 145,000 individuals directly after reaching its peak in 2008 at 162,000 employees.

In Europe, employees are much less likely to change jobs than the Americans partly due to the higher unemployment rate. For example, lost productivity was found to account for 47.1% to 67.6% of the total turnover cost in the US hospitality industry (Hinkin and Tracey, 2008), whilst voluntary turnover is almost non-existent or is very low in some parts of the world such as Singapore (Tanova and Holtom, in the press, as cited in Mwilu, 2016).

The motivation of employees involved in working in the hospitality industry is likely to be very poor because of the negative characteristics of the hospitality industry. The result of poor motivation influenced the decision to leave the organization and to seek an alternative place of work.

One of the most likely causes of high staff turnover as identified by hospitality employees is the stress, which is considered also a common feature of working in hospitality industry. The hospitality industry is characterized by temporary employment, which is associated with negative outcomes, such as variability of demand, inadequate treatment by their superiors, long or crazy working hours, job pressure, limited control over working schedule, training, fringe benefit packages, better opportunities elsewhere, physical demands of the job, and the general working conditions.

The hospitality industry has also been cited for poor implementation of best human resources retention strategies (McNamara et al., 2011). Hospitality turnover is shaped by some specific factors; the high rate of employee turnover in the industry has been linked to the low-skill requirement in most of the entry-level positions in the industry (Taylor and Finley, 2010). The low-skill requirement implies that the employees in the entry jobs receive poor payment and are also easy to quit.

Inadequate treatment by the supervisors also was identified as one of the most likely causes of high staff turnover. In addition, the work–life conflict has also been related to the high employee turnover rate in the hospitality industry. The hospitality industry is highly associated with poor work–life balance than other industries. Although work–life balance is an important factor that usually determines the satisfaction of employees with their work (O'Leary and Deegan, 2005), Blomme et al. (2010) reported that there is a lack of organizational support and dissatisfaction with the flexibility at the workplace which stimulates the work–life conflict, which, in turn, contributed significantly to turnover desires for employees within the hospitality industry. Moreover, the abnormal and crazy working hours associated with working in hospitality organizations also contributed to increasing the rate of employee turnover, especially among female workers, they are the most affected by this factor due to their responsibility of bringing up children, particularly the following birth. The same trend has been reported in many countries in the world. In India, for example, a study of the Indian hotel industry linked the abnormal and crazy working hours and the pressure culminating from multiple roles as the main factors that contribute to poor work life in the hospitality industry (Mohanty and Mohanty, 2014).

Having acceptable targets, based on precise definitions and the previously mentioned causes of turnover are meaning much to the organization, help to bring the process clearly into focus (Fair, 1992). High levels of labor turnover have become a serious problem for companies, and high level of intention turnover frustrates the companies when their staff turns out to be futile, especially after accomplishing a costly recruitment process (Hinkin and Tracey, 2000). Therefore, managing the changing employment relationship is one of the most challenging issues faced by the hospitality organizations today; high employee turnover and absenteeism within the hospitality industry offers those who can effectively manage those significant labor costs.

Being in customer service business, hospitality industry capitalizes heavily on its human resources to achieve a high standard of performance and, in turn, accomplish its competitive advantage. The hospitality industry is a high customer service-oriented business where interaction between employees and customers determines the success of the customers' experience and success of the business.

Thus, industry professionals are confronted with a tight labor supply and the need to enhance service quality; the hospitality sector is oriented to highly satisfy its customer, so the hospitality industry should have qualified and also satisfied human resources to provide excellent service to the customer because employee turnover disrupts the organization's performance. Today's hospitality industry stakeholders must look to invest in human resources rather than just minimizing labor costs (Klebanow and Eder, 1992).

In the field of tourism industry, especially the hospitality organizations, voluntary turnover of employment is significantly increasing (Phillips and Connell, 2003). Often, such type of employees who leave voluntarily and have not been determined by the employer are probably the employees that the organization would most likely to retain. The International Labor Organization's report (2001) gave the high labor turnover rate amongst those on their first employment in the hospitality industry to be at 51.7% in the United States, 30% in Asia, and 42% in the United Kingdom. So, reasons behind their leaving must be identified and analyzed seriously.

In order to analyze the labor turnover issue, there are two ways:

1. exit interviews and
2. internal analysis.

Both steps are necessary to accurately assess and diagnose turnover (Bonn, 1992).

### *7.4.1 EXIT INTERVIEWS*

Such interviews if carefully constructed can yield very useful information regarding the reasons employees leave an organization by identifying and exploring the reasons behind people leaving. In order to get more accurate information from the employee, the exit interview must be developed by someone other than the direct manager of the leavers. The reason for this is that it is unlikely to learn the truth if the line manager is asking the question, especially if the reasons behind the leaving is the poor management or leadership.

### *7.4.2 INTERNAL ANALYSIS*

The careful internal analysis and categorization of an individual's reason for leaving are important; it is only the first step in the assessment and diagnostic process.

Turnover must be analyzed in terms of internal variables of the organization. This analysis should be captured from a number of sources including personnel records, satisfaction surveys, exit interviews, and follow-up surveys. Once collected, the information can be cross-tabulated with the appropriate level of specificity to allow an accurate diagnosis of the nature and causes of turnover.

This diagnostic approach allows the employer to gain a clear picture of where problems exist. Most of the various reasons why employees leave their work can be grouped into three major categories that include economic, organizational, and individual reasons.

The next section will discuss in detail the various reasons of turnover.

## 7.5 CAUSES OF TURNOVER

Labor turnover is high in the hospitality industry, and anyone takes the responsibility of management within this environment should understand the reasons that push the employees and workers to leave their jobs in order for him to be in a better position to contain this problem. Turnover is a work rotation to achieve the conditions of the company. In addition, turnover is the changes that occur in a company due to many reasons. So, staff turnover in the hospitality organizations may be endemic, but it is not inevitable (Mwilu, 2016).

Although there is no standard framework for understanding the employees turnover process as a whole, a wide range of causes have been found useful in conceptualizing employee turnover (Sun and Law, 2007). Many scholars have studied the causes which probably lead workers decision with regard to quitting, they found that high rates of turnover in the hospitality organizations occurs for many reasons such as low-skilled and low-paying work, unsocial working hours, lack of leadership, customer service issues, labor pool, training, poor relationship with management and fellow colleagues, and harassment by managers (Musa et al., 2014), and lack of career advancement within each hospitality establishments (Hinkin and Tracey, 2000). In line with Hinkin and Tracey, Abbasi and Hollman (2000) argued that hiring practice, managerial style, lack of recognition, and lack of competitive compensation system are some of the factors causing employee separations from organizations. Most employees leave their work in the search for other fringe benefits; they leave in search for a better condition of service and career prospects.

Though debate varies, characteristics of organizations, unemployment rates, the average age of employees, gender, and racial composition are among other reasons causing employee turnover (Bennett et al., 1993). In addition to characteristics of organizations, there is the natural seasonality of the industry; according to Faldetta et al. (2013), the seasonal nature of the hospitality industry remains a significant reason in making many hospitality positions seasonal in nature, where employees are hired during high seasons and retrenched during low seasons. As managers commonly hire and fire employees based on seasonal fluctuations, managers remain ignorant of the labor-versus-demand concept; then, hotel managers remain unprepared to synchronize labor to demand (Faldetta et al., 2013); this has a negative impact on the employee morale. The low morality of service employees certainly affects customer satisfaction levels and the organization's reputation (Faldetta et al., 2013). This maximizes the financial impacts of turnover on the business (Tracey and Hinkin, 2008).

All these factors lead eventually the employee to search in other industries in order to evaluate and compare the working environment; such comparisons generate the employee intention to seek other employment opportunities (Lee, 1988).

While many leading organizations place more effort in employee retention, most are clueless. They accept employee turnover as a normal part of doing business. Such negative reactions of most of the industry' stakeholders made mitigating the turnover crisis still one of the biggest manager concerns in the hospitality industry (AlBattat et al., 2014). However, many researchers have conducted studies to examine the reasons why the turnover rate has remained high in this industry and what organizational leaders of the industry may do to change these high turnover rates (AlBattat and Som, 2013). Generally, any organizations seeking to solve this problem must analyze both the internal and external reasons for the staff turnover after compiling the information by the two ways mentioned earlier (exit interview and internal analysis).

Here, the two categories of turnover reasons are described as follows.

### *7.5.1 INTERNAL CAUSES OF LABOR TURNOVER*

Hospitality organizations often experience employee turnover caused by internal problems that occurred at the company. According to Wood and Macaulay (1998), employees' turnover is highly prevalent in the lodging industry. The following sections discuss the several internal causes of the turnover.

#### *7.5.1.1 THE PHILOSOPHY OF THE ORGANIZATION*

A principal reason that employees leave their jobs is lack of incentives. Workers may simply want a convenient working climate, recognition, or an opportunity in advance.

The Ritz Carlton Company, for example, has reduced employee turnover by establishing working philosophy focusing on workers in the first place and accordingly settling a productive working climate by focusing on quality recruitment, providing better training and orientation, establishing realistic career opportunities, and creating long-term incentive and reward systems (Barky, 1996).

#### *7.5.1.2 INADEQUATE LEADERSHIP*

Leaders are the secret weapon in keeping valued talent longer at level of performance (Iravo et al., 2012). Leadership style can control a range of factors in the work environment including stress, job satisfaction, performance, and turnover.

Chen and Silverthorne (2005) claimed that leadership style can build a climate of retention, a culture that speaks to employees in a way that encourages them to stay and demonstrate high levels of productivity; this culture can be an organization's best defense against unwanted employees' actions and so. Rehman et al. (2012) claimed that the best-suited leadership style in any organization is that it inspires employees' prospects and working ability to enhance efficiency and effectiveness in an organization. They suggested that organizations should strive to have their leadership take into considerations their styles of leadership so that labor force can feel comfortable with him/her at workplace since highly morale employees at the workplace are more productive than stressed ones.

On the other hand, inadequate/poor leadership is the main reason responsible for the failure of any business; the main culmination of ongoing poor leadership is the high employee turnover, workers who are not motivated and are burned out from a poor culture begin looking for other jobs. This is highlighted by Dailey and Kirk (1992) who asserted that inadequate management is the main factor that generates the turnover intention, and the duration the employees keep working in an organization is determined by the relationship between the management and its employees. This further escalates profitability concerns for the business. This downward spiral is often difficult to get out of since companies struggle when they lose top skills and experienced employees and must replace them with new hires, even those employees who stay get frustrated at the loss of familiar coworkers and colleagues (Kokemuller, 2017).

Inadequate management also results in low morale employees; this can result from employees feeling misdirected or uncertain about the organization and their jobs. Poor communication maximizes this issue. Overly critical managers may demean or demoralize employees who make mistakes but want to succeed. This further intensifies profitability concerns for the business which certainly will be affected negatively; the poor financial outcome is the tangible result of poor leadership. To optimize the quality, the organization needs employees committed to their jobs. Poor leaders do not inspire workers to deliver their best performance. In the long run, a culture of poor leadership immortalizes across the organization at all levels (Kokemuller, 2017). However, influencing these employees' decision to be committed and remain with the organization even when other job opportunities exist outside the organization is also the function of the leadership.

Therefore, organizations in the hospitality industry should employ effective leadership style in order to improve service provided to guests and customers and employee job satisfaction (Woods and King, 2002). Using their leadership style to motivate employees and to achieve the organizational goals (Purcell et al., 2003; Kavanaugh and Ninemeier, 2001), effective organizational and departmental leadership can achieve the development of synergy.

Namasaka et al. (2013) asserted that management should proactively and always hasten and improve the terms and conditions of services to improve the staff retention rate so as to avoid impacts caused by staff turnover, and creating a suitable work environment for employees is one of the critical roles of management (Iravo et al., 2012).

Effective leadership is one of essential factors that relates with turnover intention. Ineffective leadership occurs when employees are lacking support from their supervisor. It can cause the decrease of workers ability to adapt the stressful working environment in the organization. Hence, they have the intention to leave their job (Mobley, 1997a; Yousef, 2000).

Leadership styles can be classified according to the power that the leader bears and his or her behavior. This can be categorized into autocratic, democratic, or laissez-faire, where styles are distinguished by the influence leaders have on subordinates (Rollinson, 2005).

This classification implies three types of leadership in the work environment; these are delegating (empowerment), selling (persuasion), and telling (command) style (Fungwu et al., 2006). According to them, a telling style is adopted most frequently by the line managers if their top-level managers possess an authoritative leadership style. On the contrary, selling and delegating leadership styles are adopted most frequently by the line managers if their top-level managers possess a democratic leadership style. When managers use more selling, participating, and delegating leadership styles, the employees' organizational loyalty is higher. In contrast, the use of the telling leadership style does not strengthen the employees' organizational commitment (Fungwu et al., 2006). Regardless the style and type, the managers who treat their employees justly and in a reasonable way and supportive managers are the most desirable in work environment if we need the level of job satisfaction to increase.

Therefore, the industry authorities and professionals should make some plans to train managers in the aspects of effective leadership. This is so because the products and services provided by international hospitality establishments depend on good performance from all members.

#### *7.5.1.3 JOB INSECURITY*

Job insecurity is a major source of work stress which animates a series of negative sequences and reactions among employees. Job insecurity can result in lower job satisfaction, decreased employee well-being, a reluctance to fully commit to the organization, demotivation, and enhanced personal stress which in turn will lead to increased stress and disloyalty that end with increasing the rate of staff turnover in the organization. An employee may fear for their job when there is a lack of communication from management, particularly during periods of economic uncertainty.

If an employer suddenly decides to downsize the workforce without any clear declaration in advance about his intentions, the situation will impact all employees, which can lead to poor performance. Ultimately, it can undermine management's reputation among workforce members, lead to burnout, and cause employees to ultimately quit (Ismail, 2015).

In order to minimize job insecurity among staff members, the organization manager must provide strategic guidance to the operator and develop a plan that is communicated in advance, particularly when adopting policies aimed at reducing staff headcounts, for example, outsourcing, introducing new work practices and restructuring, staff will appreciate the clarity and may be more prepared to accept a redundancy package if such an option is available.

#### *7.5.1.4 POOR RELATIONSHIPS*

Poor relationship with coworkers, colleagues, supervisors, and/or direct managers is one of the direct causes of dissatisfaction and demotivation among workforce members. Tews et al. (2013) specifically evaluated how two types of coworker support, including emotional and instrumental, could affect employees' satisfaction, and in turnover rate, they also claimed that emotionally supportive coworkers led to higher employee retention compared to instrumental coworker support; this highlights the significant role of good relationship. According to Taylor (2002b), the job-vertical relationship is the most important relationship in work environment from the employees' perspective. The type of the employee's relationship with his/her subordinates helps in shaping the quality of their day-to-day experiences in the workplace which in turn reflect on their job satisfaction and predict how good their prospects of career development will be (Taylor, 2002a). Paille et al. (2013) claimed that trust in line managers and supervisors and the perceived support from them increases the probability of workers to stay within an organization, whereas a poor or nonexistent relationship increases the chances of voluntary turnover by the employees.

Ultimately, the poor relationship between an employee, their supervisor, and coworkers fosters a negative attitude and encourages them to quit their employment (Tutuncu and Kozak, 2007).

#### *7.5.1.5 THE ORGANIZATIONAL CULTURE*

The organizational culture is an important factor in determining employee turnover behavior (Kyndt et al., 2009). Perceived organizational climate and support could shape employees' decisions to leave or stay. Organizational culture is a descriptive term which is concerned with how the involved employees perceive the characteristics of an organization. This assessment of the organization by the stakeholders, especially the employees on its characteristics, gives a holistic picture of the organization's culture.

Their perception of the organizational culture can be shaped by the strength of the management, promotions, training practices, organizational goals, missions, suitable reward systems, and recognitions which positively decrease turnover rate of the employees in any organization (Malik et al., 2011); all these factors enhance the ability of the organizations to elicit a sense of loyalty on the part of employees, and its development of a sense of shared goals, among other factors, will influence such indices of job satisfaction as turnover intentions and turnover rate. Good management practices control the employee satisfaction, the employee feels dignified, and respected, thereby increasing their sense of self-identity and self-worth if they perceived unbiased (Hwang et al., 2014). As a result, high level of organizational commitment among the employees is recorded and then they become less likely to leave their jobs (Khalili, 2014; Karatepe and Shahriari, 2014). In turn, such culture will become the basis for shared feelings that members have about the organization, how things are done, and the expected code of behavior (Robbins and Sanghi, 2007).

Strong cultures have a greater impact on employees' behavior and are more directly related to the reduction of turnover, saying that strong culture should lead to lower employee turnover and vice versa (Kumar et al., 2012). On the other hand, the organizational climate lacking a positive culture makes the job to be unpleasant; occupational stress factors, especially unfair treatment, could lead to turnover (Hwang et al., 2014).

Hence, organizational culture is an important aspect of organizational behavior and a concept that is useful to understand how organizations function since it helps determine how well a person fits within a particular organization (Kumar et al., 2012). The effects of organizational enthusiasm and stimulating jobs on employee turnover are doubled (Mohsin et al., 2015); a fun workplace could lead to employees feeling more attached to the workplace and make them want to stay (Gin Choi et al., 2013). Staff will often stay where there is a support for fun activities, socialization with coworkers, and managers (Tews et al., 2014) even if the pay is slightly higher elsewhere as long as they have conditions that others do not/cannot provide. Good organizational culture affects not only on turnover rate but also the well-being of employees in the hospitality industry (Blomme et al., 2013).

#### *7.5.1.6 LOW PAYMENT*

Unfortunately, the hospitality industry has unacceptable conditions for its workers which lead to creating ongoing labor shortage in the organizations; unacceptable working conditions, poor training, and unsatisfactory salaries lead to high labor turnover intention (AlBattat et al., 2014). The employee may ignore the hard-working conditions if he is satisfied with the pay; however, in the hospitality industry, pay rates are often around the minimum wage, making it difficult for employees to support themselves with one job and then the need to jump into other jobs and to always be on the lookout for new job opportunities. Shaw et al. (1998) stated that payment is wage, salary, or compensation given to an employee in exchange for the services provided in an organization. Most employees feel that they are worth more than they are actually paid.

The abundant opportunities in the labor market generate higher demand for competitive financial compensation packages. Thus, when the difference becomes too great and another opportunity occurs, turnover can result. Employers should aim to develop a dynamic salary structure for staff that takes into account their job responsibilities, rewards performance, and considers income benchmarks. Compensation and extra rewards affect labor turnover in the hospitality industry (AlBattat et al., 2014). Payment has an important role in employee retention and remuneration high-quality workers. Pay has a close relationship with employee satisfaction. The influence of pay and job satisfaction affects high productivity.

Generally, money may not be a primary motivator, but it is a basic need to be fulfilled (Dobre, 2013). Many employees are motivated by both extrinsic and intrinsic rewards. In the absence of intrinsic factors such as recognition and career advancement, employees will compare the financial benefits and pursue a career with an organization that offers the best compensation package.

#### *7.5.1.7 WORK CONDITIONS*

Working conditions refer to a working environment and all existing circumstances affecting workers in the work place. These conditions include work schedules, nature of work, physical aspects, legal rights and responsibility, interactions with others, reporting times, nature of supervisors, organizational climate, and workload and work flexibility (Ali et al., 2013; Lee et al., 2015).

Employees' satisfaction with their work conditions is likely to influence them positively and cause them to stay with the organization. The employees are also likely to be more motivated and productive when they are satisfied with their work conditions. An ideal work conditions for employees can include an environment that empowers the employees and allows them to meld personal and work relationships and achieve personal needs (Timothy and Teye, 2009). However, in the hospitality industry, work conditions are very unique because of the patterns of consumer demand that imposes unsocial and irregular working hours in the form of split shifts, nightshifts, weekend shifts, or work during holiday periods such as Christmas, big festivals and events, etc. (ILO, 2010).

In poor working conditions and for long hours, hospitality employees often do their work; subsequently, they feel that they are unappreciated by either the organizations they work for or the patrons they serve, leading them to leave the industry to look for more personally fulfilling jobs. These working conditions heighten stress on workers with family responsibilities, particularly women who carry the majority of the care burden for children and household chores, as well as the elderly.

Figure 7.2 shows that workforce working in hotels and restaurants is captured to be the second highest employees having long working hours after those who are working in the agriculture sector in countries of European Union.

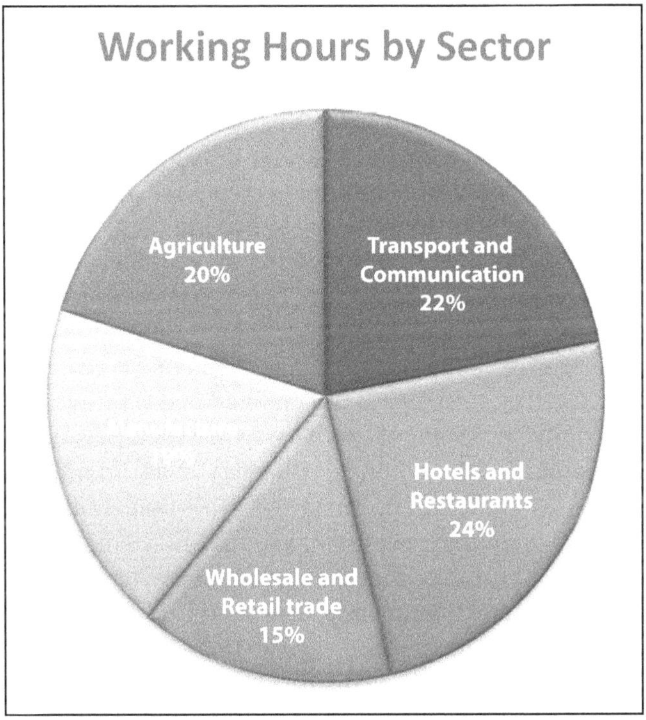


**FIGURE 7.2** **(See color insert.)** Working hours by sector.

**Source:** The Authors, based on ILO (2010a).

Most of the hospitality organizations have a very poor work–life balance since the facilities are often open throughout; then, the workers hardly get time to catch-up with their families and friends outside the job environment. Such challenging work conditions can cause increased levels of burnout and job stress amongst employees; this has created disillusionment among the staff who feel like they are over sacrificing for their jobs at the expense of their private lives (Mwilu, 2016) which can cause them to leave the organization or industry (Kokt and Ramarumo, 2015).

Jagun (2015) stated that organizations which have generous human resource policies have a very good chance to satisfy and keep their workforce members by providing them an appropriate level of privacy and good control on work environment which enhances the motivation levels to commit with the organization for the long term.

### *7.5.1.8 THE CHARACTERISTICS OF THE JOB*

Some jobs are intrinsically more attractive than others. Commonly, the attractiveness of the job is affected by many characteristics, including its repetitiveness, perceived importance, challenge, danger, and capacity to elicit a sense of accomplishment (Taylor, 2002a). However, hospitality employees are confronted with continuous risks and plenty of daily uncertainties that target the tourism industry in general (Brownell, 1998). Such uncertainty creates high levels of job stress. In addition, service providers are required to present an appropriate emotional response regardless of the circumstance. Wood and Macaulay (1991) defined emotional labor as the display of expected emotions by service employees during service encounters. Moreover, Lashley (2000) claimed that employees involved in working in hospitality organizations also experience jobs that are tightly controlled, routine, and monotonous (Lashley, 2000). Different types of employment styles are aroused; along with full-time employment, there is on-call, casual, temporary, seasonal, and part-time employment. Unfortunately, the nature of these different types is characterized by insecurity, comparatively low pay (frequently below the national average), job instability, limited growth opportunity, a high level of subcontracting and outsourcing, and a high turnover rate. So, in line with Wood and Macaulay, such work characteristics have significant psychological effects whose end result is employees leaving one job for another.

### *7.5.1.9 THE PERSONALITY OF THE WORKER*

There are factors specific to an individual personality that can shape turnover intentions. These include both personal and perceptions or expectations factors (Mobley, 1977b). Personal factors include things such as:

- changes in family situation,
- desire to learn a new skill or trade, or
- unsolicited job offers.

In addition to the factors listed above, demographic and biographical characteristics of workers are also identified as important factors in generating the intention of leaving (Mitra et al., 1992). In general, employees' turnover intention is shaped by some different determinants including:

- demographic (e.g., gender, age, educational level),
- occupational (e.g., skill level, experience, tenure, status),
- organizational (e.g., establishment size, industry, job contents, working environments), and
- individual (e.g., pay scale, reward, advancement opportunity, job security, job involvement).

Hence, the demographic characteristics of employees are on the top of factors, which causes leaving decisions. According to ILO (2010a), female workers in tourism and hospitality industries make up between 60% and 70% of the labor force; in addition, the industry also make a significant contribution of young workers. Thus, the industry accommodates a considerable number of workers with a limited level of education. Female workers at a specific time decide to leave their work because of their family responsibilities; also, many employees are young who are using hospitality jobs as a fallback or as a stepping stone to other careers. This increases the chances of the turnover.

In addition to these factors, there are also perceptions or expectations features as employees frequently hold some beliefs about the jobs and career development opportunities (Iverson and Deery, 1997). According to Lucas (1995), the turnover rate was observed to be highest amongst the newly employed staff because they often seem to have higher perception and expectations from new jobs, impatience and other personal ambitions which are rarely achieved with time. Such expectations are some of the same characteristics that predict job performance and counterproductive behaviors such as loafing, absenteeism, theft, substance abuse on the job, and sabotage of the organization's equipment or materials. These perceptions can be measured and used in employee screening to identify individuals showing the highest probability of turnover.

#### *7.5.1.10 LACK OF ENGAGEMENT*

Levels of engagement are rooted in an organization's corporate values. High employee engagement encourages a committed organizational culture and accordingly manifests high levels of loyalty among the staff of the organization. Culture is described as the "way things are done around the work environment" and engagement is "how organization staff feel about the ways things are done" (Deloitte University Press, 2016). Employees expect complete transparency in the workplace. Low engagement can result from a lack of transparency and is an important factor that influences an employee's career choices. The majority of employees will be reluctant to embrace operational changes if the benefits of these changes are not clearly explained to them; such confusing environment promotes low job satisfaction among the workforce members.

#### *7.5.1.11 LIMITED JOB SATISFACTION*

Job satisfaction is a combination of attitude and emotions, influenced by internal and external factors that the employees feel about the organization they are working in (Guan et al., 2013).

There is more than one factor that determines the level of job satisfaction for employees within the hospitality industry. These factors include (Jagun, 2015):

- the job itself,
- working conditions or environment,
- personal fulfillment (using ability in the job and work growth opportunity),
- management style,
- management beliefs,
- the relationship with the supervisor and coworkers, and
- earning good and fair compensation.

Employees are more likely to be satisfied with their work when they are participating in job-related decisions, receiving work-related information, making close friendships with their coworkers, and enjoying opportunities for promotion (Price and Mueller, 1981).

Davies et al. (2001) asserted that the commitment to the organization could be better when adapting a suitable human resource system, improving good labor relations, and settling a convenient work environment conditions. Managers or supervisors support is another facet of job satisfaction that makes the employees feel of empowerment at their work environment that in turn might also attain a higher sense of fulfillment and meaning (Wayne et al., 2013). They also highlighted the importance of performance appraisal, remuneration, and training as critical human resource practices, which contribute to satisfying the organizations' employees.

Although retention activities including job satisfaction reduce turnover and retention costs, Cascio (2014) claimed that few organizations have retention plans in place. Lack of retention plans may lead to increasing dissatisfaction level among employees; extensive studies have shown that the Mobley model (1977a) which determined and explained how job dissatisfaction can lead to increasing labor turnover rate yields seven consecutive stages between job dissatisfaction and turnover rate (Lee, 1988). Mobley believed that job dissatisfaction can lead to career shift decisions based on comparing the alternatives with the current work environment which also leads to the intention to quit causing ultimate employee turnover rates (Martin, 2011). In general, without comprehensive retaining activities in place, job dissatisfaction may persist among employees susceptible to quit their jobs (Frey et al., 2013).

### *7.5.2 EXTERNAL CAUSES OF LABOR TURNOVER*

Some external factors also have a notable contribution in labor turnover occurring in any organization; external factors exist outside the organization environment and are beyond the control of human resource managers (Nankervis et al., 1996).

The external political, social, and commercial environment can have a significant impact on the policies, practices, strategies, and plans of organizations. By analyzing the outside community and identifying the competitive points of other organizations, the proactive human resource planner can assess likely current and future changes and determine possible impact on its workforce and organizational plans.

#### *7.5.2.1 THE ECONOMY*

One of the most common reasons given by employees leaving their present work is the availability of higher paying jobs in other sectors. In an extravagant economy, the availability of alternative jobs plays a role in turnover (Wood and Macaulay, 1991).

Thus, jobs in the hospitality industry are viewed as means rather than an end. To exacerbate this situation, many other organizations which have suffered from turnover are working on human resource practices seeking to absorb these leaving employees.

#### 7.5.2.2 STRONGER BRAND VALUE

Numerous researchers confer that in such competitive market, employees favor engaging in the stronger brand organizations. Hospitality managers cannot solely use financial enticements to attract skilled employees and guarantee their commitment and loyalty. Organizations can instead engage employees by emphasizing the value of their brands. A respected brand will generate strong customer loyalty, which can be used to capture top talent from across the industry (Suikkanen, 2010).

#### 7.5.2.3 INCREASES PAY IN OTHER INDUSTRIES

Lack of balance in the distribution of wages is one of the major causes of friction between the employers and their employees (Kusluvan, 2003). In the hospitality industry, pay rates are often around the minimum wage. Also, there are huge opportunities both at home and internationally; so, employees with ambition will always be looking to improve their career prospects and will want to move about to gain more experience and responsibility and to be financially fulfilled; thus where pay levels do not compare well with the competition, the urge to leave and earn more may be overpowering (Sun and Law, 2007).

It is not easy and too often is a matter of expenditure to arrive to a fair system of awarding wages and salaries (Kusluvan, 2003) that satisfy all the employed people in the organization; so, employers follow one of two extreme approaches in the determination of wages.

At one extreme, there is a total transparency in which every employee can know what everyone else (coworkers) earns while, on the other end, are employers who not only keep secret what they pay each employee but also settle a condition of employment that salaries are not to be discussed between staff. Subsequently, it is important to recognize the relative importance of each job and remove any potential causes of dissatisfaction especially related to money. Kusluvan (2003) concludes by stating that it is vital to adopt a methodical system of evaluating jobs and its surrounding conditions so that wages and salaries are fairly distributed to all employees and workers.

#### 7.5.2.4 A STRONG LOCAL OR REGIONAL ECONOMY

Employees may leave their current employment for catching the opportunities created in strong economy that experiences continuing expansions. Phillips and Connell (2003) proposed that almost all industrialized nations and many emerging countries have experienced long economic expansions. As economies grow, job growth will continue with the economic expansions translating directly into new jobs which in turn attract the labor market intensively. Moreover, in strong economies where unemployment rates are very low, there is a problem for most service-based industries to find talented employees; low rates of unemployment in a specific sector create serious problems for employers seeking to fill job vacancies of skilled employees. According to Bolch (2001), low unemployment rates lead to increased turnover because more jobs are available. He further argued that whenever the actual unemployment rate falls to 5% level or lower, it creates labor shortage in organizations. A summary of labor turnover reasons from the literature is presented in Figure 7.3.

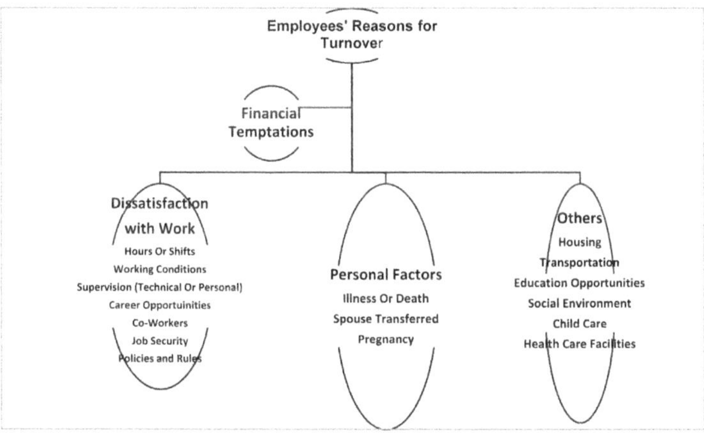


**FIGURE 7.3** Labor turnover reasons.

**Source:** The Authors

## 7.6 FACTORS AFFECTING EMPLOYEES RETENTION

High employee turnover is costly and disruptive (Bryant and Allen, 2013). Employee turnover is seen as one area of cost which can be measured and benchmarked. It is seen as a significant factor which management and industry stakeholders can influence. Thus, for an organization to realize its goals, appropriate strategies for employee recruitment and retention are essential for successful performance (Jagun, 2015).

In order to control costs associated with the workforce, employers must seek to develop appropriate retention strategies. It is becoming essential to secure and manage competent and skilled human resource as the most valuable resource of any organization because of the need for effective and efficient delivery of goods and services by organizations (Jagun, 2015). As it is defined by Jagun (2015), employee retention strategy is the organization's efforts to retain desirable employees in order to meet the business objectives.

CIPD (2014) defined retention as "the extent to which an organization retains its employees and may be measured as the proportion of employees with a specified length of service (typically one year or more) expressed as a percentage of overall workforce numbers."

Retention is important for an organization as it ensures that the organization keeps hold of its best employees, lower labor costs, thereby ensuring high levels of production and quality. If appropriate employee retention practices are adopted and implemented by organizations, employees will surely remain and work for the successful achievement of organizational goals.

Industry professionals are in need of strategies and practices to maintain an adequate labor force and improve employee satisfaction, motivation, job engagement and commitment, and work environment within the industry (Marshall et al., 2016).

Organizations today generally do recognize the important contribution that their workforces play in branding the organizations. However, they also make every effort to drive down internal costs as part of the price commitment. Understanding the factors that generate employee turnover could help corporate leaders implement initiatives to overcome this growing trend.

Some organizations invest a lot in their employees in terms of wages, compensations, induction, and training without understanding the dimensions of the dilemma. Therefore, managers at all costs must work to minimize employee's turnover. Therefore, there is an urgent need to develop a full understanding of the organizational factors that affect employee turnover, more especially their causes, what determines employee turnover, effects, and strategies that managers can put in place to minimize turnover and then start to develop initiatives. These initiatives could accompany the financial incentives; it includes, for example, family-support strategies to improve professional and community attachments and other strategies to make workforces feel more embedded and satisfied in the workplace (Wayne et al., 2013).

Generally, still, the larger issue is how often human resource managers lack the tools and strategies that might aid in preventing and managing high employee-turnover rates (Cao et al., 2013). However, high-performance work practices might work well to combat employee turnover in the hospitality industry (Karatepe, 2013; Karatepe and Vatankhah, 2014). There are six factors that if handled accurately will influence positively on employees' decision to resign from the job; these factors entail managing both the physical and moral status of the employee.

Organizational leaders must understand those factors that have a significant potential to predict and mitigate turnover consequences (Hancock et al., 2013).

## 7.6.1 LEADERSHIP

Poor leadership and especially the inability of the management to handle grievances fairly affect turnover intention indirectly through affecting negatively on staff morale, decreasing job satisfaction, and organizational commitment (Mathieu et al., 2016). Managerial inconsistencies or unfair practices impact upon line employee turnover; such practices may exist in term of managerial staff turnover, although the turnover rate of managerial employees is expected to be lower than that of operational workers (Stalcup and Pearson, 2001). For example, the results of a survey conducted by Poon (2004) from an occupationally heterogeneous sample of white-collar employees from various organizations revealed that manipulations of performance ratings arising from personal favoritism had negative effects on job satisfaction and labor turnover intention. The cost of turnover is much higher and the effect sequences of employee turnover on their coworkers seem high (Stalcup and Pearson, 2001).

Therefore, management styles could affect employees' decisions to stay or leave the organization (Kara et al., 2013). Mid-level managers' satisfaction with senior managers' supervision could affect line employees' turnover intentions (Chen et al., 2014). The formal mentoring of managers was also significantly and negatively related to the subordinates' intention to stay or to leave. Mentoring may represent a relatively inexpensive means to not only proactively influence employee attitudes and perceptions but also reduce employee turnover within the organization (Cropanzano et al., 2003; Su, 2014). In addition, transformational leadership could affect turnover intentions by motivating, inspiring, and showing empathy to their employees (Tse et al., 2013). Job retention and productivity can also be achieved through an adequate flow of information from management to employees and vice visa.

Commonly, fair treatment of employees and workers appears to translate into both employee retention and enhanced customer service, as employees are more committed to the organization and its goals, and both employee retention and customer service satisfaction affect profitability (Poon, 2004).

Practitioners and academics alike have underscored the importance of appropriate management style that includes profitability, productivity, marketing effectiveness, and customer satisfaction but also consider employee morale because of the benefits that accrue to the subordinates as well as the whole organization (Karatepe, 2013).

### *7.6.2 RECRUITMENT*

Recruitment is the sourcing process; according to Ameliya and Febriansyah (2017), recruitment is the process of getting the employee who suits the needs of the organization through the available resource.

Industry professionals took some steps in the recruitment process in order to reduce the turnover rate in their organizations; some of these steps are considered discriminative solutions; they selected to avoid some groups of workers such as the elderly, female, and disabled employees. However, some researchers considered hiring minorities groups, elderly, and handicapped is another solution to the turnover issues, especially in the back of the house positions in hospitality organizations.

Source of the new labor may be internal and external.

#### *7.6.2.1 INTERNAL LABOR*

Some management decisions such as shifting policies, rotation, and promotion procedures can generate the employees' movements among different departments in various positions within the same organization; so, the internal of the organization can be a source of employment.

#### *7.6.2.2 EXTERNAL LABOR*

External labor is hired from outside the organization; the source may be one of the following:

- College or educational institutions.
- Labor associations.
- Professional associations.
- Labor contracting companies.
- Employee's recommendation.
- Job seekers' searching.
- Job fair.

### *7.6.3 SELECTION*

Although the quality level of the new employees will determine significantly the competitiveness of the organization in the marketplace from a performance, technology, productivity, quality, and cost perspectives, also, despite the disruption and cost of turnover, many employers still view employees as replaceable commodities, especially part-time employees. The "warm body" syndrome of hiring unselectively to fill vacancies remains in place, even though the results of this practice can have devastating effects on both internal and external customers.

The employers need to choose people who are competent, compatible, and in accordance with the criteria of the organization because the success of an organization is determined by human resource. The level quality of the new employees can be measured by vocational, technical, and soft skills and also can be identified through the level of their knowledge, interpersonal creativity, and potentials (Ameliya and Febriansyah, 2017). Thus, the selection process for the new employee is an important process for the organization.

### *7.6.4 TRAINING*

The level of satisfaction that an employee feels about his organization is affected by levels of training and development to an extent. The degree that the organization adheres to conducting perfect training programs sends powerful signals to employees about the extent to which the organization trusts them and if organizations fail to deliver such induction and self-fulfillment promises, employees' sense of mutual obligations will be reduced accordingly. According to Costen and Salazar (2011), employees who feel they have the chance to learn new practices through training and development in the workplace are more satisfied with their jobs and are, as a result, more likely to remain loyal to their organization. So, learning and development is an important retention strategy establishing and supporting learning and working prospects (Govaerts et al., 2011). Lack of appropriate training in the work environment can cause what is called induction crisis that occurs when the new employees for any reason have not got the sufficient training that enables them to integrate into the team (Sun and Law, 2007). Therefore, the issues of training, skill, and quality of service are some of the important issues for the future like the past (Davidson et al., 2011). Poor induction program or a poor recruitment, with insufficient training and time spent on enabling the new employees to build strong relationships with his supervisor and coworkers, increases staff turnover and threatened quality standards and profits (Poulston, 2008). On the other hand, training programs enhance employees trust in an organization, provide ample and clear career advancement to their employees, and subsequently reduce turnover intentions (Kuria et al., 2012).

Although service sectors' employees are deserving good training programs in place on a regular basis, hospitality industry gives a little attention to training (Nolan, 2002). In such industry, poorly trained employees can turn customers away; subsequently, these customers then talk about their unhappy experience to their friends. Bad news travels fast and customers can discredit a hotel if they had a bad experience. Therefore, it can be assumed that customer turnover is also directly related to employee turnover which can become a challenge for many hospitality businesses. In the hospitality industry, it is very crucial to provide adequate training courses in order to review the needs of what is needed continuously to be fulfilled. Generally, either the formal or informal training had an important role for some reason, including the industry's global expansion through enhancing the quality of service providers, for reducing the turnover rate of employees, and needs to improve the knowledge and career paths that eventually will result to enhancing both the customer and employee loyalty.

Hence, providing training to the current employees is one of the most important ways to reduce the employees' turnover; it increases the skills and knowledge of the employee and, thus, ensures that they are comfortable in their new work environment and reduces the chances of the employees getting frustrated in performing the new tasks (Lashley and Best 2002).

### *7.6.5 COMMUNICATION*

Whether your organization has 5 or 500 employees, effective communication between the organization management and its employees is very critical; this starts with the onboarding of all new recruits till the exit interview in case they decided to leave the organization. Communication has various aspects that can impact on the employees' intention to stay or leave. According to Jones and Lockwood (2002), communication aspects include regular staff briefings, easy access to communicate with the manager, and intercommunication among all workforce members. So, communication needs to be a two-way process, not only do employees need to know what is going on, they also wish to be heard, they need to express their opinions, thoughts, and suggestions, also they need to convey their needs to their management.

Communications process within any organization can be as simple as following:

- daily briefings,
- weekly one on ones with their supervisor/manager,
- regular full staff meetings, and
- annual performance planning sessions.

In addition, management can devise other methods to receive their employees and workers' suggestions or complaints whether by face-to-face meetings or something else.

According to Jagun (2015), prevailing a good level of communication in the workplace creates a sense of belonging amongst employees and makes them feel involved and aware of the organization's missions and goals creating since they can participate in decision-making process which in returns creates a good working environment and contributes toward building a good employee–employers relationship (Noah, 2008).

In general, lack of communication leaves employee feeling disconnected from the organization. Whilst a negative staff member is considered the greatest supporter to staff turnover, a positive staff member can be the greatest contributor to your employment brand and attracting their friends/family to join work (www.hospitalityrecruitmentsolution.com.au).

### 7.6.6 CAREER GROWTH OPPORTUNITIES

Lack of career opportunities is a primary reason for high labor turnover in many organizations and industries (Diala-Mobride, 2016). In the hospitality industry, the case is more complicated because of its labor-intensive industry; thus, the high competition among the employees reduces the opportunity for individual career progression and development. In addition to the intensity of staff, less challenging jobs and low paying jobs are other factors that influence negatively on the employees' retention besides the absence of opportunities for career growth.

In a survey conducted by Diala-Mobride (2016), the results showed that about 32% of respondents stated that a lack of career opportunities in their current role was the main reason for them seeking another employment elsewhere. Employees believe that career development is a long-term proposition; so, they will seek alternative employment if they see few opportunities for career advancement with their current employer, as the issues arise because the employee's career expectations are not met by their organizations. So, the clear opportunities for career growth are one of the important factors that contribute notably in improving the employees' commitment, and this, in turn, affects positively on their performance and their retention. Career growth and development involves creating an opportunity for promotion within an organization by providing an opportunity for training and skills development that allows employees to improve their positions in the organization (Jagun, 2015).

Chen et al. (2004) developed a paper exploring the gap between career development programs and career opportunities. Their study result claimed that the larger the gap, the higher the levels of turnover intentions. As is usually the case, most employees make many transitions between jobs during their working lives. These may include both job changes within a single organization and leaving one organization to take a job in another one. In either case, there is usually the intention to grow and increase in skills, responsibility, and remuneration and/or improve the "fit" between employee skills, desires, and job requirements.

Employees are looking for a job that offers career growth opportunities and the fair compensation. So, the degree of commitment that managers have to make improvements regarding the career path and wages policy reduces the amount of the employees who had an intention to leave the work (Walsh and Taylor, 2007).

It is obvious that hospitality organizations must adopt a better improvement to maintain competitive advantages and lower their employees' turnover rates, developmental programs such as accurate career previews at the time of hiring, advancement plans, internal promotion (Prince, 2005), career advancement training programs, and capacity-building programs. Additionally, organizational support for career growth has been associated with a reduction in voluntary quit by employees as they are likely to perceive career development opportunities within the organization as high (Kraimer et al., 2011).

### 7.6.7 PAY AND COMPENSATIONS

Lack of recognition and competitive compensation systems are some of the biggest reasons for voluntary turnover in an organization (Abassi and Hollman, 2000); when the employees are extremely unsatisfied with the compensation system, the organizations face less committed staff and thus low moral performance that ends with leaving the organization.

In the hospitality industry, many employers justify that the low pay in hospitality industry organizations is a result of the low skill status of most of the employees (Chan and Kuok, 2011), this may be true; but on the other hand, this action will make the organization to lose the residual low skilled employees as well. So, the solution lies in applying for flexible and ongoing training courses and devising some adequate intensives for them. Namasivayam et al. (2006) explained that it is important for companies to understand what motivates their employees to increase retention. Sturman (2006) found that good pay can be a powerful tool for managing employees. So, some human resource managers are of the view that increased compensation and benefits should be the primary method to retain skilled workers. Total compensation satisfaction plays an important part in employee loyalty and retention.

Compensations are divided into direct (extrinsic) rewards such as salary and benefits and also indirect (intrinsic) rewards such as achieving personal goals, autonomy, and more challenging job opportunities. They further stated that compensation refers to all forms of financial returns and tangible services, benefits, and nonfinancial incentives employees receive as part of an employment relationship. The following are the suggested three categories of different benefits employee gains during his work relationship.

#### 7.6.7.1 BENEFITS

Benefits are one of the components of total compensation. Heneman and Schwab (1985) defined benefits as indirect pay or payment for "time not worked" such as health care, retirement account, and insurance. Traditionally, organizations viewed the value of benefits separate from pay. However, William et al. (2007) concluded that many employees considered benefits as an integral part of their compensation package or saw them as "entitlements."

Therefore, benefits and pay must be viewed together otherwise; employees would be dissatisfied with their total compensation.

### *7.6.7.2 FINANCIAL INCENTIVES*

Financial incentives are defined as variable pay (Zingheim and Schuster, 2008). Some examples of financial incentives are pay for performance, bonuses, commissions, profit sharing, and gain sharing (Guthrie, 2000). They generally apply to managers, except in hospitality organization; it may involve service providers as tipping. Sturman (2006) found that bonus appeared to be the most effective financial incentive that influences employee performance.

### *7.6.7.3 NONFINANCIAL COMPENSATION*

According to Mondy (2008), nonfinancial compensation is defined as "satisfaction that a person receives from the job itself or from the psychological and/or physical environment in which the person works" (p 277).

Also, nonfinancial compensation rewards may include an employee recognition program or training and development opportunities (Patton, 2009). Nonfinancial compensations may be as something simple as compliment verbal words "attaboy" (Tahmincioglu, 2004) that would leave a positive impact on the employee performance.

In general, while many factors may cause employees to leave an organization, inadequate compensation is often the cause of turnover. This, therefore, calls for a comprehensive job evaluation and compensation surveys which will help ensure equity within and without the organization by creating a compensation package in accordance with the relative worth of a job and the prevailing wage levels in the market. Table 7.1 concludes the categories of compensation that may be considered by the employer when developing a compensation package for his employees.

Employees at all levels leave the organization for greener pastures; in a study conducted by Kuria et al. (2011), they observed that 100% of the managers would leave the present organization and take up new jobs if the job offers better salary and benefits than the current one. Thus, better salaries and benefits offered at other organizations constituted one of the biggest reasons employees decided to leave the hospitality sector (Karatepe, 2013; Karatepe and Vatankhah, 2014).

**TABLE 7.1** Categories of Compensation.

| Direct compensation | | Indirect compensation | | | |
|---|---|---|---|---|---|
| **Wage** | Commissions | **Pay for vacations** | Vacations | **Security plans** | Pensions |
| | Bounces | | Holidays | | Disability aid plan |
| | Tipping | | Breaks | **Other incentives** | Brand value |
| **Salary** | Profit percentage | | Sick days | | Training courses |
| | Piece rate | **Insurance plans** | Health | | Educational incentives |
| | | | Life | | Transportation service |
| | | | | | Food services |

**Source:** The Authors

A variety of management procedures can be used to reduce the relative rate of turnover. Employees are less inclined to leave an organization that sufficiently provides for their financial and recognition needs, especially if they would be moving to another organization with the same job and similar task roles (Karatepe and Vatankhah, 2014). So, management should introduce better overtime pay and workers should be encouraged to take up any upcoming opportunity.

Mwilu (2016), for example, showed that a bonus on top of regular pay had more influence on reducing turnover intentions than regular pay rises. If an organization offers adequate promotional opportunities and competitive pay, employee turnover is likely to diminish. The employees must be involved at all levels of determining the compensation system if they are to buy it as it will be useless to claim that a compensation system is equitable; yet, the employees have no contribution of the system and have thus not accepted it.

Subsequently, if the organizations need to retain and grow its staff, clear decisions are required to be made as to what types of compensations are required; level of change is needed in salaries, reward packages, and conditions in order to recruit and keep skilled staff taking into account both the short- and the long-term impact. However, such decisions infer that the organizations are in a position to increase its compensation. Managers must, therefore, consider retention strategies that do not rely on the organization's financial ability; thus, they must seek for other solutions. The training program and career development to ensure the quality of performance (service) and the productivity also will increase the income for the employees of the service sector and will limit their intentions to leave. In addition, flexible job descriptions, job rotation, and "family-friendly" policies serve perfectly as a tool for retaining the skilled employees.

This will help alleviate the feeling of being treated inequitably in the organization, which reduces the employees' efforts and drop thoughts of leaving the organization. Such practices further suggest that not only must an organization have a very equitable system but this system must be accepted by all the workforce members. In summary, the tendency of employees to resign from the organization will be reduced if the total compensations provided by the organization competitive. Issues of recognition and salary are considered a very important issue for employees (Ameliya and Febriansyah, 2017).

### *7.6.8 MOTIVATION*

Ongoing changes in the workplace require that managers give continuous attention to motivation factors that influence worker behavior and align them with organizational goals (Musa et al., 2014). The term motivation is derived from Latin word "movere" which means to move (Dhameja and Dhameja, 2009). Motivation practices are devised basically to influence labor behavior to achieve organizational goals and objective. It determines whether an employee will do his job tasks properly. Motivation improves employees' performance.

Motivation practices can be accomplished through two types of incentives patterns; pay, financial compensations, and punishment are external incentives or motivational factors that need to be internalized in order to become effective. Internal incentives, on the other hand, are ego needs of the employee. It includes job satisfaction, job accomplishment, and prestige (Dhameja and Dhameja, 2009). Monetary and nonmonetary incentives are both critical in labor turnover and productivity (Kepner, 2001).

Motivation interacts with and ads in conjunction with other cognitive processes. In addition to monetary and nonmonetary incentives, employers today are using work conditions (job satisfaction, job security, job promotion, and pride for accomplishment) as a means of highly improving workers performance and fostering labor retention and effectiveness (Kepner, 2001). Also, there are other stimuli that can drive the employee to do better such as educational incentives. Some fast-food establishments developed strategies to combat high turnover rates, such "Educational Bonus Program" by which employees are tested on their working knowledge and skills; employees must first work their way up to the level called "expert." They obtain this level through

1. their ability to work at all of the restaurant's stations and
2. by knowing product specifications.

Once an employee becomes an "expert," he/she receives a savings account in his/her name. The organization deposits a sum of money into the account every 6 months to be used for educational purposes (Bonn, 1992). Such motivation process can be used to fight the physiological deficiencies and then activate the employees' behavior.

Generally, the needs for incentive can be many as follows:

- To increase performance and productivity.
- To psychologically satisfy a person which leads to job satisfaction and accordingly to employee commitment.
- To shape the behavior or outlook of subordinate toward work.
- To get the maximum of their capabilities so that they can be exploited and utilized maximally.

Thus, motivation process can be defined as the ability to change people's behavior. As human behavior is directed toward some goals, so motivation process can compel one to act according to the objectives set by his organization. Workers stay if their skills are fully utilized and are contributing to the achievement, of the overall goal of the organization.

## 7.7 IMPROVING RETENTION WITHIN THE HOSPITALITY INDUSTRY

While the causes of the high turnover rate in the hospitality organizations have been investigated by numerous studies, there is limited attention to the efforts or methods that can be adopted to reverse the trend and ensure the industry can retain its workforce for longer periods. The key to success in any business lies in investing in human resources. As a result of poor investment in the human resource, the organizations are suffering because they usually regard their workforce as temporary business assets. So, organizations must pay attention to labor-retention strategies. Generally, for some hotel companies, name recognition alone can be the best strategy for attracting the industry's best, brightest, and skilled employees. However, the name alone cannot prevent high turnover (Brown, 2004).

For example, the organizations' (industry) involvement in planning of internship program has been shown to be influential in the decisions of students on internship to join and stay within the hospitality industry following their graduation (Chen and Shen, 2012). Fair treatment of employees, including the use of reasonable work schedules and shifts, can also enhance the motivation and commitment of the employees. In addition, Das and Baruah (2013) advocated that the organization may use rewards as a means for motivating its employees and getting their highest performance.

Freund (2005) found that the worker–management relationship had a significant influence on employees' intentions or thinking of quitting the organization. Brown (2004) argued that for retention strategies to be effective, they must focus on providing employees with the opportunity to grow their careers in an organization with a solid business foundation.

Generally, employers may find it difficult to counter the pull of the labor markets; however, putting some efforts can reduce the overall employee turnover in addition to identifying those groups with a high intention to leave and the reasons of their leaving. The following retention strategies have been suggested as best efforts for employers to minimize the rate of their employees' turnover:

- Strategically place induction programs highlighting the organization's mission and aim for long-term employment (Pranoto, 2011).
- There must be a great emphasis on employee recruitment procedures, and retention in the hospitality-service industry (Chang et al., 2013), specially the costs associated with recruitment, selection processes, and training new employees often exceed 100% of the annual salary for the vacated positions (Bryant and Allen, 2013).
- Communicate well with employees. Especially in their first days in the organization because the most critical period of turnover cases is the first few days and weeks of the incorporation of a new employee in an organization. This is because an informed and satisfied employee is a connected employee at the workplace, therefore, will remain in their jobs (Brown, 2004; Walsh and Taylor, 2007).
- Adopting the "Three Rs" strategy: Recognize, Reward, and Repeat (Brown, 2004).
- Offer fair compensations (Walsh and Taylor, 2007), financial incentives are offered to the managerial employees; they should be offered to all employees (Namasivayam et al., 2007).
- Provision of job security via long-term contracts (Pranoto, 2011).
- Availability of supervisory and management career-path programs (Pranoto, 2011).

- Provide employees with career development opportunities (Walsh and Taylor, 2007). This is because employees are more likely to invest in their jobs if they feel the company has invested in them.
- Provision of selected benefits such as retirement plans, health insurance, etc. (Pranoto, 2011).
- Providing private or public service especially childcare services particularly for workers with family responsibilities, particularly women who carry the majority of the care burden for children and the elderly as well as for household chores (ILO, 2010).
- Measure employee satisfaction on a regular basis with the same conviction applied to measuring guest satisfaction, as the first will determine the latter (Brown, 2004).
- A confidential exit interview should be conducted with the leavers and wherever possible; this is best done by someone other than the direct manager (www.hospitalityrecruitmentsolution.com.au).

Kimosop (2007) further suggested that it is very important for employers to consider establishing social ties in the organization to promote organizational commitment. According to her, loyalty to organizations may be disappearing but loyalty to colleagues is not. Thus, by encouraging the development of social ties among key employees, organizations can often significantly reduce turnover among workers whose skills are in high demand. Retention strategies must be designed to satisfy individual employees. This, therefore, evoke emotions of compassion and community pride that generate greater organization loyalty among present and future employees (Johnson et al., 2000). In the same line, Kimosop (2007) suggested that the best way to deal with labor turnover is to tap the internal labor market. She said that since most workforces are opportunity seekers, it is important that employees feel appreciated and be made aware of the vacancies and opportunities that exist within their organization. In addition, internal postings should be readily available and easily accessible.

## REFERENCES

Abassi, S. M.; Hollman, K. W. Turnover: The Real Bottom Line, *Public Personnel Management*. *SAGE J.* **2005,** *3* (2), 333–342.

Abbasi, S. M.; Hollman, K. W. Turnover: The Real Bottom Line. *Publ. Pers. Manage.* **2000,** *29* (3), 333–342.

AlBattat, A. R.; Som, A. P. Employee Dissatisfaction and Turnover Crises in the Malaysian Hospitality Industry. *Int. J. Bus. Manage.* **2013,** *8* (5), 62–71.

AlBattat, A. R.; Som, A. P.; Helalat, A. S. Higher Dissatisfaction Higher Turnover in the Hospitality Industry. *Int. J. Acad. Res. Bus. Soc. Sci.* **2014,** *4* (2), 45–52.

Ali, A. Y.; Ali, A. A.; Adan, A. A. Working Conditions and Employees' Productivity in Manufacturing Companies in Sub-Saharan African Context: Case of Somalia. *Educ. Res. Int.* **2013,** *2* (2), 67–78.

Amankwaa, A.; Anku-Tsede, O. Linking Transformational Leadership to Employee Turnover: The Moderating Role of Alternative Job Opportunity. *Int. J. Bus. Adm.* **2015,** *6* (4), 19–25.

Ameliya, R.; Febriansyah, H. The Significant Factors of Employee Turnover, Case Study: ABC Hotel. *J. Bus. Manage.* **2017,** *6* (2), 239–249.

Asela, N.; Nasrudin, P. T.; Hasifrafidee, B. Hasbollah, Darweanna; Simpong, B. T. Types, Cause and Effects of Hotel Staff Turnover Intention: A literature Review from Hotel Industry in Malaysia. *Int. J. Manage. Appl. Sci.* **2017,** *3* (3), 120–122.

Barky, J. D. Building a Program for World-Class Customer Satisfaction Program. *Cornell Hotel Restaur. Adm. Q.* **1996,** *37* (1), 17.

Beam, J. What is Employee Turnover? (online), 2009. http://www.wisegeek.com/what-is employee-turnover.htm (accessed Oct 5, 2017).

Bennett, N.; Terry, C.; Blum, R.; Long, G.; Paul, M. R. Group and Organization Management Employee Attrition. *Group Organ. Manage.* **1993,** *18* (4), 482–499.

Bharwani, S.; Butt, N. Challenges for the Global Hospitality: An HR Perspective. *Worldw. Hospitality Tour. Themes* **2012,** *4* (2), 150–162.

Blomme, J.; Rheede, A.; Tromp, D. Work–Family Conflict as a Cause for Turnover Intentions in the Hospitality. *Tour. Hospitality Res.* **2010,** *10* (4), 269–285.

Blomme, R. J.; Sok, J.; Tromp, D. M. The Influence of Organizational Culture on Negative Work–Home Interference among Highly Educated Employees in the Hospitality Industry. *J. Quality Assur. Hospitality Tour.* **2013,** *14* (1), 1–23.

Bolch, M. The Coming Crunch. *Hum. Resour. Train. Mag.* **2001,** *196* (2628), 42–46.

Bonn, M. A. Reducing Turnover in the Hospitality Industry: An Overview of Recruitment, Selection and Retention. *Hospitality Manage.* **1992,** *11* (1), 47–63.

Brown. *Building a Culture of Retention Hotel Executive* (online), 2004. http://www.hotelexecutive.com/premium/forum (accessed Aug 24, 2017).

Brownell, J. Striking a Balance: The Future of Work and Family Issues in the Hospitality Industry. *J. Marriage Fam. Rev.* **1998,** *28* (1–2), 21–26.

Bryant, P. C.; Allen, D. G. Compensation, Benefits and Employee Turnover HR Strategies for Retaining Top Talent. *Compens. Benef. Rev.* **2013,** *45* (3), 171–175.

Cao, Z.; Chen, J.; Song, Y. Does Total Regards Reduce the Core Employees' Turnover Intention? *Int. J. Bus. Manage.* **2013,** *8* (20), 62–75.

Cascio, W. F. *Costing Human Resources: The Financial Impact of Behavior in Organizations*, 4th ed.; PWS-Kent: Boston, MA, 1991.

Cascio, W. F. Leveraging Employer Branding, Performance Management and Human Resource Development to Enhance Employee Retention. *Hum. Resour. Dev. Int.* **2014,** *17* (2), 121–128.

Chan, S. H.; Kuok, O. M. A Study of Human Resources Recruitment, Selection, and Retention Issues in the Hospitality and Tourism Industry in Macau. *J. Hum. Resour. Hospitality Tour.* **2011,** *10* (4), 421–441.

Chang, W. A.; Wang, Y.; Huang, T. Work Design-Related Antecedent of Turnover Intentions: A Multilevel Approach. *Hum. Resour. Manage.* **2013,** *52* (1), 1–26.

Chartered Institute of Personnel and Development (CIPD). Employee Turnover and Retention; CIPD: London, 2014. http://www.cipd.co.uk/hr-resources/factsheets/employee-turnover. retention.aspx (accessed Oct 12, 2017).

Chen, J.; Silverthorne, C. Leadership Effectiveness, Leadership Style and Employee Readiness. *Leadersh. Organ. Dev. J.* **2005,** *26* (4), 280–288.

Chen, L.; Shen, C. Today's Intern, Tomorrow's Practitioner? The Influence of Internship Programmes on Students Career Development in the Hospitality Industry. *J. Hospitality, Leisure, Sport Tour. Educ.* **2012,** *11* (1), 29–40.

Chen, T.; Chang, P.; Yeh, C. A Study of Career Needs, Career Development Programs, Job Satisfaction, and the Turnover Intentions of R and D Personnel. *Career Dev. Int.* **2004,** *9* (4), 424–437.

Chen, Y.; Friedman, R.; Simons, T. The Gendered Trickle-Down Effect: How Mid-Level Managers' Satisfaction with Senior Managers' Supervision Affects Line Employee's Turnover Intentions. *Career Dev. Int.* **2014,** *19*, 836–856.

Chon, K. S.; Barrows, C. W.; Bosselman, R. H. *Hospitality Management Education*; Routledge: New York, NY, 2013.

CIPD. *Employee Turnover and Retention* (online), 2005. http://www.cipd.co.uk/subjects/hrpract/turnover/empturnretent.htm?IsSrchRes=1 (accessed Oct 20, 2017).

Costen, M.; Salazar, J. The Impact of Training and Development on Employee Job Satisfaction, Loyalty, and Intent to Stay in the Lodging Industry. *J. Hum. Resour. Hospitality Tour.* **2011,** *10* (3), 273–284.

Cropanzano, R.; Rupp, D.; Byrne, Z. The Relationship of Emotional Exhaustion to Work Attitudes, Job Performance, and Organizational Citizenship Behaviors. *J. Appl. Psychol.* **2003,** *88* (1), 160–169.

Dailey, R. C.; Kirk, D. J. Distributive and Procedural Justice as Antecedents of Job Dissatisfaction and Intent to Turnover. *Hum. Relat.* **1992,** *45* (3), 305–307.

Darmon, R. Identifying Sources of Turnover Cost. *J. Mark.* **1990,** *54* (2), 46–56.

Das, B.; Baruah, M. Employee Retention: A Review of Literature. *J. Bus. Manage.* **2013,** *14* (2), 8–16.

Davidson, M. C.; McPhail, R.; Barry, S. Hospitality HRM: Past, Present and the Future. *Int. J. Contemp. Hospitality Manage.* **2011,** *23* (4), 498–516.

Davies, D.; Taylor, T.; Savery, L. The Role of Appraisal, Remuneration and Training in Improving Staff Relations in the Western Australian Accommodation Industry: A Comparative Study. *J. Eur. Ind. Train.* **2001,** *25* (7), 366–373.

Deloitte University Press. *Global Human Capital Trends* (online), 2016. https://www2.deloitte.com/content/dam/Deloitte/global/Documents/HumanCapital/gx-dup-global human-capital-trends-2016.pdf (accessed Aug 12, 2017).

Demir, C.; Colakoğlu, U.; Güzel, B. Relationship between Employee Turnover and the Location of Hotels: The Case of Kuşadasi and Izmir in Turkey. *J. Yasar Univ.* **2007,** *2* (5), 477–487.

Dhameja, S. K.; Dhameja, S. *Industrial Psychology*; S. K. Kataria and Sons: New Delhi, 2009.

Diala-Mobride, C. *How to Stop Your Best Staff Leaving*; Chartered Institute of Personnel and Development (CIPD) Middle East, CIPD, 2016 (online). http://www.cipd.ae/people-management magazine/feature-articles/stop-best-staff-leaving (accessed Aug 2, 2017).

Dobre, O. Employee Motivation and Organizational Performance. *Rev. Appl. Socio-Econ. Res.* **2013,** *5* (1), 53–60.

Doherty, L.; Manfredi, S. Women's Employment in Italian and UK Hotels. *Int. J. Hospitality Manage.* **2001,** *20*, 61–76.

Ernst and Young. *The Hospitality Sector in Europe: An Assessment of the Economic Contribution of the Hospitality Sector across 31 Countries*; Ernst and Young: London, 2013, (online). http://www.ey.com/Publication/vwLUAssets/The_Hospitality_Sector_in_Europe/$FILE/EY_The_H spitality_Sector_in_Europe.pdf (accessed Aug 10, 2017).

Fair, R. *Australian Human Resource Management: Framework and Practice*, 2nd ed.; McGraw-Hill: Sidney, 1992.

Faldetta, G.; Fasone, V.; Provenzano, C. Turnover in the Hospitality Industry: Can Reciprocity Solve the Problem. *J. Revista de Turismo y Patrimonio Cultural* **2013,** *11* (4), 583–595

Fortino, P.; Ninemeier, J. Industry in the Dark about Turnover Rate. *Lodging* **1996,** *22* (4), 25.

Freund, A. Commitment and Job Satisfaction as Predictors of Turnover Intentions among Welfare Workers. *Adm. Soc. Work* **2005,** *29* (2), 5–22.

Frey, R.; Bayón, T.; Totzek, D. How Customer Satisfaction Affects Employee Satisfaction and Retention in a Professional Services Context. *J. Serv. Res.* **2013,** *16*, 503–517.

Fungwu, T.; Hui Tsai, M.; Fey, Y.; Wu, R. A Study of the Relationship between Manager's Leadership Style and Organizational Commitment in Taiwan's International Tourist Hotels. *Asian J. Manage. Human. Sci.* **2006,** *1* (3), 434–452.

Gin Choi, Y.; Kwon, J.; Kim, W. Effects of Attitudes vs. Experience of Workplace Fun on Employee Behavior: Focused on Generation Y in the Hospitality Industry. *Int. J. Contemp. Hospitality Manage.* **2013,** *25*, 410–427.

Glebbeek, A. C.; Bax, E. H. Is High Employee Turnover Really Harmful: An Empirical Test Using Company Records. *Acad. Manage. J.* **2004,** *47* (2), 86–277.

Govaerts, N.; Kyndt, E.; Dochy, F.; Baert, H. Influence of Learning and Working Climate on the Retention of Talented Employees. *J. Workpl. Learn.* **2011,** *23* (1), 5–55.

Griffeth, R.; Hom, P. *Employee Turnover*; South/Wastern: Cincinnati, OH, 2004.

Guan, Y.; Wen, Y.; Chen, S.; Liu, H.; Si, W.; Liu, Y.; Dong, Z. When Do Salary and Job Level Predict Career Satisfaction and Turnover Intention among Chinese Managers? The Role of Perceived Organizational Career Management and Career Anchor. *Eur. J. Work Organ. Psychol.* **2013,** 23, 596–607.

Guilding, C.; Lamminmaki, D.; McManus, L. Staff Turnover Costs: In Search of Accountability. *Int. J. Hospitality Manage.* **2014,** *36*, 231–243.

Guthrie, J. P. Alternate Pay Practices and Employee Turnover: An Organization Economics Perspective. *Group Organ. Manage.* **2000,** *25* (4), 419–439.

Hancock, J. I.; Allen, D. G.; Bosco, F. A.; McDaniel, K. R.; Pierce, C. A. Meta-Analytic Review of Employee Turnover as a Predictor of Firm Performance. *J. Manage.* **2013,** *39*, 573–603.

Hartog, J.; Ophem, H. *On-the-Job Search, Mobility, and Wages in the Netherlands: What Do We Know in the Flow Analysis of Labor Markets*; Schettkat, R., Ed.; Routledge: London, 1996.

Heneman, H. G.; Schwab, D. P. Pay Satisfaction: Its Multidimensional Nature and Measurement. *Int. J. Psychol.* **1985,** *20*, 129–141.

Hiemstra, S. J. Employment Policies and Practices in the Lodging Industry. *Int. J. Hospitality Manage.* **1990,** *9* (3), 207–221.

Hinkin, T.; Tracey, J. The Cost of Turnover: Putting a Price on the Learning Curve. *Cornell Hotel Restaur. Adm. Q.* **2000,** *41* (3), 14–21.

Holston-Okae, B. L. Employee Turnover Intentions in the Hospitality Industry. *Ph.D. Dissertation*. Walden: Walden University, 2017; pp 12–54.

Hurley, R. F. An Exploratory Study of the Effect of Employee Turnover on Customer Satisfaction. In *Proceedings of the 1997 Academy of Marketing Science (AMS) Annual Conference*; Wilson, E., Hair, J., Eds.; Baton Rouge, LA: Springer International, 2015; pp 319–320.

Hwang, J.; Lee, J. J.; Park, S.; Chang, H.; Kim, S. S. The Impact of Occupational Stress on Employee's Turnover Intention in the Luxury Hotel Segment. *Int. J. Hospitality Tour. Adm.* **2014,** *15* (1), 60–77.

ILO. Developments and Challenges in the Hospitality and Tourism Sector. In *Global Dialogue Forum for the Hotels, Catering, Tourism Sector (23–24 November 2010)*; ILO: Geneva, Switzerland, 2010a.

ILO. Challenges for the Global Hospitality Industry: An HR Perspective. *Hospitality Tour. Themes* **2010,** *4* (2), 150–162.

ILO. *Human Resource Development, Employment and Globalization in the Hotel, Catering and Tourism Sector: Report for Discussion at the Tripartite Meeting on the Human Resource Development, Employment and Globalization in the Hotel, Catering and Tourism Sector*; International Labor Organization: Geneva, 2001.

Iravo, M.; Namusonge, G.; Muceke, N. Influence of Leadership Style on Academic Staff Retention in Public Universities in Kenya. *Int. J. Bus. Soc. Sci.* **2012,** *3* (21), 297–302.

Ismail, H. Job Insecurity, Burnout and Intention to Quit. *Int. J. Acad. Res. Bus. Soc. Sci.* **2015,** *5* (4), 310–324.

Iverson, R. D.; Deery, M. Turnover Culture in the Hospitality Industry. *Hum. Resour. Manage. J.* **1997,** *7* (4), 71–82.

Iverson, K. The Paradox of The Contented Female Manager: An Empirical Investigation of Gender Differences in Pay Expectation in The Hospitality Industry. *Int. J. Hospitality Manage.* **2000,** *19*, 33–51.

Jagun, V. An Investigation into the High Turnover of Employees within the Irish Hospitality Sector, Identifying What Methods of Retention Should Be Adopted. *M.Sc. Thesis*; Dublin: National College of Ireland, 2015.

Johnson, J.; Griffeth, R. W.; Griffin, M. Factors Discrimination Functional and Dysfunctional Sales Force Turnover. *J. Bus. Ind. Mark.* **2000,** *15* (6), 399–415.

Jones, P.; Lockwood, A. *The Management of Hotel Operations*; London: Cengage Learning, 2002.

Kara, D.; Uysal, M.; Sirgy, M. J.; Lee, G. The Effects of Leadership Style on Employee Well-Being in Hospitality. *Int. J. Hospitality Manage.* **2013,** *34* (1), 9–18.

Karatepe, O. M. High-Performance Work Practices and Hotel Employee Performance: The Mediation of Work Engagement. *Int. J. Hospitality Manage.* **2013,** *32*, 132–140.

Karatepe, O. M., Shahriari, S. Job Embeddedness as a Moderator of the Impact of Organizational Justice on Turnover Intentions: A Study in Iran. *Int. J. Tour. Res.* **2014,** *16* (1), 22–32.

Karatepe, O. M.; Vatankhah, S. The Effects of High-Performance Work Practices on Perceived Organizational Support and Turnover Intentions: Evidence from the Airline Industry. *J. Hum. Resour. Hospitality Tour.* **2014,** *13* (2), 103–119.

Katsikea, E.; Theodosiou, M.; Morgan, R. E. Why People Quit: Explaining Employee Turnover Intentions among Export Sales Managers. *Int. Bus. Rev.* **2015,** *24*, 367–379.

Kavanaugh, R. R.; Ninemeier, J. D. *Supervision in the Hospitality Industry*, 3rd ed.; The Educational Institute of the American Hotel and Lodging Association: Michigan, 2001.

Kenya Bureau of Statistics. *Job Opening and Labor Turnover Survey*; 2009.
Kepner, K. W. *Human Resource Management in Agribusiness* (online), 2004. http//www.Keepemployees.com/retention (accessed Oct 20, 2017).
Khalili, M. A Study on Relationship between Organizational Culture and Organizational Commitment. *Manage. Sci. Lett.* **2014,** *4*, 1463–1466.
Kimosop, D. J. Labor Turnover in Private Security Firms in Kenya: A Case Study of Future Force Security Firm. Nairobi: University of Nairobi, 2007.
Klebanow, A. M.; Eder, R. W. Cost-Effectiveness of Substance-Abuse Treatment in Casino Hotels: Human Resources. *Cornell Hotel Restaur. Adm. Q.* **1992,** *33* (1), 56.
Kokemuller, N. *Poor Leadership & Its Effects on the Staff and Company* (online), 2017. https://yourbusiness.azcentral.com/poor-leadership-its-effects-staff-company-21754.html (accessed Nov 20, 2017).
Kokt, D.; Ramarumo, R. Impact of Organizational Culture on Job Stress and Burnout in Graded Accommodation Establishments in the Free State Province South Africa. *Int. J. Contemp. Hospitality Manage.* **2015,** *27* (6), 1198–1213.
Kraimer, M.; Seibert, S.; Wayne, J.; Liden, C.; Bravo, J. Antecedents and Outcomes of Organizational Support for Development: The Critical Role of Database. *J. Appl. Psychol.* **2011,** *96* (3), 485–500.
Kumar, R.; Ramendran, C.; Yacob, P. A Study on Turnover Intention in Fast Food Industry: Employees' Fit to the Organizational Culture and the Important of their Commitment. *Int. J. Acad. Res. Bus. Soc. Sci.* **2012,** *2* (5), 9–42.
Kuria, S.; Alicc, O.; Wanderi, P. M. Assessment of Causes of Labor Turnover in Three and Five Star Rated Hotels in Kenya. *Int. J. Bus. Soc. Sci.* **2012,** *3* (15), 311–317.
Kuria, S.; Peter, W.; Alice, O. Factors Influencing Labor Turnover in Three and Five Star-Rated Hotels in Nairobi, Kenya. *Int. J. Human. Soc. Sci.* **2011,** *1* (20), 195–201.
Kusluvan, S. Multinational Enterprises in Tourism: A Case Study of Turkey. *Ph.D. Dissertation*; Strathclyde University, the Scottish Hotel School: Glascow, 2003.
Kyndt, E.; Dochy, F.; Michielsen, M.; Moeyaert, B. Employee Retention: Organizational and Personal Perspectives. *Vocat. Learn.* **2009,** *2* (3), 195–215.
Lambert, E. G.; Cluse-Tolar, T.; Pasupuleti, S.; Prior, M.; Allen, R. I. A Test of a Turnover Intent Model. *Adm. Soc. Work* **2013,** *36* (1), 67–84.
Lashley, C. *Hospitality Retail Management: A Unit Manager's Handbook;* Butterworth-Heinemann, Oxford, 2000.
Lashley, C.; Best, W. Employee Induction in Licensed Retail Organizations. *Int. J. Contemp. Hospitality Manage.* **2002,** *14* (1), 6–13.
Lee, L. E.; Marshall, R.; Rallis, D.; Moscardi, M. Women on Boards: Global Trends in Gender Diversity on Corporate Boards, MSCI, 2015. (Online) https://www.msci.com/documents/10199/04b6f646-d638-4878-9c61-4eb91748a82b (accessed Mar 4, 2019).
Lee, T. How Job Dissatisfaction Leads to Employee Turnover. *J. Bus. Psychol.* **1988,** *2* (3), 263–271.
Lee-Ross, D. *HRM in Tourism and Hospitality, International Perspectives on Small and Medium-Sized Enterprises*. London: Rewood Books, 1999.
Lucas, R. E. *Managing Employee Relations in the Hotel and Catering Industry;* London: Cassell, 1995.
Lussier, N. R. *Human Relations in Organizational Applications and Skill Building*; McGraw Hill: New York, NY, 2005.

Maddah, M. An Empirical Analysis of the Relationship between Unemployment and Theft Crimes. *Int. J. Econ. Financ. Issues* **2013,** *3*, 50–53.

Malik, M. E.; Danish, R. Q.; Munir, Y. Employee's Turnover Intentions: Is This HR Failure or Employee's Better Employment Opportunity? In *International Conference on Innovation, Management and Service*; IPEDR, IACSIT Press: Singapore, 2011; p 14.

Marshall, T.; Mottier, L.; Lewis, R. Motivational Factors and the Hospitality Industry: A Case Study of Examining the Effects of Changes in the Working Environment. *J. Bus. Case Stud.* **2016,** *11* (3), 123–132.

Martin, M. J. *Influence of Human Resource Practices on Employee Intention to Quit*; Virginia Polytechnic Institute and State University: Blacksburg, VA, 2011.

Mathieu, C.; Fabi, B.; Lacoursière, R.; Raymond, L. The Role of Supervisory Behavior, Job Satisfaction and Organizational Commitment on Employee Turnover. *J. Manage. Organ* **2016,** *22* (1), 113–129.

McNamara, M.; Bohle, P.; Quinlan, M. Precarious Employment, Working Hours, Work-life Conflict, and Health in Hotel Work. *Appl. Ergon.* **2011,** *42* (2), 225–232.

Mitra, A.; Jenkins, G. D.; Gupta, N. A Meta-Analysis Review of the Relationship between Absence and Turnover. *J. Appl. Psychol.* **1992,** *1* (3), 879–889.

Mobley, W. H. *Employee Turnover, Causes, Consequences, and Control*; Addison–Wesley: Reading, MA, 1977a.

Mobley, W. H. Intermediate Linkages in the Relationship between Job and Satisfaction and Employee Turnover. *J. Appl. Psychol.* **1997b,** *62*, 237–40.

Mohanty, K.; Mohanty, S. An Empirical Study on the Employee Perception on Work–Life Balance in Hotel Industry with Special Reference to Odisha. *J. Tour. Hospitality Manage.* **2014,** *2* (2), 65–81.

Mohsin, A.; Lengler, J.; Aguzzoli, R. Staff Turnover in Hotels: Exploring the Quadratic and Linear Relationships. *Tour. Manage.* **2015,** *51*, 35–48.

Mondy, R. W. *Human Resource Management*, 10th ed.; Pearson Prentice Hall: New Jersey, 2008.

Musa, B. M.; Ahmed, I.; Bala, A. Effect of Motivational Incentives on Staff Turnover in Hotel Industry in Gombe State, *IOSR J. Bus. Manage.* **2014,** *16* (3), 36–42.

Mwilu, J. M. Factors Influencing Employee Turnover in the Hotel Industry in Machakos Town, Machakos County. M.Sc. Thesis, South Eastern Kenya University: Kitui, Kenya, 2016.

Namasaka, D.; Poipoi, M.; Mamuli, L. Effects of Staff Turnover on the Employee Performance of Work at Masinde Muliro University of Science and Technology. *Int. J. Hum. Resour. Stud.* **2013,** *3* (1), 1–8.

Namasivayam, K.; Miao, L.; Zhao, X. An Investigation of the Relationship between Compensation Practices and Firm Performance in the US Hotel Industry. *Int. J. Hospitality Manage.* **2006,** *26*, 574–587.

Nankervis, A. L.; Compton, R. L.; McCarthy, E. T. *Strategic Human Resource Management*; National Library of Australia: Thomas Nelson, Australia, 1996.

Narayanan, A. Talent Management and Employee Retention: Implications of Job Embeddedness. *J. Strateg. Hum. Resour. Manage.* **2016,** *5* (2), 34–40.

Noah, Y. A Study of Worker Participation in Management Decision Making within Selected Establishments in Lagos, Nigeria. *J. Soc. Sci.* **2008,** *17* (1), 31–39.

Nolan, C. Human Resource Development in the Irish Hotel Industry: The Case of Small Firm. *J. Eur. Ind. Train.* **2002,** *26* (2/3/4), 88–89.

O'Leary, S.; Deegan, J. Career Progression of Irish Tourism and Hospitality Management Graduates. *Int. J. Contemp. Hospitality Manage.* **2005,** *17* (5), 421 432.
Özbağ, G. K.; Ceyhan, G.; Çekmecelioğlu, H. G. The Moderating Effects of Motivating Job Characteristics on the Relationship between Burnout and Turnover Intention. *Soc. Behav. Sci.* **2014,** *150*, 438–446.
Paille, P.; Grima, F.; Bernardeau, D. When Subordinates Feel Supported by Managers: Investigating the Relationships between Support, Trust, Commitment, and Outcomes. *Int. Rev. Adm. Sci.* **2013,** *79* (4), 681–700.
Patton, C. *Employee Rewards: Beyond the Traditional*; *Univ. Bus.* **2009,** *12* (10), 23–24.
Phillips, J. A.; Connel, G. T. *Accountability in Human Resource Management*; Butterworth Heinemann: Boston, MA, 2003.
Poon, J. Effects of Performance Appraisal Politics on Job Satisfaction and Turnover Intention. *Person. Rev.* **2004,** *33* (3), 322–334.
Poulston, J. Hospitality Workplace Problems and Poor Training: A Close Relationship. *Int. J. Contemp. Hospitality Manage.* **2008,** *20* (4), 412–427.
Pranoto, E. S. Labor Turnover in the Hospitality Industry. *Binus Bus. Rev.* **2011,** *2* (1), 597–601.
Price, J. L.; Mueller, C. W. A Causal Model of Turnover for Nurses. *Acad. Manage. J.* **1981,** *24* (3), 543–565.
Price, L. *Study of Turnover Attrition a Major Risk to COS Security*; Iowa State University Press: Ames, IA, 1977.
Prince, B. J. Career-Focused Employee Transfer Processes. *Career Dev. Int.* **2005,** *10* (4), 293–309.
Purcell, J.; Kinnie, N.; Hutchinson, S.; Rayton, B.; Swart, J. *Understanding the People and Performance Link: Unlocking the Black Box*; CIPD: London, 2003.
Rehman, S.; Mansoor, M; Bilal, R. The Impact of Leadership Styles on Job Satisfaction at Work Place. *Arab. J. Bus. Manage. Rev.* **2012,** *1* (12), 26–42.
Robbins, S. P.; Judge, T. A.; Hasham, E. S. *Organizational Behavior: Arab World Edition* (online), 2008. http://www.pearsonmiddleeastawe.com/pdfs/OB-SAMPLE.pdf (accessed Nov 10, 2017).
Robbins, S. P.; Sanghi, S. *Organizational Behavior*; Pearson Education: New Delhi, 2007.
Rollinson, D. *Organizational Behavior and Analysis: An Integrated Approach*; Pearson Education Limited: Harlow, Essex, 2005.
Shaw, J. D.; Delery, J. E.; Jenkins, G. D.; Gupta, N. An Organizational-Level Analysis of Voluntary and Involuntary Turnover. *Acad. Manage. Rev.* **1988,** *41* (5), 511–525.
Stalcup, D.; Pearson, A. A Model of the Causes of Management Turnover in Hotels. *J. Hospitality Tour. Res.* **2001,** *25* (1), 17–30.
Steed, E.; Shinnar, R. Making Employee Turnover Calculations Useful. *J. Hum. Resour. Hospitality Tour.* **2008,** *2* (1), 77–89.
Sturman, M. C. Using Your Pay System to Improve Employees' Performance: How You Pay Makes a Difference. *Cornell Hospitality Rep.* **2006,** *6* (13), 1–16.
Suikkanen, E. How Does Employer Branding Increase Employee Retention? (Undergraduate). Metropolia University of Applied Sciences: Finland, 2010.
Su, H.-W. The Factors of Turnover Intention in Hotel Industry. *IJRRAS*, **2014,** *21* (1), 31–38.
Sun, S.; Law, K. High-Performance Human Resource Practices, Citizenship Behavior, and Organizational Performance: A Relational Perspective. *Acad. Manage. J.* **2007,** *50* (3), 558–577.

Surji, K. The Negative Effect and Consequences of Employee Turnover and Retention on the Organization and Its Staff. *Eur. J. Bus. Manage.* **2013,** *5* (25), 52–65.
Tahmincioglu, E. Gifts That Gall. *Workforce Manage.* **2004,** *83* (4), 43–46.
Taylor, M.; Finley, D. Acculturation, Assimilation, and Retention of International Workers in Resorts. *Int. J. Contemp. Hospitality Manage.* **2010,** *22* (5), 681–692.
Taylor, S. *People and Organization Employee Resourcing*; Prentice-Hall: Sidney; Australia, 2002a.
Taylor, S. *The Employee Retention Handbook.* Charted Institute of Personnel and Development: London, 2002b.
Tett, R. P.; Meyer, J. P. Job Satisfaction, Organizational Commitment, Turnover Intention: Path Analyses Based on Meta-Analytic Findings. *Person. Psychol.* **1993,** *46*, 259–293.
Tews, M. J.; Michel, J. W.; Allen, D. G. Fun and Friends: The Impact of Workplace Fun and Constituent Attachment on Turnover in a Hospitality Context. *Hum. Relat.* **2014,** *67*, 923–946.
Tews, M. J.; Michel, J. W.; Ellingson, J. E. The Impact of Coworker Support on Employee Turnover in the Hospitality Industry. *Group Organ. Manage.* **2013,** *38*, 630–653.
Timothy, J.; Teye, B. *Tourism and the Lodging Sector*; Oxford: Routledge, 2009.
Tracey, B.; Hinkin, T. Contextual Factors and Cost Profiles Associated with Employee Turnover. *Cornell Hospitality Q.* **2008,** *49* (1), 12–27.
Tse, H. H.; Huang, X.; Lam, W. Why Does Transformational Leadership Matter for Employee Turnover? A Multi-Foci Social Exchange Perspective. *Leadership Q.* **2013,** *24*, 763–776.
Tutuncu, O.; Kozak, M. An Investigation of Factors Affecting Job Satisfaction. *Int. J. Hospitality Tour. Adm.* **2007,** *8* (1), 1–19.
Walsh, K.; Taylor, M. S. Developing In-House Careers and Retaining Management Talent What Hospitality Professionals Want from Their Jobs". *Cornell Hotel Restaur. Adm. Q.* **2007,** *48* (2), 163–182.
Wayne, J. H.; Casper, W. J.; Matthews, R. A.; Allen, T. D. Family-Supportive Organization Perceptions and Organizational Commitment: The Mediating Role of Work–Family Conflict and Enrichment and Partner Attitudes. *J. Appl. Psychol.* **2013,** *98*, 606–622.
White, G. L. Employee Turnover: The Hidden Drain on Profits. *HR Focus* **1995,** *72* (1), 15–17.
William, J. W.; Stanley, W.; Davis, W. S. Managing Employee Turnover: Why Employees Leave. *Cornell Hotel Restaur. Adm. Q.* **1983,** *24* (1), 11–18.
William, M. L.; McDaniel, M. A.; Ford, L. R. Understanding Multiple Dimensions of Compensation Satisfaction. *J. Bus. Psychol.* **2007,** *21* (3), 429–459.
Wood, R. H.; Macaulay, G. H. Predicting Is Difficult, Especially about the Future: Human Resources in the New Millennium. *Int. J. Hospitality Manage.* **1991,** *18* (4), 443–456.
Wood, R. H.; Macaulay, J. F. Rx for Turnover: Retention Programs That Work. *Cornell Hotel, Restaur. Adm. Q.* **1988,** *30* (1), 79–90.
Woods, R. H. *Human Resources Management Michigan*; The Educational Institute of the American Hotel and Motel Association: Orlando, FL, 1997.
Woods, R. H.; King, J. Z. *Leadership and Management in the Hospitality Industry*, 2nd ed.; Educational Institute of the American Hotel and Lodging Association: Michigan, 2002.
Yousef, D. A. Organizational Commitment: A Mediator of the Relationships of Leadership Behavior with Job Satisfaction and Performance in a Non-Western Country. *J. Manage. Psychol.* **2000,** *15* (1), 6–24.

Zeffane, R. M. Understanding Employee Turnover: The Need for a Contingency Approach. *Int. J. Manpower* **1994,** *15* (9), 22–37.

Zingheim, P. K.; Schuster, J. R. Developing Total Pay Offers for High Performers. *Compens. Benef. Rev.* **2008,** *40*, 55–59.

Zuber, A. A Career in Food Service Cons: High Turnover. *Nation's Restaurant News* **2001,** *35* (21), 147–148.

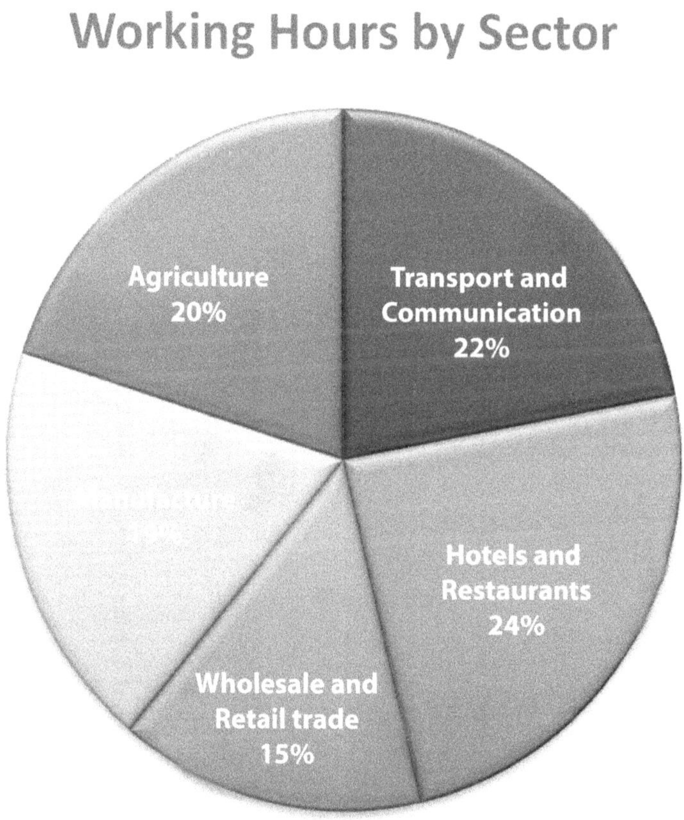


**FIGURE 7.2** Working hours by sector.

**Source:** The Authors, based on ILO (2010).

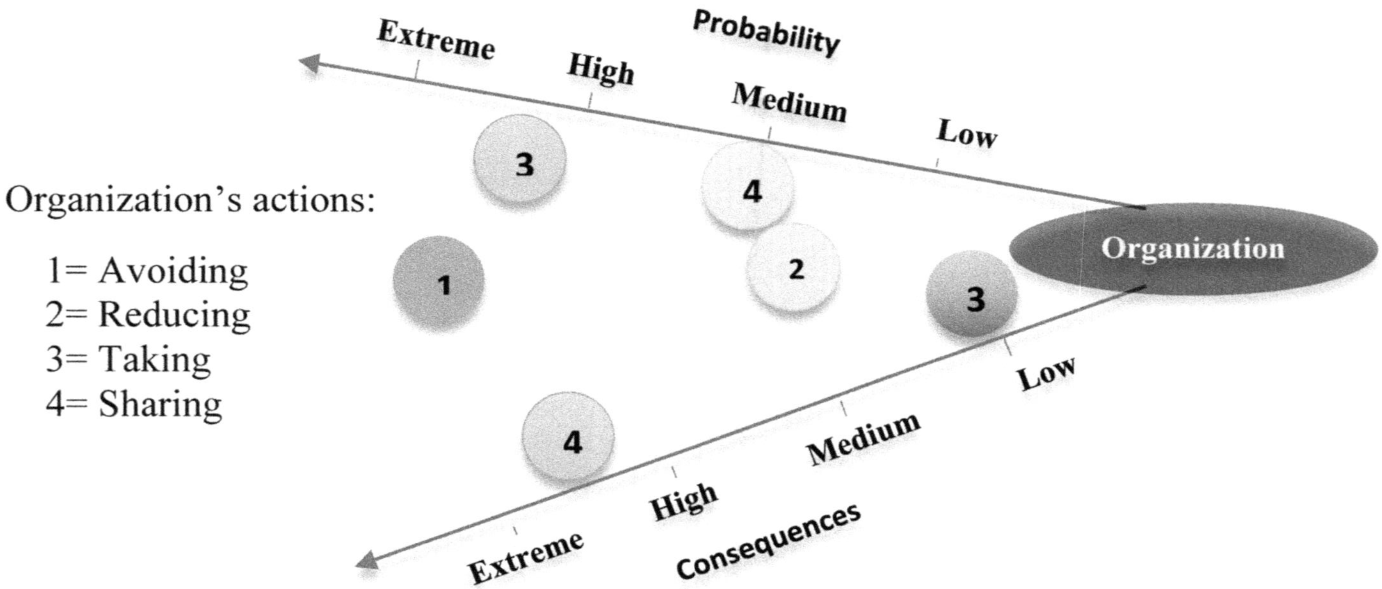


**FIGURE 9.4** Risks treatment process considering its consequences and probability.

**Source:** The Authors

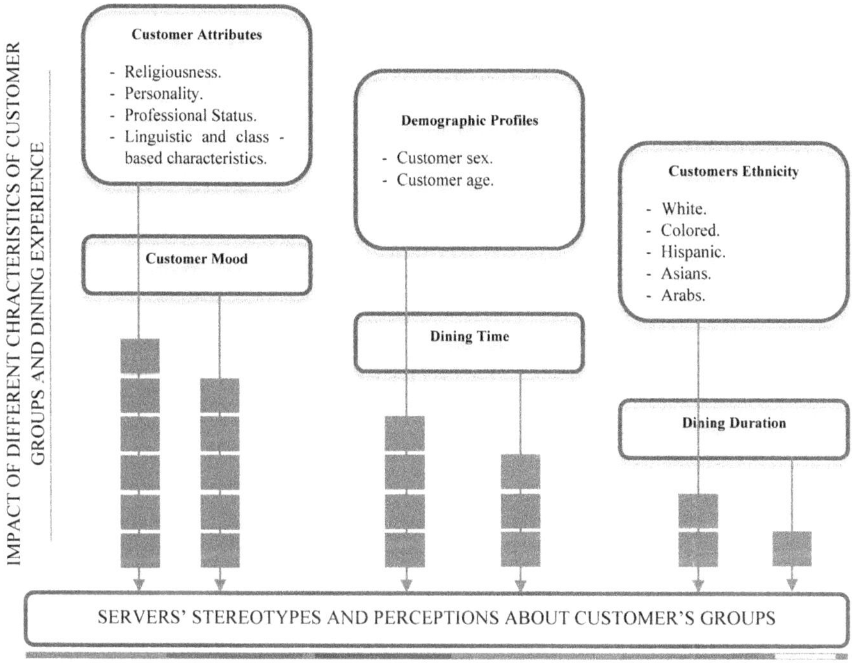


**FIGURE 10.1** Server stereotypes about customer tipping behavior.

**Source:** The Author.

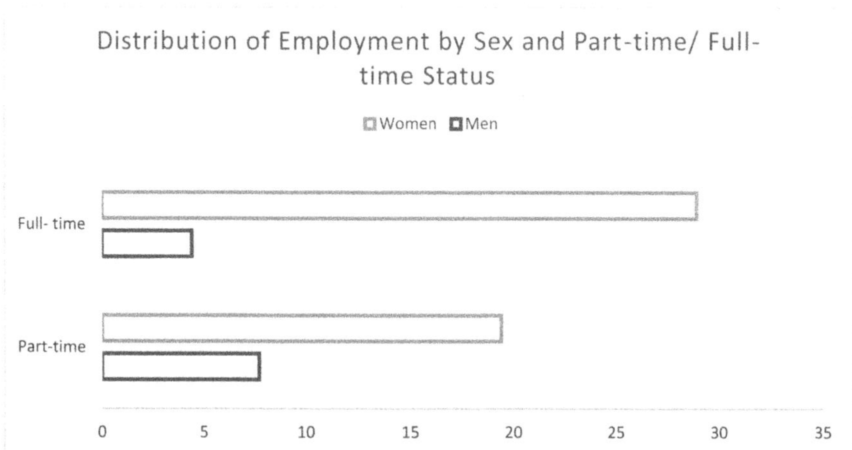


**FIGURE 13.3** The distribution of employment according to sex.

**Source:** The Authors, based on ILO (2010).

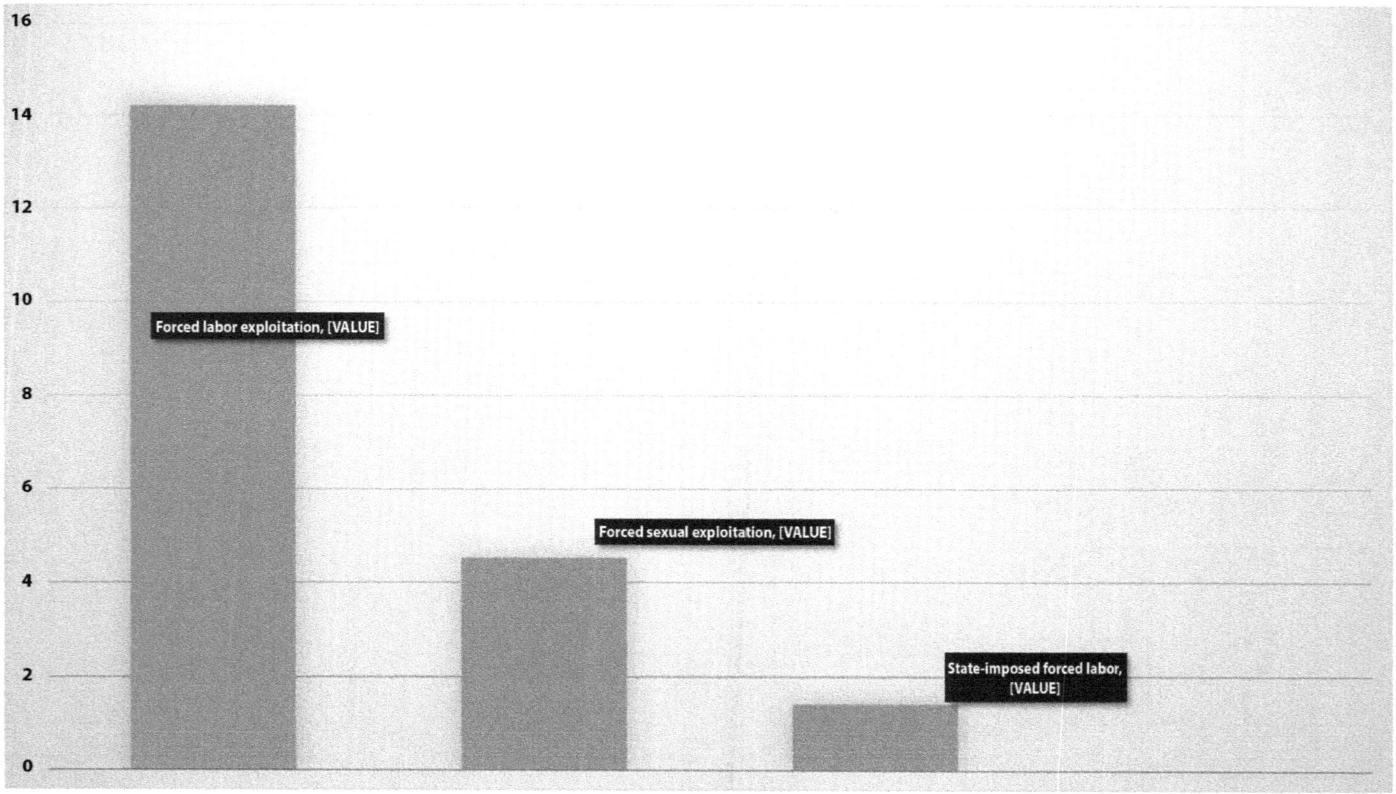


**FIGURE 14.1** Types of forced labor (in millions of people).

**Source:** The Authors based on ILO, 2012

# CHAPTER 8

# TOURISM AND SEASONALITY

*"Although seasonality phenomenon brings a lot of negative consequences for the tourist organizations, it grants the decision maker the opportunity to pause, discover more, and reflect about their business."*

## 8.1 INTRODUCTION

Tourism is defined as "a social, cultural, and economic phenomenon, which entails the movement of people to regions or places outside their usual environment for personal or business/professional purposes" (UNWTO, 2013).

The movement of people outside their countries is strongly linked to the push and pull factors that encourage people to take such a decision:

- ➢ Push factors: school and work holidays
- ➢ Pull factors: the climatic conditions in the destination country

Consequently, it can be said that tourism is a seasonal activity. The tourism industry is characterized by temporal variations in the volume of its activity, in a way that this volume increases to reach its peak in some periods of the year, but relatively decreases or stops in some other periods of the same year. This nature of things leads to the appearance of what is called "seasonality."

Seasonality is identified as one of the most noticeable characteristics of modern tourism, and most destinations experience some kind of seasonal pattern (Reece, 2010). In the same lines, Butler (2001) claimed that seasonality is considered one of the most distinctive features of tourism on a global basis that has a significant effect on tourism demand.

Although seasonality is a concept that is familiar to many, yet there is no generally accepted definition of seasonality in tourism (Koenig-Lewis and Bischoff, 2005). It could be said that there have been numerous attempts to define the seasonal concept in the tourism industry. The first definition of seasonality was given by Baron in 1973 who stated that seasonality "implies an incomplete and unbalanced utilization of the means at the disposal of the economy, and this is similar to the imbalance of the business cycle, where the economy is either overheated or running under full potential at different phases of the cycle" (cited in Oxana, 2016, p 9) while Hylleberg (1992) argued that seasonality means:

- the annual dependence movement, or,
- the systematic movement, or
- regular, intra-year tourist movement that relates to the one of the following factors:
  - changes in climatic conditions;
  - the calendar; and
  - timing of decisions, directly or indirectly, through the production and consumption decisions made by the agents of the economy.

Another definition was developed by Butler (2001), who described seasonality in tourism as "a temporal imbalance in the phenomenon of tourism, which may be expressed in terms of dimensions of elements such as numbers of visitors, expenditure of visitors, traffic on highways and other forms of transportation, employment, and admissions to attractions." Subsequently, tourism seasonality is a temporal fluctuation on a daily, weekly, monthly, or annual basis (Cooper, 2008). However, Koenig-Lewis and Bischoff (2005) pointed out that most definitions of seasonality describe it only in general terms or related to the causes but lack quantifiable definitions.

Other than the problem of vague definitions and consequences of the seasonality phenomenon in the tourism industry, some academics declared their confusion about the best measurement of the consequences of temporal variation resulted from seasonality, whether they should be expressed in terms of:

- accommodation terms (bed nights),
- destination statistical reports (total numbers of visits),
- tourist organization returns (monthly income generated), or
- economic indicators, (such as unemployment rate).

However, the adequate measure is the total numbers of visitors or bed nights. The number of staying visitors is a better indication of the potential value of tourism and return on investment than simple tourist visits, as the latter will include day visitors and cruise ship visitors who generally have lower daily expenditure and a concentrated spatial pattern of impact to a limited part of a destination.

Nevertheless, according to UNWTO (2014), the terms or units of measurement are not significant; it is the temporal extent and pattern of tourism that are generally the most important factors. In some extreme peripheral locations (e.g., sub-polar regions), the season for visitation may be only a few weeks, while very few destinations other than capital and other large cities have large-scale visitation throughout the year.

Regarding the temporal extent of seasonality in tourist destinations, there are many forms of seasonality, as follows:

- Single-peak seasonality (e.g., summer or winter): It occurs when there is an excessive seasonality, for example, summer in some Mediterranean destinations. This occurs because the seasonal pattern of demand in generating countries matches the seasonal pattern of the attractiveness in a destination region (Butler, 2001). So, it is the most extreme type of seasonality.
- Two-peak seasonality (e.g., summer and winter): It occurs when there are two seasons: a major one and a minor one; in a way that each season satisfies a pattern of demand, such as mountain regions, which attract both summer and winter tourists. The Caribbean countries are the best example of this type of seasonality (Butler, 2001).
- Non-peak seasonality (e.g., all year round): A non-peak seasonality is the one that occurs mostly in urban destinations such as Singapore and Hong Kong, where the urban center has an all-year-round use. Such destinations enjoy seasonal demand from different domestic and international visitors (Page and Connell, 2006).
- A minor peak as another seasonality pattern: A minor peak that comes between the high season and low season and offers moderate fares and rates between those of the seasons (Eastern break) (Oxana, 2016).
- Dynamic Seasonality: It is also called "multiple-demand seasonality." It is not associated with a fixed period (Derrouiche and Mebirouk, 2015).

In the same line, Baum and Hagen (1999) divided the volume of seasonal demand into three groups:

- High seasons or peak or main season.
- Shoulder season.
- Low or off-season.

Further, Shields and Shelleman (2013) classified seasonality by distinguishing four phases of seasonality: shoulder up, busy, shoulder down, and slow. Whatever the classification of seasonality is, these forms of demand variation are dynamic and may not only differ in a year but also within a month, a week, or a single day (Chung, 2009). However, the most favorable and the ideal situation that tourism organizations and operators need would be a "shoulder season," in which there is a roughly equal level of visits throughout the year, allowing the maximum use of destinations' capacity (physical infrastructure, facilities, and resources). With shoulder season, 1–2 months at the most on either side of the peak period in addition to smaller peaks of institutional holidays enable the tourist businesses to operate near capacity (Christmas and Easter or for other celebrations (e.g., Golden Week in China), and anniversaries of independence and establishment). One of the main benefits is retaining the valued human resources of the organization; such circumstances enable the employer to retain his employees on a full-time basis throughout the year and thus to obtain maximum or close to maximum returns throughout the year (UNWTO, 2014).

Generally, ensuring an equal level of visitation throughout the year requires the existence of more than one pattern of tourist activities in the destinations, for example, the presence of medical spots in mountainous regions. Baum and Lundtorp (2001) claimed that holidaymakers created another form of seasonality, which has been identified as the sporting season and is associated with at least one set of sporting activities (recreational activity and mega sports events), specifically those related to snow, including skiing, and snowboarding, in order to stimulate demand in certain regions.

Oxana (2016) stated that different tourist activities (tourism types) in different destinations are characterized by different seasonality forms, for example:

- ✓ Ski activity is mainly during winter.
- ✓ Mountain climbing activity is certainly biseasonal.
- ✓ Cultural tourism does not present patterns of seasonality.
- ✓ Wellness and spa tourism usually takes place during the middle seasons.
- ✓ Leisure tourism is at its highest during summer.
- ✓ Business tourism tends to be at its lowest during summer holidays.
- ✓ Festivals providing a cleaner image of seasonality patterns.

## 8.2 CAUSES OF SEASONALITY

In general, the universal cause of seasonality is the movement of the earth around the sun. The inclination of the earth toward the sun causes the magnifying or diminishing of the amounts of sunshine, rainfall, cloud cover, hours of daylight, and perhaps, above all, the temperature during the four conventional seasons (Spring, Summer, Autumn, and Winter) in specific places or locations. Thus, according to UNWTO (2014), the movement of people and their activities are controlled and influenced by the movement of the earth around the sun.

Increasingly, however, people have imposed their own patterns of behavior, including temporal limitations, on human activities, and these influences are best termed "institutional" or social, in that they are created and established by human social, political, religious, and economic agencies (UNWTO, 2014).

In general, because of natural and human factors, most destination areas experience an annual cycle of activity with a peak season and an off-season, which are separated by many smaller seasons. Thus, it has been accepted that seasonality in tourism occurs due to natural and institutional/anthropogenic factors (Baron, 1975 in Bigović, 2011). These causes can be interdependent and further divided into sub-categories as follows:

### *8.2.1 NATURAL FACTORS*

Nature and its forces, predominantly related to the elements of climatic conditions, such as in temperature, rainfall, snowfall, sunshine and hours of daylight (Baum and Lundtrop, 2001). As Koenig-Lewis and Bischoff (2005) recorded, all these natural factors are predictable as they are approximately constant in some particular destinations and reappear with only small changes. While destinations further away from the equator experience significant climatic changes and, in turn, greater seasonal differences, especially in peripheral regions in the Northern and Southern Hemispheres, which can lead to higher seasonality in tourism demand (Baum and Lundtorp, 2001).

### *8.2.2 INSTITUTIONAL FACTORS*

Institutionalized causes refer to human actions and policies which contribute to creating seasonality (Butler, 2001). Institutionalized seasonality is basically related to sociological and economic factors (Jafari, 2000), it is associated with economic conditions, legislation, religion, custom, and historical conventions. According to Koenig-Lewis and Bischoff (2005), institutionalized causes are not as predictable as natural and accordingly vary much more because official holiday dates may differ from time to time, thus affecting tourism demand differently.

The earliest forms of such seasonality were the religious Holy Days that celebrated events in various religious and pagan calendars such as Christmas, Easter, Saints' Days, Passover, Eid Al-fitr, Eid Al-adha, and Ramadan. Travel related to religious rituals such as pilgrimages at specific times were the earliest form of seasonality in tourism and were followed by feasts and markets at set times of the year to reflect agricultural timetables in many countries around the world (UNWTO, 2014).

Similarly, in the 19th century, in particular, the widespread of education deprived productive sectors such as agriculture from its labor, as consequently, school holidays were established to allow children time from education to assist with the harvesting of crops. These periods of leisure, or time away from school or traditional work, have become firmly established in many countries, albeit different in form in various areas, and the traditional summer school holiday period is believed to be the major institutional cause of tourist seasonality. Koenig-Lewis and Bischoff (2010) claimed in their study on accommodation businesses in Wales determines that school holidays, timing, and location as the major causes of tourism seasonality.

Therefore, high tourism demand tends to be around official and public holidays of the year that mostly fall in the summertime (Koenig-Lewis and Bischoff, 2005). Accordingly, institutionalized seasonality coincides with school, and industrial /business holidays, performance-based incentive or reward trips, and during times of festivals, races or other events that are established particularly to entice crowds.

There are some constraints that are related to the pattern of human behaviors concerning participation and visitation to tourist destinations, such constraints to travel exist in various forms. Some of these constraints are relevant to understanding why visitors come at particular times of the year and not at others. Generally, such constraints are not all absolute, they may be temporary or permanent, climatic, perceptual, financial, physical, social, cultural, and access or ability related. Thus, some of them can be controlled or mitigated.

According to UNWTO (2014), human constraints have been classified into following three categories:

1. Intrapersonal: It refers to psychological states that are relating to personal needs, social concerns (fashion, religion, or culture) (Butler, 2001), and reference group attitudes that interact with

leisure preferences. This type of constraints tends to predispose people toward certain activities and regions, and probably, specific time periods, as suitable or unsuitable.

2. Interpersonal are those relating to colleagues, friends, and family in particular and may have more impact more than preferences of a specific individual, for example, family differences over preferences.
3. Structural constraints represent factors perceived of as barriers to participation, such as inertia (routines of holiday patterns) (Koenig-Lewis and Bischoff, 2005), cost, policy issues (e.g., operating procedures, requirements), accessibility, and maybe such constraints are possible to be modified and mitigated by destination agencies.

Thus, seasonality occurs not only because people prefer spending their vacation in summer, but due to other factors that do not allow them to travel in off-peak seasons. Butler (2001) argued the importance of viewing the causes from two different perspectives: the generating area (demand) and the receiving area (supply). This can be explained further by the push and pull factors causing seasonality in a tourism destination.

The push factors include institutional (holidays), calendar (public holidays), inertia and tradition (reluctance to change holiday patterns), social pressure and fashion, and climate in generating area, while the pull factors consist of climate in the receiving area, sporting season, and events (Koenig- Lewis and Bischoff, 2005, p. 206). Generally, the holistic picture of tourism seasonality including its causes and also the push and pull factors that build the picture of a destination and influence travelers' choice are shown in Figure 8.1.

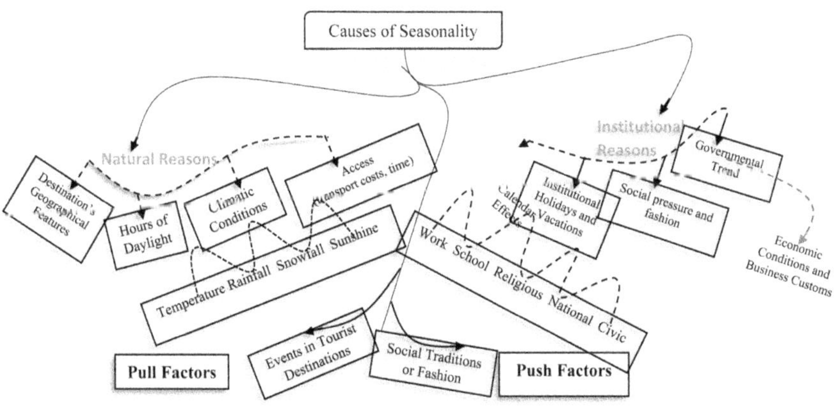


**FIGURE 8.1** Causes of seasonality.

**Source:** The Author

It can be concluded from the previous discussion that seasonality stems from the interaction of natural and institutionalized elements. However, several factors are likely to affect the future causes of seasonality.

Amelung et al. (2007) argued that climate change may influence the stability of the natural seasons. On the institutionalized level, the result of an aging population and increased mixing of working and leisure time are likely to affect seasonality in tourism.

## 8.3 IMPACTS OF SEASONALITY

According to many academics, seasonality is usually highlighted as a negative phenomenon in tourism and is managed as a weakness or a problem, not only in an economic sense, but also in a sociocultural and ecological sense as well (Bender et al., 2007; Butler, 2001; Holloway et al., 2009). It is of high importance to note that destinations that offer only in a single type of tourism and those that present the phenomenon of mass tourism, experience the higher impacts of seasonality (Baum and Lundtorp, 2001).

The impacts of seasonality can be viewed from an economic, environmental, social, and service quality perspective. The economic impacts have received most attention by both industry' stakeholders and academics, emphasizing the negative economic effects on the country of destinations and tourism operations (Butler, 2001). Some of the major economic problems are related to the loss of profit due to the inefficient use of destination full capacity, low returns on capital, difficulties with employment (small chances of recruiting and retaining full-time employees), a shortage of quality rooms during the main season, in addition to unemployment status (Chung, 2009). Thus, seasonality has been viewed as a global issue for the tourism industry with the most significant negative impact being a reduction in business revenue and cutting many jobs affiliated with tourist organizations and destinations (Oxana, 2016), as the local entrepreneurs, especially accommodation owners, suffer financially during off-peak season when the demand for products and services declines.

On the other hand, most of the researchers that have examined the phenomenon of seasonality tend to consider it as a major problem for the international tourism industry, but there are those that have expressed the opinion that seasonality has a number of positive impacts on the environment, the locals in the destination country, and cost-minded travelers. For example, Barsky and Nash (2006) argued that due to the fact that in the low season the prices in tourism-related enterprises are lower, the customers that use these services tend to be more satisfied in that period since they receive good service for less money (value for money).

The following section discusses the different impacts of seasonality phenomenon:

### *8.3.1 IMPACTS ON SERVICE QUALITY*

Regarding the negative impact that seasonality has on service quality provided by tourist destinations or organizations, there are two main facets of impacts:

1. During the peak season, the high demand for tourism services will lead to exceeding capacity for those facilities, services, congestion, overbooking, and other similar problems that will lead to lower service quality standards (in tourism-related enterprises) which in their turn will influence negatively on tourists' satisfaction (Parilla et al., 2007) and consequently on the destination image.
2. During the off-peak season, the fact that businesses have a short period (the high tourism season), this pushes the investors to adopt some actions in managing the seasonality issues that also have negative influences on service quality as follows:
    - Double their endeavors in order to achieve a high income in the periods of seasonal salability and compensate the probable losses in the off-season, thus, organizations' owners and managers tend to reduce their quality standards in order to make the most of the peak tourism demand (Andriotis, 2005), for example, the manager of food and beverage department in a hotel may decide to use low quality raw materials in preparing the menus of food and beverage outlets, or may substitutes the system of food service from selective-menu to buffet to reduce the food options.
    - It will still be difficult to maintain quality standards because the newly hired employees for the high tourism season obtained a low level of training and experience (Kandampully, 2000; Barsky and Nash, 2006). So, there is a difficulty in maintaining the quality of product and service delivery because organizations cannot retain skilled employees.

## 8.3.2 IMPACTS ON ECONOMIC STATUS

Seasonality created a very limited operating season that in turn reflected on the economic status of the whole destination and the organizations' performance and revenue. Seasonality forced tourism organizations' owners and managers to attain a whole year's income from a short intense period because of revenue swing generated from the tourists' movements.

This creates cash flow problems with loss of revenues and profits during the off-season, especially there are fixed costs facing organizations throughout the year (Koenig-Lewis and Bischoff, 2005; Shields and Shelleman, 2013), in addition to costs related to attracting, hiring, and training new employees in the peak season. For some smaller enterprises, it may prove difficult to make a living from only tourism and additional income sources are needed (Butler, 2001).

From an economic perspective, the literature recognizes substantial negative impacts on the country of tourism supply, which can broadly be divided into several areas (Butler, 2001; Page and Connell, 2006):

- capacity utilization,
- unemployment rate,
- investment and capital, and
- revenues and expenses.

Capacity utilization is a well-emphasized issue. During the peak season, the movement of tourists makes the destinations' facilities crowded and over-used, while at other times of the year they are underused. Such inefficiency in the use of resources and facilities of the destinations and its organizations are considered an unavoidable loss (Baum and Lundtorp, 2001; Annisius, 2014). It is generally recognized that remote regions in peripheral areas and higher latitudes are more likely to be negatively affected by seasonality than destinations in urban areas (Butler, 2001).

Seasonality has a significant impact on unemployment status, the low demand for tourism in the low period leads to an increase in unemployment rate in the host community (Baum and Lundtorp, 2001) as well, as most employees are recruited only for the peak season, this makes the employees feel job insecurity, that if it exists, turnover rate will maximize. In addition, Oxana (2016) described seasonal work as a repellent job opportunity because of the lack of opportunities for career progression. Koenig-Lewis and Bischoff (2005) argued that one of the greatest problems because of seasonality is the difficulty for businesses to retain fulltime, highly competent, and educated staff and in the future, it will be harder to recruit skilled labor force. Some scholars have also pointed out the problems of maintaining product and service quality because of high employee turnover and hiring low-skilled employees (Baum and Lundtorp, 2001; Duval, 2004). So, the focus is primarily on short-term employment, which in turn increases the annual cost of training seasonal staff (Getz and Nilsson, 2004; Chung, 2009).

In addition, there is another important negative effect of seasonality accompanying tourism industry that is the difficulty in attracting businessmen to invest in the tourism sector. Duval (2004) asserted that difficulties for tourism operations to gain access to capital or attract investors have been explained by the low annual returns on capital and investment, because of the short operating period of few months, and the fact that there is no guarantee of return on investment.

On the other hand, a few positive economic impacts have been discussed in the literature. It was found that seasonality provides work opportunities during low period demand for workers in other dependent industries. For instance, during the off-peak season, locals are hired to do the maintenance work on buildings, attractions or infrastructure.

Furthermore, tourism industry can be a good employer of low skilled or low educated people such as students and some specific groups that need to be hired as part-time workers such as students, housewives, and farmers (Koenig-Lewis and Bischoff, 2005). Many scholars argued that such individuals seek for the seasonal job because it pays better than alternative work that is available, and also because it allows those who wish to try other activities during the offseason to do so (Oxana, 2016). In this way, although tourism increases the cost of living during the peak seasons, but on the other hand, it also increases employment opportunity and thus the household income.

### *8.3.3 IMPACTS ON ENVIRONMENT*

The negative environmental impacts of seasonality are mainly related to the high concentration of visitors during the peak season which threats the environment in terms of the air pollution, heavy traffic, waste production (Chung, 2009). It also noted that the excessive movement of tourists causes disturbance of wildlife and overuse of natural resources; the extravagant use of water by the tourists and from the activities associated with them such as swimming pools and golf courses. In addition to the solid waste of tourist organizations that can be a major despoiler of the environment in coastal areas, rivers, lakes,and roadsides, and can also give rise to serious health risks to humans as well as wildlife.

Although there are many positive aspects of seasonality, it is worth noting that very little research has been done to explore any of them (Butler, 2001). The positive environmental impacts are mostly concentrated to the off-season. Many scholars asserted the positive effects on destinations, especially from an environmental and social viewpoint (Baum and Lundtorp, 2001; Butler, 2001; Amelung et al., 2007).

During the peak season, mass tourism, in particular, is strongly linked to negative impacts on environment, as the heavy use of the natural environment impacts on the ecological carrying capacity of a destination (Oxana, 2016); thus, seasonality is generally seen as a resting time for the environment to recover after the heavy pressure and prepare for the next tourist season (Baum and Hagen, 1999; Amelung et al., 2007). Chung (2009, p. 82) compared the off-season to "a state similar to turning off the switch for a while for preventing electronic machines from overheating."

### *8.3.4 IMPACTS ON COMMUNITY*

The overuse of infrastructure and services is leading to congestion in the streets and beaches (Traffic congestions), lack of parking, and higher prices for services are the main problems resulting from the high number of visitors who come for a short intense period (Koenig-Lewis and Bischoff, 2005). Overbooking of tourism-related businesses and generally overstrains regular infrastructure and services thus disrupting the "normal" flow of everyday life for the host community (Andriotis, 2000). Therefore, the traditional or cultural social activities can also be negatively affected (Chung, 2009).

On the other hand, similarly to the positive environmental effects, there are positive social impacts have been identified. Peak-off season not only improves the quality of the environment, but also improves the quality of life of locals. During peak-off season, the industry' stakeholders (government authorities and tourism investors) may make improvements in the construction and infrastructure of the destination. Such improvements and the enhanced amenities in destinations definitely can be used by local residents during the off-peak season. The off-season offers a resting time for the host community to recover from the high season and enjoy their resources and facilities quietly (Baum and Hagen, 1999; Amelung et al., 2007). Furthermore, off-season period is the only time that the local population can operate in what to it is a "normal" manner, and engage in their traditional social and cultural activities (Baum and Lundtorp, 2001; Oxana, 2016), local communities can preserve their own identity through time. Butler (2001, p. 11) compared it to "the light at the end of the tunnel" and suggested that the off-season is the only time when locals can engage in their normal traditional, social, and cultural activities. In addition, as has been mentioned, seasonal employment may be positive for some people and benefits society instead of unemployment.

## 8.4 CHARACTERISTICS OF TOURISM SEASONALITY

There are a number of characteristics of seasonality that enable its causes to be identified and thus may help in mitigating its occurrence or controlling its consequences (UNWTO, 2014).

### *8.4.1 REGULARITY AND CONSISTENCY*

Seasonality is characterized by its cyclicality. The high season during the warm period of the year, the cold, quiet or empty season during the cold period of the year as well as the mid-season in between both seasons (Gilbert, 1990). Its occurrence at the same time for roughly the same duration each year unlike some other negative emergencies that threat tourism industry, at both the local level such as natural disasters, political instability, security issues or epidemics, or at the global level such as economic crisis and war, make it is predictable and in a sense "reliable" in terms of it being able to be predicted and ideally alleviated. This should mean that steps to control its presence and or its effects should be easier to conceive and to implement.

### *8.4.2 COMMON CONSEQUENCES*

It is not unique to tourism, it affects other major depending economic sectors such as infrastructure, agriculture, and fishing at least equally if not more than tourism and it should be possible to learn from what has been done by professionals and operators working in those activities with respect to dealing with seasonality.

### *8.4.3 ENDOGENOUS AND EXOGENOUS CAUSES*

It is caused and influenced by both national and international factors occurring in both the country of generating and the country of destination, thus, local and external agencies and stakeholders must be involved. This may bring to mind the importance of considering the needs and requirements of both the supply and demand aspects.

## 8.5 MANAGING SEASONALITY

Combating seasonality is a difficult task and few destinations have managed to do this effectively but over the long term. Generally, in order to effectively manage seasonality, it must be accepted it and then adjusting the business, or actively try to reduce its consequences. However, it is rarely possible to achieve such changes successfully at the destination level alone, because successful intervention needs united efforts from all the industry' stakeholders. The industry' stakeholders (public and private or governmental or civilized) must attempt to reduce seasonality (Baum and Lundtorp, 2001). The importance of collaboration may be increased because fighting seasonality may require modifying peoples' leisure behavior. However, this solution may seem impossible because of the nature of tourism, tourism (as a part of leisure) is essentially about freedom of choice (in destination selected, in activities engaged in, in time of engagement in tourism) and potential tourists are not likely to accept being forced to change their behavior (UNWTO, 2014). Therefore, destinations must combine at least two or more of the strategies when controlling the consequences of seasonality (Baum and Hagen, 1999).

Although Baum and Hagen (1999) argued that there is no clear or universal solution, the literature identified several possible ways to reduce seasonality negative consequences, not all are appropriate for any specific destination. As following:

### *8.5.1 EXTENDING THE MAIN SEASON*

The most common action is to attempt to lengthen the main season at a destination. Extending the existing the peak season involves trying to stimulate demand in the low seasons using similar resources as in the main season (Baum and Hagen, 1999), most often by reducing prices charged for accommodation and services in the months immediately before and after the peak season. Pricing strategies have widely been applied in the tourism industry to combat seasonality (Wall and Mathieson, 2006; Butler, 2001).

This involves promoting seasonal pricing incentives such as discounting or special offers during low seasons to increase the demand (Chung, 2009; Shields and Shelleman, 2013). However, the success of this strategy depends on the market being flexible in its travel arrangements to be able to visit outside the peak season. Generally, the most flexible type of tourists' patterns that the industry' stakeholders must try to attract are the senior citizens as they have more flexible schedules.

Although pricing strategy is successful in some cases, the highly flexible pricing strategies may harm the overall destination image in the long term according to Baum and Hagen (1999).

### *8.5.2 MAKING THE DESTINATION UNIQUE AND PRESTIGIOUS*

This means the supplement or changes the existing offerings and facilities of the destination (festivals, shows, performances, fashion events); this is because of the human nature desire to visit the unique and prestigious places (UNWTO, 2014).

An alternative approach is to offer something unique, this may be accomplished by offering the opportunity for people to try or to see something that is going to disappear, or something occurs on long-term basis, this is the principle behind "Last chance tourism." For example, Polar Bear Tourism in Churchill, northern Canada, has achieved this, because of the fact that polar bears are apt to disappear because of global warming.

### *8.5.3 ESTABLISHING ADDITIONAL SEASONS*

Some destinations and businesses' owners and managers try to develop new tourism seasons during the low season. This can be achieved by creating events and festivals that have been recognized by Baum and Hagen as "the most common single strategy to combat seasonality" (1999). Commonly these attractions may be indoor or outdoor attractions. Events such as conferences, celebrations, concerts, sporting games, festivals, competitions, and displays are the most common attractions used in this strategy (Chung, 2009; UNWTO, 2014).

This strategy requires considerable marketing efforts, and financial costs and may take a considerable time (years) to become a permanent feature of the tourism calendar, particularly if similar events occur in neighboring destinations, so, such events mostly are established in the middle of the main peak season so that they can gain popularity, and then moved to lower seasons (Baum and Hagen, 1999). The best example of this is to create either a winter sports season to an established summer destination (Aviemore in Scotland from the mid1960s is an example), or to add a summer season to an established winter sports destination. Destinations in mountainous regions such as the Alps or the Rockies have managed to do this with considerable success, (e.g., Vail and Aspen in Colorado, St Moritz, or Innsbruck in the Alps (UNWTO, 2014).

An alternative way to add a summer season to an established winter season (which is far less common than adding a winter season to a summer one) is demonstrated in some Caribbean destinations (UNWTO, 2014). Such added attractions can also enlarge the traditional summer or winter markets and also make the destination attractive for permanent residence as opposed to summer or winter second home operations.

### *8.5.4 REVAMPING THE DESTINATION*

A destination may decide to change its image, facilities, and market completely in order to attract a new market that is not seasonal (Atlantic City, USA is the best example). Such a step is rare and requires extensive redevelopment of the destination, major investment, and excessive promotion campaigns, and sometimes legislative change (e.g., permitting activities previously not allowed). Success depends greatly on the current and future competition; however, this step is considered a significant advantage for the destination as being the first to take such a step (UNWTO, 2014).

Managing the seasonality phenomenon is not necessarily an easy task and scholars have acknowledged that there are several issues which can occur as the problem is more complex than generally thought. Butler (2001) claimed that despite the intensive efforts of industry and governments, the inflexibility of tourism increases the difficulties in overcoming seasonality, as following:

- Strategies to mitigate seasonality sometimes may have the opposite effects and increase tourism demand in the peak season instead (Getz and Nilsson, 2004; Koenig-Lewis and Bischoff, 2005).
- The destination image may be harmed if facilities and services are closed for tourists visiting during off-seasons (Koenig-Lewis and Bischoff, 2005).

Therefore, dealing with seasonality requires support from all the involved stakeholders at the destination, both from the public-and-private sectors to work together (Koenig-Lewis and Bischoff, 2005). In this case, collaboration is sometimes more beneficial than competition. However, before developing seasonality mitigation strategies, it is important to consider whether the destination is in fact economically, environmentally, and socially prepared to reduce seasonality (Butler, 2001).

## REFERENCES

Amelung, B.; Nicholls, S.; Viner, D. Implications of Global Climate Change for Tourism Flows and Seasonality. *J. Travel Res.* **2007,** *45* (3), 285–296.

Andriotis, K. Seasonality in Crete: Problem or a Way of life? *Tour. Econ.* **2005,** *11* (2), 207–224.

Annisius, D. C. Managing Seasonality in Tourism: Challenges and Opportunities for the Tourism Industryin Húsavík. BAM Thesis, Iceland, 2014.

Baron, R. V. *Seasonality in Tourism: A Guide to the Analysis of Seasonality and Trends for Policy Making*. The Economist Intelligence Unit Limited: London, 1975.

Barsky, J.; Nash, L. Hotel Seasonality Impacts Guest Experience. *Hotel Motel Manag.* **2006,** *221* (19), 14.

Baum, T.; Hagen, L. Responses to Seasonality: The Experiences of Peripheral Destinations. *Int. J. Tour. Res.* **1999,** *1* (5), 299–312.

Baum, T.; Lundtorp, S. Seasonality in Tourism: An Introduction. In *Seasonality in Tourism*; Baum, T.; Lundtorp, S.; Eds.; Oxford: Elsevier Science, 2001, pp 1–4.

Bender, O.; Schumacher, K.; Stein, D. Landscape, seasonality, and tourism: a survey with examples fromCentral Europe. In *Seasonal Landscapes*; Palang, H.; Sooväli, H.; Printsmann, A., Eds.; Dordrecht: Springer, 2007; pp 181–214.

Biederman, P. S. *Travel and Tourism: An Industry Primer*. Upper Saddle River: Pearson Education, 2008.

Bigović, M. Quantifying Seasonality in Tourism: a Case Study of Montenegro. *Acad. Turistica* **2011**, *4* (2), 15–32.

Butler, R. W. Seasonality in Tourism: Issues and Implications. In *Seasonality in tourism*; Baum, T., Lundtorp, S., Eds.; Elsevier Science: Oxford, 2001, pp 5–22.

Chung, J. Y. Seasonality in Tourism: A Review. *e-Rev. Tourism Res.*, **2009,** *7* (5), 82–96.

Cooper, C.; Wanhill, S.; Fletcher, J.; Gilbert, D.; Fyall, A. *Tourism: Principles and Practice*; Pearson Education: Harlow, 2008.

Derrouiche, S.; Mebirouk, M. B. Seasonal Concentration of the International Hotel Demand in Algeria: A Measurement and Decomposition by Nationalities. *Int. Business Res.* **2015,** *8* (7), 16–29.

Duval, D. T. When Buying into the Business, We Knew it was Seasonal: Perceptions of Seasonality in Central Otago, New Zealand. *Int. J. Tour. Res.* **2004,** *6* (5), 325–337.

Getz, D.; Nilsson, P. A. Responses of Family Businesses to Extreme Seasonality in Demand: the Case ofBornholm, Denmark. *Tour. Manag.* **2004,** *25* (1), 17–30.

Gilbert, D. Strategic Marketing Planning for National Tourism. *Tourist Rev.*, **1990,** *45* (1), 18–27.

Holloway, J. C.; Humphreys, C.; Davidson, R. *The Business of Tourism*. Pearson Education: Harlow, 2009.

Hylleberg, S. General Introduction. In *Modelling Seasonality*; Hylleberg, S., Ed.; Oxford University Press: Oxford, 1992, pp 3–14.
Jafari, J. *The Encyclopedia of Tourism*; Routledge: London, 2000.
Kandampully, J. The Impact of Demand Fluctuation on the Quality of Service: A Tourism Industry Example. *Manag. Serv. Quality*, **2000,** *10* (1), 2–10.
Koenig-Lewis, N.; Bischoff, E. E. Developing Effective Strategies for Tackling Seasonality in the Tourism Industry. *Tourism Hospitality Plan. Dev.* **2010,** *7* (4), 395–413.
Koenig-Lewis, N.; Bischoff, E. E. Seasonality Research: The State of the Art. *Int. J. Tour. Res.* **2005,** *7* (4–5), 201–219.
Oxana, K. A. Seasonality in Tourism. MSc Thesis, International Hellenic University, 2016.
Page, S. J.; Connell, J. *Tourism: A Modern Synthesis*, 2nd ed.; Thomson Learning: London, 2006.
Page, S.; Connell, J. Tourism: A Modern Synthesis, 2nd ed.; Thomson Learning, 2006.
Parrilla, J. C.; Font, A. R.; Nadal, J. R. Accommodation Determinants of Seasonal Patterns. *Ann. Tour. Res.* **2007,** *32* (2), 423–436.
Reece, W. S. *The Economics of Tourism.* Pearson Education: Upper Saddle River, 2010.
Shields, J.; Shelleman, J. Small Business Seasonality: Characteristics and Management. *Small Bus. Inst. J.* **2013,** *9* (1), 37–50.
UNWTO. Addressing Seasonality in Tourism: The Development of a Prototype, 2014. [Online] http://cf.cdn.unwto.org/sites/all/files/pdf/final_notes_richard_butler.pdf (accessed Oct 5, 2017).
UNWTO. Climate Change and Tourism-Responding to Global Challenges, World Tourism Organization, 2008.
Wall, G.; Mathieson, A. *Tourism: Change, Impacts and Opportunities*; Pearson Education: Harlow, 2006.

# CHAPTER 9

# THE HIGH VULNERABILITY OF THE TOURISM INDUSTRY TO RISKS AND EMERGENCIES

*"The risk comes from not fully knowing what you are managing and where you are standing."*

## 9.1 INTRODUCTION

Travel and tourism is regarded worldwide as the industry with the highest growth rate and the greatest potential for job creation (Business Day, 2004) and economic development worldwide. Over the past three decades, the worldwide tourist arrivals witnessed a significant global growth, which makes the worldwide travel and tourism a critical supporter to economic development and advancement. In 2012, for illustration, 1 billion tourists have traveled around the world, marking a new record for the international tourism sector that accounts for one in every 12 occupations and 30% of the world's services exports (WTO, 2013).

Along these lines, receipts from international tourism in destinations around the world developed by 4% in 2012 coming to $1075 billion. This development is equal to a 4% increment in worldwide tourist arrivals over the past year which reached 1035 million in 2011. An additional $219 billion was recorded in receipts from international passenger transport, bringing total exports created by international tourism in 2012 to $1.3 trillion (WTO, 2013).

Based on the definition of "industry" as "a group of organizations that compete directly with one another to win customers or sales in the marketplace" (Enz, 2010), the hospitality industry is defined as "a group of businesses that welcome arrivals by providing accommodation, food and/or beverages, and other entertainment facilities." The most noticeable representatives are hotels, motels, resorts, inns, and related businesses. Commonly, these organizations are bundled beneath the expression "Hospitality industry." The tourism industry and especially the hotel and restaurant subsectors are exceedingly differentiated in the sorts of businesses that work under its sponsorship.

The biggest hotel companies incorporate portfolios that contain more than 6000 hotels each and employ more than 150,000 employees in up to 100 nations. Universally, the industry is exceedingly divided, with around 20% of the workforce located within multinational enterprises compared to 80% in SMEs (ILO, 2010). Human assets play a definitive part in achieving the company objectives as they are considered the most critical asset of organizations, particularly in such competitive market as the globalization phenomenon and the amazingly quick changes influencing goods, services, people's demands, and desires-expanded competition between tourist and hospitality organizations working in different business areas. Subsequently, hospitality organizations require a high-performance administration designed to empower them to confront these pressures.

## 9.2 TOURISM AND EMERGENCY

The human dimension in the field of tourism has experienced huge challenges, triggered by the industry's vulnerability to risks and crises that undermine the organizations involved from time to time, whether it was natural crises that resulted in generating the seasonality phenomenon that in turn leads to increasing the rate of labor turnover in the industry or the man-made emergencies such as terrorist actions that aiming tourists at the tourist and hospitality organizations. Emergencies and risks do not threaten the industry they threaten millions of families depending on the industry in earning their living. According to Marshall and Alexander (2009), human resource risks are the events that prevent workforce members from fulfilling their duties, which hinders upon the organizational goal fulfillment. Risks take many forms, with disastrous consequences for the industry if they are not managed effectively (Lepp and Gibson, 2003), especially that tourism and hospitality industry receiving employees and guests from different nations and cultures, with a tendency for disasters and emergencies to occur and cause unwanted consequences (Low et al., 2010); consequently, the tourism and hospitality industry is considered a risky business.

Wang and Ritchie (2013) confirmed that the tourism and hospitality industries comprise a wide array of characteristics that make them highly vulnerable to emergency situations and then necessitates different emergency management and planning strategies. The following are some features of the industry:

- intangibility of the products,
- impossibility of production and storage of the products at the time of consumption,
- high allocation cost,
- high labor cost and fluctuation,
- vulnerability to risks and emergencies events.

While tourism demand is particularly sensitive to security and health concerns (Blake and Sinclair, 2003), researchers have clearly established that tourism is an industry that is highly vulnerable to several other intrinsic and exogenous factors. According to Paraskevas and Arendell (2007), the high vulnerability of the industry to crises (common or man-made) has a significant and terrible impact on the labor intention to proceed working in such uncertain environment. Rittichainuwat (2005) declared that low-cost destination, particularly unsafe destinations could not attract workforce to be employed. Hospitality organizations ought to build-up cross part with government authorities to avoid unnecessary data and transmit a message to avoid ambiguity (Mansfeld, 2006). Emergency situations involve a lack of knowledge of future events that have a negative impact on the business. It can be seen as the potential for loss or harm to an entity, where such an entity could be a person, a group, or an organization (Raval and Fichadia, 2007).

There are many terms that may be used to express emergency situations and may be used interchangeably such as danger, hazard, risk, crisis, and disaster. In reality, it has been suggested that the extended volume of worldwide tourism development has joined with the appeal of high-risk destinations to expose human involved in the industry whether they are workers or visitors to more noteworthy levels of danger (Drabek, 1995).

Emergencies become more frequent and complex than before affecting tourism and hospitality industry and related dependent industries (Pforr, 2006). Faulkner (2001) found an ascendant number of emergencies harming the tourism and hospitality industries. These emergencies threaten the security of any destination, as an unexpected phenomenon. Tourism is susceptible to environmental, political, economic, and social influences. For example, the volatility of world economy resulted from the financial crisis, rising prices in the commodity sector, the increasing price of oil, and fluctuations in the exchange rate reflected on the tourism industry; notably, the tourism demand has slowed down significantly. More specifically, pandemics, weather emergencies, and human-caused failures create challenges for the global tourism industry and local destinations (Calgaro and Lloyd, 2008), in addition to the credit crunch, economic disarray, mounting unemployment, and the recessionary reduction in market confidence that no one knew how long these challenges would last (Rifai, 2009). Worldwide, tourism destinations have experienced an increase in the number of both natural and man-made emergencies. Every year, more than 200 million people are affected by human-caused emergencies or man-made emergencies. This would hold a significant risk potential for tourism businesses, because it would signify a decline in the profitability of the tourism sector, leading in turn to insolvencies and job losses.

The decline in tourism industry significantly affects negatively on countries dependent on tourism, especially developing countries. According to a report released by the UNWTO (2009), the number of international tourist movements had declined slightly during the second half of 2008, a trend that continued in 2009.

Emergencies that strike the industry may arise from different reasons that expand and multiple especially in developing countries (Burns, 1999). Therefore, risks and emergency situations, that the hospitality industry may experience, arise mainly because of the following two reasons:

- problematic characteristics of hospitality operations and characteristics themselves;
- exogenous events, which can emerge from broader economic, social, and political processes or as a consequence of natural disasters.

However, the second reason is the main reason while the first reason may be considered as the motivator, where the characteristics of the industry do the action of a drop of oil in bursting a flame. The man-made faults in such a sensitive industry cause huge consequences and harm the image of organizations and destinations. So, the oldest and simplest typology of risks did not consider any factors or characteristics to become a part of creating emergency situations and only granted them into the intentional man-made emergencies and natural external causes (Rosenthal and Kouzmin, 1993). The numerous natural and human-caused disasters can significantly impact the choice of labor market members to join it and also the flow of tourists.

### 9.2.1 NATURAL RISKS/EMERGENCIES

Ichinosawa (2006) explored the impacts of natural disasters on tourism and hospitality industry and argued that such event will disturb the destination with a bad impact on local community, industry stakeholders, and economy. A prominent example of natural incidents that threaten the tourist destinations is unfavorable changing climate.

#### 9.2.1.1 CHANGING CLIMATE AND WEATHER AS AN EXAMPLE OF NATURAL RISKS

Although most researchers' studies focus on economic variables (Lim et al., 2008), climate changes have been identified as a key driver for tourism and an important tourist destination attribute (Hu and Ritchie, 1993). Climate is likely to affect both the length of the season for tourists and the expected environment; thus, tourism movements are associated with changes in climate (Sookram, 2009). Tourist destinations are exposed to natural climate variability and seasonality, this means that the profitability and viability of a business and destination are at least partly influenced by the climate. It is therefore not surprising that increasing attention has been paid to how climate change might affect tourism and hospitality industry (Wall and Badke, 1994) in terms of declining the number of arrivals to a distinct destinations or region and how these impacts can negatively influence the intentions of labor market members to join such unstable work environment.

Good weather is considered as one of the main resource or facilitator for tourism in some regions, it plays as the main tourism resource in the case of beach destinations (Kozak et al., 2008), and it acts as a facilitator that makes tourism activities possible and enjoyable (Gómez Martin, 2005). In alignment with Martin, Berrittella and others predicted that, at the international level, changes in climate would eventually lead to a loss in welfare, and that loss would be in turn disproportionately destroy many regions around the world (2006).

Therefore, climate was found to be a push factor for tourists to travel if the climatic conditions at their destination are perfect, while it is in their home countries are poor or unfavorable either in the year of travel or the previous year (Agnew and Palutikof, 2006), as it was found that the optimal temperature for attractive destination countries ranged from 21 to 24°C (Lise and Tol, 2002). Outside a certain range of temperature, the comfort of tourists will be affected so it is considered to be the most important climate variable in the analysis of tourism demand. In one of the first studies conducted on climate change and tourism, Koenig and Abegg (1997) utilized temperature to measure the effect of forecasted changes in temperature on the ski industry in Switzerland.

The study revealed that if temperatures are increased by 2°C, the Swiss ski industry function will be decreased by at least 20%, the current 85% chance of snowing will be affected and accordingly the snow line of 1.200 m will be in danger, the situation that threatens the industry functioning. This would clearly have serious implications for the growth of that sector of the industry. Along with the temperature, there is evidence to show that other weather parameters are also important such as rain, wind chill effects, humidity, radiation, and hours of sunshine (Scott and McBoyle, 2006). Some weather parameters are considered as a primary factor for the timing of travel along with its significant role in choosing the destination (Hamilton and Lau, 2005), wind and visibility are critically important for aviation and, in turn, they can be linked to transportation delays, cancellations or accidents. For example, abnormal conditions of weather in San Francisco where poor visibility in summer and rain storms in winter cause more than double cancellations and delays compared to normal conditions (Eads, 2000; Koetse and Rietveld, 2009). Moreover, according to Koetse and Rietveld (2009), the weather was found to be a cause in 70% of the aviation delays and 23% of accidents.

Stern (2006) claimed that temperature, sunshine, radiation, precipitation, wind, humidity, and fog are the most climatic factors having an impact on tourism (Stern, 2006). Other measures, such as wind speed or snow depth may also be important for specific recreational activities. Generally, these factors are significant to the tourist's assessment of his or her safety and comfort, and the tourism industry. Some tourist destinations need to take this into consideration more than others (e.g., as a result of the rising number of hurricanes in the Caribbean and along the coast of North America, earthquakes, floods, droughts, cyclones, or tidal waves).

In Fiji, for instance, the rising sea level could lead to a loss of tourism infrastructure and seriously influence the industry and the unemployment rate (ILO, 2010). The following are some of the examples that explain how climatic elements are tightly linked to tourism and hospitality industry:

- A number of heat waves have been observed in many regions in Europe especially in the North with substantial impacts on tourism. The 2003 heat wave was responsible for 15,000 deaths in France and major shifts in traditional tourist flow for this year away from the traditional resorts in the Mediterranean and toward Northern or Western beach locations (UNWTO, UNEP, and WMO, 2008).
- In Greece, as consequences of hot weather conditions in 2000, fires broke out in forest areas, causing devastating impacts on the hospitality organizations, more than a half of all tourist bookings for the next year were canceled (Scott and Lemieux, 2009).
- Drought in the State of Colorado (USA) in 2002 created dangerous wildfire conditions and tourist and visitor numbers declined by 40% in some areas, largely as a result of media coverage and perceived risks by arrivals (Scott and Lemieux, 2009).
- Poor snow conditions have also been linked to negative impacts on the personal safety of tourists. In the Swiss and Austrian Alps, accident

insurance claims by British skiers were almost double the average levels during the poor snow conditions of the 1990/1991 ski season, with approximately half listing accidents caused by exposed rocks and overcrowding on the slopes (Smith, 1993). Cold winters are also linked to higher road accident rates, whereas warmer than usual winters reduce the likelihood of accidents (Koetse and Rietveld, 2009).

– In the United States, California has experienced destructive flood events, in the first half of 2017, flooding led to evacuation of nearly 200,000 residents and damage roads and highways alone was estimated at over $1 billion (Wamsley, 2017).
– In Egypt, torrential rains hit two main tourist destinations from the Sinai Peninsula and Aswan in 2011 and 2014. In Sinai, many hotels in Taba have suffered high damages following floods. In 2014, for example, at the Miramar Taba Heights hotel, 144 out of 426 rooms were destroyed after the first floor flooded. The guests from 130 rooms in the Marriott Taba hotel were transferred to the Sofitel, and 170 rooms were closed at the Intercontinental Taba Heights Hotel (Youm 7 report).
– Hurricanes also have a severe impact on tourist destinations. Hurricanes, for example, are the most prevalent meteorological events in the United States. Hurricane Katrina in 2005 and Super Storm Sandy in 2012 caused inordinate physical and financial damage. Hurricane Katrina resulted in 1836 deaths, $81.2 billion in damages (Ryu et al., 2013).
– Damages of Hurricane Ivan occurred in Canada (September 2004) included human, environmental, and constructional damages, especially because the hurricane is categorized as a category four. An official damage assessment reported 28 persons killed, heavy damage to ecotourism and cultural heritage sites, 90% of the hotel rooms damaged or destroyed, and damage to major infrastructures such as power lines and telecommunication (Becken and Hay, 2007).

Thus, the present and the future of the tourism industry depend upon climate and environmental conditions, because they can have a dramatic effect on the competitiveness and sustainability of climate-sensitive destinations. The importance of climate has been confirmed in tourism demand studies as a significant motivation of tourist's choice to travel to a certain destination (Scott and Lemieux, 2009). Climate can be a determining factor when people choose their holiday destinations, depending on their demands for sun, snow conditions, mountains, or regions with warm weather and it can have an effect on the length and quality of tourism seasons (UNWTO, 2009).

Hence, the increasing volume of literature on the impact of climate on tourism demand is due to the recognition of the importance of the natural factors in modeling precisely the tourism demand, because they are significant influences on the tourism industry.

### 9.2.2 MAN-MADE RISKS

Man-made risks are the incidents that result from dangers involving an element of the following human elements:

- intention with a purpose of destruction,
- negligence or error, or
- threats involving a failure of a man-made system or process resulted from the limited skill or knowledge.

#### 9.2.2.1 TERRORISM ACTIONS AS AN EXAMPLE OF MAN-MADE RISKS

Many researchers in the tourism industry asserted that being safe in the destination is the main requirement for any tourist, the same is advocated for the employees and workers involved in working in a tourist destination or a city. Thus, it has been observed that organizations or areas that develop an unsafe reputation can be substituted by alternative industry or cities that are perceived as safer for both tourists and workers.

Although the major man-made threats to tourism industry are socioeconomic problems which in most cases lead to an increase in the crime rates, the threat of terrorism remains at the top of man-made threats. According to Ranabhat (2015), the number of victims of terrorism from tourists in 2014 was 32,727.

Anecdotal evidence suggests that both tourists and workers are at great risk of being victims of violence, property crimes, and terrorism in the destination or region they visit or work. The threat of danger that accompanies terrorism tends to intimidate potential tourists and workers more severely.

Today, both terrorism and tourism are global phenomena. Tourists and tourist destinations have become favorite terrorist targets. The success of travel and tourism industry does not shield it from the corrupt power of terrorism because of the frequent number of terrorist attacks on tourist destinations that led to fading the peaceful picture of travel away.

According to Enders and Sandler (2002), terrorism is "…the premeditated use or threat of use of extra-normal violence or brutality by subnational groups to obtain a political, religious, or ideological objective through intimidation of a huge audience, usually not directly involved with the policy-making that the terrorists seek to influence" (p 145–146).

The link between terrorism and tourism reveals that tourism is not only the medium of communication instigated by terrorists, but it can be the message also. So, it is evident that terrorists choose tourists intentionally for some reasons as follows:

- Their symbolic value and high profile as indirect representatives, attacking the foreign visitors brings the world attention as the news value of international tourists is too valuable (Sonmez, 1998). This is confirmed by Baker (2014) who asserted that tourism can be used as a cost-effective instrument to deliver a broader message of ideological or political opposition. It is argued that a symbiotic relationship exists between terrorist actions and media and that terrorism is both a symbolic event and a tragedy performance that is staged for the benefit of media attention (Weimann and Winn, 1994).
- Some individuals may see arrivals as a mode of neocolonialism or a danger to their social standards, traditions, and religious beliefs (Wahab, 1996; Tarlow, 2005) and also to their natural resources.
- Aziz (1995) argued that logical socioeconomic and cultural aspects are the main reason behind the terrorist actions. He claimed that friction between locals and foreign visitors is inevitable because they are separated not only by language but by social and economic gaps too. The different ideological values, class behavior, and different lifestyle that are demonstrated by tourists make them the targets of terrorism because of their tourism styles, which may demonstrate extravagant live and conspicuous consumption (Richter and Waugh, 1983).

Many scholars reported that one of the major consequences of terrorist actions is political instability (Seddighi et al., 2001; Stafford et al., 2002), which leads to the decline or disappearance of tourist arrivals in some tourist destinations. For example, the instability status of most of the Arab countries reflected on the tourism movements in most of the Middle East, there are comparatively a lower number of tourists compared to Europe.

Terrorism can be categorized according to the motivation of the terrorist groups into three different categories: nationalist, political, and religious (Kullberg in Ranabhat, 2015).

- Nationalist terrorism includes actions of extremist groups that hold extreme or fanatical views such as the separatist movements, independence fighters, and resistance movements in some regions in the world.
- All the terrorist movements can be seen as "political," so in this context political terrorism refers to extreme right or left-wing political movements.
- Religious terrorism has its roots in the religious ideology or cult movements.

The actions of such extremist groups leave a horrible impact in world community for years and that reshapes the map of tourism demand around the world, nowadays, most of the travelers turned their face away from some destinations like the Middle Eastern countries and hold their intention to new destinations such as countries of South America. According to the World Alatas (2017), at the top of countries that mostly live at peace comes Mexico at 3.723 and Paraguay at 3.84. On the contrary, the effects of terrorism are felt most strongly in the Middle East and Africa such as in Iraq at 9.96, Nigeria at 9.31, and Egypt at 7.33.

People still remember terrorist events like the explosion that killed three people in Paris in 1986, the home-made pipe bomb in Tel Aviv in 1990, the November 1997 massacre of 58 tourists at Luxor's Temple of Hatshepsut in Egypt, and the truck bombings of the United States Embassies in Kenya and Tanzania that killed 263 people in August 1998 (Pizam and Smith, 2000). Such terrorist incidents there have reduced people's propensity to travel.

The impact of terrorism on the tourist industry was dramatically demonstrated by the events of September 11, 2001. Baker (2014) mentioned that The World Travel and Tourism Council has estimated that the USA lost 92 billion dollars in travel and tourism, followed by Germany with a loss of 25 billion dollars and the UK with a loss of 20 billion. Even prior to 9/11, examples demonstrated the severe impact of terrorism on tourism, in Spain, a typical terrorist incident resulted in the reduction of 140,000 arrivals (Enders and Sandler, 1991). In 1985, a Gallup survey detailed that 79% of Americans would avoid abroad destinations that summer as a result of expanded terrorist movement at the time, and the results were that around 54% canceled their reservations (D'Amore and Anuza, 1986). In that same year, the World Tourism Organization credited a misfortune of $105 billion in tourism receipts to terrorism (Sonmez and Graefe, 1998).

The magnitude of the event, the frequency, the timing of the attack, and the types of attack effect the tourist's perception of risk, and accordingly their travel decision. On the other hand, the movements of arrivals to some of the stricken countries are restricted by policies that have been developed by governments, for example, after the 9/11 accident happened, it was more difficult to get a visa for visiting the United States for a foreigner citizen than previously (Maditinos and Vassiliadis, 2008) in order to control and provide the high level of security for civilians and tourists.

Whether it is man-made or natural emergencies, it is very important to be well prepared to mitigate the impact of emergencies and minimize losses. With no doubt that safety and security are two of the most important issues of retaining both the guests and the skilled employees. The industry must conduct recovery marketing or marketing integrated fully with crisis management activities as media coverage of terrorist actions or political instability has the potential to shape tourists' images of destinations.

Also, what increased the importance of applying appropriate safety procedures is that the core of tourism and hospitality industry is the tourist or the guest, who is looking only for comfort and then he is relatively unfamiliar with the place or area and its local safety or emergency situations, thus, they are often at greater risk than others (Murphy, 1989). Moreover, tourism industries are the source of living of many families as it hires millions of employees and workers around the world. The tourism industry is only about people and it maximizes the consequences of unpleasant actions. Thus, establishing a safety environment helps in attracting more visitors and also retaining employees.

## 9.3 EMERGENCY CLASSIFICATION AND TYPOLOGY

Risk or emergency situation is an event or set of circumstances, which can severely compromise or damage the marketability and reputation of an organization or business, its brand, or an entire tourism destination region. There are two broad categories of tourism-related emergencies which impact on organizations:

### 1. *Category one*

Emergency events that are beyond the control of the property's management:

These include natural disasters, acts of war, political upheavals, terrorism waves, epidemics, and sudden global economic downturns.

*2. Category two*

Risks which result from a failure of management action, it occurs as a result of lack of knowledge or skills required to mitigate such incidents and process or lack of contingency measures taken to deal with predictable emergencies.

These include a business collapse due to management failure, inappropriate strategic management, unethical practices, financial fraud, loss of data, destruction of the place of business due to fire or crimes without adequate backup procedures or insurance cover, and high turnover rate. It can also include service or equipment failures which compromise the reputation of the business.

Emergencies can have many faces and variable outcomes, tourist destinations for sure have to suffer most from an expected decline in tourist arrivals and its associated decline in other entertainment areas and possible extra expenditure.

In case a hospitality establishment hit by a crisis, all market players to a certain extent will experience the same consequences, labor market, certainly, will be affected significantly, high rate of employees' turnovers will be recorded, in addition, many of skilled employees will leave the labor market of the industry to other competitive industries, that in turn, will affect the competency of the labor market of the industry to the degree that made many academic and industry's professionals describe the industry labor market as a low skilled market.

James and Wooten (2005) differentiated three emergency types that affect any business:

- victim: low emergency responsibility/threat,
- accident: minimal emergency responsibility/threat,
- intentional: strong emergency responsibility/threat and two intensifying factors: emergency history and prior reputation.

In alignment with James and Wooten, individuals may experience three categories of emergency events as follows:

**Everyday events** focus on relatively frequent accidents and incidents with limited consequences, for example, an employee within his work environment can experience some events such as workplace accidents, products' mismatching, service slowness, and traffic accidents. These emergencies are, to a large extent, predictable and proceed from such things as reported accidents and statistical reports.

Most of daily risks or events arise from the fact of the hospitality industry being part of the service industry, where organizations within the service sector are faced with a wide array of potential emergency issues and this is due to both the nature of the service process itself and the extent of vague interactions between stakeholders of the industry. Generally, managers and industry stakeholders can get their experience and information about the emergency situations mainly from mishaps and disruptions in daily operations, at the same time as it is difficult to get relevant information that could provide a basis for assessment of the most serious emergencies.

**Large emergencies** focus on accidents that occur occasionally, with moderate consequences. The risks are random and vary greatly. The benchmark lies in things like individual accident investigations and claims adjustments.

**Extraordinary** emergencies focus on events that occur rarely, with destroying results. Detailed risk analyses, especially qualitative risk analyses, are required in order to carry out analyzing for the work environment internally and externally. This occurs through estimation of the likelihood ratio of full-scale emergencies.

Generally spoken, practitioners agree that the tourism and hospitality industry is prone to emergencies since major or minor events may disrupt business functions. Researchers attribute the vulnerability of hospitality properties and destinations to a wide range of emergencies and dangers coupled with the large fragmentation, yet interconnectedness, of the industry (Sawalha et al., 2013). Similarly, Wang and Ritchie (2013) confirmed that the hospitality industry comprises a wide array of services that necessitates different emergency management and planning strategies. Although hospitality properties and managers acknowledge the importance of emergency preparedness, they are often reactive in terms of response.

The first step to mitigate or diminish the risks associated with the tourist destination areas, concrete emergency classifications have to be identified, as the pragmatic approach for emergency preparation consists first of classification and the analysis of experienced and observed emergency situations in the workplace or the surrounding destination (see Fig. 9.1). Various authors have already set frameworks for an emergency typology; Rosenthal and Kouzmin (1993) viewed emergencies from a content perspective; there are one-dimensional or multidimensional typologies. Saayman and Snyman (2005) divided emergencies in the tourism industry into two categories:

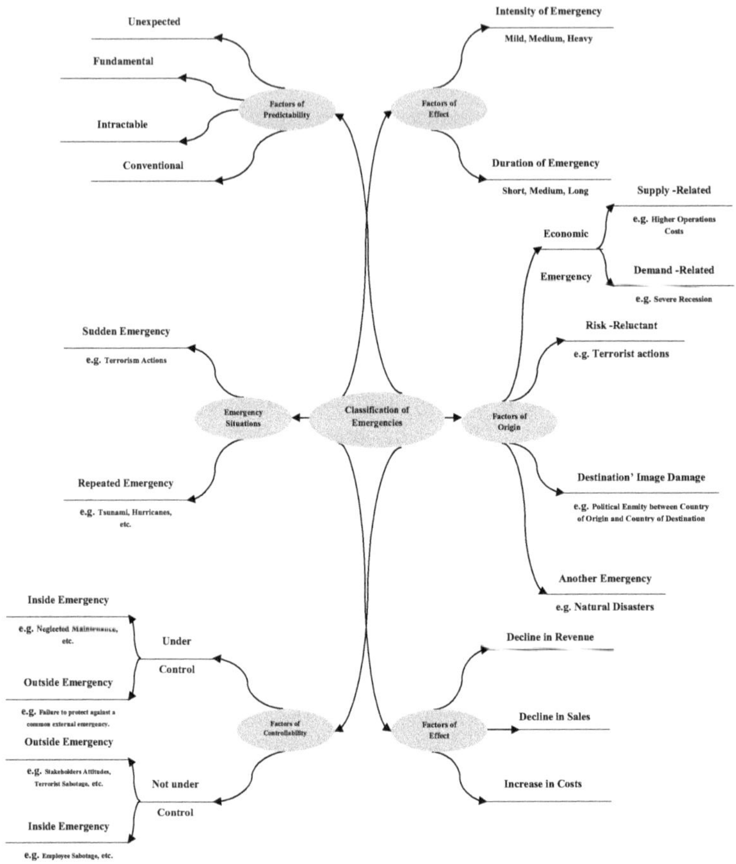


**FIGURE 9.1** Emergency situations' classification.

**Source:** The Authors

those that influence domestic tourist movement and those that influence international travel. Examples of domestic travel risks are crime, fires, fraud, complaints, low-skilled staff, bad marketing, poor maintenance of facilities and vehicles, bad management and various transport risks. The international travel risks are natural disasters (tsunamis, hurricanes, and drought), socio-demographics (ageing markets, family life-cycles, and changing structures), economics (recessions, increase in oil prices, and exchange rates), politics (sanctions and terrorism), and disease (H1N1-virus, HIV/AIDS, SARS, and Ebola). Although these risks may be present outside the borders of a destination, they nevertheless affect travelers to that destination. The application of the appropriate and most promising emergency response strategy—if nothing else—depends initially on distinguishing the emergency type.

Additionally, for an organization, it is important to constantly work on the current resilience of tourism and hospitality organizations which is identified as "ant fragility." Identifying the source and the type of emergency events that may strike the industry is very crucial in order to develop appropriate preparing procedures.

According to Gundel (2005), a classification of emergency situations is "the first step to keep them under control" and allows for analysis and planning of emergency management actions. He defines four conditions for a good typology:

1. Mutually exclusive classes,
2. Exhaustive, covering also future events,
3. Practicable, i.e. covering measures of prevention and
4. Pragmatic thus manageable.

## 9.4 EMERGENCY/RISK MANAGEMENT PROCESS

The survival of any business, including those in the tourism and hospitality industry, depends on identifying and managing emergencies. This can be done either by eliminating the source of risk entirely or, if this is not possible, by ensuring that any adverse impact that might occur will be kept to a minimum. It can, therefore, be accepted that, if risk were not controlled and managed, the industry would not grow, and jobs would not be created. In this context, Faulkner (2001) offered one of only a few proactive and strategic emergency management approaches, the so-called Tourism Disaster Management Framework, which was, for example, discussed in the context of the Katherine floods in the Northern Territory of Australia (Faulkner and Vikulov, 2001). Gray and Larson (2006) defined risk management as a proactive approach to minimizing the negative consequences of undesirable events that may occur. While Valsamakis et al. (2004) cited management guru Peter Drucker's definition of risk management as "the ability to manage the unexpected."

The management and resolution of emergencies is one of the most difficult strategic issues decision makers face because of:

- unknown variables like stakeholder perceptions,
- the lack of information about the cause,
- conditions of high uncertainty,
- time pressure, limited resources, and
- reduced control tools.

It is therefore important for organizations operating in the field of tourism industries to possess not only the ability to manage risk but also the skill and foresight to recognize it, because risk will have a tremendous bearing on the growth of the industry. Shaw (2010) goes so far as to maintain that the countries or destinations that manage emergency events best will have a competitive advantage.

Prideaux et al. (2003) and Faulkner (2001) emphasized the need for more information and the necessity for a conceptual framework to structure the cumulative development of knowledge about the effective response to such emergencies. Risk management is also seen as a proactive technique for obtaining objective information to prevent the occurrence of adverse events or to minimize their negative impact not a technique for solving the problems (Kerzner, 2001). Risk management is only a part of the quality assurance efforts required for mitigating major risk sources that may lead to the redesign or rescheduling of certain goals, policies or projects, which means additional costs meant to prevent performance and quality deterioration. The complexities involved in risk management in the tourism industry mean that it must be seen as a process that requires continuous evaluation, analysis, revision, and updating. Risk management focuses on identifying, assessing and solving risk situations before striking the business, a part of or the whole business.

According to Shaw et al. (2012), in the field of tourism, risk management is concerned with every kind of tourism industry business -tour operators, travel agents, accommodation establishments, food and beverage outlets, entertainment farms, national, provincial and local parks, entertainment facilities, festivals, airlines and guesthouses, to name but a few. Most of these businesses are interdependent and provide primarily for tourists and visitors. For example, hotels, bed and breakfast establishments and guesthouses are dependent on numbers of visitors. At the same time, if a destination could not attract a sufficient number of arrivals, these businesses accordingly would suffer.

Thus, there is a big need to adopt a strategy for identifying, analyzing, evaluating and treating the risks which may provide uncertainty around the individuals, organization, business unit or project ability to achieve their objectives. Such management process also provides a structure to ensure that identified risks are continuously monitored and reviewed. Figure 9.2 describes the standard process for risk management.

As shown in Figure 9.2, the communication and consultation procedures are a constant activity across all stages of the risk management process to

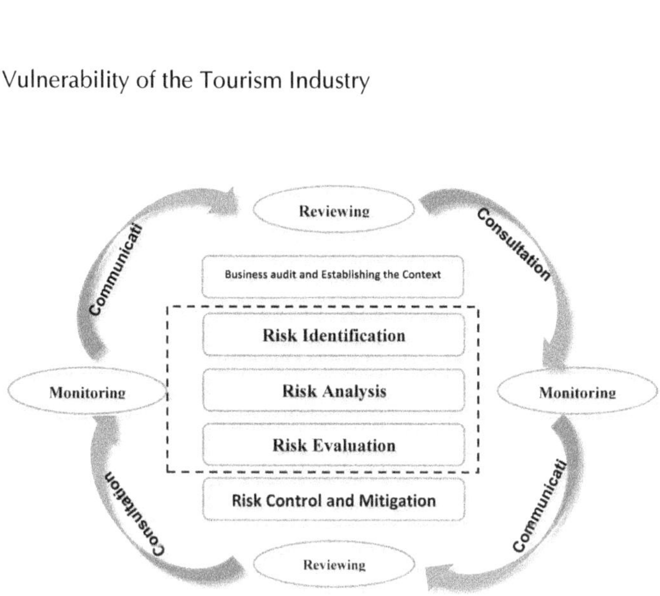


**FIGURE 9.2** Risk management process.

**Source:** The Authors

provide, share or obtain information, and to engage in dialogue with internal and external stakeholders regarding the management of risk. Along with communication and consultation, reviewing and monitoring activity must be considered at all stages.

## *9.4.1 BUSINESS AUDITING AND ESTABLISHING THE CONTEXT*

Risk management process in tourism organizations starts by auditing the current status of the business. This process must reveal the percentage of qualified personnel in the organization (Tatarusanu, 2009) in terms of their experience, educations, and critical thinking skills. In addition, all the organizational operation procedures must be reevaluated (Tatarusanu, 2009): existing policies and operation procedures, training programs, human resource policies and development, and the final outcomes.

## *9.4.2 RISK IDENTIFICATION*

There are risks associated with everything we do; doing something, or doing nothing, equally entails a risk of something happening or not happening as a result. This step in the process is designed to identify a comprehensive list of risks based on events that might create, enhance, prevent, degrade, accelerate or delay the achievement of tourism industry's objectives, and to document these possible risks in a register. Risk identification consists of identifying, analyzing and organizing into a hierarchy the potential risks resource that may threaten the organization. Such events may be identified on a list of risks, by comparing past data, employee reports, audit reports, macroeconomic and microeconomic prognoses or SWOT analysis conducted by the organization management or specialized institutions. A systematic process is necessary to ensure that all relevant sources of risk are identified. Sources of risk will change, so an important part of monitoring and review processes is to identify new hazards which have emerged for a destination or business.

Hence, risk identification may be quantitative, consisting of an objective probability estimate, based on risk-related information, with immediate application to the risk occurrence background, and quantitative, given its subjective nature and the fact that it relies on general logic arguments.

### 9.4.3 RISK ANALYSIS

Risk analysis involves an understanding of the causes and sources of risk and their positive and negative consequences. The purpose of analyzing risks is to develop a consideration of the risks your tourism organization is facing. Risk analysis means assessing risk occurrence probability and their consequences, the extent to which they may hinder the company business, according to a risk assessment list, which sets, on a scale from 1 to 10, the risk occurrence probability (1—very low, 10—very high) and their consequences (considering its severity, effect, period and involved costs). The risk may be determined by multiplying the estimated severity factor by the estimated probability factor. These risks can be assessed by using professional risk analysts who create organization-specific reports by relating risk attributes of specific areas to the particular characteristics and vulnerabilities of the organization. Research should take into account that different organizations may have very different degrees of vulnerability to risk and be affected differently. This assessment will assist in deciding which risks need to be treated and in identifying the best risk treatment strategies to apply. In addition to the degree of likelihoods, emergency events that may threaten the business may be analyzed from the following viewpoints (Tatarusanu, 2009):

- Operational effects (the inability of the company to conduct its business, sales drop, etc.),
- Financial costs,
- Legal effects (the legal consequences).

## 9.4.4 RISK EVALUATION

The purpose of risk evaluation is to assist in making decisions based on the results of risk analysis, about the risks that need treatment, and the implementation priority for these treatments in order to reduce the likelihood of a risk occurring or the potential damage arising from the risk. Evaluation process help in classifying the potential threats according to its severity and probability (see Fig. 9.3).

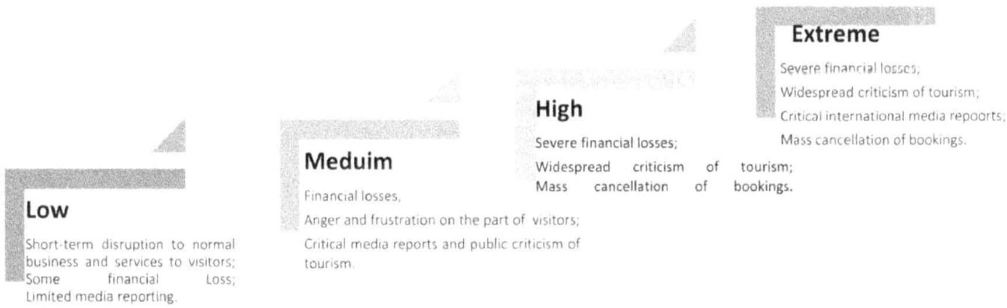


**FIGURE 9.3** Risk categories.

**Source:** The Authors

## 9.4.5 RISK TREATMENT

Risk treatment or mitigation involves selecting one or more options for controlling risks. Generally, there are a number of options when treating emergency situations: (see Fig. 9.4)

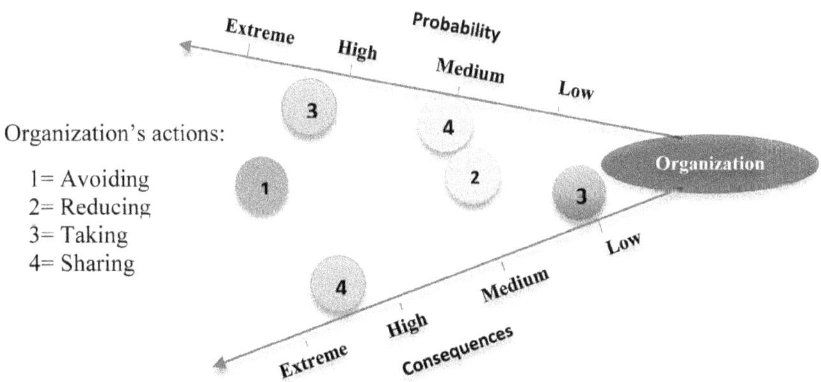


**FIGURE 9.4** **(See color insert.)** Risks treatment process considering its consequences and probability.

**Source:** The Authors

- Avoid the risk in which managers will prevent the occurrence of risks, which usually consists of giving up certain actions or modifying the operations procedures that may involve risks or reallocate some specific duties to more skilled employees. Hence, a company may decide not to perform a particular type of activity as there are not enough qualified employees.
- Reduce the risk, a risk reduction strategy relies on actions designed to decrease event occurrence probability or probable event consequences. Organizations, therefore, act by imposing restrictive safety and security measures to reduce at least man-made emergencies.
- Share the risk (e.g., obtain a specialized insurance premium, additional contract clause), also the industry' stakeholders especially the governmental institutions must have a significant part in case of emergency treatment.
- Retain or accept the risk.

In order to make the best outcomes of managing the emergencies events, all the employees and the stakeholders must be involved in the process of planning and executing the relevant proacting procedures (Tancja et al., 2014) by providing them the necessary information and decisions and keeping them constantly informed by developing good methods of communications. The next section briefly highlights their roles:

### 9.4.6 EMPLOYEES' ROLE

According to Coombs, (2011), there should be a pre-designated emergency team, multidisciplinary in nature, usually consisting of staff specializing in "public relations, security, operations, finance, legal, and human resources," and should know what tasks and responsibilities they are required to perform before, during and after the crisis.

In the field of tourism industry, Özükan (2009) claimed it is not easy to provide human resources for the tourism industry because, even though unemployment is at peak levels, most employers fail to find qualified people for the service-intensive tourism business. Subsequently, the lack of qualified staff is thus seen to be limiting the growth of the tourism industry in such unstable global market.

The lack of properly-trained personnel was found to create a gap in the skills needed for identifying and alleviating the potential risks and emergencies. Thus, employees must be highly prepared to contribute to emergency management, by being knowledgeable and trained to use organizational resources, possibly through training sessions to make them "aware of methods, procedures, and action plans to deploy when there is an imminent crisis" (Taneja et al., 2014).

Training under diverse hypothetical scenarios at least yearly will improve the skills and knowledge of team individuals and enable them to respond faster and more viable, to make more successful choices, take initiatives and improve their reaction capacities. Two key skills which must be emphasized during both the recruiting process and training system are the capacity to think creatively and to exercise leadership, since dangers or crises are unpredictable and different in nature, requiring initiatives, and frequently rigid and new management approaches.

### *9.4.7 STAKEHOLDERS' ROLE*

Stakeholders must also be involved in planning and implementing the protective procedures, by being made aware of identified potential risks through "risk communication," which includes "conveying ongoing emergency events to stakeholders, decision making within the risk management team, and organizational decisions regarding whether and what amount of information to share" (Hale et al., 2005).

Excluding employees and consumers, Tourism has four broad categories of key stakeholders: government, channels and influencers, industry participants, and suppliers. Within these groups are a number of sub-categories of stakeholders with unique needs and wants. The following Table 9.1 provides a more comprehensive view of stakeholder.

## REFERENCES

Agnew, M.; Palutikof, J. Impacts of Short-Term Climate Variability in the UK on Demand for Domestic and International Tourism. *Climate Res.* **2006,** *31*, 109–120.

Aziz, H. Understanding Attacks on Tourists in Egypt. *Tour. Manag.* **1995,** *16*, 91–95.

Baker, D. M. A. The Effects of Terrorism on the Travel and Tourism Industry. *Int. J. Religious Tour. Pilgr.* **2014,** *2* (1), 58–67.

Becken S.; Hay J. *Tourism and Climate Change: Risks and Opportunities*. Channel View Publications: Clevedon, 2007.

Berrittella, M.; Bigano, A.; Roson, R.; Richard, S. A General Equilibrium Analysis of Climate Change Impacts on Tourism. *Tour. Manag.* **2006,** *27* (5), 913–924.

Blake, A.; Sinclair, M.T. Tourism Crisis Management: US response to September 11. *Ann. Tour. Res.* **2003,** *30*, 813–832.

**TABLE 9.1** Tourism Industries' Stakeholders.

| Government | Local industry associations | Investors | Suppliers | Access providers | Media | Complementary and dependent industries | International industry associations |
|---|---|---|---|---|---|---|---|
| **Government** | | **Industry participants** | | | **Channels and influencer** | | |
| Governmental authorities that are responsible for setting policies or implementing programs | Governmental establishments with an interest or involvement in tourism industry | Current or potential investors in tourism facilities | The entity or manufacturer or individual that supplies goods and service for others | Companies and businesses that are responsible for bringing and moving tourist around within a country | Local and international media channels | Businesses and organizations that are involved in facilitating tourism activities, or those which are depending on the tourism industry | International associations and agencies representing tourism industry |
| Tourism ministry, Tourist activation authority, Hotels chambers associations, etc. | State and territory agencies | Accommodation establishments, entertainment parks, etc. | Companies that cater to hospitality establishment such as Food catering companies | Aviation companies, cruise companies, other transportation facilities | News media, specialized media, bloggers, etc. | Construction companies, Infrastructure companies, Educational and training institutions, Accounting services offices, Catering companies, etc. | WTO, IATA, WTTC, etc. |

**Source:** The Authors

Burns, P. Paradoxes in Planning: Tourism Elitism or Brutalism? *Ann. Tour. Res.* **1999,** *26*, 329–348.

Business Day. 2004. Tourism Leads to Job-Creation Change, Business Day, 2004. [Online] www.rastafarispeaks.com/cgi-bin/forum/archive1/config.pl?read=45945 (accessed Oct 22, 2017).

Calgaro, E.; Lloyd, K. Sun, Sea, Sand and Tsunami: Examining Disaster Vulnerability in the Tourism Community of Khao Lak, Thailand. *Singap. J. Trop. Geogr.* **2008,** *29* (3) 288–306.

Coombs, W. T. Crisis Management and Communications, Institute for Public Relations, 2011.

D'Amore, L. J.; Anuza, T. E. International Terrorism: Implications and Challenge for Global Tourism. *Bus. Q.* **1986,** *11*, 20–29.

Drabek, T. E. Disaster Evacuation Behavior: Tourists and Other Transients. University of Colorado: Boulder, 1996.

Enders, W.; Sandler, T. Causality between Transnational Terrorism and Tourism: The Case of Spain. *Terrorism* **1991,** *14* (1), 49–58.

Enders, W.; Sandler, T. Patterns of Transnational Terrorism, 1970–99: Alternative Time Series Estimates. *Int. Stud. Q.* **2002,** *46*, 145–165.

Enz, C. A. *Competitive Dynamics and Creating Sustainable Advantage.* In: *The Cornell School of Hotel Administration Handbook of Applied Hospitality Strategy*; Enz, C. A., Ed.; SAGE: Los Angeles, CA, 2010, pp 297–305.

Faulkner, B. Towards a Framework for Tourism Disaster Management. *Tour. Manag.* **2001,** *22*, 135–147.

Faulkner, B.; Vikulov, S. Katherine, Washed Out One Day, Back on Track the Next: A Post-Mortem of a Tourism Disaster. *Tour. Manag.* **2001,** *22*, 331–344.

Frederickson, V. Risk Management and HR executive. [Online] www.vfandco/resources/PDFs/Risk_Management.pdf (accessed 25 Oct, 2017).

Gómez Martín, Ma. Weather, Climate and Tourism. A Geographical Perspective. *Ann. Tour. Res.* **2005,** *32* (3), 571–591.

Gray, C. F.; Larson, E. W. *Project Management: The Managerial Process*, 3rd Ed.; Irwin/McGraw-Hill: Boston, Mass, 2006.

Gundel, S.. Towards a New Typology of Crises. *J. Conting. Crisis Manag.* **2005,** *13* (3), 106–115.

Hale, J.; Dulek, R.; Hale, D. Crisis Response Communication Challenges. *J. Bus. Commun.* **2005,** *42* (2), 112–134.

Hamilton, J. M.; Lau, M. The Role of Climate Information in Tourist Destination Choice Decision-Making. In *Tourism and Global Environmental Change*; Gössling, S., Hall, C. M., Eds.; Routledge: London, 2005, pp 229–250.

Hu, Y.; Ritchie, J. Measuring Destination Attractiveness: A Contextual Approach. *J. Travel Res.* **1993,** *32* (20), 25–34.

Ichinosawa, J. Reputational Disaster in Phuket: The Secondary Impact of the Tsunami on Inbound Tourism. *Disaster Prevent. Manag.* **2006,** *15* (1), 111–123.

ILO: Green Jobs in the South Pacific: A Preliminary Study, ILO, 2010.

James, E. H.; Wooten, L. P. Leadership As (Un)usual: How to Display Competence in Times of Crisis. *Organ. Dyn.* **2005,** *34* (2), 141–152.

Kerzner, H. *Project Management: A Systems Approach to Planning, Scheduling, and Controlling*, 7th ed.; Wiley: New York, 2001.

Koenig, U.; Abegg, B. Impacts of Climate Change on Winter Tourism in the Swiss Alps. *J. Sustain. Tour.* **1997,** *5* (1), 46–58.
Koetse, M. J.; Rietveld, R. The Impact of Climate Change and Weather on Transport: An Overview of Research Findings. Transportation Research Part D, 2009.
Kozak, N.; Uysal, M.; Birkan, I. An Analysis of Cities Based on Tourism Supply and Climatic Conditions in Turkey. *Tour. Geogr.* **2008,** *10* (1), 81–97.
LEPP, A.; Gibson, H. Tourist Roles, Perceived Risk and International Tourism. *Ann. Tour. Res.* **2003,** *30* (3), 606–624.
Lim, C.; Min, J. C.; McAleer, M. Modelling Income Effects on Long and Short Haul International Travel from Japan. *Tour. Manag.* **2008,** *29* (6), 1099–1109.
Lise, W.; Tol, R. Impact of Climate on Tourist Demand. *Clim. Change* **2002,** *55*, 429–449.
Low, S. P.; Liu, J.; Sio, S. Business Continuity Management in Large Construction Companies in Singapore. *Disaster Prevent. Manag.* **2010,** *19*, 2, 219–232.
Mansfeld, Y. *Tourism, Security and Safety: From Theory to Practice*; Butterworth-Heinemann: Oxford, 2006, pp 271–290.
Marshall, M.; Alexander, C. Planning for the Unexpected: Human Resource Risk and Contingency Planning, 2009. [online] www.ces.purdue.edu/extmedia/ECHouse (accessed Oct 23, 2017).
Murphy, J. F. *State Support of International Terrorism*; Westview Press: San Francisco, 1989.
Özükan, F. T. Tourism to Offer Remedy for Unemployment with 300,000 New Recruits, 2009. [online] www.todayszaman.com/tz-web/detaylar.do?load=detayandlink=172223and bolum=105 (accessed Oct 5, 2017).
Paraskevas, A.; Arendell, B. A. Strategic Framework for Terrorism Prevention and Mitigation in Tourism Destinations. *Tour. Manag.* **2007,** *28* (6), 1560–1573.
Pforr, C. Tourism in Post Crisis is Tourism in Pre-Crisis: A Review of the Literature on Crisis Management in Tourism, Curtin University of Technology, Curtin Business School, School of Management, 2006.
Pizam, A.; Smith G. Tourism and Terrorism: A Quantitative Analysis of Major Terrorist Acts and Their Impact on Tourism Destinations. *Tour. Econ.* **2000,** *6* (2), 123–138.
Prideaux, B.; Laws, E.; Faulkner, B. Events in Indonesia: Exploring the Limits to Formal Tourism Trends Forecasting Methods in Complex Crisis Situations. *Tour. Manag.* **2003,** *24*, 475–487.
Ranabhat, K. Effects of Terrorism in Tourism Industry: A Case Study of 9/11 Terrorist Attacks in World Trade Center. BAM Thesis, Centria University of Applied Sciences, 2015.
Raval, V.; Fichadia, A. *Risks, Controls, and Security: Concepts and Applications*; Wiley: New York, 2007.
Richter, L. K.; Waugh, J.W. L. Tourism Politics and Political Science: A Case of Not So Benign Neglect. *Ann. Tour. Res.* 1983, 10 (2), 313–315.
Rifai, T. UNWTO calls on Tourism Stakeholders to Join 'Roadmap for Recovery, 2009. [online] www.eturbonews.com/8222/unwto-calls-tourism-stakeholders-join-roadmap-recovery (accessed OCT 20, 2017).
Rittichainuwat, B. Understanding Perceived Travel Risk Differences Between First Time and Repeat Travelers. In 3rd Global Summit on Peace Through Tourism-Education Forum: One Earth One Family: Travel and Tourism Serving a Higher Purpose; Pattaya, Thailand, 2005.
Rosenthal, U.; Kouzmin, A. Globalizing an Agenda for Contingencies and Crisis Management. *J. Conting. Crisis Manag.* **1993,** *1* (1), 1–12.

Ryu, K.; Bordelon, B. M.; Pearlman, D. M. Destination-Image Recovery Process and Visit Intentions: Lessons Learned from Hurricane Katrina. *J. Hosp. Market. Manag.* **2013,** *22* (2), 183– 203.

Saayman, M.; Snyman, J. A. *Entrepreneurship Tourism Style*; Leisure C Publishers: Potchefstroom, 2005.

Sawalha, I.; Jraisat, L.; Al-Qudah, K. Crisis and Disaster Management in Jordanian Hotels: Practices and Cultural Considerations. *Disaster Prevent. Manag.* **2013,** *22* (3), 210–228.

Scott, D.; Lemieux, C. Weather and Climate Information for Tourism. White Paper, Commissioned by the World Meteorological Organization, 2009.

Scott, D.; McBoyle, G. Climate Change Adaptation in the Ski Industry. *Mitigat. Adapt. Strat. Global Change* **2006,** *12*, 1411–1431.

Seddighi, M. W.; Nuttall, A. L.; Theocharous H. R. Does Cultural Background of Tourists Influence the Destination Choice? An Empirical Study with Special Reference to Political Instability. *Tour. Manag.* **2001,** *22* (2), 181–191.

Shaw, G.; Saayman, M.; Saayman, A. Identifying Risks Facing the South African Tourism Industry. *South Afr. J. Econ. Manag. Sci.*, **2012,** *15* (2), 190–206.

Shaw, G. K. A Risk Management Model for the South African Tourism Industry. Ph.D. Thesis, North West University, Potchefstroom, South Africa, 2010.

Smith, K. The Influence of Weather and Climate on Recreation and Tourism. *Weather*, 1993, 48, 398–404.

Sonmez, S. Tourism, Terrorism, and Political Instability. *Ann. Tour. Res.* 1998, 25 (2), 416–456.

Sonmez, S.; Graefe, S. Determining Future Travel Behavior from Past Travel Experience and Perception of Risk and Safety. *J. Travel Res.* **1998,** 37 (2), 172–177

Sookram, S. The Impact of Climate Change on the Tourism Sector in Selected Caribbean Countries. ECLAC Project Documents Collection, Caribbean Development Report, 2009, 2, pp 204–244.

Stafford, G.; Yu, L.; Armoo, A. K. Crisis Management and Recovery: How Washington D.C. hotels Responded to Terrorism. *Cornell Hotel Restaur. Administr. Q.* **2002,** *43*, 27–40.

Stern, N. The Economics of Climate Change. The Stern Review, Cambridge University Press, Cambridge, United Kingdom, 2006.

Taneja, S.; Pryor, M.; Sewell, S.; Recuero, A. Strategic Crisis Management: A Basis for Renewal and Crisis Prevention. *J. Manag. Policy Practice* **2014,** *15* (1), 78–85.

Tarlow, P. E. Dark Tourism: The Appealing 'Dark Side' of Tourism and More. In *Niche Tourism Contemporary Issues, Trends and Cases*; Novelli, M., Ed.; Butterworth-Heinemann: Oxford, 2005, pp 47–58.

Tatarusanu, M. Human Resource Management Risks in Tourism, 2009. [Online] http://anale.feaa.uaic.ro/anale/resurse/31_M12_Tatarusanu.pdf (accessed Oct 27, 2017).

UNWTO. Tourism Highlights, 2013. [Online] http://mkt.unwto.org/publication/unwto-tourism-highlights-2013-edition (accessed Nov 20, 2017).

UNWTO (World Tourism Organization). World Tourism Barometer, 7 (2), 2009.

UNWTO, UNEP and WMO. Climate Change and Tourism: Responding to Global Challenges. Madrid: United Nations World Tourism Organization; Paris: United Nations Environment Program; Geneva: World Meteorological Organization, 2008.

Valsamakis, A. C.; Vivian, R. W.; Du Toit, G. S. *Risk Management: Managing Enterprise Risks*, 3rd ed.; Heinemann: Sandon, 2004.

Wahab, S. Tourism and Terrorism: Synthesis of the Problem with Emphasis on Egypt. In *Tourism, Crime and International Security Issues*; Pizam, A., Mansfeld, Y., Eds.; Wiley: New York, 1996, pp 175–186.

Wall, G.; Badke, C. Tourism and Climate Change: An International Perspective. *J. Sustain. Tour.* **1994,** *2* (4), 193–203.

*Wamsley, L. National Public Radio, 2017*, pp 6–10.

Wang, J.; Ritchie, B. W. Attitudes and Perceptions of Crisis Planning Among Accommodation Managers: Results from an Australian Study. *Safety Sci.* **2013,** *52*, 81–91.

Weimann, G.; Winn, C. *The Theater of Terror: Mass Media and International Terrorism*; Longman: White Plains, NY, 1994.

World Altas. Global Terrorism Index, 2017. [online] http://www.worldatlas.com/articles/the-global terrorism-index-countries-most-affected-by-terrorist-attacks.html(accessed Dec 5, 2017).

Youm 7 Report. Damages in Millions of EGP in Taba Following Last Week's Flood: Tourism Ministry, 2014. [Online] http://thecairopost.youm7.com/news/110946/news/damages-in-millions-of-egp-in-taba-following last-weeks-flood-tourism-ministry (accessed Oct 15, 2017).

CHAPTER 10

# LOW WAGES AND OVERDEPENDENCE ON TIPPING

*"In the hospitality industry, it's the customer who pays the wages, the employer only handles the money, and the employee suffers from gambling on their wages."*

## 10.1 INTRODUCTION

Low wages in addition to other factors such as bad working environment and poor management could be the highest causes of labor turnover in hospitality organizations (Haven-Tang and Jones, 2012). The development of a sound compensation plan is critical to the credibility of the management and success of a business. Several reasons highlight the importance of an effective pay system in the industry as wage compensation programs are widely used as a tool to attract, maintain, and motivate the workforce.

Pay refers to base wages or salary for work. Base pay may be expressed as an annual, weekly or hourly rate. The hourly rate is sometimes called the time rate system of payment. Under the Employment Standards Act (ESA), "wages" includes salaries, commissions or money, paid or payable by an employer to the worker for work and also money that is paid or payable by an employer as an incentive and relates to hours of work, production, performance or efficiency. Guthrie (2000) defined pay or wages that are "attached to the jobs that employees perform." Subsequently, base pay is categorized into job-based pay where the wage is related entirely on the position and length of employment rather than the employee (Armstrong, 2012). This explains the problem of wages in the hospitality industry as service providers' wages still underestimated despite their critical role in the success of service transaction with the customers and guests which leads in turn to the business success.

Unfortunately, many servers are not given any further compensation from the management except less than minimum wage (Whaley, 2011). In hospitality industry, many researchers have found that pay affects both employees' intention to leave and their level of job commitment (Ghiselli et al., 2001). In the hospitality sector, labor costs which include salary and benefits, average about a third of total revenue and 43% of all operating expenses (Quek, 2000).

Thus, organizations should invest more in human capital in order to improve the quality of the employees themselves and the service they provide, in addition, to reduce turnover as pay has been used to attract and keep the best employees. However, the employee's skills, expertise, ability, and work information should be considered when increasing their wages and the increased pay ought to happen when an employee gained job-specific certification and training courses. Generally, to be effective, an organization's pay system should address four factors (Lawler, 1989):

1. a sufficient level of rewards to fulfill basic needs of employees,
2. equity with the external labor market,
3. equity within the organization, and
4. treatment of each member of the organization in terms of his or her individual needs.

Among these factors, equity is probably the most important. The lack of equity in payment with external payment made it highly essential for servers to depend on tips for their living. Now, tipping is a major source of income for most tourism and hospitality workers. It represents the major portions of restaurant employees' wages and accounts for more than half of their income (Azar and Yossi, 2008).

## 10.2 TIPPING IN HOSPITALITY INDUSTRY

Although it is not clear how tipping originated, one form of tipping has been traced back in the nineteenth century where it arose from the practice of using boxes labeled "To Insure Promptness" which were placed in the English coffee places and inns. The label "To Insure Promptness" was abbreviated as "TIP." Customers contributed to these boxes to ensure efficient and quick services (Lynn, 2003). Some evidence suggests that tipping had its roots in the Roman Empire (Templeton, 1996). An often-repeated story is that tipping became common in Tudor England's homes where visitors paid hosts' servants for their extra effort in accommodating them.

This tipping practice spread throughout Europe, particularly in areas with a servant class. This continued on and on and by the seventeenth-century tips were accepted and even expected in numerous European establishments. However, since America did not have a servant class, this did not take off in the United States until the late 1800s, whereby wealthy Americans who had traveled to Europe started tipping as a way of showing that they were familiar with European customs (Azar, 2004). Today, Tipping is a widespread practice in many service sectors. Tipping in the increasingly service-oriented American culture has become almost omnipresent in the restaurant industry. According to Azar (2003; 2009), tips amount given to employees working in the restaurant industry in the United States of America is almost 42 billion dollars annually.

Tipping started as a sign of gratitude and status, became an incentive, and finally a norm with far less connection to anything besides behaving in a socially acceptable manner. Such manner motivated business owners to lower the wages of their employees to the point where tips were required to supplement their income.

According to Matulewicz (2013), wages excludes gratuities and money that is paid at the discretion of the employer and is not related to hours of work, production or performance. Therefore, employers pay nothing for his employees compared to other sectors or industries. Subsequently, many hospitality employees rely on tips rather than on their wages to earn a decent income. This makes tipping today is one of the significant parts of restaurant employees' income and accounts for more than half of their income (Azar and Yossi, 2008).

A tip is defined as a fee paid by customers to service providers on a voluntary basis (Ineson and Martin, 1999). While Casey (1998) defined it as money exchanged from customer to servers which is not legally required by the agreement for the purchase of the service.

Today, tipping has become a prominent element, particularly in the restaurants' industry (Brewster, 2013) under the support of employers and the current financial status of employees. However, tipping also changes from place to place. Different countries have different tipping customs. For example, tipping is forbidden in some countries, like Russia and Japan, while in the South of France, it is the sole source of restaurants' employees' income. In Europe, many restaurants add a service charge automatically to the bill. In the United States, the act of tipping is a common practice in restaurants. According to the United States Department of Labor (2016), 19 states have lower hourly wages for tipped workers; a minimum cash payment of $2.13 is the same as that required under the federal Fair Labor Standards Act. While, 21 states require bosses to pay tipped workers above government minimum wage, but lower than the full state minimum wage (Lee and Dewald, 2016).

Lu-in (2014) advocated that there are some reasons that made the establishment owners and managers insist applying tipping system in their establishments as follows:

- Motivation tool in order to stimulate servers to deliver good service.
- Control tool for server performance; service profession involves a high degree of vagueness in the performance that makes the dining experience is hard to control where the productivity of employees is not easily monitored by the employer; thus, the employers adopt such pattern payment as a control tool for his employees' performance.
- Indicator for dissatisfied customers; tipping is considered as some kind of social optimality that requires the customer and the server write a service contract in which the server strive to provide a high level of service during the experience of the customer in the restaurant, on the other side, the customer leaves an amount of tip upon the completion of this service according to his satisfaction. Thus, this norm of restaurant tipping may serve as an effective indicator of the success of the service process.

In restaurants, servers or bartenders can earn tips in a variety of ways, as follows:

- They may receive tips directly from a customer in an amount left at the discretion of the customer.
- Auto-gratuity system, where an automatic service charge, which can vary in percentage, is added to a bill.
- Tip pool system in which the employer distributes the tips among employees according to a specified formula. This system allows all employees and workers earn tip including those who are working in the back area like cooks, dishwashers, and bussers may earn tips through a tip pool system. So, tip pools are popular in the restaurant industry, but the manner through which tips are collected and redistributed varies. Sometimes tips are pooled

based on a percentage of sales, and sometimes tips are pooled based on a percentage of total tips a worker has earned. Employers or employees can manage tip pools.

Tipping is an economic phenomenon consisting of a voluntary payment by customers for service and products received. This payment created another role of the customer in the organization by tipping practices, customers directly control how much money restaurant's employees earn, and thus the role of the customer in employment relations became unavoidable. While servers perceive tip as a reward for their efforts in serving the customers in most cases, Lynn (2004) advocated that the customer and servers' perspective interests, the characteristics and factors of the tipping transaction, and the social nature of the service encounter combine to create a situation that affected by the two parties' biases, perceptions, and stereotypes. The next section discusses the relationship between the customers and the server; what motives the customer to pay extra for the servers? And how the server perceives tipping practice?

## 10.3 RELATIONSHIP BETWEEN TIPPER AND TIPPEE

Tipping practice is a significant economic phenomenon but is not readily explained by traditional economic theory. It is generally considered to be a complex social phenomenon, influenced by cultural values, traditions, and customs of the involved stakeholders (customer, servers, and the employer). Specifically, tipping involves at least two economic agents: the customer receiving service and paying the tip (the tipper) and the employees performing a service and receiving the tip (the tippee). From an economic perspective, the tipper and tippee interact in a market for tips. The relationship between customer and server implicates a variety of concerns about each party's worth, the parties' relative power and status, and their interpersonal bond.

The voluntary aspect of tipping raises questions about why rational people leave tips and about what factors determine how much they tip. Why is it that gratuities are paid at the discretion of customers after they have already received the primary services for which they are paying?

It is important to take into account that some accommodation establishments in the United States incorporate the tip in the price and demonstrate that on the menu. However, customers still commonly tip service providers even if the service is already charged with the argument being that tips which are in the form of service charge rarely get to the server.

**For the customer**, the tip provides the opportunity to recognize the service received, a chance to connect with or criticize the server performance, and an outlet to express views, emotions, and moods. The psychological theories also tried to give an explanation for the tipping phenomenon, according to Austin and Walster (1974), "equity theory" is similar to the norm of reciprocity in positing that impose people to put more into their relationship with others as long as they get what is needed from these relationships. In addition, the theory suggests that customers will feel some psychological pressure to leave larger tips the better the service they receive (Lynn and Graves, 1996).

Tipping provides a way to monitor and improve service quality by delegating the customers the function of evaluating and rewarding the service providers. In this situation, the customer is better positioned to assess service quality and provide incentives to the server (Azar, 2004). Tipping gave the customer full power over the service providers, although, this power varies according to the customer's personality and the server's dependence with regard to tips. The customer alone determines not just how much, but also whether to tip because the terms of the "implicit contract" between customer and server are not defined and the customer's obligation is neither specified nor enforceable (Azar, 2007). Tipping practice shaped the customer in a vantage position, to the extent that made the customer acts as the server's second boss, the customer has sole, unchecked discretion to make a decision of leaving tip or not.

Tips these days are meant to be a reward for a service, thus the desire of a customer to show his appreciation for the received high-quality product (service) is one of the main motivations why customers tend to tip (Azar, 2004). Accordingly, some academics and field experts supported the service quality is the main reason behind leaving a tip for the server, but, in reality, service quality is not a solid clarification for tipping, nor is it the main component that influences tipping behavior (Lynn and McCall, 2000). Studies that have found a positive relationship between service customer ratings and tip amount have nevertheless noted that the relationship is "very little" and "weaker than most people would expect" and even "so weak as to be meaningless" (Lynn, 2001). While, the relationship was very significant between tip practices and the ability of customers to demonstrate leverage practices, if customers do not have discretion because of including the tip in the price, they feel no power over the service providers (Walster et al., 1973).

Subsequently, the desire of customers to make a power play can be listed among some other motivations (Azar, 2004) as well as to show that he/she is a generous individual. On the contrary, the vulnerable economic position of the servers may be the motivation for customers to pay a tip for them; some people became accustomed to tipping to ensure the livelihood of the service industry's employees.

Another motivation why customers tend to tip is that they hope to receive the same service again in the future. Of course, this is valid for customers who intend to receive service in the future from the same organization. Better service in the future can be ensured by giving a good tip for good service. In addition, Azar (2004) claimed that people usually tip in order to conform to social norms, thus avoiding social disapproval; it was found that tipping includes the embarrassment that results from empathy for the individual giving the services and the desire to conform to social norms. Social norms can be explained in two ways. They are internal and external sources.

- External sources consist of social pressure generated by peer pressure. Dining with family members or friends may generate social pressure in terms of who is going to tip.
- Internal sources consist of a feeling of guilt and unfair behavior on the part of the individual who has failed to tip.

Other than social norms, demonstrating leverage or rewarding the server for the quality he/she strive to achieve, customers may leave tip for the service provider for many other factors such as:

- bill size,
- patronage reoccurrence,
- size of customers group,
- number of courses ordered,
- alcohol consumption,
- food ratings,
- type of restaurant,
- server appearance,
- gender of server,
- gender of customer,
- time; when meal is purchased.

Although the equity theory proposed that people are socialized by nature and need to build relationships with each other, Fernandez (2004) mentioned customer's tipping practice is an issue that is fraught with cultural misunderstanding, negative stereotypes, personal bias, inconsistent norms, and their perceptions and understanding of tipping process.

Thus, some customer may try to find devious ways to avoid following the standard guidelines or the norm of tipping 15–20% in a restaurant, the customer has the freedom to decide several factors that determine the actual amount of the tip, such as:

- where the tip will fall within the standard percentage range,
- whether to apply the chosen percentage to the pre- or post-tax amount of the bill, and
- whether to round the product of those choices up or down to an even dollar figure.

These small decisions can have a significant effect when aggregated over the economic status of the servers who are depending on the tip in their life.

Generally, the customers play an inevitable role in determining the final amount of tips, which create an unstable work environment for the employees that characterized of stress, jealous and full of conflicts among coworkers. Among possible organizational compensation strategies, tipping is unique in that the customer, not the employer, makes the major contribution to a server's wage. That way, employers and managers may feel tipping is desirable because it relieves them of some of their responsibility to compensate and motivate their labor force. However, this may result in staff feeling undervalued by the organization and create a lot of troubles in the work environment that affect business negatively.

On the other hand, servers would act in a way that would guarantee getting a good tip from the customers. Many customers assume that a tip is optional, not realizing that servers are paid close to nothing in salary, especially, employers are allowed to pay as little as $2.13 an hour on the assumption that patrons of compensations will make up the difference (Willen, 2015). Employees, especially ones who relies on tips greatly for his/her livelihoods, the tip becomes the focal point of the service encounter, because the tip affects the server's economic well-being and sometimes even his/her sense of self-worth, getting a good tip is the main target of the server in every transaction he/she makes with the customers (Dublanica, 2009).

Some employees prefer to work in such organizations that adopt such practices of payment (tipping), as they find it a good opportunity to best use their personal qualities and soft skills in stimulating customers to pay extra for them, the lack of some factors made a convenient environment for them to implement their endeavors, such as:

- the lack of employer or manager's control over their performance transaction with the customer,
- the absence of transaction costs, and
- the absence of a solid rule on how much to tip.

On the other hand, many employees are captured criticizing and complaining tipping practices and customer tipping behavior. Tipping presents the very sort of situation that promotes a kind of unpleasant sequences, for example, discrimination actions, stressful work environment, reinforcing self-fulfilling actions, and negative emotional and psychic sequences that is likely to occur at a time like the present, when overt prejudice is less acceptable and common than in the past.

Tipped service interactions make conditions for the impact of social group stereotypes, both since the customer-server relationship is regularly shaped with little opportunity for the included stakeholders to learn about one another as individuals, the ambiguous standards for behavior on both sides created an opening for unfavorable situations by both customer and server. Therefore, the involved stakeholders' respective roles and objectives require them to make decisions for which stereotypes often provide ready guidance (Lu-in, 2014). Server perceptions of customer tipping behavior motivate servers to provide superior or inferior performance based on the expected tipping behavior of customer (Barkan, 2004). Nevertheless, inexhaustible evidence shows that employees regularly hold stereotypes about specific group tipping practices, frequently paired with stereotypes about their behavior and attitudes generally as customers, that can impact the level or sort of service provided to members of stereotyped groups (Lu-in, 2014). According to McCall and Lynn (2009), understanding server perceptions on customer tipping behavior affected significantly by customers differences. Differences among customers in terms of ethnicity, sex, demographic profiles, and personality type are some of the determinants that shape the server perception of customer tipping behavior (Table 10.1).

To sum up, there are a number of ways that tipping is considered to negatively affect service quality, productivity and in turn on a restaurant's profitability. Tipping is thought to encourage autonomy, individualism, and competition in the workplace and this is counterproductive to the teamwork deemed necessary to provide excellent service.

**TABLE 10.1** Customers Differences as Determinants of Server Perceptions of Customer Tipping Behavior.

| **Differences** | **Tipping behaviors** | | **Supporters** |
|---|---|---|---|
| | **Good tipper** | **Bad tipper** | |
| Customer ethnicity | White Americans, Europeans, and Asian Arabs | Asians, blacks, and Hispanics | Clary, 1999<br>Lynn, 2004; 2006<br>McCall and Lynn, 2009 |
| Customer sex | Men | Women | Crusco and Wetzel, 1984 |
| Customer age | Older customers | Kids and adolescents | Maynard and Mupandawana, 2009<br>McCall and Lynn, 2009 |
| Customer personality | Extravertive customers | Neurotic customers | Lynn, 2009 |

**Source:** The Author

## 10.4 THE NEGATIVE CONSEQUENCES OF TIPPING

Although there are different factors affecting tips in a restaurant such as the quality of service and the type of restaurant, but the customer's attitude and personality control his/ her decision to leave a tip and the waiter's attitude and personality control his/her service performance are considered the source of unpleasant ends of service process.

### *10.4.1 DISCRIMINATION*

Discrimination remains a challenging issue in tourism and hospitality industry, without a doubt, discrimination in restaurants and other accommodation establishments often takes blatant and undeniable forms, and in some cases, has resulted in high profile litigation and multi-million-dollar settlements (Lu-in, 2014). A challenging issue that may arise is the discrimination during service transactions (Brewster and Mallinson, 2009) that tends to rely on "cues and categorizations" in which stereotypes are often used to profile undesirable individuals.

In a restaurant setting, the operation of situational discrimination is prevailing as one of the main unethical issues, "Situational discrimination" describes a paradox of modern-day discrimination. Its emergence is highly dependent on the situation, but it is more likely to occur when racial issues are obscured than when they are apparent. Consequently, discrimination is most likely to occur in situations in which it is least likely to be detected by others, the subject of discrimination, or even the actor himself. Individuals tend to discriminate in situations that are "normatively ambiguous," that is, where right and wrong behavior and actions are not clearly distinguishable, even if they would not do so in situations that are normatively clear (Lu-in, 2014).

Stereotypes can be applied to everyone. They affect employees and customers in the hospitality industry in both negative and positive ways, as follows:

### A. Servers Discriminations by Their Employers

Servers are subject to discrimination by their employers. Employers as different as restaurants have been shown to hire workforces that approximate that of their customers. Jonathan et al. (2009) claimed that some employers are much less likely to hire black men as a response to their customers' preferences who dislike black service providers.

Moreover, the hospitality industry has a history of both gender stratification and gendered service styles, some specific jobs are considered "female-friendly" which is more attractive to women than to men because of the nature of the tasks involved.

In restaurants, waiting on tables has been defined as "typical women's work"; welcoming and serving others is the core of hospitality work and women mostly perform these activities better than male counterparts, thus, such work activities are considered "feminine." Therefore, most jobs that require interacting with customers are assigned to females such as hostesses and waitresses and the cashiers. Such horizontal segregation extended to entail different types of restaurants; positions at some specific restaurants were segregated by gender, with each gender dominating in different types of restaurants and performing slightly different styles of service. Traditionally, men are staffed more in prestigious, upscale restaurants (where, not unexpectedly, wages tend to be much higher) as they are required to perform more formal service and to appear more dignified, while women have tended to work at middle- and low-range "family style" restaurants and coffee shops, where "home-style service promotes a casual, familial form of interaction and is gendered as feminine." Thus, horizontal segregation prevails in the restaurant industry (Lu-in, 2014).

### B. Servers Discriminations by Customers

Some customers tip to show their liking or empathy for the server, implicit biases might lead them to favor members of a particular racial group over others. Because tipping is spontaneous and sensitive to situational factors, customer tipping decision may be susceptible to the influence of racial-based prejudices and stereotypes, which, although invisible, often create negative ends (Lu-in, 2014). The effect of race on customer tipping behavior was confirmed in a study conducted by Lynn and his colleagues as they claimed that "consumers prefer members of their own race across many commercial contexts" (Lynn et al., 2008). They found that tipping behavior of white customers contains a situational ambiguity and implicit negative attitudes toward black servers. Their study revealed that the customers of a restaurant in Mississippi tipped black servers significantly less than white servers (17.5% vs. 20.7% and 14.6% vs. 19.4%, depending on the size of the dining party). The same way, African American customers were also founded to be tipping white servers low, this makes servers undesirable to wait on at their tables (Lynn, 2007; Lynn et al., 2008; Rusche and Brewster, 2008). In a restaurant setting, the race effect would be greater with lower ratings of service quality. Poor service quality may be used as a reason for the customers justifying their racial behaviors with the servers.

### *C. Customers Discriminations by Servers*

Tipping as a normatively ambiguous practice facilitated the reliance of customers and servers on social stereotypes whether consciously or not, during the service transaction. Such social stereotypes became the main feature of the tipped service encounter that can influence its outcome, often without being noticed.

In a restaurant setting, group-based stereotypes developed by service providers about some groups of customers are more than just (frequently inaccurate) generalizations.

According to Lu-in (2014), these inaccurate stereotypes often guide social interactions by directing servers to follow a particular path of performance or behavior and attitudes.

Servers were found to show favoritism to serve customers based on many factors such as the demographic profiles of customers, customer attributes, customer ethnicity, and dining experience's time and duration (Fig. 10.1). For example, based on the demographic profile of customers and ethnicity, servers were found preferring to serve women, elderly adults, and large parties (Harris, 1995; McCall and Lynn, 2009). Additionally, the race has been recognized as one of the factors for servers to show favoritism. White American customers, European and Caucasian customers are perceived as favorable customers by servers (Lynn, 2004). Subsequently, these groups are considered first class, while African Americans, Asians, and Hispanic customers in addition to kids are considered second class.

Once the employee assigned a class to the customer; this now begins a pattern of stereotypes that go along with that certain class. Then, employees direct better service to those customers who fit the pattern of expected large tippers (Harris, 1995). According to Brewster (2013), in a survey of 200 restaurant servers, almost 50% of the respondents confessed to giving poor service to customers that they perceived as bad tippers. Also, about 93% of the servers demonstrated that they give better service to those customers that they perceive to be good tippers.

In some cases, the customer who belongs to the upper class from the servers' point of view may not leave larger tips for the servers, however, servers still confirm with the same stereotype instead of not thinking that the stereotype is true anymore. So, after there is evidence that not all supposed upper class people leave larger than usual tips, an employee may continue to keep the same stereotype to the next one and essentially not learning a lesson. Such negative stereotypes toward some groups of customers that servers think would tip poorly impact significantly on their service delivery process. When servers keep developing favoritism to serve particular customers, avoiding less favorable customers can hinder servers' performance. The service providers would create "symbolic boundaries" between themselves and specific groups of customers according to their perceptions of these groups' tipping behavior and in turn implement "control moves" to add or reduce the value to the service to justify their stereotypes about such customers (Mallinson and Brewster, 2005).

Fernandez (2004) claimed that discrimination toward certain groups of people by servers is problematic for managers in many ways. Guests who get poor service as a result of their nationality, ethnicity or gender are probably going to spread negative word of mouth and unlikely to be repeat customers.

According to Figure 10.1, the structure and features of tipped service transactions promote employees' reliance on characteristics of customer groups (attributes, demographic profiles, ethnicity, and moods) and their dining experience (time and duration). Service providers consider stimulating the customer to leave good tips his target. Therefore, the server uses his position advantage to assess the customer groups for only determining the number of efforts he/she will put into during the service transaction. The circumstances of the transaction add more to the power of customers especially the existence of the limitations placed on employees' behavior by the standard script for their encounter, and the lack of time, attention, and motivation enhance the influence of stereotypes that the servers hold about the customers.

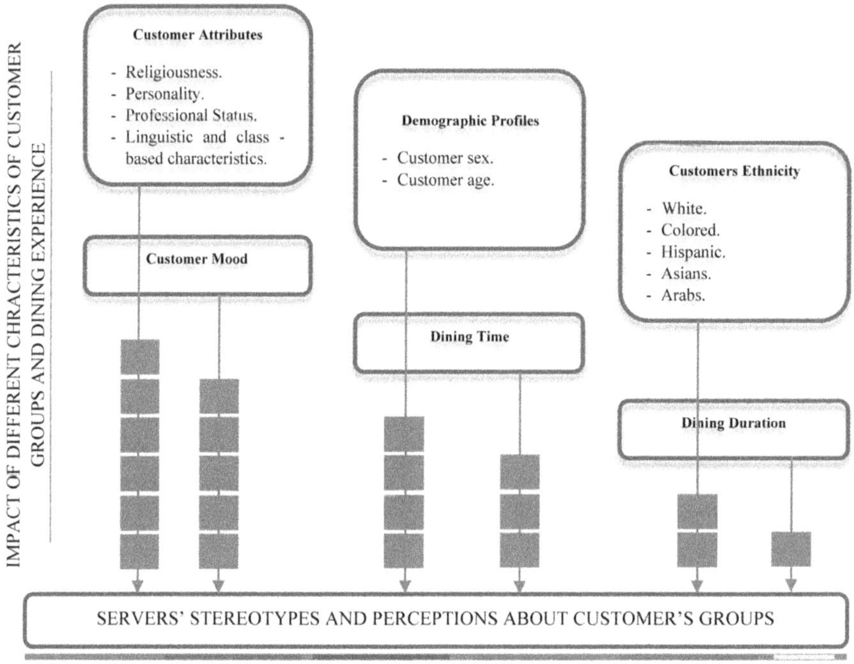


**FIGURE 10.1 (See color insert.)** Server stereotypes about customer tipping behavior.
**Source:** The Author.

Such perception of servers regarding some groups of customers' low tipping behavior can create various problems including recruiting and retaining employees at the restaurants where a majority of customers are from minority groups (Lynn and Thomas-Haysbert, 2003).

## *10.4.2 BEG POSITION*

Tipping practice gives customers so much control over servers' economic well-being, thus, it is no wonder that servers fixate on the tip in every service encounter they participate in.

During service transaction, tipping practice provides customers with means of rewarding those servers who are showing stereotype or behavior consistent with customers' preferences. Subsequently, these preferences force servers to follow or display certain types of behavior and attitude that put them in entreating position, so they may appear as if they in a beg position.

Perhaps not surprisingly, tipping behavior also varies with the mood of the customer and whether circumstances put the customer in a more positive frame of mind generally. In this case, servers would find themselves tell jokes or puzzles to entertain customers or extravagantly complimenting the customer's appearance or choice of hairstyle or touching the customers briefly on the arm or shoulder in order to change the customer's mode into better. Accordingly, the imbalance between the two parties puts the server in a vulnerable position. It is not uncommon for servers to view customers as a source of the threat. In a study entitled "vulnerability work attitude" conducted by Butler and Skipper on restaurant servers, they found that servers have a high level of insecurity to the degree that made them describe their work as "Working for tips is like gambling, there is always a risk involved" (1980). Their fear of not getting a tip from the customers shaped significantly their relationship with the customers, where the customer got the function of assessing and rewarding the service providers. In this situation, the customer is better positioned to assess service quality and provide incentives to the server (Azar, 2004), as is common, the tip is given after the service is provided, makes the relationship between server and customer similar to that of creditor and debtor (Davis et al., 1998).

A good server needs to push the right buttons in order to seduce a customer (Dublanica, 2009), servers try to manage the service transaction by drawing on a wide collection of relationship-enhancing tactics calculated to maximize the tip. In fact, and in addition to ensuring the objective indicators of service quality, the servers may use small, friendly attitudes, and gestures to build a social and emotional connection with the customer in order to get the desired amount of tip.

According to McCall and Lynn (2009), numerous research studies have shown the significant influence of such attitudes, some of which have been found to increase tips by an average of 20%, and some by as much as 40% or more.

Engaging in socially "immediate" behaviors is another way to elicit higher tips such as briefly touching the customer on the shoulder or hand, standing close to the customer, or squatting next to the table so that the server's eyes are in line with the customers (Crusco and Wetzel in Lu-in Wang, 2014).

Entertaining customers also brings bigger tips. As noted above, studies have found that customers tip more generously when they feel having a full power and enjoying a vantage position over others.

### *10.4.3 HIGH-STRESS WORK ENVIRONMENT*

Tipping practice is considered a great system for the restaurant industry because it enables the employer to cut the labor costs down by paying less than the minimum wage. But it contributes to increasing the load over the service workforce who toils in restaurants industry. In fact, servers are nearly three times as likely as other workers to experience poverty. In addition, tips are considered an uncertain benefit and vary from both customers and servers. Consequently, this puts high stress on servers resulting from their anxiety of not getting the amount of tip that compensates their low wages.

Servers seek many and hard ways to increase both the predictability of the outcome of the service interaction and their control over that outcome to reducing their vulnerable position. Service employees may play three roles during their employment in order to accomplish their task perfectly; (1) super employee, (2) expert, and (3) manager.

- As an employee, he/she first need to establish a very tight relationship with his/ her manager and also co-workers. Servers follow what the researcher has called a "crafty strategy," by which employees with special convincing and impressive communication skills can achieve their aims by indirect or deceitful methods.
  - ✓ With his/her co-workers: Servers regarded being assigned to wait on black customers as "punishment" that they tried to avoid, so, they can use their ways to convince the hostess not to assign them tables with black customers, and giving the hostess "eyes" and whispering "Not in my section. Not in my section." when she seated black customers. Sometimes fellow servers would attempt to "make deals" or "swap tables" to get out of waiting on black customers (Lu-in Wang, 2014).
  - ✓ With his/her manager: Where any restaurant, there are some sections that have the advantages of whether they are in a good location indoor or outdoor or sections that exceed other sections in seat numbers, thus, servers try also to get this such of sections by keeping a vigorous relationship with their manager.

- They may act as experts of service encounter interaction, as experts, servers predict the tip they are likely to receive from specific types of groups based on their experience of dealing with different types of customers from various races and cultural backgrounds with multi-types of dining customs and traditions.

This presumed ability allows servers to engage in "credit selection" to distinguish good credit risks from bad, which enables them to manage their expectations and determine how to approach a given customer (Butler and Kipper in Lu-in Wang, 2014) relying on their stereotypes about customers. Stereotypes about customers' tipping practices often accompany expectations about other aspects of customer behavior, such as whether customers will be difficult and demanding or easygoing and kind (Brewster and Rusche, 2012).

Generally, those who are predicted to be poor tippers are also expected to be bad customers. Bad or difficult customers not only require excessive efforts to serve them but also thereby reducing the relative payoff for the server, in addition they also impede the server's ability to attend to other customers and to quickly "turn" the table to increase the number of customers served and tips received (Brewster, 2013). Generally, over time, servers develop a "kind of specialization" on which they rely to draw these distinctions and expectations.

- If the encounter proceeds, servers can draw upon their "expert" evaluations through a third role, as "manager" of the encounter.

As managers, servers seek to control the reward structure that governs their work and affect their lives. That is, they strive to maximize their returns through their tactics, or efforts. Workers who depend on tips for a high percentage of their income "are in a sense private entrepreneur" (Lu-in Wang, 2014). However, according to Kwortnik et al. (2009), the majority of restaurants servers believe their rewards are highly affected by the quality of service they deliver, and that this belief, in turn, affects their delivery of service. Generally, servers attempt to reduce their economic uncertainty within the "patron/server interaction" in many ways. Managing the focal point of service transaction—the tipping point from the servers' point of view requires the servers to get the jump on customers by engaging in manipulative maneuvers or tactics in order to reduce their reward uncertainty.

### 10.4.4 REINFORCING SELF-FULFILLING ACTIONS

Tipping weakens the service worker's commitment to an organization and switches it to self-commitment, by promoting self-serving behaviors in the workplace (Lynn et al., 1993).

Such type of commitment imposes the servers calibrating their efforts according to their expectation of tipping; in other words, a server may provide good service and more attention for those customers who seem to tip good, while limiting the time and effort he/ she spends with tip poorly customer. According to Lu-in (2014), servers follow what the researchers have called a "self-fulfilling prophecy" strategy, in which servers make extensive efforts in serving customers if they only predicted large tip, in case of predicting a small amount of tip, service efforts will decrease significantly.

Thus, a restaurant customer who is expected to tip well will enjoy frequent dining experience from the server, asking whether she is enjoying the food or needs anything more, while customers who are expected to tip poorly "just don't get the service" (Erickson, 2004). This self-fulfilling process is not inevitable, of course. Some employees may be less influenced by stereotypes, some employees may be more aware of and resistant to their influence, and in some cases, other influences, including the parties' particular goals, might push the parties' attitudes and behaviors in other directions (Lu-in, 2014).

Therefore, the practice of tipping restaurant employees is under attack. The literature on tipping supports the idea that where tipping occurs employees have less satisfaction and commitment to the organization. Commitment is valued because it is thought to increase staff performance, improving service quality and productivity and reducing labor turnover (Paxson, 1994).

### 10.4.5 NEGATIVE EMOTIONAL AND PSYCHIC SEQUENCES

Tipping is a strange, self-defeating phenomenon. Unfortunately, tipping practices put the service employees between the hammer of employer and the anvil of the customer:

- Managers exploited the existing of tipping by lowering the wages of restaurant employees that influenced their lives negatively and made them to exert more efforts during their maneuvers with customers.
- The tip itself is emblematic of the inequality in entitlement and power between the customer and the servers, and it can affect largely not

just on the server's economic well-being, but also on his emotional state and sense of self-worth.

Getting a great tip may be a cause for celebration and a boost to the server's ego. On the other hand, being tipped ineffectively may have outsized negative impacts. Dublanica, for the case, has depicted the emotional pain and humiliation the server feels when the client denies leaving the tip as a sting; this because the client stamped the server as "not worth" the standard tip that was automatically included to the check (2009).

Being "stiffed" is worst of all. It is both a humiliation and a reminder of the server's vulnerability: "It might be noted that "getting stiffed" is rarely an event that is shared with other servers. It is not a source of prestige for the server, rather it is an indicator of the employee' inability to control the work situation" (Lu-in, 2014). This caused many service providers to break down in tears after being stiffed, "the financial consequences of not being tipped suck, but there is an emotional and psychic toll as well. Not getting a tip hurts" (Dublanica, 2009).

### *10.4.6 PROMOTING JEALOUSY AND FRICTION AMONG EMPLOYEES*

Tipping practice is influenced by prejudice. Studies have shown that female servers get tip more than males, pretty women make more than other women, and that whites make more than blacks (Willen, 2015). Thus, tipping is inequitable—effort and skill that are not necessarily matched by the reward.

These preferences have enough power to create a work environment full of envy, jealousy, and animosity.

Subminimum wage rates for tipped workers "enshrine" segregation against women and the gender pay gap, since so many servers are female. Aside from a common societal preference for physically attractive women, one clarification for why better-looking servers get higher tips than less attractive female servers appears to be the way in which male customers, in specific, react. Consistent with the above notion, researchers have found customer responds to some waitress groups more than others when they are:

- ✓ Younger women more than older women (Jackson, 1992),
- ✓ Women with attractive body than those with either small or extremely large bodies (Tantleff-Dunn, 2002),
- ✓ Blonds are perceived descent as more attractive (Miller, 2006).

- ✓ The servers wore facial cosmetics are more attractive and tipped significantly more than others (Guéguen and Jacob, 2011),
- ✓ Female servers are considered more attractive when they wear red t-shirts are than when they wear other colors (Guéguen and Jacob, 2012).

These findings indicate that male customers favor female servers whose appearance coincides with stereotypical gender preferences. This action promotes jealousy among servers. In addition, tip pooling and sharing system were found to promote friction among employees, as following (Casey, 1998):

- Between highly tipped and poor tipped staff: Good employees may feel they are supporting slack workers and these poor performers are rewarded for their lack of effort.
- Between tipped and non-tipped staff: Back-of-house employees report extreme dissatisfaction when big tips are flaunted in front of them for those who are working in front-of-house jobs.

Jealousy and frictions generate conflicts among the employees that definitely will lead to dysfunctional behavior such as low employee performance, cheating and pilferage, high staff turnover, absenteeism, and tip solicitation (Crick, 1991) that result in substantial hidden costs.

## *10.4.7 LABOR SHORTAGE IN SOME POSITIONS*

Tipped employees may not wish to be promoted to other positions if it is managerial positions and have few intentions to gain training and qualifications in the industry because positions of responsibility do not attract tips. Tipping system may be responsible for labor shrinking in some positions in hospitality establishment, any position that has a little or no direct contact with the customer lack the tipping practices advantages whether it is a managerial position or back of the house position.

Managers, in the United States, complain about the difficulty in recruiting back-of-house staff for these reasons and claim "tips and gratuities are the curse of the industry" (Raleigh, 1999, p 70). So discretionary tipping unfairly rewards only some of those who have a direct contact and responsible for guests' overall fulfillment, and pooling tips may not solve these issues if employees have a preference for this practice.

There are many voices call for abolishing tipping practices, many servers advocated that tipping is an ineffective form of compensation, as well as a form of oppression by restaurant owners and customers. For example, McKenzie (2016) claimed that tipping practice has no redeeming economic justification in the restaurant industry, with the possible exception of upscale restaurants.

Service managers must not count on tipping to motivate staff to provide good service, instead they must work for replacing it with a higher minimum hourly wage or a so-called living wage, generally described as the wage rate required to lift the living standards of a household or family with only one worker above the poverty line (McKenzie, 2016) in order to retain their skilled employees and maintain their high performance.

Ensuring living wages for the employees avoid the establishment the conflicts that may occur in the work environment and fluctuate work performance that may result in decreasing the business profitability. Raising the wages not only benefits the employees but also the organization and its customers, as follows:

### A. *For the Employee*

The leisure and hospitality industry currently have 19% of workers with hourly wages at or below the poverty level, which is higher than any other industry (Carpenter, 2016). A raise in the wage would greatly impact employees in the hospitality industry.

One of the greatest positive impacts on employees is the increase in standard of living. This is very concerning for those who have families to support and several bills to pay. According to Carpenter (2016), fair wages change both social life and work life of the employee for the following reasons:

- Fair wages would not only reduce poverty but also help to reduce income inequality. Increasing the minimum wage would put money back into the pockets of low-wage employees so that they could afford the goods and services necessary to have a positive quality of life. Raising wages at the bottom is both a fair and popular solution to fixing income inequality. Income inequality is said to cause major problems such as power differences, which can lead to corruptive performance and weak democracies.
- Another advantage to increasing the minimum wage is that it increases the level of training as well as boosts employees' morale and increases their commitment and enhances their performance.

### B. *For the Organization*

Not only does the increase in the wage affect employees but it also affects the organizations themselves. There are a few advantages of the wage hike in the hospitality industry. One of these advantages is job retention and how reduced turnover can help balance increased wage costs. Cost associated with labor turnover is very high (Heath, 2014) whether it is direct or indirect cost (Chapter 7, Effects of labor turnover). Increase in wages maintains the skilled and competent labor of the organization, as they represent the valuable asset of the business.

### C. *For the Customer*

The increased wage will not only affect employees and the organizations in the hospitality industry but also consumers. Supporters of the minimum wage believe that it will cause an economic stimulus. One study in Illinois found that raising the minimum wage to $10.65 across 4 years would bring in an additional $3.8 billion directly to families who spend the money on tipping to get extra goods and services of their choice (Hall and Gable, 2012).

Another advantage to consumers as a result of the minimum wage increase would be the improved quality of goods and services in the hospitality industry. Since so many organizations would be forced to pay higher labor costs, it makes sense that they would hire highly skilled employees who are focusing more on their products and services to increase their market share that they have.

## REFERENCES

Armstrong, M. *Handbook of Reward Management Practice: Improving Performance through Reward*, 4th ed.; Kogan Page Limited: London, 2012.

Austin, W.; Walster, E. Participant's Reactions to Equity with the World. *J. Exp. Soc. Psychol.* **1974,** *10*, 528–548.

Azar, H. O. Incentives and Service Quality in the Restaurant Industry: the Tipping-service Puzzle. *Appl. Econ.* **2009,** *41* (15), 1917–1927.

Azar, O. The History of Tipping from Sixteenth-Century England to United States in the 1910s. *J. Socio-Econ.* **2004,** *33* (6), 745–764.

Azar, O. The Implications of Tipping for Economic and Management. *Int. J. Socio-Econ.* **2003,** *30* (10), 1084–1094.

Azar, O. Why Pay Extra? Tipping and the Importance of Social Norms and Feelings in Economic Theory. *J. Socio-Econ.* **2007,** *36*, 250–255.

Azar, O. H.; Yossi, T. Behavioral Economics and Decision Making: Applying Insights from Psychology to Understand How People Make Economic Decisions. *J. Econ. Psychol.* **2008,** *29* (5), 613–618.

Barkan, R. Testing Servers' Role as Experts and Managers of Tipping Behavior. *Serv. Ind. J.* **2004,** *24* (6), 91–108.
Brewster, W. Z. The Effects of Restaurant Servers' Perceptions of Customers' Tipping Behaviors on Service Discrimination. *Int. J. Hosp. Manag.* **2013,** *32*, 228–236.
Brewster, W.; Mallinson, C. Racial Differences in Restaurant Tipping: A Labor Process Perspective. *Serv. Ind. J.* **2009,** *29* (8), 1053–1075.
Brewster, Z. W.; Rusche, S. N. Quantitative Evidence of the Continuing Significance of Race: Tableside Racism in Full-Service Restaurants. *J. Black Stud.* **2012,** *43* (4), 359–384.
Butler, S.; Kipper, J. Working for Tips: An Examination of Trust and Reciprocity in a Secondary Relationship of the Restaurant Organization. *Sociol. Q. J.* **1981,** 22 (1), 15–27.
Butler, S.; Skipper, J. Waitressing, Vulnerability, and Job Autonomy: The Case of the Risky Tip. *Work Occup.* **1980,** 7 (4), 487–502.
Carpenter, E. The Effects of Raising the Minimum Wage on the Hospitality Industry. *Undergrad. Res. J. Human Sci.* 2016, 13. [Online] http://www.kon.org/urc/v13/carpenter.html (accessed Aug 19, 2017).
Casey, B. Tipping in New Zealand Restaurants. Ph.D. Dissertation, University of Otago, Dunedin, New Zealand, 1998.
Clary, M. *Unusual Dinner Tab Brings Outcry Over Stigma of 'Dining While Black'*; Times: Los Angeles, 1999; p 33.
Crick, A. The Influence of the Tip System in the Hospitality Industry: A Pilot Study. *Caribb. Finance Manag.* **1991,** *7*, 19–30.
Crusco, A. H.; Wetzel, C. G. (1984). The Midas touch: The Effects of Interpersonal Touch on Restaurant Tipping. *Personal. Soc. Psychol. Bull.* **1984,** *10*, 512–517.
Davis, S.; Schrader, B.; Richardson, T.; Kring, J.; Kieffer, J. Restaurant Servers Influence Tipping Behavior. *SAGE J.* **1998,** *83* (1), 223–226.
Dublanica, S. Waiter Want: Thanks for The Tip – Confessions of A Cynical Waiter, 2009, pp 109–110.
Erickson, K. To Invest or Detach? Coping Strategies and Workplace Culture in Service Work. *Symbolic Interact.* **2004,** *27* (4), 549–572.
Fernandez, G. A. The Tipping Point Gratuities, Culture, and Politics. *Cornell Hotel Restaur. Administr. Quart.* **2004,** *45* (1), pp 48–51.
Ghiselli, R. F.; Lalopa, J. M.; Bai, B. Job Satisfaction, Life Satisfaction, and Turnover Intent. *Cornell Hotel Restaur. Administr. Q.* **2001,** *42* (2), 28–37.
Guéguen, N.; Jacob, C. Clothing Color and Tipping: Gentlemen Patrons Give More Tips to Waitresses with Red Clothes. *J. Hosp. Tour. Res.* **2012,** *20*, 1–4.
Guéguen, N.; Jacob, C. Enhanced Female Attractiveness with Use of Cosmetics and Male Tipping Behavior in Restaurants. *J. Cosmetic Sci.* **2011,** *62*, 283–288.
Guthrie, J. P. Alternate Pay Practices and Employee Turnover: An Organization Economics Perspective. *Group Organ. Manag.* **2000,** *25* (4), 419–439.
Hall, D.; Gable, M. The Benefits of Raising Illinois' Minimum Wage, 2012. [Online] http://www.epi.org/publication/ib321-illinois-minimum-wage/ (accessed Oct 20, 2017).
Harris M. Waiters, Customers, and Service: Some Tips about Tipping. *J. Appl. Soc. Psychol.* **1995,** *25* (8), 725–744
Haven Tang, C.; Jones, E.. Local Leadership for Rural Tourism Development: A Case Study of Adventa, Monmouthshire, UK. *Tour. Manag. Perspect.* 2012, 4, 28–35.

Heath, J. *Effect of Wage on Employment;* 2014. [Online] http://news.cincinnati.com/article/20140126/EDIT01/301260016/Effect-wage-employment (accessed Nov 21, 2017).

Ineson, M. E.; Martin, J. A. Factors Influencing the Tipping Propensity of Restaurant Customers. *J. Retail. Consumer Serv.* **1999,** *6* (1), 27–37.

Jackson, L. A. *Physical Appearance and Gender: Sociobiological and Sociocultural Perspectives*; State University of New York Press: Albany, NY, 1992.

Jonathan S.; Leonard.; David I.; Levine.; Giuliano, L. Customer Discrimination, 2009. [Online] http://moya.bus.miami.edu/~lgiuliano/customer_discrim_apr09.pdf (accessed Dec 5, 2017).

Kline, S.; Hsieh, Y. Wage Differentials in the Lodging Industry: A Case Study. *J. Human Resour. Hosp. Tour.* **2007,** *6* (1), 69–84.

Kwortnik, R.; Lynn, M.; Ross, W. Buyer Monitoring: A Means to Insure Personalized Service, *J. Market. Res.* **2009,** *46* (5), 573–583.

Lee, P.C.; Dewald, B. Tipping Practices of Chinese Tourists in US Restaurants: An Exploratory Study. *J. Tour. Hosp. Manag.* **2016,** *4* (2), 17–34.

Lu-in, W. At the Tipping Point: Race and Gender Discrimination in a Common Economic Transaction. *Va. J. Soc. Policy Law* **2014,** *21* (1), 101–166.

Lynn, M. Determinants and Consequences of Female Attractiveness and Sexiness: Realistic Tests with Restaurant Waitresses. *Arch. Sex. Behav.* **2009,** *38*, 737–745.

Lynn, M. Ethnic Differences in Tipping: A Matter of Familiarity with Tipping Norms. *Cornell Hotel Restaur. Administr. Q.* **2004,** *45*, 12–22.

Lynn, M. Geo-Demographic Differences in Knowledge About the Restaurant Tipping Norm. *J. Appl. Soc. Psychol.* **2006,** *36*, 740–750.

Lynn, M. Race Differences in Restaurant Tipping: A Literature Review and Discussion of Practical Implications. *J. Foodserv. Bus. Res.* **2007,** *9* (4), 99–113.

Lynn, M. Tip Levels and Service: An Update, Extension and Reconciliation. *Cornell Hotel Restaur. Administr. Q.* **2003,** *44*, 139–148.

Lynn, M.; McCall, M. Gratitude and Gratuity: A Meta-Analysis of Research on the Service-Tipping Relationship, 2000. http://scholarship.sha.cornell.edu/articles/152 (accessed Sept 5, 2017).

Lynn, M.; Sturman, M.; Ganley, C.; Adams, E.; Douglas, M.; McNeal, J. Consumer Racial Discrimination in Tipping: A Replication and Extension. *J. Appl. Soc. Psychol.* **2008,** *38* (4), 1045–1060.

Lynn, M.; Thomas-Haysbert, C. Ethnic Differences in Tipping: Evidence, Explanations, and Implications. *J. Appl. Soc. Psychol.* **2003,** *33* (8), 1747–1772.

Mallinson, C.; Brewster, Z. W. 'Blacks and Bubbas': Stereotypes, Ideology, and Categorization Processes in Restaurant Servers' Discourse. *Discourse Soc.* **2005,** *16* (6), 787–807.

Matulewicz, K. Customers, Tips, and Law: Gender and the Precariousness of Work in BC restaurants, 2013. https://www.upf.edu/documents/3298481/3410076/2013-LLRNConf_Matulewicz.pdf/83a2ed5f-4f99 43ac-b625-8c2374a6dac1 (accessed Oct 5, 2017).

Maynard, L. J.; Mupandawana, M. Tipping Behavior in Canadian Restaurants. *Int. J. Hosp. Manag.* **2009,** *28* (4), 597–603.

McCall, M.; Lynn, A. Restaurant Servers' Perceptions of Customer Tipping Intentions. *Int. J. Hosp. Manag.* **2009,** *28*, 594–596.

McCall, M.; Lynn, M. Techniques for Increasing Servers' Tips: How Generalizable Are They? *Cornell Hosp. Q.* **2009,** *198*, 201–207.

McKenzie, R. "Should Tipping be Abolished?", National Center for Policy Analysis, 2016 http://www.ncpa.org/pdfs/st382.pdf (accessed Oct 21, 2017).

Miller, C. Perceived Differences Between Blonde and brunette Females: Intelligence, Promiscuity and Attractiveness. M.Sc. Thesis, University of Northern Colorado, Greely, CO, 2006.

Paxson, M. A Review of the Organizational Commitment Literature as Applied to Hospitality Organizations. In *Progress in Tourism, Recreation and Hospitality Management*; Cooper, C., Lockwood, A., Eds.; John Wiley and Sons: Chichester, 1994; Vol. 5, pp 211–228.

Quek, P. Controlling Labor Costs, 2000. [Online] http://www.hotel online.com/Trends/PKF/Special/LaborCosts_Feb00.html (accessed Oct 3, 2017).

Raleigh, P. Tips and Gratuities Don't have to be the Curse of the Industry. *Nation's Restaurant News*, 1990, 33 (37), 70.

Rusche, S. E.; Brewster, Z. W. 'Because they Tip for Shit!': The Social Psychology of Everyday Racism in Restaurants. *Sociol. Compass* **2008,** *2* (6), 2008–2029.

Tantleff-Dunn, S. Biggest Isn't Always Best: The Effect of Breast Size on Perceptions of Women. *J. Appl. Soc. Psychol.* **2002,** *32*, 2253–2265.

Templeton, D. Is it Service or Custom that Tips the Scales? *Sonoma Indep.* **1996,** 24–30.

United States Department of Labor. Wage and Hour Division (WHD) Minimum Wages for Tipped Employees. [Online] http://www.dol.gov/whd/state/tipped.htm (accessed Oct 3, 2017).

Walster, E.; Berscheid, E.; Walster, G.W. New Directions in Equity Research. *J. Personal. Soc. Psychol.* **1973,** *25*, 151–176.

Whaley, J. E. What's in a Tip? An Exploratory Study of the Motivations Driving Consumer Tipping Behavior. Ph.D. Dissertation, Auburn University, United States, Alabama, 2011.

Willen, M. Why Tipping Is Unethical, 2015. [Online] https://talkingethics.com/2015/01/04/why-tipping-is unethical/ (Sep 28, 2017).

CHAPTER 11

# WORKFORCE DIVERSITY IN THE TOURISM AND HOSPITALITY INDUSTRY

*"Diversity means integration. If it is well managed, it will mean strength."*

## 11.1 INTRODUCTION

With increasing globalization and migration, managing diversity in organizations is becoming more and more important. There is a necessary need to actively deal with diversity in organizations and to determine advantages and disadvantages for various organizations (Dietz and Petersen, 2006; Kochan et al., 2003; McKay et al., 2009; Podsiadlowski et al., 2013). Its origin is complex and related to the social, economic, and political forces that have and continue to occur across the world (Phillips, 2012). The notion of workforce diversity originated in the US-based organizational literature because, having defined itself early as country of immigrants, the United States had to contend with diversity from its beginning (Barak, 2014). In the scientific literature, diversity started receiving attention in the 1990s (Nishii and Mayer, 2009). Beziibwe (2015) said that the origin of workforce diversity was influenced by the foundation of workforce diversity initiatives in the early days of the industrial revolution.

In recent years, the growing diverse work force in organizations has led scholars to boost increased attention to the issue of workforce diversity (Gupta, 2013). Workforce diversity reminds that people differ in many ways, visible or invisible, mainly age, gender, marital status, social status, disability, sexual orientation, religion, personality, ethnicity, and culture (Shen et al., 2009). Visible diversity refers to characteristics that are observable or easily detectable attributes such as race, gender, or physical disability, and invisible diversity refers to underlying attributes such as religion, education, and tenure with the organization (Barak, 2014, p 132). Diversity is considered as one of the few tools of business management that combines financial performance and social ethics (Nadine, 2017). Workplace (also called workforce) diversity can be characterized as an organization, in which employees possess distinct elements and qualities, differing from one another. "These different elements include employees' beliefs, values, and actions that vary by gender, ethnicity, age, lifestyle, and physical abilities. Managing these elements can create an old way of staffing-related problems that are the focus for human resource departments" (Foma, 2013, p 402). *"Workforce diversity seeks to assess the diversity of all persons in the work environment, including but not limited to, employees, customers, business partners, and consultants"* (Mattews, 2016, p 163).

The increasing diversity of both tourists and workers in the tourism industry has led to a necessity need for those people in the sector to have skills to manage this diversity (Feighery, 2012), so managing diversity becomes one of the most important factors in achieve organization competitiveness (Rahmawati, 2012). Hospitality and tourism industry presents a unique opportunity to understand new cultural experiences for both workers and the tourists. It is important for the personnel to understand and appreciate different cultures to enhance their interactions with tourists of different cultures, religions, races, creeds, colors, ages, genders, and sexual orientations.

For this reason, organizations that are plying their trade in this industry must attempt to train their personnel to appreciate and accommodate people from diverse backgrounds around the world. As such, workplace diversity not only facilitates clear understanding of different cultural, social, and economic perspectives, but also enhances the delivery of adequate services through good communication and observation (Merchant, 2017). Diversity requires a type of organizational culture in which each employee can endeavor his or her career aspirations without being stopped by gender, race, nationality, religion, or other factors that are irrelevant to performance (Bryan, 1999). Many organizations are finding that diversity can be a source of competitive advantage in the marketplace, in addition to the fact that hiring and promoting in such a way as to enhance diversity is simply the right thing to do. Organizations with a diverse workforce are also able to understand different market segments better that are less diverse organizations. Organizations with diverse workforces are generally more creative and innovative than other organizations (Griffin, 2007).

The organization should create such a working environment that will improve the motivation, satisfaction, and obligation of diverse people.

Performance criteria must be clearly and objectively established, effectively communicated, and used on objective criteria without any bias. Identify desirable and undesirable behaviors that must be based on performance feedback discussions involving a diverse workforce (Henry and Evans, 2007).

Diversity could be considered as a source of strength to the organizations, while others concluded that diversity could be considered as a source of weakness (Shaban, 2016). Hiring employees from various backgrounds and experiences in tourism and hospitality industry may cause a positive or negative impact on organizational performance and productivity, so this study tries to identify the benefits and challenges that may face the organizations.

## 11.2 DEFINITION OF DIVERSITY AND WORKFORCE DIVERSITY

Diversity has been a corporate buzzword for many years (Hankin, 2005). There is no general definition of diversity, so there are many ways to define diversity. Diversity is a complex, multidimensional concept. It is a plural term with different perceptions in different organizations (Mwinami, 2014). Workforce diversity has become an important issue in today's companies, as they are becoming increasingly diverse with respect to their workforce (Rao and Bagali, 2013). *"Diversity" is not a synonym for the equal employment opportunity, nor is it another word for affirmative action, though either or both of those may aid diversity. Instead, diversity refers to the vast array of physical and cultural differences that constitute the spectrum of human differences"* (Hunsaker and Alessandra, 2008, p 82).

There are many definitions of diversity:

- According to Cummings and Worley (2009), Diversity can be defined as the ways that people are similar or different. Diversity also refers to the mix of gender, age, disability, cultures, ethnic backgrounds, and lifestyles that describe an organization's workforce and potential labor pool. And workforce diversity defined as an approach to include and support diverse persons in all the organizational positions by using diversity and inclusion activities (Sims, 2016).
- Diversity is the coexistence of employees from different sociocultural backgrounds within the company. Diversity includes cultural factors such as race, gender, age, color, physical ability, ethnicity, etc. The broader definition of diversity may include age, national origin, religion, disability, sexual orientation, values, ethnic culture, education,

language, lifestyle, beliefs, physical appearance, and economic status (Ande, 2014).

- Diversity also can be defined as the "acknowledgement, understanding, accepting, valuing, and celebrating differences among people with respect to age, class, ethnicity, gender, physical and mental ability, race, sexual orientation, spiritual practice, and public assistance status" (Wambui et al., 2013).
- *"Diversity represents the multitude of individual differences and similarities that exist among people."* This definition underscores three important issues about managing diversity (Abrahams and Ruiters, 2008, p 328):

  ✓ *There are many different dimensions or components of diversity. This implies that diversity pertains to everybody. It is not an issue of age, race, or gender. It is not an issue of being heterosexual, gay, or lesbian. Diversity pertains to the host of individual differences that make all of us unique and different from others.*

  ✓ *Diversity is not a synonymous with differences. Rather, it encompasses both differences and similarities. This means that managing diversity means that managing diversity entails dealing with both simultaneously.*

  ✓ *Diversity includes the collective mixture of differences and similarities, not just pieces of it. Dealing with diversity requires managers to integrate the collective mixture of differences and similarities that exists within organizations.*

- Workforce diversity means a workforce made up of people with different human skills or who belong to various cultural groups. From the perspective of individuals, diversity refers to all the ways, in which people differ, including dimensions such as age, race, marital status, physical ability, income level, and lifestyle (Daft and Lane, 2016).

  Workforce diversity is a complicated phenomenon to manage in an organization (Henry and Evans, 2007).
- Diversity can be divided into demographic diversity, organizational diversity, and sociocognitive diversity (Chin and Park, 2013):

  ✓ Demographic diversity such as age, gender, ethnicity, and nationality. These are readily detectable attributes that can be easily characterized individuals.

  - ✓ Organizational diversity: Diversity also involves the organizational context that adds to the diverse perspectives of the group dynamism such as occupation and functions of the workers, seniority in the company, and hierarchical ranking within the organization.
  - ✓ Socio-cognitive diversity includes cultural and religious values, beliefs, knowledge level, and personality characteristics.

- Workforce diversity can also be defined as *"the division of the workforce into distinction categories that (a) have a perceived commonality within a given cultural or national context, and that impact potentially harmful or beneficial employment outcomes such as job opportunities, treatment in the workplace, and promotion prospects—irrespective of job—related skills and qualifications"* (Ozbilgin et al., 2015, p 3).

## 11.3 FACTORS FOR THE RISE OF WORKFORCE DIVERSITY

Immigration, the increase in global organizations, and the increasing number of women entering the organizational workforce have led to greater and greater workplace diversity. These factors may cause the workforce diversity. These factors include:

- Globalization: It has transformed society, economics, and politics, greatly influencing demographics within the workplace. Not only are today's workers more diverse (Johnson, 2017), but many organizations came under the pressure of new competitors and they had to work with new types of consumers and different human resources; they were unready to face the diversity both within their branches and in their markets (Mwinami, 2014).
- Migration: Its flows are just one of the main factors contributing to population and workforce diversity. Many young people traveled from developing countries to developed countries for looking a job, this caused more diverse employees, for example, USA's workers from many countries such as Asia, Arica, Europe, etc.
- Women's work: Today's women have a good opportunity to become well educated and have a good position, so the workplace has changed and becomes more diverse.
- Aging population.

- Political diversity.
- Status diversity.

Figure 11.1 indicates the factors that cause diversity.

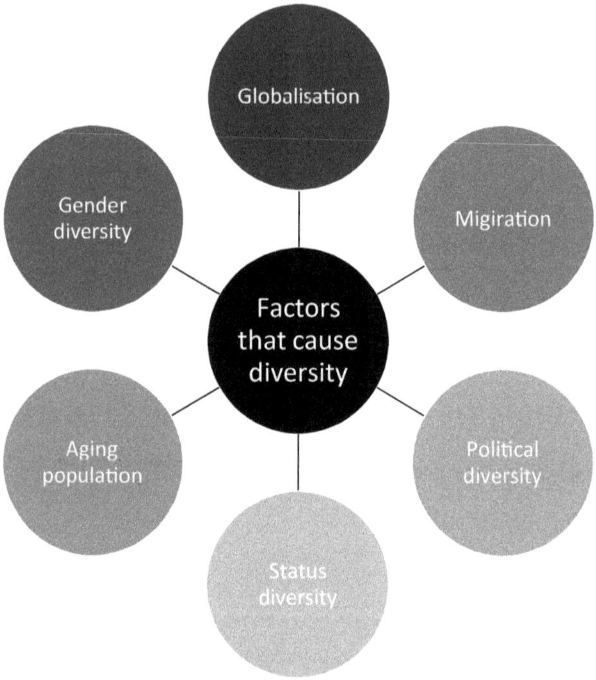


**FIGURE 11.1** The causes of diversity.

**Source:** The Author.

## 11.4 CATEGORIES OF DIVERSITY

Diversity can be categorized as follows:

1. Bal and Bozkurt (2014) have described workforce diversity using the following dimensions: social category diversity, informational diversity, and value diversity. Social category diversity is illustrated as differences in demographic characteristics such as age and race. Informational diversity refers to the diversity of backgrounds such as

knowledge, education, experience, tenure, and functional backgrounds. Value diversity involves differences in personality and behaviors.

2. There are three categories of diversity can be identified in organizational settings, namely (Carelse, 2013, p 15):
   - functional diversity, which refers to differences based on organizational uses and tasks,
   - business diversity, which refers to products and services offered, and
   - workforce diversity, which implies different types of employees with a different type of attributes. At a minimum, these attributes would be:
     - occupational diversity, which includes ranges of jobs related to the organizational mission,
     - professional diversity, which refers to the training issues and the certification required for job performance, and
     - social diversity, which could include differences and characteristics that identify the social identity of a person, such as gender, race, ethnicity, religion, sexual orientation, physical ability, family, economic, educational, and geographic backgrounds and status.

3. Mwinami (2014) also categorizes diversity in four levels:
   - diversity as racial/ethnic/sexual balance,
   - diversity as understanding other cultures,
   - diversity as culturally divergent values, and
   - diversity as broadly inclusive (cultural, subcultural, and individual).

4. Nelson and Quick (2013, p 333) put another classification of diversity:
   - Surface level:
     - Social category differences: race, ethnicity, gender, age, religion, sexual orientation, and physical abilities.
   - Deep level:
     - Differences in knowledge or skills: education, functional knowledge, information or expertise, training, experience, and qualities.
     - Differences in values or beliefs: cultural settings and ideological beliefs.
     - Personality differences: cognitive style, affective disposition, and motivational factors.

   - Organizational/community status differences: tenure or length of service and title (work function, seniority, discipline, etc.).
   - Differences in social and network ties: work-related ties, friendship ties, community ties, and in-group memberships.
5. According to another categorization, diversity is divided into employee differences in terms of three categories. The categories include demographic, organizational, and sociocognitive diversity. The first category is demographic diversity such as age, gender, ethnicity, and nationality. The second category is organizational diversity. It is important to note that workforce diversity is not limited to the physical or social attributes of the organizational context that adds to the diverse perspective of the group dynamism.

Organizational diversity may include the occupation, functional, or job files of the workers such as marketing. The last category, sociocognitive diversity, involves cultural and religious values, beliefs, knowledge level, and personality characteristics (Bal and Bozkurt, 2014). Table 11.1 summarizes the categorization of diversity.

There are many types of workplace diversity as listed below (Wambui et al., 2013):

- **Age:** Brown (2008) stated that increased diversity may also provide many challenges for human resource management; as the workforce ages, for example, employers will have to struggle with higher healthcare costs and pension contributions. Employees will need to accept that benefits are in sync with the vision of the organization; consequently, their responsibility will increase basically.

Robbins et al. (2009) argued that the relationship between age and job performance is likely to be an issue of increasing importance during the next decade for at least three reasons, namely: (1) the common belief that job performance declines with increasing age; (2) the workforce is aging, hence the employees are either forced to work longer because of financial reason or they choose to work longer because they live longer and healthier lives; and (3) a worldwide shortage of highly skilled staff forces companies to re-employ older people. Age diversity can have both advantages and disadvantages for the organizations. Some of age diversity disadvantages and advantages are (Saxena, 2014):

**TABLE 11.1** Diversity Categorization.

| **Summarization of categorization of diversity** | |
|---|---|
| **First categorization** | – Social category diversity<br>– Informational diversity<br>– Value diversity |
| **Second categorization** | – Functional diversity<br>– Business diversity |
| **Third categorization** | Diversity as racial/ethnic/sexual balance<br>Diversity as understanding other cultures<br>Diversity as culturally divergent values<br>Diversity as broadly inclusive (cultural, subcultural, and individual) |
| **Fourth categorization** | **Surface level:**<br>Social category differences: race, ethnicity, gender, age, religion, sexual orientation, and physical abilities<br>**Deep level:**<br>Differences in knowledge or skills: education, functional knowledge, information or expertise, training, experience, and abilities<br>Differences in values or beliefs: cultural background and ideological beliefs<br>Personality differences: cognitive style, affective disposition, and motivational factors<br>Organizational/community status differences: tenure or length of service, title (work function, seniority, discipline, etc.)<br>Differences in social and network ties: work-related ties, friendship ties, community ties, and in-group memberships |
| **Fifth categorization** | **Demographic diversity:** such as age, gender, ethnicity, and nationality<br>**Organizational diversity:** includes the occupation, functional, or job portfolios of the employees such as marketing<br>**Socio-cognitive diversity:** includes cultural and religious values, beliefs, knowledge level, and personality characteristics |

**Source:** The Author.

**Age diversity disadvantages:**

- Conflict: When managers fail to manage generational gaps amongst workers, conflicts are likely to evolve and consequently reducing the productivity of workers.

- Communication problems: An increasing age heterogeneity may result in poor communication, less interaction, and reduced employee performance because of differing values and preferences.

**Age diversity advantages:**

- An age heterogeneous workforce yields a host of multiple skills, cultured styles, morals, and preferences that may cause increased productivity.
- The perceptions, cognitive models, and interpretations of an age-diverse workforce are various and, consequently, if brought together may result in a larger pool of knowledge, a larger problem-solving toolbox and increased employee performance.

❖ **Gender:** Genders are defined as a range of differences between man and women, extending from a biological to the social constructionism. Abbas and Hameed (2010) suggest that there are following three dimensions of gender discrimination: gender discrimination in hiring, gender discrimination in promotion, and gender discrimination in the provision of goods and facilities. Organizations prefer to hire male workers compared with women because they are perceived to have better performance and ability to manage their tasks.

The significant amount of workforce diversity remains ineffective if gender issues are not first known and managed well. According to Abbas and Hameed (2010), females do not have an upper hand when it comes to hiring compared with men. There is also women discrimination in supervisor salary or getting a promotion. A female supervisor who replaces male supervisor gets a lower salary level. Other than that, it shows that gender discrimination affects employee's performance as well as organizations productivity. Failure of communication among different gender may lead to negative performance in an organization (Elsaid, 2012). According to Morna (2004), gender is the notion that seeks to recognize the importance of women in this male-dominated world by bringing them into the mainstream participation in all fields of the public. It also analyzes women, not as submits but equal partners in contributing toward women's representation in decision-making processes and supporting the democratic principals in this changing world. It is further stated that gender refers to the social roles allocated respectively to women and men societies at particular times. Such roles and the differences between them are conditioned by a variety of political, economic, ideological, and cultural factors and are characterized in most societies by incommensurate power relations.

**Race and ethnicity:** Ethnicity can be used as a substitute for cultural background and diversity in ethnicity can be expected to be positive for innovative performance, since it expands the viewpoints and perspectives in the firm. Ethnicity might be positively associated with innovation; a high degree of diversity in ethnicity might be negative since it can create conflict and groups due to social categorization (Kyalo and Gachunga, 2015).

Most people across the globe do identify themselves according to an ethnic group. The race has been studied broadly in organizational behavior, particularly as it relates to employment outcomes such as personnel selection, performance evaluations, pay, and workplace discrimination. Some points around race research are discussed (Robbins, 2009) as follows:

- In employment positions, there is a flair for individuals to prejudice colleagues of their own race in performance evaluations, promoting decisions, and pay raises.
- Employers who use mental ability tests for selection, promoting, training, and similar personnel decisions are concerned that these tests results may be racially unfair.
- The opportunity of inherent genetic group differences in cognitive ability is a contentious issue, and different views in this regard will certainly continue to be discussed.

❖ **Educational diversity:** Tracy and David (2011) found that employers usually reject hiring employees whose training, experience, or education is judged to be employed. On the other hand, this meant that education is very important to workers. Most organizations implement educational diversity initiatives to motivate and encourage employees to work effectively with others so that organizational targets are achieved (Jomo and Jomo, 2015). An employee will be more productive and innovative depending on the level of their education (Daniel, 2009). An employee's educational background can be a significant indicator of their knowledge, skills, and capability (Jomo and Jomo, 2015). Educational diversity can negatively influence decision-making consensus in top management teams thereby resulting in poor performance. Furthermore, educational diversity tends to increase the level of inconvenience and conflict that may lead to decreased social communication and performance in teams (Zhuwao, 2017).

❖ **Physical ability/disability:** According to Bendix (2010), people with disabilities are defined as people who have long-term or recurring physical or mental weakness, which basically limits their prospects of entry into or advancement in employment. Common disabilities involve limited hearing or sight, limited mobility and mental and emotional shortages. Many persons experience worry around workers with disabilities, especially if the disability is severe. However, the manager can set the tone for proper treatment of workers with disability. This is important as people with disability now fall within the so-called "designated group" (Grobler et al., 2006). Swanepoel et al. (2008, p 550) indicate that "*The Act places a duty on designated employers to provide reasonable accommodation for people with disabilities, such as modifying or adjusting a job or the working environment that will enable them to have access to, participate in or advance in employment, to ensure that they enjoy equal opportunities and are equitably represented in the workforce of a designated employee.*" The organizational implication of the disability tends to represent both opportunity and adjustment. Training is required to increase managers' awareness of the opportunity and to create an environment where accommodation requests can be made without fear. Employing disabled workers, however, means a need for more comprehensive health care, new physical workplace systems, and new attitudes toward working with the disabled and challenging jobs that use a variety of skills. Organizational development interventions, including work design, job planning and development, as well as performance management, can be used to integrate the disabled into the workforce. For example, traditional approaches to job design can simplify work to permit physically handicapped workers to complete a complex task.

Career planning and development programs need to focus on making disabled workers aware of career opportunities. "*A career path, performance management intervention, goal setting mentoring, and coaching that aligns the workforce's characteristics are important to develop these workers*" (Cummings et al., 2009, p 477).

There are also some types of workforce diversity:

- religion,
- physical appearance,
- culture/socio,

- cultural differences,
- problem-solving ability,
- critical thinking ability,
- team building ability,
- income,
- music enjoyed,
- type of books read,
- TV shows enjoyed,
- experiences when being raised,
- language,
- capability for cmpathy,
- ability to be kind,
- ability to motivate people,
- ability to work with others,
- job description,
- listening ability,
- conflict resolution ability,
- level of self, and
- awareness.

## 11.5 DIMENSIONS OF WORKFORCE DIVERSITY

A common misconception about diversity is that only certain persons or groups are included under this term. In fact, just the opposite is true; diversity is multidimensional. It emphasizes acceptance and respect for differences and similarities (Clemons, 2006, p 24).

When considering workplace diversity and achieving connectivity to our customers, we need to take into account both the primary dimensions of diversity, which are those things that we see in people, and the secondary dimensions, which are those things that we do not see. It is in the dimensions we do not see that many of the uniquc talents of persons are found (Gravel and Sylvio, 2014).

Dimensions of diversity are divided into primary and secondary types. The primary dimensions are core characteristics of everyone that cannot be changed: age, race, gender, physical and mental abilities ethnic heritage, and sexual orientation (Reece, 2012). These differences are often using to self-identify and to describe themselves and often shape conversations (IVY Planning Group, 2015). The secondary dimensions are the differences we acquire and sometimes dismiss or modify over time, based on the life decisions we make. The secondary dimensions of diversity are those that enhance one's life experiences (IVY Planning Group, 2015). They involve a person's work experience, health habits, religious beliefs, education and training, first language, family status, organizational role and level, communication style, and socioeconomic status (Reece, 2012).

The dimensions of workplace diversity alter and influence organizational work and functionality. Workplace diversity plays many roles within an organization, on an interpersonal, intrapersonal, and structural participation level. The dimensions of workplace diversity play a pivotal role in the organization, which influences organizational policies which creates and contributes to stifling differences among employees. Workplace diversity often affects employee job satisfaction based on factors of equity related to performance appraisals, which affect salary fluctuations and career mobility. Lack of performance often results in disciplinary action or terminations; however, if concerns develop about employees perceiving disciplinary procedures ineffective, which result in the equity continuum being labeled as inaccurate. The equity balance is affected by unfair practices such as overt discrimination against a particular race, gender or people with disabilities, which affect the organizations' diversity climate (Veldsman, 2013, p 21–22).

The blend of secondary and primary dimensions adds depth to each person and helps shape his or her values, priorities, and perceptions throughout life (Reece and Reece, 2017, p 333). Figure 11.2 shows the workforce dimensions.

## 11.6 MANAGING DIVERSITY

A big problem with diversity is the fact that many people, including management, have the wrong background about what diversity is (Banhegyi et al., 2009).

The misconceptions about diversity are (Banhegyi et al., 2009, pp 32–33) as follows:

- Diversity is not culture: Managing diversity does not mean teaching people about what other cultures are like. This approach will only reinforce stereotypes, which is precisely one of the things diversity management is trying to get rid of.
- Diversity is not affirmative action: While affirmative action is necessary to correct past imbalances, it cannot be seen as diversity. Affirmative

action is government initiated, whereas diversity is totally natural. Affirmative action is imposed by law on people and organizations.

- Diversity is not an absence of standards: Diversity does not mean that anything at all is acceptable in the organization. It is very important for management to create boundaries or a framework within which all workers from different cultural backgrounds can function.

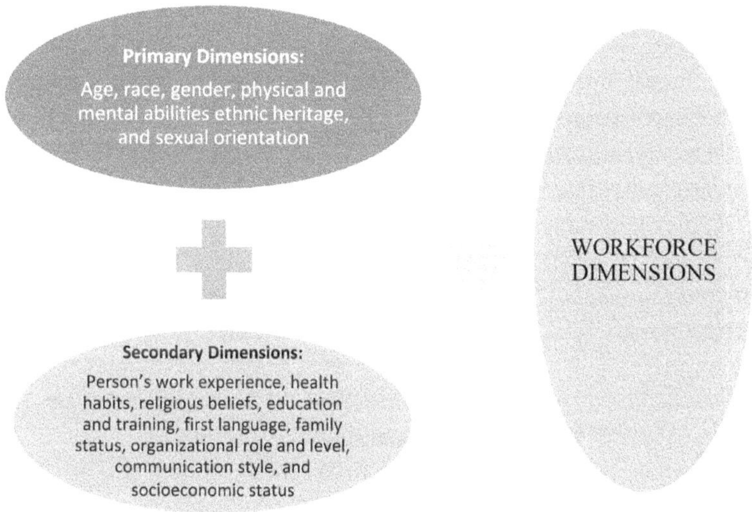


**FIGURE 11.2** The workforce dimensions.

**Source:** The Authors.

Many firms' leaders are now beginning to believe that diversity has important bottom-line benefits. Diversity in the workforce can be a competitive advantage because various viewpoints can facilitate unique and innovative approaches to problem-solving, that way increasing creativity and innovation which in turn, leads to better organizational performance (Otike et al., 2015).

While diversity provides many benefits to the organization, it also makes them face challenges so, it is essential for managers and employees to understand how to manage diversity (Management Training Specialists, 2014). Managing diversity can be defined as *"the challenge of meeting the needs of a culturally diverse workforce and of sensitizing workers and managers to differences associated with gender, race, age, and nationality in an attempt to maximize the potential productivity of all employees"* (Ellis and Sonnenfield, 1994, p 82). Managing diversity means to minimize its potential to a performance barrier while maximizing its potential to enhance organizational performance (Peters, 2008). Managing diversity means also *"managing opposing opinions, constant contradictions, continuous oppositions, different perceptions, emotions, relative understandings, difficult actions, and conflicts inherent in human nature"* (Nadine, 2017, p 564). Managing diversity is not only concerned the moral issues but it also about competitiveness, maximizing benefits, or human effectiveness (Peters, 2008).

Managing diversity can create a competitive advantage. Potential benefits include better decision making, higher creativity and innovation, greater success in marketing to foreign and domestic ethnic minority communities, and a better distribution of economic opportunity (Cox, 1991; Cox and Blake, 1991; Henry and Evans, 2007).

Managing diversity includes building specific skills and creating policies and roles that increase the best work behaviors and attitudes from each worker (Foma, 2013).

Diversity management aims to improve the competitiveness, innovation, and performance of the company by capitalizing on (Nadine, 2017):

- the diversity of the people (gender, age, origin, religious beliefs, sexual orientation, physical and mental conditions),
- the functionality of the organization (international settlements, business, and culture), and
- the style of interaction and mode of thinking (formations, training, and communication).

Part of the aim of managing diversity ensures employees have every opportunity available that the organization offers for self-progression and achievement. However, the challenge of diversity management is that employees have multiple spheres of diversity (Brooks, 2007).

### *11.6.1 DEFINITION OF DIVERSITY MANAGEMENT*

*"Managing diversity does not mean controlling or containing diversity, it means enabling every member of your workforce to perform to his or her potential"* (Thomas, 2005, p 87).

The idea that diversity can be managed originated in the 1960s and since then following three approaches have been identified: (1) Golden rules, which assert that treatment of everyone in the same way and treating others as you want to be treated, (2) "Right the wrong" approach, which takes the form affirmative action and finally, (3) Value of difference approaches, which recognize that differences occur but does not want people to be associated with the predominant culture (Otike et al., 2015).

Managing diversity refers to the planning and implementing of systems and practices in an organization that maximizes the potential of workers to participate to organizational goals and develops their personal abilities without being hindered by group identities such as race, gender, age, physical ability, or ethnic group. Managers should not be threatened by people's differences or their diversity. They should realize that people's differences could be an asset to the organization and pack away their preconceived ideas about the value that previously disadvantaged employees can bring to it (Banhegyi et al., 2009).

Workplace diversity management is broadly defined as the systematic and planned commitment by the organization to recruit, reward, and promote a various mix of employees (Bagshaw, 2004). Diversity management is defined as the process aimed to both maintain and create a positive work environment, where all individuals' similarities and differences are valued, so that all persons can maximize their contributions to organizations' objectives and goals (Patrick and Kumar, 2012).

Harris et al. (2007) also defined diversity management as the planning and implementation of organizational systems and practices that maximizes the advantages of diversity and minimizes the disadvantages. Diversity management can also be defined as the creation of an inter- and intranational environment within which these different aspects approached and sensitivities are incorporated and developed to manage diversity in such a way that the full potential (productivity and personal aspirations) of individuals and institutions may be realized optimally (Greybe and Uys, 2001). Managing diversity means enabling the diverse workforce to do its full potential in a fair work environment, where no one group has an advantage or disadvantage (Torres and Bruxelles, 1992). The management of any organization should analyze the factors affecting their employee's performance to increase it. However, they need to set and apply polices and roles to ensure this diversity will success (Alghazo and Al Shaiban, 2016).

Effective managers are aware that certain qualities are necessary for creating a successful and diverse workforce. First, managers must understand discrimination and its consequences on employees. Second, managers must recognize their own cultural favors and prejudices (Mwinami, 2014). Diversity is not about differences among groups, but rather about differences among individuals. Everyone is unique and does not represent or speak for a particular group. Finally, managers must be willing to change the organizational structure if necessary.

Mismanaged diversity can have long-reaching impacts on employee satisfaction and productivity. Employees who perceive themselves as valued members of their organization are harder working, involved, and innovative. Mismanagement can have negative consequences, such as preventing workers' abilities and motivation. This leads to poor performance. Thus, when an organization ignores the importance of workforce diversity, conflict can emerge and neither the corporation nor its employees will realize their potential (Goetz, 2001). Mismanaged workforce diversity may lead to a dissatisfied workforce and low productivity in an organization, this is because when employees feel that they are being distinguished based on their gender, social class, sexual orientation, and ethnicity, they decide to engage in disruptive activities that may be a barrier of key strategic objectives (Onyango, 2015).

Diversity management has following three key components (Barak, 2016, p 48):

- "Diversity management is voluntary: Equal rights legislation is enforced through sanctions (monetary fines or incarceration), and affirmative/positive action policies are enforced through incentives (government contracts), but diversity management is self-initiated by the companies themselves. It is not enforced or coerced but is entirely voluntary.
- Diversity management uses a broad definition of diversity: Whereas both equal rights legislation and affirmative or positive action policies specify the groups that are to benefit from the laws or public policies, companies that implement diversity management often use broad and open definitions of diversity.
  One of the reasons for this comprehensive and often vague definition is that they make diversity programs inclusive and reduce potential objections from members of the majority group.
- Diversity management aims at providing tangible benefits to the company: Diversity management is seen as a business strategy aimed at tapping into the full potential of all employees in the company in order to give the company a competitive advantage, whereas in the past, employees of different backgrounds (e.g., race/ethnicity or gender) were labeled as unqualified by managers if they did not conform to values and norms of the majority. The logic of diversity management is that it

allows every member of the organization to bring to the workplace his or her unique perspective, benefiting the organization."

### *11.6.2 CAUSES AND REASONS FOR DIVERSITY MANAGEMENT*

Causes of diversity management are globalization, the emergence of the network cultures, cost-cut, simplification, positive action, uncertainty, and fear. The following are generic reasons why organizations implement a management diversity process (Mfene, 2010): benefiting from a range of skills that the organization never had before; attracting and keeping the best talent; promoting greater productivity as a result of employee job satisfaction; developing enhanced creativity, innovation, and problem-solving, as well as the accompanying timely responses to diverse customers; and utilizing all persons to the maximum, and creating improved relations and communication between organized labor and management.

Organizations can succeed at diversity if the organization made an initiative to create, manage, and value the diverse workforce has the full support of the top management (Hayes, 1999; Jackson et al., 1992; Henry and Evans, 2007). Robbins et al. (2009) clears that although the approaches to managing diversity may vary from region to region or even from one company to another, the following key elements have emerged that should be integrated into any diversity management initiative:

- The organization should assign this work to a senior manager (Jackson et al., 1992). The organization must give concerns for diversity to HRM (Human Resources Management) decisions around recruitment, selection, placement, successful planning, performance management, and rewards (Otike et al., 2015; Cascio, 1998).
- The organization should present such a working environment that could increase the motivation, satisfaction, and commitment to diverse people. In addition, performance standards must be clearly and accurately established, effectively communicated and used on objective criteria without any prejudice, identify desirable and undesirable behaviors that must be based upon performance-feedback discussions involving a diverse workforce (Otike et al., 2015).
- The strategy (diversity or otherwise) must be based on the will of the human resources, strength, and culture of the organization. Managers

must understand their organization's culture first and then implement diversity strategies according to that culture (Hayes, 1999).

- Training and development programs will improve the skills in dealing with the day-to-day diversity problems. This will help managers to be aware of how strong relations impact on stereotypes of groups and on perceptions of persons and the expectations (Henry and Evans, 2007).
- Communicating with various cultures: It will contribute to managing a diverse workforce. A person will be able to understand how cultural and ethnic differences shape the conflict process and coming up with conflict decision strategies. That will be able to deal with cultural differences (Otike et al., 2015).
- Creation of the support system to minimize isolation and discrimination: This can be achieved through the encouragement of a formal system and informal networks (Henry and Evans, 2007). The reason for diversity training programs is often misunderstood at all levels. So, it is important to first understand what diversity is and what the organization hopes to achieve by managing it more effectively (Otike et al., 2015).
- Capitalize on the current diversity within your organization by ensuring that you include both senior and line managers on your diversity training courses as well as employees from different functions and departments (Bagshaw, 2004). And finally, the diversity training, this would create the awareness of what the concept of workforce diversity is, and the saving of clear information needed to create behavior changes that are required to effectively manage and work within a diverse workforce (Otike et al., 2015).
- Mentoring programs in which experienced advisors are hired for a period of times in order to advise employees on the whole concept of workforce diversity and the reasons why diversity should be managed effectively in the workplace (Henry and Evans, 2007).
- Introduce a clear business case for diversity initiatives and link with changing demographics and social changes. This gives diversity a context that enhances understanding (Bagshaw, 2004).
- Obtain visible management support: Experience has shown that an important success factor for diversity management. Organizations that had successfully adopted diversity programs had strong support from top management that placed high vantage on diversity close to other competing organizational goals (Robbins et al., 2007).

- Assessment of individual's beliefs about work rules, being able to identify work values of others from different cultural backgrounds and examination of the leadership assumptions from a multicultural perspective (Henry and Evans, 2007).
- Diversity needs identification the particular need can be identified using scientific needs analysis tools such as diversity reviews or focus groups (Robbins et al., 2007).

Van der Walt and du Plessis (2010) indicated that when employers implemented diversity management completely it benefited both the employer and employee:

- The workforce is aging, and the employer can benefit from this.
- The companies' consumers will also become more diverse.
- Employees will want to work in the company.
- Consumers will want to purchase from these companies.
- Employer will be able to select from a bigger group of very qualified persons.
- The company will attract new stakeholders and business partners that would like to be embraced in the company.

Organizations could also benefit from managing diversity, organizational diversity can benefit the organization as follows (Mfene, 2010):

- It enables a wide range of various views to be present in an organization, including views that might challenge the status quo from all sides.
- It focuses and strengthens an organization's bottom values.
- Diversity is pragmatic in organizational change.
- It stimulates social, economic, mental and emotional growth.
- It helps an organization understand its position in the global community.

If organizations do not accept implementing diversity management, the organization will be faced with higher employee turnover, which will lead to an increase in recruitment and selection cost.

This means that employees will not stay with the organization long time, which in turn will cause the organization to continuously recruit new employees. The organization will also incur unnecessary training costs because of the high turnover of persons. It is consequently important that organization should embrace diversity to be more creative and innovative in their product and service delivery to clients (Mfene, 2010).

### *11.6.3 HOW TO EFFECTIVELY MANAGE CULTURAL DIVERSITY?*

The effective diversity management provides many advantages to the performance of organizations by encouraging workers to work together and allowing the use of employees' all skills and abilities. The discovery of creativity, more qualified personnel selection, reduction of costs, increase in management efficiency, and the ability of organization to adapt and provide flexibility to continue this activity are some of those contributions.

Beside those organizational benefits, organizations that value differences and create the opportunity for its members to use their potential fully provides individual contributions such as comfort and confidence to employees, morale, job satisfaction, effective communication, teamwork, high performance, and loyalty (Ordu, 2016).

In order to successfully control your multicultural workforce, you should first be aware that majority and minority cultures do not always share experiences. Also, the following strategies can help you face cultural barriers and enjoy advantages from cultural diversity (Vietnam Manpower, 2016):

- Building programs and policies that improve awareness of cultural diversity.
- Improving positive attitudes toward cultural differences.
- Recognizing the same points of view and relations among different ethnic groups.
- Being flexible in communication skills.
- Clearing personal concerns and confusions when encountering cultural barriers.
- Establishing cultural diversity committees.

To enhance diversity management for effectively managing workforces there are a few guidelines presented as follows (Veldsman, 2013, pp 25–26):

1. Ensure management accountability: Managers who are responsible for hiring and training staff need to be held accountable for their success or failure at creating a diverse staff. In the corporate world promotions and pay raises should depend on a manager's proven success at managing a diverse staff.
2. Re-examine the organization's structure, culture, and management systems: Organization's need to self-reflect and examine their systems regarding recruitment, performance appraisal criteria, promotion, and career development programs for bias.

3. Pay attention to the numbers: Those responsible for recruiting and managing staff need to constantly monitor the diversity statistics of their staffs, and be managed around those statistics by CEOs.
4. Provide training: Training is essential for staff to understand the importance of diversity goals and to learn how to successfully manage and work with a diverse staff.
5. Develop mentoring programs: Mentoring relationships are crucial to retaining a diverse staff and communicating organizational expectations concerning promotions and advancement.
6. Promote internal identity or advocacy groups: Internal caucuses of women, people of color, gays and lesbians, or people with disabilities can provide an important forum for support, camaraderie, mentoring, resolving conflict, and influencing organization policy and procedures.

Managing diversity should be an integrated part of the culture of the organization (Baumann, 2015).

- Confirm that all your internal policies and plans from hiring to promotions are based on employee performance. Avoid tenure, ethnic background, or any other kind of category into your human resources' policies. Managing a diverse workplace begins with strong policies of equality from the organization.
- Hiring employees must base on the quality of his experience, his education, and skills, not age or any other category.
- Encourage diversity when establishing teams and organizing special work groups within the organization.
- Deal serious with prejudice or discrimination complaints. Encourage workers to report all cases of discriminatory behavior, and have a clear process in place for dealing with these complaints.
- Holding training courses for employees to know the benefits of diversity and discuss how they can manage diverse in the workplace effectively.

## 11.7 WORKFORCE DIVERSITY MANAGEMENT STRATEGIES

With workforce diversity, managers need to shift their way of application and change from treating every staff member alike to realizing the differences in the workforce whereby responding to the differences in ways that ensure employee motivation and retention and high performance.

The strategy (diversity or otherwise) must be based on the will of the human resources, strength, and culture of the organization (Hayes, 1999). Managers must recognize their company's culture first and then implement diversity strategies according to that culture (Kirton and Greene, 2015).

This requires implementation of programs such as training and creating environments that can utilize the full potential of the entire workforce (Kinyanjui, 2013).

- Recognition: You must realize that people have differences may be physical, generational, or cultural, and you cannot show that these obstacles have been broken down. Instead, celebrate the differences among your employees, and encourage them to let their individualities show. An employee's worth comes from more than his ethnicity or age (Ryan, 2017).
- Communication in Workforce Diversity Management: Communicating with employees begins when management commits to the four-step process for Managing Diversity for Success.
  The technique used to communicate will vary depending on the number of employees and locations (McArthur, 2010). Communication is very important in a workplace as it is the backbone of productivity and relationships for the success of the organization (Mayhew, 2010).
- Fairness: Acting fairly enables you to successfully deal with diversity in your workplace. For example, do not schedule an obligatory meeting that falls on a religious holiday (Ryan, 2017).
- Focus on Yourself: Diversity is an issue that you must manage in the workplace, and it starts with managing your own attitude and behavior (Ryan, 2017).
- Employee Assessments: When the manager of an organization prepares assessments between employees, he must also examine his employees' attitudes and behavior, particularly how they work with others. If he discovers that an employee only delegates tasks to people of a certain race, or if an employee discounts the ideas of people below or above a certain age, it is your responsibility to address the issue (Ryan, 2017).
- Encourage Interaction: Encourage employees to work with others in a team work of different backgrounds or generations. Setting these types of interactions encourages your employees to learn more about communication styles, talents, and goals—their own and those of their co-workers (Ryan, 2017).

**FIGURE 11.3** Workforce diversity management strategies.

**Source:** The Author.

## 11.8 ADVANTAGES OF DIVERSITY IN THE WORKFORCE

Diversity is beneficial to both organizations and employers. Although organizations are interdependent in the workplace, respecting personal differences can increase productivity. Diversity in the workplace can reduce complaints and increase marketing opportunities, recruitment, creativity, innovation, and business image (Esty et al., 1995). Some of these advantages are listed as follows:

- High level of Productivity, innovation, and creativity: When management takes care of its workers by offering proper reparations, health care, and employee estimate, it enables workers to feel they belong to the organization unheeding of their cultural background by remaining loyal and hardworking which helps to increase the organization's productivity and profit (Bedi et al., 2014).

- A multicultural organization is better suited to serve a diverse customer in a more increasingly global market. Such firms have a better understanding of the needs of the legal, political, social, economic, and cultural environments of foreign societies (Saxena, 2014).
- Increased problems-solving skills (Robbins et al., 2007), multicultural organizations are found to be better at problem solving, have better ability to find various solutions, and are more likely to display multiple perspectives in dealing with complex issues and complaints (Saxena, 2014), because organizations employing a diverse employee can provide a major variety of solutions.
- Diversity in the workplace is beneficial as by implementing it organization can reduce absenteeism, turnover and do not lose people with special skills, or human capital (Bozhko, 2014).
- Employees from diverse backgrounds bring various skills and experiences in suggesting innovative ideas that are flexible in adapting to fluctuating markets and customer demands (Saxena, 2014).
- Generating fresh ideas (Greater openness to new ideas): Organizations may need new ideas such ideas may come from hiring employees from many diverse backgrounds. Successful organizations make the best use of the collective knowledge of their employees, and such collective knowledge is enhanced by including people with different experience and backgrounds. Marketers have found that many innovative ideas for new products have come from their employees with diverse backgrounds (Yong Kim, 2017).
- Learning and growth: Diversity at the workplace creates an opportunity for employee's personal growth. When workers are being exposed to new cultures, ideas, and perspectives, it can help each person to reach out and have a clearer insight of their place in the global environment and thus their own surroundings. Mismanaged diversity may prevent employees from improving their abilities, skills, and increasing their motivation to get things done, thereby decreasing their job satisfaction, job performance, and organizational productivity.
- In contrast, well-managed diverse environment may provide companies with an opportunity to increase organizational effectiveness by maximizing individual potentials, combining individual talents, increasing productivity, and promoting innovation (Yong Kim, 2017).
- Effective Communication: Workplace diversity can widely strengthen an organization's relationship with some specific group of customers by making communication more effective. A customer service personnel can be paired-up with customers from their specific area

or location, making the customer feel at home with the representative and consequently with the company (Bedi et al., 2014).
- Diverse Experience: Employee and their co-workers that come from a diverse background bring some amount of unique perceptions and experience during teamwork or group tasks. Collecting the diverse skills and knowledge of culturally distinct employees together can widely benefit the company by strengthening the realization and productivity of the team to adapt to the changing conditions (Bedi et al., 2014).
- Consumers may find the services and products with high quality, which are necessary for them, as workforce that produced them is very diverse and can cover many different needs (Bozhko, 2014).

## 11.9 DISADVANTAGES OF WORKFORCE DIVERSITY

Diversity if not well managed has disadvantages. Many people feel threatened by working with people of different age, sex, or culture. First, there is an increase in the cost of training. This increase comes from costs associated with seminars, programs, and lectures given to promote diversity in the corporation. These types of training are given to all levels of staff within the organization. They teach employees how to accept the personalities with different background and ideas, thoughts of others. These programs also teach one how to deal with conflicts and prejudice in a professional and civil manner (White, 1999).

Failure to handle and manage diversity can cause a lot of problems for an organization (Nataatmadi and Dyso, 2005).

- The first significant importance is financial cost caused by high turnover, absenteeism, and complaints (Nataatmadi and Dyso, 2005). For example, a diverse workforce may require language and cultural-awareness training to facilitate communication into the workplace and local society (Baum, 2006). This increase can also come from costs associated with seminars, programs, and lectures given to promote diversity in the corporation. These types of training are given to all levels of staff within the organization. They teach employees how to accept the personalities with diverse backgrounds and ideas or thoughts of others. These programs also teach one how to deal with conflicts and prejudice in a professional and civil manner (White, 1999).

- Organizations lose all the money invested in training and seminars when a dissatisfied worker leaves the work (Nataatmadi and Dyso, 2005).
- Poor individual and organizational productivity is another disadvantage. This happens when people feel unappreciated, so they become less innovative and creative. They will waste because of poor communication and misunderstandings (Nataatmadi and Dyso, 2005).
- Increased incidents of conflict: Conflicts arise when two or more persons differ or disagree on a situation. In diverse workplace, the most common conflicts arise from feelings of excellence, ignorance, or fear, and result in pejorative comments or nods. If management ignores such incidents, productivity suffers (Baum, 2006). Prejudice feelings or pejorative comments cause a lack of acceptance. This can produce negative dynamics such as racism, stereotyping, and culture conflicts (White, 1999).

  Unfortunately, diversity in an organization can also create conflict. This can arise when (Griffin, 2007, p 209–210):

  - "An individual think that someone else has been hired, promoted, or fired because of her or his diversity status.
  - Diversity is misunderstood or misinterpreted or consists of inappropriate interactions among people of different groups.
  - There is an environment of fear, distrust, or individual prejudice. Members of the dominant group in an organization may worry that newcomers from other groups pose a personal threat to their own position in the organization.
  - People are unwilling to accept people different from themselves. Personal bias and prejudices are still very real among some people today and can lead to potentially harmful conflict."

Table 11.2 clears the advantages and disadvantages of diversity.

## 11.10 DIVERSITY TRAINING

*"During the 1970s, 1980s, and 1990s, many employers instituted diversity training programs as a way of demonstrating their commitment to diversity and proactive compliance with equal employment opportunity regulations. Successful diversity programs, used mentoring rather than training workshops, and had a diversity manager or task force that was responsible for increasing the number of women and minorities in good jobs"* (Landy

and Conte, 2010, p 531). As organizations embrace diversity, investments are required in training managers and employees to understand diversity. Diversity training should be a part of an overall strategy of the organization to develop and value diversity as awareness programs alone will not achieve diversity objectives (Mathews, 1998). High-quality diversity awareness training is one human resource function that enhances the effective integration of diverse group members. Awareness training builds a common understanding of the value of diversity, assisting in building social unity so that it improves individual and organizational outcomes (Bal and Bozkurt, 2014). *"Diversity training has a slightly different purpose. It attempts to bring about workplace harmony by teaching people how to get along better with diverse work associates"* (Dubrin, 2012, p 65–66).

**TABLE 11.2** Advantages and Disadvantages of Diversity.

| Advantages | Disadvantages |
|---|---|
| High level of productivity, innovation, and creativity | High turnover, absenteeism, and lawsuits |
| A multicultural organization is better suited to serve a diverse customer in a more increasingly global market | High costs |
| Increased problems-solving skills | Poor individual and organizational productivity is the second disadvantage. This happens when people feel unappreciated, so they become less innovative |
| By implementing diversity organization can reduce absenteeism, turnover and do not lose talent people, or human capital | Increased incidents of conflict. Conflicts arise when two or more individuals differ or disagree on a situation |
| Generating fresh ideas (Greater openness to new ideas) | |
| Increasing learning and growth | |
| Effective communication. | |
| Diverse experience (employee and their co-workers that come from a diverse background bring to the table some amount of unique perceptions and experience during teamwork or group tasks) | |
| Consumers may find the services and products, which are necessary for them, as workforce that produced them is very diverse and can cover many different needs | |

**Source:** The Author.

Training and development programs will improve the skills in dealing with the day-to-day diversity problems. This will help managers to be aware on how power relations impact on stereotypes of individuals and on perceptions of persons and the expectations. Intercultural communication will help in managing a diverse workforce. A person will be able to understand and realize how cultural and ethnic differences shape the conflict process and coming up with conflict decision strategies. We will be able to negotiate outcomes with cultural differences in mind. Mentoring programs, involvement of experienced advisors and other helps for a period of years are needed. This mentor should be able to advise employees on the whole concept of workforce diversity and the reasons why diversity should be managed in the workplace. Assessment of one's beliefs about work values is the ability to identify work values of others from different cultural backgrounds and check of the leadership presuppositions from a multicultural perspective (Kirton and Greene, 2015).

## 11.11 WORKFORCE DIVERSITY IN TOURISM AND HOSPITALITY

*"Hospitality businesses are notorious employers of cheap, relatively docile and insecure migrant labor"* (McDowell, 2011). *"In recent years the hospitality and tourism workplace has become more diverse"* (Rood, 2010, p 81). Globalization has enhanced the diversity experienced in the hospitality and tourism industry because of its multicultural nature. Many migrants possess high levels of skills and experience while being willing to take up positions offering comparatively poor pay and conditions.

Tourism-sector employees often have less protection than in other fields of the economy, while a core permanent worker, who are well educated and skilled, hold managerial positions. The tourism sector is characterized by low pay, part-time, seasonality, a notoriously high turnover rate, and low levels of unionization among workers (Tchibozo, 2013).

Tourism includes the movement of people from their usual surroundings to places of interest either within the country or across international borders for leisure, business, fun, or adventure. Hospitality, on the other hand, includes providing services such as travel, accommodation, and entertainment to meet the needs of tourists. Hospitality and tourism aims at optimizing the experience of tourists in cultural environments that differ from those of their home countries or regions (Merchant, 2017). The tourism and hospitality industry has typically employed many minorities as well as other persons who are seeking a part-time job or short-time job (not a career). Hotels, restaurants, clubs, foodservices operators in noncommercial facilities, and others compete with potential employers in other industries for individuals without specialized knowledge or skills to work at beginning fare rates in entry-level positions (Hayes and Ninemier, 2009). In a globalized world, hotels, restaurants, and travel organizations will hire more employees and serve more customers from diverse cultural backgrounds. Understanding those who are culturally different will present a global challenge to the tourism and hospitality organizations that struggle to be better in a global marketplace (Reisinger, 2009). The workforce structure in the hospitality and tourism establishments is vast and diverse. Indeed, it is necessary to employ people from all nationalities to feed workplace diversity that predicts positive influence and enhanced productivity in the hospitality and tourism industry. Workplace diversity also enables businesses in the hospitality and tourism industry to feed and describe a positive image of inclusive equal employment opportunities for all without regard to race, gender, or nationality (Merchant, 2017). Hospitality and tourism present a unique opportunity to understand new cultural experiences for both employees and the tourists. It is necessary for the personnel to understand and appreciate different cultures to enhance the nature of their communications with tourists of different cultures, religions, races, creeds, colors, ages, genders, and sexual orientations. It is for this reason that businesses plying their trade in this industry must pursue to train their personnel to appreciate and accommodate people from diverse backgrounds around the world.

As such, workplace diversity not only facilitates easy understanding of different cultural, social and economic perspectives but also enhances the delivery of satisfactory services through communication and observation (Merchant, 2017). *"An organization's success and competitiveness depend upon its ability to embrace diversity and realize its benefits. When organizations actively assess their handling of workplace diversity issues and develop and implement diversity plans, there are multiple benefits for the organization. In essence, cultural diversity creates cultural competence for the organization. It has several ways of providing a competitive edge and increased productivity in the hospitality business"* (Devine *et al.*, 2007, p 122). *"Operators in the tourism sector must deliver their services to an increasingly broad range of clients from a diverse range of cultural backgrounds. The increasing diversity of both tourists and workers in the industry has resulted in a greater need for those people in the sector to possess skills to manage this diversity"* (Aitken and Hall, 2001, p 1).

Managing workforce diversity is a primary challenge in today's hospitality industry. Since several diversity groups such as minorities, disabled people, and women are looking for an employment opportunity, it is a chance for the hospitality industry to benefit from such a trend to expand the experience of the workforce. Most of the hospitality organizations realize the moral and economic urgency of diversity management and have already started implementing practices and policies for diversity groups. However, when an organization disregards the importance of implementing diversity, conflict can appear and neither the employees nor the hotel will perceive their potential. It is applicable for every hospitality organization to realize that the establishment of workforce diversity is the only path to obtain a sustainable competitive advantage (Theodoridis, 2017). Inherent in the service transactions of tourism is the essential contact between the producer (travel agency, hotel, etc.) and the customer of the service, and the cultural diversity of employees is likely to have an important impact on the service encounter. As another sector of the economy, the "business case for diversity" is also adopted by organizations in the tourism sector. Therefore, it is responsible to suggest that for many tourism-sector organizations, the cultural diversity of their workforce is a key consideration in assessing their ability to engage with emerging tourism marketing, as well as to service their current customer (Tchibozo, 2013).

Hospitality and tourism employees who estimate diversity have some essential beliefs that form the organization for their mindset (Hayes and Ninemier, 2009) are as follows:

- Valuing diversity needs a change in corporate culture, and these change efforts never end.
- When diversity is valued, benefits increase to employees and to the organization.
- Trying to implement diversity efforts should include everyone because every staff member makes diverse attitudes, backgrounds, and experiences to the job.

*"Without diversity in the workplace, hospitality corporations run the risk of becoming monoculture organizations that see things from a very limited perspective. Establishing diversity in the workplace is not limited to laws that pertain to the hiring of women, disabled people, gay men and lesbians and minority ethnic groups. Additionally, it is not limited to managing or even honoring differences between people, but it is about considering those differences and allowing them to work in the best possible way for the benefit of both the organization and the worker." Significant cultural differences do exist and play a role in work and life with people from other cultures but that*

*is the fact in every globalized organization. In fact, as the economy becomes increasingly global, the workforce of any organization will become increasingly diverse. Organizational competitiveness and success will depend on the ability to effectively manage cultural diversity in a workplace and communicate effectively across cultures"* (Okoro and Washington, 2012, p 58).

### *11.11.1 BENEFITS OF DIVERSITY IN THE HOSPITALITY AND TOURISM INDUSTRY*

Workplace diversity in the hospitality and tourism industry is subsequently a key factor in facilitating cultural exchange on a global market. There are some benefits to expanding diversity into the management workforce (Baumann, 2015):

1. The tourism industry presents a unique opportunity to learn new different cultural experiences for both employees and tourists. Personnel needs to be trained in the respect and appreciation of differences to boost the nature of their interactions with guests of various cultures, religions, races, creeds, colors, ages, genders, and sexual orientations.
2. Only individuals with a diverse background in higher management positions can design a corporate vision that not only facilitates understanding of different cultural and social behaviors but also improves the delivery of satisfactory services through interaction and observation.
3. In such competitive environment, diversity at higher levels, which should be the most visible face of the corporation, also enables organizations in the hospitality and tourism industry to nurture and describe a positive image of inclusiveness equal employment opportunities for all without regard to race, gender, age, nationality, or any other diversity marker.
4. Diversity in the hospitality and tourism industry is significant. Recruitment from a skilled pool also needs a clear vision of diversity. If employers in hospitality and tourism continue to carry a reputation for a lack of diversity at a senior level, talented employees from minority groups will be hesitating to enter the industry. People will certainly not gravitate toward organizations that have a track record of discrimination.

4. Studies highlight that developing a diverse workforce can create a competitive advantage for a business, improving staff moral while increasing levels of worker retention. In the hospitality industry specifically, where customers are coming from across the globe, a diverse workforce allows employees to bring a stronger cultural insight and understanding of the customers they are serving.
5. With the amazing growth of social media, the hotel and tourism industry are one of the most exposed industries out there. Any detail or any complaint can go viral in a matter of minutes. Organizations need to be prepared to deal with such type of reputation crisis which hurts their branding efforts.

### *11.11.2 THE IMPORTANCE OF DIVERSITY FOR HOTELIERS*

Diversity occurring in hospitality gains many important benefits. Exposure to cultural exchanges among hospitality workers and guests offers increased opportunities to develop a vital tourism industry, especially in light of business globalization. Consequently, employers and their associates are able to readily understand and accept the idea of equal employment opportunity, overcoming inherent stereotypical concepts (Reynolds, 2017).

There are many reasons why hoteliers should focus on diversity in their hiring and employment practices:

- Diversity helps employee spirit. When people believe that their employer values their differences, and is committed to hiring and promoting them fairly while still respecting their various backgrounds and experiences, they are generally more motivated and more loyal workers.
- Having a diverse workforce ensures the presence of different views and ideas. When a staff member uses the benefit of his own background to improve hotel methods or contributes to discussion of workplace practices, hoteliers can only benefit.
- A hotel that builds a reputation for being committed to diversity may very well find itself a popular choice for job applicants. A hotel that shows that it values diversity will have its pick of the brightest and most talented employees.

### *11.11.3 CULTURAL DIVERSITY IN HOSPITALITY AND TOURISM*

*"Cultural diversity can be referred to as the variety of human groups, societies or cultures in a specific region, or in the world all together. Cultural diversity indicates a mixture of both individuals and groups with dissimilar backgrounds, beliefs, characteristics, customs, traditions, and values. It categorizes people with diverse race, ethnicity, nationality, religion, or language among various groups within a community, organization, or nation. For example, a wide range of multicultural people can be found in the United States. With one third of multicultural and multiethnic people, the United States is a melting pot of all different cultures around the world. There are, for example, African Americans, American Indians, Caucasians, Hispanics and Asian Pacific Islanders. All these people have their own ways of life and own identities that discrete from others. Minority cultural groups are increasingly extending across the country. Especially within the last decade, 2000-2010, the minority groups have increased 9.7 per cent"* (Korjala, 2012, p 20).

*"Cultural diversity is vital for companies in the long term. It especially is important for hospitality industry organizations to identify cultural diversity in advance when growing internationally. Unfortunately, there are companies who go international without a strategic plan and get surprised by the cultural issues which their international business encounters"* (Peterson, 2004, p 78).

## 11.12 CONCLUSIONS

1. In recent years, managing diversity in organizations is becoming more and more vital. Diversity is considered as one of the few tools of business management that combines financial performance and social ethics.
2. Workforce diversity uses some dimensions:
   a) Social category diversity, informational diversity, and value diversity. Social category diversity is explained as differences in demographic characteristics such as age and race. Informational diversity refers to the diversity of backgrounds such as knowledge, education, experience, tenure, and functional backgrounds. Value diversity involves differences in personality and attitudes;
   b) surface level (social category differences), deep-level (differences in knowledge or skills, differences in values or beliefs,

personality differences, organizational/community status differences, and differences in social and network ties; and

c) diversity is divided into employee differences in terms of three categories. The categories include demographic diversity, organizational diversity, and sociocognitive diversity.

3. Hiring employees from various backgrounds and experiences in tourism and hospitality industry may cause a positive or negative influence on organizational performance and productivity.
4. A big problem with diversity is the fact that many people, including management, have the wrong background about what diversity is. The misconceptions about diversity are: Diversity is not culture, diversity is not affirmative action, and diversity is not an absence of standards (Banhegyi et al., 2009).
5. When employers implemented diversity management completely, it helped both the employer and employee (Van der Walt and du Plessis, 2010): The companies' consumers will also become more diverse, employees will want to work in the company, customers will want to purchase from these companies, and the company will attract new stakeholders and business partners that would like to be involved in the company. Organizations could also benefit from managing diversity. Organizational diversity can benefit the organization as follows (Mfene, 2010): It enables a wide range of various views to be present in an organization, including views that might challenge the status quo from all sides, it focuses and strengthens an organization's bottom values, diversity is pragmatic in organizational change, it stimulates social, economic, mental, and emotional growth, and it helps an organization understand its position in the global community.
6. To successfully control your multicultural workforce, you should first be aware that majority and minority cultures do not always share experiences. Also, the following strategies can help you face cultural barriers and enjoy advantages from cultural diversity (Vietnam Manpower, 2016): Building programs and policies that improve awareness of cultural diversity, improving positive attitudes toward cultural differences, recognizing the same points of view and relations among different ethnic groups' members, being flexible in communication skills, clearing personal concerns and confusions when encountering cultural barriers, and establishing cultural diversity committees.
7. Diversity in tourism and hospitality industry: Workplace diversity in the hospitality and tourism industry is subsequently a key factor

in facilitating cultural exchange on a global market. There are some benefits to expanding diversity into the management workforce (Baumann, 2015) as follows: The tourism industry presents a unique opportunity to learn new different cultural experiences, diversity in the hospitality and tourism industry is significant. Recruitment from a skilled pool also needs a clear vision of diversity. If employers in hospitality and tourism continue to carry a reputation for a lack of diversity at a senior level, talented employees from minority groups will be hesitating to enter the industry, diversity helps employee spirit, having a diverse workforce ensures the presence of different views and ideas. When a staff member uses the benefit of his own background to improve hotel methods or contributes to discussion of workplace practices, hoteliers can only benefit. A hotel that builds a reputation for being committed to diversity may very well find itself a popular choice for job applicants. A hotel that shows that it values diversity will have its pick of the brightest and most talented employees, and a diverse staff will help a hotel better understand and serve the needs of its guests, who are probably a diverse group themselves! A satisfied guest is frequently a loyal guest, and one who will tell friends and family about their experiences (good and bad), this called a word of mouth.

## REFERENCES

Abbas, Q.; Hameed, A. Gender Discrimination and Its Effect on Employee Performance or Productivity. *Appl. Hum. Resour. Manag. Res.*, **2010,** *6* (1–2), 75–76.

Abrahams, E.; Ruiters, R. Industrial Psychology: Selected Topics. In *Introduction to Psychology*; 2nd ed.; Nicholas, L., Ed.; UCT Press: Cape Town, 2008; p 328.

Aitken, C.; Hall, C. Migrant and Foreign Skills and Their Relevance to the Tourism Industry. *Tour. Geogr.* **2001,** *2* (1), 66–86.

Alghazo, A. ; Al Shaiban, H. The Effects of Workforce Diversity on Employee Performance at an Oil and Gas Company. *Am. J. Bus. Soc.* **2016,** *1* (3), 148–153.

Ande, A. A. Comparative Study of Workforce Diversity in Service and Manufacturing Sectors in India. *Int. J. Res. Bus. Manag.* **2014,** *2* (3), 1–8.

Bagshaw, M. Is Diversity Divisive? A Positive Training Approaches. *J. Ind. Commer. Train.* **2004,** *36* (4) 153–157.

Bal, Y.; Bozkurt, S. *Globalization and Human Resources Management: Managing the Diverse Workforce in Global Organizations*; IGI Global, 2014; pp 1339–1351.

Banhegyi, S.; Bates, B.; Booysen, K.; Bosch, A.; Botha, M.; Botha, S.; Cunningham, P.; Goodman, S.; Ladzani, W.; Lotz, O.; Musengi, S.; November, M.; Southey, L.; Smith, A.; Visser, C.; Vries, L.; Williams, O.; Botha, D.; Krause, B. *Business Management: Fresh Perspective*; Pearson Education South Africa: Cape town, South Africa, 2009; pp 32–33.

Barak, M. *Managing Diversity: Toward a Globally Inclusive Workplace*, 3rd ed.; Sage Publications: USA, 2014; pp 121–152.

Baum, T. *Human Resource Management for Tourism, Hospitality and Leisure (An International Perspective)*; Thomson Learning, 2006; pp 164–171.

Baumann, S. Six Benefits of Top Management Diversity in the Hospitality and Tourism Industry (Online). http://latinasinbusiness.us/2016/05/27/6-benefits-management-diversity-hospitality-tourism-industry/ (accessed Aug 20, 2017).

Bedi, P.; Lakra, P.; Gupta, E. Workforce Diversity Management: Biggest Challenge or Opportunity for 21st Century Organizations. *IOSR J. Bus. Manag.* **2014,** *16* (4), 102–107.

Bendix, S. *Industrial Relations in South Africa*; Juta and Co. Ltd: Claremont, Cape Town, 2010.

Beziibwe, A. S. Relationship Between Workplace Diversity and Organisational Performance. PhD Dissertation, Uganda Technology and Management University, Uganda, 2015.

Bozhko, O. Managing Diversity at the Organizational Level. PhD Dissertation, Luiss Guido Carli University, 2014; pp 16–20.

Brooks, F. Racial Diversity on Acorn's Organizing Staff 1970–2000. *Adm. Soc. Work* **2007,** *31* (1), 27–48.

Brown, S. L. Diversity in the Workplace: A Study of Gender, Race, Age, and Salary Level. *Acad. Manag. J.* **2008,** *44* (3), 533–545.

Bryan, J. H. The Diversity Imperative. In *Executive Excellence;* Sage: New Delhi, 1999; p 6.

Carelse, K. *Employees' Perceptions Toward Workplace Diversity in a Financial Institution Operating in the Western Cape*. B.A.M Thesis, University of The Western Cape, 2013; pp 15–42.

Cascio, W. F. *Managing Human Resources: Productivity, Quality of Work Life, Profits*; McGraw-Hill: Boston, MA, USA, 1998.

Chin, H. Y.; Park, H. J. What are the Key Factors in Managing Diversity and Inclusion Successfully in Large International Organizations? 2013. http://digitalcommons.ilr.cornell.edu/cgi/viewcontent.cgi?article=1044&context=student (accessed Aug 20, 2017).

Clemons, H. *7 Steps (Achieving Workforce Diversity Step-by-step)*; The HLC Group: USA, 2006; p 24.

Cox, T. The Multicultural Organization. *JSTOR* **1991,** *5* (2), 37–47.

Cox, T.; Blake, S. Managing Cultural Diversity: Implications for Organizational Competitiveness. *JSTOR* **1991,** *5* (3), 45–56.

Cumming, T. G.; Worley, G. W. *Organization Development and Change*; Nelson Education: Canada, 2009.

Daft, R.; Lane, P. *The Leadership Experience*, 7th ed.; Cengage Learning: Boston, MA, 2016; p 329.

Daniel, C. The Effects of Higher Education Policy on the Location Decision of Individuals: Evidence from Florida's Bright Futures Scholarship program. *Reg. Sci. Urban Econ.* **2009,** *39*, 553–562.

Devine, F.; Baum, T.; Hearns, N.; Devine, A. Managing Cultural Diversity: Opportunities and Challenges for Northern Ireland Hoteliers. *Int. J. Contemp. Hosp. Manag.* **2007,** *19* (2), 120–132.

Dietz, J.; Petersen, L. Diversity management. In *Handbook of Research in International Human Resource Management*; Stahl, G., Björkman, I., Eds; Edward Elgar Publishing: Cheltenham, 2006; pp 223–243.

Dombai, C.; Verwey, S. The Impact of Organizational Culture as a Context of Interpersonal Meaning on the Management of Organisational Diversity. *Cummunicare* **1999,** *18* (2), 104–131.

Dubrin, A. *Essentials of Management*, 9th ed.; South-Western Cengage Learning: USA, 2012; pp 65–66.

Ellis, C.; Sonnenfield, J. *Diverse Approaches to Managing Diversity. Hum. Resour. Manag.* **1994,** *33* (1), 82.

Elsaid, A. The Effects of Cross Cultural Work Force Diversity on Employee Performance in Egyptian Pharmaceutical Organizations. *J. Bus. Manag. Res.* **2012,** *1* (2), 162–179.

Esty, K.; Griffin, R.; Schorr-Hirsh, M. *Workplace Diversity. A Manager's Guide to Solving Problems and Turning Diversity into a Competitive Advantage*; Adams Media Corporation: Avon, MA, USA, 1995.

Feighery, W. Cultural Diversity and the School-to-work Transition: A Relational Perspective. In *Cultural and Social Diversity and the Transition from Education to Work,* 17th ed.; Tchibozo, G., Ed.; pringer: London, 2012, pp 55–86.

Foma, E. Impact of Workplace Diversity. *Rev. Integr. Bus. Econ.* **2013,** *3* (1), 402–410.

Goetz. Workforce Diversity. 2001 (Online). http://academic.emporia.edu/smithwil/001fmg456/eja/goetz.html (accessed Oct 20, 2017).

Gravel, M.; Sylvio, A. *Workplace Diversity (How to Get It Right)*; USA, 2014 (Online). https://books.google.com/books?id=-IlWDQAAQBAJ&pg=PT35&lpg=PT35&dq=When+considering+workplace+diversity+and+achieving+connectivity+to+our+clients,+we+need+to+take+into+account+both+the+primary+dimensions+of+diversity,+which+are+those+things+that+we+see+in+people,+and+the+secondary+dimensions,+which+are+those+things+that&source=bl&ots=8RsFad3LjD&sig=P8v2RNZseWf9lXKzN2TXrlMY-JE&hl=en&sa=X&ved=0ahUKEwjNtMKs1IvXAhUJ2mMKHbSfBT4Q6AEIJjAA#v=onepage&q=When%20considering%20workplace%20diversity%20and%20achieving%20connectivity%20to%20our%20clients%2C%20we%20need%20to%20take%20into%20account%20both%20the%20primary%20dimensions%20of%20diversity%2C%20which%20are%20those%20things%20that%20we%20see%20in%20people%2C%20and%20the%20secondary%20dimensions%2C%20which%20are%20those%20things%20that&f=false (accessed Oct 20, 2017).

Greybe, L.; Uys, F. M. Strategies for Diversity Management. *J. Public Adm.* **2001,** *36* (3), 185–201.

Griffin, R. *Principles Management*; Library of Congress Control: USA, 2007; pp 209–442.

Grobler, P.; Wärnich, S.; Carrell, M.; Elbert, N.; Hatfield, R. D. *Human Resource Management in South Africa*; Thomson Learning: London, 2006.

Gupta, R. Workforce Diversity and Organizational Performance. *Int. J. Bus. Manag. Invent.* **2013,** *2* (61), 36–44.

Hankin, H. *The New Workforce: Five Sweeping Trends That Will Shape Your Company's Future*; AMACOM: USA, 2005; p 67.

Harris, C.; Rousseau, G. G.; Venter, D. J. L. Employee Perceptions of Diversity Management at a Tertiary Institution. *J. SAJEMS* **2007,** *10* (1), 51–71.

Hayes, D.; Ninemier, J. *Human Resources Management in the Hospitality Industry*; John Wiley and Sons, Inc.: USA, 2009; pp 16–17.

Hayes, E. Winning at Diversity. In *Executive Excellence*; Sage: New Delhi, 1999; p 9.

Henry, O.; Evans, A. Critical Review of Literature on Workforce Diversity. *Afr. J. Bus. Manag.* **2007,** *12*, 72–76.

Hickman, D. The Effects of Higher Education Policy on the Location Decision of Individuals: Evidence from Florida's Bright Futures Scholarship Program. *Reg. Sci. Urban Econ.* **2009,** *39*, 553–562 (Online). https://www.colorado.edu/Economics/papers/Wps-09/wp09 09/09-09Hickman.pdf (accessed Oct 20, 2017).

Hunsaker, P.; Alessandra, T. *The New of Managing people*; Free Press: USA, 2008; p 82.

IVY Planning Group. In *Dimensions of Diversity*; 2015 (Online). http://www.ivygroupllc.com/executive leader/dimensions-of-diversity/ (accessed Aug 25, 2017).

Jackson, B. W.; La Fasto, F.; Schultz, H. G.; Kelly, D. Diversity. *Hum. Resour. Manag.* **1992,** *31* (1–2), 21–34.

Kayalo, J.; Gachunga, H. Effect of Diversity in the Workplace on Employee Performance in the Banking in Industry in Kenya. *Strateg. J. Bus. Change Manag.* **2015,** *2* (53), 145–181.

Kinyanjui, S. Innovative Strategies for Managing Workforce Diversity in Kenyan Leading Corporations in Present Global Scenario. *Int. J. Bus. Manag.* **2013,** *8* (15), 20–32.

Kirton, G.; Greene, A. M. *The Dynamics of Managing Diversity: A Critical Approach*; Routledge Publication: USA, 2015.

Kochan, T.; Bezrukova, K.; Ely, R. The Effects of Diversity on Business Performance: Report of the Diversity Research Network. *Hum. Resour. Manag.* **2003,** *42*, 2–21.

Korjala, V. Cultural Diversity in Hospitality Management: How to Improve Cultural Diversity Workforce. B.A.M thesis, Turku University of Applied Science, Turku, 2012; pp 18–32.

Landy, F.; Conte, C. *Work in the 21st Century: An Introduction to Industrial and Organizational Psychology,* 3rd ed.; Blackwell Publishing: USA, 2010; p 531.

Mathews, A. Diversity: A principle of Human Resource Management. *Publ. Personal Manag.* **1998,** *27* (2), 175–185.

Mattews, J. A Perspective on How Counseling Curricula Can Enhance Workforce Diversity Practices. In *Developing Workforce Diversity Programs, Curriculum and Degrees in Higher Education*; Chaunda, S., Scott, J., Eds.; IGI Global: USA, 2016; p 163.

Mayhew, R. Communication and Diversity in the Workplace, 2010. [Online] https://smallbusiness.chron.com/ (accessed Jan 14, 2019).

McArthur, E. *Managing Diversity for Success*; 2010 (Online). http://workforcediversitynetwork.com/res_articles_managingdiversity_mcarthur.aspx (accessed Nov 13, 2017).

McDowell, L. *Working Bodies: Interactive Service Employment and Workplace Identities*; Wiley: USA, 2011.

McKay, P. F.; Avery, D. R.; Morris, M. A. A Tale of Two Climates: Diversity Climate from Subordinates' and Managers' Perspectives and Their Role in Store Unit Sales Performance. *J. Person. Psychol.* **2009,** *62* (4), 767–791.

Merchant, P. *Workplace Diversity in Hospitality and Tourism*; 2017 (Online). http://small-business.chron.com/workplace-diversity-hospitality-tourism-15436.html (accessed June 17, 2017).

Mfene, P. N. Enhancing Supervisor and Subordinate Communication in Diversity Management. *Afr. Insight J.* **2010,** *40* (2), 141–152.

Morna, C. L. *Gender in Southern African Politics Ringing up the Changes*, 2004 (Online). http://www.genderlinks.org.za/item.php?i_id=42 (accessed Oct 20, 2017).

Mwinami, S. An Assessment of the Effect of Workplace Diversity on the Employee Performance at Tanseco. M.Sc. Thesis; Mzumbe University, 2014; pp 6–35.

Nadine, S. Managing Cultural Diversity: The Case of Small and Medium Tourism Enterprises (SMTE). *Eur. Sci. J.* **2017,** *13*, 562–574.

Nataatmadi, I.; Dyso, L. *Managing the Modern Workforce: Cultural Diversity and Its Implications*, 2005 (Online). http://www.irma-international.org/viewtitle/32666/ (accessed Nov 20, 2017).

Nelson, D. and Quick, J. *Organisational Behavior: Science, the Real World and You*, 18th ed.; CENGAGE Learning: USA, 2013; p 333.

Nishii, L. H.; Mayer, D. M. Do Inclusive Leaders Help to Reduce Turnover in Diverse Groups? The Moderating Role of Leader Member Exchange in the Diversity to Turnover Relationship. *J. Appl. Psychol.* **2009,** *94* (6), 1412–1426.

Okoro, E.; Washington, M. Workforce Diversity and Organizational Communication: Analysis of Human Capital Performance and Productivity. *J. Divers. Manag.* **2012,** *1* (7), 57–62.

Onyango, W. The Link Between Demographic Workforce Diversity Management, Employee Retention and Productivity: A Case of the Civil Society Organizations in Homabay County, Kenya. *J. Culture Soc. Develop.* **2015,** *8*, 12–19.

Ordu, A. The Effects of Diversity Management on Job Satisfaction and Individual Performance of Teachers. *Edu. Res. Rev.* **2016,** *11* (3), 105–112.

Otike, F.; Messah, O.; Mwalekwa, F. Effects of Workplace Diversity Management on Organizational Effectiveness: A Case Study. *Eur. J. Bus. Manag.* **2015,** *3* (2) (Online). https://www.researchgate.net/publication/267995664_Effects_of_Workplace_Diversity_Management_on_Organizational_Effectiveness_a_case_study (accessed Aug 20, 2017).

Ozbilgin, M.; Tatli, A.; Jonsen, K. *Global Diversity Management (An Evidence-based Approach)*, 2nd ed.; PALGRAVE: England, 2015; p 3.

Patrick, H.; Kumar, V. *Managing Workplace Diversity: Issues and Challenges*; SAGE Open: India, 2012; Vol. 2 (3), pp 346–351.

Peters, B. *Managing Diversity in Intergovernmental Organisations*; Springer: Germany, 2008; p 76.

Peterson, B. *Cultural Intelligence: A Guide to Working with People from Other Cultures*; Nicholas Brealey Publishing: Yarmouth, 2004.

Phillips, K. L. *War! What is It Good for? Black Freedom Struggles and the US Military from World War II to Iraq*; University of North Carolina Press: USA, 2012.

Podsiadlowski, A.; Gröschke, D.; Kogler, M. Managing a Culturally Diverse Workforce: Diversity Perspectives in Organizations. *Int. J. Intercult. Relat.* **2013,** *37* (2), 159–175.

Rahmawati, P. *Managing Diversity: The Gap Between Theories and Practices in the Hospitality Industry*; 2012 (Online). https://sustainabletourismforbali.wordpress.com/2012/05/08/managing-diversity-the gap-between-theories-and-practices-in-the-hospitality-industry/ (accessed Oct 17, 2017).

Rao, S.; Bagali, M. Workforce Diversity and Management: An Empirical Study on Relationship Between Diversity Management Practices, Obstacles and Acceptance of Gender Diversity Among Employees in IT Industry; Bangalore. *IOSR J. Bus. Manag.* **2013,** *16* (2), 12–25.

Reece, B. A.; Reece, M. *Effective Human Relations: Interpersonal and Organisational Applications*, 13th ed.; Cengage Learning: USA, 2017; p 333.

Reece, B. *Human Relations: Principles and Practices*, 7th ed.; South-Western Cengage Learning: USA, 2012; pp 141–164.

Reisinger, Y. *International Tourism: Cultures and Behavior*; Elsevier: USA, 2009; pp 31–35.

Reynolds, M. Diversity in the Hospitality Industry (Online). https://yourbusiness.azcentral.com/diversity-hospitality-industry-24394.html (accessed Oct 20, 2017).

Robbins, S. P.; Judge, T. A.; Odendaal, A.; Roodt, G. *Organisational Behavior: Global and Southern African Perspectives*; Pearson Education: Cape Town, 2009.

Robbins, S.; Odendaal, A.; Roodt, R. *Organisational Behavior (Global and Southern African Perspectives)*; Creda Communication: Cape Town, 2007; pp 241–267.

Rood, A. Understanding Generational Diversity in the Workplace: What Resorts Can and are Doing? *J. Tour. Insight* **2010,** *1* (1), 80–89.

Ryan, T. Five Strategies for Dealing with Diversity in the Workplace, 2017 (Online). http://smallbusiness.chron.com/5-strategies-dealing-diversity-workplace-18106.html (accessed Oct 26, 2017).

Saxena, A. In *Workforce Diversity: A Key to Improve Productivity*, Symbiosis Institute of Management Studies Annual Research Conference (SIMSARC13), 2014; Elsevier; pp 76–85.

Shaban, A. Managing and Leading a Diverse Workforce: One of the Main Challenges in Management. *Procedia Soc. Behav. Sci.* **2016,** *230*, 76–84 (Online). https://www.researchgate.net/publication/308739249_Managing_and_Leading_a_Diverse_Workforc One_of_the_Main_Challenges_in_Management (accessed Aug 26, 2017).

Shen, J.; Chanda, A.; D'Netto, B.; Monga, M. Managing Diversity Through Human Resource Management: An International Perspective and Conceptual Framework. *Int. J. Hum. Resour. Manag.* **2009,** *20* (3), 235–251.

Sims, A. Workforce Diversity Curriculum Design Considerations for Diversity Certificates and Study Abroad Experiences. In *Developing Workforce Diversity Programs, Curriculum, and Degrees in Higher Education*; Scott, A. C., Sims, J., Eds.; IGI Global: USA, 2016; pp 117–139.

Swanepoel, B. J.; Erasmus, B. J.; Schenk, H. W. *South African Human Resources Management. Theory and Practice*; Juta and Co. Ltd.: Cape Town, 2008 (Online). file:///C:/Users/ABDALLAH/Downloads/Carelse_MSC_2013.pdf (accessed June 17, 2017).

Tchibozo, G. Leveraging Diversity to Promote Successful Transition. In *Cultural and Social Diversity in the Transition from Education to Work;* Tchibozo, G., Ed.; Springer, 2013; pp 3–20.

Theodoridis, D. Workforce Diversity as a Guiding Light Toward SHRM: Exploring Managers' Views Regarding Workforce Diversity, Its Impact on Recruitment and Selection Practices, and the Role of Sustainable HRM within Organizations. MSc Thesis, 2017; pp 25–29.

Thomas, R. *Building on the Promise of Diversity*; American Management Association: USA, 2005; p 87.

Torres, C.; Bruxelles, M. Capitalizing on Global Diversity. *HR Magazine*, 1992; pp 30–39.

Tracy, R. L.; David, E. M. Choosing Workers' Qualifications: No Experience Necessary? *Int. Econ. Rev.* **2011,** *34* (3), 479–502.

Van der Walt, S.; du Plessis, T. Leveraging Multi-generational Workforce Values in Interactive Information Societies. *S. Afr. J. Inform. Manag.* **2010,** *12* (1), 1–7.

Veldsman, D. Perceptions of Diversity Management in a Public-sector Organization/ Government Institution within the Western CAPE. PhD Dissertation, 2013; pp 20–26.

Vietnam Manpower. How to Effectively Manage Cultural Diversity at Workplace in Hospitality Industry; 2016 (Online). http://vnmanpower.com/en/cultural-diversity-management-in-hospitality industry-bl261.html#7qiSTMWEUW2vxK6H.99 (accessed July 28, 2017).

Wambui, T.; Wangomble, T.; Muthura, M.; Kamau, A.; Jackson, S. Managing Workplace Diversity: A Kenyan Perspective. *Int. J. Bus. Soc. Sci.* **2013,** *4* (16), 199–218.

White, R. D. *Managing the Diverse Organization: The Imperative for a New Multicultural Paradigm;* 1999 (Online). https://pdfs.semanticscholar.org/0dde/79c3247f1fc5eba423973837dccd747704c5.pdf (accessed May 6, 2017).

Zhuwao, S. Workforce Diversity and Its Effect on Employee Performance in a Higher Education Institution in South Africa. M.Sc. Thesis, School Of Management Sciences at the University Of Venda, 2017; pp 1–30.

# CHAPTER 12

# TECHNOLOGICAL CHANGE RESISTANCE

*"Decisions about technology are decisions about leaving the cumbersome thoughts and ways of yesterday behind in exchange for tomorrow's operation improvement, not about sacrificing human assets."*

## 12.1 INTRODUCTION

Change is like most other things in life that tend to occur slowly and in an unsymmetrical way that leads to change in ways and methods adopted, attitude, the way of thinking and is often considered as a reaction to pressure that can no longer be positioned. It is the same with both individuals and organizations (Honey, 1988). New technologies and rising customer demands increase the pressure to make changes. Hospitality industry was one of the first industries to attempt to put into practice new technology aimed at improving business performance and in turn customer service (Piccoli et al., 2003). Change helps organizations to navigate successfully and facilitate growth. A number of researchers have stressed the importance of change in organizations (Honey, 1988; Manuela and Clara, 2003; Price and Chahal, 2006; Stjernholm and John, 2005).

## 12.2 TECHNOLOGY INNOVATIONS: NEW AND EMERGING TRENDS IN TOURISM INDUSTRY

The word technology has been derived from the Greek words "techne" meaning art or skill and "logia." In the context of day to day practice, "technology" is a distinct word referring to the use and knowledge of humanity's tools and techniques. Technology is one of the central and most critical components related to efficient operations management in an organization. It can be defined as the application of science (the combination of the scientific method and material) to meet an objective or solve a problem. It is also a body of knowledge used to create tools, develop skills, and extract or collect materials (Molinero, 2012). While the term technology change means the overall process of the invention, innovation, and diffusion of technology or processes (AL-Ameri, 2013).

As the world is being ushered into the information age, adoption of technology innovations is rapidly increasing. Technological development is contended to drastically modify the nature of the hospitality organization's distribution channels subsequently redrawing the nature of the organization–customer interaction and, moreover, reshaping the nature of the organization's connections with competitors (Nemec Rudez and Mihalic, 2007).

In the private sector, labor costs are assumed to decrease when tasks that are presently performed by human labor are "off-loaded" to nonhuman working devices. This inclination to "offload" mental or physical tasks from humans to computers is informed by the expectation that such offloading will free newly unencumbered minds and bodies to perform other, more creative, tasks. The more we can offload routine physical and mental chores to technological aids, the more physical and mental power we will be able to store up for the deepest, most creative, or most complex tasks. Technology change is a most important initiator that allows people to do innovative things that have not been done before or would have done in a less efficient manner (AL-Ameri, 2013).

Therefore, the introduction of new technology has become vital in all sectors so as to reduce cost and compete with the national and internal markets (Mark, 1987), embracing new technologies with modern techniques and approaches empower a business to create effective results in terms of production and performance (AL-Ameri, 2013). In view of Yuan et al. (2005), technology innovation or change has a positive significant influence on organizational performance.

Generally, organizations attempt to adopt technology for many reasons.

- Cost reduction in operating the business.
- Greater marketing capability since of its speed and affect (Buhalis, 2008), making modern distribution channels empowers the organization to put through with new, often more youthful, and value customers (MacFarland, 2012) subsequently producing higher levels of profitability.
- Improved customer service emerging from greater customer knowledge and faster reaction times (Luck and Lancaster, 2003), the rapid identification of new customer requirements and expectations, it

became to be conceivable for the advancement of more profound level competitive advantage (Nemec Rudez and Mihalic, 2007).

- Enhancing customer loyalty, new technology has also developed the relationship between service organizations and their customers as data mining of customer databases (Siguaw et al. 2009) offers hotels the opportunity to develop in-depth customer profiles and match service offerings based on the customers' profiles and needs.

In general, new technology has enabled service organizations to improve their performance through the gathering of customer information at different and novel customer contact points (Peelen et al. 2009). For example, hotels gather information, as customers book over the internet, and hotels are enabled to review their own performance through internet-based reviews, such as Trip Advisor.

Market competitiveness challenges made changing the way that organizations work is exceptionally basic. Hospitality organizations nowadays proceed to reply to market competitiveness challenges through utilizing new technology facilities as a frame of advancement (Sigala, 2011). For case, the utilize of call centers to handle hotel customer inquiries has empowered the cutting of costs inside the hotel organization, and the liberation of employees to engage with the core competencies of the hotel, improving and developing the customer relationship (Lin and Hwan Yann, 2007). Each organization uses different forms of technology for their business that has an essential and basic impact on the nature, design, structure, and work of an organization. Numerous positive and valuable changes have taken place these days in the working environment in terms of competency and adequacy with the invention of new technologies.

### *12.2.1 INFORMATION TECHNOLOGY IN TOURISM*

Information technology (IT) is defined as the collective term given to the most recent improvement in the mode (electronics) and machines (computers and communication technology) utilized for securing, handling, analysis, storage, retrieval, spread, and application of information (Haque and Rahman, 2012).

As the world is being introduced into the data age, selection of the IT is quickly expanding. Improvement of IT has revolutionized economies and organizations. Today, the travel and tourism industry is one of the most significant users of internet technology, which has become one of the most important communication tools for travelers as well as travel and tourism enterprises. Internet application and other technological innovations have influenced tourism in a variety of ways and resulted in fundamental changes in the industry structures and traveler behaviors.

The Internet has changed the world into a global village that can be explored at the click of a mouse. It gives potential tourists quick access to the textual and visual structure on destinations all through the world. The Internet has, moreover, become a basic tool in business to business and business to consumer transactions, the distribution of products, and organizing of business partners and is an instantaneous means of accessing knowledge on all kinds of subjects including travel and tourism information. Information is promptly accessible 24/7, and the transparency of details empowers consumers to make more informed choices.

This ease of access and depth of information has stimulated the rise of a new breed of travel customers who are independent and prefer to look for occasions themselves online, rather than through travel operators. Thus, the Internet became the primary source of tourist destination information. The specific elements of such information needs are the following (Jadhav and Mundhe, 2011).

- ✓ Quality of facilities and their standard costs including exchange rates.
- ✓ Geographical information on the area, landscape, climate, etc.
- ✓ Accommodation, food outlets, and shopping facilities.
- ✓ Availability and accessibility of transports' means.
- ✓ Activities and entertainment facilities.
- ✓ Social traditions, culture, and other extraordinary highlights of the place.
- ✓ Seasons of the visit and other special features.

The internet also offers tourism destination and businesses the means to make information and booking facilities available to millions of consumers around the world at a relatively low cost, while at the same time enabling them to cut down drastically on amounts invested in the production and distribution of promotional materials.

By using IT, firms can develop and deliver the right product to the right customer, at the right price and place, without over depending on intermediaries. An example of this is the global destination systems (GDS). GDS system is created with the purpose of reducing the rush at reservation counters and to minimize the role of intermediaries.

A system containing information about availability, prices, and related services for airlines, car companies, accommodation establishments, restaurants, rail companies, etc., and through which reservations can be made and tickets can be issued. A GDS also makes some or all of these functions available to subscribing travel agents, booking engines, and airlines. The GDS leaders are Amadeus, Apollo/Galileo/Worldspan, Sabre. These GDS are important technology solutions for information management and are used primarily by travel agencies and airlines.

## 12.3 LABOR AND TECHNOLOGICAL CHANGES

More recently, hospitality organizations have been presented with both the opportunities and challenges created by the adoption of new technologies. According to Baggio et al. (2011), early attempts by both the field experts and academics were characterized by a heavy focus on the associated benefits of the new technology with a limited attention to the contextual implementation of the technology and often outright neglect of the managerial, employee and stakeholder challenges, and resistance actions involved. Despite high levels of technological innovation in the industry over the past 20 years, there remain deep challenges both in terms of preparing employees to adopt new technology (Sigala, 2011) and in developing appropriate managerial models through which to visualize and to shape the technology toward the generation of sustainable competitive advantage (Daghfous and Barkhi, 2009). When technology is presented to the working environment, employees are not expected to learn how to utilize modern technology but are instead expected to be replaced by it. Technologically driven unemployment, like unemployment in common, tends to weaken the mental wellbeing of those influenced by it. Organization-wide change often goes against the values held by the staff of the organization—how employees believe things should be done. Kailash and Thomas (1998) are of the opinion that adopting new technology is a challenging task for organizations as it alters job system and the role and responsibilities of employees and can lead to unfavorable consequences for employees. Often, organization-wide change is difficult and provokes strong resistance because people are afraid of the unknown, they do not share a vision of the future, or they do not understand the need for change.

The key point to bear in mind when contemplating any technologically actuated change in the work process is that the presentation of the technology does not just give a substitute for a few separated components of a work. It also changes the character of the occupations that are left for the people to perform and then impacts the roles, attitudes, and aptitudes of the individuals who take part in it (Nicholas, 2014).

Technological change can also lead to changes in job satisfaction, stress, working conditions, productivity, and operational efficiency.

Generally, resistance to change should be expected in following such cases (Dent and Goldberg, 1999; Jiang et al., 2000).

- When change is undertaken without involving employees and workers from all work levels;
- Situations where change includes many interpretations;
- When employees feel strong forces hindering them from the change;
- When extraordinary pressure is put on workers to make the change(s) instead of clearly directing them to adapt steadily to the change; and finally
- When change is made on personal gains grounds as opposed to the benefit of the organization.

## 12.4 TECHNOLOGY CHANGE AND LABOR RESISTANCE

Employers assume that human beings are unreliable and inefficient and strive to give humans as small a role as possible in the operation of systems. Technological changes made workers function as mere monitors, passive watchers of screens. Such human monitors are bored by their job, lack the capacity to sustain situational awareness, and become deskilled. The assumption that the human becomes the weakest link in the system, thus, turns into a self-fulfilling prophecy (Brown, 2015). New technology innovation, new policies, new operations methods, and new organizational structure may be faced by some types of resistance; resistance to change has been recognized as one of the important factors that can influence the success of the business. Although the decision to automate typically derives from the presumed ability of automation to enhance speed and efficiency, about half to two-thirds of all major organizations' change efforts fail, and resistance is the little-recognized but critically important contributor to that failure (Maurer, 1996). Negative reactions arise from the fact that automation changes the nature of the work that humans are left to perform. The tasks that humans are left to perform are often less challenging or engaging.

Egan and Fjermestad (2005) defined resistance as the intended behavior with the purpose of preventing the implementation or use of a new system or to prevent the system designers from achieving their intended change.

While according to Manuela and Clara (2003), resistance is defined as a phenomenon that affects the change process by delaying its beginning or hindering its implementation or affecting its efficiency which, in turn, increases cost. Hence, resistance is the action that tries to keep the status quo and to avoid change.

There are three levels of resistance to change. These types can be broken down into three groups: organization-level resistance, group-level resistance, and individual-level resistance.

Understanding these different types of resistance can help in understanding the ways to reduce resistance and to encourage compliance with the required changes.

- ✓ Organizational level resistance includes resistance to change due to organizational culture, power and conflict, structure, and differences in functional orientations.
- ✓ Group level resistance includes resistance to change due to group thinking, group cohesiveness, escalation of commitment, and also group norms (Paul et al., 2006).
- ✓ Individual level resistance includes resistance to change due to selective perception and retention, uncertainty and insecurity, and employee habits (Goldberg et al., 1999).

Job loss can impact employees who retain their jobs after the introduction of a labor-saving device. Morris and Phelps (1999) pointed out that resistance happens since it undermines the status quo or increases the fear and anxiety about real or imagined consequences. As claimed by Paul et al. (2006), employees with low skills and tolerance levels will be in the first line in resisting change because of their limited ability to develop the new skills and new behavior that are required for the new circumstances resulting from the introduced change (Paul et al., 2006), which subsequently threatens personal security and confidence in an ability to perform. Also, the resistance actions arise because of employees' fear of learning new skills and fear or inability to adapt. Resistance usually happens when employees doubt or have past feelings of hatred or resentments toward their bosses or supervisors who lead the change and when they have distinctive understandings or assessments of the situation (Block, 1993). As Strickland (2000) stated, "individuals stand up to change since they encounter a loss of identity, of belonging."

Resistance changes depend on two main factors to a critical extent:

1. the treatment that employees receive during the change process; and

2. the relationship between employees and their supervisors and managers.

Managers often have difficulty in determining the real reason why subordinates resent or resist a change. They may feel that the subordinates are just being stubborn or selfish when the real reason may be entirely different and even fully justified.

However, Peters and Watermann (2004) claimed that job security and new opportunities for promotion are the greatest concern in the minds of employees which need to be addressed as job loss cause more than a mere temporary setback as workers displaced by automation are at high risk for long-term unemployment. Thus, psychological dynamics play an important role in change challenge whether by motivating employees to comply with the change or develop the opposite attitude.

Schoor (2003) listed some more specific factors that contribute to resistance to change. Understanding the reasons for resistance to change can help managers prevent disaster and improve the change's chances for success. There are many reasons why employees may react negatively to change as following.

1. **Behavior factors:**

   A. **Self-interest,** when workers see the changes as harmful in one way or another, particularly (Yuh-Shy, 2000):

      - Security: A concern about job loss through a reduction in workforce members as a result of automation inclusions.
      - Self-esteem: Occurs when individuals who feel they should have been asked were not asked for their ideas concerning the change.
      - Money: A concern about the loss of money through a reduction in financial compensations (salary, pay, benefits, or overtime).
      - Creation of burden: Changes sometimes add more efforts whether it mentally or physically and, with it, long hours, confusion, mistakes, and other negative results. The initial stages of automation and computerization, for example, can result in additional problems at first. If the change will obviously require more effort with little accomplished as a result, employees are apt to resent and indeed stand up to it, especially if no financial incentives accompany the extra effort.
      - Perception of criticism: whether or not the change is really criticizing the things that were already done or the way in which they were done, workforce individuals may see the change as an

individual criticism. For illustration, a individual in obligation who has created or formulated a certain system or method will very likely take it personally in case somebody needs to change it.

**B. Demographic and social factors:**

- Good working conditions: Anxiety about being moved to a less desirable work environment or location.
- Bad timing: The response of employees to changes happening in their workplace varies according to the time. If it comes at a time when employees are as of now enduring from issues, the change is ordinarily loathed and likely stood up to by those who are gathered to execute it. So, the timing of a change is exceptionally imperative to its acceptance.
- Freedom: The employees may feel instability in the case of a new boss; they may think that a new boss will limit their personal freedom with closer supervision that provides less opportunity for decision-making.

**C. Psychological factors:**

- Psychological concerns: Anxiety is very commonly observed among those faced with the introduction of new technology in the workplace particularly when the organization promotes the notion of "button pusher" instead of a "skilled craftsman," a concern about ending up with jobs that no longer require their abilities and skills. Even workers who initially exhibit an open and receptive attitude toward the new technology often find their ability to understand it hindered by anxiety and/or frustration precipitated by its introduction.
- Lack of respect and satisfaction: When employees have a lack of respect and/or negative attitude toward the person or department responsible for making the change, there is a strong tendency to resent and resist the change because their feelings do not allow them to look at the change objectively.
- Negative perception: Employees with a negative perception of the organization, the job, and/or the boss are very apt to resist change, no matter what it is.
- Lack of proper communication: The dictator tone can make negative feelings. In some cases, change is requested in such a way that the individuals stand up to it, essentially since they do

not like being told what to do. This feeling can too happen in case employees are told what to do but not told why.
- Secondhand information: Some individuals are very sensitive about the way they learn of the change. If they found out about it from a secondhand source, they might resist it until they hear it "from the horse's mouth."
- The destabilization impact caused by the introduction of new individuals who are not familiar with the organization's culture and operations.

**2. Management factors:**

**A. Fear of loss of power:**

- Responsibility: A concern that jobs will be diminished to modest assignments without responsibility.
- Authority: A concern about a loss of power and authority over the subordinates because of a reorganization takes place or a new boss who decides to choose to pull back or reduce authority.
- Job status: Concern about loss of job title, responsibility, obligations, or authority that will result in a loss of status and recognition from others, such as when another layer of management is embedded between a subordinate and his or her manager.
- Challenge to authority: Some supervisor may challenge the management to test their power of control by simply refusing to implement a change.

**B. The cost of change is high:**

- More harm than good: Sometime employees may be more aware of operation mechanism than their managers, and then they may feel the change is a mistake and it will cause more unpleasant consequences. In some cases, this response is advocated, it is especially common when employees at the lower levels of an organization feel that top management makes changes without knowing what's going on "down on the line."
- No need: This type of resistance occurs when employees do not see any reason for the change, and there is no wrong with the way things are now.

In this way, resistance to change can be predictable, and employees tend to see the changes in the organization in a global context. If such resistance is not adequately addressed at both an occupational or organizational level, it may compromise the intellectual and/or emotional capacity of the employees to adequately adjust to the introduction of a new technology. In globalizing a business, organizations' management must take care of employees by informing them the benefits of change, motivating them, and making them aware of the importance of change and its benefits in the organization.

In such scenario, the organization manager's message should be that our staff is our greatest asset, and, with technology development, the aim is to enhance product (service) quality, reduce costs, increase profitability, and enhance productivity. During this process, management has to take the initiative in communicating with the employees directly (Peters and Watermann, 2004).

Then, while some employees resent and/or resist change, others accept and welcome it accordingly. The degree to which these opposites occur depends to a significant extent on management competency in addition to other many factors that help in gaining consensus to start a change; the best way to avoid resistance is to assure employees by supporting them and motivating them, involving them and explaining clearly why the change is taking place and what the benefits are that they are going to receive. The degree the employees will accept change is determined by expectations that an outcome may be attained, and the degree of value placed on the outcome in the employee's mind; thus, employees may accept or welcome change when they see a clear benefit to doing so (Porter and Lawler, 1968). In addition, if the employees have a positive attitude toward the person or the department from which the change comes, they will be more likely to accept and even welcome the change.

Therefore, an individual's attitude toward change comes from his or her perception of the outcomes of a change, compared with the individual's goals and values. Reasons for a positive reaction to change primarily are generated by gains that such changes make for the employees such as (Yuh-Shy, 2000):

- Participation: Involvement of those affected by a change in strategy will reduce organizational resistance and create a higher level of psychological commitment among employees towards the proposed changes. Also, participation leads to qualitatively better strategic decisions (Kim and Mauborgne, 1998).

- Clear vision: Presenting a clear vision and a sense of direction of the job that has to be performed, the employees' feelings of insecurity about losing their job, or any of the incentives they already enjoy will decrease.
- More security: A perception of greater security in a job, perhaps, because more of technical or soft skills will be used.
- More financial benefits: A hope for a salary increase, more compensations, or profit-sharing system, or more overtime.
- Less time and effort: If the change actually makes the job easier and requires less time and effort.
- More authority: A hope for promotion to a position of greater authority, or a new boss who allows more authority than was available under the previous boss.
- More prestige: An employee who dreams of a new title, a new office, or a special assignment that carries with its status and prestige see changes the ideal opportunity for this.
- More responsibility: A job change that provides new responsibility, or a new boss who assigned more responsibility than the previous one did.
- Building trust: One of the more modest strategies to enhance labor commitment and mitigate resistance is to build a supportive employee and management relationship.
- Better working conditions: A hope for a new and reliable equipment, new work schedule, or other conditions that make the job easier or more enjoyable.
- Increased personal satisfaction: A hope for a greater feeling of achievement because of a chance to use their abilities more to eliminate some of the obstacles that had stood in the way of personal performance.
- Effective communication: The way the manager or supervisor tells his employees to do things affect significantly on their response and reaction to what is needed.
- A new challenge: The desire of more fulfilling work.

Managing with resistance effectively depends on an ability to represent the change precisely, to depict the source of resistance, and to select and actualize procedures suitable for addressing and overcoming that source instead of blaming each other for the disappointment of the initiative (Argyris, 1990). In addition, process checking can be exceptionally supportive in ensuring that the contributors to change are completely included and committed, and also in avoiding the issues that can "turn off" other functions of the organization (Ali, 2012).

## REFERENCES

Ahmed, S. Technology Organizations. *Int. J. Res. Bus. Manag.* **2014,** *2* (7), 73–80.

AL-Ameri, M. Assessing Resistance to Technological Change for Improved Job Performance in the UAE (Public Sectors). Ph.D. Thesis, University of Salford, 2013.

Ali, M. A. The Role of Digital Certificates in Contemporary Government Systems: The Case of UAE Identity Authority. *Int. J. Comput. Sci. Eng. Inf. Technol. Res.* **2012,** *2* (1), 41–55.

Argyris, C. *Personality and Organization*; The University of Chicago Press: Chicago, 1990; pp 156–158.

Ashford, S. J.; Rothbard, N. P.; Piderit, S. K.; Dutton, J. E. Out on a Limb: The Role of Context and Impression Management in Selling Gender-Equity Issues. *Adm. Sci. Q.* **1998,** *43*, 23–57.

Ashforth, B. E.; Macl, F. A. The Power of Resistance: Sustaining Valued Identities. In *Power and Influence in Organizations*; Kramer, R. M., Neale, M. A., Eds.; Sage: Thousand Oaks, CA, 1998.

Baggio, R.; Mottironi, C.; Corigliano, M. Technological Aspects of Public Tourism Communication in Italy. *J. Hosp. Tourism Technol.* **2011,** *20* (2), 105–119.

Block, P. Flawless Consulting. In *Managing Organizational Change*; McLennan, R., Ed.; Prentice Hall: Englewood Cliffs, NJ, 1989.

Brower, R. S.; Abolafia, M. Y. The Structural Embeddedness of Resistance Among Public Managers. *Group Org. Manag.* **1995,** *20*, 149–166.

Brown, A. O. *Technology-induced Workplace Change*; 2015 (Online). http://www.aoop.org/resources/Technology%20Induced%20Workplace%20Change.pdf (accessed Aug, 2017).

Bryant, M. Talking About Change: Understanding Employee Responses Through Qualitative Research. *Manag. Decis.* **2006,** *44* (2), 46–258.

Buhalis, D.; Law, R. Progress in Information Technology and Tourism Management: Twenty Years on and Ten Years After the Internet: The State of e-Tourism Research. *Tourism Manag.* **2008,** *29* (4), 609–623.

Cheng, L., Yang, C. and Teng, H. An Integrated Model for Customer Relationship Management: An Analysis and Empirical Study. *Hum. Factors Ergonom. Manuf. Service Indu.* **2012,** *2* (1) 1–20.

Daghfous, A.; Barkhi, R. The Strategic Management of Information Technology in U.A.E. Hotels: An Exploratory Study of TQM, SCM and CRM Implementation. *Technovation* **2009,** *29* (9), 588–595.

Dent, E.; Goldberg, S. Challenging "Resistance to Change." *J. Appl. Behav. Sci.* **1999,** *1* (35), 25–41.

Egan, R. W.; Fjermestad, J. In *Change and Resistance, Help for the Practitioner Change*, Proceedings of the 38th International Conference on System Sciences; New Jersey Institute of Technology: Newark, 2005.

Graham, J. Principled Organizational Dissent: A Theoretical Essay. *Res. Org. Behav.* **1986,** *8*, 1–52.

Gronroos, C.; Ojasalo, K. Service Productivity: Towards a Conceptualization of Transformation of Inputs into Economic Results in Services. *J. Bus. Res.* **2005,** *67* (4), 414–423.

Ham, S.; Kim, W.; Jeong, S. Effect of Information Technology on Performance in Upscale Hotels. *Int. J. Hospitality Manag.* **2005,** *24* (2), 281–294.

Haque, I.; Rahman, A. Information Technology in Tourism Industry: What more Needed? *Int. J. Eng. Sci. Paradigms Res.* **2012,** *1* (1), 111–117.

Honey, P. The Management of Change. *Manag. Serv.* **1988,** *32*, 14–16.

Huh, H.; Kim, T.; Law, R. A Comparison of Competing Theoretical Models for Understanding Acceptance Behavior of Information Systems in Upscale Hotels. *Int. J. Hospitality Manag.* **2009,** *28* (1), 121–134.

Jadhav, V. S.; Mundhe, S. D. Information Technology in Tourism. *Int. J. Comput. Sci. Inf. Technol.* **2011,** *2* (6), 2822–2825.

Jiang, J. J.; Muhanna, W. A.; Klein, G. User Resistance and Strategies for Promoting Acceptance Across System Types. *Inf. Manag.* **2000,** *37* (1), 25–36.

Kailash, J.; Thomas, L. Impact of Information Technology on Users Work Environment: A Case of Computer Aided Design System Implementation. *Inf. Manag.* **1998,** *34*, 349–360.

Kegan, R.; Lahey, L. The Real Reason People Won't Change. *Harvard Business Review* 2001; pp 85–92.

Kim, W. C.; Mauborgne, R. Procedural Justice, Strategic Decision Making and the Knowledge Economy. *Strategic Manag. J.* **1998,** *19*, 323–338.

Lin, Y.; Hwan-Yann, S. Strategic Analysis of Customer Relationship Management. *Total Quality Manag. Bus. Excell.* **2007,** *14* (6), 715–731.

Luck, D.; Lancaster, G. E-CRM: Customer Relationship Marketing in the Hotel Industry. *Manag. Audit. J.* **2003,** *18* (3), 213–231.

Manuela, P. V.; Clara, M. F. Resistance to Change: A Literature Review and Empirical Study. *Manag. Decis.* **2003,** *42* (7), 148–155.

Mark, J. A. Technological Change and Employment: Some Results from BLS Research. *Monthly Labor Rev.* **1987,** *110* (4), 26–29.

Maurer, R. Using Resistance to Build Support for Change. *J. Qual. Particip.* **1996,** *19*, 56–63.

McFarland, A. *Tourism Marketing Strategies for the Under Thirties*, Paper Presented at THRIC Conference, Europa Hotel, Belfast, June 5, 2012.

Mintzberg, H.; Waters, J. A. Of Strategies, Deliberate and Emergent. *Strateg. Manag. J.* **1985,** *6*, 257–272.

Molinero, C. *What is Technology*? 2012 (Online). http://prezi.com/hktxqvq10z-v/what-is-technology/ (accessed Oct 3, 2017).

Morrison, E. W.; Phelps, C. C. Taking Charge at Work: Extra Role Efforts to Initiate Workplace Change. *Acad. Manag. J.* **1990,** *42*, 403–419.

Nemec Rudez, H.; Mihalic, T. Intellectual Capital in the Hotel Industry: A Case Study from Slovenia. *Int. J. Hosp. Manag.* **2007,** *26* (1), 188–189.

Nicholas, C. *The Glass Cage: Automation and Us*; Norton and Company: New York, NY, 2014.

O'Toole, J. *Leading Change: Overcoming the Ideology of Comfort and the Tyranny of Custom*; Jossey Bass: San Francisco, CA, 1995.

Paul, M. S.; Mike, S.; Rodger, M. Employee Involvement, Attitudes and Reactions to Technology Changes. *J. Leadersh. Organ. Stud.* **2006,** *12* (3), 85–100.

Payne, A.; Frow, P. A Strategic Framework for Customer Relationship Management. *J. Mark.* **2005,** *69* (4), 167–176.

Peelen, E.; Van Montfort, K.; Beltman, R.; Klerkx, A. An Empirical Study into the Foundations of CRM Success. *J. Strateg. Mark.* **2009,** *17* (6), 453–471.

Piccoli, G.; O'Connor, P.; Capaccioli, C.; Alvarez, R. Customer Relationship Management: A Driver for Change in the Structure of the U.S. Lodging Industry. *Cornell Hotel Restaur. Adm. Q.* **2003,** *4* (8), 73–81.
Porter, L. W.; Lawler, E. E. *Managerial Attitudes and Performance*; Dorsey Press: Homewood, IL, 1968.
Price, A. D. F.; Chahal, K. A Strategic Framework for Change Management. *Constr. Manag. Econ.* **2006,** *12* (3), 203–217.
Sagie, A.; Koslowsky, M. Organizational Attitudes and Behaviors as a Function of Participation in Strategic and Tactical Decisions: An Application of Path-goal Theory. *J. Org. Behav.* **1994,** *15* (1), 37–47.
Schoor, A. In *Learning to Overcome Resistance to Change in Higher Education: The Role of Transformational Intelligence in the Process*, Proceedings of HERDSA 2003 Conference, University of South Africa, Pretoria, 2003.
Shapiro, D. L.; Lewicki, R. J.; Devine, P. When do Employees Choose Deceptive Tactics to Stop Unwanted Organizational Change? *Res. Negot. Organ.* **1995,** *5*, 155–184.
Sigala, M. E-CRM 2.0 Applications and Trends: The Use of Perceptions of Greek Tourism Firms of Social Networks and Intelligence. *Comput. Hum. Behav.* **2011,** *27* (2), 655–661.
Siguaw, J.; Enz, C.; Namasivayam, K. Adoption of Information Technology in U.S. Hotels: Strategically Driven Objectives. *J. Travel Res.* **2009,** *39* (2), 192–201.
Spector, P. E. Perceived Control by Employees: A Meta-analysis of Studies Concerning Autonomy and Participation at Work. *Hum. Relat.* **1986,** *39*, 1005–1016.
Stjernholm, A. M.; John, P. U. Technology Innovation, Human Resource and Dysfunctional Integration. *J. Manpow.* **2005,** *26* (6), 488–501.
Strickland, D. Emotional Intelligence: The Most Potent Factor in the Success Equation. *JONA* **2000,** *30* (3), 112–117.
Yuan, L.; Yongbin, Z.; Yi, L. The Relationship Between HRM, Technology Innovation and Performance in China. *Int. J. Manpow.* **2005,** *27* (7), 679–697.
Yuh-Shy, C. *Individual Resistance from Employees to Organizational Change*; 2000 [Online] http://www.jgbm.org/page/19%20Dr.%20Chuang,Yuh-Shy.pdf (accessed Oct 5, 2017).

CHAPTER 13

# LABOR DISCRIMINATION

*"Think female workers, think hostess and servers" and*
*"think men, think managers and travelers"*
*"Think migrant worker, think service and cleaning jobs" and*
*"think native, think management and supervision positions"*
*"Think old workers, think back-line jobs" and*
*"think young workers, think front-line jobs"*
*Such kinds of stereotypes and prejudices stand*
*against the advancement of any business.*

## 13.1 INTRODUCTION

Tourism has experienced a growth to become one of the fastest growing economic sectors in the world. Jobs in tourism are always attractive and highly respected. Job opportunities arising out of the growing tourism industry cover a range of sectors and activities, including transport and travel, retail, hospitality, accommodation, visitor attractions, and the performing arts. Such sectors and activities involve a diversity workforce of vulnerable groups which can often be underrepresented in the labor market, for example, women, youth, and disabled.

Diversity of the workforce involves acknowledging, understanding, accepting, and valuing of differences among people in terms of culture, ethnicity, gender, sexual orientation, ability, disability, age, education background, appearance spiritual practice, geographical background, income, marital status, and other individual qualities (Baum, 2007). From a broader viewpoint, diversity in workforce is becoming an increasingly appreciated way for the success, sustainability, and competitiveness of any organization. Accordingly, diversity management has been offered as an emerging tool to gain many organizational benefits, such as lower turnover and absenteeism leading to mitigating labor shortage, continuing production flow, increased sales, reduced cost, increased creativity, innovation, and system flexibility.

On the other hand, diversity brings some issues to the workplace due to the significant differences among workers such as (Nayab, 2010):

- **Launching divergent beliefs by force:** The most common diversity issue in the workplace is religious and spiritual beliefs and also political beliefs. Launching such beliefs causes a challenge; so, management needs to ensure employees do not force their religious or political beliefs on others, and strive to ensure employees keep their beliefs independent of work.
- **Gender discrimination**: Recent years have witnessed an increase in segregation issues in aspects such as hiring, remuneration, promotions, etc.
- **Sexual harassment**: This takes many shapes such as making unwanted jokes or offensive words, touching or any other unsought bodily contact, unwanted flirting, transmitting or posting e-mails or pictures of a sexual or other harassment-related nature, displaying sexually suggestive objects, pictures, or posters, and the like.
- **Racial discrimination**: Hiring or promoting individuals belonging to a certain race, color, religion, sex, or national origin is considered a main cause of hindering the success of any organization.
- **Negative attitudes toward workers with disabilities**: One of the biggest diversity issues in the workplace is negative prejudices and stereotypes that lead to a negative attitude of some employees against workers with disabilities.

  This translates to various forms of discrimination, and if people in the management also inculcate such negative attitudes it affects hiring, firings, promotions, and other functions of the organization.

Such diversity-related challenges require strong management that seeks to set up an organizational cultural climate based on appreciating the worker difference and fighting the discrimination attitudes. Discrimination occurs when a person, or a group of people, is treated less favorably than another person or group because of their background or certain personal characteristics.

Within any organization, discrimination can take one of the three forms (Hollinshead et al., 2003):

- Individual discrimination—individual discrimination concerns prejudice demonstrated by one individual against another.

- Structural discrimination—structural discrimination results in certain groups being excluded due to certain negative stereotypes about their role and ability in accomplishing tasks flawlessly.
- Organizational discrimination—organizational discrimination reflects commonly held beliefs about the suitability of certain groups for certain jobs.

The pervious forms of discrimination can be direct or indirect (Tomei, 2003).

- Direct discrimination takes place where an employee is treated less favorably because of a protected characteristic they possess on the grounds of age, gender, race, etc., than an employee of a different age, gender, race, etc. (Daniels, 2004). Direct discrimination in all its forms could involve a decision not to employ someone, to dismiss them, withhold promotion or training, offer poorer terms and conditions, or deny contractual benefits because of a protected characteristic (Acas, 2016).
- Indirect discrimination takes place when an employer applies an unjustifiable criterion to different groups (e.g., based on age, gender, and race) which negatively affects one group, resulting in a person from the disadvantaged group being unable to comply with the criterion (Daniels, 2004).

There is much research in the literature on the subject of *age* discrimination (Martin and Gardiner, 2007) in employee selection and wages, *race*-related discrimination (Mathis and Jackson, 2000), *gender*-based discrimination (Haar and Spell, 2003; Burgess, 2003), and *disability*-based discrimination (Mathis and Jackson, 2000). This chapter discusses discrimination based on gender, age, race, and disability in detail for the following reasons:

- The *aging* of the labor force is one of the elements affecting labor force diversity in developed countries (Burke and Ng, 2006). This situation will cause sectors, particularly hotel management, fast food chains, and retail sales, to encounter serious employee difficulties (Mathis and Jackson, 2000; Martin and Gardiner, 2007).
- The existence of *racial diversity* in the labor force is another factor affecting labor force diversity.
- Labor force diversity is also affected by the inclusion of the *disabled* in the labor force (Mathis and Jackson, 2000).
- The increasing rate of *women's participation* in the labor force is one of the elements affecting labor force diversity worldwide (ILO, 2009).

## 13.2 AGE DISCRIMINATION

Discrimination based on age is not a new phenomenon. People have experienced discrimination because of their age for hundreds of years. Such type of discrimination is a form of oppression which arises from a social construction of old age (Biggs, 1993). Far too little has been done to change the mindset and attitudes created by this discrimination affecting the basic human rights of older employees although much has been done to change attitudes regarding racism and sexism (Ibbott et al., 2006). MacGregor (2006) argued that there is poor feedback from civil society organizations to the existence of ageism, especially in the United States and Canada. Organizations such as the Canadian Association for Retired Persons (CARP) and the American Association of Retired Persons (AARP) attempt to bring change in regard to issues affecting old-age workers. Unfortunately, their efforts seem to be making little progress in convincing those in power of the seriousness of age discrimination. Endeavors at legislating policies are consistently met by opposition, exceptions, lack of enforcement, and simple lack of interest by lawmakers (Macgregor, 2006). As a result of ignoring ageism issue, old workers are underrepresented in the workforce as a whole in tourism and hospitality industries, with only 14% of employees being 50 years old and older (People 1st, 2006).

Butler (1969) developed the term ageism to describe discriminatory attitudes, behaviors, actions, and policies against people because of their age.

Many researches on ageism in employment uses the age-band of 50 and above to refer an older worker; however, age discrimination affects people of all ages and now affects individuals in their thirties and forties (Wersley, 1996). Butler and Lewis (1973) developed one of the earliest definitions of ageism, stating that it represents the prejudices and stereotypes that are applied to older individuals on the basis of their age. In some communities and societies, the "old" are venerated (Minois, 1989) but, in business society, older workers are treated with absurdity and hostility.

Ageism limits an older person's life chances due to restrictions being placed on them as a result of stereotypical assumptions about their role and abilities (Thompson, 2003) that legitimize the use of age as a sign to deny older people opportunities and resources (Bytheway, 1995).

This hostility continues to the present day and negative views of older people represent a challenge to the fair and equitable treatment of older people in society, work, and other spheres of life. For example, Gringart et al. (2005) surveyed 128 employers about their attitudes toward older employees and found that discrimination in hiring was a direct result of negative attitudes and stereotypes about older workers and thus most employers were "not very likely to hire older workers." Berger (1999) found that employers' attitudes have also been linked to organizations' size characteristics. For example, employers from large organizations (with 20 or more employees) had more negative attitudes toward older workers than those from small enterprises.

Older female workers often were found to experience gender discrimination coupled with age discrimination (McMullin and Berger, 2006).

As with stereotyping and discriminatory actions central to other forms of inequality (e.g., race and gender), employers also draw on ageism stereotypes justifying what they claim to be cost savings for the business (Valletta, 1999). There is a perception that older workers are not interested in working in lower paid/skilled jobs, do not have the physical strength to work in some hospitality environments and will "put off" customers. Along with the employers' belief that the older employee will lose his accumulated work experience due to his old age (Adler and Hilber, 2009), there are other reasons associated with old age still in the mind of employers when treating with old-age workers as shown in Table 13.1.

However, according to Bonn (1992), there is no evidence to back up most of the abovementioned claims, he claimed that older workers are often more stable, reliable, and better at dealing with people (customers and coworkers) than are younger employees.

Also, older workers are usually able to spend more time with customers and can often build better relations with diverse customers. Some organizations use the experience of their older workforce members as a resource for training new employees.

**TABLE 13.1** Reasons of Ageism.

| Ageist stereotypes | Cost-savings technique |
|---|---|
| Less creative | Skill obsolescence |
| Less flexible | Knowledge obsolescence |
| Less trainable | Less productive (health problems) |
| Less interested in new technology | Circumventing pension payouts |
| Less interested in working with younger people | Decreasing wages |
| Do not attract customers | Long-term investment (younger workers) |

**Source:** The Author.

In addition, in the tourism context, older workers are doing their job task better than what is expected from them (Capita Consulting, 2011), here are the justifications:

- *Wages*: Although income is important, old workers have high flexibility regarding wages because of most of them are motivated by the need to get out of the house and interact with others; enthusiasm for a particular enterprise; and a deep-rooted desire to be needed and valued.
- *Health absence*: Older workers have less short-term sickness absence. Older workers with chronic diseases or long-term illness tend to leave the labor market altogether.
- *Unsuitable environment*: Older workers are more able to treat customers than younger, especially in the field of food and beverage as they have got enough experience which enables them to read what their customers exactly need and in turn make them the most proficient of managing customers of restaurants and bars.
- *Do not attract customers*: In general people perceive the product of older workers with trust, sales increase where staff are of diverse ages.
- *Less interested in working with younger workers/teams*: Older and younger workers learn from each other.
- *Commitment*: Older workers often exhibit higher job commitment, less turnover, and lower rates of absenteeism than do younger workers.

In the same line, Capita Consulting (2011) identified the value and benefits of retaining older workers, particularly in such work that have special characteristics of challenges that make retaining young workers a costly and hard process, such as:

- Seasonal work.
- Part time/flexible working options.
- Customer facing.
- Demand for high levels of customer service.
- Retention challenges.

Subsequently, these unique characteristics support the recruitment of older workers who are looking for flexible working arrangements and have good interpersonal skills, in addition to the following advantages:

- Have lower levels of turnover significantly reducing recruitment costs,
- Have high soft skills that enable them to deal with customers in very good manners, based on years of life experience,
- Have a broad range of skills and experience, offering opportunities to mentor new recruits,

- Have lower levels of short-term sickness and fewer accidents, based on their work experience,
- Have high flexibility to accept challenging working schedules (holidays and big events) compared to younger workers, and
- Have good ability to manage and cope with stress.

Ageist actions and discrimination result in lower levels of overall organizational commitment for older employees, particularly for high-skilled older workers, it leads to significant job displacement, involuntary exit from the labor market, and downward mobility upon reemployment (Hirsch et al., 2000), in addition, ageist actions push old workers out of a particular workplace or full-time employment. We explicitly refer to this as a "push" rather than voluntary self-selection because ageist treatment causally precedes a given employee's decision to leave (Snape and Redman, 2003).

In order for employers to deal with the impending worker shortage, they need to change their ageist attitudes toward older workers and avoid discriminating against them in the workplace. Much age discrimination in the workplace is subtle (Cooper and Torrington, 1981) and appears to be deeply embedded in the policies, practices, and cultures of many organizations (Hollywood et al., 2003), hiring practices are the most common area for age discrimination. Attempts have been made to create legislation to counteract ageism, but little progress has been made. Even with legislation in place in the area of employment, only a small number of court cases are ever resolved. In the United States in 2005, of the 16,585 age discrimination complaints submitted to the Equal Employment Opportunity Commission (EEOC), 63% were discarded due to insufficient grounds for complaint. Successful intervention resolved only 1.2% of cases, while 18% were resolved without going to court (Dennis and Thomas, 2007).

Therefore, civil society organizations and legislation alone cannot be expected to fundamentally change peoples' perceptions of older workers but can act as a catalyst to foster change. Barriers to older worker employment in the sector are cultural and must be challenged effectively.

## 13.3 RACE DISCRIMINATION

Migrant workers play an important role in labor markets and contribute to the economies and societies of both their home and destination countries. They spur development through the creation of new enterprises, and strengthen ties between their countries of origin and destination via the transfer of technology and skills. The International Labor Organization (ILO, 2013) estimated that, in 2014, there were 232 million international migrants worldwide who were outside their home country for at least 12 months and approximately half of them were estimated to be economically active (i.e., being employed or seeking employment).

The movement of migrant is always accompanied by national origin discrimination. National origin discrimination involves treating people unfavorably because they are from a particular country or part of the world, because of ethnicity or accent, or because they appear to be of a certain ethnic background (even if they are not). Such discrimination is defined by the International Convention on the Elimination of All Forms of Racial Discrimination as "any distinction, segregation, restriction or preference based on race, color, descent, or national or ethnic origin which has the purpose or effect of nullifying or reducing the exercise of human rights and fundamental freedoms, on an equal footing, in the political, economic, social, cultural, or any other field of public life." National origin discrimination also can involve treating people unfavorably because they are married to (or associated with) a person of a certain national origin. Also, people may be inflicted the discrimination even if they are the same origin.

According to Acas (2016), race discrimination can be made up of two or more of the following elements:

- *Color*: It is strongly linked to the geographical origin to which migrants belong.
- *Ethnic origin*: An ethnic group will usually have characteristics that set it apart from other groups such as:
  - cultural traditions,
  - language,
  - literature,
  - religion, and
  - geographical origin.
- *National origin*: The history of the area can be key factors.
- *Nationality*: Usually the recognized country of which the employee is a citizen.

In businesses context, according to Manhica et al. (2015), organizations' managers usually prefer to hire employees from particular ethnic groups because of some specific skills, abilities, or simply seen as professional in doing some jobs. However, such "ordering" tends to be categorically determined, heavily influenced by the sex, ethnicity, or other characteristics of those who usually do the job in question.

Waldinger and Lichter (2003) refer to such matching as the "hiring queue" in which ethnic workers and employees' groups seen as having the most needed job requirements higher than others. For example, ethnic restaurants seek chefs or waiters of particular ethnic origin. This might be a demand for particular skills that only migrant workers can be expected to have, as when ethnic restaurants.

There are two distinct groups supporting hiring employees from specific subgroups of different national origins, the second one is an obvious example of how such groups of workers experience discrimination in their work only because they belong to different races (Table 13.2).

Depending on the kind of tasks and jobs that need to be filled, the employers have followed one of the following employment approaches (Waldinger and Lichter, 2003):

- Some employers will seek to develop a stable and competent work force, to reduce the costs of constant recruiting, training, and turnover-related costs.
- Others may value the flexibility entailed in employing casual employees.

**TABLE 13.2** Employers' Perspectives Toward Ethnic Employment.

| **Adopting employees of different races** | |
|---|---|
| **Skills** | **Marginalized position** |
| Desirable job attributes (work in peace and are not troublemakers) | They are not in a position that allows them to demand stable employment or more suitable working conditions |
| High certain skills | Willing to take jobs that the majority employees and workers would not accept |
| Highly motivated | Willing to accept lower pay |
| More flexible | Willing to work in worse conditions (e.g., long and crazy working hours) |

**Source:** The Authors.

As the migrant labor desire to seek employment and livelihoods is at the core of the migration, employers of the second type found their lost in such type of labor.

The employers see the migrant position as flexible and willing to work under any circumstances. Consequently, the existence of such short-term employment opportunities in the secondary labor market matches the employers' aspirations of migrant workers who intend to return home with quickly earned money, and who do not seek permanent residence and employment (Piore, 1979); however, it is not necessarily so that migrants are not concerned with stability (Tyldum, 2015).

The high flexibility of migrant labor in accepting to join any kind of work conditions is the normal result of their vulnerable position. Figure 13.1 sheds light on the two reasons contributed to shape their position.

This makes them always subject to employment-related abuse and exploitation, as employers aware of these reasons commonly exploit their vulnerability and treat them as low-cost labor rather than humans that are equally entitled to the same rights as the workers from the more economically developed countries.

Migrant workers from the developing countries are particularly vulnerable to violations of their right to decent work because many migrate due to poverty and the inability to earn or to produce enough to support themselves

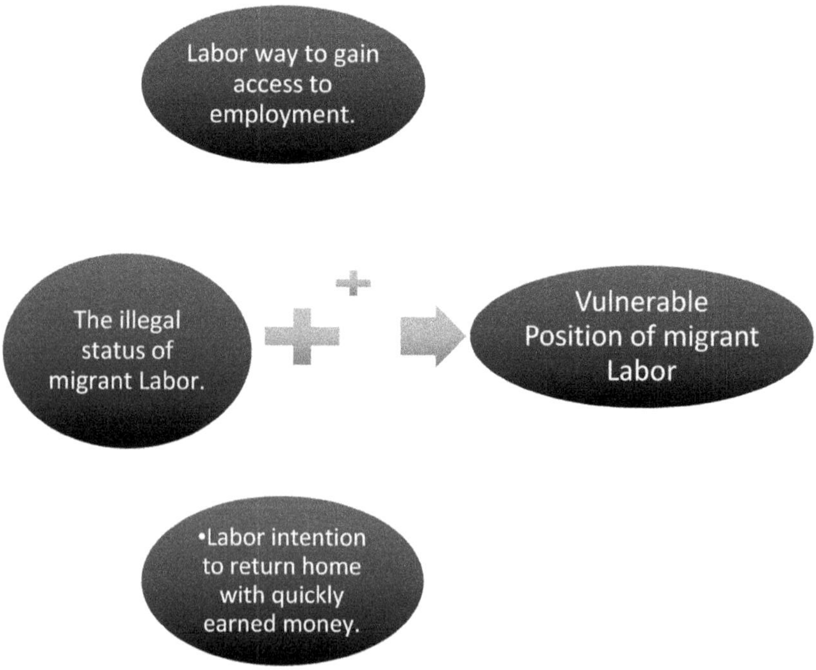


**FIGURE 13.1** Migrant labor status' equation.

**Source:** The Authors.

or their family (UN: 1990) According to ILO (2013), the scale of remittances flowing to developing countries, now over 400 billion dollars a year.

In order to gain access to employment, migrant labor depends mainly on social contacts and networks (for instance, information, positions and assignments tend to be transmitted through friendship, kinship, and collegial ties within ethnic networks). Friberg (2011) asserted that ethnic networks may be a resource for gaining access to employment in secondary jobs, but that social mobility into better, more stable jobs usually connected to other factors.

The conditions surrounding the migrant employees make them subject to negative attitudes from their employers and an easy prey for discriminations actions. Consequently, migrant labor finds themselves trapped behind walls of discrimination, xenophobia, and racism.

## 13.4 EMPLOYEES WITH DISABILITIES

As being one of the diversity dimensions, disability deserves a detailed investigation in order to better recognized and subsequently effectively managed. Employees with disabilities (EWD) in the tourism industry has been largely ignored, except for a few studies while the special needs of tourists with disabilities and their potential benefits to the tourism industry have been studied relatively well (Bengisu and Balta, 2010).

According to US Department of Justice, individual with a disability is someone who "has a physical or mental impairment that substantially limits one or more major life activities or has record of such an impairment is regarded as having such an impairment" (USDJ, 1990). According to Groschl (2007), disability can be viewed from the ecological model, which uses medical criteria to define disability and views disability as a cause of disease, impairment, incapacity, or pathology (Masala and Petretto, 2008). The so-called social perspective conceptualizes the disability as a dynamic process, considering the interaction of personal characteristics with the physical, social, and psychological environment (Masala and Petretto, 2008). The social model does not deny a person's impairment but places disability in a social, economic, and political context and highlights the role of the barriers faced in daily life (Barnes and Mercer, 2008). Some authors prefer the social model, although medical measures are still necessary for classification of disabilities since there are no other useful and scientific alternatives.

Generally, according to the European Commission, people are considered impaired/handicapped when their physical function, their mental ability, or their psychological health deviates from the age-typical condition without much doubt for longer than 6 months and when therefore their participation in society is diminished (European Commission, 2004).

In a survey conducted by Burcu (2007) in Turkey involved a large scale of people with disabilities (PWD), he found that about one-third of the respondents "made peace with their disabilities," and another third did not consider themselves different from the rest of the society according to their self-evaluation. Unfortunately, PWD in many countries face staggering challenges; they are significantly excluded from the labor market and accordingly, this makes them unable to find and maintain suitable jobs, which leads them eventually to exclusion from the social life (Barnes and Mercer, 2008).

Even if they managed to get a job, discrimination and prejudice actions follow PWD during their career advancement path. Always, PWD lies on the vulnerable side when compared with employees without disabilities who have similar professional qualifications and skills. In the tourism context, a number of EWD receive lower hourly wages than do employees without disabilities despite working late or rotating shifts (Presser and Altman, 2002). Meager et al. (1998) conducted a survey in the United Kingdom with 2000 PWD of working age; the results showed that PWD are more likely to end up their career cycle soon in lower skilled occupations.

The reason according to the response of 1321 Turkish PWD is being them constantly pitied by other people, being treated with scorn, and being rejected from the society (Burcu, 2007) that trouble them and affect their commitment and consequently the turnover rate. According to Berthoud (2008), Job possibilities of PWD are reduced significantly compared to others and PWD from ethnic minorities in particular are more likely to be unemployed (Meager et al., 1998). Not only is this unacceptable from an ethical point of view, but it is also economically irrelevant (Ross, 2004).

The society and employers commonly have a prejudiced image of PWD. This provides important clues about some of the challenges that PWD face in daily life and in the work environment. The negative stereotypes that the organizations hold about PWD limit their intention to hire them, in addition to the several challenges they may face in understanding legal definitions and implications of hiring them (Groschl, 2007). Lack of information and fear in the society are identified by Daruwalla and Darcy (2005) as some of the common deficiencies that contribute to the negative attitudes of the employers (Daruwalla and Darcy, 2005).

Additional training, need for retraining, more supervision, and additional costs for accommodations are concerns employers have when working with EWD.

Various researchers have determined productivity, anticipated low-performance levels, mobility, absenteeism, and appearance as the reasons responsible for the employers' negative attitudes toward PWD (Gonzales, 2009).

Discomforts with the process of interviewing PWD, negative attitudes from coworkers were additional issues that prevented employers from penetrating into the disability community. In their study, Schur et al. (2005) argued that the corporate culture influence on the employers' decision to hire EWD, the corporate culture plays a significant role in the creation of attitudinal, behavioral, and physical barriers for employees or job seekers with disabilities. Gonzales (2009) also claimed that barriers and negative perceptions have been shown to grow further if the PWD is a woman or from an ethnic minority.

Despite the negative stereotype that shaped EWD as not qualified employees or cannot work as hard as employees without disabilities, employers consistently rate them average or above average in performance, quality and quantity of work, flexibility, and attendance (Bureau of Labor Statistics, 2011). In their study, Donnelly and Joseph (2012) cited that employees with physical or cognitive disabilities perform at the same (or higher) level as the rest of the employees following adequate training in a hotel. As long as adequate education, devices and equipment are provided to EWD (visually impaired) they can perform many challenging jobs (Bengisu et al., 2008). Therefore, in the work environment, hiring EWD is surrounding with some difficulties and benefits as shown in Table 13.3.

It was found that some employers had positive attitudes and were more willing to hire and integrate PWD into the workforce more than others, for example, some researchers found significant differences between attitude by gender; females totaled higher as compared to males indicating that women had more favorable attitudes toward PWD than their male counterparts (Perry et al., 2008). Generally, employers who have a positive attitude in hiring PWD have some specific characteristics as following (Daruwalla and Darcy, 2005; Perry et al., 2008):

- Own disability,
- Past working experience (employers who had worked in the past with PWD),
- Frequent exposure, and
- Female employers.

**TABLE 13.3** Advantages and Disadvantages of Hiring EWD.

| **EWD** |
|---|
| **Positive** |
| *Production*: High commitment, stability, and devotion that make them productive as any other workers as long as they got trained about their job-related problems and solutions |
| *Loyalty*: EWD are more loyal than others that result in a low rate of labor turnover that leads to reducing the labor-related costs because of the long-term contracting |
| *Motivation*: Their vital need to escape from the social isolation that may beat them if they responded to the surrounding negative hints make EWD more motivated to work than others |
| *Business image*: As a sign of respecting others, EWD employment may improve the organization' image |
| *Customers' support*: Customers may demonstrate understanding and compassion for workers with disabilities. Most of the customers may change their spending patterns based on a company's employment of EWD. Such treatments may seduce employers to place EWD in front-line jobs |
| *Savings*: Governmental assistance and funds for disability training programs |
| **Negative** |
| *Specific jobs*: EWD needs certain types of jobs tailored specifically for them, for example, employees with orthopedic disabilities need:<br>- No heavy physical efforts jobs<br>- No dynamics or moving jobs |
| *Learning problems*: Employees with some kind of disabilities find it harder to learn new skills |
| *Costs*: Accommodating EWD is relatively expensive while additional settings, training, supervision, and flexible work schedules were also required. McCary (2005) found that the perceived costs for making accommodations as well as time-intensive training were major concerns |
| *Inflexibility*: Changes in work routines and having different supervisors can negatively affect the performance of employee with learning disabilities (Ruggeri-Stevens and Goodwin, 2007) |
| *Risks*: Some kind of disability pose extra risks in the workplace such as employees with epilepsy |
| *Unreliability*: Employees with mental health problems are unreliable |
| *Teamwork performance*: The performance of the workforce may be affected because of the lack of communication between EWD and employees without disabilities this may because workforces ignore to accept EWD as colleagues |
| *Extra burden*: Dealing with the EWD requires special treatment that may be considered an overload burden on their coworkers and the customers (if they work in front-line jobs) |
| *Physical appearance*: Usually, in the service sector, the employer prefers the appearance, physical looks, and self-presentation skills of customer-facing employees over hard or technical skills |
| Lack of related work experience, knowledge, and skills |

**Source:** The Authors.

Presser and Altman (2002) indicated that, because hotels and restaurants often look for part-time employees, hospitality work schedules facilitate the incorporation of EWD, providing for an arrangement beneficial for employee and employer. Especially, the upcoming years hold the hope for EWD, a greater portion of the available disabled workforce will be helped to overcome their disability for three main reasons (Donnelly and Joseph 2012):

- Medical advances have enhanced the ability to diagnose disabilities earlier and better treatments mean more PWD can join work effectively.
- Second, technological advances in assistive technology allows for more disabilities to be effectively accommodated at an affordable price.
- Unemployed PWD also tend to have very high levels of education, demonstrating that, as a whole, they are well-educated and qualified to work.

These reasons may help in changing the negative attitudes of employers; also, it was shown that it is possible to change the personal attitudes of nondisabled persons toward PWD through disability awareness training programs (Daruwalla and Darcy, 2005).

Therefore, in order to eliminate discrimination against individuals with disabilities, efforts must be placed to make employers aware of the advantages of hiring PWD (Ruggeri-Stevens and Goodwin, 2007), in addition to activating the legislation of PWD employment. Moreover, according to (Groschl, 2007), an improvement in employer education and enhanced communication between EWD and those without disabilities, might lead to hiring and better engagement of this sector of the population.

## 13.5 GENDER DISCRIMINATION

Recent years have seen an emergence of studies that explore the role of women in the labor force and the expansion of the internationally hospitality workforce (Baum, 2007).

Many countries have a high presence of the feminine labor force in tourism this is because of the high demand for unqualified workers, especially for young women. Although the participation and involvement of women in the tourism sector are being encouraged and women's participation has increased directly and indirectly in the tourism industry, but today tourism represents a double-edged opportunity, as they face discriminative practices in terms of gender inequality and women's empowerment, as the tourism and hospitality sectors are dominated by women and managed by men; in fact it is very common as the service sector is largely populated by women and they are more present especially at the lower level.

In America, more than 50% of the people who are employed in the tourism sector are women. According to UK Essays (2015), one in every 15 people all over the world is employed in the tourism sector and half of them are women.

### *13.5.1 WOMEN IN HOSPITALITY INDUSTRY*

In order to maintain its glamorous image, the tourism industry is considered to be oriented toward recruiting young female workers. Likewise, the perceived glamour of tourism work is thought to be a key factor in attracting women into the workforce. Other than the image of the industry, the participation of women in work life is a respectable indicator of a country's economic development. Such economics provides more opportunities for women to participate public business or in self-employed home-based work.

In tourism economies, the tourism industry is considered as "female-friendly" (Obadić and Marić, 2009), this may be because of the following two reasons:

1. It is more attractive to women than to men because of the nature of the work involved and type of employment;
   - *Nature of work*: Women are better in these jobs in the service industry because they have more patience. Customers prefer to deal with females because they find it easier to talk to them. Women are more relaxed than men. This gives the priority for women when the organization feels labor shortage, so, the nature of the tourism and hospitality industry made the jobs an easy-access for women.
   - *Type of employment*: Women are seeking flexible-hour jobs in order to accommodate their family commitments (Jordan, 1997), consequently, part-time jobs that dominate employment pattern in the industry is primarily attributable to women's preference. This pattern of employment allows for workers to earn an amount of money and at the same time to take care of the family.

2. Previously, service sector positions were less prestigious than those in manufacturing and were thus dominated by women. In the market economy, work experience in the expanding service sector became an advantage for many women, while many men had to struggle for jobs in the declining industrial or agricultural sectors. Thus, women workers predominated in some jobs. Women in tourism had more chance to be employers in hotels and restaurants sector than there are in other sectors. For example, there are more ministerial positions in tourism held by women than in other areas.

Unfortunately, today, the not rosy side of tourism labor market exists. Despite tourism industry is a labor intensive one that provides different jobs opportunities from high-skilled jobs to unskilled jobs. But, female workers are often concentrated in low status, low paid, and precarious jobs in tourism industry. Women are still under-represented in the managerial structures of these sectors (Witz and Savage, 1992). They are still not being paid as much as men and they are not receiving the same level of education and training and services as men. The view of tourism employment as glamour environment and positively attractive provides employers with a useful explanation for the number of women working in poorly paid jobs within the industry. Their justification is that women are happy to accept the poor conditions because the work is glamour.

In some countries, these gendered differences are very significant and as a result, gender discrimination represents a huge problem. Globally, the overall percentage of women's participation in the tourism labor force is around 55% (Baum, 2013). The countries with the lowest female participation in tourism employment are situated in North Africa or the Middle East. In the Middle East and North Africa region, women remain untapped resources comprising 49%of the total population, representing more than half of the university graduates in some countries; however, they make up just 28% of the labor force (World Bank, 2004).

Among supply-side factors impacting women labor in some countries is cultural and religious aspect that strongly affect overall access to employment, which is also reflected at a sectoral level (Baum, 2013), religion is a key determinant of Muslim and Hindu women work, as they are having a significantly lower participation rate especially in tourism and hospitality sector than those of different religious backgrounds (H'madoun, 2010). However, Hayo and Caris (2013) claimed that traditional identity and the perception of family roles of the women is a more meaningful explanation than religious identity; the traditional social norms that is measured by the thoughts and attitudes of both the family members and neighbors toward women working especially in tourism and hospitality industry reduce critically the participation of women (Jordan et al., 2011). It is also argued by Carvalho (2010) that peer's attitudes are as vital as the household members attitudes.

In addition, marital status determines women contribution in labor market of the industry. In particular, it is found that married females have higher probabilities of participation than singles, divorced, or widow females. In contrary, in Yemen, for example, unmarried women are more likely to participate in the workforce than married women or women in urban areas.

This suggests that norms about women's role outside the home may be more strictly enforced after marriage and in more conservative, rural societies. On the other hand, singles have lower probabilities of participation as they are supported by their families, and thus, have fewer incentives to be economically active (Livanos et al., 2009). Similarly, the so-called marriage premium effects are confirmed by Thrane in case of more than 100,000 Norwegian tourism employees. Married employees typically earn a higher wage rate than their unmarried counterparts (Thrane, 2008).

Generally, such determinants lose much of its effects in case of education; higher educational level means family support and holds an implicit approval of working, in the same line, Chamlou et al. (2011) argued that women with higher education are more likely to participate, based on the data collected in Amman. In Morocco, Taamouti and Ziroili (2010) examined the relationship between individual factors and female work, concluding that for urban women, education is the main determinant of labor market participation.

In fact, employment provides women with a real opportunity to enhance the quality of their lives, as higher expenditure has a positive impact as female members would be expected to contribute financially in order to afford the necessary expenditure.

In summary, gender equality is a precondition for sustainable growth, employment, competitiveness, and social cohesion. According to ILO (2010), gender equality means the demand to assure equal conditions for both men and women—their full rights to benefit from economic, political, cultural, and social development. However, it is worldwide known that employment across a wide spectrum of industries is segregated by sex. The jobs that women do are different from those done by men (horizontal segregation) and women work at lower levels than men in the occupational hierarchy (vertical segregation) (Jordan, 1997). Therefore, supporting economic sectors that employ large percentages of women, such as service sector, will help improve the relative economic status of women.

### 13.5.2 GENDER STEREOTYPING IN THE WORLD OF HOSPITALITY INDUSTRY

The tourism industry plays a significant role in employment of women, because it offers greater opportunities for women; women have possibilities to work in small-scale and informal types of tourism businesses, particularly home-based business such as those providing bed and breakfast accommodation or simple meals outlets because such work does not necessarily compromise women's other productive duties within the household (Kattara, 2005).

At the same time, tourism can provide a number of entry points for currently inactive women. There is a potential for the creation of various employment and self-employment opportunities, especially in seasonal employment.

Women, it is argued, seek these jobs in order to accommodate their family commitments. Along with opportunities, tourism also brings risks and challenges to different groups of women in different tourism subsectors (accommodation and food, air transport, travel agencies and tour operators, etc.). Historically, women were generally seen as home-makers and thus not only was their unpaid work in the home not considered "work," their paid work was also viewed as nonessential (Denton et al., 2000). McDonald (2006) used the term "invisible" when referring to the position of women within the topic of work and retirement. Such negative stereotypes about women located women in seasonal and part-time jobs at the lower end of the pyramid of tourism and hospitality employment (Richter, 1994), for instance, it is familiar that hotel domestic workers, waitress, and cooks were generally female, while the majority of tour guides, taxi drivers, boat operators, and maintenance workers were male. Furthermore, mass tourism is frequently predestined for maintaining traditional beliefs and notions about female gender roles by segregating employment such that women's domestic skills and what are believed to be (feminine characteristics) become commodities (Mckenzie Gentry, 2007). Such stereotypes are confirmed by the social construction that allowed national governments and tourist organizations to describe women in a service role, while men in supervisor and administrative positions. This is confirmed by Leontidou (1994) who claimed that the traditional gender distinctions have promoted the image of men as travelers and women as hostesses. Many studies focusing on the tourism and hospitality sector has highlighted the specific issues experienced by women in this area, where only a few senior managers, and fewest number in top management, are female. Some studies suggest that women have only limited access to well-paid, skilled, and managerial positions. The gender-based wage differential is also well documented for the different occupations and is persistent across cultural boundaries (Gray and Benson, 2003).

Although the wage gap between women and men narrowed to 78% as 60 years ago, women earned 59 cents on the dollar (Polachek et al., 2015), but throughout the world men still earn more than women. For example, in Spain, Munoz-Bullon studied gender inequality especially with regard to wage inequalities in the hotel and restaurant subsector and found out that male workers earn on average 6.7% higher monthly wages than their female counterparts. In relation to the discrimination component he also noted that men generally occupy jobs that require high qualifications, and in subsectors where wages are higher (restaurants vs. tour guides in Spain) men are more often hired with open-ended contracts (Munoz-Bullon, 2008).

Along with pay differential, gender discrimination most explicitly appears in forms of occupational gender segregation that are frequently linked to traditions and stereotypes (Hakim, 1992).

Smith et al. (2003) confirmed that gender stereotypical attitude is not simply a reflection of the individual but rather emerges in the form of deeply rooted traditional epistemological sexist believes, that are common believe patterns in the society, where men are traditionally the travelers and leaders, whereas women are servers and subordinates. Generally, norms and beliefs dictate certain behavior that governs the relations and positions of individuals in social life that reflects significantly on working live (Smith et al., 2003). In tourism and hospitality industry, Purcell (1996) developed a well-known analysis of the effects of negative stereotypes about women on her work life, he argued that there are three main factors determining employers to recruit women for particular types of work: labor price, sex, and gender (Mullins, 1998). Thus, "women's job" fall predominantly into one of those three categories; typically, a woman will be hired when the employer need to cut labor costs, and assign her to perform those roles which are perceived as feminine, such as welcoming the guests, cleaning the rooms, and serving the food and drink, while a man will do the repair work and manage the hotel. Stereotyping can have negative impacts to women's advancement in the workplace, since negative stereotypes of women offer many questions that surrounding the female workers:

- How their employers perceive them?
  Their perception definitely influences on:
  - Selecting them for further training and development opportunities and

  - Their growth opportunity or mobility in their career.
- How their coworkers perceive their work?
  Their perception definitely influences on:
  - Their engagement and commitment that will reflect on their performance.
- How the customers perceive their work?
  Their perception definitely influences on:
  - The quality of service they offer.
- How the society perceive their work?
  Their perception definitely influences on:
  - Basically, will determine to work or not.

The consequences of such negative stereotypes created the so-called occupational gender segregation, that represents a widespread phenomenon throughout the world and refers to unequal distribution of women and men among different jobs and as such limits promotion opportunities for women. Abundant evidence suggests that women's employment in the tourism and hospitality industry is segregated both horizontally and vertically, with the majority of women located in subordinated positions, receiving lower levels of payment.

Considering the vertical gender pyramid, women have occupied lower levels in the industry with few opportunities for upward mobility, while men dominate the key managerial positions. Vertical segregation, sometimes called "glass ceiling," means the existence of obvious and subtle barriers that lead to absence of female workers in all the management level positions (Elliott and Smith, 2004). The concept is sometimes presented as "stinky floor" that prevents women to be promoted to the higher levels of organizational pyramid (Baum, 2013). However, there is also a horizontal segregation because more women are employed within the sector than men while earning less (Campos-Soria et al., 2011) because women are disproportionately represented in lower skills and lower paid jobs within the sector (Baum, 2013).

Horizontally, women and men are placed in different occupations—women are employed as receptionists, waitresses, room attendants, cleaners, travel agency sales persons, etc., on the other hand, men are employed as barmen, porters, gardeners, maintenance staff, etc., (Parrett, 2004). Even when getting to the management position, women are subject to more experience vertical exclusion. The vertical segregation at the managerial level (Ng and Pine, 2003) include assigning women middle managers in housekeeping, front desk, personnel and training, and conference and banqueting, whereas male managers are in finance and control, property and security and purchasing, the latter more likely to lead to the general manager's job. In such way, tourism industry segregates women into areas of employment which commercialize their perceived domestic skills and "feminine" characteristics.

The vertical and horizontal occupational structure of women workforce in the industry created three main stories depicting the women in the tourism and hospitality industry (Fig. 13.2):

- First, gender-contingent jobs

Gender-contingent jobs which happen to be mainly done by women but for which the demand for labor is gender-neutral (Purcell, 1996). Women work in such jobs as a result of employers' pursuit of cutting labor costs rather than gendered preferences; they want cheap workers, and women have historically identified a low-paid labor, partly because their status as a "family member" rather than as "breadwinners."

- Secondly, gender-typified jobs

It is common in tourism and hospitality industry that "the right kind of personality" is a more important employment prerequisite than formal

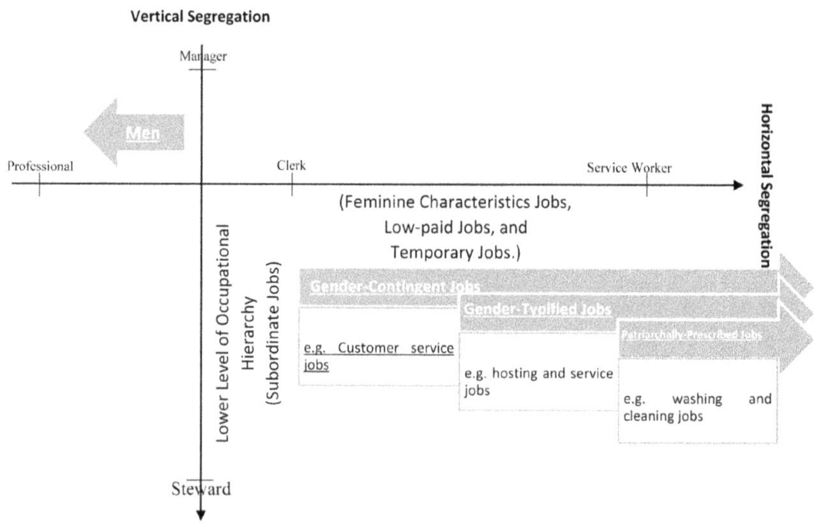


**FIGURE 13.2** Women's work in tourism and hospitality industry.

**Source:** The Authors.

qualifications. In case of the female workers, personality tends to be used as a synonym for sexual attractiveness (Purcell 1996; Weichselbaumer, 2003) where sexuality or other attributes assumed to be sex-related are explicit or implicit components of the job specification.

This notion is confirmed by women themselves, in a case study conducted in an English hotel by Biswas and Cassell (1996) and found that women felt that they were viewed as sex objects (e.g., receptionists and sales and marketing staff).

- Finally, patriarchally-prescribed jobs

Patriarchal prescriptions, though, is a distinct and equally powerful tendency, deriving from perceptions that male dominance in the home and in the public sphere and women's dependency are normal and that these norms derive from "natural" differences between them. Hence, this approach believes in inherent aptitudes that women possess in caring for the comfort and welfare of others and preparing and serving food calls (Purcell, 1996).

Accordingly, people in particular jobs and the jobs themselves have the characteristics of only one gender.

Women in the hospitality industry are widely employed in subordinate jobs for their nurturing and/or sexual attributes. However, they also have been excluded from some occupations within the tourism industry due to traditional ideologies of gender and social sexuality which is very stereotyped._Moreover, segregated treatment of women has been reported in selection, pay, and career development prospects.

### *13.5.3 THE STATUS OF WOMEN IN TOURISM INDUSTRY*

The tourism industry is characterized by its employment seasonality. Therefore, so-called "seasonal unemployment" made tourism an attractive opportunity for female. Exactly that feature made tourism industry an attractive opportunity for women who could combine work with family responsibilities and other duties (Ghodsee, 2003).

Seasonal, part-time, and casual employment allows women to combine these various commitments with paid work outside their homes. Moreover, because many tourism sector jobs require only basic and highly transferable skills, easy access jobs made women may move in and out of the sector with relative ease (Obadić and Marić, 2009). However, the seasonality of such employment is often criticized by the researchers, which also tends to offer low-paying, low-skill opportunities with little chance for advancements.

Subsequently, gender discrimination is a common attitude in tourism and hospitality industry in spite of the fact that gender equity legislative framework remains in force for decades. Numerous respondents in different studies mentioned that age and sex were important factors governing work in tourism (Mckenzie Gentry, 2007).

In fact, the tourism industry has shown a wide adoption of segregation occupation. In the industry women frequently carry out the most undesirable and lowest status work, in addition they face direct discrimination since women are statistically underpaid compared to men even if they are equally positioned (Foubert, 2010). The marginalized status of women in tourism and hospitality industry is interlinked basically to (Burrell et al., 1997; Brownell, 1994; Davidson and Cooper, 1992; Knutson and Schimdgall, 1999; Ng and Pine, 2003; UK Essays, 2015):

- The discriminatory preferences of employers and customers,
- Gender stereotyping,
- Recruitment processes,
- Work regulations,
- Patriarchal hierarchies,
- Lack a role model,
- Lack of mentoring,
- Lack of networking options,
- The reconciliation of work and home life,
- Family and peers for women in the workplace,
- The hidden societal and attitudinal barriers "the glass ceiling," and
- Educational levels.

These factors reflected on women's work in forms of exploitative and underpaid employment (Kiani, 2009). In developing countries, for example, women mainly work in lower paid clerical and cleaning jobs while men mostly work as hotel and restaurant managers, machine operators, and gardeners (Kattara, 2005). In Singapore, only two females out of 77 occupied the general manager position in the hospitality sector (Kattara, 2005). The same case in Egypt, the women observed to be less likely in top managerial positions in five-star hotels (UNWTO, 2010).

The barriers to women's advancement in hospitality properties were identified as gender relationship at work as they often lack the opportunity to socialize with the top male managers and therefore do not benefit from the mentoring received by their male colleagues, in addition to discrimination, lack of mentor support, and lack of network access. Moreover, family responsibilities were seen as the main barrier to women's progression to senior in hotels and restaurants, the difficulty in combining this type of work with family responsibilities, given the requirement to work shifts and long hours (Kara et al., 2018). Accordingly, a high percent of most of women in tourism and hospitality industry work as part-time workers, because the flexibility it can give to women who may be required to spend more time working in their homes (with family or care responsibilities).

In Britain, accommodation and food and beverage are the dominant employment subsectors within the tourism and hospitality industry. These subsectors are characterized by a female-dominated workforce, nearly three quarters of which is employed part time (Parrett, 2004). The share of part-time women employment in EU-27 in 2006 was 25% (European Commission, 2007). Figure 13.3 shows the distribution of employment according to sex in the EU-27 by part-time/full-time status, in which it is noticeable that percentage of women working part-time is higher than males.

The types of employment were reviewed in hotel and restaurant establishments: full-time, part-time, and casual. Women are likely than men to work as part-time employees (ILO, 2010). Also, three levels of employment status were reviewed in hotels and restaurants sector: professional, clerk, and service worker. Kattara (2005) noted that women are more likely than men to work at clerical level in the hotels and restaurants sector and less likely than men to reach the professional level.

**FIGURE 13.3 (See color insert.)** The distribution of employment according to sex.

**Source:** The Authors, based on ILO (2010).

The airline industry is another example of a segregated sector. Compared to men, women dominate sales, ticketing, and flight attendant positions, while men dominate the majority of airline CEOs, mangers, and pilots. Approximately 80,000 pilots worldwide, about 4000 are now women (5%) (Kattara, 2005). Another sector of tourism industry is tour guiding which is often regarded as a desirable profession in developing countries due to the generous tips provide by foreign tourists. In many countries, tour guiding is another area that has been hard for women to enter. In many societies, the profession is male-dominated, and women tour guides have faced significant discrimination (Kattara, 2005).

### *13.5.4 WOMEN CAREER ADVANCEMENT PATH IN HOSPITALITY AND TOURISM INDUSTRY*

Tourism employment is gendered in nature and the problem with this segregated employment is that women's low status within their societies is reinforced and magnified in the mass industry (Jordan, 1997). Despite that women being the majority of higher education graduates in tourism, men hold upper-management and decision-making positions more often than women do, besides earning better salaries (Costa, 2014). In key managerial positions, where the income is subject to individual negotiations, women tend to earn 20–30% less than men.

The proportion of men in leadership positions almost doubles that of women. Women are very much underrepresented in top-level occupations, especially in executive positions. (Santos, 2006). Women do not invest in their own capital because they are less aware of the benefits (Baum, 2013). Subsequently, the career paths of women are also different from men, female workers during her work life make fewer moves and number of positions (Blayney and Blotnicky, 2011) in spite of that women were rated higher on interpersonal behaviors than were males at the middle and executive levels (Martin and Kromkowski, 2003) and females were found to be more oriented toward supporting and maintaining relationships with stakeholders than men (Hisrich and Brush, 1994).

#### *13.5.4.1 OCCUPATIONAL GENDER SEGREGATION*

Many of the women perceived tourism to be an industry which is still male-dominated at senior management levels, despite the number of women employed. They do not agree that a climate of equal opportunities already exists (Jordan, 1997).

Although men and women in managerial positions use different techniques and demonstrate different competencies and women predominate in hospitality workforce as research indicates (Burgess, 2000). Women continue to be underrepresented in senior positions and general management roles and when it comes to women in leadership roles the sector falls short of other industries that do not demonstrate the same advantage (Sayers, 2012). They are still underrepresented in management roles due to facing formal and informal exclusionary practices and prejudices of required male characteristics in order to be successful. Even when getting to the management position, women are subject to experience exclusion practices (Koenig et al., 2011). For example, Biswas and Cassell (1996) conducted a case study on the gender divisions of labor in an English hotel and found that men occupied higher status roles than women.

Evidence comes from Baum and Cheung (2015) as following:

- Women hold less than 40% of all managerial and supervisory positions in the international hospitality industry,
- Women hold less than 20% of general management roles,
- Women are identified as owners of less than 20% of hospitality business and only around 10% of hotels worldwide, and
- Women make up between 5% and 8% of corporate board numbers of publicly quoted hospitality businesses.

Hence, women inclusion in the hierarchical levels of tourism labor market unfortunately still facing some existing barriers. A report on women's place in the tourism industry commissioned in the United Kingdom found that only a small minority of women managers were able to achieve top managerial positions. Burrell et al. (1997) and McKenzie-Gentry (2007) indicated that women managers only represent 3% of the total staff in hotels in Belize. Ramos-Mir et al. (2004) advocated that tourism industry in Spain face the same problem in the in the Balearic Islands. All of this research reveals existing of the glass ceiling that blocks the entry of women into highly paid jobs. Wentling (2003) also found similar results in the United States. Women were "plateauing" at middle management positions, at which level they could only act as implementers of decisions, rather than as decisions makers. In the United States, in hotels over 500 rooms, the "pink-collar ghetto" still exists where only 2.6% of the hotel managers were identified as women (Wood and Viehland, 2000), the same notion exists in Canada; Maxwell (1997) claimed that there is an absence of significant representation of women in management level and the hospitality industry is one with a long-established history of male dominancy. Catalyst (2008) reported that although the overall labor force is 46.9% female, women in management in 2006 represent 36.4% as in Canada. Only 26.4% of senior management jobs are female and only 14.4% occupy a position as a Financial Post Corporate Officer.

In the Caribbean, the same case exists where most of the top managerial staff are men who brought in from North America or Europe because they felt that Caribbean's did not have the experienced and skilled male labor needed to serve in upper-level management. Also, managerial positions at the lower end of the hierarchy went also for men but these levels for Caribbeans men who were trained by the hotels and worked their way into positions such as executive housekeeper and food and beverage manager (Mckenzie Gentry, 2007), while, women are excluded.

As long as gender segregation persists, and women's work is devaluated, there will be more opportunities for advancement and higher earnings on the side of men (Reskin and Bielby, 2005). Still the negative perceptions and prejudices that the male managers and professionals have against female constitute the strong challenge that hinders women's upward mobility in workplace. Although there is such stereotyping in the industry, studies show that female students are more committed to careers in hospitality and tourism and seem to better fit success in this sector than do their male classmates and colleagues as women tend to be strong in idea generation and innovation according to a comparison on the basis of differences in the characteristics of women as managers and male managers (Rosnener, 1995). Tourism companies run by a woman is frequently more successful than those managed by man. Also, Johansen (2007) found that women are more successful than men in using the reactor and the prospector strategy. This may be the nature of women that tend to be more interactive and use valuable input and advice rather than make decision on their own.

Other studies have also found that men tend to be more concerned with positions of dominance and formal power and women like to use a more interactive style and are open to more feedback from colleagues and associates to find innovative ideas (Johansen, 2007). In summary, longitudinal research data testify in favor of success of women, even without start-up capital female tourism managers out-perform the organizations run by men in terms of organization growth and subsequently raising national employment rates and creating wealth. So, it is recommended that tourist companies should promote women to leadership positions (Alonso-Almeida, 2013), in order to make this recommendation real women must be able of "wearing two different hats—one at work and one at home" till the several attempts to achieve gender equity make results.

### 13.5.5 GENDER SEGREGATION REASONS

Many empirical studies have focused on analyzing the causes of women exclusion in tourism and hospitality industry. Here are some reasons that enhance the women stereotype in tourism labor market:

### 1. Glass ceiling

The term was earlier used by Morrison et al. (1987) in their book "Breaking the Glass Ceiling: Can Women Reach the Top of America's Largest Corporations?" That gave new insight to the issues women face in their journey to top managerial positions. The term of the "glass ceiling" has been widely discussed in relation to the obstacles faced by female managers in their desire to get to the top. The glass ceiling has been described as hidden discriminatory societal and attitudinal barriers that hinder the career progression of women (Bird et al., 2002), then it refers to the failure of women and other minority groups in climbing up the corporate ladder, despite seeing the top jobs, but still not reaching them due to segregation barriers. So, when it comes to studying the barriers to the advancement of women in tourism and hospitality industry three important factors must be appreciated: the glass ceiling, the intersection between gender, and other diversity characteristics (Mooney and Ryan, 2009). Li and Leung (2001) claimed that an important predictor of the existence of the glass ceiling is female managers' lack of connection to professional and old boy networks. Mooney and Ryan (2009) identified four glass ceiling barriers to women's advancement in the hospitality industry, namely:

- *Odd and long working hours*

  The long working hours are a major challenge for women because many have significantly more family responsibilities than their male counterparts. Relating to the work life, this was particularly a challenge for women in their late 20s and early 30s, who are more likely to be married and with children. So, most women who progressed to the top were single, signaling to young women that if they wanted career progressing, they had to sacrifice a partner or children.

- *Old boy's network*

  The "old boy's network" or the "old boy club," indicate to the informal networks in the workplace that women difficult to penetrate which limit her work performance as such skills shortage hinder the professional contact with the professionals of the industry. Li and Leung (2001) suggested that female managers should establish their own networks to overcome the isolation in a male dominated corporate environment. Their networks could serve as informal communication, support, and mentorship systems that effectively counterbalance men's groups.

- *Think male*

  Due to the reasons associated with marriage and childbearing compared with women, males are favored when the organization call for hiring as they perceived as more reliable and less likely to leave the job or the industry.

- *Geographical mobility*

  Men had greater liberty for mobility than women because men's mobility is less restricted by their children's care.

## 2. *Social norms*

Social norms are the result of men's perception of women and also women's perception of themselves; women perfectly perform cleaning and service-related duties, this is the common norm of female workers that lead to over-representation of women in lower professional category, lower responsibility positions, and lower status and income (Elliott and Smith, 2004; Jordan, 1997); whereas maintenance, bartending, gardening, and higher responsibility level jobs are mostly taken by men in tourism sector which means that still social norms are important factor of segregation patterns.

## 3. *Stereotypical assumption*

The culture of occupational gender segregation in hospitality and tourism industry is promoted by organizations themselves due to managing recruitment process in accordance to stereotypical stance of women's appropriate work roles (Jordan, 1997). A significant portion of employers make recruitment decision on stereotypical assumption about specific jobs that suit only men or women and thus occupation gender segregation occurs (Burrell et al., 1997). Women were concentrated in "mothering" and in "glamorous" roles. Women felt that they were viewed as maternal home-makers (e.g., chambermaids, breakfast waitresses, and hostesses) (Biswas and Cassell, 1996).

### 4. *Cultural values*

The role played by cultural values in influencing the career progression of women in management jobs is highly recorded.

For example, Li and Leung (2001) argued that cultural values in Singapore play a role in restricting women's access to professional and old boy networks. Because of such exclusion, female managers have limited opportunity to socialize with powerful executives who could help their business development that lead to reinforcing their career growth.

### 5. *Sexism practices*

Traditionally, women were believed to be successful only in nonleadership positions, therefore they have been assigned lower position posts of lower earnings, no prestige, and power and in this direction Sayers (Mkono, 2012) claimed that it is sexism that causes anchoring prejudices about women's abilities to take the responsibility of others (management positions) as women were perceived by both male and female managers as less likely to possess the qualities, attitudes, and temperaments required to succeed as a manager. In the same line of argument, Schein (2007) asserted that the characteristics required for success are viewed as being possessed by men rather than women, and this is why managerial work is dominated by males.

### 6. *Unethical leadership policy*

In contemporary work settings, feminine leadership is more effective than the leadership of men (Koenig et al., 2011), as they are equally qualified in terms of academic qualifications and above all, they practice transformational leadership which defines many successful organizations (Alonso-Almeida, 2013). In the hotel industry in Canada, it was found that women manage successfully the majority of the small-sized hospitality properties (Blayney and Blotnicky, 2010).

On the other hand, one of the main disadvantages that is adjacent to men leadership is the negative stereotypes they often hold about female workers that eventually result in occupational gender segregation. Gender segregation leads to unequal treatments in terms of career rewards and upward mobility for male and female workers (Reskin and Bielby, 2005). Consequently, gender divisions of labor in the hotel industry became undeniable (Biswas and Cassell, 1996).

Although female tourism employees generally achieve higher levels of education than male counterparts do but gender still plays an important role in wage levels because still receive on average 20% lower wages than their male colleagues.

Hence, under the leadership of men, occupational gender segregation, in general, is strongly proved. For example, in most tourism organizations, promotion systems operate on the basis of informal and nonwritten criteria and the decisions that senior management makes about promotion usually depend on middle managers' recommendation. Such promotion procedures further contribute to gender segregation (Jordan, 1997). Therefore, there is a need for establishing fair promotion processes. When career advancement to the managerial position is subject to discretion and preferences it definitely will influence strongly on women's career dynamics (Eurofound, 2010).

## *7. Work–life imbalance*

In tourism and hospitality industry, jobs are accused of interrupting female workers' life because of the variability of the demand cycle due to seasonality differences that demand unsocial working hours.

Working conditions in hospitality and tourism sectors are frequently challenging, employees facing a heavy workload and constant pressure although there are considerable differences between countries and between different segments (Eurofound, 2010). In New Zealand and Australia, research on women in the hotel industry concluded that long working hours is among factors causing a significant imbalance in the life of female workers (Mooney and Ryan, 2008).

## *8. Nature of work*

In tourism and hospitality context, many employees and employers claimed that the nature of some occupations may be responsible for occupational segregations. Purcell (1996) concluded from his interviews with employees and employers in Italy and the United Kingdom that jobs in the hospitality industry were contingently gendered. There are some types of jobs that require the presence of female smile and other jobs need to an acceptable extent the strong (rigid) practices, while most back-line jobs require physical abilities and consequently, such jobs are restricted for men.

Women are segregated into those areas of employment which require their domestic skills and their "feminine" characteristics (Kinnaird et al., 1994). According to Burrell et al. (1997), cleaning and reception in hotels in the United Kingdom, France, Spain, and Italy are occupational areas where women predominate, as employers considered that women were better at such jobs than men. Even if the women worked in some areas such as the kitchen, they are more likely to work in washing up and cleaning rather than cooking. Also, women work in reception area, for example, is still limited due to the need for security at night or for carrying heavy suitcases, which stereotypically excludes women.

On the other hand, the maintenance, bar, and kitchen departments in hotels are dominated by men (Ramos-Mir et al., 2004). In the same line, Burrell and his colleagues found that bar jobs are dominated by men in Spain, the United Kingdom, and France, but are more evenly distributed in Italy. They also found that there is a high proportion of men in kitchen-related jobs in France and the United Kingdom. In Spain, this proportion is more equivalent, whereas women dominate in Italy. Hence, nature of work is a good reason for employers to justify their decisions of segregation.

### *13.5.6 TACKLING WORKPLACE DISCRIMINATION*

Both quantitative and qualitative investigation studies suggest a need to tackle informal workplace custom and practice and unwritten rules that contribute to unfair discriminatory practices. Employers must take into their consideration only the qualities and skills required to fill job vacancies regardless the gender of the job applicants (ILO, 2009). The equal treatment of men and women in terms of fair salary levels that are needed to increase the level of job satisfaction of both male and female employees (Kara et al., 2012) ensure the success of the organization by maintaining its competent and skilled employees.

Organizations' success depends on employee commitment and loyalty. Equal opportunity practice might contribute to talent identification and consequently organization success (Baum, 2013). For example, Wood et al. (2009)

concluded that employer use of standardized job application forms, rather than CVs, may be a practical action for enforcing the gender equity policy and consequently help in tackling racial discrimination in recruitment practice.

In order to avoid discriminatory practices in the recruiting process, there are two most significant points to consider as follows (Yeşiltaş et al., 2013):

– *Business necessity and job matching*

  It is expected that the qualifications expected by the employer of the applicant to demonstrate job-related performance are genuinely related to the job.

– *Main occupational qualifications*

  If the organization or employer included in the job criteria certain characteristics such as gender, religion, or ethnicity, this would normally be assessed as discriminations if these characteristics are not "vital requirements of the job."

Ensuring the equal opportunity policy is in itself insufficient but necessary when coping with gender discrimination. Organizations with such a policy are more positive to women with the climate of trust created within a highly supportive work environment.

The positive climate is commonly beneficial to the organization and to the employees because it conveys equal opportunities for all and makes a sound basis for organizations' success (Baum, 2013). It is also recommended that organizations should promote male careers of jobs traditionally dominated by women and vice versa in order to avoid occupational gender segregation as Demir (2007) found a negative relationship between the ratio of female coworkers and women turnover. It was seen that women workers would like to work more with their female coworkers, and were more satisfied and tried to quit less from their jobs.

Guerrier (1986) argued that if women do not aspire to attain senior management posts in hotels this is an acknowledgment of the way such positions are represented and the segregation practices that result in lack of opportunities they may perceive. So, Baum (2013) recommended making steps to identify talent not on the gender basis but rather on transparent access to higher organizational positions for both members. Moreover, Baum (2013) claimed that policies that encourage suitable childcare provisions are needed to improve the vulnerable status of female workers in work environment, that will ensure that women while on leave remain in touch with the organization.

## REFERENCES

Acas. *Race Discrimination: Key Points for the Workplace*; Help and Advice for Employers and Employees; 2016 (Online). ww.acas.org.uk (accessed Oct 23, 2017).

Adler, G.; Hilber, D. Industry Hiring Patterns of Older Workers. *Res. Aging* **2009,** *31* (1), 69–88.

Alonso-Almeida, M. M. Influence of Gender and Financing on Tourist Company Growth. *J. Bus. Res.* **2013,** *66* (5), 621–631.

Aslund, O.; Skans, O. N. Will I See You at Work? Ethnic Workplace Segregation in Sweden, 1985–2002. *Indus. Labor Relat. Rev.* **2010,** *63* (3), 471–493.

Barnes, C.; Mercer, G. Disability, Work, and Welfare: Challenging the Social Exclusion of Disabled People. *Work Employm. Soc.* **2008,** *19* (3), 527–545.

Bartol, K.; Martin, D.; Kromkowski, J. Leadership and the Glass Ceiling: Gender and Ethnic Group Influences on Leader Behaviors at Middle and Executive Managerial Levels. *J. Lead. Organ. Stud.* **2003,** *9* (3), 8–19.

Baum, T. Human Resources in Tourism: Still Waiting for Change. *Tourism Manag.* **2007,** *28* (6), 1383–1399.

Baum, T. *International Perspectives on Women and Work in Hotels, Catering and Tourism*; GENDER Working Paper 1/2013, Bureau for Gender Equality and Sectoral Activities Department, International Labor Office, Geneva, Switzerland, 2013.

Baum, T.; Cheung, C. *Women in Tourism and Hospitality: Unlocking the Potential in the Talent Pool;* Hospitality Industry White Paper, 2015.

Bengisu, M.; Balta, S. Employment of the Workforce with Disabilities in the Hospitality Industry. *J. Sustain. Tourism* **2010,** *19* (1), 35–57.

Bengisu, M.; Izbirak, G.; Mackieh, A. Work Related Challenges for Visually Impaired Individuals in Turkey. *J. Vis. Impair. Blind.* **2008,** *102* (5), 284–294.

Berger, E. D. Managing Age Discrimination: An Examination of the Techniques Used When Seeking Employment. *Gerontologist* **2009,** *49* (3), 317–332.

Berthoud, R. Disability Employment Penalties in Britain. *Work Employm. Soc.* **2008,** *22* (1), 129–148.

Bird, E.; Lynch, P. A.; Ingram, A. Gender and Employment Flexibility within Hotel Front Offices. *Serv. Indus. J.* **2002,** *22* (3), 99–116.

Biswas, R.; Cassell, C. Strategic HRM and the Gendered Division of Labor in the Hotel Industry. *Person. Rev.* **1996,** *25* (2), 19–34.

Blayney, C.; Blotnicky, K. The Impact of Gender on Career Paths and Management Capability in the Hotel Industry in Canada. *J. Hum. Resour. Tourism Hosp.* **2010,** *9* (3), 233–255.

Blayney, C.; Blotnicky, K. The Impact of Gender on Strategic Typology in the Hotel Industry in Canada. *Glob. J. Bus. Res.* **2011,** *5* (2), 107–117.

Bonn, M. A. Reducing Turnover in the Hospitality Industry: An Overview of Recruitment, Selection and Retention. *Hosp. Manag.* **1992,** *11* (1), 47–63.

Brownell, J. Women in Hospitality Management: General Managers' Perceptions of Factors Related to Career Development. *Int. J. Hosp. Manag.* **1994,** *13* (2), 101–117.

Burcu, E. *Being an Individual with Disabilities in Turkey: A Study on Principal Sociological Characteristics and Problems [in Turkish]*; Hacettepe University Publications: Ankara, Turkey, 2007.

Bureau of Labor Statistics. *Persons with a Disability: Labor Force Characteristics Summary*, 2011 (online). http://www.bls.gov/news.release/disabl.nr0.htm (accessed Aug 5, 2017).

Burgess, C. Gender and Salaries in Hotel Financial Management. *Women Manag. Rev.* **2003,** *18* (1/2), 50–59.

Burgess, C. Gender and Salaries in Hotel Financial Management: It's Still a Man's World. *Women Manag. Rev.* **2003,** *18* (1/2), 50–59.

Burgess, C. Hotel Accounts: Do Men Get the Best Jobs? *Int. J. Hosp. Manag.* **2000,** *19* (4), 345–352.

Burke, R. J.; Eddy, N. G. The Changing Nature of Work and Organizations: Implications for Human Resource Management. *Hum. Resour. Manag. Rev.* **2006,** *16*, 86–94.

Burrell, J.; Manfredi, S.; Rollin, H.; Price, L.; Stead, L. Equal Opportunities for Women Employees in the Hospitality Industry: A Comparison between France, Italy, Spain And The UK. *Int. J. Hosp. Manag.* **1997,** *16* (2), 161–179.

Butler, R. Ageism: Another form of Bigotry. *Gerontologist* **1969,** *9*, 243–246.

Butler, R.; Lewis, M. *Aging and Mental Health: Positive Psychological Approaches*; C. V. Mosby Press: Saint Louis, 1973.

Campos-Soria, J. A.; Ortega-Aguaza, B.; Ropero-Garcia, R. Gender Segregation and Wage Difference in the Hospitality Industry. *Tourism Econ.* **2009,** *15* (4), 847–688.

Campos-Soria, J. A.; Marchante-Mera, A.; Ropero-García, M. A. Patterns of Occupational Segregation by Gender in the Hospitality Industry. *Int. J. Hosp. Manag.* **2011,** *30*, 91–102.

Capita Consulting. The *Case for Recruiting and Retaining Older Workers: A Business Imperative for the Hospitality Sector*; 2011 (Online). https://www.instituteofhospitality.org/Knowledge_Pack_HOSPITALITY_Dec2011_v2 (accessed Oct 20, 2017).

Capita Consulting. *The Case for Recruiting and Retaining Older Workers: A Business Imperative for the Hospitality Sector*, 2011. https://www.instituteofhospitality.org/Knowledge_Pack_HOSPITALITY_Dec2011_v2 (accessed Aug 25, 2017).

Carvalho, J. P. *Veiling: Discussion Paper Series*; Department of Economics, University of Oxford, 2010; p 491.

Catalys. *Women in Management in Canada*; 2008 (Online). http://www.catalyst.org/publication/247/women-in-management-in-canada (accessed Aug 5, 2017).

Chamlou, N.; Musi, S.; Ahmed, H. *Understanding the Determinants of Female Labor Force Participation in the Middle East and North Africa Region: The Role of Education and Social Norms in Amman*. AlmaLaurea, 2011; p 31.

Cooper, C.; Torrington, D. *After FORTY: The Time for Achievement?* John Wiley and Sons: Chichester, 1981.

Costa, C.; Carvalho, S.; Casador, Z.; Breda, Z. Future Higher Education in Tourism Studies and the Labor Markets: Gender Perspectives on Expectations and Experiences. *J. Teach. Travel Tourism* **2012,** *12* (1), 70–90.

Daniels, H. *Employment Law for HR and Business Students*; CIPD: London, 2004.

Daruwalla, P.; Darcy, S. Personal and Societal Attitudes to Disability. *Ann. Tourism Res.* **2005,** *32* (3), 549–570.

Davidson, M. J.; Cooper, C. L. *Shattering the Glass Ceiling: The Woman Manager*. Paul Chapman Publishing Ltd.: London, 1992.

Demir, C. Colakoğlu, U. and Güzel, B. Relationship Between Employee Turnover and the Location of Hotels: The Case of Kuşadasi and Izmir in Turkey. *J. Yasar Univ.* **2007,** *2* (5), 477–487.

Dennis, H.; Thomas, K. Ageism in the Workplace. *Generations* **2007,** *31* (1), 84–89.

Denton, F. T.; Fretz, D.; Pencer, B. G. *Independence and Economic Security in Old Age*. UBC Press: Vancouver [B.C.], 2000.

Donnelly, K.; Joseph, J. Disability Employment in the Hospitality Industry: Human Resources Considerations. *Cornell HR Review*, 2012; pp 1–14 (Online). http://digitalcommons.ilr.cornell.edu/chrr/27 (accessed Aug 5, 2017).

Elliott, J. R.; Ryan, A. S. Race, Gender, and Workplace Power. *Am. Sociol. Rev.* **2004,** *69*, 365–386.
Eurofound. *Addressing the Gender Pay Gap: Government and Social Partner Actions*; Dublin, 2010.
European Commission. *Public Health. POMONA 2: Health Indicators for People with Intellectual Disabilities*; 2004 (Online). http://ec.europa.eu/health/ph_projects/2004/action1/action1_2004_14_en.htm (accessed Oct 21, 2017).
European Commission. *Employment of Women in the Tourist Accommodation Sector; Industry, Trade and Services; Population and Social Conditions*; Eurostat DATA in Focus, 2007.
Foubert, P. *The Gender Pay Gap in Europe from a Legal Perspective*; Publications Office of the European Union: Luxembourg, 2010.
French, W. *Human Resources Management*, 3rd ed.; Houghton Mifflin Company: USA, 1994.
Friberg, J. H. Culture at Work: Polish Migrants in the Ethnic Division of Labor on Norwegian Construction Sites. *Ethnic Racial Stud.* **2011,** *35* (11), 1914–1933.
Ghodsee, K. State Support in the Market: Women and Tourism Employment in Post-socialist Bulgaria. *Int. J. Politics Culture Soc.* **2003,** *16* (3), 465–482.
Gilbert, J. A.; Stead, B. A.; Ivancevich, J. M. Diversity Management: A New Organizational Paradigm. *J. Bus. Ethics* **1999,** *21* (1), 61–76.
Gonzales, M. L. Getting to Know Reality and Breaking Stereotypes: The Experience of Two Generations of Working Disabled Women. *Disabil. Soc.* **2009,** *24* (4), 447–459.
Gray, S. R.; Benson, P. G. Determinants of Executive Compensation in Small Business Development Centers. *Nonprof. Manag. Lead.* (Wiley Periodicals, Spring) **2003,** *13*, 213–27.
Gringart, E.; Helmes, E.; Speelman, C. P. Exploring Attitudes Toward Older Workers Among Australian Employers: An Empirical Study. *J. Aging Soc. Polic.* **2005,** *17* (3), 85–103.
Groschl, S. An Exploration of HR Policies and Practices Affecting the Integration of Persons with Disabilities in the Hotel Industry in Major Canadian Tourism Destinations. *Hosp. Manag.* **2007,** *26*, 666–686.
Guerrier, Y. Hotel Manager: An Unsuitable Job for a Woman? *Serv. Indus. J.* **1986,** *6* (2), 227–240.
H'madoun, M. *Religion and Labor Force Participation of Women;* Faculty of Applied Economics, University of Antwerp, 2010.
Haar, J.; Spell, C. Contemporary Issues Regarding Work-family Policies. In *Human Resource Management: Challenges and Future Directions*; Wiesner, R., Millett, R., Eds.; John Wiley and Sons: Australia, 2003; pp 44–56.
Hakim, C. Explaining Trends in Occupational Segregation: the Measurement, Causes and Consequences of the Sexual Division of Labor. *Eur. Sociol. Rev.* **1992,** *8* (2), 127–152.
Hayo, B.; Caris, T. *Female Labor Force Participation in MENA Region: The Role of Identity*; Philipps Universität Marburg, 2013.
Hirsch, B. T.; Macpherson, D. A.; Hardy, M. A. Occupational Age Structure and Access for Older Workers. *Indus. Labor Relat. Rev.* **2000,** *53* (3), 401–18.
Hisrich, R. D.; Brush, C. The Women Entrepreneur: Management Skills and Business Problems. *J. Small Bus. Manag.* **1994,** *32*, 30–37.
Hollinshead, G.; Nicholls, P.; Tailby, S. *Employee Relations*, 2nd ed.; Prentice Hall: Harlow, 2003.
Holywood, E.; Brown, R.; Danson, M.; McQuaid, R. *Older Workers in the Scottish Labor Market: A New Agenda*, Scotecon; Stirling, 2003.
Ibbott, P.; Kerr, D.; Beaujot, R. Probing the Future of Mandatory Retirement in Canada. *Can. J. Aging* **2006,** *25* (2), 161–178.

ILO. *Labour Migration and Development: ILO Moving Forward*; Background Paper for Discussion at the ILO Tripartite Technical Meeting on Labour Migration, Geneva, 2013.

ILO. *Developments and Challenges in the Hospitality and Tourism Sector*; Global Dialogue Forum for the Hotels, Catering, Tourism Sector, Geneva, Switzerland, 2010.

ILO. *ABC of Women Worker's Rights and Gender Equality*; Geneva, 2009.

Johansen, M. The Effect of Female Strategic Managers on Organizational Performance. *Public Organ. Rev.* **2007,** *7* (3), 269–279.

Jordan, F. An Occupational Hazard? Sex Segregation in Tourism Employment. *Tourism Manag.* **1997,** *18* (8), 525–534.

Kara, D.; Uysal, M.; Magnini, V. Gender Differences on Job Satisfaction of the Five-star Hotel Employees: The Case of the Turkish Hotel Industry. *Int. J. Contemp. Hosp. Manag.* **2012,** *24* (7), 1047–1065.

Kattara, H. Career Challenges for Female Managers in Egyptian Hotels. *Int. J. Contemp. Hosp. Manag.* **2005,** *17* (2/3), 238–251.

Kiani, K. A. Determinants of Female Labor Force Participation. *ASEAN Mark. J.* **2009,** *1* (2), 117–124.

Kinnaird, V.; Kothari, U.; Hall, D. Tourism: Gender Perspectives. In *Tourism: A Gender Analysis*; Kinnaird, V., Hall, D., Eds.; Wiley: New York, 1994.

Knutson, B. J.; Schmidgall, J. Dimensions of the Glass Ceiling in the Hospitality Industry. *Cornell Hotel Restaur. Admin. Q.* **1999,** *40* (6), 64–75.

Koenig, A. M.; Alice H. E.; Abigail A. M.; Ristikari, T. Are Leader Stereotypes Masculine? A Meta-Analysis of Three Research Paradigms. *Psychol. Bull.* **2011,** *137*, 616–642.

Lee, B. Legal Requirements and Employer Responses to Accommodating Employees with Disabilities. *Hum. Resour. Manag. Rev.* **1996,** *6* (4), 231–251.

Leontidou, L. Gender Dimensions of Tourism Sub-cultures and Restructuring. In *Tourism: A Gender Analysis*; Kinnaird, V., Hall, D., Eds.; Wiley: New York, 1994.

Li, L.; Leung, R. W. Female Managers in Asian Hotels: Profile and Career Challenges. *Int. J. Contemp. Hosp. Manag.* **2001,** *13* (4), 189–196.

Livanos, I.; Yalkin, C.; Nunez, I. Gender Employment Discrimination: Greece and the United Kingdom. *Int. J. Manpow.* **2009,** *30* (8), 815–834 (Emerald Group Publishing Limited).

MacGregor, D. Neglecting Elders in the Workplace: Civil Society Organizations, Ageism and Mandatory Retirement. *Can. J. Aging* **2006,** *25* (3), 243–246.

Manhica, H.; Östh, J.; Rostila, M. Dynamics of Unemployment Duration Among African Migrants in Sweden. *Nordic J. Migration Res.* **2015,** *5* (4), 194–206.

Martin, E.; Gardiner, K. Exploring the UK Hospitality Industry and Age Discrimination. *Int. J. Contemp. Hosp. Manag.* **2007,** *19* (4), 309–318.

Masala, C.; Petretto, D. R. From Disablement to Enablement: Conceptual Models of Disability in the 20th Century. *Disabil. Rehabil.* **2008,** *30* (17), 1233–1244.

Mathis, L. R.; Jackson, H. J. *Human Resources Management*, 9th ed.; South Western College Publishing: USA, 2000.

Maxwell, G. Hotel General Management: Views from Above the Glass Ceiling. *Int. J. Contemp. Hosp. Manag.* **1997,** *9* (5/6), 230–236.

Mc Kenzie Gentry, K. Belizean Women and Tourism Work: Opportunity or Impediment? *Ann. Tourism Res.* **2007,** *34* (2), 477–496.

McCary, K. The Disability Twist in Diversity: Best Practices for Integrating People with Disabilities into the Workforce. *Divers. Factor* **2005,** *13* (3), 16–22.

McDonald, L. Gendered Retirement: The Welfare of Women and the "New" Retirement. In *New Frontiers of Research on Retirement*; Stone L. O., Ed.; Statistics Canada, Unpaid Work Analysis Division: Ottawa, 2006; pp 137–164.
McKenzie-Gentry, K. Belizean Women and Tourism Work. Opportunity or Impediment? *Ann. Tourism Res.* **2007,** *34* (2), 477–496.
McMullin, J. A.; Berger, E. D. Gendered Ageism/Age(ed) Sexism: The Case of Unemployed Older Workers. In *Age Matters: Re-aligning Feminist Thinking*; Calasanti, T. M., Slevin, K. F., eds.; Routledge: New York, 2006; pp 201–223.
Meager, N.; Bates P.; Dench S.; Honey S.; Williams M. *Employment of Disabled People: Assessing the Extent of Participation*; Department for Education and Employment Research Report RR69; Department for Education and Skills Publications: Nottingham, UK, 1998.
Minois, G. *History of Old Age: From Antiquity to the Renaissance*; The University of Chicago Press: Chicago, 1989.
Mkono, M. Women in Hotel Management in Zimbabwe: Career Ambitions, Progression Tactics, and Career Challenges. *Tourismos* **2012,** *7* (2), 165–181.
Mooney, S.; Ryan, I. A Woman's Place in Hotel Management: Upstairs or Downstairs? *Gender Manag.* **2009,** *24* (3), 195–210.
Mullins, J. L. *Managing People in the Hospitality Industry*; Longman: Harlow, 1998.
Munoz-Bullon, F. The Gap Between Male and Female Pay in the Spanish Tourism Industry. *Bus. Econ.* **2008,** *13*, 08–55.
Näre, L. Ideal Workers and Suspects. *Nordic J. Migrat. Res.* **2013,** *3* (3), 72–81.
Nayab, N. *Common Diversity Issues in the Workplace*; 2017. http://www.brighthub.com/office/human-resources/articles/91541.aspx (accessed Dec 2, 2017).
Ng, C. W.; Pine, R. Women and Men in Hotel Management in Hong Kong: Perceptions of Gender and Career Development Issues. *Int. J. Hosp. Manag.* **2003,** *22*, 85–102.
Obadić, A.; Marić, I. The Significance of Tourism as an Employment Generator of Female Labor Force. *Signif. Tourism* **2009,** *18* (1), 93–114.
Paez, P.; Arendt, S. W. Managers' Attitudes Towards Employees with Disabilities in the Hospitality Industry. *J. Hosp. Tourism Admin.* **2014,** *15* (2), 172–190.
Parrett, L. *Women in Tourism Employment: A Guided Tour of the Greenwich Experience*; Research Report; London Thames Gateway Forum, 2004.
People 1st. *Skill Needs Assessment for the Hospitality, Leisure, Travel and Tourism Sector*, UK Report; People 1st: London, 2006.
Perry, T. L.; Ivy, M.; Conner, A.; Shelar, D. Recreation Student Attitudes Towards People with Disabilities: Considerations for Future Service Delivery. *J. Hosp. Leisure Sport Tourism Educ.* **2008,** *7* (2), 4–14.
Piore, M. J. *Birds of Passage: Migrant Labor and Industrial Societies*; Cambridge University Press, 1979.
Polachek, S. W.; Zhang, X.; Zhou, X. A Biological Basis for the Gender Wage Gap: Fecundity and Age and Educational Hypogamy. *Gender Converg. Labor Mark.* **2015,** 35–88.
Presser, H. B.; Altman, B. Work Shifts and Disability: A National View. *Month. Labor Rev.* **2002,** *125* (5), 11–24.
Purcell, K. The Relationship Between Career and Job Opportunities: Women's Employment in the Hospitality Industry as a Microcosm of Women's Employment. *Women Manag. Rev.* **1996,** *11* (5), 17–24.

Ramos-Mir, V.; Rey-Maqueira J.; *Tugores-Ques, M.* In *Determinants of Gender Wage Differentials in the Hospitality Industry in the Balearic Islands. The Role of Gender Segregation*, International Tourism Research Conference, Palma de Mallorca, Spain, 2004.

Reskin, B. F.; Bielby, D. D. A Sociological Perspective on Gender and Career Outcomes. *J. Econ. Persp.* **2005,** *19* (1), 71–86.

Reskin, B. F.; Denise, D. B. A Sociological Perspective on Gender and Career Outcomes. *J. Econ. Persp.* **2005,** *19* (1), 71–86.

Richter, L. K. Exploring the Political Role of Gender in Tourism Research; In *Global Tourism: The Next Decade;* Theo bold, W., Ed.; Butterworth Heinemann: Oxford, 1994.

Roscigno, V. J.; Mong, S.; Byron, R.; Tester, G. Age Discrimination, Social Closure and Employment. *Soc. Forces* **2007,** *86* (1), 313–334.

Rosener, J. B. *America's Competitive Secret: Utilizing Women as a Management Strategy*; Oxford University Press: New York, 1995.

Ross, G. F. Ethics, Trust and Expectations Regarding the Treatment of Disabled Staff Within a Tourism/Hospitality Industry Context. *Hosp. Manag.* **2004,** *23* (5), 523–544.

Ruggeri-Stevens, G.; Goodwin, S. Learning to Work in Small Businesses: Learning and Training for Young Adults with Learning Disabilities. *Educ. Train.* **2007,** *49*, 745–755.

Santos, L. D.; Varejao, J. *Employment, Pay and Discrimination in the Tourism Industry*; FEP Working Papers, 2006.

Sayers, R. C. The Cost of Being Female: Critical Comment on Block. *J. Bus. Ethics* **2012,** *106* (4), 519–524.

Schein, V. E. Women in Management: Reflections and Projections. *Women Manag. Rev.* **2007,** *22* (1), 6–18.

Schur, L.; Kruse, D.; Blanck, P. Corporate Culture and the Employment of Persons with Disabilities. *Behav. Sci. Law* **2005,** *23* (1), 3–20.

Sheldon, P. J. *The Tourism Education Future Initiatives*; Routledge: New York, USA, 2014.

Smith, C.; Usha, R.; Aida, N.; Lawrence, H.; Reynaldo, M. *The Importance of Women's Status for Child Nutrition in Developing Countries*; Research Report 131; Washington DC: International Food Policy Research Institute, 2003.

Snape, E. D.; Redman, T. Too Old or Too Young? The Impact of Perceived Age Discrimination. *Hum. Resour. Manag. J.* **2003,** *13* (1), 78–89.

Taamouti, M.; Ziroili, M. *Individual Determinants of Female Labor Participation in Morocco*; 2010.

Thompson, N. *Promoting Equality: Challenging Discrimination and Oppression*, 2nd ed.; Palgrave MacMillan: Basingstoke, 2003.

Thrane, C. Earning Differentiation in the Tourism Industry: Gender, Human Capital and Socio Demographic Effects. *Tourism Manag.* **2008,** *29*, 514–524.

Tomei, M. Discrimination and Equality at Work: A Review of the Concepts. *Int. Labor Rev.* **2003,** *142* (4), 401–418.

Tucekr, H. Undoing Shame: Tourism and Women's Work in Turkey. *J. Tourism Cultural Change* **2007,** *5* (2), 87–105.

Tyldum, G. *The Social Meanings of Migration*. Ph.D. Thesis, University of Oslo, Oslo, 2015.

UK Essays. *Women in the Workforce Sociology Essay* 2015 (Online). https://www.ukessays.com/essays/sociology/women-in-the-workforce-sociology-essay.php (accessed Aug 21, 2017).

United Nations. *The Rights of Migrant Workers, Office of the High Commissioner of Human Rights*; Geneva, Switzerland (Online). http://www.unhchr.ch/html/menu6/2/fs24.htm (accessed Aug 20, 2017).

UNWTO. *Global Report on Women in Tourism*; World Tourism Organization (UNWTO) and the United Nations Entity for Gender Equality and the Empowerment of Women, Madrid, Spain, 2010.

Valletta, R. G. Declining Job Security. *J. Labor Econ.* **1999,** *17* (4), 170–96.

Waldinger, R. D.; Lichter, M. I. *How the Other Half Works: Immigration and the Social Organization of Labor*; University of California Press: Berkeley, 2003.

Weichselbaumer, D. Sexual Orientation Discrimination in Hiring. *Labor Econ.* **2003,** *10* (6), 629–642.

Wersley, R. *Age and Employment: Why Employers Should Think Again About Older Workers*; Age Concern England: London, 1996.

Whiteneck, G. G.; Harrison-Felix, L. C.; Mellick, D. C.; Charlifue, S. B.; Gerhart, K. A. Quantifying Environmental Factors: A Measure of Physical, Attitudinal, Service, Productivity, and Policy Barriers. *Arch. Phys. Med. Rehabil.* **2004,** *85* (8), 1324–1335.

Witz, A.; Savage, M. The Gender of Organizations. In *Gender and Bureaucracy*; Savage, M., Witz., A., Eds.; Blackwell Publishers/The Sociological Review: Oxford, 1992.

Wohland, P.; Rees, P.; Norman, P.; Boden, P.; Jasinska, M. *Ethnic Population Projections for the UK and Local Areas*; 2010 (Online). http://www.geog.leeds.ac.uk/fileadmin/downloads/school/research/projects/migrants/WP_ETH_POP PROJECTIONS.pdf (accessed Aug 10, 2017).

Wood, R.; Viehland, D. Women in Hotel Management: Gradual Progress, Uncertain Prospects. *Cornell Hotel Restaur. Admin. Q.* **2000,** *41* (6), 51–54.

Woods, R.; Viehland, D. Women in Hotel Management. *Cornell Hotel Restaur. Admin. Q.* **2000,** *4* (5), 51–54.

World Bank. *Jobs or Privileges: Unleashing the Employment Potential of the Middle East and North Africa*, 2014.

Yeşiltaş, M.; Temizkan, R.; Temizkan, M. P.; Arslan, O. E. Discrimination in Job Application Forms of Hospitality Industry. *J. Bus. Res. (Turkish)* **2013,** *5* (3), 18–36.

# PART IV
# Labor Rights

CHAPTER 14

# LABOR TRAFFICKING IN THE TOURISM AND HOSPITALITY INDUSTRY

*"The reason why the world is living in hatred is that people who are created to be loved, are trafficked, while things that are created to be used, are loved."*

## 14.1 INTRODUCTION

Around the world, millions of men, women, and children are being exploited. Trafficking of human beings (THB) is one of the fastest growing criminal issues in the world, generating over $32 billion profits in a year (Polaris Project, 2012). The United Nations has identified at least 510 issues of human trafficking that flows around the world. THB victims can be trafficked within their own country (origin) or internationally (destination country), within their work environment, or outside its boundaries. The use of force, fraud, or coercion to compel an employee to do a work, to provide a service, or to have sex against his/her will is considered trafficking. In other words, it is a form of modern day slavery—victimizing the employees under the slogan of flag of work responsibilities.

In Europe for instance, Eastern European countries and the Balkans tend to be origin countries of trafficking and those within Northern and Western Europe are normally the most vulnerable destination countries to THB, whereas Southern European countries tend to be used when victims are in transit from Asia, Africa, and the Americas. Although most of the reported victims of THB have been trafficked away from their home countries in the destination countries, an increasingly notable number of victims are trafficked close to their homes, within the regions or even within their country of origin, and their exploiters are often fellow citizen (Datta and Bales, 2013). Human trafficking includes trafficking for labor and sexual purposes. The International Labor Organization (ILO) estimated 21 million victims of trafficking worldwide and they are forced into labor (2012). Additionally, more women and children are believed to be victims of human trafficking compared to men. According to the ILO (2014), about 11.4 million victims of trafficking are women and girls. Minors under the age of 18 years induced into commercial sex are victims of sex trafficking—regardless of whether the trafficker used force, fraud, or coercion.

In reality, trafficking happens regardless of the age, race, and place, in developed countries and developing ones, in international companies, and local ones with migrants or native young or old and male or female individuals. Labor trafficking occurs in a range of different circumstances, and labor trafficking is the result of poverty and a weakening social fabric in sender countries. It comes in the form of discrimination against vulnerable groups including women and ethnic minorities.

According to a 2008 US Health and Human Services report, there are some common characteristics that make labor vulnerable to traffickers (Walters and Davis, 2011):

- They lack high-education levels.
- They come from developing countries or communities with poverty, corruption, and high crime rates.
- They have social problems, for example, the lack of family support (e.g., are orphaned, runaway/throwaway, homeless, have family members collaborating with traffickers).
- They have histories of physical and/or sexual abuse.

## 14.2 HUMAN TRAFFICKING

The key element of trafficking relationship is the abuse of power; using the threat or force or other forms of coercion, abduction, fraud, or deception in order to recruit, transport, transfer, or harbor of persons who are in vulnerable positions (COMBAT, 2016). Trafficking is slightly different from smuggling according to the two separate Palermo protocols, where smuggling implies a degree of acquiescence between the transporting agent and the smuggled person, whereas trafficking implies an absence of such consent, during at least some stage of the trafficking cycle (ILO, 2002).

Although there are significant differences between THB and human smuggling, the underlying issues that give rise to these illegal activities are often similar. Generally, severe poverty, lack of economic possibilities, public unrest, and political uncertainty are factors that all contribute to an environment that encourages human smuggling and trafficking in persons.

It may be difficult to make a determination between smuggling and trafficking in the initial phase. Trafficking often involves an element of smuggling, specifically the illegal crossing of a border. In some cases, the victim may believe they are being smuggled but are really being trafficked, as they are unaware of their fate.

The United Nations Office on Drug and Crime's definition (UNODC) holds the same meaning of human trafficking as "The recruitment, transportation, transfer, harboring or receipt of persons, by means of threat, use of force or other means of coercion, of abduction, of fraud, of deception, of the abuse of power or of a position of vulnerability or of the receiving or giving of payment and (includes human rights abuses such as debt bondage, deprivation of liberty, and lack of control over freedom and labor) (…) to a person having control over another person, for the purpose of exploitation" (UNODC, 2014).

Some groups are considered more vulnerable or likely to be trafficked such as the following groups:

1. migrant workers,
2. female workers,
3. low educated workers,
4. children and young people,
5. war or political refugees, and
6. immoral or unethical work group (those who are involved in dirty works, e.g., prostitution, adultery, robbery, fraud, etc.)

Based on UNODC's definition given to trafficking in Persons Protocol, trafficking has three constituent elements relating to what is done, how it is done, and why it is done. The following section lists the act, the means, and the purpose of trafficking activity (UNODC, 2014):

**The act** (what is done):

- Recruitment
- Transportation
- Transfer
- Harboring or reception of victims

**The means** (how it is done):

- Threat or use of force
- Coercion
- Abduction

- Fraud
- Deception
- Abuse of power or vulnerability
- Giving payments or benefits to a person in control of the victim

**The purpose** (why it is done):

- Exploiting the prostitution of others
- Sexual exploitation
- Forced labor
- Slavery or similar practices
- The removal of organs

Relating to the last element of trafficking process (the purpose of trafficking), EU member states—22 members states provided data for all 3 years—between 2010 and 2012 with the purpose of investigating the answer of "why trafficking is done?," the results revealed that the majority of THB victims are trafficked for two main purposes, as follows (Eurostat 2015):

- Sexual exploitation (66%)
- Forced labor (20%)
- Other forms of trafficking (13%)

Trafficking specifically targets the trafficked person as an object of criminal exploitation. The purpose from the beginning of the trafficking enterprise is to profit from the exploitation of the victim. It follows that fraud, force, or coercion all plays a major role in trafficking.

From the above discussion, the different types of exploitation can be concluded as follows (Eurostat, 2015):

- **Sex trafficking:**
    - Sexual exploitation
    - Forced marriage

- **Labor trafficking (slavery practices and domestic servitude):**
    - Forced labor
    - Bonded labor

- **Child trafficking:**
    - Illegal adoption

- **Others:**
  - Coerced organ donation or removal
  - Forced begging

Therefore, there are three major—but not mutually exclusive—forms of human trafficking: sex trafficking, child trafficking, and labor trafficking. Forced begging and removal of organs are considered to some extent some rare forms of trafficking. The next section will address the major forms of human trafficking.

### *14.2.1 SEX TRAFFICKING*

*Sex trafficking is a type of modern slavery that exists throughout globally. Sex trafficking occurs when someone uses unethical methods to cause a commercial sex act with an adult or to force a minor to commit a commercial sex act.* The US Trafficking Victims Protection Act of 2000 defines sex trafficking as "(…) the recruitment, harboring, transportation, provision, or obtaining of a person for the purpose of a commercial sex act (….)." Further, "…the commercial sex act is induced by force, fraud, or coercion, or in which the person induced to perform such act has not attained 18 years of age." It is important to note that this definition clearly states that anyone engaged in a commercial sex act, who is younger than 18 years old, is by definition a trafficking victim, regardless of circumstances.

Sex trafficking is an issue the hospitality and tourism industry faces around the globe. In New York City, for example, 45% of commercially abused victims were exploited in hotels in the forms previously mentioned, especially escorting service and exotic stripping (Reid, 2012). Types of sex trafficking may include

- escort services,
- forced prostitution,
- child sex trafficking/tourism,
- forced dancing/stripping, and
- pornography.

Based on the International Labor Union, Carolin et al. (2015) claimed that an estimated 4.5 million victims are forced into sexual labor, with 98% of the victims being identified as female. Social relations play a major role in directing the victims to get involved in such activities; female victims of sexual trafficking may be involved into sexual activities through what they may know, like a boyfriend. Generally, traffickers find their victims through the following ways:

- Clubs or bars
- Social network
- Home neighborhood
- School

Often, social interruptions and the absence of family role in the life of the victims are considered the main pushing factor that lures them into sexual trafficking; on the other side, the trafficker or the pimp's promises of love, home, protection, opportunity, or adventure are considered pull factors.

Carolin et al. (2015) estimated the business that a trafficker or a pimp can make from this trade; a trafficker/pimp can make $150,000–$200,000 per child each year and the average pimp has four to six girls.

Many countries banned prostitution; 39 countries have laws making prostitution illegal, and 12 countries have limited laws allowing some aspects of prostitution, while circumstances of many countries pushed them to consider prostitution a legal work; in 49 countries around the world, prostitution is legal (Carolin et al., 2015).

### *14.2.2 CHILD EXPLOITATION*

Child exploitation is a sort of trafficking that is likely to be hazardous to the health and/or physical, mental, spiritual, moral, or social development of children and can impede their education. Traffickers and pimps often focus on young victims between the ages of 12 and 14 years old, the market demand for young victims, as they argued. The gullibility makes the children and young kids more vulnerable to be victims of trafficking (Walters and Davis, 2011). Around the world, especially in developing countries, child victims are sacrificed to sex trafficking for short-term financial earnings (Leth, 2005). Horrendous conditions make the child human trafficking tasks easy. It was reported that one in three teens on the street will be lured into prostitution within 48 h of leaving home (Mitchell et al., 2010). Thus, through the world, over one million children are trafficked for sex trade.

Child victims are subject to abuse from their traffickers, as they consider them only useful in the sex industry for a short period of time; subsequently, they are prone to sturdy violence from those involved in trafficking (Newman, 2011). Children may be dropped when they are no longer attractive or young enough, further victimized in other ways or, in some cases, killed to prevent disclosure. This discarding of "useless victims" creates a need for new prostitutes and children—an endless cycle of supply and demand (Walters and Davis, 2011).

In the United States, for example, minors under the age of 14 represent 11% of minors sold for sexual purposes. Victims between the ages of 14 and 17 in the United States are the largest percentage of juvenile victims who are sold for sexual activities (Mitchell et al., 2010).

Other than sex trafficking, child may be exploited in work environment, where some industries are considered attractive for them; once they enter the industry, they experience numerous types of exploitations, starting with the right to choose what suit them and ending with the wages they get. For instance, tourism industry attracts 218 million children (Sharma et al., 2012); the characteristics of tourism employment impose them to work for long hours under pressure circumstances at very low wages and this definitely affects their lives negatively (see Chapter 2, Child labor).

### *14.2.3 LABOR TRAFFICKING*

The term trafficking implies crucially the use of compulsion and limits the freedom and choice afforded to the victims. Today, 3 out of every 1000 people worldwide are in forced labor (ILO, 2012). *Forced labor* is a situation in which victims are compelled to work against their own will in unacceptable working conditions, under the threat of violence or some other form of punishment, their freedom is restricted, and a degree of ownership is exerted. Like sex trafficking, the definitions of labor trafficking are not uniform across organizations, governments, or researchers. Labor trafficking can be defined as "(...) the recruitment, harboring, transportation, provision, or obtaining of a person for labor or services, through the use of force, fraud, or coercion for the purpose of subjection to involuntary servitude, peonage, debt bondage, or slavery" (ILO, 2005).

Traffickers often rely on some specific ways to exploit the employees, starting with the right to choose what suit them and ending with the wages they pay. Labor traffickers basically handle the labor law in order to restrict employees' benefits and exploit them by providing them low wages, even if they worked longest hours in dangerous working conditions without proper safety precautions or standards.

It was identified a simple typology with three broad forms for the purpose of estimating the magnitude of forced labor (ILO, 2001) as follows (Fig. 14.1):

- Forced labor imposed by the state, which includes the following subcategories:
    - Military groups
    - Rebel groups
    - Mandatory participation in public works
    - Prison labor
- Forced commercial sexual exploitation (CSE), which includes women, men, and children who have been forced by private agents into commercial sexual activities or into prostitution.
- Forced labor for economic exploitation, which comprises all forced labor imposed by private companies and organizations in sectors other than the sex industry. It includes forced labor in services, industry, and agriculture, as well as in some illegal activities.

According to ILO (2002), labor trafficking occurs in a range of different circumstances, when

- The employment itself is illegal.
- The conditions of work are worse than those prescribed by law.
- The job seekers reach to a country where there are barriers to legal migration.
- The individual is below the minimum age of employment.

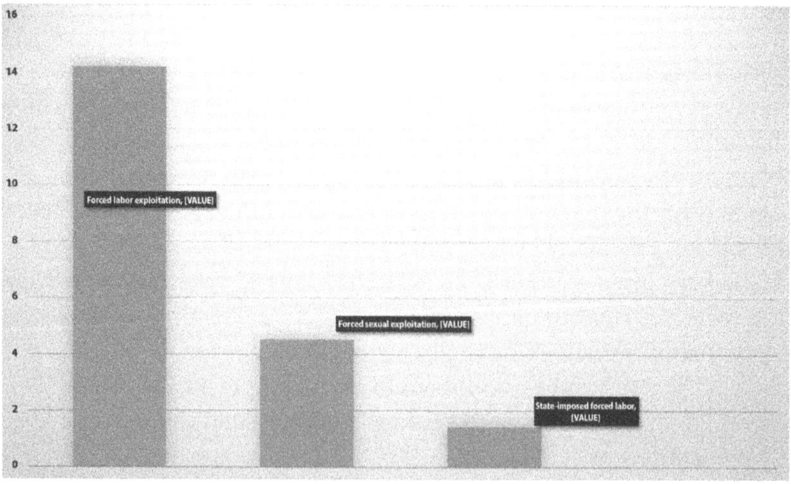


**FIGURE 14.1 (See color insert.)** Types of forced labor (in millions of people).

**Source:** The Authors based on ILO, 2012.

Victims of labor trafficking are not a homogenous group of people. Victims are young children, teenagers, men, and women. Some of them enter the state legally and some of them work in legal occupations, whereas others enter or work illegally. The ILO (2005) has suggested some elements that, either separately or together, can indicate forced labor:

- Threats, for example, victims may be blackmailed by traffickers using the victims' illegal status as an undocumented immigrant or their participation in an "illegal" industry.
- Actual physical harm.
- Victims are often kept isolated to prevent them from getting help.
- Restriction of movement and confinement to the workplace or to a restricted area.
- Debt bondage.
- Withholding of wages or excessive wage reductions, which violate previously made agreements.
- Retention of passports and identity documents (the workers can neither leave nor prove their identity and status).

Recognizing potential red flags and knowing the signs of labor trafficking victims are key steps in recognizing more victims and helping them find the assistance they need. Table 14.1 tabulates the most common forms and signs of labor trafficking.

**TABLE 14.1** Trafficking Forms and Signs.

| Forms | Signs |
|---|---|
| • Commercial sex with under eighteens | • Abnormal behavior |
| • Hard/humiliating working environment and conditions | • Changes in personality or behavior |
| • Low payment | • Avoidance of interaction with others, especially about personal matters |
| • Stressful tasks | • Poor physical health/poor hygiene |
| • Limited movements, their movements are being controlled (feel that they cannot leave) | • Poor information about their work |
| • Long and crazy hours jobs (sleep deprivation) | • Fatigue |
| | • Malnourishment |
| | • Suffer injuries |
| | • Psychological upset (show fear or anxiety) |

**Source:** The Authors

## 14.3 LABOR TRAFFICKING IN THE HOSPITALITY INDUSTRY

Human trafficking is a global issue, which has not been fully addressed by stakeholders. There is a lack of awareness of how victims are moved through hospitality and tourism businesses to work as slaves whether in a tough working environment or to work as prostitutes. Human trafficking is a crime in which traffickers exploit others for profit or personal benefits. Around the world, there has been a growing focus on the use of hospitality organizations as vehicles for human trafficking through its conscious or unconscious participation in sex trafficking of men, women, and children.

The high privacy and anonymity that hospitality organizations strive to offer to guests may be considered the unconscious participation of the industry that the traffickers highly appreciate as it helps them to hide their crimes. As criminals, traffickers tend to seek the path of no or low resistance. Unfortunately, many hospitality organizations, hotels in particular, offer these "low or free resistance pathways," often without their knowledge. This makes the accommodation establishment a low risky environment, where hotel staff and also the community are not aware of the signs of human trafficking, and particularly for the purposes of child sexual exploitation. Traffickers use all available resources or venues to help facilitate their ways to crimes; they take advantage of the privacy and amenities offered by hotels and motels (Polaris Project, 2012). It was reported by the National Trafficking Resource Center (United States) that hotels and motels are the second most popular location of trafficking for sexual exploitation.

Another type of trafficking, which occurs in hospitality enterprises, is labor trafficking. Employees can be forced to work in hotels by illegal subcontracting companies. Also, it was reported by Polaris Project (2012) that immigrant workers from overseas are coerced by some hotel franchise owners to work under threats of an actual physical exploitation. Some international companies and businesses entice immigrant labor under "fraudulently recruiting contracts" in which employees are recruited for one purpose and forced to engage in some other job. In the USA in 2015, there were thousands officially reported trafficked victims; a significant percentage occurred in hospitality organizations (hotels and restaurants). It was reported by the National Trafficking Resource Center (United States) that restaurants and bars are two of the most popular venues for labor exploitation.

### 14.3.1 WHY IS THE HOTEL INDUSTRY VULNERABLE TO THB?

Traffickers are individuals and organizations who trade in humans as commodities (Walters and Davis, 2011). All hospitality organizations, regardless of their size, brand, or location, are vulnerable to THB.

Traffickers are benefiting from the lack of awareness around this issue within the hotel industry. All too often, they continue to exploit their victims unchecked because personnel, managers, and executives do not know what to look for. There are a number of characteristics that hospitality organizations and its operational practices are characterized of, which make them particularly vulnerable to human traffickers and their victims. These characteristics can be categorized as follows.

#### A. Management Style

- In case of hotel chains, the ownership of the hospitality property is separated from the management.
- The wrong belief about the consequences of adopting the code of conduct, for example, the management of the property wrongly believe that by approving the code of conduct for the protection of children from sexual exploitation, the business or hotel reputation will be affected negatively; this may be because that by endorsing that paper, the management admit that there may be a problem in their organizations relating to ethics and this affects its customers who primarily seek security and safety (www.thecode.org).

#### B. Organizational Culture

There is often confusion between labor trafficking and sex trafficking, where the latter is not considered a criminal offence in many countries and accepted within hotels. Thus, hospitality organizations are routinely used for sex trafficking where victims are compelled to provide commercial sex to paying customers. Hotel owners/managers sometimes offer extra "services" to guests, especially VIP guests, which may be commissionable, and management and staff share in the proceeds. These services are usually internal "service" to minimize the risk to guests; female workers may be ordered to stay at a hotel where customers come to them (in-call), or they are required to go to rooms rented out by the customers (out-call).

Such unethical practices promote or establish an organizational culture, which considers revenue generation at the expense of ethical or moral behavior. As a result, employees may have a customer orientation and willingly respond to customer requests or demands without ethical boundaries

(COMBAT, 2016), whereas those who resist or report suspected incidents of trafficking lack the protection and may be forced to resign. Consequently, employees fear retribution from their supervisors or managers complicit in trafficking if they report any suspected incidents and such practices become usual matter in the organization.

### C. *Technological Systems*

Automated reservation and check-in systems in hospitality organizations made the entry to the hotel very easy with to some extent less monitored actions (COMBAT, 2016).

- Automated reservation systems, often using a third party to make reservation, enable traffickers to enter and escort victims to these organizations for exploitation.
- Mobile and automated check-in systems mean that the check-in process and room access are not fully controlled.

### D. *Operational Procedures*

The nature of hospitality organizations' work that seeks to ensure high level of comfort and entertainment for customers may reach to the degree of leniency with customers who break the rules as a sign of extravagant welcoming and appreciation.

For example, many hotels do not require full identification for all guests and customers entering or staying in a property, especially if children are accompanying adults. Such extravagant procedures provide a level of protection for traffickers.

Following are some of the operational procedures that offer free resistance pathways for traffickers within the hospitality organizations (COMBAT, 2016):

- Many hotels do not require all guests to sign in or register at check-in, particularly if they are VIP or children accompanying an adult.
- Unlimited use of "do not disturb" signs means that guests are allowed to remain invisible to staff for extended periods of time.
- Accepting payment for accommodation and other services by cash makes traffickers and their victims harder to trace.

### E. *Employment Practices*

Globally, there are 40.3 million people estimated to be living in slavery. For the hospitality sector, there is a lack of precise data. However, according to a recent study, there are more than one million victims of modern slavery in the European hospitality sector annually (COMBAT, 2016).

Some of the issues that were identified during the employment practices that give rise to such situations of labor abuse include

- Recruiting low or unskilled labor where their knowledge of legislation or labor rights is very limited.
- Recruiting foreign workers of culturally diverse backgrounds where language barriers may prevent reporting and/or an understanding of their rights, in addition to their vulnerable status that limits them to ask their rights.
- The absence of trade union representation in many countries to support staff members.
- Anti-THB training and awareness is conducted only to comply with organization policy without taking the issue seriously or implementing clear measures to address it.

### F. *Outsourcing Strategies (COMBAT, 2016)*

- Contractual outsourcing of services and products to suppliers who may have unethical practices.
  - Housekeeping, maintenance, or gardening services
  - All the raw materials and other supplies
- The use of global supply chains which are complex and unreliable and therefore difficult to control.

### G. *The Excessive Tasks Required for Jobs*

Fair working efforts and working time are a key component of decent work. The excessive and/or atypical efforts and hours can be detrimental to physical and mental health and impede the balance between work and family life. Most of the jobs in hospitality organizations, especially hotels, require extra efforts to accomplish many tasks within very limited time; department of food and beverage and room division are considered the main two areas where their staff suffer from excessive tasks and duties—for example, housekeepers are required to clean and tide a hospitality unit (room) in less than 30 min (maybe 15 min). Following are the lists of the tasks and duties required from two employees who belong to the two divisions mentioned before.

- **Food and beverage division (Busboy)**
  - Clean tables and ensure that fresh tablecloths and mats are provided.

- Remove dirty dishware, glassware, and flatware, and deliver it to the washing area.
- Clean and polish tables and furniture and mop and sweep floors.
- Clean up spilled food and ensure that floors and tables surfaces are sanitized.
- Serve water to newly seated customers and inform them that they will be assisted by a server shortly.
- Provide servers with information of new customer arrival, especially in peak hours.
- Assist servers in serving beverages, condiments, and coffee.
- Ensure that each table has enough supply of napkins and tissue paper.
- Keep an eye out for customers looking for service and assist them with their questions.
- Make sure that the restaurant area is clean at all times.
- Ensure that buffet tables are properly bussed and supplied as soon as any item runs out.
- Supply cabinets and serving areas with items such as napkins, napkin rings, ketchup, mustard, and extra sets of flatware.
- Serve entrees such as rolls, butter, and bread and ensure that there is constant supply of ice and drinking water for customers.
- Clean and organize plates in the kitchen and expedite orders on request from waiters and servers.
- Ensure that adequate restaurant supplies such as linen, condiments, and napkins are available at all times.
- Assist in cleaning tables after each course and bussing them with fresh plates and glasses.

- **Room division (Housekeeper)**
  - Keeping all areas of the entity, including all toilets, clean and tidy. This includes washing, dusting, polishing, vacuum cleaning, and sweeping as appropriate.
  - Ensuring that all cleaning equipment/materials are maintained in a safe, clean, and efficient working environment. Where an item of equipment requires repair, this should be reported to the administrator.
  - Ensuring that the manager is aware of the need for replacement materials and equipment for the satisfactory performance of the duties.
  - Wear protective uniform in accordance with health and hygiene regulations and infection control guidelines.

- Maintaining a friendly contact with customers respecting their right to choice, dignity, privacy, and confidentiality at all times.
- Laundry (where domestic rules allow and by agreement with employee).
- Sorting, washing, load, and unload machines taking care to use correct temperatures depending on types of textile.
- Sluicing of linen where necessary, hand-washing as required.
- Ironing of clothing and linen as required.
- Ensure working within the infection and safety control guidelines.
- To undertake such other duties as may be determined from time to time within the general scope of the job.
- To be responsible for your own health and safety and that of anybody else who may be affected by your acts or behaviors.

In addition to the above, there are some general requirements that apply to all jobs in the hospitality organizations:

- Participation in staff meetings.
- Participation in training activities.
- Participation in quality assurance programs.
- All duties must be carried out to comply with:
  - notification of accidents and other health and safety requirements;
  - statutory legislation, in particular hygiene regulations;
  - nationally and locally agreed codes of good practice;
  - fire precautions; and
  - equal opportunity principles and the trust's antidiscriminatory policy.

Once again, the question still exists, can anybody accomplish these tasks within less than 30 min and at the same time finish a specific number of rooms (usually 15–20) during the work shift, or as a busboy, to handle all the tables in the sections assigned to him, before and after the customers use the table? Unquestionably, this is considered a notable type of labor trafficking occurring in the field of tourism and hospitality industry.

## 14.4 WHY IS IT IMPORTANT TO COMBAT THB IN THE HOSPITALITY INDUSTRY?

It is important to remember that trafficking for both sexual and labor exploitation occurs in hotels. Hospitality organization can potentially be considered "guilty" in an incident of human trafficking regardless of whether hotels:

- are unknowing or unconscious participants,
- adopt a "head in the sand" approach and ignore trafficking hints, or
- are willing participants who may or may not share in the trafficking returns.

Hotels and other hospitality businesses have been identified as a convenient environment for sexual and labor exploitation; so, it is important for all staff members, before training, to bc aware of the trafficking consequences and look for and spot the signs or signals of THB, regardless of their position or department.

Some owners or managers might hesitate in announcing their initiatives and actions to combat trafficking in their organization for fear of alienating community, customers, and investors; however, there is clearly more potential damage resulting from a lack of action. One only has to look at the volume of the negative image that companies received after the implication of some of their hotels in THB.

Lack of actions against human trafficking can cause significant damage. The reporting of a single human trafficking incident can result in (Crane, 2013)

- a negative impact on the hospitality organization reputation;
- business interruptions by law enforcement organizations;
- business interruptions due to public protests;
- arising criminal or civil lawsuits;
- an erosion of customer trust in the hotel/brand;
- decrease in stakeholders' trust;
- negative impact on staff morale, motivation, and commitment; and
- decline in business profitability.

Therefore, the hospitality industry cannot afford to ignore this crime of exploitation and, in fact, should take steps to end it. Hospitality organizations must have an ethical and moral obligation to combat THB.

As corporate social responsibility has grown in importance, organizations should have become more mindful of human rights, labor rights, and anticorruption and more committed toward their community and environment. They are consequently calling for the support and involvement of their staff members in the fight against human trafficking (Kangaspunta, 2015). If hospitality organizations strengthen their antitrafficking policies, it would promote antitrafficking efforts of law enforcement and regulators.

Moreover, hospitality staff must be trained and well equipped to detect instances of trafficking. With training and awareness about human trafficking, hospitality organizations are in a unique and critical position to (COMBAT, 2016)

- identify potential victims of human trafficking,
- detecting the trafficking activities,
- report situations to the law enforcement organizations immediately, and
- deter future situations of human trafficking at properties.

It is so important to train employees how to detect the trafficking issues and how to identify the trafficker; but at the same level of importance, it is also important that there are clearly defined reporting procedures that staff can use without fear of punishment. Generally, some of the indicators tourism employees must be aware of include (Carolin et al., 2015)

- A trafficker pays for services in cash one day at time.
- Call a third party to finish the procedures.
- Always try to remove himself from any liability.
- Escort his victim everywhere.
- Control all or most money and identification papers of his victim.
- Reserving adjacent rooms.
- Showing up late or unusual hours.
- Trafficker/victim interaction could include:
    - use inappropriate nicknames,
    - trafficker uses offensive slang,
    - openly frightens or physically assaults victim, and
    - inconsistency in story.
- The trafficker and the victim usually insist on little or no services (housekeeping and food service).
- The trafficker and the victim also have little or no luggage/personal stuff.
- Their rooms are accustomed by men.
- Usually, the trafficker and the victim request extra number of towels and linens.
- The trafficker may request room with access to exits.
- Use online services websites mostly (e.g., backpage.com).

By actively combating THB, hospitality organizations demonstrate to stakeholders (community, investors, customers, employees, and suppliers) that they support human and labor rights as well as anticorruption initiatives.

Such actions can help to enhance stakeholder trust in the business or the brand and improve value. Proactively addressing human trafficking can, therefore, help organizations to mitigate against legislative, regulatory, and financial business risks (Tuppen, 2013).

## 14.5 WHAT HAS BEEN DONE WITHIN THE TOURISM INDUSTRY AGAINST THB?

When trafficking incidents occur in hotels, they are therefore subject to criminal and civil obligations.

Even though THB is a criminal activity in 146 countries, condemnation rates of traffickers across the globe are low. Although these rates vary by country, in Europe, only 44% of prosecutions result in condemnation (Kangaspunta, 2015). In fact, these rates are lower than other serious illegal conviction rates. Thus, many argue for additional legislation, which imposes organizations to disclose their antitrafficking policies and activities.

Generally, there are four possible reasons why conviction rates for THB remain low including (COMBAT, 2016):

- the lack of training on detecting the signs of trafficking,
- a low level of reporting of traffickers and victims (which may not reflect the reality of the situation),
- the dark nature of the crime (victims are often seeing to hide the crime and the reliance on others to testify in court), and
- the limited capacity or resources to investigate trafficking incidents and corruption.

According to WTO, since the early 1990s, various measures in fighting CSE of children have been taken by the tourism industry. Tourism industry associations are developing policies for their organizations, for example:

- The Universal Federation of Travel Agents' Associations was the first tourism industry association who has adopted The Child and Travel Agents' Charter (1994).
- WTO Statement on the Prevention of Organized Sex Tourism (1995).
- The International Hotel and Restaurants Association, adopted in 1996, a resolution in which they "recommend to all their members" to "(…) adapt measures and policies to prevent the use of their enterprises for

the commercial sexual exploitation of children" and "to prevent ease of access to child prostitution or child pornography."

Relating the governmental movements, the European Parliament and European Commission have realized the gravity of the problem of the CSE of children. The following measures have been taken by the European Commission:

- preparation of a training system for organization staff,
- preparation of label folders for guests, and
- preparation of an in-flight video.

Also, the French government released a tourism project, depicted as "Grande Cause National 1997," that has summarized in an effective way what hospitality organization can do to join the fight against the CSE of children:

- The hotel's policy should clearly state the hotel's intention and position with regard to the trade in child sex. The hotel shall also make this understood among its personnel and provide them with knowledge on how to detect the trafficking issues and how to handle them.
- Hotel management should provide information to its staff and customers regarding national laws and the penalties imposed for the sexual abuse of children.
- The hotel's security staff should be trained to detect and handle guests or personnel who sexually abuse a child, particularly on the hotel's premises.
- Staff members must report immediately to the police or some other authority.
- Cooperate with the relevant labor unions and human right organizations.
- Work actively as a precautionary activity by building up links with police, social authorities, and other organizations that may be interested in such issues.
- Prevent children from entering the hotel alone via bars, restaurants, lobby, or reception.
- Imposing full control over check-in systems and accessing the hotel's facilities.

## REFERENCES

Carolin, L.; Lindsay, A.; Victor, W. Sex Trafficking in the Tourism Industry. *J. Tour. Hospitality* **2015,** *4* (4), 1–6.

COMBAT. *Trafficking in Human Beings in the Hotel Industry*, 2016. www.brookes.ac.uk/microsites/combat-human-trafficking (accessed Sept 14, 2017).

Crane, A. Modern Slavery as a Management Practice: Exploring the Conditions and Capabilities for Human Exploitation. *Acad. Manage. Rev.* **2013,** *38* (1), 49–69.

Datta, M. N.; Bales, K. Slavery in Europe—Part 1: Estimating the Dark Figure. *Hum. Rights Q.* **2013,** *35* (4), 817–829.

Eurostat. *Trafficking of Human Being* (online), 2015. https://ec.europa.eu/anti trafficking/sites/antitrafficking/files/eurostat_report_on_trafficking_in_human_beings__2015_edition (accessed Nov 12, 2017).

ILO. A Global Alliance against Forced Labor. *Global Report under the Follow-Up to the ILO Declaration on Fundamental Principals and Rights at Work*; Geneva: ILO, 2005.

ILO. *Profits and Poverty: The Economics of Forced Labor*, 2014 (online). http://www.ilo.org/wcmsp5/groups/public/---ed_norm/-declaration/documents/publication/wcms_243391.pdf (accessed Sept 5, 2017; accessed Nov 28, 2017).

ILO. *Stopping Forced Labor, Global Report under the Follow-up to the ILO Declaration on Fundamental Principles and Rights at Work*; Geneva: ILO, 2001.

International Labor Office (ILO). *Forced Labor, Child Labor and Human Trafficking in Europe: An ILO Perspective* (online), 2002. file:///C:/Users/ABDALLAH/Downloads/labor.pdf (accessed Sept 19, 2017).

International Labor Organization. *21 Million People Are Now Victims of Forced Labor, ILO Says*; Geneva: International Labor Organization, 2012.

Kangaspunta, K. *Was Trafficking in Persons Really Criminalized? Anti-Trafficking Review* (online), 2015. file:///D:/My%20Documents/Downloads/100-218-1-PB.pdf (accessed Dec 21, 2017).

Leth, I. Child Sexual Exploitation from a Global Perspective. In *Medical, Legal and Social Science Aspects of Child Sexual Exploitation*; Cooper, S. W.; Estes, R. J.; Giardino, A. P.; Kellogg, N. D.; Vieth, V. I., Eds.; St. Louis, MO: GW Medical Publishing, 2005.

Mitchell, J.; Finkelhor, D.; Wolak, J. Conceptualizing Juvenile Prostitution as Child Maltreatment: Findings from the National Juvenile Prostitution Study. *Child Maltreat.* **2010,** *15*, 18–36.

Newman, W. J.; Holt, B. W.; Rabun, J. S.; Phillips, G.; Scott, C. L. Child Sex Tourism: Extending the Borders of Sexual Offender Legislation. *Int. J. Law Psychiatry* **2011,** *34*, 116–121.

Polaris Project. *Human Trafficking in Hotels and Motels Victim and Location Indicators* (online), 2012. http://www.twolittlegirls.org/ufiles/Hotel%20and%20Motel%20Indicators%20AAG.pdf (accessed Nov 5, 2017).

Reid, J. A. Exploratory Review of Route-Specific, Gendered, and Age-Graded Dynamics of Exploration: Applying Life Course Theory to Victimization in Sex Trafficking in North America. *Aggression Violent Behav.* **2012,** *17*, 257–271.

Sharma, A; Kukreja, S.; Sharma, A. Impact of Labor Laws on Child Labor: A Case of Tourism Industry. *Int. J. Adv. Manage. Econ.* **2012,** *1* (3), 47–57.

Tuppen, H. *Addressing Human Trafficking in the Hospitality Industry* (online), 2013. http://www.greenhotelier.org/know-how-guides/addressing-human-trafficking-in-the-hospitality industry/ (accessed Sept 14, 2017).

UFTAA. Child and Travel Agents Charter, 1994.

U.S. Congress. *Victims of Trafficking and Violence Protection Act of 2000*, n.d.; pp 106–386. Available at: http://www.state.gov/documents/organization/10492.pdf (accessed Sept 19, 2017).

U.S. Department of State. *U.S. Department of State Foreign Affairs Manual Volume 9 Visas*; Washington, DC: U.S. Department of State, 2012.

UNODC. *Human Trafficking* (online), n.d. http://www.unodc.org/unodc/en/human-trafficking/what-is human-trafficking.html (accessed Sept 19, 2017).

Walters, J.; Davis, P. H. Human Trafficking, Sex Tourism, and Child Exploitation on the Southern Border. *J. Appl. Res. Child.: Inform. Policy Child. Risk* **2011,** *2* (1), 9–11.

World Tourism Organization. *Code of Conduct for the Protection of Children from Sexual Exploitation in Travel and Tourism: Background and Implementation Examples*, Available at: https://www.unicef.org/lac/code_of_conduct.pdf (accessed Nov 22, 2017).

# CHAPTER 15

# SOCIAL JUSTICE, HUMAN RIGHTS, AND LABOR RIGHTS

*"Labor rights are a fundamental pillar of social justice and economic development."*

## 15.1 INTRODUCTION

All employees have basic rights in the workplace—including the right to privacy, fair wages, and freedom from prejudice. A job candidate also has certain rights even prior to being hired as an employee. Those rights include the right to be free from discrimination based on age, gender, race, national origin, or religion during the hiring process.

## 15.2 HUMAN RIGHTS

The classic definition of human rights refers to the universal moral right held by all individuals, something which all human beings, everywhere, at all times ought to have, something of which no one may be deprived without a grave affront to justice, something which is owing to every human being simply because he is human (Cranston, 1973).

The term "human rights" is used to refer to a wide spectrum of rights necessary for a human to live a life with dignity. The primary element recurring throughout each of these definitions is universality. Human rights are commonly understood as the inherent fundamental rights to which a person is entitled simply because he or she is a human being (Sepulveda et al., 2004).

Although most academics locate the foundations of human rights discourse in the period of the enlightenment, arguably the modern idea of human rights did not emerge until after the Second World War (Nickel, 2009). Following the war, there was a commitment to an international organization (the United Nations [UN]) which would impose certain standards of decency on the world's governments, although the UN understood in 1948 the urgent need to institute a set of values that individuals and societies around the world should respect and circulated by releasing the Universal Declaration of Human Rights (UDHR) that is considered the first universal statement on the basic principles of an alienable human rights. Then, the UN defined human rights as it is inherent in our nature as human beings whatever the nationality, place of residence, sex, national or ethnic origin, color, religion, language, or any other status, the foundation for the quality of life in which individual dignity and worth receives due respect and protection and as the foundation for freedom, justice, and peace (UNO, 1948, preamble). Therefore, we are all equally entitled to our human rights without discrimination.

However, Cole and Eriksson (2010) claimed that universally, still there is no accepted definition of human rights. The confusion and ambiguity surrounding defining human rights back to the end of the 19 centuries when Maritain (1971) claimed that it is so difficult to give examples of "natural rights" as it varies from culture to culture. In 1993, Turner tried to clarify natural rights by dividing human rights to natural rights and civil rights (Turner, 1993):

- Natural rights are owned by all human beings and are derived from nature. Human rights are considered the offspring of natural rights, which themselves evolved from the concept of natural law. Eventually, this concept of natural law developed into natural rights; this change reflected a shift in emphasis from society to the individual. Although natural law provided a basis for controlling excessive state power over society, natural rights gave individuals the ability to press claims against the government (Renteln, 1988). Natural rights scholars have confirmed the existence of specific rights—most notably the right to self-preservation and the right to property. The idea of fundamental rights is connected to theories of Natural Law and is thus ultimately depends on the belief that value is inherent in the structure of the universe.
- The civil rights are derived from membership in society formed out of a social contract and are thus distinct from the natural rights. Under this conception, civil rights can be changed because it is derived from society rather than God or nature. They depend on specific levels of social organization and wealth and hence cannot be claimed by the members of a society as a legacy.

Also, many organizations and researchers begun to set their own definitions of human rights; Donnelly (2003) defined human rights as those basic standards without which people cannot live in dignity, whereas Green Hotelier's definition was the fundamental principles and standards that aim to secure dignity, freedom, and equality for all people (2014).

According to Wasserstrom (1979), the definition of human rights posits four necessary requirements:

- First, it must be possessed by and only all human beings.
- Second, it must be owned equally by all human beings.
- Third, because human rights are owned by all human beings, we can rule out any of those rights that one might have in virtue of occupying any particular situation or relationship.
- Fourth, if there are any human rights, they have the extra characteristic of being assertable, in a manner of speaking, "against the whole world."

Finally, human rights have their structure in the twin concepts of equality and dignity (Liver and Miller, 2006).

## 15.3 GENERATIONS OF HUMAN RIGHTS

There are three overarching kinds of human rights norms (Lopes, 2010; Vasek, 1977):

- Civil-political rights:
    - physical and civil security (e.g., no cruelty, slavery, inhumane treatment, arbitrary arrest; equality before the law),
    - civil-political choices or empowerments (e.g., freedom of thought, conscience, and religion; freedom of assembly and voluntary association; political participation in one's society).

- Socioeconomic rights:
    - provision of goods satisfying social needs (e.g., food, shelter, health care, education),
    - provision of goods satisfying economic needs (e.g., work and fair wages, an adequate living standard, a social security net).

- Cultural or collective-developmental rights:
    - the self-development of communities (e.g., their political status and their economic, social, and cultural development),

- rights of ethnic and religious minorities (e.g., to the enjoyment of their own cultures, languages, and religions).

The first two are incorporated in Articles 22–27 of the Universal Declaration. They represent likely claims of individual persons against the state and firmly accepted norms identified in international agreements and conventions. The final type, which represents potential claims of peoples and groups against the state, is the most debated and lacks both legal and political recognition. Arguably, this separation reinforced the existing gap between civil and political which were seen as "universal, paramount, categorical moral rights" and economic and social rights which had a much lower status, with some authors proclaiming them not to belong to the human rights scheme at all (Donnelly, 2003).

Civil and political rights deal with freedom and participation in political life like the rights to life, liberty or political participation, etc. They are strongly individualistic and negatively built to protect the individual from the state. Thus, civil and political rights are considered very clear and precise, which therefore can be applied immediately. Also, the right to form and join a trade union and the right to privacy were categorized as civil and political rights (Lopes, 2010).

It imposes merely negative obligations on the states, which do not attempt to apply and implement the human rights. Conversely, economic, social, and cultural rights and socioeconomic rights ensure equal conditions and treatment.

They are not rights directly possessed by individuals but constitute positive duties upon the government to respect and fulfill them, whereas cultural or collective development constitutes a broad class of rights that have gained acknowledgment in international agreements and treaties but are more contested than the preceding types.

Economic, social, and cultural rights are considered those which have been expressed in vague terms (e.g., the right to housing, clothing, the right to education, the right to work, the right to decent working conditions, or the right to strike) and, imposing only positive obligations on the states, restricted to the existence and availability of resources and consequently involved a progressive realization and implementation (Lopes, 2010; Mantouvalou, 2011).

The precedence of civil and political rights over economic, social, and cultural rights is one of the reasons why human rights have not been acknowledged as an area that applies to tourism projects and activities. The implication of this was that some of these were viewed as real human rights, whereas others were presented as aspirational goals (Mantouvalou,

2011). Despite such classification, it is, however, undeniable that countries' obligations to respect, protect, promote, and fulfill human rights universally apply to all sort of rights. Hence, there is increasing argument that human rights must be treated holistically (to include civil and political as well as economic and social rights). There is no logical distinction between the two groups of rights. For example, political and civil rights require government obligations and responsibility to be realized, and not all civil and political rights apply to all human beings equally (Mantouvalou, 2012).

Therefore, the primary responsibility for the realization of human rights rests with the state under the international law. The responsibility requires three sets of roles (Eide, 2004):

- to respect the freedom and dignity of the individual,
- to protect them against third parties, and
- to provide access to welfare covering basic needs such as food, shelter, education, and health.

Human rights responsibilities under international law extend beyond governments to private companies in positions of power over workers and communities.

## 15.4 LABOR RIGHT AS HUMAN RIGHTS

The right to work has been spearheaded by the International Labor Organization (ILO) since its creation in 1919. Work provides an element of human dignity as well as provides the remuneration important for securing an adequate standard of living (Smith, 2007). Labor rights are a relatively new addition to the modern corpus of human rights. The modern concept of labor rights dates to the nineteenth century after the creation of labor unions following the industrialization processes.

So, human rights may be viewed as a foundation for the labor law, and sometimes workers' rights are considered the human right. Whether it is a labor law foundation or something else, human rights has become increasingly important and pervasive for a number of reasons:

- First, human rights have dominant status and political impacts on both the authority and community. Human rights claims can, therefore, be used by civil society organizations, labor rights movements, and

even business organizations to gain public support for their activities (Kolben, 2010) that thrust the government also to adopt. Claims based on the human rights discourse mean that labor movements can move away from economic arguments and special interest and toward a position based on ethics and morality which transcends any controversy over the (detrimental) impact of unions on the economy.
- Second, human rights have significant normative power. Subsequently, "the claims that relate to human rights are often strong enough to win most of the time when they compete with other considerations" (Nickel, 2009). Labor rights, which gain this status, are not easily denied. An excellent example of this is the current status of antidiscrimination law, which is increasingly based on the notion that discrimination in work environment is a breach of human rights.

Fundamental principles of labor rights and human rights are set out in the ILO's Constitution of 1919 and in the Declaration of Philadelphia of 1944 (appended to the Constitution).

Labor rights and human rights are normally discussed as if they were two separate entities. But according to many researchers, labor rights are considered a human right. Ssenyonjo (2010), in his answer to the question whether labor rights are human rights followed the positive perspective and was satisfied that the answer is positive. Looking at the UDHR, which is a nonbinding but enormously influential document, Ssenyonjo (2010) claimed that the several human rights are labor rights:

- **Article 4 of the UDHR prohibits slavery and servitude:**
  - the right to work,
  - the right to choose freely the work type, and
  - the right to claim fair wages.
- **Article 23 confirms that everyone has**
  - the right to work;
  - the right to work in a job freely chosen;
  - the right to receive equal pay;
  - the right to get decent compensation for work performed, which should guarantee a dignified life for himself and his family;
  - the right to work in healthful work environment; and
  - the right to form and join trade unions.
- *Article 24 guarantees a right to rest and leisure, including reasonable limitations of working hours, as well as holidays with pay.*

Listing these provisions confirms that labor rights not only are human rights but that there is an extensive list of these rights in human rights law.

To find another positivist answer to the question whether labor rights are human rights or not, the answer this time turn to the ILO, the expert branch of the UN in the field of labor rights (Swepston, 2003).

The ILO predates all the human rights agreements and organizations; it was formed in 1919 as part of the League of Nations to protect worker's rights, which shows that labor issues became a matter of international concern before human rights. The ILO later became incorporated into the UN. The UN itself backed labor rights by incorporating several issues into three articles of the United Nations Declaration of Human Rights, which is the basis of the International Covenant on Economic, Social, and Cultural Rights (Articles 6–8), that are described as follows:

- Article 6 confirms that everyone has the right to recognition everywhere.
- Article 7 guarantees equality for all without any discrimination.
- Article 8 gives everyone the right to an effective solution by the competent national courts for acts violating the fundamental rights granted him by the constitution or by law.

On the other side, despite the ILO did not explicitly present the documents adopted under its auspices as human rights documents for many decades (Jenks, 1960), it adopted binding conventions that incorporated labor standards and nonbinding recommendations that further detailed this list of standards.

But in recent years, the ILO endorsed a list of labor rights as human rights. In 1998, it adopted the Declaration of Core Labor Standards. The Declaration binds all ILO Member States, irrespective of whether they have ratified the relevant conventions, and contains five core rights:

1. the prohibition of all forms of forced labor,
2. the abolition of child labor,
3. the elimination of discrimination in employment,
4. freedom of association, and
5. the right to collective bargaining.

Although the ILO had understood the need of labor for a law, the ILO, in turn, introduced the fundamentals of labor rights; however, its declaration is being criticized significantly and gave rise to very heated debates in academic literature (Langille, 2005a). By listing these rights as fundamental human rights, the ILO left a number of other labor rights outside the scope of the Declaration.

However, ILO ignored some labor issues, to illustrate the problem; the decision of the ILO to pick four labor rights only as fundamental human rights, while leaving others outside the scope of the declaration, was criticized for excluding traditional and important socioeconomic rights, such as the right to a minimum wage (Heenan, 2004).

## 15.5 DEVELOPING A HUMAN RIGHTS POLICY

Adopting a human rights policy is a precursor to a company's human rights due diligence toward meeting its responsibility to respect human rights. Developing a human right policy provides the basis for embedding the responsibility to respect people through all business functions and should be approved at a most senior level and communicated internally and externally. It is important that the policy to be considered more than just a statement of intent—it must have governance consequences, that is, it indicates how management will implement and monitor the policy.

Human rights policies explicitly use the words "human rights" but can either be stand-alone statements or expressed within the organization statements of business principles, codes of conduct, or other value-related statements and documentation (United Nations Global Compact, 2015).

The human rights policy sets out how the organization respects human rights by having policies and processes in order to identify, prevent, mitigate, and account for how it addresses its adverse human rights impacts. Many human rights policies also explain the company's commitment to support human rights, that is, to make a positive contribution to promote or advance human rights, in addition to the minimum requirement to respect human rights.

Another definition was developed by United Nations Global Compact (2015) as a company's public expression of its commitment to meet its obligation to respect internationally recognized human rights standards. At least, this means the rights set out in the International Bill of Human Rights and the principles concerning fundamental rights set out in the ILO's Declaration on Fundamental Principles and Rights at Work. The rights to freedom not only include rights to work and to join a trade union but also the right to rest, to leisure (tourism), and freedom of movement (to travel). Freedom from poverty is also a human right (Pogge, 2007). Corporations have a duty to avoid complicity in human rights violations and must protect their employees' rights to privacy, to participate in politics and culture, religion, and education and first of all to guarantee their rights of equality, well-being, and health. The UN' norms on the responsibilities of transnational companies and other business enterprises with Regard to Human Rights note:

- Corporations have the obligation to promote, secure the fulfillment of, respect, ensure respect of, and protect human rights recognized in international as well as national law.
- Corporations shall guarantee freedom of association and effective recognition of the right to collective bargaining.

Human rights support everything we do, from the way staff are treated, their working conditions, to how customers are treated, in the supply chain and how goods and services for the organizations are produced, in the communities where the organization is located and in the way the property or the business is run.

According to United Nations Global Compact (2015), organizations adopt human rights policy for *three* reasons:

### *1. A universal responsibility*

Businesses have the responsibility to consider international human rights standards regardless of whether they are operating in an area of weak governance obligations or domestic regulations that do not comply with international human rights, or in a more stable context.

The very process of developing a human rights policy can have positive managerial results. Many organizations reported that developing the policy helped to

- generate in-house managerial capacity,
- build leadership commitment around human rights, and
- raise awareness and understanding of the company's human rights impacts.

### *2. Commercial purposes*

Demonstrating respect for ethical issues such as human rights and social responsibility is increasingly becoming a common international business practice in order to prove business good intention. Such intention or practices serve the organizations to achieve its commercial purposes, as following:

- *To gain a competitive advantage:* Many organizations believe that showing respect for ethical concerns such as human rights and social responsibility gives them a competitive advantage over competitors that overlook the area.
- *To build trust with stakeholders and address their concerns:* Good practices especially in the fields of human right and environmental issues enhance the stakeholders trust in the organization's business.

Many organizations also find that external stakeholders become more willing to engage constructively with them when they have such policies and approaches in place.

*3. Legal concerns*

The responsibility to respect human rights is not a legal duty imposed on organizations by treaty, but it is not a law-free zone either. The provisions of many international human rights treaties are embedded in most countries law (e.g., safety, health, antidiscrimination), and many governments have adopted the Rome Statute of the International Criminal Court, which—depending on the provisions of their own criminal code—may mean that they are empowered to prosecute companies for certain international human rights violations.

## 15.6 PROVISIONS ON HUMAN RIGHTS FOR WORKERS

Human rights policies/position statements often include provisions on the human rights of workers who directly or indirectly perform work linked to the organization. The human right policy in the organizations varies as follows:

- The organization size will affect the level of detail the organization goes into.
  For small organizations, these issues may already be covered under existing employee codes of conduct. Some offer a short sentence on key labor rights issues that outline their commitment.
  Others refer that additional detail is to be found in the large organizations policies related to their stakeholders.
- The way of management in dealing with the employees and workers; some companies publicly disclose more than others.

Key human right-related areas regularly covered in human rights policy documentation include (United Nations Global Compact, 2015):

1. *"Accessibility for persons with disabilities,*
2. *Child labor/minimum age workers/worst forms of child labor,*
3. *Employment relationship,*
4. *Equality,*
5. *Fair wages/compensation,*
6. *Forced/bonded/compulsory labor,*
7. *Health and safety,*
8. *Maternity protection,*
9. *No harsh or degrading treatment/harassment,*
10. *Non-discrimination,*
11. *Right to form or join a trade union and to bargain collectively,*
12. *Right to strike,*
13. *Working conditions—including working hours."*

## 15.6.1 KEY LABOR RIGHT-RELATED ARTICLES

Labor and employment laws give guidelines to the workplace and define what employees and employers are responsible for. These laws are crucial because they enable businesses to devote more of their focus to productivity and profitability rather than giving constant energy and resources to problem-solving. The following are some significant articles related to labor rights (United Nations Global Compact, 2015):

### *Child Labor*

Children under 18 are not allowed to work in operations or jobs requiring excessive efforts nor in activities that may be hazardous to their health or safety.

### *Fair Wages/Compensation*

Business owners must pay at least the minimum wage or the appropriate prevailing wage, whichever is higher, comply with all legal requirements on financial aspects, and provide any fringe benefits required by law or contract. If the compensation paid does not satisfy the workers' basic needs and provide some discretionary income, our business partners are required to take appropriate actions that seek to progressively realize a level of compensation that does.

### *Forced/Bonded Labor*

Business owners must not use forced labor. No employee may be coerced to work through force or intimidation of any form, or as a means of political oppression or as punishment for holding or expressing political views.

### *Health and Safety*

Nobody should be at great risk/danger because of their work. Everybody has the right to go home in the same state as they come to work. Members of the public are also entitled to expect to make sure work activities do not harm them. Employers must be committed to reduce the risk of serious harm associated with work activities and to keep their employees healthy.

### *Discrimination*

Business owners/managers must respect each individual's human rights and not discriminate on the basis of race, color, religion, beliefs, sex, age, social status, family origin, physical or mental disability, or sexual orientation nor commit other violations of human rights. Such discrimination will not be permitted. They also must be resolute in supporting human rights in everything they do. Ignorance and inaction do not constitute excuses for discrimination.

### *Working Conditions*

Employers must handle all employees fairly and honestly regardless of where they work. All staff must have a written contract of employment, with agreed terms and conditions, including notice periods on both sides. All personnel are allowed to reasonable rest breaks, access to toilets, rest facilities and potable water at their place of work, and holiday leave in accordance with the legislation of the country where they work. All employees must be provided with appropriate job skills training courses.

Governments are primarily responsible for guaranteeing that everyone enjoys their human rights. Traditionally, human rights were understood as a liberation from others interference, except where such interferences can be clearly justified in law (Liver and Miller, 2006). In other words, the main duties arising from human rights rely not on the individuals but on states, its authorities, or agents (Sepulveda et al., 2004).

And as such, it was conceived that countries had only a negative obligation to refrain itself from interfering in citizen's right to have a life with dignity. However, developments on the doctrine of state responsibility under international human rights influenced to a great extent the traditional idea of human rights as a freedom from governments' interference.

Human rights activism demands that the human dignity of all people be recognized and respected. As a result of the bad situation of human rights around the world, some nongovernmental organizations that advocate human rights grew significantly in the last few years, including Human Rights Watch, Amnesty International, World Organization against Torture, Freedom House, International Freedom of Expression Exchange, Anti-Slavery International, etc. (George and Varghese, 2007). It was admitted that human rights principles impose not only negative obligations but equally positive obligation for every government that undertakes to adhere to a human rights regime.

In fact, all human rights involve a combination of negative and positive duties. However, human rights generate at least four levels of duties, namely, to respect, protect, promote, and fulfill—and these responsibilities universally apply to all rights (Lopes, 2010).

## 15.7 THE HUMAN RIGHTS AND TOURISM

Although human right is an area of examination that can potentially address many issues associated with tourism, not more than a handful of studies have been conducted relating the two. One important reason as to why issues like human rights have been traditionally ignored by tourism researchers could be that the dominant typology of tourism was that of an "industry" rather than that of a "system." Such industry unfortunately creates "master–servant" relationships.

The tourism industry's product, which is used as a trade export item at international level, is the live collection of natural and human resources, wildlife, culture, history and heritage, and social exchange. Thus, the destinations, organizations, and infrastructures facilitating travel are subject to the wider sociopolitical, ecological, economic, and technological impacts (Leiper, 1990). Note that the very first component of Leiper's attraction collection is the human element. Hence, ethical principles, in addition to environmental sustainability governing the industry's behavior in host destinations, should be at the forefront of companies' behavior (George and Varghese, 2007).

In fact, the majority of international tourism is managed by multinational organizations and influential economic actors that generated significant political and economic impact, especially in developing countries (Hemingway,

2004). They have significant advantages over local institutions with access to financial, electronic, information, and communication systems, as well as political lobbying powers (Mowforth et al., 2008). They constantly watch the environment to exploit changes in international costs and demand patterns, and having no distinct loyalty can switch to a different destination as it suits them. Therefore, tourism (especially to less economically developed countries) is based on unequal relations. Rather than mitigating the poverty, tourism can exacerbate existing unequal, exploitative relationships and the poorest families and members of communities often feel the burdens hardest, frequently at the expense of their human rights.

That way of relation enhanced the typology of the tourism industry that is based on the gratification of the "self" at the expense of the "other." Accordingly, the industry stakeholders' groups develop negative perceptions toward each other as following (George and Varghese, 2007):

- Tourists find that other stakeholders (the community and the organization) violate their human rights.
- Residents of the destination areas find their human rights being violated by the visitors and the industry.
- Employees find that both their employers and the tourists disregard their dignity.

However, the rights of tourists to travel were considered more important than labor and destination locals' rights, even when travel agents suspected tourists of traveling for sex with minors. Lovelock's conclusion, "Tourism strongly supports the rights of the tourists" (2008), is echoed by George who suggested, "the rights of tourists are over-stressed and the rights of other stakeholders, especially the local community members are under-stressed or ignored" (2008).

In one way, economic benefits are also uncertain, tourism support to develop states' economy, while in another way, it may destroy the basic rights of people, especially the local people at the destinations (Dann and Seaton, 2001) in addition to breaking the environmental standards (see Chapter 6, External ethical issues).

Most of the profits from tourism flow back to such nations communities who sacrifice their natural, cultural, and social resources to make the tourism product successful, receive either an unfairly low return or suffer from a deterioration of their livelihood as a result of negative environmental, social, and cultural effects from the tourism activity. Tourism is frequently under investigation for its harsh environmental impacts (as this is a part of the sustainability concept) but not from a human rights perspective, despite the direct and negative impact that tourism can have on the rights of the local residents in the destinations to attain a decent standard of health and well-being.

Finally, the relationship between tourism and human rights is extremely important to be understood. The tourism–human rights nexus is shaped in three different perspectives (Table 15.1):

a) tourism itself as a human right,
b) tourism as a tool for realization of human rights, and
c) tourism as leading to human rights violations (Lopes, 2010).

The industry believes that it cannot give superior service to the visitors and at the same time protect the rights of their employees. The conception of tourism in the form of a master–servant relationship is the major reason why the human rights of residents are violated (Wickens, 2002). In their resistance to this order of things, employees and residents may violate the human rights of tourists.

## 15.8 THE HUMAN RIGHTS–TOURISM INTERFACE

The UDHR, adopted by the UN General Assembly on December 10, 1948, consists of 30 articles, which outline the perspective of the UN on the human rights guaranteed to all people in the world.

Although tourism was not widely understood as an area where the human rights declaration could find an implementation, its ramifications for tourism are far and wide.

In fact, some of the objectives of UDHR highlighted in its preamble are the social objectives of tourism as well: for instance, UDHR speaks of the role of human rights protection in strengthening the development of friendly relations between nations; similarly, one of the main goals of tourism is achieving international harmony and peace (D'Amore, 1988).

Also, a few of the articles of the UDHR are more direct in their application to tourism human rights than to any other sector, for example, Article 13, which states that everyone has the universal right to freedom of movement, and, Article 24, which states that everyone has the universal right to rest, leisure, and holidays with pay.

Table 15.2 examines some of the more relevant UDHR articles separately in their implications for tourism practice.

**TABLE 15.1** Tourism–Human Rights Nexus.

| Tourism itself as a human right | Tourism as a tool for realization of human rights | Tourism as leading to human rights violations |
|---|---|---|
| | **Activity** | |
| Everyone has the right to rest and leisure, including reasonable limitation of working hours and cyclic vacations with pay and this is nearly the purpose of tourism. Therefore, tourism is beyond doubts the primary activity that gives meaning to this human right element<br>It contributes to the application of the right to freedom of movement. According to UDHR, everyone shall have the right to liberty of movement within the territory of a country and shall be free to leave any state including his own | The UN WTO considers tourism as an important vehicle to achieve economic growth and prosperity. Tourism plays a crucial role in poverty alleviation and improving the facilities of destinations communities, since it contributes significantly to development of infrastructure, including transport and communications, water supply, energy, and health services | Tourism is based on the gratification of the "self" at the expense of the "other" (George and Varghese, 2007) |
| | **Impact** | |
| Rest and leisure with dignity are essential for a human life<br>Tourism creates a unique environment for development and friendly relations among nations—which are some of the main purposes sought by humanity when adopting the UDHR (Lopes, 2010) | Tourism is in a good position to support and promote the human right to equality and nondiscrimination, as provided by international human rights instruments. As tourism provides a unique opportunity for interaction amongst human beings from the most diverse background, regardless of their age, race, language, color, sex, religion, political, or other opinions, national or social origin, property, birth, or another status, etc.<br>Such interaction opportunities enhance international understanding, peace, universal respect, and awareness of human rights and fundamental freedoms for all | Specific labor and residents' groups like women and children are particularly affected by the negative influences of tourism activities. Absence of legal protection and the lack of labor rights, especially in developing countries, are considered as factors that permit discriminatory practices against women workers to occur in the tourism field (Hemingway, 2004). In addition, sex tourism industry is experiencing a boom worldwide accompanied by a rise in child prostitution/exploitation (Slob and Wilde, 2006)<br>Also, in many countries, child labor is common in the tourism industry, particularly in the informal sector (George and Varghese, 2007)<br>Generally, tourism industry violates labor rights in a horrible way, amongst the human rights abuses within the tourism industry; lack of effective labor protection for seasonal workers, low payment, and discriminatory and unfair labor practices |

**Source:** The Authors.

**TABLE 15.2** The Human Rights–Tourism Interface.

| Article | Topic | Interface |
|---|---|---|
| Article 1 | All human beings are born free and equal in dignity and rights. They are endowed with reason and conscience and should act toward one another in a spirit of brotherhood | Brotherhood |
| Article 2 | Everyone is entitled to all the rights and freedoms set forth in this declaration, without distinction of any kind, such as race, color, sex, language, religion, political or other opinion, national or social origin, property, birth, or other status | Equality |
| Article 3 | Everyone has the right to life, liberty, and security of person | Liberty |
| Articles 4 | Condemning slavery of all forms | Equality |
| Articles 5 | No one shall be subjected to torture or to cruel, inhuman, or degrading treatment or punishment | Equality |
| Articles 6–11 | UN's commitment toward a nondiscriminatory international legal framework | Equality |
| Article 12 | No one shall be subjected to arbitrary interference with his privacy, family, home, or correspondence, or to attacks upon his or her honor and reputation | The destination's community privacy |
| Article 13 | The right to freedom of movement and residence within the borders of each state | Rest and leisure |
| Article 23 | Everyone has the right to work, to free choice of employment, to just and favorable conditions of work, to claim decent wages, and to protection against unemployment | Labor rights |
| | It also lists the right to form or join trade unions as one of its subclauses | |

**Source:** The Authors, based on UDHR.

## 15.9 LABOR LAW

In parallel with the Industrial Revolution, labor law arose as the relationship between the worker (employee) and employer shifted from small-scale production to large-scale factories. Workers sought better conditions and the right to join or avoid joining a labor union, while employers sought a more flexible and less costly workforce. Therefore, the state of labor law at any time is both the product of and a component of struggles between various social forces.

According to some academic researchers, "there is no comprehensive and conceptionally consistent definition of labor law." But one thing still certain: it is not always helpful to view labor law as being primarily a set of laws issued by a government. In many institutions, much of what governs conduct in the work environment are the content of contracts, informal understandings, and formal instructions that originate within the work place.

Harry Arthurs (2007) advocated that "the law of the workplace is still largely generated from within," where are the internal features of the work environment:

- work-place culture,
- the ethical climate,
- custom and practice,
- the employment contract,
- the works rule book or employee handbook, and
- collective agreements.

These internal sources often form the core of the rules governing the employment relationship and subsequently constitute the legislation that organizes the relation between the two involved entities. Hence, we look at the legislation, it is not only "labor laws" that rule the workplace. In many times, we must look to constitutional law or the general civil code or civil statutory laws, the "common law," and even the criminal law. A labor law legislation will usually be read together with these sources. Subsequently, Brian Langille refers to the collision of legislations concepts, legal frameworks, and diverse points of reference that make up the subject we know as labor law as "a slice of life" (Langille, 2005b) rather than a unified separate legal concept. Legislation becomes relevant only to fill gaps or ensure minimum standards related to workforce life.

In almost every country, the basic feature of labor law is that the rights and obligations of the worker and the employer are mediated through a contract of employment between the two. This has been the case since the collapse of feudalism. Labor law must cover the common terms and conditions of labor issues such as:

- Minimum wage
- Living wage
- Hours
- Health and safety
- Discrimination
- Dismissal
- Child labor

There are two explanations of the purpose of labor law that workers can feel immediately comfortable with (Langille, 2005b):

- To fix the imbalance of power between the worker and the employer: by protecting workers' right to organize in trade unions and to develop in place protective policies, which prevent the employer from dismissing the worker without a reasonable cause. Labor law, therefore, sets up and preserves the processes by which workers are empowered to negotiate from an equal position or, at least, of less inequality.
- To control working conditions: by placing an acceptable restriction on the organizations in order to set up a minimum standard over issues such as working time, health and safety, and pay. These legislations law limits the degree to which the more powerful party (employer) can abuse the weaker (worker).

But it is worth to clarify that the former purpose represents the law as a tool to promote worker empowerment, while the latter represents a form of worker protection. These two different purposes of the law as a mean to intervene in the bargaining relationship have both delivered real benefits to working people in numerous issues, and both have been—and continue to be—goals attempted by the trade unions.

A third rationale sometimes approved as a purpose of labor law is

- To regulate the labor market: the government may choose to implement legislation to place either maximum or minimum limits on wages or working hours, either nationally or in particular sectors or industries.

And, a fourth answer

- To control trade union freedom: labor law is also used as a tool to limit and control trade unions.

To sum up, legislation on working conditions includes acts dealing with subjects like wages, hours of work, rest days, restrictions on employment of women and young persons, safety, health, and welfare. Such legislations set up certain standards, which are then enforced through appropriate inspection procedures and penal measures. Generally, the standards laid down in the various acts of labor law are minimum standards, with provision for exemptions in certain suitable cases, leaving a space through collective bargaining or industrial adjudication to improve these standards in appropriate cases according to the stakeholders' interest.

### *15.9.1 LABOR RIGHT IN TOURISM—HOSPITALITY INDUSTRY*

Labor rights are entitlements that relate specifically to the role of being a worker. Some of these rights are exercised individually and others collectively. Employee rights and employer awareness of areas of conflict and sensitivity are some of the significant issues in tourism industry. The labor issues in tourism industry are upon four areas:

1. hiring,
2. investigation of employee misconduct,
3. firing, and
4. postrecruiting decisions by management (Ward, 1989).

Since tourism is one of the largest industries in the world, the magnitude of the impacts of human rights violations upon its employees cannot be whiled away.

It is unacceptable for tourist organizations to profit from illegal and exploitative practices and then refuse to acknowledge their legal and ethical responsibilities. Tourist organizations have a responsibility to ensure that their business is not tainted by human rights abuses of their employees. Thus, the right to work emphasizes the need to promote employment for all, but not just any kind of employment. Jobs and livelihoods have to be decent for the right to be fulfilled (ILO, 1996). Decent work entails (UN, 1948, 1966)

- a right to work in a job freely chosen;
- a just remuneration;
- a right to fair working conditions:
    - protection of privacy,
    - a right to be protected from arbitrary,
    - unjustified dismissal, and
    - a right to strike;
- equal remuneration for work of equal value;
- safe and healthy working conditions;
- equal opportunity for everyone to be promoted in his employment;

- rest and leisure;
- reasonable limitation of working hours;
- periodic holidays with pay; and
- the right to form and to join trade unions.

These rights may be based on different foundations, such as freedom, dignity, or capability. Employees and workers feel jealous about the king-like treatment accorded to the customers while their own basic needs are unmet and resulting in their opportunistic behavior. While the tourists relax in the sunshine around the world and the customers rest in their suites, life is far from paradise for the waiters, cleaners, cooks, porters, drivers, receptionists, and other staff working to make the holidays happy and carefree.

Working conditions in the tourism industry, especially for those who fall in the lower echelons of the hierarchy, are notoriously exploitative (Murrmann, 1989). Gender discrimination of the employees is one of the main issues that upset the employees, including sexual exploitation of female staff is a major allegation against the tourism industry.

These conditions keep employees and workers in poverty and violate the labor standards laid out in national and international legislation. Many a time, even international tourism and hospitality chains appoint local employees and offer them poor wages, below than that of similar employees of domestic firms in the other sectors. Employees, especially the seasonal workers, should have the human right to ask for adequate social protection. Many firms abandon the employees in the lean season and their families have to swim through the entire off-peak season through utter poverty and misery. It would have been wiser if these firms send them for training and development during the lean season or provide them alternate employment instead of sacking them (Claudio, 1992).

Employment in the frontline in tourism is renown to be underpaid and highly stressful (Hall and Brown, 2006). Tourism Concerns research into tourism labor (Beddoe, 2004) suggests that workers suffer from

- unpaid overtime;
- overdependence on tips;
- stress, lack of secure contracts;
- poor training;
- lack of promotion opportunities for locally employed people;
- insecure, short-term contracts;
- low wages and high costs;

- long working hours and high work intensity, leading to fatigue;
- poor management practices, including bullying and favoritism, racial and gender discrimination;
- high labor turnover, exhaustion, and inadequate training, giving cause for concern about safety;
- employers who are hostile or resistant to trade union organization; and
- collective bargaining.

Forced or compulsory labor is classified as slavery and prohibited in the International Covenant on Civil and Political Rights (UN, 1966).

On the other side, Green Hotelier (2014) developed a detailed list of some key areas where human rights may be prevalent for the hospitality organization' business and those within its business boundary who may be responsible for managing this function.

- **Workplace (human resources, general managers, corporate responsibility)**
  - transparent contracts (in language worker understands),
  - fair and equal pay,
  - holiday entitlement and rest,
  - fair treatment (e.g., bullying and harassment),
  - accessibility,
  - diversity and inclusion,
  - discrimination (e.g., sex, race, color, creed, sexual orientation),
  - freedom of speech,
  - freedom to associate,
  - worker/management dialogue,
  - grievance procedures,
  - maternity,
  - religious observation,
  - health and safety,
  - training and development opportunities.

- **Supply chains (procurement, corporate responsibility)**
  - child labor,
  - bonded/trafficked labor,
  - working conditions, including labor standards and health and safety,
  - diversity,
  - impact on communities.

- **Communities where operating (development, human resources, corporate responsibility)**
  - access to work,
  - access to water,
  - access to land,
  - access to employment,
  - land concession,
  - pollution (water, air, solid waste),
  - community dialogue,
- **Customers (customer relations, data management, account managers, corporate affairs, corporate responsibility, general managers, secretariat)**
  - discrimination,
  - data protection,
  - privacy,
  - health and safety,
  - accessibility.
- **Governance (secretariat, corporate affairs, compliance, legal)**
  - bribery and corruption,
  - transparency,
  - partner companies (owners, investors, etc.).

Another issue is the industry encouraging employees to apply the knowledge–skill–attitude set that they have acquired in one organization: this, in addition to be a support to the human right to work at a place and job of one's choice, will benefit the industry in general and the employee concerned in particular (Malloy and Fennell, 1998). As a reaction to issues related to human rights in the specific case of tourism, some noted that there are some advocacy groups that stemmed up such as Tourism Concern, End Child Prostitution in Asian Tourism, Equitable Tourism Options, Ecumenical Coalition of Churches for Tourism, etc. Governments feel that tourism is a quick fix solution to the ailments related to tax revenue and foreign exchange reserve and extract maximum from the tourism enterprises, which pass the same onto the tourists with an added premium.

As a whole, all the governmental and nongovernmental organizations must unite to settle the human rights down and promote the implementation of the human rights articles in business environments.

## 15.10 SOCIAL JUSTICE

How the good and bad things in life are distributed among the members of the human society is the straightforward definition of the meaning of social justice that is provided by the political theorist David Miller in 1999 (Miller, 1999). The laborer could not be viewed separately from society. Thus, this social status should be guaranteed by legislation. Social movement influenced critically in the creation of early labor law, which encouraged the development of civil law to include the labor force. According to Rodgers (2013), in Germany for instance, antidiscrimination legislation was instigated early in the development of employment law, recognizing that the government should be involved in the guarantee of group, as well as individual status. In a similar way, legislations were created in France during the period of the Social movement (1900–1968), in order to create legal protections for labor force on the grounds of public policy. As such, worker contracts become "socialized" and labor law became dominated by role of government power in the regulation of the employment relation.

By contrast, in the United Kingdom, the focus was on the specific nature of the employment relationship. In particular, labor theorists referred to problems associated with the unequal relationship between organization and employees and the need to challenge this unequal distribution of power in order to achieve social justice for the employees. It was felt that if workers were to challenge the lack of social power in their work environment and employment relationship, then this could only be achieved through the "spontaneous that of management" (Rodgers, 2013).

So, social movement has a significant role in the creation and the development of the ILO (Hendrickx, 2013). This organization was formed in 1919 as part of the peace project at the end of the First World War. Its constitution explained the importance of creation of labor standards in the achievement of that social justice, and the importance of the social justice to that mandate.

The consideration and the involvement of various social groups in the design and implementing the labor law will result in achieving the social justice. Social justice is not only about a set of abstract legal rights which had little to do with the experience of general society, but it means that the law could expand to meet social equality and was not constrained by the liberal commitment to nonintervention. This gave a space for the development of labor law to meet the social compromise of the early twentieth century. New legal forms came to the fore, which recognized the interdependent activities of stakeholders and a need to coordinate those activities in the "public interest." However, the relationship between human rights and social justice nowadays is not straightforward, this may be because:

1. Social justice has been considered as outdated, and increasingly there are arguments that human rights are calling the same claims of social justice.
2. Some activists and labor unions representatives of the second generations view social rights as opposed to civil and political rights. Many labor rights, if they can be viewed human rights at all, sit far better with the economic and social rights. For example, it could be argued that minimum wage legislation has more in common with the character of a social rather than a civil or political right (Collins, 2011).

Despite this conflict, the importance of social justice was identified in ILO constitution, and also, the labor standards creation was spotted as the significant tool in achieving and settling the social justice. The seven policy concerns in the constitution discerned three priorities in the ILO in terms of "social justice."

1. work as a source of livelihood and fulfillment,
2. prevention of exploitation, and
3. workers protection against the difficulties of working in dangerous or inadequate environments.

Work represents a social value; thus, this recognition ensures treating the workers as a human and guard them against the treatment as a commodity or an article of commerce. Social justice, therefore, not only required a redistribution of power from employers to employees but also meant the recognition of the value of work to all stakeholders and to the social system as a whole.

In addition, the distribution of income and wealth is the "good" most commonly referred to in discussions of social justice. However, many various results come up according to the country of origin when googling social justice, but there are two common approaches to settle the social justice in work environment; this depends largely on the type of the organization and the employee status; the material and nonmaterial approaches were identified in Table 15.3.

**TABLE 15.3** Social Justice Approaches.

| Material | Nonmaterial |
|---|---|
| One key element of social justice is the just distribution of income and wealth in any particular society is that all its members have sufficient material resources to live with dignity and to flourish. Some questions must be considered about the wealth of our whole society, about the rich as well as the poor. Unequal societies must successfully manage their social problems and try to solve them | The distributional paradigm of social justice thus covers a wide area, stretching beyond traditional concerns with the distribution of income and wealth to embrace nonmaterial dimensions of social justice. Thus, understanding the domination and oppression should be the starting point for a conception of social justice (Fraser, 1997) |
| When the distributional debate moves beyond the issue of poverty, the question arises as to whether the goal is a meritocratic or egalitarian conceptualization of social justice. However, the equality of opportunity is the main prerequisite for social justice (Lister, 2007) | Although the redistribution paradigm (wealth and income) is concerned with economy in justice, the recognition paradigm addresses cultural or symbolic injustice (Lister, 2007) |

**Source:** The Authors.

Therefore, although it is important to develop policies to help employees move out of low paid jobs, the negative typology associated with these jobs must also be tackled, as social justice is not just about opportunity but also about equity and about a fair distribution of rewards (Lister, 2007).

## REFERENCES


Arthurs, H. Compared to What? Draft Paper Delivered in Honor of the 40th Anniversary of the UCLA Comparative Labor Law Project, 2007.

Beddoe, C. *Labor Standards, Social Responsibility and Tourism*; Tourism Concern: London, 2004.

Claudio, S. E. Unequal Exchanges: International Tourism and Overseas Employment. *Community Dev. J.* **1992,** *27* (4), 402–410.

Cole, S.; Eriksson, J. Tourism and Human Rights. In *Tourism and Inequality: Problems and Prospects*; Cole, S., Morgan, N., Eds.; CABI International: London, UK, 2010; pp 107–125.

Collins, H. Theories of Rights as Justifications for Labor Law. In *The Idea of Labor Law*; Langille, B., Davidov, G., Eds.; Oxford University Press: Oxford, 2011.

Cranston, M. *What Are Human Rights?* The Bodley Head Ltd., 1973.

D'Amore, L. "Tourism: The World's Peace Industry. *J. Trav. Res.* **1988,** *27* (1), 35–40.

Dann, G. M.; Seaton, A. V. Slavery, Contested Heritage, and Thana Tourism. *Int. J. Hospitality Tour. Admin.* **2001,** *2* (3/4), 1–29.

Donnelly, J. *Universal Human Rights in Theory and Practice*, 2nd ed.; Cornell University Press: Ithaca, NY, 2003.

Eide, A. *Making Human Rights Universal: Achievements and Prospects* (online), 2004. http://www.uio.no/studier/emner/jus/humanrights/HUMR4110/h04/undervisningsmateriale/eide.pdf (accessed Aug 28, 2017).
Fraser, N. *Justice Interruptus*; New York and London: Routledge, 1997.
George, B.; Varghese, V. Human Rights in Tourism: Conceptualization and Stakeholders Perspective. *Electr. J. Bus. Ethics Organ. Stud.* **2007,** *12* (2), 40–48.
Green Hotelier. Know How Guide: Human Rights and the Hotel Industry. *International Tourism Partnership* (online), 2014. http://www.fairtrade.travel/source/websites/fairtrade/documents/Green_Hotelier_Know-How_Guide_Human-Rights_2014.pdf (accessed Aug 15, 2017).
Hall, D.; Brown, F. *Tourism and Welfare Ethics, Responsibility and Sustainable Well-being*; Oxford: CABI, 2006.
Heenan, J. A. Shrinking the International Labor Code: An Unintended Consequence of the 1998 ILO Declaration on Fundamental Principles and Rights at Work? *J. Int. Law Policy* **2004,** *36*, 101–141.
Hemingway, S. The Impact of Tourism on the Human Rights of Women in South East Asia. *Int. J. Hum. Rights* **2004,** *8* (3), 275–304.
Hendrickx, F. Foundations and Functions of Contemporary Labor Law. *Eur. Labor Law J.* **2012,** *3* (2), 108–110.
ILO. *About the ILO* (online), 1996. http://www.ilo.org/global/About_the_ILO/lang--en/index.htm (accessed Aug 31, 2017).
Jenks, C. W. *Human Rights and International Labor Standards*; Steve and Sons: Richmond, VA, 1960.
Kolben, K. Labor Rights as Human Rights? *Va. J. Int. Law* **2010,** *50*, 449–462.
Langille, B. What Is International Labor Law For? International Institute for Labor Studies, ILO: Geneva, 2005a; p 5.
Langille, B. Core Labor Rights—The True Story (Reply to Alston). *Eur. J. Int. Law* **2005b,** *16* (3), 409–437.
Leiper, N. Tourist Attraction Systems. *Ann. Tour. Res.* **1990,** *77* (3), 367–384.
Lister, R. Social Justice: Meanings and Politics. *Benefits J. Poverty Soc. Justice* **2007,** *15* (2), 113–125.
Liver, A.; Miller, J. Global Tourism—A Hobbesian Covenant? The Right to Development vs. Indigenous Property Rights. In *Turk-Kazakh International Tourism Conference* (online), 2006. http://ertr.tamu.edu/index.php?option=com_contentandview=articleandid=979:global-tourism-a hobbesian-covenant-the-right-to-development-v-indigenous-property-rightsandcatid=132:turkkazakh-international-tourism-conference-andItemid=64 (accessed Aug 13, 2017).
Lopes, E. C. *Human Rights in Tourism: Effectiveness of the Legal Framework for Tourism in Mozambique upon the Realization of the Right to Development of Local Communities*; Pretoria: University of Pretoria, 2010.
Lovelock, B. Ethical Travel Decisions. Travel Agents and Human Rights. *Ann. Tour. Res.* **2008,** *35* (2), 338.
Malloy, D. C.; Fennell, D. A. Codes of Ethics and Tourism: An Exploratory Content Analysis. *Tour. Manage.* **1998,** *19* (5), 453–461.
Mantouvalou, V. Support of Legalization. In *Debating Social Rights*; Gearty, C., Mantouvalou, V., Eds.; Hart Publishing: Oxford, 2011; pp 90–98.
Mantouvalou, V. Are Labor Rights Human Rights. *Eur. Labor Law J.* **2012,** *3* (2), 151–166.
Maritain, J. *The Rights of Man and Natural Law*; Gordon Press: New York, NY, 1971.
Miller, D. *Principles of Social Justice*; Harvard University Press: Cambridge, Mass, and London, 1999.

Mowforth, M.; Charlton, C.; Munt, I. *Tourism and Responsibility: Perspectives from Latin America and the Caribbean*; Routledge: London, 2008.
Murrmann, S. K. Employer Rights, Employee Privacy and Aids: Legal Implications to Hospitality Industry Managers. *J. Hospitality Tour. Res.* **1989,** *13* (3), 147–157.
Nickel, J. Making Sense of Human Rights, 2nd ed.; Blackwell Publishing: London, 2009.
Pogge, T. Introduction. In *Freedom from Poverty as a Human Right*; Pogge, T., Ed.; 2007 (online). http://www.realadventures.com/listings/1128334_Omo-Valley-Tours-to-Ethiopia-Pharez-Ethiopian-Tour_(accessed Aug 30, 2017).
Renteln, A. D. The Concept of Human Rights. *Anthropos* **1988,** *83* (4), 343–364.
Rodgers, L. *Human Rights, Social Justice and Labor Law*; Labor Law Research Network, University of Toronto: Toronto, 2013.
Sepulveda, M.; Banning, T.; Gudmundsdottir, G. D.; Chamoun, C. *Human Rights, Ideas and for Human Rights Education Project*; University for Peace HERP Publications: San José, Costa Rica, 2004.
Slob, B.; Wilde, J. *Tourism and Sustainability in Brazil: The Tourism Value Chain in Porto de Galinhas, Northeast Brazil;* SOMO—Centre for research on Multinational Corporations, 2006.
Smith, R. K. *Textbook on International Human Rights*, 3rd ed.; Oxford University Press: Oxford, 2007.
Ssenyonjo, M. Economic, Social and Cultural Rights: An Examination of State Obligations. In *Research Handbook on International Human Rights Law*; Joseph, S.; McBeth, A., Eds.; Edward Elgar: Northampton, MA, 2010, p 36.
Swepston, L. The International Labor Organization's System for Human Rights Protection. In *Human Rights: International Protection, Monitoring, Enforcement*, 2nd ed.; Symonides, J., Ed.; UNESCO/Ashgate: Farnham, UK, 2003; p 91.
Turner, B. S. Outline of a Theory of Human Rights. *Sociology* **1993,** *27* (3), 489–512.
United Nations Global Compact. *A Guide for Business: How to Develop a Human Rights Policy*, 2nd ed.; Office of the United Nations High Commissioner for Human Rights: Geneva, 2015.
United Nations. *The Universal Declaration of Human Rights* (online); United Nations: New York, 1948. http://www.webworld.unesco.org (accessed Aug 15, 2017).
United Nations. *International Covenant on Civil and Political Rights*; Office of the High Commissioner of Human Rights: Geneva, Switzerland, 1966 (online). http://www2.ohchr.org/English/law/ccpr.htm (accessed Aug 5, 2017).
Vasek, K. *Human Rights: A Thirty-Year Struggle: The Sustained Efforts to Give Force of Law to the Universal Declaration of Human Rights*; UNESCO Courier: Farnham, UK, 1977; pp 30–11.
Ward, L. M. Employee Rights and Their Impact on Personnel Decisions by Managers in the Hospitality Industry. *J. Hospitality Tour. Res.* **1989,** *13* (3), 137–145.
Wasserstrom, R. Rights, Human Rights, and Racial Discrimination. In *Rights*; Lyons, D., Ed.; Wadsworth Publishing Company: Belmont, 1979; pp 46–57.
Wickens, E. The Sacred and the Profane: A Tourist Typology. *Ann. Tour. Res.* **2002,** *29* (3), 834–851.

# INDEX

## E



## G

## R



## S

For Product Safety Concerns and Information please contact our EU representative GPSR@taylorandfrancis.com
Taylor & Francis Verlag GmbH, Kaufingerstraße 24, 80331 München, Germany

www.ingramcontent.com/pod-product-compliance
Ingram Content Group UK Ltd.
Pitfield, Milton Keynes, MK11 3LW, UK
UKHW022212190926
475702UK00003B/318
*9781771887311*